Religion and Democracy in the United States

Religion and Democracy in the United States

DANGER OR OPPORTUNITY?

Alan Wolfe and Ira Katznelson
Editors

RUSSELL SAGE FOUNDATION
NEW YORK
PRINCETON UNIVERSITY PRESS
PRINCETON AND OXFORD

Published by Princeton University Press, 41 William Street, Princeton, New Jersey 08540
In the United Kingdom: Princeton University Press, 6 Oxford Street, Woodstock,
Oxfordshire OX20 1TW
and Russell Sage Foundation, 112 East 64th Street, New York, New York 10065
press.princeton.edu
russellsage.org

Library of Congress Cataloging-in-Publication Data

Religion and democracy in the United States : danger or opportunity? / Alan Wolfe
and Ira Katznelson, editors.
p. cm.
Includes bibliographical references and index.
ISBN 978-0-691-14728-4 (hardcover : alk. paper) — ISBN 978-0-691-14729-1
(pbk. : alk. paper) 1. United States—Religion. 2. Democracy—United States.
3. Democracy—Religious aspects. I. Wolfe, Alan, 1942– II. Katznelson, Ira.
BL2525.R455 2010
322'.10973—dc22
2010009116

British Library Cataloging-in-Publication Data is available

This book has been composed in Sabon

Printed on acid-free paper. ∞

Printed in the United States of America

1 3 5 7 9 10 8 6 4 2

CONTENTS

CONTRIBUTORS

ALLISON CALHOUN-BROWN is an associate professor of political science at Georgia State University.

ROSA DELAURO is a member of the U.S. House of Representatives for the state of Connecticut (D-CT).

BETTE NOVIT EVANS is professor emeritus of political science at Creighton University.

JAMES L. GIBSON is the Sidney W. Souers Professor of Government in political science at Washington University in St. Louis. He is also a professor of African and African American Studies and director of the program on Citizenship and Democratic Values Weidenbaum Center on the Economy, Government, and Public Policy.

JOHN C. GREEN is a distinguished professor of political science at the University of Akron. He is also a Senior Fellow with the Pew Forum on Religion & Public Life.

FREDRICK C. HARRIS is a professor of political science and director of the Center on African-American Politics and Society at Columbia University.

AMANEY JAMAL is an assistant professor of politics at Princeton University.

IRA KATZNELSON is the Ruggles professor of political science and history at Columbia University.

GEOFFREY C. LAYMAN is an associate professor of political science at the University of Notre Dame.

DAVID L. LEAL is an associate professor of government and director of the Irma Rangel Public Policy Institute at the University of Texas at Austin.

DAVID C. LEEGE is professor emeritus of government and international studies at the University of Notre Dame.

NANCY L. ROSENBLUM is the Senator Joseph Clark Professor of Ethics in Politics and Government at Harvard University.

KENNETH D. WALD is a distinguished professor of political science at the University of Florida at Gainsville.

Clyde Wilcox is a professor in the Government Department at Georgetown University.

Alan Wolfe is a professor of political science and director of the Boisi Center for Religion and American Public Life at Boston College.

ACKNOWLEDGMENTS

OUR FIRST DEBT is owed to the American Political Science Association for initiating and supporting the Task Force on Religion and Democracy in the United States that produced this book. A discussion of the purposes, process, and composition of the Task Force can be found in chapter 1 of the volume.

None of our work would have been possible without the support of the wonderfully thoughtful and efficient staff of the APSA in Washington, DC, especially the tireless work of Robert Hauck, its Deputy Director and Liaison to the Task Force. He participated in our deliberations, handled the group's daunting logistics (bringing us together four times over two years), and smoothed the process toward publication.

We also owe a special debt to the Russell Sage Foundation. We warmly thank its President, Eric Wanner, for the decision to join with APSA to underwrite the meetings of the Task Force meetings, and for his keen interest in the subject of our deliberations.

This volume is co-published by the Foundation, where Suzanne Nichols, its Director of Publications, has worked hand in hand with Chuck Myers and his colleagues at Princeton University Press, who deserve our thanks for their patience and for selecting outstanding reviewers whose comments improved all the chapters.

Mark Lilla and John DiIulio offered the benefit of their wisdom and helped us frame the questions we asked at the early stage of work. Susan Richard, at Boston College, played an indispensable role in the preparation of the manuscript.

Religion and Democracy in the United States

INTRODUCTION

Rosa DeLauro

To be sure, I am not a political scientist or theologian; nor do I study religion's role in politics with an academic's eye. But as a public official, a Democrat, and a Catholic, I do experience it firsthand on an almost daily basis. And so this article is not to be any kind of final analysis but rather something closer to a work in progress: I intend to offer a snapshot of my own faith and its effect on my work as a policy maker today. In the process, I hope to provide a practitioner's opinion on the role that religion ought to play in American democracy.

Religion is an integral part of our national discourse, and there is no doubt that it has played a key role in the last three presidential elections. It is clear that the perspectives and influence of religious communities weigh heavily on our policy debates, whether the issue is poverty, war, the environment, stem-cell research, or reproductive health. Often, this can be a constructive thing: these trends, in no small part, moved Catholic Democrats in the House of Representatives, including me, to draft a Statement of Principles declaring that our faith does have bearing on the broad range of issues that we champion in the Congress and in our communities. It also moved me to work with my colleague, Representative Tim Ryan of Ohio, to draft legislation that seeks common ground on the sensitive issue of abortion.

Other recent developments at the intersection of religion and public life, however, give me reason for concern: legitimate scientific conclusions manipulated toward ideological ends; religiously affiliated organizations allowed to discriminate with taxpayer dollars; and a communion controversy that flared up in 2004 and continues to threaten every Catholic politician's ability to participate in our faith's most sacred ritual. Indeed, too often religious faith has been used cynically as a political weapon and an election-day wedge. Our challenge today—in the Congress, in academia, and even for those in the Church's hierarchy—is to respond by presenting a better alternative.

As a result, I believe that religious faith can and should inform the work of our democracy. It can and should restore government's moral role in society—as long as it respects and promotes the dignity of every human person, calls us to work for the common good, unifies us into a community, and works within the confines of our Constitution and a pluralistic society.

Although these are simple and clear goals, it is also important to recognize that we pursue them in a complicated world and one that is experiencing a significant rise in religious extremism and intolerance. In his essay "Theologies of Democracy in a New Century," E. J. Dionne expressed the dilemma this way: "Religion can create community, and it can divide communities. It can lead to searing self-criticism, and it can promote a pompous self-satisfaction. It can encourage dissent and conformity, generosity and narrow-mindedness."

Those conflicting religious tendencies to unite and divide us are, in the public sphere, essentially tied up with government's own contradictory impulses—its potential to bring people together and its history of tearing them apart. We policy makers and elected officials have a responsibility to confront and grapple with these tensions, to navigate this complicated territory deliberately and thoughtfully. And in the end, if we are able to integrate our religious principles into a public way of life—in other words, put our faith into action—we will then surely bring our faith and values into our public service.

Whether I realized it or not, that process began for me at an early age. I attended Catholic schools from kindergarten through college, where I learned to nourish my mind and my heart—to reach out, to work hard, to fulfill my potential, and to be whatever I wanted to be. But my Catholic upbringing and education also taught me the importance of trying to make a difference in my community and in the lives of our neighbors. In a bigger sense, it taught me the importance of giving something back to my world and to the people of that world.

Growing up Catholic in the 1960s

As the daughter of Italian immigrants growing up in New Haven's Wooster Square neighborhood, I saw that it was the Church that bound us together as a community—in our schools and in our hospitals. Practicing our faith was important in my family. My father received communion daily and lived his faith with commitment. Our local parish was our community center where people gathered to share their lives and help one another. Every night around my family's kitchen table, I saw how the Church could serve as the nexus between family and community. And I witnessed firsthand how my parents helped solve our neighbors' problems.

Both my mother and father went on to serve as elected officials on the New Haven City Council—my mom for thirty-five years, finally retiring at age eighty-five as its longest-serving member. From their example, I learned the vital connections among family, faith, responsibility, and working for the common good. It was the idea that the values I learned at home and at church reached beyond those two places. I saw that we could effect positive change at the community level. With that experience also came the understanding that government can and must play a critical role in lifting people up, helping them to make the most of their own abilities and to meet their responsibilities to one another.

In many ways, my own story is hardly unique. I believe that these shared values have helped guide America's policy makers over the course of our nation's history. Indeed, many of the economic and social achievements of the past century have their roots in a vision of opportunity and community and in a recognition of our obligations to one another. From the GI Bill to Medicaid and Medicare; from Head Start to food stamps; from the child tax credit to the Family Medical Leave Act, each was motivated by the need to ensure the common good.

I often point to the example of Social Security and the philosophy behind it, born in part out of FDR's appreciation for Catholic social teaching and Monsignor John Ryan's advocacy based on the social letters of Pope Pius XI and particularly Pope Leo XIII's *Rerum Novarum,* which served to inspire the progressive politics of the day. It read: "Among the several purposes of a society, one should try to arrange for . . . a fund out of which the members may be effectually helped in their needs, not only in the cases of accident, but also in sickness, old age, and distress."

Social Security is the public policy embodiment of those teachings—a declaration that our human rights are realized in community. Such sentiments are also expressed by FDR's own words to the Congress in 1934: "We are compelled to employ the active interest of the Nation as a whole through government in order to encourage a greater security for each individual who composes it."

For FDR, Social Security was one way we could promote and maintain our shared values, rewarding work and ensuring a decent retirement for those who have worked a lifetime. And by encouraging younger generations to take responsibility, Social Security reinforced the idea that, in America, we do not leave every man or women to fend for himself or herself—and we do not tolerate the impoverishment of our senior population. In America, we meet our shared responsibility to one another.

By the time I came of age in the 1960s, these principles, this idea of the common good, had already taken hold both on the national stage and in my own heart and mind. This was a decade of great cultural and social change—a period that saw the civil rights movement, the Vietnam War, and the Great Society as well as the Second Vatican Council.

Of course, the decade began with the election of a new kind of leader, President John F. Kennedy. Indeed, if President Kennedy inspired a whole generation to take their civic duties seriously, he also created our operating norms for questions of faith in public life when he broke down the barriers that kept Catholics from the highest office of the land.

On September 12, 1960, then-Senator Kennedy answered skeptics worried about his Catholicism in a now-famous speech to the Greater Houston Ministerial Association. He said simply, "I believe in an America where the separation of church and state is absolute—where no Catholic prelate would tell the President . . . how to act and no Protestant minister would tell his parishioners for whom to vote."

He continued, "I believe in an America that is officially neither Catholic, Protestant, nor Jewish—where no public official either requests or accepts instructions on public policy from the Pope, the National Council of Churches, or any other ecclesiastical source." His election affirmed the principle that our public life is enriched by the diversity of views and values that are nurtured in civil society and that are arbitrated in politics to a national conclusion.

I remember the tremendous optimism that accompanied so many momentous steps under Kennedy's leadership to control nuclear arms, advance racial and gender equity, and ameliorate poverty. Both those goals and the values underpinning them would ultimately inspire me and my generation to bring our Catholic identities and values into our public lives for decades to come.

During the same period that our nation elected its first Catholic President, the Church undertook its own transformation. With the Second Vatican Council, we were called to integrate all aspects of our lives—called to live out our Christian vocation in the world and to address the urgent social and economic problems of our time. The temporal order of our lay lives was at once interconnected with our vocation as Christians.

As written in the Pastoral Constitution on the Church in the Modern World, *Gaudium et Spes,*

> Let there, then, be no such pernicious opposition between professional and social activity on the one hand and religious life on the other. Christians who shirk their temporal duties shirk their duties towards his neighbor, neglect God himself, and endanger their eternal salvation. (GS43)

After the Second Vatican Council, things would never be the same, not just with the liturgical changes brought about by the Council but also in the way we understood church as "people of God" and the role of the laity. It was a profound call to be active participants in public life and agents of Christian living *in* the world, not away from it.

That made sense to me: I had seen it as a child. As committed Catholics, my parents lived out their faith in this way. They helped their neighbors, understanding that community was central and being in the right relationship with others was a sign of an active faith. They believed that faith was more about action and works than about words. The model

I grew up with is the model that inspired me to follow a life in public service.

The Politics of Division: The Election of 2004

A lot changed in the four decades that followed Kennedy's presidency and the Second Vatican Council—nothing more so than the relationship between faith and politics.

Whether you supported him or not, it is hard to deny that President George W. Bush's comfort with evangelical language and principles has affected our public discourse. Ever since he responded, in 1999, that Jesus Christ was the political philosopher and thinker with whom he most identified, it was clear that religion would become integral to the politics of his administration.

This was not the case when I came of age politically. According to the Pew Forum, in 1968, only 40 percent of Americans believed their houses of worship should express views on day-to-day social and political questions; 53 percent believed organized religion should keep out of politics. But something changed. Nearly three decades later, by the late 1990s, those numbers had flipped: 54 percent felt their churches had a role in politics, while only 43 percent said they should refrain from discussing politics from the pulpit.

Of course, by now the marriage of convenience between the religious right and the Republican Party has been well documented. But as Democratic members of Congress, we struggled to recognize and respond to that phenomenon. And by 2004, a new religious discourse reached its height of influence at the same time that many Democratic leaders had fallen out of practice in communicating their faith and connecting with religious communities. I never imagined how dramatically those trends would affect the way we elect a president.

To be sure, none of this came about overnight. The issue of abortion, for example, had long been at the center of discussions surrounding faith and politics. For years, many of my colleagues had lived with the issue in the most vivid ways. Since taking office, I had consistently voted to maintain a woman's right to choose an abortion—affirmed by the U.S. Supreme Court; guaranteed in the U.S. Constitution; and supported by the majority of American voters.

Yet because of my legislative record on this one issue, I had been asked to resign from the board of a Catholic Women's High School and was even disinvited from events including a communion breakfast at a local parish. These incidents were hurtful. Although I did not challenge the Church's teaching on this critical issue, I was troubled by the Church's decision to use abortion and make it the sole issue of importance.

In the years preceding 2004, I had worked to raise awareness among my colleagues about faith's implications not just on one issue but on the broad range that we deal with as legislators. In an effort called *Public Voices,* I convened a series of panels and meetings on faith, values, and politics featuring columnist Ron Brownstein, journalist Joe Klein, political theorist Alan Wolfe, Rev. Jim Wallis, Michael Novak of AEI, and Will Marshall of the Progressive Policy Institute. I hosted dinners in my home for my colleagues—all with the hope that some would recognize that, as Democrats, we had to communicate the values and faith that informed our work: we had to make the connection explicit; if not, others would do it for us. Unfortunately many of those meetings saw scant attendance.

Then one day in December 2003, shortly before Christmas, Rep. Nick Lampson of Texas and I discussed our common backgrounds growing up in Italian Catholic households, and before long we were talking about the current state of politics in our religion. We shared a similar frustration, and that spontaneous conversation led to us to bring our colleagues together in the hope of starting a dialogue about the role of our faith in our public lives. That is how we began our unofficial Catholic working group, inviting many guests from the faith and political worlds to speak to us and help us not only to tackle key and controversial issues but also to begin a discussion within our own Caucus.

Uniting us at these meetings as Catholics and Democrats was an understanding of the vital connection between faith and public service—the Catholic tradition we all had grown up with had given each of us a commitment to make a difference engaging in the social and political realm.

These conversations helped me to crystallize my own thoughts. I realized that I had never felt the need to "resolve" my religious faith with my career as a public servant. My church is part of who I am and what I value. Until the presidential election of 2004, it did not occur to me that my church would not be joyful about what I was trying to achieve for people from my role as a legislator.

Yet, for all our advancement and work guided by Catholic social teaching, we increasingly came to find ourselves, especially during the 2004 election, subject to scrutiny from some in the Church hierarchy and the media on but a single issue—abortion. That scrutiny took the form of a handful of bishops threatening to withhold the sacrament of communion based on one's support for a woman's right to choose. For many of us, first inspired by John F. Kennedy—a president who insisted that his religion would not dictate his politics—this threat served as a wake-up call.

Even if this line in the sand were the work of a few bishops, we understood it was time to take a stand. Their decision to single out some of us for our pro-choice position on abortion while failing to show significant interest in all we were doing to advance life and the Church's rich tradition of social justice felt out of balance. We worried it would be ultimately damaging to the Church we loved. In a letter to Cardinal McCarrick in May 2004, forty-eight House Democrats wrote,

> As Catholics, we do not believe it is our role to legislate the teachings of the Catholic Church. For any of us to be singled out by any bishop by the refusal of communion or other public criticism because we vote in what we believe are the requirements of the United States Constitution and laws of our country, which we are sworn to uphold, is deeply hurtful. We would remind those who would deny us participation in the sacrament of the Eucharist that we are sworn to represent all Americans, not just Catholics.

We felt a need to make clear that although some of us differ on the issue of abortion, each and every one of us was committed to the basic principles that are at the heart of Catholic doctrine. As such, when we met with Cardinal McCarrick after sending the letter, our message was simple, frank, and respectful: Democrats had no intention of ceding our faith to those who would use it as a political weapon or to exclude us from our own Catholic tradition. We expressed our belief that religion was being used as a divisive tactic and that the Church's leadership should not embrace that kind of strategy.

We found Cardinal McCarrick to be a caring and spiritual pastor—someone who represented the Church's teaching but at the same time understood the hurt and confusion we were experiencing. Later, we were encouraged when Cardinal McCarrick, speaking at a meeting among Bishops at a Denver conference, expressed concern that if withholding Holy Communion from politicians became a practice, "the sacred nature of the Eucharist might be turned into a partisan political background. Our task force does not advocate the denial of Communion for Catholic politicians or Catholic voters in these circumstances . . . We do not want to encourage confrontations at the altar rail with the body of the Lord Jesus in our hands."

We may have been successful in preventing the church from endorsing such a radical stance as denial of communion at large. Yet the politicization of Catholicism proved effective for the Bush campaign in the 2004 election—from threatening to deny communion to pro-choice politicians like John Kerry to a concerted effort by the Republican Party to use the Church as a political organizing tool in key battleground states. And the result was a serious defection among Catholics to vote Republican. Democrats lost the Catholic vote 52 to 47 percent, with 14 percent of white Catholics who voted for Bill Clinton in 1996 choosing *not* to vote for John Kerry.

With those results and the new reality they signaled, our unofficial Catholic working group, including Members on both sides of the abortion debate, began to realize the need to engage in a more reflective process. In the first six months of 2005, we held numerous sessions with academics, Catholic thinkers, and theologians to help us process, reflect, and decide on a path of action

That led us to loudly challenge the Administration's federal budgets that consistently proposed to cut essential programs for working families and the poor. For many of us, brought up in the tradition of Catholic social teaching, the federal budget should reflect our values and advance the moral responsibilities of government. Yet, in reality, these budgets, especially those following President Bush's reelection in 2004, *offended* the common good. Budget after budget, the Administration's proposals targeted important agencies such as the Department of Health and Human Services squarely behind the bulls eye for drastic cuts.

The budget released in early 2005, for example, increased tax cuts for the wealthy by $106 billion over five years while it dramatically cut funding for vital human needs programs. Among the most damaging were $10 billion taken from Medicaid as well as $212 billion in cuts to domestic discretionary spending over five years—including funding for child nutrition, student loans, pensions, vocational rehabilitation, Head Start, and child care. The Church would no doubt send letters to Congress against these cuts. It understood that the Bush budgets represented a threat to working people with the lowest incomes and sent the wrong message to the world about our nation's values.

Yet we felt the need to go beyond simply highlighting the connection between budgets and values. One morning in July 2005, we gathered to discuss what to do next and what to do about the fact that Democrats were still being portrayed as godless heathens by those who disagreed with our political views.

We Catholic Democrats had been meeting for nearly two years. We had already written Cardinal McCarrick and met with him. And we felt a strong and deep conviction that much was at stake for the country as well as for our tradition of religious pluralism. The time had come to speak up and speak clearly on this complex and highly personal matter, to make clear that ours was a vibrant moral agenda that speaks to a broad array of issues informed by our faith, and to do so with a newfound boldness and energy.

So we drafted the following statement of principles, which was signed by fifty-five Catholic Democrats:

Statement of Principles
By Fifty-Five Catholic Democrats in the
U.S. House of Representatives

As Catholic Democrats in Congress, we are proud to be part of the living Catholic tradition—a tradition that promotes the common good, expresses a consistent moral framework for life and highlights the need to provide a collective safety net to those individuals in society who are most in need. As legislators, in the U.S. House of Representatives, we work every day to advance respect for life and the dignity of every human being. We believe that government has moral purpose.

We are committed to making real the basic principles that are at the heart of Catholic social teaching: helping the poor and disadvantaged, protecting the most vulnerable among us, and ensuring that all Americans of every faith are given meaningful opportunities to share in the blessings of this great country. That commitment is fulfilled in different ways by legislators but includes: reducing the rising rates of poverty; increasing access to education for all; pressing for increased access to health care; and taking seriously the decision to go to war. Each of these issues challenges our obligations as Catholics to community and helping those in need.

We envision a world in which every child belongs to a loving family and agree with the Catholic Church about the value of human life and the undesirability of abortion—we do not celebrate its practice. Each of us is committed to reducing the number of unwanted pregnancies and creating an environment with policies that encourage pregnancies to be carried to term. We believe this includes promoting alternatives to abortion, such as adoption, and improving access to children's healthcare and child care, as well as policies that encourage paternal and maternal responsibility.

In all these issues, we seek the Church's guidance and assistance but believe also in the primacy of conscience. In recognizing the Church's role in providing moral leadership, we acknowledge and accept the tension that comes with being in disagreement with the Church in some areas. Yet we believe we can speak to the fundamental issues that unite us as Catholics and lend our voices to changing the political debate—a debate that often fails to reflect and encompass the depth and complexity of these issues.

As legislators, we are charged with preserving the Constitution, which guarantees religious freedom for all Americans. In doing so, we guarantee our right to live our own lives as Catholics, but also foster an America with a rich diversity of faiths. We believe the separation of church and state allows for our faith to inform our public duties.

As Catholic Democrats who embrace the vocation and mission of the laity as expressed by Pope John Paul II in his Apostolic Exhortation,

Christifideles Laici, we believe that the Church is the "people of God," called to be a moral force in the broadest sense. We believe the Church as a community is called to be in the vanguard of creating a more just America and world. And as such, we have a claim on the Church's bearing as it does on ours.

To be clear, we were aware that some would accuse us of political opportunism—of trying to broaden the Democratic Party's appeal by reframing the abortion debate. But I believe our statement came out of a deeper reality than that. I know it came from a desire to rescue the Catholic faith as we had lived it from those who would take it from us. It came from the experiential recognition that others were defining us by seeking to dissolve the connection between our party's public priorities and the values that have always guided them.

And so as much as the statement was an acknowledgment that faith does matter in today's public discourse, more importantly it was a means for us to define *ourselves*—to declare that our Catholic faith has bearing on the broad range of issues that we champion here in the Congress and in our communities. It was a way to communicate to the public not only the principles that guide us but also to make explicit their policy implications on everything from increasing access to education for all and pressing for real health care reform to taking seriously the decisions to go to war and to reduce poverty.

The document was also motivated by a broad agreement that so many of the decisions being made by this Congress have clear social and moral implications that directly contradict our values as Catholics. These include decisions that have benefited the few at the expense of the larger community and have made it harder for parents to raise their children and balance the pressures of work and family. This latter issue includes everything from our lack of investment in health care to neglect of child care and education.

Our Statement of Principles offered a powerful tool to engage a potentially polarizing landscape in a constructive way. It marked the beginning of a newfound unity among Catholic Democrats in Congress and also started a long overdue conversation about how we should be communicating our faith. But the greatest challenge ahead lay in translating that unity from principles to practice, finding common ground not just in big statements but on real policy solutions.

Toward a Politics of Unity

We knew our statement would evoke a mixed response. In the National Catholic Reporter Sister Joan Chittister saw a complicated history behind our words: "We are into theological stew like we haven't seen for decades. Take one part 'primacy of conscience,' add one part 'people of God,' salt with 'as much bearing on the church as the church has on ours' and stir. Depending on how you see it, that is either a recipe for renewal or a recipe for revolution."

For her, that struck a chord: "From where I stand, it seems to me that the laity of the church has heard the church's recognition of the 'lay vocation.' And, furthermore, they are beginning to take it seriously."

But certainly, not everyone embraced our efforts. The religious right failed to see our Statement of Principles outside of the usual black-and-white framework they had grown accustomed to and instead pushed back against the idea that anyone serious about her faith could also be a serious member of the Democratic Party. The Catholic League ridiculed our words and announced that we were "driven by fear." Yet, that is not how we felt at all. Instead, it seemed as if there were something new and exciting on the horizon, and the politics of division were about to change.

Throughout 2006, Congressman Tim Ryan of Ohio and I worked together to introduce *The Reducing the Need for Abortion and Supporting Parents Act* in September of that year. Although one might call Congressman Ryan "pro-life" or antiabortion, and I am staunchly in favor of a woman's right to choose, we both recognized something elemental about the abortion debate—that it was time to forge consensus and find common ground. We recognized that a majority of the American people still support *Roe v. Wade*. And despite our differences, we both want to see fewer abortions, not more—and we understood that the first step toward making that possible was helping women never to have to come to that decision in the first place.

Our bill focused on the need to reduce abortion in our country while at the same time it provided supports for new parents to strengthen their families. The bill's language makes clear that those of us who support the right to choose do not "celebrate abortion," as some have suggested. It simply says that absent prevention, absent contraception, and absent family planning, you simply cannot reduce the rate of abortion. In addition our bill asserts that there is much positive action we can take in this arena by improving access to safe, affordable, and effective contraceptive methods; by restoring the Medicaid entitlement to coverage of Family Planning Services; and by providing grants to states to reduce teen pregnancy.

It also creates an environment that encourages pregnancies to be carried to term, promoting alternatives to abortion, such as adoption, as well as improving access to children's health care and child care. By providing a comprehensive approach to this issue—from increased funding for child care assistance to after-school programs to nutritional support through food stamps—our legislation promotes real parental responsibility once the child is born. And it does so by reducing the economic pressures that can sometimes cause a woman to decide against carrying a pregnancy to term.

Of all the important goals this legislation can help us reach, perhaps the most important is simple forward progress beyond the question of legality and toward actually reducing the need for abortion. Our goal has been to break the stalemate and show that Catholics not only are ready to take action on this critical issue but are ready to lead.

The fact is that by the second half of the second Bush term, the religious right's influence had begun to wane. As the president's popularity and credibility began to unravel—which some would say started with his failed and misguided drive to privatize Social Security and the government's botched response to Hurricane Katrina—Democrats were able to regain the Congress in the midterm elections of 2006 and begin to set a new direction for the country.

Again, E. J. Dionne described it as "part of a larger decline of style of ideological conservatism that reached high points in 1980 and 1994 but suffered a series of decisive—and I believe fatal—setbacks during George W. Bush's second term."

This decline created an opportunity and an urgency for Democrats to provide an alternative. And in a significant way, religious Democrats learning the lessons of the 2004 election were in a much better position to tell their story and share their experiences.

Indeed, with the new majority in Congress came new opportunities to push forward the common-ground agenda on abortion we Catholic Democrats and others had been working toward. We sought new ways to make our legislation a reality. And in Representative David Obey, Chairman of the Appropriations Committee, we found someone who understood what Tim Ryan and I were trying to achieve. With his support, we were able to include several new programs and increased funding in the fiscal year 2008 Health and Human Services Spending Bill—for programs such as Title X, Healthy Start, teen pregnancy prevention, adoption awareness, after-school programs, and child-care programs for new parents attending college, just to name a few. This was welcome news after more than six years of stagnant funding in these areas.

What is more, this was evidence that we were not just going to talk about common ground but that we could actually find our way there as policy makers. So by the time the Democratic Party, now led by Senator Barack Obama, approved its platform in 2008 in Denver, it included new language specifically about reducing the need for abortion:

> The Democratic Party also strongly supports access to affordable family planning services and comprehensive age-appropriate sex

> education which empower people to make informed choices and live healthy lives. We also recognize that such health care and education help reduce the number of unintended pregnancies and thereby also reduce the need for abortions.
>
> The Democratic Party also strongly supports a woman's decision to have a child by ensuring access to and availability of programs for pre- and postnatal health care, parenting skills, income support, and caring adoption programs.

An effort that began not long ago as an informal conversation and a working group among my peers was now essentially codified by our party as integral to its core philosophy. It certainly marked new territory for our party.

But beyond the abortion issue, there was also a new understanding that attacks from the right would not go unanswered. When the Catholic League's President Bill Donohue described Barack Obama's Catholic council as a bunch of "Catholic dissidents" for diverging from the Vatican line, as Democrats, we refused to take the insult silently. We pushed back publicly. I signed a letter with more than three dozen elected officials, academics, and community leaders; in it we called out Donohue directly for his history of divisive rhetoric:

> Mr. Donohue, your work to fight legitimate cases of anti-Catholic bigotry in this country should be applauded. But when you smear other Catholics with whom you disagree, you betray your own cause. Our measure of what it means to be a "good" Catholic is not defined by the narrow pronouncements of partisan operatives; but rather by the rich teachings of our Church and our informed consciences.

But playing defense was only half the battle. And if the Obama campaign was engaged in responding to the politics of division by not letting any attack go unanswered, they were also busy crafting something much bigger and lasting—a new narrative of unity. And our new conversation about faith would be a part of it.

This narrative was not entirely new—it was the culmination of a process. Of course, we know those themes had taken root during Obama's star-making 2004 Democratic Convention speech. But it was not long before they began to really take flight. In 2006 before the Call to Renewal Conference in Washington, we could see the blueprint coming to life:

> When we ignore the debate about what it means to be a good Christian or Muslim or Jew; when we discuss religion only in the negative sense of where or how it should not be practiced, rather than in the positive sense of what it tells us about our obligations towards one another; when we shy away from religious venues and religious broadcasts because we assume that we will be unwelcome, others

will fill the vacuum, those with the most insular views of faith, or those who cynically use religion to justify partisan ends.

And so two years later, by the time we had reached the general election, it was the Democrat, not his Republican opponent, who was widely considered to be the so-called "faith" candidate. And he would call on that faith differently—not to divide people but to bring them together.

Obama turned away from the hot-button culture wars and instead has turned consistently to the big challenges of these historic times to apply the values and guidance of his faith. Like our Catholic Working Group, he made the point that honoring his core beliefs was less about standing in the right place on a few narrowly defined issues and more about moving forward on a broad range of issues that affect people's families every day.

"My faith teaches me that I can sit in church and pray all I want, but I won't be fulfilling God's will unless I go out and do the Lord's work," Obama said shortly after becoming the presumptive nominee in June 2008.

And he captured a growing desire in the American people to get the big things right. A Faith in Public Life poll released the week after the 2008 election showed that religious voters want a broad agenda. Only 20 percent of evangelicals and 12 percent of Catholics say an agenda focused primarily on abortion and same-sex marriage best reflects their values. All religious groups in 2008 ranked the economy as their top priority.

During the fall of 2008, I traveled to battleground states such as Michigan, Pennsylvania, and Ohio to campaign for Barack Obama. And everywhere I went—senior centers, community centers, and diners, with small groups of undecided voters or at big rallies of Obama supporters, with groups of Catholic voters or often Italian-American gatherings—people everywhere wanted to hear our plan to steer the economy back in the right direction: health care and education, vibrant communities, and a strong safety net. With America facing an economic crisis greater than any since the Great Depression, a middle class hit hard by job insecurity, stagnant wages, rising health care costs, and a financial market in crisis, they wanted a leader who shared their values, understood their aspirations, and honored their hard work.

In November 2008, Obama won 54 percent of Catholic votes—an increase of 7 percent over John Kerry's showing in 2004. And even though he only won 26 percent of evangelical and born-again voters, that number was up 5 percent from 2004 as well. To me the results served as an affirmation that voters were searching not for just one or two divisive issues to dominate the public discourse but for political and policy debates to be framed in terms of values shared by all Americans. I believe this understanding represents the foundation that our nation's new leadership has set out to build on today.

I know that as we try to restore our economy and, with it, the middle class, no investment is more critical than the one we make in our human capital—the investment we make in our *one* human family and our society's ability to give its people work and purpose and willingness to take care of its most vulnerable.

The relationship between faith and politics has changed significantly since the 1960s when I first considered its impact on my life and our democracy. But people continue to hunger for authentic leadership that promises to strengthen our communities and make opportunity real. It has always been that way—a simple yearning for leaders who share a common purpose for the common good. Growing up in Wooster Square, I saw it around our dinner table. In 1960, I saw it in John F. Kennedy inspiring a nation to dream, to sacrifice, and to serve. And I see it right now, even in these challenging days, a new hope and honest faith that hard work will mean progress once again.

PART I

Religious Pluralism and American Democracy

Chapter 1

POLITICAL SCIENCE, DEMOCRACY, AND RELIGION

Alan Wolfe

Political Science Catches Up

"Scarcely any political question," wrote Alexis de Tocqueville in one of the most widely cited sentences in *Democracy in America*, "arises in the United States that is not resolved, sooner or later, into a judicial question."[1] If he were writing today, Tocqueville might be tempted to say that however any political question ends up, it originates as a religious one. Scarcely an election takes place or a policy is proposed before someone brings religion into the conversation. Some celebrate its presence, while others condemn it, but both agree that to understand what is happening in American politics, religion has to be accounted for.

Since at least the writings of Seymour Martin Lipset, Tocqueville's analyses of democracy have been elevated to the status of social science classics, joining the ranks of Marx, Weber, and Durkheim.[2] Every time we talk about voluntary associations, public opinion, self-interest rightly understood, or the tyranny of the majority, we echo themes first touched on by our French visitor. Tocqueville's reputation as a social theorist can be exaggerated because he was not a systematic thinker and never really compared the United States to other countries. But his recognition of the power of the democratic forces being unleashed in the first decades of the nineteenth century lives on.

Much the same could be said for Tocqueville's writings on religion. Just as he was a Frenchman writing about America, Tocqueville was a Catholic discussing the pervasive influence of Protestantism. "There is no country in the world where the Christian religion retains a greater influence over the souls of men than in America," he proclaimed, a statement that not only reflects the Second Great Awakening that immediately preceded his visit but extends to the many religious revivals that have taken place since.[3] Every time we talk about the importance of the local congregation, the voluntaristic impulses of America's faith traditions, or the tendency of American religions to grow by recruiting new members, we are indebted to Tocqueville's analysis.

Tocqueville may have been the most insightful visitor to explore the relationship between democracy and religion in the United States, but he was by no means the only one. Max Weber came to this country in the early years of the twentieth century to visit the St. Louis World's Fair, and he too kept his eyes and ears open during his visit. In an essay on the Protestant sects that seemed so prevalent in American life—and to which Tocqueville had also called attention—Weber argued that, especially in newly settled regions of the United States, religion acted as a kind of moral credit agency. "Admission to the local Baptist congregation," he wrote, "follows only upon the most careful 'probation' and after closest inquiries into conduct going back to early childhood."[4] Economic enterprise required conditions of trust, but social newness did not give people appropriate cues about who could be trusted and who should be shunned. Into the vacuum flowed the local congregation. People would prove their worthiness to each other by demonstrating their faith in God.

With historical predecessors as illustrious as Tocqueville and Weber, it might seem axiomatic that the social sciences in general, and political science in particular, would have developed a long-standing interest in religion. Yet something closer to the opposite actually took place: as religion became more important in American public life, the study of religion by American political scientists went into a tailspin. During the 1950s, for example, Billy Graham's career as a public evangelist took off; the man spoke at huge rallies, not only in rural parts of the country but in the heart of Manhattan at Madison Square Garden. At the same time, conservative Catholics, concerned primarily about Soviet influence over such countries as Poland or Italy from which their families had originally come, formed political organizations determined to push the United States in a right-wing direction, especially with respect to its foreign policy. Yet the only major work done by a social scientist during this period, Will Herberg's *Protestant, Catholic, Jew*, was written by a political activist (first of the left, then of the right) teaching at Drew University in New Jersey.[5] At more prestigious universities, scholars, having endorsed the so-called secularization thesis, simply assumed that as the United States became more modern, religion would lose its influence. In addition, the 1950s saw the spread of quantitative techniques and behavioral approaches in American political science, and the study of religion, as subjective an area of interest as one can imagine, seemed difficult to reconcile with the objectivity so important to scholarship at that time.

As a consequence of these trends, religion was assigned a second-class status among subjects explored by American political scientists. Given what was happening in America in the decade that followed the 1950s—the election of a Catholic to the White House in 1960, the Goldwater campaign of 1964, and the first stirrings of the Christian Right, the March on Washington for civil rights led by a Baptist preacher from Georgia, Buddhists setting themselves on fire in Vietnam to protest the war, and the outbreak of spiritual fervor associated with the counterculture—the gap between the political scientists and the public only widened. In their examination of articles published in the *American Political Science Review*, for example, Kenneth D. Wald and Clyde Wilcox found that, over the course of its life, the journal on average published one article on religion every three years, and although there had been a slight uptick in more recent years (twenty-five articles dealing with religion in the period between 1960 and 2002), the attention devoted to the subject remained minimal.[6] The reason, they argued, cannot lie in the fact that political scientists had retreated into some kind of cave unaware of the real world around them because more articles on gender and race, two other subjects of wide and increasing interest during the post–World War II period, were published than articles on religion. Nor was the cause for neglect characteristic of social science in general; sociologists paid more attention to religion in their flagship journals than did political scientists. Despite the fact that larger numbers of Americans, unlike Western Europeans, continued to attend church and to have their political behavior influenced by their religious preferences, political scientists were unwilling to give religion its due.

A general dearth of scholarly articles on the subject, moreover, constituted just one area of general neglect. Political science departments are typically organized by fields of interest such as American politics, comparative politics, international relations, and political theory. The subject of religion can be taught in any of them. Yet undergraduate courses on religion and politics during the 1950s and 1960s in any of these fields were few and far between. To cite only one example, Wellesley College offered no undergraduate courses on religion at all from 1989 until 1996; starting in the latter year, it began offering "Religion and American Politics" and added courses on religion and ethnic conflict in 2000. One might think the situation would be different at Boston College, where I teach, because BC is a Jesuit/Catholic university with a distinct religious mission. To some degree it is, as BC offered one course in the earlier period on church-state relations. But it was not until the mid-1990s that a regular undergraduate course on "Religion and American Politics" was added to the curriculum. Just as political scientists were engaged in relatively little research on religion during this period, they were also not focused on religion when it came to teaching.

To be fair, it should be pointed out that a tendency to ignore religion could also be found in other fields in which the subject deserved more widespread treatment, none more so than journalism. It is not that newspapers ignored religion, but from the end of World War II until the early 1970s, they treated it in roughly the same way they treated movies: listing services taking place over the weekend or reporting on church-sponsored charitable affairs. One study, for example, showed that, in Mark Silk's summary of its findings, "by 1975 religious news space had reached its lowest ebb in [*New York*] *Times* history."[7] It became a common complaint among religious activists, including those who would become leaders of the religious right, that the media was dominated by secularists who showed little interest in them or the faiths for which they spoke. At least for a time, there seems to have been some truth in their complaints.

In more recent years, the trends I have been describing have begun to change, in some cases dramatically so. Many newspapers, responding to the obvious importance of the subject, started hiring full-time religion reporters and assigning them to cover political developments; between 1972 and 1982, according to yet another study, the number of column inches in American newspapers devoted to religion more than doubled.[8] Such a rate of growth in religion coverage is difficult to sustain, and in just the past few years the competitive pressures on newspapers stemming from the rise of the Internet and decreases in readership have led to cutbacks in this area.[9] Still, media coverage of religion remains at a high level. Significant support, moreover, exists for such coverage. The Templeton Foundation now offers an annual prize for religion reporting. The Pew Forum on Religion and American Public Life carries out extensive surveys, conducted in conjunction with academic political scientists, that are featured prominently in the media. The Religion and Ethics Newsweekly sponsors programs on public television and does its own reporting. No one could credibly claim that religion is currently undiscovered territory in the U.S. media. If anything, newspapers and television go out of their way to find religious angles on stories that, at first glance, do not seem to have one, including stories on shopping malls and day-care centers.[10]

A similar reversal of the cycle is fortunately taking place in political science. The American Political Science Association (APSA) allows members to define areas of interest, and religion is now among the most popular of these designations. The "Religion and Politics" section, which was founded among APSA members to further research on the subject, is among the fastest growing in the discipline; 335 people joined the section in 1989 as compared to 628 in 2007. (By way of contrast, the section on "Federalism and Intergovernmental Relations" declined from 506 to 296; "Urban Politics" dropped from 347 to 344; and "Political Psychology" increased from 292 to 426.)[11] The section, in addition, has begun to publish a scholarly journal, *Religion and Politics*. Not unsurprisingly, more political science departments are teaching courses on religion and politics. Of the five colleges surveyed in the Boston area, three, Boston College, Brandeis University, and Harvard University, currently feature undergraduate courses dealing with religion.

As part of this renewed interest in religion among political scientists, Ira Katznelson of Columbia University, president of the APSA in 2005–06, convened a task force on the subject of "Religion and Democracy in the United States." APSA task forces have had a long history, going back to the publication of *Toward a More Responsible Two-Party System* in 1950. In more recent years, task forces have been convened on inequality and American democracy, political violence and terrorism, difference and inequality in the developing world, civic education, and interdisciplinarity.

The aim of an APSA task force is to bring together prominent scholars dealing with a specific subject in order to pool their expertise and to write a report bringing the best knowledge on the topic to the general informed public. Katznelson asked me to chair the task force on religion and democracy. The following, each of whom has written a chapter for this volume, agreed to serve: Allison Calhoun-Brown, Georgia State University; Bette Novit Evans, Creighton University; James L. Gibson, Washington University; John C. Green, University of Akron and Pew Forum; Fredrick C. Harris, Columbia University; Amaney Jamal, Princeton University; Geoffrey C. Layman, University of Notre Dame; David L. Leal, University of Texas; Nancy L. Rosenblum, Harvard University; Kenneth D. Wald, University of Florida; and Clyde Wilcox, Georgetown University.

In assembling this task force, Katznelson and I sought to bring together scholars in three areas of the discipline: the study of American politics using primarily empirical methods; political philosophy; and constitutional law. No effort was made to ascertain the faith commitments (or lack of them) of any of the members; our objective was neither to apologize for religion or specific religions nor to join those writers well known for their criticisms of people of faith. Our intent was to select political scientists whose publications had made them leaders in the emerging field of religion and politics and to ask them to share with each other the insights yielded by their respective approaches.

Our specific focus was on the relationship between religion and democracy in the United States, asking ourselves many of the same questions that Tocqueville posed to us many years ago: Is religion healthy for democracy because it encourages civic participation and the expression of ideas or dangerous because it is associated with sectarianism and dogmatism? If religion, as our founders believed, reinforces morality, can we have a common morality in the absence of a dominant religion? How is religious pluralism best managed? Has separation of church and state posed religion against democracy or helped the two reinforce each other? In what ways will religion's role in American democracy be shaped by the inclusion of religious voices outside the Judeo-Christian tradition?

The task force met six times between 2006 and 2007. As each member developed a topic on which to write, all members engaged in extensive discussion with each other. The result, we hope, is an edited volume with more coherence than one sometimes finds in books of this sort. In particular, members made every possible effort to integrate their findings with people whose approach differed from their own, for example, by linking empirical findings with the approaches of political philosophy—and vice versa. In what follows, I offer an overview of the main conclusions that our task force reached.

Religious Pluralism and American Democracy

"With equal pleasure," wrote John Jay in *Federalist* #2,

> I have as often taken notice that Providence has been pleased to give this one connected country to one united people—a people descended from the same ancestors, speaking the same language, professing the same religion, attached to the same principles of government, very similar in their manners and customs, and who, by their joint counsels, arms, and efforts, fighting side by side throughout a long and bloody war, have nobly established general liberty and independence.[12]

Some of what he said was true: Americans were indeed similar in their customs at the time of the founding. But they did not all belong to same religion: Jews were present in the United States from the start, and one of the original colonies, Maryland, was inhabited primarily by Catholics. Religious pluralism has been a fact of life in the United States since the time of its creation.

The extent of religious diversity in the present-day United States, of course, is much greater than it was in John Jay's time. The gold standard on the issue of religious diversity is the "U.S. Religious Landscape Survey" released by the Pew Forum on Religion and Public Life in June 2008. Its findings are striking: 78.4 percent of Americans identify themselves as Christians of one denomination or another, which seems to suggest the dominance of just one tradition in this country. But that figure is deceiving. In fact, those claiming to be Protestant constitute a bare majority of 51.5 percent, while 4.7 percent belong to non-Christian religious traditions such as Judaism, Islam, or Buddhism, and 16.1 percent of Americans consider themselves unaffiliated. Such numbers, moreover, capture a picture frozen in time and in that sense do not convey just how fluid the religious identification of Americans can be. By Pew's estimate, 44 percent of Americans are religious switchers (if one includes changing from one Protestant denomination to another). When the effects of recent immigration are added to the picture, the religious pluralism of the United States becomes even more striking. True, the percentage of Muslims uncovered by Pew was low (0.6 percent), although, as Amaney Jamal argues in her essay in this volume (see chapter 3), this estimate is most likely too low. But Pew also found robust numbers of Buddhists and Hindus. As the Pew study underscores, not only does the United States lack a majority religion, it lacks anything even close to one.[13]

Some sense of the changing demographics of American religion, as well as the implications of these trends for American politics, is offered by John Green in his chapter for this book (chapter 2). Green takes 1960, the year in which Americans for the first (and only) time elected a Catholic to the presidency, as a point of historical comparison. The fact that 33.9 percent of Americans in 1960 were mainline Protestants is striking; here was a group sufficiently large in size to offer at least a glimmer of what it would be like to serve as an established religion. These, after all, were years in which there existed much talk about an American "establishment," the bulk of whose members—university presidents, U.S. Senators, corporate CEOs—were white Anglo-Saxon Protestants.[14] The single largest group of Catholics, moreover, were, in Green's terms, "traditionalists," reflecting the fact that pre–Vatican II Catholics lived in predominantly ethnic parishes emphasizing respect for authority and traditional gender roles. The two largest Christian groups, in other words, projected images of stability and continuity in 1960, if in very different ways. Although exceptionally diverse, American religious life at that time was also well organized. As Herberg had emphasized in his 1955 book, Americans of that era placed a great deal of emphasis on belonging; religion served, among other things, as a source of identification of community.

At the same time, the 1960s would become known for the attacks on that establishment, symbolized by "the best and the brightest" whose arrogance led the country into war—and in that way came under attack both from the New Left and the emerging New Right.[15] Challenged in the most dramatic fashion, the leading figures of the mainline Protestant establishment—John Lindsay, mayor of New York; Kingman Brewster, president of Yale; National Security Advisor McGeorge Bundy—lost the authority they once embodied.[16] Also at the same time the Second Vatican Council took the first steps toward modernizing Catholicism in ways that would begin to undermine more traditional ways of life; as Green's data suggest, the percentage of traditional Catholics was cut in half between 1960 and 1984 while centrist and modernist Catholics expanded. The political consequences of both of these developments would prove enormously important. On the one hand, the demise of the New England Protestant establishment prefigured the transformation of the Republican Party into a Southern and Western party with a far more conservative face. On the other, post–Vatican II Catholicism would prove to be both more theologically liberal but also more politically independent, breaking the link between Catholics and urban political machines and removing from the ranks of reliable Democratic voters those who were economically liberal but culturally conservative. If one is seeking an explanation of why the United States elected a liberal Democrat in 1960 and a conservative Republican in 2004, the changes in these two important religious groups ought to be viewed as major factors.

As Green's chapter suggests, the demographics of American religion look very different in 2004 compared to those of 1960: there were both more evangelicals and more unaffiliated people in the former year compared to the latter. Not surprisingly, religious diversity is accompanied by a significant amount of political diversity: three-quarters of traditionalist evangelicals believe that American democracy is based on Christian values, for example, compared to slightly more than a third of unaffiliated secularists, an accurate reflection of how Americans can be polarized over an important issue. Yet on the crucial question of religious diversity itself, there is less diversity of opinion: surprising agreement exists across the religious divide, for whereas 90 percent or more of the more liberal groups see the benefits of religious pluralism, so do 74 percent of the most conservative group. Religious pluralism is not only a fact of American public value, it is also a widely endorsed value.

The true test for American religious pluralism may emerge from groups outside the Judeo-Christian tradition, especially, in the wake of September 11, 2001, Muslims. In her contribution to this volume, Amaney Jamal provides important data on this issue. Relying on the first systematic poll of Muslim Americans ever taken in this country, Jamal demonstrates the extent to which Muslims share the same democratic values as non-Muslims in the United States. Generally speaking, Muslims tend to be socially and morally conservative but economically more liberal. Few of them endorse radical actions such as suicide bombings. They attend mosque in roughly the same rate that Christians attend churches. Although a significant number of them put more emphasis on their religion than their country (47 percent), so do a similar number of Christians (42 percent). Most important for the issue of religious pluralism, they associate with people from many religious backgrounds: a mere 12 percent of Jamal's respondents led lives essentially contained within the Muslim community. In perhaps the only somewhat jarring note, 26 percent of them believed that Muslim Americans should remain distinct from the larger American society, but otherwise, Muslim Americans are very much like immigrant groups from non-Protestant backgrounds in the past: wanting to hold onto their traditions even as they adjust themselves to the demands of a highly pluralistic society. Especially in contrast to Western Europe, where both anti-Muslim sentiment and support for radical Islam are greater, religious pluralism, which was once more or less confined to the Judeo-Christian tradition, can be expanded to include other religious groups.

How can pluralism best be managed in the United States? This is the question that preoccupies Bette Novit Evans in her chapter (chapter 4). It is a widely accepted conclusion among scholars of American constitutional law that the U.S. Supreme Court has failed to find consistent principles for resolving the tensions built into the First Amendment.[17] Evans offers a more optimistic take. The First Amendment, she argues, is part and parcel of a much broader approach to pluralism represented by such institutional realities as the separation of powers and federalism. The way we conduct things here is to do them in ways that prevent any one group or person from monopolizing power to further parochial interests. Not all are pleased with this widespread commitment to pluralism; in the 1960s and 1970s, liberals favored more centralized authority in the presidency, for example, whereas in more recent years conservatives have done so. Arguments over the merits of pluralism are as constant as pluralism in America is permanent.

Yet there is little doubt that America's pluralist political culture makes the management of religious diversity possible. Evans discusses religious traditions such as the Amish and some ultra-Orthodox Jewish sects that seek to seal themselves off from the rest of society; generally, although not always, we seek to accommodate such groups and, in so doing, to send the message that our polity is strong enough to absorb the concerns of groups at the margins. At the same time, Evans continues, pluralism helps to check the power of majority religions in specific states or regions from imposing their views on subjects such as the teaching of creationism on those who belong to minority religions or no religion at all. When we add the important fact that courts themselves serve to reinforce pluralism because they are one political institution among three, the pluralistic bias in our constitutional system is further reinforced. No one institution tells us what to do just as no one institution tells us what to believe.

The conclusion at which Evans arrives is important to reiterate. From time to time one hears calls in the United States for a greater emphasis on common American values. This in itself is not dangerous and reflects an understandable desire to overcome the fractiousness and partisanship that characterize American life. Yet for those who believe that religion offers the most appropriate language for moral conversation, calls for a common morality can lead to calls for a common religion. This is a trap the United States avoided at its founding when it opted to separate church and state. And it is a trap that must be avoided now when religious diversity is even more extensive than it was then. It is not the job of the task force on Religion and American Democracy of the American Political Science Association to make a normative case on behalf of religious pluralism. But it is very much our role as students of American politics to call attention to pluralism as a fact of life of the American political system. Given our history, our Constitution, and such present realities as immigration, we will always be religiously pluralistic. Finding the best way to manage our pluralism is a task that should properly engage the attention of both scholars of American politics and American citizens.

Religion and Democratic Values

When Tocqueville came to the United States in the early 1830s, he left behind a continent in which the histories of religion and politics had long been intertwined. France, Tocqueville's own country, had perfected the notion of the divine right of kings: the monarchy's claim to political legitimacy was based on the notion that the king spoke on behalf of God. Leading religious figures such as Cardinal Richelieu became simultaneously leading political figures, using their power in one realm to reinforce their influence in the other. Even after the French Revolution toppled the monarchy, France remained an overwhelmingly Catholic country shaped by the Church's deep involvement with politics. It was not until the early years of the twentieth century that France broke the long-established link between political and religious authority. What the political philosopher Mark Lilla calls the Great Separation, the rejection of a political theology that rooted the ultimate authority of the state in the authority exercised by God, took centuries to work itself out on the European continent.[18]

Although the Protestant Reformation had first promised a break with the Catholic tradition of blending religious and political authority, even Europe's Protestant countries were slow to make the great separation. Martin Luther, fearful of the radical movements that took his appeal to individual conscience too literally, moved in the direction of political authoritarianism. John Calvin, his fellow Protestant reformer, created a theocracy in his city-state of Geneva. The Church of England was officially Protestant but also the church of the realm. To this day, even Denmark, perhaps the most secular country in the world, retains a Lutheran established church. Church and state had too many overlapping interests—both sought legitimacy, codified law, punished dissent, and claimed authority—to wander off in different directions. There always existed antagonism and conflict between them, but it was caused primarily by their attempts to occupy the same space.

The American Revolution constituted the first, and to this day the most important, attempt to create separate realms for political power and religious salvation. In part this was because some of the founders, such as

Thomas Jefferson, were quite familiar with the dangerous ways religion and politics had interacted in Europe. Jefferson was a deist, someone who believes that God set the world in motion only then to refrain from playing a role in the course it took. So, too, were all the other early presidents of the United States, up to and including the fifth one James Monroe, the only exception being the Unitarian—and thus unconventional Christian—John Adams.[19] These were men who had been touched by the Enlightenment.[20] Religion, in their view, was all too frequently associated with ignorance, bigotry, and sectarianism to be trusted with official state power in the new republic.

At the same time, as a number of important scholars have demonstrated, separation of church and state came to the United States at the urging of numerous believers as well.[21] Influenced in part by John Locke, who was both a liberal theorist and a devout Christian, they argued that religion needed distance from government in order to thrive.[22] Just as avoiding the inefficiencies of mercantilism would allow the free market to flourish, bypassing the inefficiencies of a state church would allow churches to grow by recruiting new members, all attracted because religion would appeal to them personally. The delinking of church and state, in their view, would be good for religion by fostering good religion. The pure air of religious freedom would produce more authentic devotion.

Both Enlightenment-influenced liberals and free-market Protestants were raising what contemporary political scientists would call an empirical question: Does religion promote sectarianism, or does it encourage tolerance? This is the kind of question that political scientists can answer with empirical tools. Three of the chapters in this book try to do just that.

In his chapter (chapter 5), James Gibson notes that social scientists over many decades have found a pronounced relationship between religiosity and intolerance; if tolerance means, as he puts it, allowing "all ideas, even repugnant ones, to enter into the marketplace of ideas and compete for the hearts and minds of the citizenry," then on one important measure religious people manifest intolerance: they are less likely than nonbelievers to extend a welcome to atheists in the public square. For a religious person, this makes a certain mount of sense: if you passionately believe that only Jesus saves, you do not want to give equal credit to the ideas of someone who does not believe in Jesus. If such a point has a certain theological credibility, however, it lacks liberal-democratic credibility, for as citizens, we are obligated to make room for the ideas of people who believe other things than we do.

When John Green compared the religious population of the United States in 1960 and 2004, he found more religious traditionalists in the latter year (see chapter 2). Because Gibson finds that religious traditionalism is associated with intolerance, we would therefore expect that levels of intolerance may be higher now than they were a half-century ago. That this may be the case is supported by the data Gibson has collected, for, as he puts it, "those who believe most of the problems of this world are the result of people moving away from God are, *ceteris paribus*, more intolerant." Of course it is true that nonreligious people can also be intolerant; support for hate crimes laws and speech codes reflects a tendency on the part of the secular left not to tolerate the views of those they condemn as haters and bigots. Gibson has nonetheless told us something we need to know: a society containing many religious traditionalists may be a better one in some ways (if you believe that people need to seek God), but it will likely fail the strong test of encouraging broad tolerance among all its citizens.

The question, however, does not end here. People do learn tolerance, especially when they come into contact with people unlike themselves. Many institutions encourage people to broaden their horizons, and these include not just universities and workplaces but political institutions such as parties and even single-interest groups. Both Clyde Wilcox (chapter 6) and Geoffrey Layman (chapter 7) address the issue of whether heightened levels of participation in politics on the part of conservative Christians lead them to become more tolerant and thereby to become more respectful of the norms of liberal democratic citizenship.

Wilcox has been studying conservative Christians for three decades, and some of his findings are troubling from the standpoint of democratic theory. In his chapter for this volume, for example, Wilcox compares general donors to the Republican Party with those who are explicitly conservative Christian and finds "that we have reason to be worried about the democratic values of Christian right members." As Gibson has also discovered, deeply traditionalist activists within the Republican ranks have little positive to say about atheists, Muslims, and others whom they regard as enemies in the theological and cultural wars they believe themselves to be fighting. When people take the words of the Bible as the literal truth and then seek to enter politics, as Wilcox points out, their apocalyptic sensibility stands in sharp contrast to the give and take of democratic proceduralism.

Still, Wilcox is correct to remind us that the Christian Right is not an unchanging entity. Not that long ago, conservative Protestants were explicit in both their anti-Catholicism and anti-Semitism. This is no longer the case, as conservative Protestants have found common cause with Catholics over abortion and have united with conservative Jews over support for Zionism. One doubts that a similar acceptance of Muslims will occur in the future among Christian conservatives, for, as Jamal points out, non-Muslims in America know very little about Islam, yet 36 percent of them nonetheless believe that Islam encourages violence.

Yet Muslims are people of the book and also happen to have culturally conservative values. It may be political alliances rather than any change of heart that led conservative Protestants toward greater acceptance of Catholics and Jews, but tolerance is tolerance wherever it is found. It would be a step toward democratic inclusion if conservative Christians were ever to move toward a similar alliance with Muslims.

Geoffrey Layman's research also confirms this general conclusion that religious sectarianism can be modified by the experience of political activism. Unlike Wilcox, who studied religious activists who had become politically involved, Layman examined political activists who were religious. His work involves delegates to party conventions, people who, although generally not determining who will be their party's nominee, work hard enough for their party to come to the conventions and participate. Layman confirms a trend toward greater polarization between the parties than has been analyzed by others; activists in both parties tend to be recruited from the more extreme elements known as the party base.[23] He also, much as did Gibson and Wilcox, finds less attachment to democratic norms among the extremists of the Republican Party than among their secular counterparts in the Democratic Party. Democracy requires that passion and commitment be accompanied by adherence to pragmatic norms, but those attracted to the Republican Party through their religious activism tend to have less pragmatic views toward politics than others and are therefore less likely to view compromise, the quintessential activity of democratic bargaining, as legitimate.

Layman, however, finds that over time these attitudes tend to change; it is those with the least experience attending conventions who tend to be the most purist in their views. If Layman is right, and there is every reason to believe he is, mere participation in an ideologically skewed institution such as a party convention can have a moderating effect over time, even if such trends are less pronounced among conservative religious activists than they are among secularists on the left. The more one is involved in politics, the greater the tendency to adapt to political norms, including those respecting compromise.

The political scientist Jon Shields has argued that political participation on the part of conservative Christians helps inculcate democratic values.[24] All these papers suggest that this can be true or not true depending on when activists were motivated; those attracted to politics before and after the period of greatest influence of the Christian Right, Wilcox shows, tend to be more tolerant. This suggests that in the future Christian conservatives may bring to politics a less harsh and judgmental temperament than the generation that preceded them. Evidence that this is happening can be found in an extensive survey of evangelical Christian college students conducted by Corwin Smidt and James Penning.[25]

Although identifying as conservative and Christian, these students were more interested in social justice than their parents and, most importantly for our purposes, indicated degrees of tolerance similar to people in all other religious categories. A fair conclusion to all this literature would be this: traditionalist religious views are associated with intolerance but not in any fixed psychological sense, as historical and politics contexts can moderate intolerance's effects.

The conclusion that seems to follow from this work is that both the liberal deists and the religious believers who did so much to shape the founding of the American experiment had it right. The former had reasons to worry that too close an identification of religion and politics does result in intolerance and dogmatism; religious people do tend to have strong views, and when they make them known, especially when they are new to politics, they do so with the zeal of purists. But the early evangelicals who argued that separation of church and state would be good for religion were also correct; political participation does encourage people to grow, and as they grow, their views become more capacious and accommodating of others, and this in turn contributes to the stability that democracy needs to protect all freedoms, including religious freedom.

Political Diversity and American Religion

Certainly since the days of Tocqueville, and also since the time of Will Herberg, the United States has become far more diverse, not only in terms of religion but with respect to gender identity, ethnicity, and race. The years since 1960 have not only witnessed the relative declining influence of mainline Protestants and the rise of the Christian Right, they have also been accompanied by the civil rights movement, the growth of feminism, increased immigration, demands by gays and lesbians for marital equality, and other, less pronounced, efforts on the part of groups to have their identity accepted as legitimate by the majority. The term "identity politics" was unknown in 1960 when John F. Kennedy won his race for the presidency. Its use was widespread, and its political consequences significant, when John F. Kerry lost his in 2004. As the philosopher Charles Taylor explains, one of the most significant demands made on modern polities is a demand for recognition.[26] Accept us for who we are, advocates of these movements ask, not as who you want us to be.

With respect to substantive issues, one can explain the rise of the Christian Right as a reaction against the politics of recognition. The one issue that did more than any other to launch the Christian Right was abortion; *Roe v. Wade*, which legalized abortion in all fifty states, as I have indicated above, brought conservative Catholics and conservative Protestants together in a political alliance seeking the overturning of that decision. Because *Roe* itself was strongly supported by so many feminists, who in turn viewed a woman's right to choose as a fundamental right, abortion politics quickly turned into a conflict over worldviews: one side, influenced by the liberatory movements of the 1960s, insisted on personal autonomy; the other, reacting against those movements, spoke on behalf of obedience to authority and respect for traditional values. As Kenneth Wald and David Leege show in their contribution to this volume (chapter 11), cultural politics was fueled by "entrepreneurs" who mobilized widespread discontent over social change to advance their agenda.

Churches themselves became part and parcel of these transformations. Many of America's religious denominations—Catholicism, conservative Protestantism, Orthodox Judaism—have not been open to the idea of women serving as clergy, and despite widespread gains in gender equality over the past few decades, have not significantly changed their practices. Other identity-based movements, especially those advocating for equal rights for homosexuals, have met strong resistance in numerous religious communities; even the mainline and liberal Episcopal church found itself deeply divided over the ordination of a gay bishop. At a time when even conservative institutions such as the military and the prison system found themselves accommodating the politics of identity, churches, with a few notable exceptions, did not.

Yet the relationship between religion and the politics of identity has proven to be more complicated than this initial sketch indicates. Consider the experience of the black church in America. The large majority of African-Americans belong to denominations that can in religious terms be properly described as evangelical. Just like their white counterparts, they have strong views about the literal truth of the Bible, and on some of the leading social issues of the day, such as gay rights and abortion, they lean toward the right. True of the historically dominant African-American denominations, this is even more true of the Pentecostalist wave sweeping through so many African-American communities. And even African-Americans who adhere to faiths outside the Christian tradition, especially those attracted to Islam, share the same socially conservative and theologically more orthodox views of those who remain tied to Protestantism.

At the same time, African-American religious leaders have historically identified more with the Democratic Party. African-American voters, not surprisingly, are also heavily Democratic in their political identity, a tendency made even stronger by the election of Barack Obama in 2008. African-Americans represent one group for which the politics of recognition and the politics of religion did *not* come into conflict: prophetic religious voices, clergy leadership, and church attendance all became linked to the cause of racial justice and equality. Evangelical in tone,

African-American religion, as Fred Harris points out in this volume (chapter 8), drew on the Social Gospel tradition associated with liberal Protestantism in its general outlook on the world. Martin Luther King Jr. was both a Baptist from the South (as well as the son of a generally conservative preacher) and a seminary-trained student who learned the lessons of liberal Protestantism in the North. Compared to others, moreover, King, while generally leftist in his views, was something of a moderate. Under the leadership of thinkers such as James Cone, a black liberation theology movement developed in the 1970s and 1980s that drew on elements of Marxism and Third World anticolonialist movements. Liberals who objected to the close association between conservative Christians and the Republican Party looked the other way, or even expressed their support, when black Christians formed alliances with the Democratic Party. From their point of view, African-American religion was too steeped in traditions of justice and equality to be ignored.

Harris's chapter calls attention to the growing influence of prosperity gospel preachers in the world of African-American religion. Preaching the importance of letting Jesus into your life so that you can improve your material standing, the prosperity gospel, as Harris points out, relying on the work of political scientist Michael Dawson, substitutes an individualistic ethic for a communal one: you are to be judged by how you improve yourself, not what you do for fellow African-Americans, including the very poor. The rise of the prosperity gospel portends dramatic changes in the role that African-American religiosity will play in American politics. On the one hand, it is more likely that we will see prominent black preachers, especially those attracted to the prosperity gospel, aligning themselves with the Republican Party, even under an Obama presidency. At the same time, the appeal of the prosperity gospel depends on the actual amount of prosperity one can find among African-Americans. A severe depression, which would have a disproportionate impact on recent members of the middle class, including African-Americans, could swing the pendulum back to the social gospel tradition. Whatever happens, however, racial identity and religious identity will continue to be intertwined, each giving support to the other.

The relationship between women and American religiosity has also proven itself to be more complicated than it at first seemed. Despite the fact that so many conservative religions assign second-class roles to women, women have been instrumental in the rise of conservative religion; as Allison Calhoun-Brown points out in her chapter (chapter 9), women tend to be more devout than men by every measure of religious devotion, from church attendance to belief in the Bible's inerrancy. A number of ethnographic studies of women's religiosity uncover a curious finding: even in conservative religions where women are treated as second-class citizens, women themselves experience through their faith a sense of empowerment.[27] It may matter less what religious denominations say about women than what they offer women. Whereas men find a sense of fulfillment in work and politics, women are more likely to do so in church.

Calhoun-Brown offers a careful and well-researched analysis of the consequences of women's involvement in religion for their sense of efficacy. She makes a distinction between two kinds of efficacy: personal efficacy, or a feeling of self-confidence and a willingness to take on tasks, and political efficacy, confidence that one can make one's voice heard in the larger society. One might think that church attendance would increase personal efficacy while decreasing the political kind, for the messages in so many churches, especially conservative ones, emphasize women's dependence on men and in that sense treat women as less than equal in public life. Yet Calhoun-Brown found the exact opposite. Frequent female church attendance often leads women to devalue their own personal efficacy, but it also increases their political sense of self-worth. The appropriate conclusion would be that institutions matter. Just as participation in nominating conventions moderates the purist views of deeply devout activists, participation in church contributes to the development of social skills that, in turn, increase political efficacy.

It is true, as Calhoun-Brown concludes, that any decrease in personal efficacy associated with religious involvement is a problem for democracy, for without personal efficacy there can be no genuine sense of empowerment. For this reason, feminists have been correct to view the power and influence of religion in America as threatening to the ideal of gender equality. At the same time, however, political efficacy is also necessary for democratic success: so long as people believe that their voices matter and that they can influence what government does, conditions of political legitimacy are met even if those same individuals may not feel very successful in their personal lives. If we believe that we are still a long way away from gender equality, there are some aspects of religious involvement in politics that set the cause back and some others that advance it. Determining which ones work and which ones do not is more important than either condemning religion because it harms women or praising it because it keeps them in their place.

What will be the relationship between religion and politics when the majority of America's single largest religious denomination, the Catholic Church, is Latino? We do not know exactly when this will happen, but as David Leal reminds us in his chapter (chapter 10), Latinos are the largest minority group in the United States, remain strongly Catholic despite conversions to Protestantism among younger generations, and are exceptionally devout; by one estimate cited by Leal, as much as 85 percent of the Catholic segment of the U.S. population will be Latino by the mid-twenty-first century. One of the most important political developments influencing American politics in the last two decades of the twentieth century was the fact that so many Catholic voters, no longer tied to the Democratic Party, simultaneously moved to the suburbs and began to identify themselves as independents. It seems increasingly obvious that one crucial political development of the new century is that the differences between urban and suburban white Catholics will pale in comparison to the influence of Hispanics. Republican stalwarts such as Karl Rove, George W. Bush, and John McCain all have recognized this fact, and they have urged their party to soften its anti-immigration stance to accommodate voters who are clearly conservative in their moral and religious views. (McCain later changed his views.) Yet they have not won their party over, and it is likely that Hispanic Catholics will, like the Catholic immigrants of previous years, lean toward the Democratic Party.

For political scientists, the increasing importance of Hispanic Catholics allows a close-up examination of identity in the making. In his chapter, Leal focuses on some of the more fascinating aspects of this process. Latinos, Leal points out, have, in contrast to earlier immigrant groups in the American experience, rarely controlled the institutions of the Catholic Church. They are more numerous and influential in some parts of the country than in others. They typically are working-class and union members rather than wealthier suburbanites. Given all these facts, does their religious identification smooth the path toward increased political participation? It is clear from Leal's chapter that religion can serve as an inspiration for organizers such as César Chávez and Ernesto Cortés, who help bring benefits to ordinary people. (President Obama's experience as a community organizer and the traditions they embody became issues in the 2008 presidential campaign.) Nonetheless, Catholicism tends to be more hierarchical than one finds among many Protestant denominations, raising the possibility that Latino Catholics may not develop the civil skills in sufficient amounts to increase their rates of participation. Leal cites evidence on both sides of this question. Still, there seems no reason to conclude that Catholicism per se creates obstacles to participation; poverty has more to do with why people do not participate in politics than faith.

Latinos, it should also be pointed out, not only reflect diversity, they are themselves diverse. There is no reason why members of a group this large will all approach politics in the same way when they or their parents and grandparents come from so many different countries. As the Latino proportion of the U.S. population expands, we will see diversity within diversity: the differences between Puerto Ricans and Cubans will be as large as the differences between Latinos and Anglos. The United States is a vast laboratory for ethnic, racial, and religious diversity, and all of these forms can be seen among those with Hispanic backgrounds.

It is ironic that so many of those who lament the fact that the United States lacks the ethnic and racial homogeneity of the past hope that religion can offer a source for a more unified morality when religion itself is part and parcel of the diversity that America has become. The reality is that the ferment produced by the rise of identity politics in the 1960s and 1970s, far from coming to an end, will extend itself to include religious groups in the near future. One can already see conservative Christians adopting the mantle of victimhood and minority rights used during the civil rights movement of the 1960s as they argue that the United States is dominated by secular humanists whose commitment to political correctness seeks to marginalize them. Yet it is a victory for free speech when conservatives who, in the past, might have argued against John Stuart Mill embrace his ideas when they seek the liberty to proclaim their dislike of homosexuality or their opposition to feminism. In a similar way, liberal democracy ought to welcome the fact that conservative religious believers view themselves as one more element in America's rainbow coalition of groups seeking recognition for their identity. The rights of all minorities are best protected when all groups are minority groups, a situation we increasingly face in the United States.

Religion and Cultural Conflict

For a number of decades now, the most common metaphor used to describe the themes that dominate campaigns, elections, and governance in the United States is the existence of a culture war. The divide that *Roe v. Wade* revealed—involving those who insist on tradition, authority, and respect for law on the one hand and those who stand for individual rights and personal autonomy on the other—was extended well beyond abortion to include such issues as prayer in schools, gay rights, stem-cell usage, and the "right to die." Whether the culture gap was deep or exaggerated became the subject of extended debate.[28] Yet it seems increasingly clear that culture war themes are lessening in importance in recent years. The 2008 election in particular, which was dominated by the economic crisis that took place in the fall of that year, suggests that Americans are at the moment more engaged with pocketbook issues than with the state of their culture. This by no means suggests that culture war themes will disappear; the vice-presidential nominee of the Republican Party in 2008, Alaska Governor Sarah Palin, made them central to her campaign. But they are unlikely to monopolize American campaigns the way they did in the 1980s and 1990s.

The culture war, nonetheless, raises important questions about the functioning of American democracy. Prominent among them are these: Are issues such as abortion or gay rights less amenable to bargaining and compromise than those dealing with labor or the environment? Are the passions unleashed by partisans in culture war conflicts dangerous to the stability democracy requires if it is to be effective? Does the prominence of "single-issue" politics produce excessive sectarianism? Will those concerned with culture war issues suffer disruptive disappointments when the utopian goals they seek cannot be achieved in the give-and-take of real politics? Does a culture war contain the potential to turn itself into a civil war?

The centrality of questions such as these to political science can be traced back to the decades just after World War II. I have already mentioned that political scientists during this earlier period paid little scholarly attention to religion. At the same time, they paid considerable attention to the conditions for stable democracy. These were years in which scholars from a number of disciplines argued that the United States faced an "end of ideology" due to the exhaustion of extreme views associated with totalitarian movements.[29] America was a consensus society, ran one common refrain, and, when compared to extremism, consensus was no bad thing. It was during this era that Alexis de Tocqueville had his greatest impact on American political science. Inspired by him, social scientists found ways to argue that class conflict, and all its attendant instabilities, could be avoided. Stability, indeed, became something of a watchword during this era. The success of a political system was measured not by how it managed conflict but by how it avoided it.

One of the key texts of the era was Anthony Downs's *An Economic Theory of Democracy*, first published in 1957.[30] The leaders of political parties are rational actors, Downs argued, more concerned about winning elections than ideological purity. Politicians understand that they need to have strong appeal within their party to obtain its nomination, but once nominated, they then need to appeal to independent voters in the center of the political spectrum. As they do, they will take care to moderate any ideological positions necessary to achieve the nomination, thereby guaranteeing that general elections will feature politicians trained in the art of moderation. The way politics was conducted in the 1950s gave strong credence to Downs's claims. The two parties in Great Britain were so similar to each other that *The Economist* coined the term "Butskellism" to characterize the general agreement between Tory Rab Butler and Labor's Hugh Gaitskell. Meanwhile in the United States, Dwight D. Eisenhower governed as a centrist along with support from leading Democrats in Congress. The most disruptive conflicts took place within the parties rather than between them: Republican isolationists preferred Robert Taft to Eisenhower, and Southern and Northern Democrats took opposite positions on civil rights.

The first signs of the impending downfall of the Downs model took place in 1964, when an outright conservative, Barry Goldwater, won the

Republican nomination. Goldwater would go on to lose the election by a landslide, of course, but before long, the conservative faction of the party that selected him would become the majority current within the party. Activists inspired by their religious convictions were at the heart of this revival; the term used to describe them was that they constituted the "base" of the Republican Party. Arguably the man most responsible for the role played by "the base" in recent American politics, Karl Rove, relied on a theory about how democracy works quite distinct from that of Anthony Downs. Appeal to the extremes rather than the moderate middle, Rove urged George W. Bush, but so long as you mobilize as many of those on the extremes as you can, you will still win. Strategists will be debating Rove's ideas for decades to come. On the one hand, George Bush did win two elections by appealing to the base. On the other, one of those victories was too close for comfort, and Rove's tactics were exhausted by 2008. Nonetheless, the questions posed by Rove's success remain, and one of the objectives of the APSA task force was to try to shed light on them.

Kenneth Wald, a task force member, co-authored a chapter for this volume with David Leege addressing this issue directly (see chapter 11). Wald and Leege, building on the research of the latter, do not find the "culture war" model particularly helpful in understanding recent politics in the United States. Influenced by Aaron Wildavsky, they instead talk about how cultural concerns become politicized.[31] People will always have views about the health of their culture, and often such views will cause them great concern. But little of this matters for politics unless cultural concerns are mobilized. Cultural politics is best understood, therefore, not as populistic rages of anger coming from below but as efforts on the part of political entrepreneurs to discover what is on the minds of mobilizable citizens and to mobilize them. To do so, these political operatives develop appropriate symbols, exploit available technologies, and attempt to build workable majorities. Mobilizing cultural differences, unlike, say, mobilizing economic ones, often leads to a passionate form of politics relying on emotional appeals based on resentment and victimization. But in comparison to situations in other countries in which religious and cultural differences lead to violence and civil conflict, such as one finds in the Balkans, the politics of cultural differences is not all that different from politics in other realms of public life.

Wald and Leege therefore warn against those who view the so-called culture war as an alarming development that threatens liberal democratic political stability. Their most important insight is their challenge to the notion that cultural politics inevitably becomes zero-sum contests in which a victory for one side can only come with a defeat for the other. In fact, as the work of Morris Fiorina and his colleagues has demonstrated empirically, even the most publicized of culture war issues, abortion, is amenable to compromise in the sense that the majority of Americans prefer a solution somewhere between the two extremes.[32] Cultural conflicts, moreover, can be, as Wald and Leege point out, prescriptive rather than proscriptive, offering ideas about how we ought to live as well as insisting on punishment for those whom we presume to live wrongly. And just because someone cares deeply about an issue such as abortion or gay rights does not mean an automatic adherence to single-issue politics: people care about many things that can be pursued in many different ways. Like Bette Novit Evans, Wald and Leege picture the United States as a pluralistic society with many inputs and outputs. It is precisely this pluralism that allows cultural politics the space to operate as other forms of politics, thereby avoiding the potential for violent conflict.

Writing from within the tradition of normative political theory, Nancy Rosenblum comes to a similar conclusion in her chapter for this volume (see chapter 12). How should a liberal democratic society accommodate the views of strong religious believers? The answers given by political theorists tend to congregate around two kinds of responses. One, which Rosenblum calls the logic of congruence, claims that a democratic polity requires groups that are themselves democratic to function well. Associations are, from this point of view, training grounds for the obligations of democratic citizenship. Through our participation in the groups that compose civil society, we learn to get along with others and to see the world from a broader perspective. The problem with strong religious associations is that they place little or no emphasis on this kind of democratic responsibility and for this reason do not encourage liberal democratic civic virtues. Particular policy prescriptions follow from this perspective; we ought, for example, not to grant exemptions to religious groups from general requirements, such as not engaging in racial or gender discrimination, that apply to all other groups. Democracy treats all of its citizens equally. Just as we should not discriminate against religion, we should not discriminate in favor of it either.

Against this view Rosenblum discusses what she calls the logic of autonomy. Believers exist in two worlds: this one, in which they find themselves inevitably engaged with their fellow citizens, but another as well in which their obligations are to God. Democracy must make room for those with strong faith commitments because if does not accord respect to their beliefs, it violates things that those citizens consider sacred, and it loses the capacity of witness and judgment that strong believers bring to the affairs of the day. We should think of religious groups as semiautonomous in the sense that they ought to be free to govern their own affairs as much as possible. Policy implications follow from this view as well: if society in general is committed to the principle of gender equality but one of its constituent groups prohibits women from entering the clergy, the group ought to be allowed to fulfill its religious mission as it best sees fit.

From the standpoint of democratic citizenship, there are problems with both perspectives, which Rosenblum explores at length. She nonetheless believes that although liberal political philosophers are generally sympathetic to the logic of congruence, American democracy can tolerate a certain degree of autonomy. As befits the themes explored in this volume, Rosenblum's conclusion is more empirical than theoretical. She does not search for a solution that would satisfy Kantian principles of universality in the sense that they would be correct for all times and places. Instead, in Tocquevillian fashion, she argues that American religion at this time and place is sufficiently moderate, and that American pluralism at this time and place is sufficiently vigorous, not to be threatened by demands for autonomy. Because all religions in America are minority religions, more respect for autonomy can be granted than if one religion were a majority one.

When answers to philosophical conundrums are based on empirical factors, those conditions can change, in which case the solution will have to change as well. But there is little prospect for any of the conditions discussed by Rosenblum to change in a direction that would work against her reasoning: American religion is likely to become even more diverse in the future, and the constitutional rules under which we operate resist changes in a more unitary direction. The research conducted by many of the task force members, moreover, suggests that the high point of Christian Right influence over U.S. politics has been reached. Even if the culture war continues, it is unlikely to expand. There can be little doubt that the extremist politics produced by the culture war proved to be a challenge for American democracy. And there can be little doubt that this challenge was met.

Conclusion

Scholarship on religion has now become something of a growth industry in American political science, a development that came late but, given the importance of religion in the world, is surely welcome. We hope that the work of the APSA Task Force on Religion and Democracy in the United States will stimulate even more work in the area. But our purpose in this book—indeed the purpose of our task force—was neither to synthesize existing research nor to call for the expansion of research into new areas. Instead, we wanted to take stock of what political scientists have learned about the role religion has played in American democracy and to share those findings with the general educated reading public.

In retrospect, I believe that what stand out from the Task Force's work are both the existence of widespread agreement on the dangers that religious zeal poses for democracy as well as the strong resources that American democracy has at its disposal to ward off those dangers. It is an undeniable fact that the United States contains a considerable number of people who have deep religious convictions and who, at least in recent years, have sought to influence public policy in accord with those convictions, in many cases by becoming activists in and voters for the political party that sought their support. If you are one of these people, you are likely to believe that, in bringing your convictions to the public square, you are exercising your rights. If you happen to be a secular person who believes that people of faith are ignorant and misguided, however, you will likely fear this development and be worried that your rights will be violated if religious-inspired majorities impose their way of life on people with whom they disagree. The only way a democratic society can include both is by finding ways for them to live together.

Our work suggests that such ways do exist. From the standpoint of democracy, it is far better to have citizens with strong views inside the tent, even if conflict results, than angry and alienated ones outside, where the potential for violence always looms. We have found strong believers, especially on the conservative Christian end of the political spectrum, to be more intolerant and less willing to compromise than the ideal of democracy citizenry expects. For this reason, our findings resemble those of 1950s social science, which was also concerned with intolerance and sectarianism.[33] In those earlier years, liberals, having witnessed totalitarianism in the 1930s, war in the 1940s, and McCarthyism in the 1950s, properly wondered whether intolerant and authoritarian views were compatible with democracy. Should liberals today share their concerns? After all, not only can one still find intolerant people in the United States, but, unlike in 1964, when conservatives lost their bid for national office, they have at points controlled all branches of government forty years later.

Yet the very success of conservative politics is what makes the participation of deeply religious individuals less of a threat to democracy than many earlier social scientists believed. A recurring theme running through these chapters finds that institutions are important for shaping individual attitudes. Much as de Tocqueville suggested, the institutions of democracy further democratic citizenship. They do not necessarily do so by making everyone a liberal or a democrat; they are not strong shapers of individual character in that sense. Their more important roles are two: religion encourages people to develop personal self-confidence; and religious political activism leads to the acceptance of the need for bargaining and compromise. A liberal democracy does not need, and should not want, all its citizens to be liberal democrats. Its political needs are more modest than that: it requires citizens who want to win but who have learned that from time to time that they must suffer defeat.

The 2008 presidential election, which brought the Democratic Party back to power and signified a shift from conservatism to liberalism, suggests that the highpoint of the Christian Right has passed. Will those who sought influence through their strong religious convictions accept their political defeat? The question remains at this point an impossible one to answer; we are in no better position than anyone else to glimpse into the future. But based on our research and deliberations, we are persuaded that although what Wald and Leege call the politics of cultural differences can be intense, American democracy can accommodate them. We should be thankful that in the last few decades of the twentieth century religious Americans made demands on their political system. Some of their demands were met, and others were not. But democratic rules of the game need to be challenged so that democracy can be reinvigorated. They were and it has been.

Notes

1. Alexis de Tocqueville, *Democracy in America*, Henry Reeve edition, Phillips Bradley, trans. (New York: Knopf, 1966), volume I, 280.

2. Seymour Martin Lipset, *Political Man: The Social Bases of Politics* (Garden City, NY: Doubleday, 1960).

3. Ibid, 303.

4. Max Weber, "The Protestant Sects and the Spirit of Capitalism," in *From Max Weber: Essays in Sociology*, Hans Gerth and C. Wright Mills, editors and translators (New York: Oxford University Press, 1946), 305.

5. Will Herberg, *Protestant, Catholic, Jew: An Essay in American Religious Sociology* (Garden City, NY: Doubleday, 1955).

6. Kenneth D. Wald and Clyde Wilcox. "Getting Religion: Has Political Science Discovered the Faith Factor," *American Political Science Review* 100 (November 2006), 523–529.

7. Robert B. Petit, "Religion through the Times: An Examination of the Secularization Thesis through Content Analysis of *The New York Times*, 1855–1975," unpublished doctoral thesis, Columbia University, cited in Mark Silk, *Unsecular Media: Making News of Religion in America* (Urbana: University of Illinois Press, 1995), 35.

8. Glenn Himebaugh and Scott Arnold, "We Now Cover Faith, Not Bazaars," *Bulletin of the American Society of Newspaper Editors* (October 1982), 26, cited in Silk, 35.

9. Andrew Walsh, "The Twilight of the Religious Beat," *Religion in the News*, 11 (Fall 2008), 20–21.

10. Francine Parnes, "Religion Journal; Yes. God is Everywhere, Even at the Local Mall," *New York Times*, March 2, 2002; Diana B. Henriques, "In God's Name: As Exemptions Go, Religion Outweighs Regulation," *New York Times*, October 8, 2006.

11. I am grateful to Sean Twombly of the APSA for gathering this information.

12. James Madison, Alexander Hamilton, and John Jay, *The Federalist Papers*, Isaac Kramnick, editor (Harmondworth: Penguin, 1987).

13. "U.S. Religious Landscape Survey," *Pew Forum on Religion and Public Life*, June 2008.

14. Richard Rovere, *The American Establishment, and Other Reports, Opinions, and Speculations* (New York: Harcourt, Brace & World, 1962); E. Digby Baltzell, *The Protestant Establishment: Aristocracy and Caste in America* (New York: Random House, 1964).

15. David Halberstam, *The Best and the Brightest* (New York: Random House, 1972).

16. The best treatment of this phenomenon is Gregory Kabaservice, *The Guardians: Kingman Brewster, His Circle, and the Rise of the Liberal Establishment* (New York: Henry Holt, 2004).

17. See, for example, Stephen D. Smith, *Foreordained Failure: The Quest for a Constitutional Principle of Religious Freedom* (New York: Oxford University Press, 1995).

18. Mark Lilla, *The Stillborn God: Religion, Politics, and the Modern West* (New York: Knopf, 2007).

19. David L. Holmes, *The Faiths of the Founding Fathers* (New York: Oxford University Press, 2005). See also Brooke Allen, *Moral Minority: Our Skeptical Founding Fathers* (Chicago: Ivan R. Dee, 2006).

20. Darren Staloff, *Hamilton, Adams, Jefferson: The Politics of Enlightenment and the American Founding* (New York: Hill & Wang, 2005).

21. Steven Waldman, *Founding Faith: Politics, Providence, and the Birth of Religious Freedom in America* (New York: Random House, 2008); Mark De-Wolfe Howe, *The Garden and the Wilderness: Religion and Government in American Constitutional History* (Chicago: University of Chicago Press, 1967); William Lee Miller, *The First Liberty: America's Foundation in Religious Freedom,* expanded and updated edition (Washington, DC: Georgetown University Press, 2003); and Philip Hamburger, *Separation of Church and State* (Cambridge, MA: Harvard University Press, 2002).

22. John Dunn, *The Political Thought of John Locke: An Historical Account of the Argument of the "Two Treatises on Government"* (Cambridge: Cambridge University Press, 1969).

23. David W. Brady and Pietro S. Nivola, *Red and Blue Nation: Characteristics and Causes of America's Polarized Politics* (Washington, DC: Brookings Institution, 2006).

24. Jon A. Shields, "Between Passion and Deliberation: The Christian Right and Democratic Ideals," *Political Science Quarterly* 12 (2007), 89–113.

25. Corwin E. Smidt and James M. Penning, *Evangelicalism: The Next Generation* (Grand Rapids: Baker, 2002).

26. Charles Taylor, *Multiculturalism and the Politics of Recognition: An Essay* (Princeton, NJ: Princeton University Press, 1992).

27. See, for example, Christel J. Manning, *God Gave Us the Right: Conservative Catholic, Evangelical Protestant, and Orthodox Jewish Women Grapple with Feminism* (New Brunswick, NJ: Rutgers University Press, 1999); and Brenda

Brasher, *Godly Women: Fundamentalism and Female Power* (New Brunswick, NJ: Rutgers University Press, 1998).

28. See James Davison Hunter and Alan Wolfe, *Is There a Culture War? A Dialogue on Values and American Public Life* (Washington, DC: Brookings Institution, 2006).

29. Lipset, *Political Man*; Daniel Bell, *The End of Ideology: On the Exhaustion of Political Ideas in the Fifties* (New York: Free Press, 1962).

30. Anthony Downs, *An Economic Theory of Democracy* (New York: Harper & Row, 1957).

31. Aaron Wildavsky, "Choosing Preferences by Constructing Institutions," *American Political Science Review* 18 (March 1987), 3–21.

32. Morris P. Fiorina, with Samuel J. Abrams and Jeremy Pope, *Culture War? The Myth of a Polarized America* (New York: Pearson Education, 2006).

33. T. W. Adorno, Else Frenkel-Brunswik, and Daniel J. Levinson, *The Authoritarian Personality* (New York: Harper, 1950); Samuel Stouffer, *Communism, Conformity, and Civil Liberties: A Cross-Section of the Nation Speaks Its Mind* (Garden City, NY: Doubleday, 1955).

Chapter 2

RELIGIOUS DIVERSITY AND AMERICAN DEMOCRACY

A View from the Polls

JOHN C. GREEN

THE REELECTION OF President George W. Bush in 2004 led many Americans to rediscover the political relevance of religion.[1] To some people, Bush's strong support from religious voters—especially his fellow Protestants—was deeply troubling. Thus, they might well have appreciated the following campaign appeal:

> I believe it would be tragic—and I repeat, tragic—not only for the United States at home but for the picture of the United States presence abroad, if this election were determined primarily, or even substantially, on religious grounds.[2]

However, this appeal was not issued in the 2004 election but in the 1960 campaign, and it came not from a Bush critic but from a Protestant predecessor, Richard M. Nixon, the 1960 Republican presidential nominee.[3] A better-known statement to this effect came from the 1960 Democratic nominee, John F. Kennedy, in response to concerns about his Catholic faith. After noting that he was not "the Catholic candidate for President" but rather the Democratic Party's candidate "who happens also to be Catholic," he warned:

> If this election is decided on the basis that 40 million Americans lost their chance of being President on the day they were baptized, then it is the whole nation that will be the loser, in the eyes of Catholics and non-Catholics around the world, in the eyes of history, and in the eyes of our own people.[4]

Both Nixon's and Kennedy's 1960 statements pointed to the perils of faith-based politics, in this case, the long-standing tensions between Protestants and Catholics. But these concerns did not prevent either candidate from pursuing religious voters or benefiting from their ballots in the close contest. And this pursuit of faith-based votes had some promising consequences, including the election of the first (and only) Roman Catholic to the White House.

More than forty years later other presidential candidates commented on both the perils and promise of faith-based politics in a context similar to that of 2004. Republican Mitt Romney, much like Kennedy, addressed concerns about his Mormon faith in 2007: "A person should not be elected because of his faith nor should he be rejected because of his faith." But then he noted the value of religion in politics, albeit from a conservative perspective:

> It is important to recognize that while differences in theology exist between the churches in America, we share a common creed of moral convictions. And where the affairs of our nation are concerned, it's usually a sound rule to focus on the latter—on the great moral principles that urge us all on a common course. Whether it was the cause of abolition, or civil rights, or the right to life itself, no movement of conscience can succeed in America that cannot speak to the convictions of religious people.[5]

And the eventual 2008 Democratic Party nominee, Barack Obama, expressed similar sentiments in a 2006 speech, but from a liberal perspective. In responding to an accusation that "Jesus Christ would not vote for Barack Obama" because of his liberal political views, he recalled the role of faith in reform movements throughout American history:

> Frederick Douglas, Abraham Lincoln, Williams Jennings Bryan, Dorothy Day, Martin Luther King—indeed, the majority of great reformers in American history—were not only motivated by faith, but repeatedly used religious language to argue for their cause. So to say that men and women should not inject their "personal morality" into public policy debates is a practical absurdity. Our law is by definition a codification of morality, much of it grounded in the Judeo-Christian tradition.[6]

Taken together, all these comments cover a range of common perspectives on religion and American democracy.[7] On the one hand, some observers worry about the perils of faith-based politics. They fear it will be a source of irreconcilable conflict in a pluralistic society that will erode public support for democratic values. But on the other hand, some observers stress the promise of faith-based politics, seeing it as a source of common purpose, an integral part of American pluralism, and a source of support for democratic values. Instead, they worry about the exclusion of religion from public life.

At root, these perspectives reflect the great diversity and dynamism of American religion. After all, faith-based conflict requires the presence of a variety of religious groups in sufficient numbers to be politically relevant. But the mere existence of such religious diversity and dynamism is only part of the story, and the politicizing of faith-based differences is also important. This chapter investigates these issues with a "view from the polls," both in the sense of employing public opinion surveys and also by focusing on actual voting for president, by far the most common expression of American democracy.

This investigation begins with a description of the variety and sizes of religious groups in the American electorate in 1960 and 2004, finding a great deal of religious diversity in both years as well as substantial change between those years. It next turns to how these religious groups voted for president in these elections and the contribution their votes made to partisan alignments. Here, too, there was substantial change in how religious communities were politicized: in 1960, the major party coalitions were alliances of ethno-religious groups, based in religious traditions (where the Protestant-Catholic cleavage was prominent); by 2004, the party coalitions had been restructured by the effects of religious traditionalism (where a division between religious conservatives and liberals was prominent). But in both elections, such faith-based divisions were part of a broader web of cross-cutting cleavages, including differences based in income and gender. The discussion then reviews the politics of the faith-based partisan alignments in 1960 and 2004, including issue positions and support for prominent faith-based social movements.

The investigation concludes with evidence on potential religious sources of political conflict and the distribution of democratic values among religious groups. In terms of potential religious sources of conflict, there is a high level of support for religious pluralism across the religious landscape but also evidence of differences rooted in religious particularism and support for civil religion. In terms of the distribution of democratic values, there is a high level of general support for majority rule, minority rights, and citizen participation, but there is also evidence that faith-based conflict can erode public support for such values. However, the very diversity and dynamism of American faith-based politics may mitigate such erosion.

In sum, the impact of religious diversity in American democracy is complex, changeable, and contingent on political circumstances. Nixon and Kennedy in 1960, as well as Romney and Obama circa 2008, all had reasonable concerns about the perils of faith-based politics, but they also had reasons to be optimistic about the promise of such politics as well.

American Religious Diversity and Dynamism

The great diversity and dynamism of American religion make it difficult to describe, and scholars have found two concepts useful in addressing this difficulty: *religious tradition* and *religious traditionalism* (Layman 2001; Green 2007a). These concepts capture key aspects of religion that were relevant to the presidential vote in 1960 and 2004 and thus helpful in illustrating the contours of faith-based politics.

The concept of a *religious tradition* taps the belonging aspect of religion, the religious communities with which individuals are affiliated. A religious tradition can be defined as a set of denominations, religious movements, and congregations with similar beliefs, behaviors, and origins (Kellstedt and Green 1993). Such defining characteristics include religious doctrines and normative practices as well as an orientation toward the present, future, and past—and the nature of "tradition" itself. Indeed, many religious traditions in the United States developed from debates over the definition of the proper faith (Finke and Stark 2005).

Religious traditions have often been defined in part by race and ethnicity, drawing on distinctive ethno-religious groups (Swierenga 2007). Among the most enduring of such groups is the Black Protestant tradition, a product of slavery and segregation (Lincoln and Mamiya 1990). Other prominent examples of ethno-religious groups included Irish Catholics, Dutch Calvinists, and Polish Jews. Assimilation into American society has reduced the distinctiveness of many such communities, but new ones continue to appear, such as Mexican Catholics, Korean Pentecostals, and Nigerian Muslims. A good example of the combined effects of these factors is the mainline Protestant tradition, the core of which is a set of denominations with similar beliefs and practices but originally drawn from multiple streams of European immigration (Green 2007b).

Throughout most of American history, religious tradition has been the primary means by which religion was connected to democratic politics, and especially to the presidential vote. Beginning in the early nineteenth century, some religious traditions supported Democratic presidential candidates, others backed first the Whigs and then the Republicans, with still others divided between the major parties (McCormick 1974). Such ethno-religious coalitions were important into the twentieth century, with perhaps the best known example being Franklin D. Roosevelt's New Deal coalition. In the New Deal era, the Democrats were supported by Catholics, Jews, southern evangelicals, and black Protestants. At the same time, the Republicans were backed by various kinds of mainline Protestants (Kellstedt et al. 2007). Social welfare issues played a critical role in assembling coalitions from these diverse religious groups (Petrocik 2006).

Religious traditionalism taps the believing and behaving aspects of religion and can be defined as the extent to which individuals partake of the defining beliefs and practices of the tradition with which they affiliate (Green 2007a, ch 2). Despite the best efforts of religious communities to inculcate their adherents with the proper faith, there are inevitably religious differences among them. Such differences can become a source of tension within a tradition or its components, particularly if reinforced by shifting social conditions. The resolution of such tensions can change the character of a religious tradition over time, and, if they are not resolved, such tensions can lead to the development of new religious traditions (Finke and Stark 2005).

In the second half of the twentieth century, differences in traditionalism have been associated with a "restructuring" of American religion (Wuthnow 1988, 1996; Kohut et al. 2000). Two rival groups developed within most religious traditions, one variously labeled "orthodox," "conservative," or "traditionalist," and the other called "progressive," "liberal," or "modernist." The unaffiliated population is often thought of as part of this restructuring, reinforcing the less traditional side of these disputes (Wuthnow 1989). Religious moderates or "centrists" were part of the new structure as well because not all members of the religious traditions actively participated on one or another side of this new structure. A good example of this development is the conflict within a mainline Protestant denomination, the Episcopal Church in the United States, over the ordination of the first openly gay bishop (Moore 2006). Supporters of the ordination sought to redefine traditional beliefs and practices in response to modern attitudes of inclusion, while opponents sought to maintain traditional beliefs and practices in the face of such circumstances.

By the 1980s, scholars observed that religious traditionalism had become politicized, with religious beliefs and practices influencing the presidential vote independently of membership in religious traditions (Layman and Green 2005). These changes added new groups to the religious elements of the major party coalitions. The Republicans gained support from the more traditional elements of many religious traditions, including groups aligned with the Democrats, but they lost support among the less traditional within their existing religious constituencies. A similar set of changes occurred within the Democratic coalition. Cultural issues played a major role in this restructuring of the major party coalitions (Hunter 1991).

The ethno-religious and restructured coalitions involve different kinds of faith-based conflict. For ethno-religious coalitions, the primary conflict is among religious traditions, such as the Protestant-Catholic divisions in the 1960 election. Such conflict may reflect the power of religious affiliation in pluralistic politics. But for restructured religious coalitions, the primary conflict is degrees of traditionalism, such as the disagreements between religious conservatives and liberals in the early twenty-first century. Such conflict may reflect the power of religiosity in an ideologically polarized politics. All else being equal, either kind of division constitutes a source of political peril, eroding public support for democratic values.

But all else is rarely equal in American politics, so that faith-based conflict, whatever its source, may not uniformly erode public support for democratic values, and even if it does, the effects of such erosion on the operation of democratic institutions may not be severe. As Bette Evans notes elsewhere in this volume (see chapter 4), the existence of diverse religious communities means that electoral majorities are likely to be "coalitions of minorities" that require extensive cooperation among disparate allies to be successful. And, religious diversity aside, broader heterogeneity of American society means that members of religious communities are likely to be embedded in a web of cross-cutting cleavages in politics. In classic Madisonian fashion, both of these features can mitigate the erosion of democratic values by religious conflict, allowing for a promising faith-based politics.

Religious Traditions and Traditionalism, 1960 and 2004

Just how diverse was American religion in 1960 and 2004, and how dynamic was the religious landscape between these elections? Table 2.1 reports an estimate of the size of the major religious groups in both years (expressed as a percentage of the voting-age population). These groups are defined by religious tradition (in **bold**) and where practicable by religious traditionalism (in *italics*), separating out *traditionalists* (with the most traditional beliefs and behaviors), *centrists* (moderate levels of traditional belief and behavior), and *modernists* (the least traditional). Individuals unaffiliated with organized religion are divided in an analogous fashion into "unaffiliated believers" and "unaffiliated seculars"; black Protestants, Latino Protestants, and Catholics are defined in part by race and ethnicity. The final column of the table reports change in the relative size of these groups between 1960 and 2004. These estimates come from surveys with unusually rich religion measures that can be compared over time (see the appendix for the details of the surveys employed and how the religious categories were defined).

Table 2.1 shows that American religion was very diverse in 1960 and had become even more so by 2004, revealing the dynamism of American religious communities.[8] The first two religious traditions in the table, mainline and evangelical Protestants, were made up of historically white churches (i.e., of European origin). Mainline Protestants were the largest religious tradition in 1960, accounting for about one-third of the voting-age population. Centrist mainline Protestants were the single largest category in 1960 but still rather small in relative terms (just 14.6 percent of the total). Traditionalist mainliners were slightly smaller (12.3 percent), with modernist mainliners a distinct minority within their tradition but still a relatively large group overall (7.0 percent).

By 2004, mainline Protestants had decreased sharply in relative terms, falling to about one-sixth of the voting-age population. Although all the

TABLE 2.1
Variety and Size of Religious Groups, 1960 and 2004

	Percentage of voting-age population		
	1960	2004	Change 1960–2004
Mainline Protestants	**33.9**	**16.4**	**–17.5**
Traditionalist mainline	*12.3*	*4.0*	*–8.3*
Centrist mainline	*14.6*	*6.2*	*–8.4*
Modernist mainline	*7.0*	*6.2*	*–0.8*
Evangelical Protestants	**21.7**	**25.1**	**3.4**
Traditionalist evangelical	*10.7*	*12.8*	*2.1*
Centrist evangelical	*7.2*	*6.9*	*–0.3*
Modernist evangelical	*3.7*	*5.5*	*1.8*
Latino Protestants	*	2.6	2.6
Black Protestants	**11.0**	**9.3**	**–1.7**
Roman Catholics	**21.4**	**22.0**	**0.6**
Traditionalist Catholic	*10.6*	*5.2*	*–5.4*
Centrist Catholic	*6.6*	*6.1*	*–0.5*
Modernist Catholic	*4.1*	*6.2*	*2.1*
Latino Catholics	*	*4.5*	*4.5*
Other Christians	**2.0**	**2.8**	**0.8**
Liberal faiths	**1.1**	**1.2**	**0.1**
Jews	**2.3**	**1.9**	**–0.4**
Other world religions	*	**1.4**	**1.4**
Unaffiliated	**6.6**	**17.3**	**10.7**
Unaffiliated believers	*	*4.9*	*4.9*
Unaffiliated seculars	*6.6*	*12.3*	*5.7*
Total	**100.0**	**100.0**	

Source: 1964 Anti-Semitism Study (*N* = 1975); 2004 National Survey of Religion and Politics (*N* = 2730).

* Less than 1 percent.

mainline Protestant subgroups had become smaller, traditionalists and centrists decreased far more than the modernists. The decline of mainline Protestantism was by far the largest change recorded in table 2.1. Scholars have offered a number of explanations for this massive shift, ranging from religious factors, such as the deleterious effects of less traditional beliefs (Kelley 1972) to demographic factors, such a decline in birth rates (Hout et al. 2001); politics may have played a role as well (Hout and Fischer 2002).

Evangelical Protestants accounted for about one-fifth of the voting-age population in 1960 and increased to about one-quarter by 2004. In both years, the traditionalists were the largest group of evangelicals, and in 2004 they were the largest single category in table 2.1 (12.8 percent). Over this period, modernist evangelicals also increased in size, while centrist evangelicals declined slightly. As with the decline of mainline Protestants, evangelical growth may reflect a combination of religious, demographic, and political factors.

The next two categories in table 2.1 represent racial and ethnic minorities among Protestants, contemporary examples of important ethno-religious groups. Black Protestants are the historic African-American churches. In 1960, this tradition made up a little more than one-tenth of the adult population and declined to a little less than one-tenth by 2004. Latino Protestants are best thought of as ethnic subtraditions of Protestantism, with the largest portion coming from evangelical denominations. In 1960, Latino Protestants were too few to measure in surveys, but by 2004 they made up 2.6 percent of the adult population. (For more information on black Protestants, see chapter 8 in this volume by Fredrick Harris.)

Roman Catholics accounted for about one-fifth of the voting-age population in 1960, and the traditionalist Catholics were the most numerous (10.6 percent). And in 2004, Catholics were about the same size overall, but this occurred largely because of the growth of Latino Catholics. Like their Protestant counterparts, Latino Catholics were too few to measure in 1960 but had grown to 4.5 percent of the adult population in the 2004 survey.[9] (For more information on Latino religious groups, see chapter 10 in this volume by David Leal.)

By 2004 non-Latino Catholics declined to a little more than one-sixth of the voting-age population. Like mainline Protestants, traditionalist Catholics decreased the most, but in contrast, modernist Catholics increased in relative size. Here declining birth rates appear to be the chief explanation for the change in the relative number of white Catholics (Hout et al. 2001), but other factors may have contributed as well.

What about the well-known European ethno-religious groups in 1960 and 2004? In 1960, 14.2 percent of the voting-age population reported being born in Europe or with at least one European-born parent (6.2 percent Protestant and 8.0 percent Catholic). In 2004, just 5 percent of the voting-age population met this criterion.[10] These figures reveal the assimilation of ethnic Europeans into the major religious traditions and American society in general.

The next four categories in table 2.1 cover a variety of smaller religious groups. The "Other Christians" was a composite category of small Christian traditions such as Mormons and the Eastern Orthodox. It accounted for 2 percent of the voting-age population in 1960 and grew to nearly 3 percent in 2004. Another composite category was the "liberal faiths," which included Unitarian-Universalists, Wiccans, and New Age adherents, accounting for about 1 percent in 1960 and slightly more in 2004. In 1960, Jews made up more than 2 percent of the voting-age population and had declined to less than 2 percent by 2004. Another composite group was "Other World Religions" such as Muslims, Buddhists, Hindus, and other non-Christian groups. In 1960, this category was not measurable in surveys, but by 2004 it made up more than 1 percent of the voting-age population. (For a further look at one of these groups, American Muslims, see chapter 3 in this volume by Amaney Jamal.)

The final "religious" tradition in table 2.1 is the unaffiliated population, individuals who reported no connection to organized religion. In 1960, the unaffiliated were one-fifteenth of the voting-age population, and by 2004, they had expanded to more than one-sixth. This change included large gains in the unaffiliated seculars (nonreligious people) but also a sharp increase among the unaffiliated believers (individuals who reported religious beliefs and practices but no affiliation). The growth of the unaffiliated reflects many of the factors associated with the decline of mainline Protestants and white Catholics.

Table 2.1 reveals that in a strictly religious sense, there was no *natural* majority of religious people in the voting-age population in either 1960 or 2004, and even the largest religious groups were relatively small minorities at the national level. There may have been (and may still be) something like religious majorities at the regional and local levels (evangelicals in the rural South, Mormons in Utah, and Jews in parts of Brooklyn, NY), but such patterns simply add a geographic element to the overall religious diversity. So from the point of view of democracy, any successful combination of religious groups will be a coalition of minorities. This point is reinforced by the dramatic changes in variety and size of religious groups between 1960 and 2004.

However, *electoral* majorities at the national level were (and can be) constructed around commonalities among religious groups. For example, a "Protestant," "Christian," or "religious" majority can be assembled by bringing together religious groups otherwise divided by tradition and/or traditionalism. Such coalitions of minorities are likely to be fragile and owe their existence as much to politics as to religion. But in the eyes of non-Protestants, non-Christians, or the nonreligious, such coalitions of minorities may well appear monolithic and exclusive. Indeed, whether faith-based coalitions appear perilous or promising is likely to depend on one's religious and political location in American society.

Religious Diversity and the Presidential Vote, 1960 and 2004

One way to assess the political impact of religious diversity and dynamism on American democracy is to review the presidential vote in the

1960 and 2004 elections. This comparison offers a good illustration of the complex, changeable, and contingent nature of faith-based politics in the United States. As we have seen, religion was especially prominent in both campaigns, and thus they both represent good examples of faith-based voting.[11] It is important to note, however, that every presidential election has its unique features, and there is considerable variation in the impact of religion. For example, the religious elements of Franklin D. Roosevelt's victory in 1944 resembled those of Kennedy's 1960 win, but Kennedy did much better among Catholics than FDR. Meanwhile, the faith-based vote in 2008 resembled that of 2004, but Barack Obama received especially strong support from a wide variety of ethno-religious minorities compared to George W. Bush.[12] Table 2.2 lists the 1960 and 2004 two-party presidential vote and reported voter turnout by the religious categories listed in table 2.1.

The 1960 Election

In 1960, all the Catholic groups in table 2.2 voted strongly Democratic, providing their co-religionist, John F. Kennedy, with more than seven in ten of their ballots. Modernist Catholics (84.3 percent) were the most Democratic, followed by the traditionalists (79.8 percent), with modernists reporting the highest turnouts among Catholics (70.8 percent). The Democrats also won a large majority of Jews (93.3 percent), the group with the highest reported turnout (76.9 percent), and black Protestants (84.0 percent), the group with the lowest turnout (43.6 percent). Three-fifths of the unaffiliated seculars voted Democratic as well. Note that Kennedy drew substantial support from some of the mainline and evangelical Protestant groups (especially in the South).[13]

Meanwhile, all the white Protestant groups voted strongly Republican in 1960. Nearly two-thirds or more of mainline Protestants backed Richard M. Nixon, who received the most ballots from modernist mainliners (74.7 percent), while traditionalist mainliners reported higher turnout (75.9 percent). Evangelical Protestants also voted Republican in 1960, especially traditionalist evangelicals (70.6 percent), which was Nixon's second strongest constituency. However, evangelicals turned out at a substantially lower rate than mainline Protestants. The GOP also won small majorities of two composite categories, other Christians and liberal faiths (groups that reported relatively high levels of turnout). Nixon did relatively poorly with the remaining religious groups.

Several things are worth noting about the 1960 voting patterns. First, the ethno-religious elements of the New Deal era coalitions were still largely intact, with the exception of evangelical Protestants. But the defection of evangelicals in 1960 may have reflected ethno-religious politics, being in part a reaction to a Catholic candidate at the top of the

TABLE 2.2
Religious Groups and the Presidential Vote, 1960 and 2004

	Percentage two-party vote					
	1960			2004		
	Kennedy	Nixon	*Turnout*	Kerry	Bush	*Turnout*
Mainline Protestants						
Traditionalist mainline	34.9	65.1	*75.9*	39.5	60.5	*76.3*
Centrist mainline	34.6	65.4	*73.0*	49.6	50.4	*69.8*
Modernist mainline	25.3	74.7	*64.2*	59.0	41.0	*63.9*
Evangelical Protestants						
Traditionalist evangelical	29.4	70.6	*54.8*	13.5	86.5	*68.1*
Centrist evangelical	42.7	57.3	*49.3*	27.4	72.6	*56.1*
Modernist evangelical	35.6	64.4	*58.4*	46.8	53.2	*58.3*
Latino Protestants	*	*	*	37.1	62.9	*49.3*
Black Protestants	84.0	16.0	*43.6*	82.8	17.2	*50.4*
Roman Catholics						
Traditionalist Catholic	79.8	20.2	*63.9*	29.0	71.0	*71.7*
Centrist Catholic	71.4	28.6	*70.2*	48.6	51.4	*70.3*
Modernist Catholic	84.3	15.7	*70.8*	66.3	33.7	*59.2*
Latino Catholics	*	*	*	68.6	31.4	*43.1*
Other Christians	43.3	56.7	*74.4*	20.0	80.0	*59.2*
Liberal faiths	46.7	53.3	*70.0*	75.0	25.0	*78.8*
Jews	93.3	6.7	*76.9*	73.3	26.7	*86.5*
Other world religions	*	*	*	82.4	17.6	*44.7*
Unaffiliated						
Unaffiliated believers	*	*	*	64.3	35.7	*46.7*
Unaffiliated seculars	61.0	39.0	*60.2*	74.2	25.8	*54.3*
All	**50.1**	**49.9**	***63.1***	**48.9**	**51.1**	***60.8***

Source: 1964 Anti-Semitism Survey (*N* = 1975); 2004 National Survey of Religion and Politics (*N* = 2730).

* Less than 1 percent.

Democratic ticket. In this regard, the voting of European ethno-religious groups is instructive: Catholic and Protestant ethnics each voted more strongly Democratic and Republican, respectively, than their assimilated co-religionists (data not shown). Second, religious tradition was quite important to the vote, and traditionalism was less so, with only modest and idiosyncratic differences among traditionalists, centrists, and modernists. And third, the level of reported turnout showed no clear pattern by religious tradition or traditionalism.[14] It was these patterns that informed Nixon's and Kennedy's comments about faith-based voting in 1960.

The 2004 Election

The 2004 voting patterns present a sharp contrast to those of 1960. For one thing, the Catholic groups no longer voted uniformly Democratic. Although John F. Kerry received two-thirds of the ballots of his co-religionists among modernist Catholics (down from 1960), he lost the traditionalists and centrists. However, modernist mainline Protestants had switched parties (59.0 percent Democratic), as did the composite category of liberal faiths (75.0 percent). Kerry also made gains among modernist evangelicals, although they remained largely in the Republican column. The Democrats also gained support from unaffiliated seculars and benefited from most of the new religious groups: other world religions (82.4 percent), Latino Catholics (68.6 percent), and unaffiliated believers (64.3 percent). The Democrats continued to receive strong support from black Protestants and Jews, but at a lower level than in 1960. With just a few exceptions, the religious groups who voted for Kerry reported turning out at rates lower than the nation as a whole, often showing declines from 1960.

The Republicans experienced changes by 2004 as well. George W. Bush's strongest constituency was traditionalist evangelicals (86.5 percent), substantially more Republican than in 1960. Bush also made gains in winning the centrist evangelicals but lost ground in securing the backing of modernist evangelicals. The GOP also picked up substantial support among traditionalist Catholics (71.0 percent) and centrist Catholics (51.4 percent) but received fewer votes while winning traditionalist mainline (60.5 percent) and centrist mainline Protestants (50.4 percent). In addition, the composite category of other Christians became markedly more Republican, and Bush won one of the new groups in the table, Latino Protestants.

Several things are worth noting about the 2004 voting patterns as well. First, the New Deal–era ethno-religious coalitions had largely vanished by 2004, and the party coalitions had been substantially restructured. Second, religious tradition was less important to the vote than in 1960, and traditionalism was more important: in the three largest Christian traditions, the traditionalists were always the most Republican, and the modernists the most Democratic, with the centrists always falling in between.[15] A similar pattern held for the unaffiliated believers and the unaffiliated seculars. Third, reported turnout varied by traditionalism as well, with traditionalists always reporting higher turnout than modernists and the unaffiliated. It was these patterns that informed Romney's and Obama's comments about faith-based voting after 2004.

Religious Diversity and Major Party Coalitions, 1960 and 2004

If nothing else, the 1960 and 2004 presidential votes show the complexity and changeability of faith-based politics in American democracy. These patterns can be seen clearly in the relative contribution the religious groups made to the major party coalitions in each election—and the dramatically different coalitions of minorities that elected Kennedy and Bush reveal the contingent nature of faith-based politics. Table 2.3 takes these patterns a final step, presenting the percentage of each presidential candidate's ballots provided by the religious groups, with the final column reporting the shifts in each religious group's relative contribution to the Democratic and Republican vote between 1960 and 2004.

Party Coalitions in 1960

In terms of religious groups, the largest source of Democratic presidential votes in 1960 was traditionalist Catholics, accounting for about one-sixth of the total. This figure reflects the fact that traditionalist Catholics were relatively numerous (see table 2.1), even though they did not cast the most Democratic votes or report the highest turnout (table 2.2). All the Catholic groups combined for about one-third of Kennedy's ballots. Black Protestants were the second largest source of Democratic votes in 1960, at about one-eighth. Taken together, all of the mainline Protestant groups accounted for one-quarter of Kennedy's ballots, while all evangelicals made up about one-eighth. Jews and unaffiliated seculars combined for about one-eighth of the Democratic vote as well.

The religious elements of the 1960 Republican presidential coalition are easier to describe: all the mainline Protestant groups made up more than one-half of all Nixon's ballots, and adding in evangelical Protestants brings the total from white Protestant categories to almost four-fifths of the Republican vote. Centrist and traditionalist mainliners were the first and second largest source of Republican support, each providing roughly one-fifth of the total. Meanwhile, all the Catholic groups made up less than one-tenth of the GOP vote in 1960. These figures reveal the reality behind Nixon's and Kennedy's statements about the perils and promise of faith-based voting.

Party Coalitions in 2004

The religious elements of the Democratic presidential coalition were even more diverse in 2004 than in 1960. The single largest source of Kerry's ballots was the unaffiliated seculars, at more than one-sixth, replacing traditionalist Catholics as the most important element of the Democratic

TABLE 2.3
Religious Groups and Major Party Vote Coalitions, 1960–2004

	1960		2004		Change 1960–2004	
	Kennedy	Nixon	Kerry	Bush	Democratic	Republican
Mainline Protestants						
Traditionalist mainline	10.4	19.5	4.2	6.2	–6.2	–13.3
Centrist mainline	11.9	22.5	7.3	7.1	–4.6	–15.4
Modernist mainline	3.8	11.4	7.7	5.1	3.9	–6.3
Evangelical Protestants						
Traditionalist evangelical	5.9	14.3	4.4	26.7	–1.5	12.4
Centrist evangelical	5.1	6.9	3.2	8.2	–1.9	1.3
Modernist evangelical	2.6	4.7	4.5	4.9	1.9	0.2
Latino Protestants	*	*	1.6	2.6	1.6	2.6
Black Protestants	12.7	2.4	13.2	2.6	0.5	0.2
Roman Catholics						
Traditionalist Catholic	15.9	4.0	3.9	9.0	–12.0	5.0
Centrist Catholic	9.6	3.9	6.7	6.8	–2.9	2.9
Modernist Catholic	6.9	1.3	8.1	3.9	1.2	2.6
Latino Catholics	*	*	4.4	1.9	4.4	1.9
Other Christians	2.1	2.7	1.1	4.3	–1.0	1.6
Liberal faiths	1.1	1.3	2.2	0.8	1.1	–0.5
Jews	4.5	0.3	4.1	1.4	–0.4	1.1
Other world religions	*	*	1.7	0.4	1.7	0.4
Unaffiliated						
Unaffiliated believers	*	*	4.5	2.4	4.5	2.4
Unaffiliated seculars	7.5	4.8	17.2	5.7	9.7	0.9
Total	100.0	100.0	100.0	100.0		

Source: 1964 Anti-Semitism Survey ($N = 1975$); 2004 National Survey of Religion and Politics ($N = 2730$).
* Less than 1 percent.

coalition. If the unaffiliated believers were added in, unaffiliated votes exceeded one-fifth of the total Democratic vote—roughly three times larger than in 1960. Black Protestants were once again the second largest Democratic constituency, at one-eighth of the total, only slightly larger than in 1960. If Latinos and the composite category of other world religions were included, then these racial and ethnic minorities totaled about one-fifth of the Democratic vote as well.

In 2004, the combination of all non-Latino Catholics accounted for a little more than one-sixth of the Democratic vote, and the sum of all mainline Protestant groups was about the same size. Both figures were substantially lower than in 1960. However, modernist groups were a larger portion of the Democratic vote in 2004, with all such groups making up one-fifth of Kerry's ballots, compared to about one-eighth of Kennedy's in 1960. Jews and all the evangelical categories were roughly as important to the Democratic coalition in both elections.

The faith-based elements of the Republican presidential coalition were also more diverse by 2004. The largest source of Republican votes was traditionalist evangelicals, providing more than one-quarter of all Bush's ballots, nearly twice as many as for Nixon in 1960. All the evangelical categories summed to about two-fifths of the Bush vote. Meanwhile, all mainline Protestants made up a little less than one-fifth of the GOP vote in 2004, less than one-half of their contribution in 1960. Much of this change reflects the sharp decline in the relative size of mainline Protestants (see table 2.1) as a percentage of the population. Nonetheless, the Republican coalition still drew some three-fifths of its supporters from the white Protestant categories in 2004.

Traditionalist Catholics were the second largest Bush constituency in 2004 (9.0 percent), and all Catholics made up about one-fifth of his vote total. All the other religious categories summed together for the remaining one-fifth of the GOP ballots. The traditionalist groups were quite important to Bush in 2004, with the sum of these groups providing more than two-fifths of the Republican vote. However, this figure was only slightly higher than in 1960, with gains among traditionalist evangelicals and Catholics largely replacing losses among traditionalist mainline Protestants. Here, too, one can see the reality behind Romney's and Obama's comments about the perils and promise of faith-based politics.

Religious Diversity and Partisan Alignment, 1960 and 2004

Thus, the diverse religious groups played important—but often quite different—roles in the 1960 and 2004 presidential elections. The results of the previous tables are usefully summarized in table 2.4, which presents a "net Democratic alignment" score for each religious group.

The net party alignment score displays two things at once. First, the sign of the score shows how each religious group "lined up" in partisan voting (as in table 2.2), with a positive number showing a net bias in the Democratic presidential vote and a negative number showing a net bias in the Republican presidential vote. Second, the magnitude of the score shows the net contribution of each religious group to its party's presidential ballots (as in table 2.3), with the larger figure representing a higher proportion of the vote cast.[16] In essence, the net alignment score

TABLE 2.4
Religious Groups and Net Democratic Alignment, 1960 and 2004

Net Democratic alignment (1960)		Net Democratic alignment (2004)	
Net Democratic		**Net Democratic**	
Traditionalist Catholic	11.9	*Unaffiliated seculars*	11.5
Black Protestants	10.3	*Black Protestants*	10.6
Centrist Catholic	5.7	*Modernist Catholic*	4.2
Modernist Catholic	5.6	*Jews*	2.7
Jews	4.2	*Modernist mainline*	2.6
Unaffiliated seculars	2.7	*Latino Catholics*	2.5
		Unaffiliated believers	2.1
		Liberal faiths	1.5
		Other world religions	1.3
Net Republican		**Net Republican**	
Liberal faiths	–0.2	*Centrist Catholic*	–0.1
Other Christians	–0.6	*Centrist mainline*	–0.2
Centrist evangelical	–1.8	*Modernist evangelical*	–0.4
Modernist evangelical	–2.1	*Latino Protestants*	–1.0
Modernist mainline	–7.6	*Traditionalist mainline*	–2.0
Traditionalist evangelical	–8.4	*Other Christians*	–3.2
Traditionalist mainline	–9.1	*Centrist evangelical*	–5.0
Centrist mainline	–10.6	*Traditionalist Catholic*	–5.1
		Traditionalist evangelical	–22.3
Absolute difference*	**22.5**	**Absolute difference***	**33.8**

Source: 1964 Anti-Semitism Survey (N = 1975); 2004 National Survey of Religion and Politics (N = 2730).

*The absolute difference in alignment scores between the top and bottom religious groups in each year.

summarized the patterns in tables 2.1, 2.2, and 2.3. This summary measure will simplify the following discussion of the politics of faith-based groups.

The different order of the religious groups in the 1960 and 2004 columns of table 2.4 starkly reveals the change in the faith-based alignments. In 1960, traditionalist Catholics were most fully aligned with the Democrats by this measure, followed by black Protestants, centrist and modernist Catholics, and Jews. For the Republicans, centrist mainline Protestants were most fully aligned, and the next four groups were traditionalist mainliners and evangelicals and modernist mainliners and evangelicals. All the remaining religious groups were less fully aligned with the major parties, with some nearly evenly divided between them.

In 2004, the faith-based alignments were quite different. The unaffiliated seculars were the most fully aligned with the Democrats, followed by black Protestants, modernist Catholics, Jews, and modernist mainline Protestants. On the Republican side, traditionalist evangelicals were the most fully aligned, and the next four groups were traditionalist Catholics, centrist evangelicals, the composite category of other Christians, and traditionalist mainliners. Here, too, the remaining religious groups were less fully aligned with the major parties, and some were nearly evenly divided.

Table 2.4 also illustrates the restructuring of the ethno-religious coalitions between 1960 and 2004. The bottom row of the table provides a simple measure of the intensity of faith-based politics in these elections: the absolute difference between the net alignment scores of the religious groups most fully aligned with the Democrats and Republicans. The 2004 figure was substantially larger than the 1960 figure (33.8 to 22.5), suggesting greater faith-based polarization in 2004 (Dionne 2008) caused by the greater impact of traditionalism on the presidential vote.

Demography and Faith-Based Alignments

This net alignment score allows an important question to be addressed immediately: to what extent did the partisan alignment of religious groups in 1960 and 2004 reflect other demographic characteristics, such as income and gender, the impact of which on presidential voting is well established? The simple answer is that the faith-based alignments were not just a product of other demographic factors. Multivariate analysis of the 1960 and 2004 presidential vote shows that many of the religious groups had an independent impact on the presidential vote when the effects of the other demographic factors were taken into account.[17] In fact, the religious groups showed considerable internal demographic diversity,[18] so that faith-based political cleavages were embedded in a web of cross-cutting cleavages in electoral politics.[19]

Figures 2.1a and 2.1b illustrate this pattern of cross-cutting cleavages by plotting for 1960 and 2004, respectively, the percentage of each religious group that was above the median income (dotted line) and the percentage that was female (dashed line). For each year, the religious groups are listed in order of alignment (solid line) from the most Democratic to the most Republican.[20] These figures show a complex relationship among income, gender, and the political alignment of the religious groups.

For example, in 1960 there was substantial variation in income and gender across the faith-based alignments (fig. 2.1a). The religious groups most aligned with each party (traditional Catholics and centrist mainliners) had essentially the same level of income. Likewise, Jews (aligned with the Democrats) had the highest income, while black Protestants (also aligned with the Democrats) had the lowest income. As a consequence,

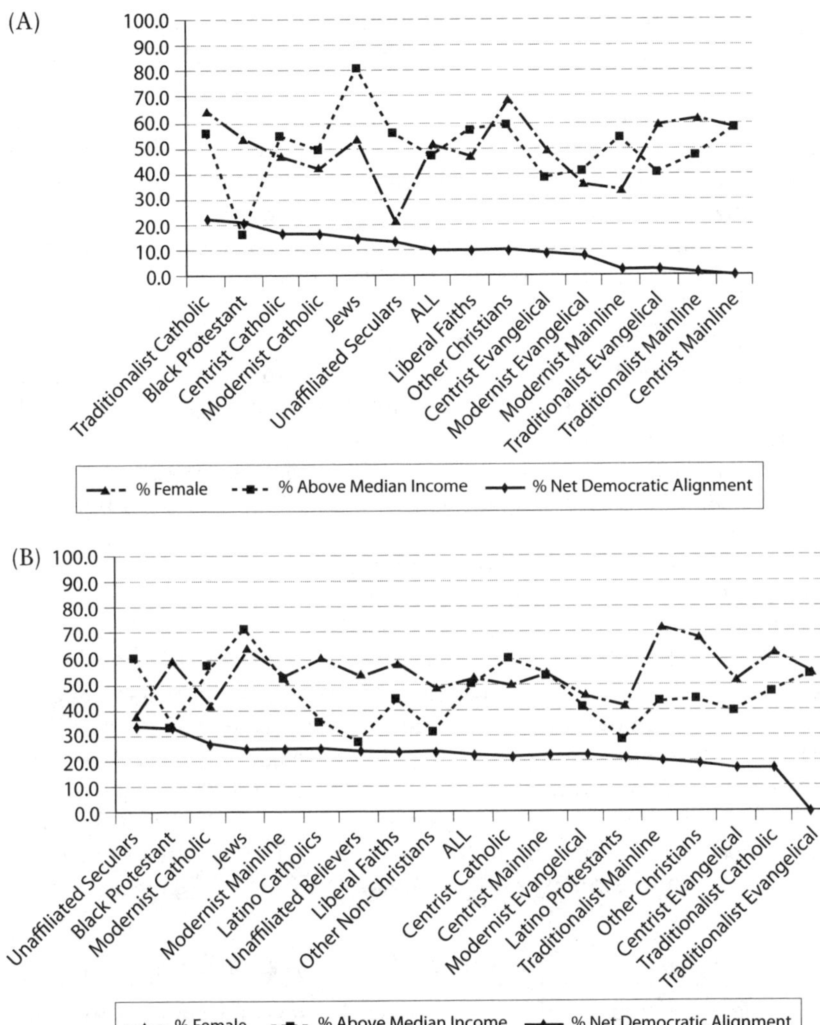

Figure 2.1. (A) Partisan alignment, income, and gender by religious groups, 1960. Source: 1964 Anti-Semitism Survey ($N = 1975$). (B) Partisan alignment, income, and gender by religious groups, 2004. Source: 2004 National Survey of Religion and Politics ($N = 2730$).

there was only a modest negative correlation between the level of income and the order of net Democratic alignment ($r = -0.06$). A similar situation occurred for the percentage of women, where the unaffiliated seculars were the least female and the Catholic traditionalists were among the most, but both groups were aligned with the Democrats. As a consequence, the correlation between the percentage of women and the order of alignment of the religious groups was very small ($r = -0.02$).

A more complex pattern occurred in 2004 (fig. 2.1b). Income showed a weaker pattern than in 1960: the percentage above the median income for traditionalist evangelicals (the group most aligned with the Republicans) was only slightly less than that of the unaffiliated seculars (the group most aligned with the Democrats). The groups with the highest income (Jews and unaffiliated seculars) were both aligned with the Democrats, while groups with the lowest incomes (black Protestants and the Latinos) were also aligned with the Democrats. Hence, the correlation between the level of income and Democratic alignment was very small ($r = -0.02$). Interestingly, gender showed a stronger relationship to faith-based alignments in 2004 than in 1960, with the Republican-aligned traditionalist groups having more women than the Democratic-aligned unaffiliated and modernist groups ($r = -0.08$). (For information on gender and the politics of religious groups, see chapter 9 by Allison Calhoun-Brown in this volume.)

Thus, to the extent that income and gender had independent effects on the presidential vote, they could modify the political impact of religion. So, for example, if high income encouraged a Republican vote, then high-income members of a religious group were more likely to vote Republican than their less-well-off co-religionists—even if the religious group was aligned with the Democrats. And if women were more likely to vote Democratic, then women even in Republican religious groups were likely to vote more Democratic than their male co-religionists. The differences between 1960 and 2004 are instructive: faith-based alignments in 2004 cut across income levels more fully than in 1960, but at the same time, gender was more strongly associated with faith-based alignments.

The Politics of Faith-Based Alignment, 1960 and 2004

How did the change in faith-based voting alignments occur between 1960 and 2004? Figure 2.2 provides an illustration of the pattern of change over time, plotting the alignment measure for four illustrative religious groups: traditionalist evangelicals and Catholics, unaffiliated seculars and modernist mainline Protestants. Because detailed religious measures are not available in surveys across this long span of time, membership in these four groups was estimated from available data.[21]

The first thing to notice about figure 2.2 is the overall pattern of change: the unaffiliated seculars (dotted-and-dashed line) and modernist mainline Protestants (dashed line) moved toward greater Democratic alignment over the period, while the traditionalist evangelicals (dotted line) and traditionalist Catholics (solid line) moved toward greater Republican

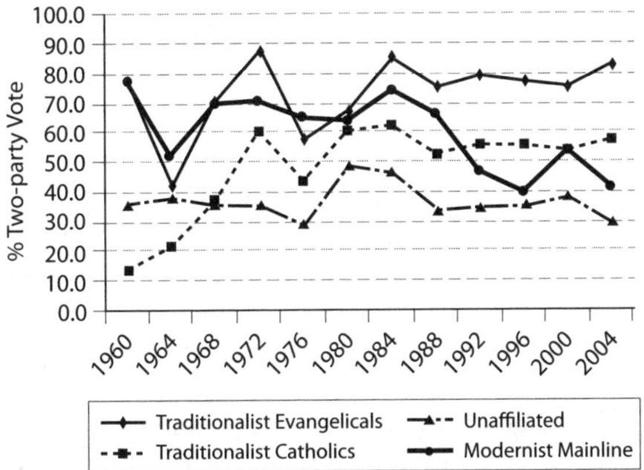

Figure 2.2. Religious groups and Republican presidential vote, 1960–2004. Source: 2004 ANES Cumulative File.

alignment. These patterns become clearest after 1988, suggesting the impact of systemic political factors on faith-based alignments. A likely cause is the rise of cultural conflict between 1960 and 2004 (Layman 2001).

But note that there is considerable fluctuation in the patterns for all four religious groups. Some of these fluctuations parallel the election results, with most groups moving toward the Democrats in good Democratic years (such as 1964) and toward the Republicans in good Republican years (such as 1972). These patterns suggest that the alignment of religious groups was in part contingent on particular presidential candidates and campaigns. Other fluctuations appear to be peculiar to each religious group. For example, the traditionalist evangelicals and Catholics showed more volatile patterns on their way to a Republican alignment in 2004, whereas the unaffiliated seculars and modernist mainliners showed a steadier shift toward Democratic alignment. Such patterns suggest that special values and circumstances of these religious groups were at work as well. In either case, these shifts may reflect political activism by members of these religious groups, both within the major party activist corps and outside of it. (On the role of religion among major party activists, see Geoffrey Layman, chapter 7 in this volume; on the role of religious activists in political change, see Ken Wald and David Leege, chapter 11 in this volume.)

These patterns over time illustrate both the complexity and the changeability of religious groups in presidential elections. Moreover, they point to the contingent impact of political circumstances on the creation, maintenance, and operation of faith-based alignments in presidential elections. Although it is beyond the scope of this chapter to assess the impact of all of these factors over time, it is worth looking at two such factors in the 1960 and 2004 elections in a little more detail: issues and social movements.

Issues and Faith-Based Alignments

Figures 2.3a and 2.3b plot liberal positions on social welfare and cultural issues across the faith-based alignment in 1960 and 2004, respectively. Both topics have long been associated with religious communities and party coalitions, with social welfare issues playing an important role in ethno-religious coalitions and cultural issues having an important impact on the restructured coalitions.

Figure 2.3a looks at 1960. Here the social welfare issue is federal government provision of health care for the elderly (dotted line), with the liberal position being support for such a program.[22] Note that the religious groups most aligned with the Democrats were also the most in favor of the enactment of such a health care program, and those aligned with the GOP less so. The high point occurred for black Protestants and the low point for modernist mainline Protestants, so that the correlation between health care for the elderly and Democratic alignment was substantial ($r = 0.23$).

The cultural issue displayed in figure 2.3a is an assessment of the state of the country's morals, with the liberal position being that morals were "getting better" in the country (dashed line).[23] Here, too, a positive view of the nation's morals was higher among the groups aligned with the Democrats and lower among religious groups aligned with the GOP. But the slope of this line is shallower than that for health care ($r = 0.13$). In fact, this relationship resulted in large part from groups that were outliers: the high scores of black Protestants and liberal faiths and the low scores of the composite category of other Christians and traditionalist evangelicals.

Somewhat different patterns occurred in 2004 (fig. 2.3b). Here the social welfare issue was the level of government spending (dotted line), with the liberal position being increased spending.[24] Although this was not the same issue as in 1960, support for entitlement programs for the elderly was closely associated with support for increased government spending in 2004. Support for a larger public sector was more common among religious groups aligned with the Democrats than for groups aligned with the GOP. But compared to 1960, this relationship had a smaller slope, a more uneven pattern, and a lower correlation with alignment ($r = 0.12$). The high points were for Latino Catholics and black and Latino Protestants; the low points were traditionalist evangelicals and traditionalist and centrist mainline Protestants.

The cultural issue in 2004 is abortion (dashed line), and a pro-choice position counted as a liberal response (fig. 2.3b).[25] Although this was not

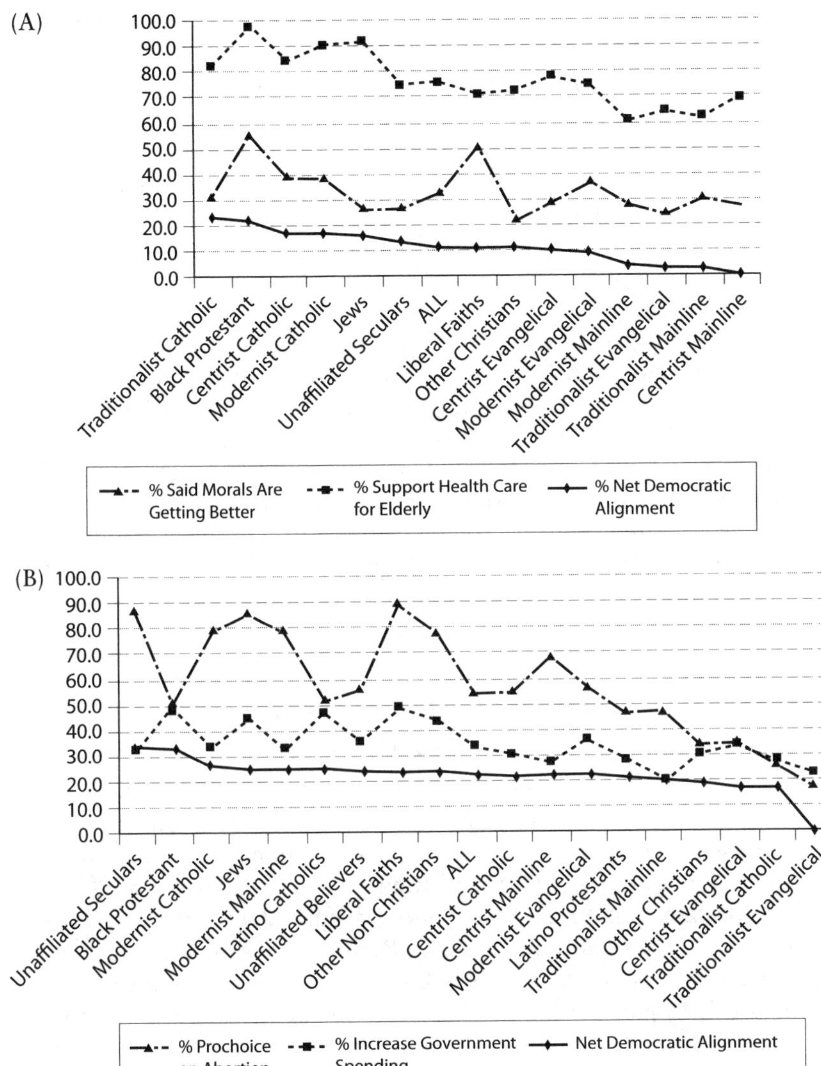

Figure 2.3. (A) Partisan alignment, social welfare, and cultural issues by religious groups, 1960. Source: 1964 Anti-Semitism Survey (N = 1975). (B) Partisan alignment, social welfare, and cultural issues by religious groups, 2004. Source: 2004 National Survey of Religion and Politics (N = 2730).

the same issue as the state of morals displayed for 1960, abortion attitudes were highly correlated with support for "moral values" in 2004. This relationship shows a steeper slope than government spending in 2004 or views of morality in 1960. It also had a higher correlation with the alignment order of the religious groups ($r = 0.38$). The strongest pro-choice groups were Jews, the liberal faiths, and unaffiliated seculars; the least pro-choice groups were traditionalist evangelicals and Catholics and the composite category of other faiths. But note that black Protestants and Latino Catholics were markedly less pro-choice than other groups with a similar alignment score, whereas all mainline Protestant groups were more pro-choice than other similarly aligned religious groups.

These patterns suggest that the changes in the issue agenda played an important role in faith-based alignments. Although social welfare issues mattered in both elections, they were more important to the ethno-religious coalitions of 1960 than to the restructured coalitions of 2004. Culture issues mattered in both years as well but were more important to the restructured coalitions of 2004 than to the ethno-religious coalitions of 1960. Of course, between these two elections important policy changes had occurred: Medicare was enacted into law by Congress, and abortion was legalized by the Supreme Court.

Social Movements and Faith-Based Alignments

An important feature of American politics between 1960 and 2004 was the activity of social movements closely connected to the religious community and frequently led by clergy. One was the civil rights movement that pursued rights for African-Americans in a number of ways, and another was the rise of the Christian Right, a series of movements focused on various kinds of "traditional values." Figures 2.4a and 2.4b plot support for the civil rights and Christian Right movements across the faith-based alignments in 1960 and 2004, respectively.

Figure 2.4a plots approval of the percentage of the religious groups that felt warm toward the NAACP, one of the principal civil rights organizations and quite active in the 1960s.[26] The NAACP was fairly popular, with better than two-fifths of the respondents reporting warm feelings toward it. As one might expect, black Protestants scored highest in this regard, with the lowest score coming from modernist evangelicals. Overall, the Democratic-aligned groups were more supportive than the Republican-aligned groups, so that the responses were positively correlated with the 1960 alignment measure ($r = 0.16$).

Figure 2.4a also plots approval of the John Birch Society (dashed line). This organization was part of the Christian anticommunist movement

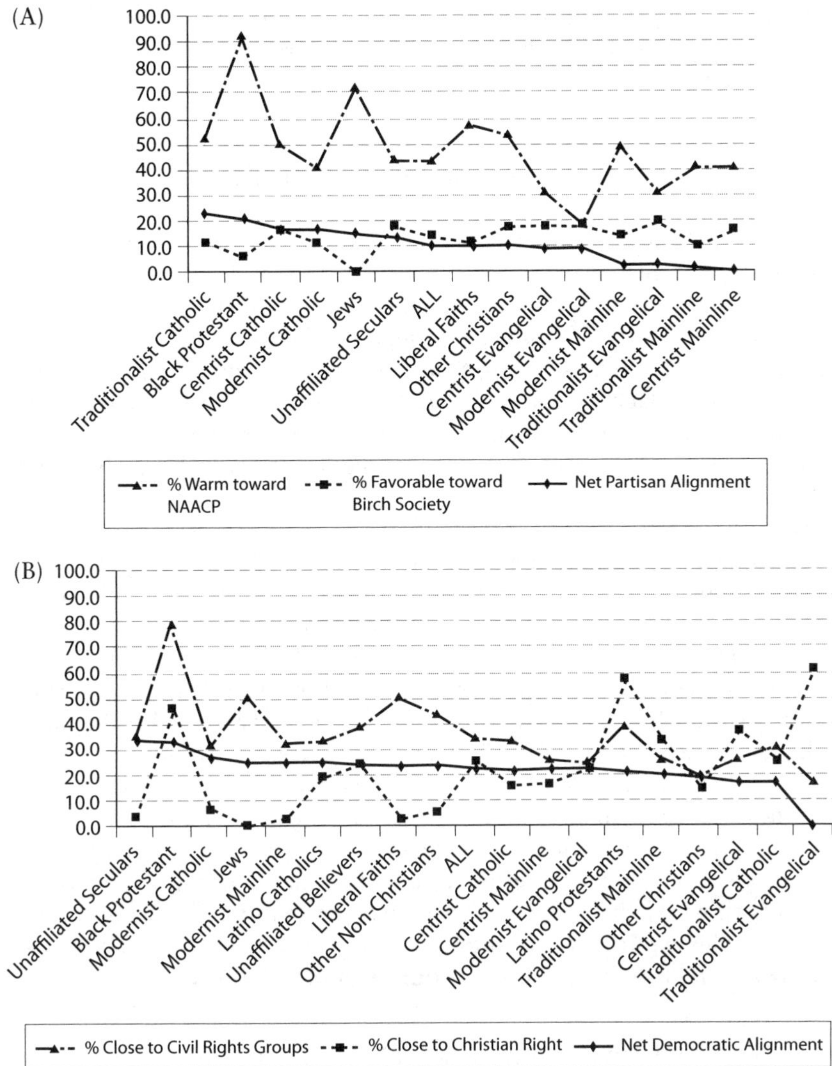

Figure 2.4. (A) Partisan alignment and social movements by religious groups, 1960s. Source: 1964 Anti-Semitism Survey (N = 1975); 1964 NES (N = 1531). (B) Partisan alignment and social movements by religious groups, 2000s. Source: 2004 National Survey of Religion and Politics (N = 2730); 2000 National Survey of Religion and Politics (N = 6000).

and especially active in the early 1960s.[27] Note that there was relatively little support for the Birch Society across the religious groups, but the support that existed was concentrated among the Republican-aligned groups led by traditionalist evangelicals. Lower levels of support were found among the Democratic-aligned groups, with Jews having the lowest score. Overall, the correlation with the 1960 alignment was modest ($r = -0.05$).

Figure 2.4b looks at similar measures in the 2000s. The first of these is the respondents' proximity to "civil rights groups," a generic reference to groups that continued to pursue rights for African-Americans into the twenty-first century.[28] This measure suggests that these organizations remained fairly popular, showing a similar pattern of support to that in the 1960s, when black Protestants were the most supportive of civil rights organizations and traditionalist evangelicals the least supportive. The correlation of this measure with 2004 alignment was a bit higher than the 1960 measure ($r = 0.20$).

Figure 2.4b also plots proximity to the Christian Right.[29] Overall, there appears to have been more support for the Christian Right in 2004 than for the Birch Society in 1964, with the strongest backing coming from traditionalist and centrist evangelicals, but with considerable support from Latino and black Protestants as well; the lowest support was found among unaffiliated seculars, Jews, and the liberal faiths. And support for the Christian Right was more highly correlated with the 2004 alignment measure than the 1960 measure ($r = -0.29$). (For a discussion of Christian Right activists, see Clyde Wilcox, chapter 6 in this volume.)

These patterns suggest that such social movements were important ingredients in faith-based alignments in both years, but as with issue positions, support for these movements became more firmly connected with faith-based alignments in the twenty-first century. These movements fostered the explicit mobilization of some religious groups for political purposes and thus were potential sources of faith-based conflict.

Religious Diversity and Faith-Based Political Conflict

Thus, the faith-based partisan alignments in 1960 and 2004 were in part contingent on broader political conflicts. But what about potential *religious* sources of political conflict, such as might be fostered by faith-based social movements, and their impact on the alignment of religious groups? Table 2.5 reports the percentage agreement across the faith-based alignment with three statements about the role of religion in public life, each of which is potentially controversial: religious pluralism, civil religion, and religious particularism.[30] These data come from 2003, and some fragmentary survey data allow for a comparison to the 1960s. Taken together,

TABLE 2.5
Religious Groups and Views of Religion and Public Life, 2003

	Percentage agreeing		
	Religious diversity good for America	America strong because of faith in God	American democracy based on Christianity
Unaffiliated seculars	84.2	50.9	37.4
Black Protestants	82.6	80.9	54.0
Modernist Catholic	91.1	70.5	45.0
Jews	94.9	56.7	23.7
Modernist mainline	94.0	82.0	55.0
Latino Catholic	81.2	82.9	52.4
Unaffiliated believers	80.3	77.2	47.2
Liberal faiths	97.9	38.3	27.7
Other world religions	81.0	58.6	32.8
All	**85.5**	**79.4**	55.4
Centrist Catholic	91.5	84.5	58.5
Centrist mainline	94.1	90.2	68.6
Modernist evangelical	91.1	84.0	56.4
Latino Protestants	76.7	85.0	56.7
Traditionalist mainline	82.3	93.5	62.1
Other Christians	80.6	81.7	55.9
Centrist evangelical	84.3	90.2	68.2
Traditionalist Catholic	91.6	92.4	66.4
Traditionalist evangelical	74.0	94.7	75.7

Source: 2003 Religious Diversity Study (*N* = 2000).

they reveal both the peril and promise that faith-based politics can present to American democracy.

Religious Pluralism

In 2003, more than four-fifths of Americans agreed that "religious diversity has been good for America" (first column table 2.5). This statement is an example of religious pluralism: the notion that religious diversity is a desirable thing (Wentz 1998), a view often seen as a prerequisite for democratic politics (Hutchinson 2007). Support and opposition to pluralism can be an important source of conflict in a religiously diverse society.

As table 2.5 shows, there was only modest variation in support for religious pluralism across the faith-based alignment. The highest-scoring groups were the liberal faiths (97.9 percent) and Jews (94.9 percent), both aligned with the Democrats, while the lowest groups were traditionalist evangelicals (74.0 percent) and Latino Protestants (76.7 percent), groups aligned with the Republicans. However, these low scores were nonetheless quite high, and religious pluralism was only modestly associated with the alignment measure ($r = 0.05$). Thus, a positive evaluation of religious diversity was the consensus position overall and among the religious groups.

Although not a strictly comparable measure, an "index of cultural diversity" based on 1964 survey questions showed a similar pattern, with a high level of agreement across the religious groups.[31] This pattern is supported by a related survey question, "America owes much to immigrants," that was asked in 1964 and 2003.[32] Immigration has been a major source of religious diversity in the United States, although views on the subject involve many other factors besides religion. Responses to this question were overwhelmingly positive in both years, and the pattern was nearly identical across the religious groups. Like religious pluralism, these items were only weakly correlated with political alignment in 1960 and 2004. These findings suggest that most religious groups have been accustomed to the great religious diversity that has characterized the United States for some time.

If religious Americans may have long valued religious diversity in general, then what about specific kinds of diversity, such as relations between particular religious traditions? The available evidence is mixed for both 1960 and 2004.[33] On the one hand, mutual dislike among Protestants, Catholics, and Jews appears to be relatively low in the present period and to have declined substantially since the 1960s. For example, a 2003 survey found that fewer than one-tenth of the most traditional evangelical Protestants said they would not vote for a "generally qualified" Catholic presidential candidate nominated by their own political party, and the comparable figure for the most traditional mainline Protestants was even lower. In contrast, a survey taken in 1959 found that more than one-half of the most traditional evangelical Protestants and more than one-third of the most traditional mainline Protestants would not vote for a Catholic nominee of their party. The analogous figures in 2003 for opposing a Jewish nominee were about one-tenth of the most traditional evangelicals and mainliners, whereas in 1959 the figures were about three in ten for both groups.

However, a mild reverse trend may have occurred regarding evangelical Protestants. In 1959, virtually all religious groups said they would vote for a Baptist nominee of their party, a Protestant denominational family mostly located in the evangelical tradition (in fact, Americans elected

Baptists to the White House in 1948 and 1976). However, in 2003, about one-sixth of Americans said they would not vote for an "evangelical Christian" candidate, including one-tenth of Catholics, one-sixth of Jews, and more than one-quarter of the unaffiliated. Other studies find considerable hostility to "Christian fundamentalists" in the public at large, a term often applied to evangelicals (Bolce and De Maio 2007).

In addition, hostility to newly prominent religious groups is evident in recent times: in 2003 more than one-third of Americans said they would not vote for a Muslim presidential candidate from their party, and in 2007 about one-sixth said they would not vote for a Mormon.[34] Such opposition was more common among the most traditional religious groups but present among other groups as well. The mixed nature of these data is well illustrated by views toward voting for an atheist: in 2003 one-half of Americans said they would not vote for an atheist nominee of their party, and in 1959 the figure was about three-quarters. But overall, hostility to religious groups was more strongly linked to political alignment in 1959 than in 2003. This change is consistent with the lessened importance of religious tradition in the restructured party coalitions in 2004 compared to the ethno-religious coalitions in 1960.

Civil Religion

In 2003, nearly four-fifths of Americans agreed with the statement "America has been strong because of its faith in God" (second column in table 2.5). This statement is a version of American "civil religion," a nonsectarian belief that God has a special relationship with the United States, and a view that has often been seen as a source of national unity (Lipset 1997). Support or opposition to civil religion can be an important source of conflict in a religiously diverse society.

As one might expect, the unaffiliated seculars (Democratic alignment) were among the least likely to agree with this statement of civil religion—but one-half agreed with the statement nonetheless. The group with the lowest level of agreement was the composite category of liberal faiths (38.3 percent), and the highest level of agreement was found among the traditionalist groups aligned with the GOP (better than 90 percent). Although there is wide agreement with this statement of civil religion, it was still correlated with the 2004 political alignment ($r = -0.27$). Thus, the picture is mixed: civil religion may have become as much a point of national disunity as unity.

There is reason to believe that civil religion was also widely accepted in 1960 as well. Indeed, John F. Kennedy's inaugural speech in 1961 has been identified as a prime example of civil religion (Bellah 1967). Although not strictly comparable, a 1964 survey question asked about passing a hypothetical law to require that the president of the United States "believe in God."[35] Three-fifths of the respondents supported such a law, with the strongest support also coming from traditionalists and the least support from the less traditionally religious and non-Christians. More recent survey findings on whether the president should be a person of faith show a similar pattern.[36] But unlike 2003, these views were not correlated with partisan alignment in 1960, a change that fits with the restructured party coalitions rather than ethno-religious coalitions.

Religious Particularism

In 2003, a little more than one-half of Americans agreed with the statement "Our democratic form of government is based on Christianity" (third column in table 2.5). This statement is an example of religious particularism—and in fact, Christian particularism. Although there may be some truth to this statement from a historical point of view (Heclo 2007), it can also be understood as claiming a privileged position in politics for a particular religion or set of related religious traditions.[37] Like religious pluralism and civil religion, support or opposition to forms of religious particularism can be a source of conflict in a religiously diverse society.

The traditionalist groups aligned with the Republicans were most likely to agree with this statement, whereas the non-Christian groups aligned with the Democrats were the least likely. However, it is worth noting that the level of agreement with this measure of religious particularism was markedly lower than for the measure of civil religion, overall and across the religious groups. It was also less correlated with alignment ($r = -0.21$). Perhaps religious diversity itself militates against religious particularism, even in this general form.

Some indirect evidence suggests that many Americans may have agreed with this kind of religious particularism in the 1960s as well. For example, in 1964 nearly three-fifths of Americans favored prayer in public schools,[38] at about the time the U.S. Supreme Court ruled this practice unconstitutional. Support for school prayer was then greatest among the traditionalist groups and least among the less traditionally religious and non-Christian groups. There continued to be majority public support for school prayer in the early twenty-first century, with a similar pattern across the religious groups.[39] But once again these views were not linked to partisan alignment in the 1960s as they were in the 2000s.

Taken together, these attitudes reveal both peril and promise in explicitly religious conflict in politics. Religious particularism appears to be, and to have been, a more serious flash point than views on religious pluralism per se, especially in the restructured party coalitions of the twenty-first century. And civil religion may have an impact similar to religious particularism. But these views can also be a source of agreement across

TABLE 2.6
Religious Groups and Basic Democratic Values, 2004

	Percentage who strongly agree that democracy requires		
	Politicians take citizens' views into account	Government protects rights of minorities	Opportunities for participation
Unaffiliated seculars	72.1	60.3	61.6
Black Protestants	70.7	77.1	63.7
Modernist Catholic	81.5	63.0	53.8
Jews	76.2	83.3	39.0
Modernist mainline	76.5	57.4	48.5
Latino Catholic	74.7	69.6	55.7
Unaffiliated believers	61.8	57.4	54.4
Liberal faiths	79.2	60.9	45.8
Other world religions	62.2	67.6	54.1
All	**74.2**	**61.7**	**54.9**
Centrist Catholic	65.2	61.8	42.2
Centrist mainline	82.6	56.2	55.4
Modernist evangelical	81.1	61.6	62.2
Latino Protestants	61.9	40.0	55.0
Traditionalist mainline	74.5	59.6	40.4
Other Christians	78.1	58.1	35.5
Centrist evangelical	75.7	54.1	60.6
Traditionalist Catholic	70.7	63.9	49.4
Traditionalist evangelical	77.9	51.5	55.9

Source: 2004 General Social Survey (*N* = 1490).

faith-based alignments, especially the widespread recognition of American religious diversity. It is worth noting that these general attitudes were less strongly correlated with faith-based alignments than cultural issues in 2004.

Religious Diversity and Public Support for Democratic Values

If religion can be a unique source of political conflict, what impact might such conflict have on public support for democratic values? A first step toward answering this question is to gauge general public support for democratic values. Table 2.6 reports the percentage of each religious group that strongly agreed that three values were "very important" to "people's rights in a democracy" in 2004: (1) "politicians take into account the views of citizens before making decisions" (a rough proxy for majority rule); (2) "government authorities respect and protect the rights of minorities"; and (3) "people be given more opportunities to participate in public decision making."[40] Unfortunately, there are no comparable survey measures for the 1960s, but what evidence does exist suggests a similar pattern of opinion.

First, three-quarters of Americans strongly agreed that democracy requires politicians to pay attention to the views of citizens (first column table 2.6), and here there was only modest variation among the religious groups. For instance, seven in ten unaffiliated seculars (most aligned with the Democrats) strongly endorsed this statement, and so did nearly eight of ten traditionalist evangelicals (most aligned with the Republicans). Interestingly, the groups with the lowest level of agreement were found toward the middle of the partisan alignment: unaffiliated believers (61.8 percent), the composite category of other world religions (62.2 percent), centrist Catholics (65.2 percent), and Latino Protestants (61.9 percent). Strong commitment to this version of majority rule was not correlated with alignment ($r = 0.02$).

Second, three-fifths of Americans strongly agreed that democracy required the government to protect the rights of minorities (second column table 2.6), and here there was somewhat more variation across religious groups. The groups most in agreement were Jews (83.3 percent), black Protestants (77.1 percent), and Latino Catholics (69.6 percent), all aligned with the Democrats. And the groups least in agreement were Latino Protestants (40.0 percent), traditionalist evangelicals (51.5 percent), and centrist evangelicals (54.1 percent), all aligned with the Republicans. Strong commitment to this version of minority rights was more strongly correlated with alignment, but in the opposite direction ($r = -0.10$).

Third, a majority of Americans strongly agreed that democracy requires opportunities for citizen participation (third column table 2.6), and on this matter there was considerable variation among the religious groups. However, the groups most and least in agreement were found on *both* sides of the partisan alignment. The most supportive groups included black Protestants (63.7 percent), modernist evangelicals (62.2 percent), unaffiliated seculars (61.6 percent), and centrist evangelicals (60.6 percent). And the least supportive groups included the composite category of other Christians (35.5 percent), Jews (39.0 percent), traditionalist mainline Protestants (40.4 percent), and centrist Catholics (42.2 percent). As a consequence, strong commitment to this version of citizen participation was not correlated with alignment ($r = 0.03$).

On balance, the patterns in table 2.6 provide a positive assessment of the general support for democratic values among religious groups in 2004. Strong commitment to majority rule neared the level of consensus, and although strong commitment to minority rights was somewhat lower and less widespread, it was still backed by a large majority of the public. Strong commitment to citizen participation was more problematic from the point of view of a functioning democracy, with just a simple majority in agreement and considerable variation across the religious groups. The fact that these views were not strongly connected to the faith-based alignment may reduce concern somewhat.

Of course, these patterns reflect support for democratic values in general, not in specific circumstances. Could public support for these values be eroded by religious conflict? Some survey evidence suggests this pattern may be the case. Figure 2.5a illustrates this possibility for minority rights in a 2005 survey,[41] plotting first the general support for minority rights from table 2.6 (dotted line) and then the percentage of each religious group that would not ban demonstrations or rallies by any of four unpopular groups (dashed line): "religious fundamentalists," "radical Muslims," "Communists," and "people who are against all churches and religion."[42] The difference between these two lines provides an estimate of the potential erosion of general democratic values as a result of the political conflict involving these unpopular groups across the faith-based alignment.

Three features of figure 2.5a are worth noting. The first is the widespread pattern of large differences between the general support for minority rights and unwillingness to ban demonstrations by unpopular minorities. This potential erosion of support for minority rights includes nearly every religious group. The second is the association of such erosion with the faith-based alignment: the groups aligned with the GOP showed the largest level of potential erosion, largely because of the views of traditionalist groups, and especially traditionalist evangelicals (here the correlation with alignment order was –0.06, similar to that for the general measure of minority rights in table 2.6). In fact, religious traditionalism is linked to intolerance in the public, as James Gibson documents elsewhere in this volume (chapter 5). Both of these patterns may be problematic from the perspective of a functioning democracy.[43]

A third feature of figure 2.5a is more positive from the perspective of democracy: the level of erosion is widely distributed across partisan alignment, with both the Democratic and Republican coalitions containing a mix of religious groups with lower and higher levels of erosion. In practical terms, this means that groups with different levels of support for democratic values are closely allied with one another and thus may have incentives to moderate their political behavior, if not their views. This welter of groups and values is consistent with the mitigating effects of coalitions of minorities and cross-cutting cleavages on political conflict.

Of course, protection of minority rights is not the only democratic value that might be undermined by religious conflict. Figure 2.5b looks at the potential erosion of majority rule, plotting the general support for

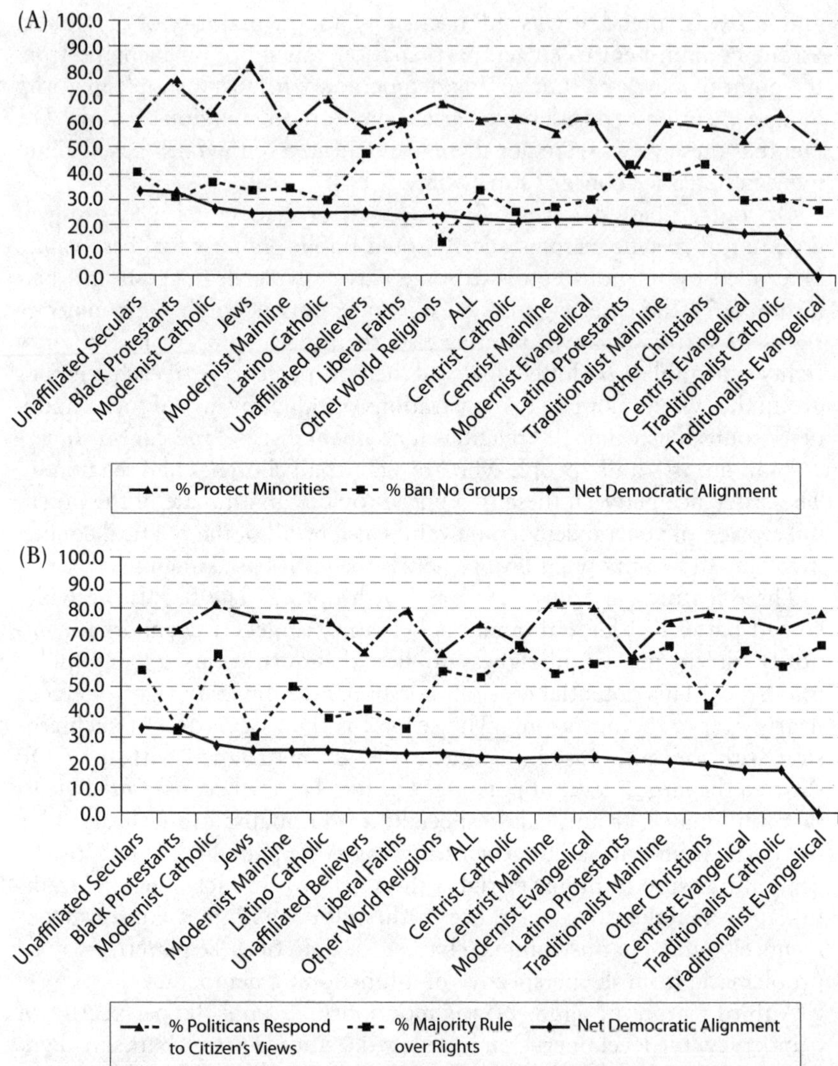

Figure 2.5. (A) Partisan alignment and potential erosion of support for minority rights by religious groups. Source: 2005 CID Survey (*N* = 1001); 2004 General Social Survey (*N* = 1490). (B) Partisan alignment and potential erosion of support for majority rule by religious groups. Source: 2005 CID Survey (*N* = 1001); 2004 General Social Survey (*N* = 1490).

this value from table 2.6 (dotted line) as well as the percentage of each religious group that gave priority to majority rule over protecting minority rights in a separate survey in 2004 (dashed line).[44] Here, too, the difference between these lines provides an estimate of the potential erosion of public support for majority rule.

Note that in figure 2.5b the level of potential erosion is smaller and less widespread than for minority rights in figure 2.5a, and it shows the opposite association with alignment, with the Republican-aligned groups tending to show less erosion than the Democratic-aligned groups (the correlation with alignment order was 0.10, in the same direction but larger than the general correlation of majority rule with alignment in table 2.6). In the context of religious diversity, such support for majority rule may also provide incentives for cross-pressured partners in the coalitions of minorities to modify their behavior, also mitigating the erosion of democratic values.

Religious Diversity and American Democracy

What has this "view from the polls" revealed about religious diversity and American democracy? In terms of religion, it has documented the great variety of religious groups in the United States, and it has illustrated the dynamism of such religious groups over time. In terms of politics, it has shown that religious groups have been politicized in different ways under different circumstances, and, at least in 2004, religious groups showed mixed, if on balance positive, support for democratic values. In 1960, a diverse set of religious groups rooted in religious traditions provided the basis for the ethno-religious party coalitions. By 2004, the set of religious groups had changed in variety and size, with religious traditionalism restructuring party coalitions. In both cases, these alliances were coalitions of religious minorities embedded in a broad set of cross-cutting cleavages. In this context, the variegated support for democratic values among religious groups is further evidence of the diversity of American faith-based politics. In sum, the role of religion in American democracy is complex, changeable, and contingent on political circumstances.

These conclusions reveal some of the perils of faith-based politics, whether these be the Protestant-Catholic tensions that Nixon and Kennedy warned about in the 1960 presidential campaign or the disputes between religious conservatives and liberals that worried many observers in 2004. Religion can be a potent source of political conflict, turning even closely related religious communities into antagonists and rendering sources of national unity into sources of disunity, including the potential to erode public support for democratic values.

But there is also promising evidence for faith-based politics and democracy, both in the narrow sense of building political majorities in a pluralistic society and in the broader sense of bringing important concerns into public affairs—as eloquently described by Romney and Obama in the prelude to the 2008 presidential campaign. Such concerns include considerable support for democratic values, but in a classic Madisonian fashion, the very diversity and dynamism of faith-based politics may mitigate the erosion of support for democratic values, allowing religious diversity to make a positive contribution to democracy. This evidence is consistent with the view that there may be something exceptional about American faith-based politics. Perhaps, as Mark Lilla (2007) has argued, the unique history of the United States has produced the unusual combination of a high level of political freedom for people of many faiths with a relatively peaceful and democratic politics among them. If so, American faith-based politics represents something of an achievement in light of human history and the experience of other countries. It is in this sense that a description of faith in American politics may be, as Nancy Rosenblum argues in chapter 12 of this volume, a description of faith in American politics itself.

Appendix: Religious Groups in 1960 and 2004

The data for the 1960 election came from the 1964 Anti-Semitism Survey (Glock et al. 1979) and the data for the 2004 election came from the 2004 National Surveys of Religion and Politics (Green et al. 2007). The virtue of these surveys is that they contained a set of similar religion items that were used to calculate the religious groups on religious tradition and traditionalism. The Anti-Semitism Survey contained a measure of the 1960 presidential vote, and these data were weighted to accurately reflect the 1960 presidential vote and turnout.

The religious traditions were calculated from a detailed measure of religious affiliation using a standard classification of the denominations or congregations (see Kellstedt and Green 1993; Layman 2001; Green 2007a, ch 2; and Steensland et al. 2000). Black Protestants and Latinos were separated on the basis of race and ethnicity. Religious traditionalism was calculated on the basis of five belief and behavior measures common to both surveys (worship attendance; belief in God; life after death; the devil; and "Jesus is the only way to salvation"). The items were combined into a factor-based index and adjusted so that each religious tradition had the same mean score in both years. The index was then partitioned within the three largest traditions based on levels of religious salience to create the traditionalist, centrist, and modernist categories. Every effort was made to make the 1960 and 2004 categories as comparable as possible.

TABLE 2.7A
Religious Categories, 1960

	Percentage of adult population	Certain belief in God	Weekly worship attendance	Highest religious salience
Mainline Protestants				
Traditionalist mainline	12.3	97.1	73.3	70.0
Centrist mainline	14.6	68.9	37.0	22.1
Modernist mainline	7.0	44.9	18.0	19.6
Evangelical Protestants				
Traditionalist evangelical	10.7	98.6	79.7	84.4
Centrist evangelical	7.2	86.7	26.6	42.0
Modernist evangelical	3.7	50.7	13.7	28.8
Latino Protestants	*	*	*	*
Black Protestants	11.0	85.3	50.7	71.0
Roman Catholics				
Traditionalist Catholic	10.6	98.6	93.8	76.3
Centrist Catholic	6.6	77.3	62.6	34.8
Modernist Catholic	4.1	61.7	46.3	31.7
Latino Catholics	*	*	*	*
Other Christians	2.0	82.5	67.5	70.0
Liberal faiths	1.1	52.4	42.9	47.6
Jews	2.3	41.3	13.0	23.9
Other world religions	*	*	*	*
Unaffiliated				
Unaffiliated believers	*	*	*	*
Unaffiliated seculars	6.6	30.0	2.3	6.2
Total	**100.0**	**76.6**	**50.6**	**48.8**

Source: 1964 Anti-Semitism Survey ($N = 1975$).
* Less than 1 percent.

Although this categorization process is complex, it was remarkably robust, with a wide range of alternative measures, methods, and cut-points producing essentially the same results (see Green et al. 2007 for more details; for other versions of these categories, see Guth et al. 2006; Green and Waldman 2006; and Green 2004). Because the categories used in this chapter are calculated for purposes of comparing the two data sets over time, they differ somewhat from other versions of the categories calculated using more religion items. Tables 2.7a and 2.7b show the religious content of the categories in 1960 and 2004.

TABLE 2.7B
Religious Categories, 2004

	Percentage of adult population	Certain belief in God	Weekly worship attendance	Highest religious salience
Mainline Protestants				
Traditionalist mainline	4.0	100.0	72.2	61.1
Centrist mainline	6.2	95.5	30.1	30.4
Modernist mainline	6.2	55.1	10.9	12.6
Evangelical Protestants				
Traditionalist evangelical	12.8	100.0	93.9	73.2
Centrist evangelical	6.9	95.7	34.4	49.5
Modernist evangelical	5.5	76.4	25.5	32.3
Latino Protestants	2.6	91.4	65.7	67.0
Black Protestants	9.3	94.7	59.0	67.2
Roman Catholics				
Traditionalist Catholic	5.2	100.0	84.8	62.2
Centrist Catholic	6.1	98.8	52.9	32.0
Modernist Catholic	6.2	59.5	15.4	11.7
Latino Catholic	4.5	89.4	46.9	51.1
Other Christians	2.8	93.7	70.3	62.2
Liberal faiths	1.2	66.0	21.3	28.3
Jews	1.9	53.9	23.7	25.7
Other world religions	1.4	70.2	42.9	42.1
Unaffiliated				
Unaffiliated believers	4.9	92.9	10.7	28.4
Unaffiliated seculars	12.3	22.7	1.0	4.3
Total	**100.0**	**79.8**	**43.1**	**41.0**

Source: 2004 National Survey of Religion and Politics ($N = 2730$).

When other data sets were employed in the analysis (such as in tables 2.5 and 2.6 and figs. 2.5a and 2.5b), the religious traditions were defined in the same fashion, and a factor-based index of the most similar religious beliefs and behaviors was calculated, adjusted to the mean scores of each religious tradition, and then partitioned to match the size of the categories in the 1960 or 2004 categories. On some occasions, only worship attendance was available for these purposes, in which case, the categories are described as "most traditional" (reported weekly attendance) and "less traditional" (less than weekly attendance).

Notes

1. As Alan Wolfe notes in the introduction, political scientists rediscovered the political relevance of religion in the 1980s; see Smidt et al. (2009) for a good summary of the subsequent research that complements this volume. On religion and the 2004 campaign, see Green et al. (2006).

2. I am indebted to Shaun Casey of Wesley Seminary for this material; see Casey (2009) for a fuller account of religion in the 1960 campaign.

3. Nixon was a Protestant from a Quaker background.

4. "Address to the Greater Houston Ministerial Association," http://www.americanrhetoric.com/speeches/jfkhoustonministers.html. Accessed July 2008.

5. "Faith in America," http://www.npr.org/templates/story/story.php?storyId=16969460. Accessed July 2008.

6. "Call to Renewal Keynote Address," http://obama.senate.gov/speech/060628-call_to_renewal. Accessed July 2008.

7. For a good summary of these concerns, see Wald and Calhoun-Brown (2007, ch 12).

8. Table 2.1 understates the level of American religious diversity because of the many specific denominations found within many of these religious categories. For a very detailed portrait of American religious diversity, see the Pew Forum on Religion and Public Life, "U.S. Religious Landscape Survey," http://religions.pewforum.org/. For a fuller discussion of the many aspects of such religious diversity, see Wuthnow (2005).

9. The 2004 survey may underestimate the Latino population; see a joint report of the Pew Hispanic Center and the Pew Forum on Religion and Public Life, "Changing Faiths: Latinos and the Transformation of American Religion," http://pewforum.org/surveys/hispanic/. Accessed October 2007.

10. The 1960 data come from the 1964 Anti-Semitism Survey and the 2004 data from the General Social Survey.

11. There were other similarities as well. Both elections were quite close in the popular vote, with comparable levels of voter turnout and one victory for each party. In both elections the Democratic nominees were Catholic and U.S. Senators from Massachusetts (John F. Kennedy and John F. Kerry), whereas the Republican nominees were Protestants from the West with strong ties to the White House (Richard M. Nixon of California, the sitting vice-president, and George W. Bush of Texas, the son of a former president).

12. On the faith-based vote in 1944 see Green (2007a, 39), and for 2008 see Green (2009a).

13. Evangelicals in the South and especially the Deep South voted more Democratic in 1960 than their co-religionists elsewhere in the country. However, southern voters made up a relatively small portion of the 1960 electorate because of lower voter turnout and the fact that the South made up a relatively small portion of the 1960 voting-age population.

14. However, frequency of worship alone was modestly associated with higher turnout in the 1960 data.

15. The tendency of traditionally religious people to vote more Republican than their less traditional counterparts held for nearly all religious communities in 2004, albeit often by small margins (Green 2007a, ch 3).

16. The net Democratic alignment score was calculated by subtracting the Republican column in Table 2.3 from the Democratic column for each religious group. For example, in 1960 the net Democratic alignment score for traditionalist Catholics was 11.9, which is equal to the Kennedy figure of 15.9 minus the Nixon figure of 4.0.

17. This conclusion is based on a binary logistic regression of the Republican vote using these categories and standard demographic variables in 1960 and 2004. For similar results for 2004, see Olson and Green (2008, ch 1).

18. Calculation of a Lieberson/Sullivan Social Diversity Index (Lieberson 1969) showed a very high level of diversity for all the religious groups and very little variation among them.

19. See Green (2007a, ch 5) for more evidence on religion, demography, and cross-cutting cleavages.

20. For purposes of this and other figures, the partisan alignment measure was converted into positive numbers by setting the most Republican score equal to zero and increasing the other scores accordingly.

21. This time series uses the American National Election Cumulative File (American National Election Study 2005). The religious traditions were defined by denominational affiliation as in the previous tables, but the traditionalists were measured as regular worship attendees, modernists by less regular attendance, and the unaffiliated seculars as nonattendees. These results are quite similar to estimates using additional religious measures (Green 2009b).

22. This item came from the 1964 Anti-Semitism Survey and was a dichotomous "agree-disagree" variable.

23. This item came from the Anti-Semitism Survey and was a five-point Likert scale item concerning the state of morals in the country. The figure plotted is the percentage of respondents who said morals were "getting better."

24. This item came from the Fourth National Survey of Religion and Politics and was a five-part Likert scale item on government spending and services. The figure plotted is the percentage of respondents who supported increased government spending and services.

25. This item came from the Fourth National Survey of Religion and Politics and was a four-part question on abortion. The figure plotted is the percentage of respondents who said abortions should be legal in all or most circumstances.

26. This measure comes from the 1964 National Election Study and is a thermometer rating of the NAACP. The measure plotted is the top two-fifths of the scale, which was asked only to respondents who reported having heard about the NAACP.

27. This measure came from the 1964 Anti-Semitism Survey and is a five-point approval rating of the Birch Society, which was asked only to respondents who reported having heard of the Birch Society.

28. This measure came from the 2000 National Survey of Religion and Politics and was a five-point proximity scale. The data plotted are the percentages of each group that reported being "close" or "very close."

29. This measure came from the Fourth National Survey of Religion and Politics and was a five-point proximity scale. The data plotted are the percentage of each group that reported being "close" or "very close."

30. These items come from 2003 Religion and Diversity Survey (*N* = 2910) conducted by Robert Wuthnow. For more details, see Wuthnow (2005). These items were five-point Likert-scale items.

31. This scale was part of the 1964 Anti-Semitism Survey.

32. This item was found both in the Anti-Semitism Survey and the Religion and Diversity Survey.

33. These data come from a June 2003 survey by the Pew Research Center and the Pew Forum on Religion and Public Life, and from a December 1959 Gallup survey (AIPO622). The level of traditionalism was estimated by frequency of worship attendance; Evangelical Protestants were estimated on the basis of religious beliefs and demography.

34. See Pew Forum on Religion and Public Life, "Public Expressed Mixed Views of Mormonism, Islam," September 25, 2007, http://pewforum.org/surveys/religionviews07/.

35. This item comes from the 1964 Anti-Semitism Survey.

36. This item was asked in the 2004 National Survey of Religion and Politics.

37. By the same token, an assertion that American democracy was based entirely on nonreligious principles could be seen as a similar claim of privilege for secular or nonreligious Americans.

38. This item comes from the 1964 Anti-Semitism Study.

39. Examples are the school prayer items asked in the 2000 General Social Survey.

40. These items come from a battery asked in the 2004 General Social Survey.

41. These data come from the Citizen, Democracy, Involvement (CID) Survey Project (Howard et al. 2005).

42. The CID asked the respondents if they would support a ban on a demonstration by each of these four groups. The measure in figure 2.5a is the percentage of each group that did not agree to the ban for any of the groups.

43. There is some evidence that traditionalists became more tolerant between 1960 and 2004. For example, in the Anti-Semitism Survey, 53.7 percent of the traditionalist evangelicals favored removing a book by an atheist from the public library, and in 2004, a nearly identical question in the General Social Survey found that 41.4 percent held this view. In both years, traditionalist evangelicals were the most likely to approve of removing a book by an atheist. This 12.3 percentage point change was greater than the 8.9 percentage point change for the public as a whole. By way of comparison, in 1964 Jews were the least likely to favor this action, with 10.5 percent, and in 2004 Jews still had among the lowest scores, at 6.7 percent.

44. This item comes from the CID and reads: "For democracy to work best, the will of the majority must be followed OR For democracy to work best, the rights of minorities must be protected."

References

American National Election Study. 2005. The 1948–2004 ANES Cumulative Data File [computer file]. Ann Arbor, MI: Inter-university Consortium for Political and Social Research.

Bellah, Robert N. 1967. "Civil Religion in America." *Journal of the American Academy of Arts and Sciences* 96 (1): 1–21.

Bolce, Louis, and Gerald De Maio. 2007. "Secularists, Antifundamentalists, and the New Religious Divide in the American Electorate." In *From Pews to Polling Places,* ed. J. Matthew Wilson, 251–76. Washington, DC: Georgetown University Press.

Casey, Shaun A. 2009. *The Making of a Catholic President*. New York: Oxford University Press.

Dionne, E. J. 2008. "Polarized by God? American Politics and the Religious Divide." In *Red and Blue Nation?* Vol. I., eds. David W. Brady and Pietro S. Nivola, 175–205. Washington, DC: Brookings Institution.

Finke, Roger, and Rodney Stark. 2005. *The Churching of America 1976–2005*. New Brunswick, NJ: Rutgers University Press.

Glock, Charles, Gertrude Selznick, Rodney Stark, and Stephen Steinberg. 1979. Anti-Semitism in the United States, 1964 [computer file]. Ann Arbor, MI: Inter-university Consortium for Political and Social Research.

Green, John C. 2004. "The American Religious Landscape and Political Attitudes: A Baseline for 2004." Pew Forum on Religion and Public Life. http://pewforum.org/docs/index.php?DocID=55.

———. 2007a. *The Faith Factor: How Religion Influences the Vote*. Westport, CT: Praeger Press.

———. 2007b. "Protestantism, Mainline." In *Encyclopedia of Politics and Religion*, ed. Robert Wuthnow, 735–38. Washington, DC: CQ Press.

———. 2009a. "What Happened to the Value Voters?" *First Things* March, 42–48.

———. 2009b. "The Faith-Based Politics in American Presidential Elections: Trends and Possibilities." In *The Future of Religion in American Politics*, ed. Charles W. Dunn, 209–28. Lexington, KY: University of Kentucky Press.

Green, John C., and Steve Waldman. 2006. "Tribal Politics." *The Atlantic* January/February, 10–14.

Green, John C., Mark J. Rozell, and Clyde Wilcox, eds. 2006. *The Values Campaign: The Christian Right in American Politics*. Washington, DC: Georgetown University Press.

Green, John C., Lyman A. Kellstedt, Corwin E. Smidt, and James L. Guth. 2007. "How the Faithful Voted: Religious Communities and the Presidential Vote." In *A Matter of Faith: Religion in the 2004 Presidential Election*, ed. David E. Campbell, 5–36. Washington, DC: Brookings Institution Press.

Guth, James L, Lyman A. Kellstedt, Corwin E. Smidt, and John C. Green. 2006. "Religious Influences in the 2004 Presidential Election." *Presidential Studies Quarterly* 36 (June): 223–42.

Heclo, Hugh. 2007. *Christianity and American Democracy.* Cambridge, MA: Harvard University Press.

Hout, Michael, and Claude S. Fischer. 2002. "Why Americans Have No Religious Preference: Politics and Generations." *American Sociological Review* 67:165–90.

Hout, Michael, Andrew Greeley, and Melissa J. Wilde. 2001. "The Demographic Imperative in Religious Change." *American Journal of Sociology* 107:468–500.

Howard, Marc Morjé, James L. Gibson, and Dietlind Stolle. 2005. "The U.S. Citizenship, Involvement, Democracy Survey," Center for Democracy and Civil Society (CDACS), Georgetown University.

Hunter, James. 1991. *Culture Wars: The Struggle to Define America*. New York: Basic Books.

Hutchinson, William R. 2007. *Religious Pluralism in America*. New Haven: Yale University Press.

Kelley, Dean. 1972. *Why Conservative Churches Are Growing*. San Francisco, CA: Harper & Row.

Kellstedt, Lyman A., and John C. Green. 1993. "Knowing God's Many People: Denominational Preference and Political Behavior." In *Rediscovering the Religious Factor in American Politics,* eds. David C. Leege and Lyman A. Kellstedt. Armonk, NY: M. E. Sharpe, 53–71.

Kellstedt, Lyman A., John C. Green, James L. Guth, and Corwin E. Smidt. 2007. "Faith Transformed: Religion and American Politics from FDR to George W. Bush." In *Religion and American Politics: From the Colonial Period to the Present,* 2nd ed., eds. Mark A. Noll and Luke E. Harlow, 269–95. Oxford: Oxford University Press.

Kohut, Andrew, John C. Green, Scott Keeter, and Robert Toth. 2000. *The Diminishing Divide: Religion's Changing Role in American Politics*. Washington, DC: Brookings Institution.

Layman, Geoffrey C. 2001. *The Great Divide: Religious and Cultural Conflict in American Party Politics*. New York: Columbia University Press.

Layman, Geoffrey C., and John C. Green. 2005. "Wars and Rumors of Wars: The Contexts of Cultural Conflict in American Political Behavior." *British Journal of Political Science* 36(1):61–89.

Lieberson, Stanley. 1969. "Measuring Population Diversity." *American Sociological Review* 34:850–62.

Lilla, Mark. 2007. *The Stillborn God: Religion, Politics, and the Modern West.* New York: Knopf.

Lincoln, C. Eric, and Lawrence Mamiya. 1990. *The Black Church in the African American Experience*. Durham, NC: Duke University Press.

Lipset, Seymour Martin. 1997. *American Exceptionalism: A Double-Edged Sword*. New York: W. W. Norton & Company.

McCormick, Richard L. 1974. "Ethno-Cultural Interpretations of Nineteen-Century American Voting Behavior." *Political Science Quarterly* 89:351–77.

Moore, Martha T. 2006. "Episcopal Church Torn by Gay Issue as More Parishes Leave." *USA Today*, March 2.

Olson, Laura R., and John C. Green, eds. 2008. *Beyond Red State, Blue State: Electoral Gaps in the Twenty-first Century American Electorate*. Upper Saddle River, NJ: Prentice Hall.

Petrocik, John R. 2006. "Party Coalitions in the American Public: Morality Politics, Issue Agendas, and the 2004 Election." In *The State of the Parties,* 5th ed., eds. John C. Green and Daniel Coffey, 279–89. Lanham, MD: Rowman & Littlefield.

Smidt, Corwin E., Lyman A. Kellstedt, and James L. Guth. 2009. *The Oxford Handbook of Religion and American Politics*. New York: Oxford University Press.

Steensland, Brian, Jerry Z. Park, Mark D. Regnerus, Lynn D. Robinson, W. Bradford Wilcox, and Robert D. Woodberry. 2000. "The Measure of American Religion: Toward Improving the State of the Art." *Social Forces* 79:291–318.

Swierenga, Robert P. 2007. "Ethno-religious Political Behavior in the Mid-Nineteenth Century: Voting, Values, and Cultures." In *Religion and American Politics: From the Colonial Period to the Present,* 2nd ed., eds. Mark A. Noll and Luke E. Harlow, 145–68. Oxford: Oxford University Press.

Wald, Kenneth D., and Allison Calhoun-Brown. 2007. *Religion and Politics in the United States* 5th ed. Lanham, MD: Rowman & Littlefield.

Wentz, Richard E. 1998. *The Culture of Religious Pluralism.* Boulder, CO: Westview Press.

Wuthnow, Robert. 1988. *The Restructuring of American Religion.* Princeton, NJ: Princeton University Press.

———. 1989. *The Struggle for America's Soul: Evangelicals, Liberals, and Secularism.* Grand Rapids, MI: Eerdmans.

———. 1996. "Restructuring of American Religion: Further Evidence." *Sociological Inquiry* 66:303–29.

———. 2005. *America and the Challenges of Religious Diversity.* Princeton, NJ: Princeton University Press.

Chapter 3

MUSLIM AMERICANS

Enriching or Depleting American Democracy?

AMANEY JAMAL

SINCE 9-11, Muslim Americans have increasingly been viewed as suspicious entities in American society. Not only is there a pervasive and dominating fear that Muslims have violent tendencies aimed at destroying all things American, but even those Muslims who profess allegiance to America are thought inherently incapable of sharing core American democratic values because they embrace a rigid and intolerant Islamic faith. Thus, not only are Muslim Americans viewed as other conservative religious groups, like the Christian Right, as groups that uphold inherently intolerant and regressive beliefs; this group is also viewed as anti-American and as people who, through the use of violence, can undermine American freedom and democratic liberties altogether. We have seen the manifestation of these stereotypes in both policy and popular discourses. In fact, these two overarching themes structure the interactions between mainstream society and the Muslim population.

Although the horror of 9-11 has in many ways shaped these negative interactions, the catastrophic event has raised the opportunity to better understand the Muslim-American experience before and after 9-11. In the first-ever national poll of Muslim Americans, the Pew Research Center found that Muslim Americans are very much a mainstream religious minority in the United States.[1] They share many of the same religious values of the general American public. Mostly middle class, Muslim Americans are concerned with issues similar to those that occupy the general American population. Yet, differences emerge between the two populations as well. Muslim Americans are more worried about the effects of 9-11 on their own communities and are more critical of U.S. foreign policy in the Middle East.

These survey findings not only provide us with the unique opportunity to compare Muslim Americans to the general population but also offer us the ability to better understand significant patterns and variations that emerge within the sample of Muslims. This chapter first offers an overview of the Muslim-American community. Where applicable, it also makes comparisons to the larger mainstream U.S. population. The study then examines the ways in which two sets of issues mediate patterns of Muslim-American political engagement. The following suppositions guide this line of inquiry.

First, from a mainstream standpoint, Muslims are often seen as different and threatening. There is wide belief that the Islamic religion is antidemocratic. To examine these claims more carefully, it is imperative to look at the effect of Muslim religiosity and identity on levels of political engagement. Are more observant Muslims less likely to participate politically? Are religious Muslims more likely to remain marginalized from mainstream society? Do they shy away from participation in the "secular" institutions of the state? What about those individuals who strongly identify as Muslim? Are they more likely to remain on the outskirts of the mainstream and to resist assimilation?[2] Are they more likely to hold values that are anti-American? Second, complementing this line of inquiry, what are the concerns that emanate from within the Muslim community? How do levels of real and perceived discrimination mediate patterns of political engagement? This chapter will simultaneously address these two sets of issues. First, however, we begin with an overview of the American Muslim community.

The American Muslim Community

The American Muslim community today stands at around 6 million individuals.[3] Sixty-five percent of the community is foreign born, whereas 35 percent of American Muslims were born in the United States. Muslim immigrants come from at least sixty-eight different countries: 24 percent of the Muslim population directly emigrated from Arab countries; 18 percent came from Pakistan or another South Asian country, and 8 percent came from Iran. Another 5 percent of the Muslim community came from Europe, and 4 percent from Africa. Another 6 percent immigrated from other countries. Thirty-nine percent of the Muslim population in the United States is relatively new, having arrived after 1990. And among native-born Muslims, slightly more than half (57 percent) are African-American. Twenty-five percent of the community converted to Islam, and 75 percent of native-born Muslims were born into the faith. One-fifth of the native-born (or 7 percent of the entire sample) population is second-generation immigrant. Muslims immigrate to the United States for a variety of reasons. Education and economic opportunities are cited by almost equal percentages of the population (26 percent and 24 percent, respectively). Twenty percent of the Muslim population say that they came to the United States to escape conflict and persecution in their home country, and 77 percent of all Muslim immigrants are U.S. citizens. No single racial group constitutes a majority among the Muslim-American population—39 percent describe themselves as white, 26 percent black, 20 percent Asian, and 16 percent as of mixed race.

Income and Education

Muslim Americans generally resemble the mainstream population when we examine their levels of education and income. More than a fifth (22 percent) of the Muslim population is enrolled in college classes. These percentages extend to both the foreign-born and immigrant communities. However, a somewhat larger proportion of Muslims have not finished high school (21 percent) than is true for the public at large (16 percent).

Economically, family income among Muslim Americans is roughly comparable with that of the general U.S. population. Among U.S. adults, 44 percent report household incomes of $50,000 or more annually, as do 41 percent of Muslim-American adults. At the highest end of the income scale, Muslim Americans are about as likely to report household incomes of $100,000 or more as are members of the general public (16 percent for Muslims compared with 17 percent among the general public). Roughly a third of both Muslim Americans (35 percent) and adults nationwide (33 percent) report household incomes of less than $30,000.

These impressive levels of economic integration stand in direct contrast to the experience of Muslims in Europe. Surveys of Muslim populations in Great Britain, France, Germany, and Spain conducted in 2006 as part of the Pew Global Attitudes Project found Muslims to fare much worse than their average European counterparts. For example, 53 percent of Muslims in Germany reported family incomes of less than €18,000 annually, compared to only 25 percent of Germans overall. A similar trend exists in France. In Great Britain, 61 percent of Muslims reported incomes of less than £20,000 annually, compared to only 39 percent of the general public. And 73 percent of Spanish Muslims report incomes of less than €14,500, compared with half of the Spanish public nationwide.

All in all, the Pew Survey of Muslim Americans found the community to be highly assimilated and successful. Not only do Muslim Americans resemble the general population in terms of income and education distribution, but the Muslim-American community today is also highly satisfied and happy. The community's level of satisfaction resembles those levels of the general population; compared to 49 percent in the general population, 42 percent of Muslim Americans are satisfied.

Differences, however, do emerge between the Muslim-American and general populations. Muslims tend to be more socially conservative than the general population. For example, 61 percent of Muslims said homosexuality should be discouraged, compared to 38 percent in the general population. However, despite their social conservatism, they are strong advocates of bigger government. For example, 70 percent of Muslims, compared to 63 percent of the general population, believe the government should do more to help the needy. The support of Muslims for big government extends also to the terrain of ethics: 59 percent of the Muslim-American community believes the government should do more to protect "morality" in society, whereas 37 percent of the general population supports this intervention.

The Muslim-American population and the general population are most divided on matters relating to U.S. foreign policy. Only 35 percent of the Muslim population thinks the United States made the right decision to go to war in Afghanistan. An even smaller 12 percent thinks we made the right decision in going into Iraq. The general population is more supportive of the government's decision to go to war—61 percent supported the war in Afghanistan, and 45 percent supported the war in Iraq. These foreign policy assessments extended to George W. Bush's approval rating, with only 15 percent of the Muslim population approving of the way Bush was handling his job; in the general population, a larger 35 percent approved of the way Bush handled his job. Of those Muslim Americans who voted in the 2004 national election, only 14 percent chose Bush, with the vast majority—71 percent—voting for John Kerry.

Not only are Muslims more critical of U.S. foreign policy, but these assessments extend to the War on Terror as well. Whereas 67 percent of the general population believes the War on Terror is a sincere effort to curb terrorism, only 26 percent of the Muslim population believes this to be the case. The two populations are closer in their profiling assessments concerning the War on Terror; 54 percent of the Muslim community believes that the War on Terror singles out Muslims, whereas 45 percent of the general population believes this is the case. However, they diverge on the degree to which it bothers them—74 percent of Muslims say it bothers them a lot, compared to a much smaller 52 percent in the general population. On such matters as the Arab-Israeli conflict, we see greater agreement: 61 percent of Muslim Americans believe that a way can be found for Palestinians and Israelis to coexist. This percentage is shared by the general population, with a slightly higher 67 percent believing peaceful coexistence is possible.

On political participation scores and measures, we see another set of similarities and differences. Most notably, Muslim Americans are far less likely to identify as Republican; further, they were less supportive of George W. Bush than the general population. Of the Muslim-American population, 37 percent identified as Democratic, whereas 34 percent of the general population did so. Although comparable percentages identified with the

Democratic Party, only 7 percent of the Muslim population—compared to 24 percent of the general population—said they were Republican. In the 2004 election, only 14 percent of the Muslim community voted for Bush, whereas 50 percent of the general population did so. As we have seen, though, the Bush Administration's War on Terror and unpopular foreign policy did not resonate well with the Muslim-American community.

Muslim Americans: Political Engagement and 9-11

Since the events of 9-11, Muslim Americans have been portrayed as both victim and suspect. The general American population both sympathizes with and remains wary of this religious minority. In this conundrum, Muslim Americans have come to play a new dual role in the post–9-11 environment. Today they find themselves both having to take a defensive stance toward Islam as they also attempt to secure their status as an American minority group. Unlike other minorities, however, there is deep concern within the larger society about whether Muslims respect and appreciate democracy. Will Muslim absorption and integration threaten democracy more largely?

The events of 9-11 have only heightened the urgency of these questions. It is indeed unfortunate that Muslim Americans have come to be known to millions of other Americans through this lens of terrorism. It is also through this very lens that Muslim Americans continue to engage mainstream America. Muslims know that they are perceived to be a highly suspicious minority group, that their patriotic loyalties are being tested day in and day out. Although 9-11 is several years removed from us, this prism of interaction, it appears, will continue to structure engagement between Muslims and the mainstream public for years to come.

Thus, American Muslims today find themselves having to represent and speak for Muslims across the globe—often having to explain the more grotesque and demoralizing topics of sectarian violence in Iraq, suicide bombings in Palestine, or the limited rights women enjoy in Saudi Arabia. Muslims in America have become accustomed to explaining to the average listener that Islam does not condone these actions, the religion has been hijacked, and it certainly is not the Islam that Muslim Americans embrace. In fact, when Muslim Americans vigorously condemn the repulsive headlines that dominate the news, it is often assumed that an "Americanizing" effect, rather than ingrained Muslim orientations, mediates these more "moderate" viewpoints. Although we see that Muslim Americans are far more moderate than Muslims across the globe, worry and mistrust persist.

The Pew Survey reveals that Muslim Americans are more moderate on questions pertaining to violence than other Muslims in Europe and across the Muslim world. The percentage of U.S. Muslims who feel suicide bombings are justifiable and those who have favorable views of al-Qaeda are remarkably low—especially when these percentages are compared to those for other Muslims in other countries. In Europe, 16 percent of the Muslim population of France, 16 percent of the Muslim population in Spain, and 15 percent of Britain's Muslim population felt suicide bombings are often or sometimes justified. Compared to the 8 percent of U.S. Muslims who felt so, European Muslims, then, are twice as likely to see suicide bombings as justifiable. When compared to their counterparts in the Muslim world, the U.S. percentage is small. In Nigeria, 49 percent of the population reported that suicide bombings are often or sometimes justifiable, with another 29 percent in Jordan in agreement; 28 percent of Egyptians feel that suicide bombings are often or sometimes justifiable, and among Turks, 17 percent shares the view. In Pakistan, only 14 percent can see themselves justifying suicide bombings, and among Indonesians, another 10 percent will say that they are often or sometimes justified.[4] The results of these surveys reveal, if anything, that among the U.S. Muslim community, one finds the lowest percentage of Muslims who believe suicide bombings are justifiable to "defend Islam." Not only does the U.S. Muslim population overwhelmingly denounce suicide bombings, but the Pew report also finds that only 5 percent (1 percent very favorable and 4 percent somewhat favorable) of U.S. Muslims have favorable opinions about al-Qaeda.

Although some might argue that the moderation of values among Muslim Americans can be attributed to assimilation theories predicting that the values of immigrants will, over time, come to resemble those of the mainstream society, there are other factors that shape these perspectives as well. First, Muslim Americans enjoy great freedom to practice their own religion in the United States. Second, and as the Pew report documents, the Muslim-American community has enjoyed considerable socioeconomic success in the United States as well. In other words, Muslim Americans are very much invested in the structures that allow them religious freedom and economic prosperity. Muslim Americans are direct beneficiaries of American democracy and therefore are invested in preserving the status quo.

Muslim Americans and the "Other Within"

9-11 solidified the prism through which mainstream society views its Muslim minority group and vice-versa. Although mainstream society sympathizes with Muslims, it continues to worry whether Muslims are so different that they could harm democracy either by espousing violence and holding on to illiberal values or by becoming a marginal, disaffected, and balkanized group that remains on the fringes of democratic society. For mainstream society, it appears, consistent reassurance is needed to quell concerns about Islamic religiosity and identity. Reassurance is also needed by Muslims. As Muslims continue to engage mainstream society, there is a strong desire to know that the community will not be singled out and denied the opportunities to practice its civic rights and responsibilities. Muslim Americans fear that 9-11 has dealt them a tremendously significant blow—one that they may never overcome. These concerns and worries mediate the ways in which mainstream society and the Muslim American population interact with one another today. Yet, to what extent do Muslim religiosity, identity, and discrimination shape patterns of political engagement? Before we turn to this question, the next section offers an overview of these dimensions.

Discrimination: Real and Perceived

The events of 9-11 exposed the deep misunderstanding that exists about Muslims and Islam more broadly. Mainstream Americans knew very little about the religion prior to 9-11. What little they did know was often based on the portrayals of the popular media—where Muslims were seen as terrorists well before 9-11. The horrific events of that day simply reinforced and solidified an existing perception. A long history of misrepresentation and the promotion of violent stereotypes about Muslims mark the popular American media.[5] As Susan Akram says, "Muslims and Arabs are consistently absent from that desirable group of ordinary people, families with social interactions, or outstanding members of communities such as scholars or writers or scientists." This process of stereotyping, Akram goes on to say, "has been so complete and so successful that film critics, most Americans and social commentators have barely noticed" (Akram 2002). Muslim Americans have often lamented the fact that the media is not fair when it comes to the way their community is represented. The Pew survey finds that 57 percent of the Muslim-American population believes the media is unfair and biased against them.

Through the lens of these types of portrayals, the American mainstream has come to learn about Islam and Muslims. A July 2005 Pew survey revealed[6] that 36 percent of the American population believes Islam encourages violence; another 36 percent reported that they have unfavorable opinions about Islam; and 25 percent say they had no opinion about the religion at all. When asked whether they knew what Allah and the Quran stood for, only half of the U.S. population could identify Allah as the word Muslims use to refer to God and the Quran as their holy book. In fact, those Americans who knew what Allah and the Quran stood for were more likely to have favorable opinions about Islam and Muslims.

It is against this backdrop that Muslim Americans continue to strive to exercise their political rights and voices. When asked by the Pew survey of 2007 to identify the most important problem facing U.S. Muslims today, 60 percent of response patterns among Muslims centered on issues pertaining to discrimination, misunderstandings, and stereotyping. Specifically, 19 percent reported that discrimination, racism, and prejudice were major problems. Another 15 percent reported the major challenge centered on their image as terrorists. Fourteen percent indicated that ignorance and misconceptions about Islam continue to be problematic. And 12 percent added that generalizations and stereotypes about all Muslims are of great concern. In fact, 53 percent of Muslims believe it is much more difficult to be a Muslim in the United States today, after the events of 9-11.

The Pew survey also reveals that, specifically because of their faith, 37 percent of the Muslim population in the United States worries about job security, 31 percent worries about being monitored, and 51 percent worries that women who wear the *hijab* (Muslim headscarf) are subjected to unfair treatment. A full quarter of the Muslim population has fallen victim to acts of discrimination. Twenty-six percent of U.S. Muslims report non-Muslims acting suspicious of them; 15 percent of Muslims have been called offensive names; and 9 percent of Muslims say they have been singled out by law enforcement. Yet, discrimination is not the only mode through which Muslims interact with mainstream society. A full third of the Muslim population reports members have been the recipients of support since the 9-11 attacks from members of the mainstream population. Nevertheless, as the response patterns indicate above, Muslim Americans remain rather vulnerable to the ways in which the mainstream society views and treats them.

Religiosity

The Muslim-American population is as religious as its Christian counterpart. Forty percent of Muslim Americans attend mosque at least once a week. Christians in the general population report a 39 percent weekly attendance rate. Whereas 30 percent of Muslims take part in social activities at their mosques, 40 percent of the general population report doing so at their churches. Ninety percent of Muslims report that religion is very important or important in their lives, and 83 percent of the general population agreed. Sixty-one percent of the Muslim population prays daily, compared to 64 percent of the general population. Eighty-six percent of Muslims believe the Quran is the word of God, but 60 percent of Muslims believe there is more than one way to interpret Islam. Ninety-six percent of those sampled believe in one God, Allah, and 94 percent of them believe in the prophet Mohammad. Three-fourths believe that giving *zakat* (charity) and fasting during the month of Ramadan are very important.[7]

The Pew Research Center defines Muslim religious commitment as attending mosque at least once a week, praying all five *salah* prayers,[8] and reporting that religion is "very important" in their lives. According to this definition, nearly one-quarter (23 percent) of Muslim Americans have a high level of religious commitment. About as many (26 percent) have a relatively low level of religious commitment, rarely engage in these practices, and generally regard religion as less important in their lives. A majority of Muslim Americans (51 percent) fall somewhere in between.[9]

Identity

Muslim Americans are well integrated even while they remain devout and committed to their identities. When asked whether they consider themselves "Muslim first" or "American first," 47 percent reported that they considered themselves Muslim first, with another 28 percent saying American first; 18 percent volunteered to say both equally. That close to half the Muslim population chose to cite their religion as a primary marker of identity is similar to a finding that emerged when this same question was asked of Christians in the general population. There, 42 percent said they considered themselves Christian first. Christians, however, were more likely to identify as American as well, with 48 percent professing this primary identity.

Although Muslims are more likely to identify as Muslim first, they are also likely to associate with people from different religious backgrounds. Muslims do not socialize only with members of their own community. Only 12 percent of Muslims reported that all of their friends were Muslim. The remainder indicated that they have other friends from other backgrounds.[10]

Muslim Americans believe they can balance their religious commitments and life in the United States. When asked whether they felt there is a conflict in being a devout Muslim and living in a modern society, 63 percent did not believe there was a conflict. In the general population that number is at 42 percent. Finally, Muslims are more likely to favor integration rather than segmentation or marginalization. When asked whether Muslims coming to the United States today should mostly adopt American customs and ways of life, 43 percent of respondents said yes. However, 26 percent of respondents agreed with this statement: "Muslims coming to the United States today should mostly try to remain distinct from the larger American society." Another 16 percent volunteered that Muslims should try to accomplish both.[11]

Tests

How do levels of religiosity, chosen markers of identity, and perceptions of discrimination shape levels of American Muslim political engagement? More specifically, how do these factors shape the four patterns of political behavior and attitudinal predispositions important for our analysis here—voting, support for al-Qaeda, attitudes about assimilation, and levels of life satisfaction? Two popular strands of inquiry guide these tests. The first strand emanates from concerns held by mainstream society: Do Muslims who are more religious and who see themselves as Muslim first exhibit qualities that may be seen as undemocratic or threatening to democracy? Are they more likely to resist political participation? Are they more likely to support violent groups such as al-Qaeda? Are they more likely to be less satisfied and believe Muslims should remain distinct? For mainstream society, Muslim religion and identity are markers of "otherness." Do these markers matter for political engagement?

Although popular perceptions seem to hold that higher levels of Islamic religiosity may threaten democracy, it is important to note that existing theories on the role of religion in promoting useful political engagement maintain that religiosity—and especially church attendance—need not come at the expense of democracy. Scholars have long paid significant attention to the role of religious institutions in the political mobilization of citizens (Harris 1994; Verba et al. 1995; Wuthnow 1999; Jones-Correa and Leal 2001). Studies capturing the dynamics of church involvement have highlighted the power of the institution for mobilizing congregants. Verba and colleagues found that churchgoers are more likely to be engaged in political activities. Churches can potentially increase individual levels of civic skills, political efficacy, and political knowledge. They write, "The acquisition of such civic skills is not a function of SES [socioeconomic status] but depends on the frequency of church attendance and denomination of the church one attends."[12] This overflow from the religious to the political sphere has been documented in several studies analyzing the role of churches in political life (Peterson 1992; Calhoun-Brown 1996; Smidt 1999; Greenberg 2000). Some of these studies posit that instead of merely increasing levels of civic involvement, religious institutions can also serve as conduits for direct political mobilization. As Rosenstone and Hansen point out, "Involvement in organizations . . . promotes political participation by making people susceptible to mobilization. Politically, organizations stand between national and local political leaders and ordinary citizens."[13] In fact, new studies have found that civic skills gained in churches do not influence levels of political participation indirectly. Rather, churches influence political participation by directly recruiting congregants into political processes (Djupe and Grant

2001). In short, religiosity and church attendance can bolster political engagement in ways useful for democracy. Yet, current scholarly work stands at odds with common popular accounts of the link between Muslim religiosity and political engagement.

Further, in popular discourse there is also much concern about Muslim identity pronouncements. Here is it assumed that Muslim Americans who characterize themselves primarily as Muslim are more likely to lack loyalty to American democracy. This contention also undermines existing theoretical works on the subject matter. Although there is concern among scholars that a plethora of ethnic identities can have a negative impact on American cultural assimilation (Huntington 2004), critics of these formulations (de la Garza et al. 1996; Citrin et al. 2007) argue that ethnic identities should not threaten identification with American culture, values, and political institutions. They find that ethnic identities can be accompanied with strong patriotic commitments to the United States and its political institutions. However, the fear that Muslim identity and religiosity may impede democracy remains a strong concern of the general American population.

This strand of inquiry, deriving from mainstream American concerns, contrasts with voices emerging from within the Muslim community. In this second strand, members of the community are more likely to consider the impact of discrimination on patterns of political engagement rather than that of religiosity and identity on democracy. Muslim community leaders worry that discrimination may generate marginalization within the community. Discrimination, yet another reminder of Muslim "otherness" in the United States, can plausibly create barriers to participation. Yet, the scholarship is rather divided on the link between discrimination and political engagement. Scholars who have studied group consciousness and collective identity, for example, have found that discrimination promotes empowerment in ways that bode well for political engagement (Miller et al. 1981; Leighley 1996; Jamal 2005). Yet, others worry that groups who are discriminated against might become more disaffected and disadvantaged. Sears et al. refer to this as the "black discrimination model" (Sears et al. 2003; Schildkraut 2005).

To reconcile these conflicting accounts about the sources of and factors that may bolster or stifle political engagement, it is vital to test these claims empirically. Not only will these tests tell us if and how religiosity, identity, and discrimination matter for political engagement, but they will also help us to reconcile much of the confusion surrounding theoretical and popular accounts of minority and Muslim political integration. Further, the findings will also shed light on the mechanisms that may contribute to the dissatisfaction and alienation of Muslim Americans in ways that may pose problems for democracy more generally.

In order to conduct these tests, I used four dependent variables—political participation, support for al-Qaeda, assimilation, and satisfaction—to capture the different dimensions of political engagement.

Political Participation: Voting

I first examine levels of political participation as demonstrated by the vote. Democracy requires the active and formal participation of all its citizens. Citizens who do not participate risk becoming marginalized. Interest representation requires active engagement with the political process. Do religiosity, identity, and discrimination mediate voting patterns? Are religious Muslims more likely to vote? Can religiosity and mosque attendance enhance participation among Muslims as it does for Christians? Or does religiosity not matter at all? Similarly, what role does identity play? Are those Muslims who see themselves as Muslim first less likely to participate? Finally, what role does discrimination play in influencing the vote? Does discrimination empower or disempower Muslims?

Support for Terrorism: al-Qaeda

Second, I examine whether and how religiosity, identity, and discrimination mediate attitudes toward al-Qaeda. Although support for al-Qaeda is extremely low among American Muslims, with only 1 percent having very favorable views and another 4 percent having somewhat favorable views of the organization, it is important to understand the characteristics of those who hold positive evaluations for the group. Examining religiosity is important because much of the post–9-11 scrutiny of Muslim Americans has concentrated on mosques with the assumption that religious Muslims are more likely to be engaged in terrorism. Specifically, I ask whether those Muslims who are more religious, who see themselves as Muslim first, and who have been or worry about being discriminated against tend to have more favorable opinions about al-Qaeda.

Assimilation: Should Muslims Adapt or Remain Distinct?

Third, I explore whether religiosity, identity, and discrimination among Muslim Americans shape attitudes about assimilation. Does religiosity breed a desire to remain less integrated? What about those Muslims who see themselves as Muslim first? Are they more likely to want to remain distinct? Could discrimination play a role? If Muslims attempting to integrate are met with discriminatory responses, will they become more likely to resist assimilation?

Satisfaction: Are Muslims Satisfied with the Way Things Are Going in This Country?

Fourth, how do levels of religiosity, identity, and discrimination mediate levels of satisfaction? Are religious people less satisfied living in a more secular society like the United States? What about those individuals who see themselves as Muslim first? Do levels of discrimination truly structure levels of satisfaction with life the United States?

Tests and Findings

I conducted logistical regression analysis to test many of the claims outlined above. To measure the vote, I used a question asked in the Pew Survey: "In the 2004 presidential election between George W. Bush and John Kerry, did things come up that kept you from voting, or did you happen to vote?" This variable is coded dichotomously with a simple yes or no response. To tap into support for al-Qaeda, I relied on the following question: "Overall, do you have favorable or unfavorable opinions of al-Qaeda?" Those who reported very favorable or somewhat favorable responses were placed in one category. Those who responded with unfavorable sentiments toward the group were placed in another category. Third, to tap into levels of satisfaction, Muslim Americans were asked "Overall, are you satisfied or dissatisfied with the way things are going in this country today?" Respondents were able to choose between being satisfied or dissatisfied. Finally, to gauge whether Muslims want to integrate more or remain distinct, I used the following question: "Which statement comes closer to your view: 'Muslims coming to the United States today should mostly adopt American customs and ways of life' or 'Muslims coming to the United States today should mostly try to remain distinct from the larger American society'?"

In all the models, I controlled for the following demographic factors: age, gender, income, education, and birth place (whether the respondent is an immigrant or United States born). In order to test whether identity, religiosity, and discrimination are linked to the dependent variables described above, I used the following measures. To capture religiosity, I adopted the scale constructed by the Pew research center to measure religious commitment (discussed above). This scale consists of prayer, mosque attendance, and the importance of religion in one's life.[14] To measure identity, I borrowed one question from the Pew survey, which asks respondents whether they see themselves as Muslim or American first. The measure of discrimination was also based on a single question: "Have you ever been discriminated against?" Finally, to tap into worries about discrimination or levels of perceived discrimination, I constructed another index variable relying on three questions: (1) "How worried are you about not being hired for a job or promoted because of your religion?" (2) "How worried are you about your telephone calls and e-mails being monitored by the government because of your religion?" and (3) "How worried are you that women who wear the *hijab* in public will be treated poorly because it identifies them as Muslim?"[15] My findings are shown in table 3.1.

The factors that shape voting patterns among Muslim Americans appear to be demographic in nature. Specifically, those Muslims who are older, more educated, and born in the United States are more likely to have exercised their right to vote. These findings about education, age, and U.S. birth support what we already know about other immigrant groups and the general population. Education serves as a key resource enhancing political efficacy and knowledge in ways that bode well for political participation more broadly. Further, older people are more likely than younger people to vote. Birth in the United States also facilitates voting because although immigrants may have to learn about the political process and in fact obtain citizenship rights, the U.S.-born population is already equipped to exercise the right to vote. Discrimination, identity, and religiosity have no significant effect on whether Muslims vote or not. In other words, these factors neither promote nor depress voting behavior.

When we examine support for al-Qaeda, we discover an intriguing finding. In this model, there are two significant variables: education and immigration status. Those less educated are more likely to support al-Qaeda, a pattern found among other Muslim communities cross-nationally as well. But more surprising is the finding that Muslims born in the United States are more likely to have favorable attitudes about al-Qaeda than Muslims born abroad. Although a very small percentage of immigrant and American-born Muslims are likely to support al-Qaeda, 0.06 percent and 3.6 percent, respectively, American Muslims are more likely to support al-Qaeda than their immigrant counterparts (see table 3.2). Even when race is controlled for, this finding persists. Perhaps this is because Muslims born abroad are more likely to comprehend the negative impact of al-Qaeda on the lives of citizens in the region; in other words, the results might suggest that ideological position is a function of physical experience—the more removed from the violence on the ground, the more the organization can be idealized. Further, not only does al-Qaeda harm people's lives in the Muslim world, but its presence also attracts those who are fighting the War on Terror, thereby exposing people and nations to horrible war scenarios. Although the percentage of those holding favorable views of al-Qaeda is quite low

TABLE 3.1
Logistic Regression Analysis: Political Engagement Vote, Favorable Opinions of al-Qaeda, Satisfaction, and Muslim Distinction

	Model 1	Model 2	Model 3	Model 4
	Vote 2004	Favorable opinions about al-Qaeda[a]	Satisfaction	Muslims should remain distinct
Gender (female)	0.153	–0.071	–0.419	0.265
	(0.298)	(0.653)	(0.266)	(0.276)
Income (low–high)	–0.002	–0.075	–0.010	–0.064
	(0.074)	(0.113)	(0.066)	(0.070)
Age (low–high)	0.042***	–0.008	–0.030**	–0.008
	(0.013)	(0.023)	(0.011)	(0.010)
Education (low–high)	0.342***	–.485**	0.004	–0.185*
	(0.099)	(0.182)	(0.082)	(0.091)
Immigrant status (immigrant)	–0.648*	–1.389**	1.296***	–0.783***
	(0.317)	(0.587)	(0.312)	(0.277)
Muslim first	–0.076	–0.567	0.054	1.123***
	(0.326)	(0.617)	(0.298)	(0.280)
Religiosity scale (low–high)	–0.033	–0.225	0.023	0.084
	(0.053)	(0.127)	(0.042)	(0.050)
Discriminated against	0.130	0.496	–0.290	0.144
	(0.347)	(0.722)	(0.320)	(0.307)
Worry index (low–high)	–0.007	0.093	–0.282***	0.011
	(0.055)	(0.115)	(0.049)	(0.049)
Constant	–2.018	4.316**	–3.262***	1.409
	(1.189)	(1.635)	(1.014)	(1.024)
Observations	615	661	750	774
Percentage predicted correctly	69%	—	69%	78%

Robust standard errors in parentheses; *significant at $p < 0.05$; **significant at $p < 0.01$; ***significant at $p < 0.001$.

[a] *Note:* because only 5 percent of the Muslim-American sample has a favorable opinion of al-Qaeda, I also utilize a rare event logit for this model for robustness purposes. All the findings are robust. Further, percentage predicted correctly is not calculated for this equation because of the small number of positive observations.

(5 percent, compared to 95 percent who don't hold favorable opinions toward the group),[16] it certainly stands against conventional knowledge that immigrants are less likely to hold favorable views of the organization. Most antiterror policies have disproportionately focused on those Muslims coming from abroad. That the U.S.-born population is more

Table 3.2
Probability Shifts between Immigrant and Second-Generation Muslims

	Vote 2004	Support al-Qaeda	Satisfaction	Muslims should remain distinct
American-born Muslims (compared to immigrant Muslims)[a]	12% Difference Immigrant: 69% American born: 81%	3% Difference Immigrant: 0.06% American born: 3.6% *American born 6 times more likely*	24% Difference Immigrant: 38% American born: 14% *Immigrants more than twice as likely to be satisfied*	14% Difference Immigrant: 17% American born: 31%

[a] Controlling other independent variables at their means.

likely to have favorable opinions of the organization stands at odds with popular perceptions. American-born Muslims should, according to assimilation models, be more integrated and hold the views of ordinary Americans. This finding might indeed stand against assimilation and acculturation models of incorporation. American-born Muslims who have favorable opinions about al-Qaeda may be more likely to identify with the organization as a means of asserting their hyphenated American identity. Whereas first-generation immigrants are more likely to seek and desire socioeconomic incorporation, second-generation immigrants are more likely to be invested in asserting their ethnic identities (Portes and Rumbaut 2001).

This finding is supported when we look at the results of the model examining those who believe Muslims coming to this country should remain distinct. Those with lower education and those who consider themselves Muslim first are more likely to support the statement. Further, the American-born Muslim population, compared to the immigrant Muslim population, is also more likely to believe that Muslims should remain distinct by a likelihood of 14 percent (see table 3.2). Those less educated may be more marginalized and as a result support less assimilation. Those who think of themselves as Muslim first are also more likely to desire a distinct identity disassociated from the mainstream. The evidence appears to suggest that while asserting a Muslim identity does not matter for voting patterns, opinions about al-Qaeda, or levels of general satisfaction, it does matter for attitudes about assimilation. Those who consider themselves Muslim first are more likely to desire less assimilation. But most surprising, again, is the finding that U.S.-born Muslims are more likely to desire distinction. One can argue that American Muslims are more likely to want to assert their own identity—one that is separate from the mainstream. Yet and once again, this stands contrary to what we know about cohort effects on acculturation and assimilation. The U.S.-born population should be more "American" than its predecessors. Although more research is needed to understand these findings, it may appear that U.S.-born Muslims believe remaining distinct is more appealing if not more advantageous than incorporation. Perhaps they, as U.S.-born citizens, have the highest expectations of what citizenship rights should afford them. As a result, they are most affected by the overall climate, which sees and views Muslims as outsiders. Table 3.3 shows that U.S.-born Muslims are in fact more likely to report that they have been discriminated against than their immigrant counterparts by a margin higher than 100 percent.[17]

These findings substantiate what other scholars have learned while studying the tendencies among the second generation. Portes and Rumbaut (2001) argue that "segmented assimilation" represents many of the

TABLE 3.3
Discrimination Rates and Birth Place

	Discriminated against (No)	Discriminated against (Yes)	Total
Born in United States	59%	41%	100%
Immigrant	82%	18%	100%

trajectories shaping the incorporation of the second generation in the United States. "Unequal modes of incorporation," they maintain, shape the extent to which immigrants may enrich society or find that their aspirations are blocked, becoming therefore more poised to experience downward mobility. In a subsequent study, Portes and Rumbaut further examined the sources of downward mobility among second-generation immigrants. They found that there are elements of dissonant acculturation linked to these experiences. They labeled this process, drawing on the earlier work of Irving Child, "reactive ethnic formation." Groups that experience significant levels of "extreme discrimination and derogation of their national origins are likely to embrace them ever more fiercely; those received more favorably shift to American identities with greater speed and less pain" (Portes and Rumbaut 2001). Thus, how the second generation is received determines the extent to which the second generation adopts oppositional attitudes toward the mainstream. This has consequences for social mobility more generally.[18]

Finally, when we examine the sources that influence levels of satisfaction, we find a similar trend to that documented above. Muslims born in the United States are less satisfied with life in the United States than are immigrants. In fact, immigrants are almost twice as likely to be more satisfied than American-born Muslims (31 percent to 14 percent). Again, this confirms much of the speculation about this finding (see table 3.2). The index variable capturing worry about specific discriminatory outcomes shapes levels of satisfaction as well; those most worried are least satisfied. Finally, the younger generation appears to be more satisfied than the older generation. Again, what emerges in this analysis is a story about dissatisfaction among those groups that, according to our conventional wisdom, should be more satisfied. The U.S.-born Muslim population should be afforded opportunities and privileges that their immigrant counterparts don't possess; that they are systematically less satisfied illustrates that, at some level, they are either most disappointed with life in the United States or they have higher expectations than their immigrant counterparts.

Conclusion

The Pew Survey results reveal that there are significant similarities between the Muslim and Christian populations in the United States. These similarities encompass all facets of political, social, religious, and civic life. However, differences emerge as well, especially when we examine response patterns pertaining to evaluations of U.S. foreign policy in the Middle East. The markers of distinction that relegate Muslims to an elusive category of "other"—identity, religiosity, and discrimination—are not systematically pertinent in explaining patterns of Muslim-American political engagement. Religiosity is not significant in any of the equations. There is nothing unique about Islamic religiosity, rituals, or practice that either promotes or depresses support for al-Qaeda, attitudes about assimilation, levels of satisfaction, or the exercise of one's right to vote. Discrimination is important in one of the models that examine levels of satisfaction. Those who worry more about the impact of discrimination are more likely to be dissatisfied. Furthermore, identity matters in only one of the equations as well: those who see themselves as Muslim first believe that Muslims should remain more distinct from the mainstream. Yet, this identity is not salient for support of al-Qaeda, voting behavior, or levels of satisfaction. The particularity of Muslims—their identity and their levels of religiosity—have little bearing on political and social integration. Muslims are far more likely to resemble the mainstream population in many of its characteristics.

Most surprising is the systematic finding that emerges in three models: American-born Muslims are more likely to have favorable views of al-Qaeda, be less satisfied, and support a distinct Muslim identity. Something appears to have gone wrong with the acculturation/assimilation script. Second- and third-generation immigrants should have less favorable opinions about al-Qaeda, be more satisfied, and desire more integration than their immigrant counterparts. That U.S.-born Muslims are more likely to consider themselves victims of discrimination (table 3.3) lends credence to the argument that American-born Muslims are becoming more and more disaffected as a political and social community.[19] It could be the case that the U.S.-born Muslim population feels the burden of a post–9-11 backlash in ways that the immigrant population does not. It is not that the U.S.-born population has suffered more, but perhaps it is less likely to tolerate the backlash. The immigrant population may accept the backlash as the price of enjoying a more prosperous life in America.

Although the democratic acculturation script might appear to have gone wrong when the incorporation trajectory of the second generation is examined, the findings might also suggest that this disaffection of the second generation is indeed part and parcel of the Americanization process. To be American is to better understand and assert one's rights and to voice dissent in the face of nondemocratic treatment. Certainly, the second generation appears to be more likely to resist such treatment, assert its identity, and voice its discontent. The findings of this chapter corroborate studies of the second generation among Latinos and Asian Americans. It is the second generation members that are more likely to be assertive of their rights. Indeed, the process of voice and dissent is one of the great pillars of American democracy. In this regard, Muslim Americans, it appears, are joining other immigrant groups in laying claim to the American democratic experience.

Appendix: Data Questions and Coding Used in Logistical Regression Analysis

1. Satisfaction: Overall, are you satisfied or dissatisfied with the way things are going in this country today?
   A. Satisfied
   B. Dissatisfied
2. Which comes closest to your view?
   A. Muslims coming to the United States today should mostly adopt American customs and ways of life.
   B. Muslims coming to the United States today should mostly try to remain distinct from the larger American society.
   C. Both
   D. Neither
   E. Don't know/Decline to answer
3. How worried are you . . .
   About not being hired for a job or promoted because of your religion?
   A. Very worried
   B. Somewhat worried
   C. Not too worried
   D. Not worried at all
   E. Not sure/Decline to answer

   About your telephone and e-mails being monitored by the government because of your religion?
   A. Very worried
   B. Somewhat worried
   C. Not too worried
   D. Not worried at all
   E. Not sure/Decline to answer

That women who wear the headcover or *hijab* in public will be treated poorly because it identifies them as Muslim?
A. Very worried
B. Somewhat worried
C. Not too worried
D. Not worried at all
E. Not sure/Decline to answer

4. Thinking more generally—not just about the past 12 months—have you ever been the victim of discrimination as a Muslim living in the United States?
A. Yes, I have been the victim of discrimination.
B. No, I have not been the victim of discrimination.
C. Don't know/decline to answer

5. On average, how often do you attend the mosque or Islamic center for *salah* and *Jum'ah* prayer?
A. More than once a week
B. Once a week for *Jum'ah* prayer
C. Once or twice a month
D. A few times a year, especially for the *Eid*
E. Seldom
F. Never
G. Don't know/Decline to answer

6. How important is religion in your life?
A. Very important
B. Somewhat important
C. Not too important
D. Not important at all
E. Don't know/Decline to answer

7. Concerning the daily *salah* or prayer, do you, in general . . .
A. Pray all five *salah* daily
B. Make some of the five *salah* daily
C. Occasionally make *salah*
D. Only make *Eid* prayers
E. Never pray
F. Don't know/Decline to answer

8. Do you think of yourself first as an American or first as a Muslim?
A. American
B. Muslim
C. Both (Volunteer)
D. Neither (Volunteer)

9. Overall, do you have a favorable or unfavorable opinion of al-Qaeda?
   A. Very favorable
   B. Somewhat favorable
   C. Somewhat unfavorable
   D. Very unfavorable
   E. Don't know/Decline to answer

10. Last year, that is in 2006, was your total family income from all sources before taxes . . .
    A. Less than $20,000
    B. Over $20,000; below $30,000
    C. Over $30,000; below $50,000
    D. Over $50,000; below $75,000
    E. Over $75,000; below $100,000
    F. Over $100,000

11. What is the last grade or class that you completed in school?

12. In the 2004 presidential election between George W. Bush and John Kerry, did things come up that kept you from voting, or did you happen to vote?
    A. Yes, voted
    B. No, didn't vote
    C. Other/Don't know

Notes

1. Pew Research Center, Muslim Americans: Mostly Middle Class and Mainstream, available at http://www.allied-media.com/AM/mosque_study.htm. May 2007.

2. By focusing on the assimilation experiences of Muslim Americans, this chapter is predominantly concerned with the Muslim immigrant experience.

3. The Pew Research Center estimates that the U.S. Muslim population is at 2.5 million. Muslim Organizations such as the Council on American Islamic Relations (CAIR) place the size of the community near 10 million. Most scholars who work on the Muslim-American community place the number at close to 6 million.

4. The Great Divide: How Westerners and Muslims View Each Other: 13 Nation Pew Global Attitudes Survey. Pew Research Center, 2006. See http://pewglobal.org/reports/pdf/253.pdf.

5. See Michael Suleiman, "Stereotypes, Public Opinion and Foreign Policy: The Impact on Arab-American Relations," *Journal of Arab Affairs* April 2002; Daniel Mandel, "Muslims on the Silver Screen," *Middle East Quarterly* Spring 2001; Mark Tessler and Dan Corstange, "How Should Americans Understand Arab Political Attitudes: Combating Stereotypes with Public Opinion Data from the Middle East," *Journal of Social Affairs* Winter 2002; Jack Shaheen, "Bad

Arabs: How Hollywood Vilifies a People," *The Annals of the American Academy of Political and Social Science* July 2003; Fawaz Gerges, "Islam and Muslims in the Mind of America," *The Annals of the American Academy of Political and Social Science* July 2003.

6. http://people-press.org/reports/display.php3?ReportID=252.

7. All data presented here comes from the Muslim American Report: Middle Class and Mostly Mainstream. Pew Research Center, 2006. http://pewresearch.org/assets/pdf/muslim-americans.pdf.

8. Muslims are required to pray five times a day at dawn (*fajr*), noon (*thuhr*), afternoon (*asr*), early evening (*maghrib*), and night (*isha*).

9. See Pew Report on Muslim Americans, available at http://pewresearch.org/assets/pdf/muslim-americans.pdf.

10. Ibid.

11. Ibid.

12. Verba et al. 1995, 282.

13. Rosenstone and Hansen 1993, 87.

14. These dimensions of religiosity have a Cronbach's alpha of 0.70.

15. These dimensions of worry have a Cronbach's alpha of 0.65.

16. It is not known what levels of the general population support al-Qaeda. If we were to survey the general mainstream population, we might find that 5 percent of the general population, too, have favorable opinions of al-Qaeda. Surprisingly, after the Oklahoma City bombings in 1995, a hypothetical question was asked of the mainstream population: "Is it ever justified for citizens to take violent action against the United States government?" Nine percent of Americans said yes. "Two Stories Found in One Poll" ABC News. May, 23, 2007. http://abcnews.go.com/GMA/story?id=3203514.

17. Some might assume that these findings tell us more about the African-American Muslim experience. When I control for race, however, I find no independent effect of blackness on these data. It appears that these findings are pertinent among all U.S.-born Muslims, blacks and nonblacks alike.

18. Portes and Rumbaut found that Mexican Americans in California (while intense debates about immigration reform ensued in the 1990s) developed many of the reactive ethnic formation attributes. Patricia Fernandez-Kelly and Schauffler also find this pattern applicable to the Nicaraguan-American experience as well (Fernandez-Kelley and Schauffler 1994).

19. Others might argue that immigrants are not as forthcoming as the U.S.-born community in their responses about support for al-Qaeda or their desire to remain distinct. But this argument, although plausible, is not substantiated by the available evidence. When examining one of the more neutral dependent variables—Levels of Satisfaction—we still find that immigrants are more satisfied than the U.S. born.

References

Akram, S. 2002. "The Aftermath of September 11, 2001: The Targeting of Arabs and Muslims in America." *Arab Studies Quarterly* Spring:61–118.

Calhoun-Brown, A. 1996. "African American Churches and Political Mobilization: The Psychological Impact of Organizational Resources." *The Journal of Politics* 58(4):937–54.

Citrin, J., A. Lerman, M. Murakami, and K. Pearson. 2007. "Testing Huntington: Is Hispanic Immigration a Threat to American Identity?" *Perspectives on Politics* 5(1):31–48.

de la Garza, Rodolfo, A. Falcon, and F. C. Garcia. 1996. "Will the Real Americans Please Stand up: Anglo and Mexican American Support for Core American Political Values." *American Journal of Political Science* 40:335–51.

Djupe, P., and T. Grant. 2001. "Religious Institutions and Political Participation in America." *Journal for the Scientific Study of Religion* 40(2):303–14.

Fernandez-Kelley, P., and R. Schauffler. 1994. "Divided Fates: Immigrant Children in a Restructured US Economy." *International Migration Review* 28(4):662–89.

Gerges, F. July 2003. "Islam and Muslims in the Mind of America." *The Annals of the American Academy of Political and Social Science* 588:73–89.

Greenberg, A. 2000. "The Church and the Revitalization of Politics and Community." *Political Science Quarterly* 115(3):377–94.

Harris, F. 1994. "Something Within: Religion as a Mobilizer of African American Political Activism." *Journal of Politics* 56(1):42–68.

Huntington, S. 2004. *Who Are We? The Challenges to America's National Identity*. New York: Simon & Schuster.

Jamal, A. 2005. "The Political Participation and Engagement of Muslim Americans: Mosque Involvement and Group Consciousness." *American Politics Research* 33(4):521–44.

Jones-Correa, M., and D. Leal. 2001. "Political Participation: Does Religion Matter?" *Political Research Quarterly* 54(4):751–71.

Leighly, J. 1996. "Group Membership and the Mobilization of Political Participation." *Journal of Politics* 58(2):447–9.

Mandel, D. Spring 2001. "Muslims on the Silver Screen." *Middle East Quarterly* 8(2), http://www.meforum.org/26/muslims-on-the-silver-screen.

Miller, A., P. Gurin, G. Gurin, and O. Malanchuk. 1981. "Group Consciousness and Political Participation." *American Journal of Political Science* 25(3):494–511.

Peterson, S. 1992. "Church Participation and Political Participation: The Spillover Effect." *American Politics Quarterly* 20(1):123–39.

Pew Research Center. July 26, 2005. "Summary of Findings: Views of Muslim-Americans Hold Steady after London Bombings," available at http://people-press.org/reports/display.php3?ReportID=252 (accessed September 28, 2007).

———. May 22, 2007. "Muslim Americans: Middle Class and Mostly Mainstream," available at http://pewresearch.org/assets/pdf/muslim-americans.pdf (accessed September 28, 2007).

Portes, A., and R. G. Rumbaut. 2001. *Legacies: The Story of the Immigrant Second Generation.* Berkeley: University of California Press.

Rosenstone, S., and J. M. Hansen. 1993. *Mobilization, Participation and Democracy in America.* New York: Macmillan.

Rumbaut, R. G., and A. Portes. 2001. *Ethnicities: Children of Immigrants in America.* New York: Russell Sage Foundation.

Schilkraut, D. 2005. "The Rise and Fall of Political Engagement among Latinos: The Role of Identity and Perceptions of Discrimination." *Political Behavior* 27(3):285–312.

Sears, D., M. Fu, P. J. Henry, and K. Bui. 2003. "The Origins and Persistence of Ethnic Identity among the 'New Immigrant' Groups." *Social Psychology Quarterly* 66(4):419–37.

Shaheen, J. July 2003. "Reel Bad Arabs: How Hollywood Vilifies a People." *The Annals of the American Academy of Political and Social Science* 588:171–93.

Smidt, C. 1999. "Religion and Civic Engagement: A Comparative Analysis." *Annals of the American Academy of Political and Social Science* 565:176–92.

Suleiman, M. April 1982. "Stereotypes, Public Opinion and Foreign Policy: The Impact on American-Arab Relations." *Journal of Arab Affairs* 1(2):147–66.

Tessler, M., and D. Corstange. Winter 2002. "How Should Americans Understand Arab Political Attitudes: Combating Stereotypes with Public Opinion Data from the Middle East." *Journal of Social Affairs* 19(76):13–34.

Verba, S., K. Schlozman, and H. Brady. 1995. *Voice and Equality: Civic Voluntarism in American Politics*. Cambridge, MA: Harvard University Press.

Wuthnow, R. 1999. "Mobilizing Civic Engagement: The Changing Impact of Religious Involvement." In *Civic Engagement in American Democracy*, eds. T. Skocpol and M. Fiorina. Washington, DC: Brookings Institution.

Chapter 4

THE CONSTITUTIONS OF RELIGIOUS PLURALISM IN THE UNITED STATES

Bette Novit Evans

Introduction

By all measures the United States is among the most religiously intense and diverse nations in the world. Our daily newspapers regularly chronicle the disastrous consequences of religious intensity and diversity across the globe. Although the United States has not been free from religious bigotry, hatred, and even violence, overall it has an enviable record for both religious freedom and peace. Mark Lilla, in a *New York Times Magazine* article, describes the American success as "a miracle":

> As for the American experience, it is utterly exceptional: there is no other fully developed industrial society with a population so committed to its faiths (and such exotic ones), while being equally committed to the Great Separation. Our political rhetoric, which owes much to the Protestant sectarians of the 17th century, vibrates with messianic energy, and it is only thanks to a strong constitutional structure and various lucky breaks that political theology has never seriously challenged the basic legitimacy of our institutions. Americans have potentially explosive religious differences over abortion, prayer in schools, censorship, euthanasia, biological research and countless other issues, yet they generally settle them within the bounds of the Constitution. It's a miracle.[1]

The American experience is indeed exceptional, but it is not miraculous. The United States is blessed with both a religious and a governmental pluralism that have established the conditions for our relative success in a world tormented by religious conflict. Journalist Thomas Friedman recently expressed the situation with characteristic sharpness:

> The world is drifting dangerously toward a widespread religious and sectarian cleavage—the likes of which we have not seen for a long, long time. The only country with the power to stem this toxic trend is America. People across the world shall look to our example of pluralism, which is like no other.[2]

How has the United States been able to avoid the toxic consequences of interreligious conflict and tyranny? Like Friedman, I find the answer in pluralism, and in particular, in the confluence of both a pluralist pattern of religious diversity and a Madisonian fragmentation of governmental power that characterizes structural pluralism. Let me set out the argument from the outset: the combination of America's intense singular religiosity and diversity poses serious challenges both to peace and to religious liberty. The search for guiding principles to resolve religious conflicts has proven elusive.[3] Even so, American social and political structures have combined to create reasonable success in managing our unwieldy religious landscape. The very unwieldiness of our religious life and the "messiness" of our fragmented political power have helped prevent the "toxicity" Friedman described.

This chapter describes the confluence of these two kinds of pluralism. The first section describes the current pattern of American religious pluralism, including dangers of polarization and the special challenges arising at the margins of the pluralist consensus. The second section describes the fragmentation of American political institutions. The third section illustrates these patterns with examples from religion clause jurisprudence, primarily issues arising under the Free Exercise clause. I have selected specific Free Exercise cases that illustrate the ways religious groups relate to the society as a whole—from those that seek to remain thoroughly insular to those that seek to remain a distinctive practice while being otherwise totally integrated into the wider society. The converse of this story could be told by looking at Establishment Clause cases, which illustrate the impact of public support for religiosity on groups who do not share the dominant vision; however, for the most part, Free Exercise litigation provides much more direct illustration. Following that section, the concluding one offers some comparisons and normative prescriptions for maintaining the conditions of pluralism.

The American commitment to religious liberty is symbolized by the opening words of our Bill of Rights: "Congress shall make no law respecting an establishment of religion or prohibiting the free exercise thereof. . . ." These words are traditionally divided into the Establishment Clause, which prohibits state-sponsored or imposed religious obligations and the Free Exercise Clause, which protects religious expression from state penalties or burdens. These clauses are embedded in the whole of the First Amendment, which protects not only the freedom of religion, but also speech, press, and assembly. What all of these have in common is that they are ways people acquire and share information—not only on serious political, scientific, artistic, religious, and cultural matters but also on frivolous and even pernicious ones. Together, they prevent government from monopolizing the role of definer of meanings and values. I have argued elsewhere, and I continue to believe, that the "core meaning" of the religion clauses is that they foster a multiplicity of meanings for the members of a society and hence counter the twin dangers of anomie (the absence of meanings) and a monopoly of meanings.[4] Thus, the First Amendment symbolizes and legitimates for Americans the expectation that meanings are gained from multiple sources, in which no source has a natural preeminence.

Of course, the religion clauses perform other important functions. They help depoliticize religious controversies. By separating religious and governmental institutional powers, the Establishment Clause in particular impedes sectarian conflicts from spilling over to cause civic ones. Along with the other First Amendment guarantees, these guarantees also promote the independence of the institutions and associations that can challenge the hegemony of government.[5] There is reason to believe that the separation of church and state is at least partly responsible for the vigor of American religious life by requiring churches to compete for the loyalty of members and their resources.[6]

Beyond their context in the First Amendment, the religion clauses are located within the Bill of Rights as a whole and within the Madisonian Constitution itself. Thus, they are a part of the institutional framework created by the Constitution. Of course, constitutions can be nothing more than "words on paper," or in Madison's words, "parchment guarantees," without the matrix of institutional, cultural, demographic, economic, and social conditions that underlie them. These "parchment guarantees" have proven far more powerful than some of their authors might have expected, but words alone do not create practices. Religious liberty has succeeded because it is consistent with the pluralism of our major social institutions.[7] Americans' memberships, identities, and authority patterns tend to be plural and crosscutting rather than monolithic or segmented, and the fragmentation of power in American government reinforces and sustains social pluralism. The Madisonian system of fragmented governmental institutions, reinforced by the patterns of American religiosity, creates the context in which the religious freedom guarantees are embedded. Religious liberty is thus constitutional in the broad sense that it is a part of "the way a society is constituted." Although these institutional features are deeply embedded, they are neither immutable nor permanent, and a certain vigilance is necessary to protect and preserve them. The United States has been exceptionally fortunate (and I emphasize *fortunate* rather than particularly *virtuous* or *brilliant*) in the fact that the conditions of pluralism have coincided.

A complete discussion of pluralism would have to include many factors beyond the religious landscape. A full pluralism depends on overlapping commitments based on economic and professional interests, geographic and ethnic identities, friendships, voluntary associations, and countless other factors to blunt the sharp lines of religious divisions. Above all, growing economic inequalities severely undermine the web of connections essential to pluralism; I would venture that no pattern of religious overlap could overcome pervasive and persistent economic cleavages, which have accelerated in recent years. Our focus on religious pluralism should not obscure the broader requirements for a full pluralism.

Religious Pluralism and Its Challenges

Religious pluralism requires diversity; political pluralism requires dispersed powers. But although both may be necessary conditions, they are not sufficient conditions. Mere diversity or mere dispersion might create a segmented rather than a pluralistic social constitution. Think of a segmented society as constructed like the segmented worms we all studied in high school biology—or perhaps more pleasantly, like a string of beads. Each segment is discrete and divided from the others. Where religious (or other identifiable) groups settled in distinct and identifiable conclaves and stayed in them over the generations, they create segmentation in the way that produces identifiable Suni and Shia neighborhoods and villages in Iraq, or Serbian or Muslim towns in Bosnia, or Protestant and Catholic neighborhoods in Northern Ireland. Where religious divisions are reinforced by economic or ethnic or linguistic or historical divisions, the segmented whole becomes fragile. In contrast, pluralistic societies such as the United States are characterized by overlapping lines of identity and cleavages.[8]

The pattern of American religiosity reflects both diversity and overlap. In spite of the mythology about "our Puritan fathers," America has always been religiously diverse; among the earliest settlers were not only Puritans but also Anglicans, Baptists, a few Catholics and Quakers, a tiny community of Jews, Muslim and animist slaves, and many with no particular religious convictions at all—not to mention the entire indigenous population whose beliefs were not even recognized as "religious." Our nation never had a single religious majority. In fact, historians tell us that the guarantee against an establishment of religion was adopted precisely because no single denomination was strong enough to impose its will on all the others, but every one feared that some other one might eventually try to establish itself as the national church.[9] The great wave of immigration at the end of the nineteenth century brought more Catholics and Jews along with German Lutherans, and a mid-twentieth-century wave brought a sizable population of Hindus, Muslims, and Buddhists.[10] In almost every group, the first immigrants tended to settle in homogeneous enclaves—we can easily think of the Irish Catholic,

Italian Catholic, and Eastern European Jewish neighborhoods of New York City at the turn of the last century, and of the German Lutheran settlements in the Upper Midwest, of Muslim settlements in Detroit, and of more recent Buddhist communities of Southeast Asian immigrants. Michael Foley and Dean Hoge document a dramatic increase in ethnic churches among these populations.[11] If previous patterns continue, these ethnic enclaves do not persist over generations, and distinctive religious groups become dispersed among the general population. Over time, as Catherine Albanese has shown, distinctive immigrant religions adapt to the American experience and show a striking convergence.[12] From an observer's perspective, then, American religious diversity is remarkable. However, from the perspective of religious minority members, the distinctions among other religions tend to blur, sharpening their own sense of difference or otherness.

For the most part, social class lines do not cleanly divide American religions. The time has long past when social scientists could rank religious denominations by economic stratification, with Episcopalians on top and Pentecostals on the bottom. The economic mobility across religious groups means that economic divisions among Americans do not cut along the same lines as denominational ones but tend to overlap them. And geographic mobility has had the same impact on the physical dispersion of religious groups—for example, Southern Baptists are no longer southern.

American religious institutions have been in constant flux since colonial times. Finke and Stark have described a continuing pattern of the growth of noninstitutionalized sects, their evolution into institutionalized churches, and then their relative decline as newer sects arise in the social space they have abandoned.[13] By the mid-nineteenth century, American religious diversity was characterized by the variety of Protestant denominations. By the mid-twentieth century, Will Herberg captured (some say helped create) it in his book *Protestant/Catholic/Jew*.[14] More recently, we use the more inclusive term "Abrahamic Religions," but the influx of Hindus, Buddhists, and members of other Eastern faiths since the mid-1960s may have already made that term seem parochial. Moreover, denominational divisions, once so much a part of the American religious landscape, have ceased to operate as important social markers. Robert Wuthnow, among others, has documented the decline in denominational separateness over the past half-century as well as church mergers and the concomitant rise in cross-denominational organizations.[15] Many of the fast-growing megachurches avoid denominational attachments altogether and portray themselves as nondenominational. But even as they do, many of these churches have created their own federations, which themselves function as denominations.[16] Mark Noll aptly describes some of these changes:

> free flowing Pentecostal and charismatic styles will go on spreading their influence far beyond the explicitly Pentecostal churches. The most important Christian schisms will increasingly follow theological ideological lines rather than denominational ones. Especially as the historical Catholic-Protestant chasm continues to narrow, Christians will be aligned to fellow believers from other denominations according to shared convictions.[17]

Observers debate whether this "restructuring" enhances or threatens pluralism. In 1991, James Davison Hunter's book *Culture Wars* warned of an increasing polarization of American society into two opposing and mutually exclusive camps.[18] He defines the split as "not theological or ecclesiological" but one that reflects profound differences over "how to order our lives" and, ultimately, over moral authority. On one side is orthodoxy, with its commitment to externally definable and transcendent authority, and on the other side is progressivism, for which moral authority is based on reason and/or subjectivity. This cleavage cuts across traditional denominational lines, dividing conservative and progressive elements of the same denomination and uniting religious groups that have historically had little overlap. If Hunter proves to be right, this polarization is profoundly "religious" in the sense that religion is about comprehensive meanings.[19]

There is troubling evidence that the restructuring of American religion supports Hunter's thesis and thus undermines pluralism. New cross-denominational organizations split traditional and progressive traditions, not among denominations but within many of the major ones—creating the kind of polarization about which Hunter warned. Adding to the seriousness of this possible polarization is the loss of bridges between the two traditions. Mainline liberal Protestantism and its educational institutions long served as a bridge between orthodox Christianity and "secular humanism." The dramatic decline of mainline Protestantism may be an indication that the bridge is disappearing, leaving the society culturally polarized.

Three contemporary examples seem to illustrate Hunter's conclusion. Despite a long history of Protestant-Catholic antagonism, today conservative Protestants and Catholics are strong coalition partners in opposition to legalized abortion and gay marriage. Likewise, despite a long history of antagonism between Protestants and Jews, elements of both communities have joined in support of Israel—albeit for very different reasons. And Mormons, long detested by traditional Protestants, are now their valued coalition partners on many conservative political causes. And Jews and Muslims, with the bitterest disagreements on Middle Eastern politics, make common cause in fighting religious discrimination in the United States. And all of these groups are active in coalitions with nonreligious interest groups fostering their policy initiatives. For better or worse, American politics has been transformed by the growth of coalitions across religious traditions and between religious interest groups and nonreligious ideological, economic, and other kinds of organizations. Pessimistically, this realignment may have reduced the multiplicity of denominational divisions to a single ideological one.

On the other hand, an optimistic interpretation is that these cross-denominational coalitions foster compromise and cooperation. A wide range of empirical studies continue to find Hunter's predictions overly pessimistic and to conclude, in Alan Wolfe's words, that we remain "one nation, after all."[20] In the optimistic interpretation, the coalition building keeps the religious landscape fluid, prevents religious groups from seeing each other as permanent enemies, and thus helps prevent the kinds of religious warfare that have plagued so much of our world.

Further complicating this picture is the fact that much of religion in the United States is practiced as individual spirituality, outside of any religious institution. This is not a new phenomenon. In the mid-1960s, sociologist Thomas Luckmann described religious individualism as *The Invisible Religion*.[21] And in the 1970s, Robert Bellah made famous the term "Sheilaism" (quoting a respondent named Sheila who constructed her own religion) to describe the individualized composite of beliefs and practices people create from the cafeteria of possibilities in our society.[22] Most recently, Alan Wolfe has described the anti-institutional bias of American religiosity,[23] while numerous scholars describe the "shopping cart" approach many Americans take to creating their distinct individual religions.[24] The noninstitutional nature of so much American religion adds further complexity. The fact that a significant amount of American religiosity cannot be captured within any particular denomination or other social grouping further blurs any simple lines of demarcation among religions, and the "cafeteria" nature of individually constructed beliefs and practices creates additional affinities across traditions.

Along with individualized religions and blurred denominational lines, there is a blurring of distinctions between religious and secular institutions in general. Churches themselves have become multifunctional. The days when churches were open only for Sunday morning services are long past. Today religious institutions sponsor schools, book clubs, health clinics, social service agencies, athletics, child care centers, shelters, and food services; to support them, churches become major employers and have large financial interests. As such, they are subject to numerous government regulations, such as labor laws, zoning and historical preservation laws, tax policy, political campaign regulation, child protection, and school certification laws and are drawn into politics, not only on matters of conscience but often on the most mundane of regulatory matters. And as a result, these religious institutions often find themselves allied with nonreligious institutions that provide the same functions or share common interests. Furthermore, many religious-oriented organizations, including schools, universities, hospitals, and social service agencies, become centers of power in their own right, challenging governmental hegemony by proposing and instituting their own policy initiatives. Religious organizations have many resources for effective political action, including organization and leadership and social cohesion, and religious groups have established an important presence among professional lobbyists.[25] As a result, religious institutions contribute to the multiplicity of power sources in a community, preventing the kinds of political monopolies that Madison feared.

I began by positing that the religion clauses are best understood as a part of the general American pattern of fostering alternate sources of meaning and identity in the society at large and that they are an important part of the larger web of divisions and overlaps that characterize a pluralistic society. The pluralist vision is profoundly modern in that it accepts, celebrates, and fosters the mixture of partial, crosscutting, and overlapping meanings and identities.[26] This vision appeals to many, but certainly not to all Americans. It does not appeal to those who believe that religious conscience or authority should be the preeminent source of identity and meaning or to those who believe the state should exercise that monopoly.[27] Thus, the pluralist vision runs contrary to the Platonic vision of a unified society in which people can live seamless lives.[28] The mosaic of overlapping meanings, structures, and institutions that pluralists find attractive is a source of pain and a symptom of pathology to those who seek a coherent social reality. Sociologist of religion Frank Lechner, describing all kinds of religious fundamentalism, notes that a common theme is the critique of the differentiated society.

> The threat of modernity lies not so much in a new kind of theology, but rather in institutional differentiation, compartmentalization, and cultural pluralism—social life becomes horribly complex, and there no longer seems to be one true common culture. Thus . . . the response to this threat is to revitalize the true faith and to dedifferentiate—to make all institutions operate on sound value principles, to implement the sacred world view across the board and to deprivatize religion.[29]

Groups devoted to a unified social reality may seek to withdraw into insular communities that maintain their own integrated *nomos*, or they may try to transform the society at large in conformity with their vision. The Amish, the Hasidim, and other separatist groups exemplify the first strategy; they challenge pluralism by demanding a much stronger kind of separateness—the kind I earlier called "segmentation." Transformative groups are illustrated most dramatically in the various Islamacist movements, which demand that Shari'a and religious customs be incorporated into the law of the state. In the United States, various Christian movements, such as R. J. Rusdoony's Christian Reconstructionism, seek to institute Biblical prescriptions as the law of the United States.[30] Mark Lilla has described the persistent appeal of political theologies and reminds us that they have been the norm in human history and that our preference for separating religion and the rest of social life has been a recent Western innovation.[31]

We might expect that the most challenging constitutional controversies under the religion clauses have been brought by groups that do not fit comfortably into the pluralist pattern. And although some controversies do involve groups at the margins of pluralism, many do not. One might hypothesize that groups genuinely at the margins lack the financial and organizational resources, or simply the political efficacy, to use the judicial process effectively. The third section of this chapter returns to the issue of insularity and integration, using contemporary religion clause jurisprudence as a lens to view the pluralist strategies for managing religious conflicts.

The Institutional Pluralism of American Government

Every student of American government learns that the U.S. Constitution creates a jurisdictional fragmentation almost unparalleled in institutional design. Despite the dramatic increase in presidential power, no single governmental body is capable of enforcing any dominant meaning. Federalism fragments power geographically, and the separation of powers reinforces this fragmentation at every level. The goal is to prevent both the creation of permanent majorities and the accumulation of power in any governmental institution. Thus, the Constitution created not only an extended and federal republic, with its numerous separate and independent governments, but also the separation and "blending" of powers among the three branches of the national government, so that no single one could act without the acquiescence of the others. The fragmented institutional structure created by the Constitution deprives the partisans of any "culture war" of a comprehensive battlefield.[32] The fragmentation of political power and redundancy of functions within government multiply the points of access for groups attempting to influence public policy, thus enhancing citizen impact on government. Even the representative institutions are designed to hamper each other, and these are themselves balanced against nonrepresentative institutions such as the judiciary and by private centers of power totally outside of government.[33]

Pluralist interpreters of American government reject any simplistic dichotomy between "majority rule/minority rights" found so often in discussions of constitutional rights.[34] They focus instead on the multiplicity of actors able to influence outcomes because of fragmented power and multiple access points. Pluralists understand policies as results of temporary coalitions of those whose interests are a stake in the particular issue. Public decision making is almost always a minority phenomenon; what makes the situation democratic is that the coalition of minorities is fluid. The distribution of power within government helps to provide access to many different groups; those who may be disadvantaged in dealing with one institution may find more favorable access in another. Legislative bodies are attentive to certain kinds of interests and courts to others; federal agencies have particular constituencies, whereas state agencies, city councils, and other institutions are receptive to others. Both elective and nonelective branches of government are constituted to provide access to some different combination of interests, and the judiciary is simply another policy-making branch of government, with its own constituencies and procedures. Democracy results from the multiplicity of access points for different interest groups.

Of course, my description of American institutional pluralism is an idealized description of American politics. In practice, political and economic inequalities skew the public agenda and undermine these optimistic assumptions. Some groups have the resources to set the public agenda or to be favored coalition partners, whereas others are so weak, disorganized, or disfavored that they are not sought as coalition partners at all; still others are excluded entirely from effective participation, so that their interests are never represented. The resulting distortion of equal representation provides one of the best justifications for the role of the courts in protecting minorities who are systematically excluded from effective electoral representation.[35] Nevertheless, the fragmented nature of American policy making remains a constant and profoundly affects the way our religious liberty guarantees are argued and practiced in the United States. Perhaps Hunter's anticipated culture war has been muted by the fact that there is no institutional capacity for a system of meanings to dominate and because neither our constitutional nor our religious structures condition us to expect systematic and comprehensive meanings.

Federalism multiplies American institutional fragmentation by fifty—and in fact, by much more, because the states themselves are divided into countless semi-independent institutions and, as Madison hoped, different religious majorities.

> It is of great importance in a republic, not only to guard the society against the oppression of its rulers, but to guard one part of the

> society against the injustice of the other part. Different interests necessarily exist in different classes of citizens. If a majority be united by a common interest, the rights of the minority will be insecure. There are but two methods of providing against this evil. The one by creating a will in the community independent of the majority . . . [a heredity authority, which Madison rejects]; the other by comprehending in the society so many separate descriptions of citizens as will render an unjust combination of a majority of the whole, very improbable if not impractical. . . . Whilst all authority in it will be derived from and dependent on the society, the society itself will be broken into so many parts, interests, and classes of citizens that the rights of individuals or of the minority will be in little danger from interested combinations of the majority.[36]

For Madison, an "extended republic" with its federal structure was particularly important for preventing oppressive national majorities.

> The influence of factious leaders may kindle flames within their particular States, but will be unable to spread a general conflagration through the other States: a religious sect may degenerate into a political faction in a part of the Confederacy, but the variety of sects dispersed over the entire face of it, must secure the national Councils against any danger from that source. . . .[37]

Recent evidence from the American Religious Identification Survey confirms Madison's expectations, as Gary Gilden explains:

> State constitutions may be a more reliable guarantor of non-mainstream liberty because of the religious composition of the particular state. A faith with a decided minority status nationally may have clusters of congregants in an individual state that exert more significant power to inform or influence political outcomes in that state. The ARIS survey found "with respect to religion in particular, states differ considerably in the religious make-up of their populace. That diversity is likely to contribute as much as any other source of social variation to differences in their cultural and political climate." For example, while Baptists comprise 55 percent of the population in Mississippi, they constitute but 4 percent of the population in Massachusetts. Lutherans and Catholics, composing 65 percent of the population in North Dakota, may display substantial political sway in that state. By contrast, their combined 26 percent of the population in the State of Washington exceeds by a mere one percent those professing no religion. Furthermore, as Professor Berg has noted, "geographical numbers do not tell the whole story of whether a group is vulnerable to political or legal pressure. . . . [A] group may be small and still have power as a political or cultural elite."[38]

Even almost a century after the expansion of national powers, the bulk of ordinary policy is still made at state and local levels—a fact that has substantial impact on religious policy making. In the first instance, most state-church controversies originate in some local practice, often a very mundane one. And in the final instance, when other avenues of resolution have failed and parties take recourse to the courts, the federal courts are not the only avenue of appeal. Especially since the U.S. Supreme Court backed away from an active role in protecting religious minorities in the *Smith* and *Boerne* cases, many plaintiffs prefer to rely on state constitutional protections and state courts for vindicating their rights—a point to which we shall return.

Managing Challenges to Religious Pluralism Seen through the Lens of Religion Clause Jurisprudence

The foregoing general description of Madisonian pluralism is probably familiar to most undergraduate students of American government, but we sometimes forget how these patterns shape religion clause jurisprudence. First of all, we must remember that the vast majority of religious conflicts never end up in courts at all. Many are solved through very local political processes—by negotiation among the parties, or by employers and administrators, including public school teachers and principals, and military officers or by legislatures from city councils and state legislatures to the U.S. Congress. Many are not solved at all and either fester beneath the surface in communities or simply fade away as parties move on to other agendas. To bring an issue to the courts requires time, commitment, and money beyond the reach of most persons; hence, the cases that reach the appellate courts are often financially sponsored by advocacy groups. These groups have long recognized courts as important points of access for influencing political policy, and many have become important players in the distribution of power. This, too, is consistent with the Madisonian vision.

Once these issues are in the courts, legal dialogue tends to be phrased in terms of principles and doctrines, particularly on competing understandings of the accommodation of religion. From a pluralist perspective, the doctrinal debates boil down to arguments about which governmental institutions should make decisions about accommodation. Very roughly, arguments about religious accommodation focus on the extent to which the right to free exercise of religion requires government to exempt religious adherents from policies that burden their beliefs or practices. Establishment Clause arguments often center on the extent to which government may voluntarily accommodate religious interests. Establishment Clause accommodation problems usually begin when politically successful religious groups have already achieved accommodation from legislative or executive officials, and opponents challenge the accommodation as an unconstitutional establishment of religion. Free Exercise challenges most often begin when other decision makers have failed to make an accommodation that a religious believer argues should be required as a matter of constitutional right. Constitutional scholars frequently treat these kinds of issues entirely separately, but both controversies really boil down to arguments about which institutions have the responsibility for making accommodation decisions. Often these issues are overlaid with questions about federalism, such as when federal courts may or should override the decisions made by state officials, whether legislative, administrative, or judicial. In any case, the issues grow out of the fact that our system of government consists of such a variety of governmental decision makers, whose authority is always in tension.

We often assume that religion clause complaints are brought mostly by minority religious groups, because majoritarian ones are able to protect their interests within other parts of the political process. The general notion is that religious minorities use the Free Exercise Clause to claim rights denied by the majority and make Establishment Clause claims when majorities have used political power to benefit majoritarian religious interests. A brief sampling of religion clause cases demonstrates a more complex pattern. Often religious minorities do seek protection under the religion clauses against majority oppression or insensitivity, but as often, individuals or groups we associate with the religious mainstream seek protection under the Free Exercise Clause against perceived burdens. This pattern reinforces Robert Dahl's original insights that our system is better understood as coalitions of minorities.[39] Local majorities who may be successful in local environments are often less so in wider venues, which is exactly what Madison anticipated. Even tiny minorities, as we shall see in the *Kiryas Joel* case, may be locally powerful. Even truly insular groups, as we shall see in our very first example, are not truly insular in a pluralist society; conflicts arise because they almost inevitably interact with the broader culture.

We begin with the relatively simple problem of an insular religious group that simply wishes to be left alone—represented by the landmark 1972 case of *Wisconsin v. Yoder*: [40] The Amish, a conservative branch of the Mennonite Church, live in separate communities, practice material simplicity, and adhere to strict biblical teachings. When consolidated schools began replacing the local schools in their rural community, they perceived a threat to the future of their religious culture. Although willing to educate their children through the eighth grade in local schools, they rejected further secular education as imparting worldly values in conflict with their religious ones. Their refusal to send their children to school after the eighth grade violated Wisconsin's law requiring school attendance through age sixteen. Several Amish parents, including Yoder, challenged Wisconsin's compulsory education law. The Amish argued that secondary schooling would endanger their own salvation and that of their children and cause disintegration of their communities. Upholding their claim, the Supreme Court ruled that the Constitution demanded exemptions from state laws for religiously motivated behavior except when there was a compelling state interest to the contrary.

Chief Justice Warren Burger, writing for the Court, adopted the compelling state interest test for balancing state interests against religious freedom claims: "Only those interests of the highest order and those not otherwise served can overbalance legitimate claims to the free exercise of religion." The Court recognized that Wisconsin had compelling justifications for compulsory education but concluded that the state's purposes would not be sacrificed by granting the Amish an exception. Considering the exemplary record of productivity and self-sufficiency, the Court found that traditional Amish vocational education was quite successful in preparing its children for productive and independent lives. Thus, the justices concluded that Wisconsin has no compelling interest in forcing the Amish to continue conventional education up to age sixteen and ruled that they had a constitutional right to be exempt from the law's requirements.

What the Amish wanted, and ultimately received, was an exemption from an otherwise valid state law in order to remain insular. Although the *Yoder* case was an important Free Exercise landmark and a victory for minority religions, the situation it represents is not a common one. Much more common conflicts arise when members of religious groups want to maintain some distinctive aspect of their religious practices while participating in the mainstream culture in other ways and thus need accommodation in order to live in both worlds simultaneously. An excellent example is the 1986 case of *Goldman v. Weinberger,*[41] in which Capt. Goldman sought the right to keep his head covered in accordance with Orthodox Jewish practice while still serving as an Air Force officer, whose regulations required being bareheaded indoors. Captain Goldman had been informally accommodated by his superior officers, but after the infraction was challenged, he was essentially faced with a choice between his military career and his religious obligations. Captain Goldman's claim to a right of religious accommodation was rejected by a divided Supreme Court, largely out of deference to military authority. Justice Rehnquist, writing for a divided majority, hinted that Capt. Goldman would just have to choose between his military career and his favored head covering. That is precisely the *opposite* of the pluralist idea, in which Captain Goldman would be able to be a loyal Air Force officer *while* being an Orthodox Jew. Subsequently, the U.S. Congress adopted a law permitting certain kinds of religious attire to be worn with military uniforms. This case reinforces two important aspects of pluralism: First,

Capt. Goldman's efforts to live both as an Orthodox Jew and as a military officer represent the pluralist vision of overlapping memberships, identities, and loyalties. Second, the outcome involved a number of different institutions, including the military bureaucracy, federal courts, and ultimately the U.S. Congress.[42]

Not only individuals but also religious institutions find themselves caught between religious distinctiveness and participation in the wider culture. When that distinctiveness conflicts with a core value of the larger society, the conflict is serious indeed.[43] The 1972 case of *Bob Jones University v. United States* illustrates this tension.[44] Bob Jones University is a private, religiously affiliated university. Originally enrolling only white students, it briefly admitted only married black students. In 1975 it abandoned racially exclusive enrollment and substituted a policy prohibiting interracial dating or marriage. These racial policies all reflected theological beliefs of its founder and administration, who understood racial separation as a religious injunction. In order to preserve its independence from government requirements regarding racial integration, the college did not accept federal aid in any form. It did, however, maintain a tax-exempt status as a nonprofit institution, which allowed contributors to receive tax exemptions for money donated to the college. During the same period, the federal government determined that racial integration was a value to be pursued by a wide variety of public tools, including the tax code, and the Internal Revenue Service (IRS) adopted a ruling that denied tax-exempt status to institutions practicing race discrimination Thus, in 1976 the IRS revoked the university's tax-exempt status on the grounds that its racial policies conflicted with a major federal policy.[45] The university responded by asserting that the IRS lacked both the statutory and constitutional power to deny tax exemptions to a religious university that practiced religiously motivated race separation.[46] The university insisted on a constitutional right to continue to practice its religiously motivated vision of racial separation while still maintaining the benefit of a tax-exempt status. Their challenge forced the courts to consider whether the denial of a government benefit, such as tax-exempt status for an action motivated by sincere religious belief, violates the Free Exercise Clause. In an eight-to-one decision, the Court ruled that it did not. Applying the compelling state interest test, the majority found the "overriding governmental interest" in eliminating racial discrimination sufficiently compelling to justify whatever burdens the university suffered—especially because the university could continue to practice its religious tenets without governmental benefits.[47]

An unusual and interesting situation occurred when an insular group was able to extract a major concession from the political process, and that concession was challenged on Establishment Clause grounds. The peculiar case of *Board of Education of Kiryas Joel School District v. Grummet*[48] reminds us that even small minority religious factions may be politically powerful enough in local arenas to secure concessions legislatively—indeed, that is exactly what Madison expected. This case also illustrates the supremely Madisonian processes involved in managing religious conflicts. This 1994 Supreme Court case is a virtual "poster child" of institutional pluralism. Its story began during the 1970s, when the village of Kiryas Joel was carved out of the existing Monroe Woodbury district in New York in such a way that its population consisted almost entirely of members of the very insular Satmar Hasidic sect of Judaism. The villagers educated most of their children in private religious schools but felt unable to provide the full range of rehabilitative services in private schools for their disabled children. A 1985 Supreme Court decision had prohibited states from providing these kinds of services on the grounds of private religious schools because doing so violated the Establishment Clause.[49] Being unable or unwilling to undertake those expenses privately, members of the Satmar community decided to send their children to public schools for rehabilitative services in the nearby town of Woodbury. But parents worried that the cultural differences would pose traumatic hardships on their already disabled children and that the children would also encounter practices forbidden by their religious faith. So the villagers reached an agreement with the Woodbury school district to secede and create a school district consisting almost exclusively of members of the Satmar sect. The New York legislature accommodated the village by creating its own public school district.[50]

From a pluralist perspective, the village of Kiryas Joel was acting appropriately in exercising its political power to persuade the legislature to grant this unusual accommodation. Likewise, the state legislature was responding appropriately to constituent interests in granting it. Constitutional doctrine is not the highest priority of either interest groups or legislative bodies. Local taxpayers and members of the State Board of Education represented a different perspective and different priorities—including religiously neutral criteria for administering state educational services. When they challenged the creation of a religiously constituted public school district, the dispute passed out of the legislative process and into the judicial system, where other priorities became dominant. Both New York courts and the U.S. Supreme Court found the plan unconstitutional, ruling that the Establishment Clause forbids "religious gerrymandering." Interestingly, Justice Souter's majority opinion suggested some administrative solutions to the problems his ruling created. Subsequently, the New York legislature followed his suggestion and passed a new statute, creating a general right for communities to create smaller school districts out of larger ones under certain conditions. The New York Supreme

Court struck down this law.[51] But the story did not end there. In 1997, the Supreme Court overturned its 1985 decision regarding special education facilities in private schools, which had made the special district seem necessary in the first place.[52] Once rehabilitative services could be legally offered at religious schools, the issue was resolved.

The Kiryas Joel narrative illustrates how religious establishment controversies are interwoven with the complicated relationships among institutions. Actors at various stages of this case included both local and national institutions, and public and private ones, included the governing bodies of Kiryas Joel and the surrounding town of Woodbury, religious and secular interest groups, state educational agencies, the New York State legislature, New York State courts at various levels, and the U.S. Supreme Court. The conflicting legislative and judicial solutions reflect the advantage of redundancy—allowing not only second opinions but often third and fourth ones as well. However one may judge the substantive outcomes, this case provides an excellent example of the multiple opportunities for access and redress within a Madisonian system.[53]

No discussion of religious controversy would be complete without consideration of the landmark 1990 case, *Employment Division, Department of Human Resources of Oregon v. Smith*,[54] which transformed Free Exercise jurisprudence, or of the subsequent developments that have deeply implicated federalism and state power into the management of religious conflict. Although the *Smith* case has significance far beyond the accounts that follow, I intend to recount them specifically as narratives about institutional pluralism.

Alfred Smith and Galen Black were fired from their jobs in a private drug rehabilitation program in Oregon when it was discovered that they used peyote as part of religious ritual of the Native American Church of which they were members. They applied for unemployment compensation, but the state unemployment office denied their application on the grounds that they had been fired for work-related misconduct. Smith and Black appealed the denial of state benefits, and both the appellate and state Supreme Court decided in their favor. The Oregon Supreme Court ruled that religious exercises could not be considered as misconduct for purposes of denying state benefits, citing a consistent pattern of U.S. Supreme Court decisions. The state petitioned for *certiorari* to the U.S. Supreme Court, which vacated the state judgments and remanded the case to the Oregon courts to determine whether state law prohibited sacramental use of peyote and whether the state constitution protected sacramental peyote use. On remand, in 1988, the Oregon Supreme Court concluded that Oregon law (unlike those of twenty-three other states and the federal government) "makes no exception for the sacramental use," but also noted that if the state should ever attempt to enforce the law against religious practice, that prosecution would violate the Free Exercise Clause of the U.S. Constitution.

The U.S. Supreme Court again granted *certiorari,* and in April 1990 it overturned the Oregon court's decision. Writing for a six-justice majority, Justice Antonin Scalia upheld the unemployment board's decision to refuse compensation, ruling that doing so did not violate Smith's constitutional right to free exercise of religion. In the majority's view, the Free Exercise clause is breached only when laws specifically *target* religious practice for unfavorable treatment. Because Oregon's drug law was generally applicable, and in no way intended to disadvantage Native American religions, it did not violate the Free Exercise Clause. The constitutional guarantee of Free Exercise is met simply by a formal neutrality; it prohibits only laws that on their face discriminate against a religion. Moreover, a five-member majority (Justice Sandra Day O'Connor concurred on other grounds) ruled that religious exemptions to generally applicable laws are not constitutionally required by the Free Exercise Clause and that such laws need not be justified by a compelling state interest.

Justice Scalia's controversial opinion specifically addressed institutional issues—specifically, *which* institutions should have the authority for granting religious accommodations. He clearly recognized that the majority's ruling limits judicial protection of religious exercise, leaving religious accommodation to the political process. "Values that are protected against government interferences through enshrinement in the Bill of Rights are not thereby banished from the political process." He readily admitted that "leaving accommodation to the political process will place at a relative disadvantage those religious practices that are not widely engaged in; but that unavoidable consequences of democratic government must be preferred to a system in which each conscience is a law unto itself." In short, the majority preferred to place religious protection in the hands of elective institutions rather than in nonelective courts. The Oregon legislature was certainly free to have granted an exemption for religious peyote use, but it was not constitutionally required to do so.

Justice Sandra Day O'Connor, concurring in the result, would have maintained the compelling state interest test, but she believed that Oregon's interest in combating use of hallucinogenic drugs was sufficiently compelling to justify the burden to Smith's and Black's religious exercise. Along with the dissenters, she also rejected the majority's position that violations of Free Exercise are limited to laws intentionally targeting religious practice and would have maintained the long-standing understanding that the First Amendment protects religious exercise both from laws specifically targeting religion and from generally applicable laws. By retaining the compelling state interest standard, she would have retained the role of courts in adjudicating religious claims rather than returning many of them to the political process. Without serious judicial scrutiny, the fate of minority religions would indeed be left up to the political process, which is precisely what the Bill of Rights is intended to prevent. "The very purpose of a Bill of Rights was to withdraw certain subjects from the vicissitudes of political controversy, to place them beyond the reach of majorities and officials and to establish them as legal principles to be applied by the courts."

The four dissenters argued passionately that all laws—both intentional and incidental—that burden religious freedom are subject to the compelling state interest test and argued that Oregon had failed to show a compelling reason for denying members of the Native American church exemptions from the law. After vigorously defending the compelling state interest standard, the dissenters argued that both the majority and Justice O'Connor had struck the balance incorrectly: "It is not the State's broad interest in fighting the critical 'war on drugs' that must be weighted against respondents' claim, but the State's narrow interest in refusing to make an exception for the religious, ceremonial use of peyote." From this perspective, the dissenters concluded that virtually nothing is lost by granting the exemption—especially considering that both federal law and that of twenty-three states exempt sacramental use of peyote from criminal prosecutions, without reported problems.

Shortly after this decision, the state of Oregon amended its controlled substances laws to exempt ritual peyote use from prosecution. Moreover, the decision in *Smith* produced the unusual effect of creating "strange bedfellows" among its critics; mainstream religious groups, the fundamentalist right, marginal religious movements, and the libertarian left were uncharacteristically united in decrying not only the specific outcome, but the implications of Justice Scalia's jurisprudence for religious rights within a religiously plural society. Shortly after the decision, a diverse number of religious advocacy groups and constitutional scholars petitioned the Court for a rehearing on the issue of the compelling state interest doctrine, but the petition was denied.

At the same time, religious interest groups and constitutional scholars mounted a significant campaign to urge Congress to adopt legislation reversing the effects of the *Smith* decision. In November 1993 Congress enacted the Religious Freedom Restoration Act (RFRA), with the intention of restoring the compelling state interest test. The key section of the bill provided that government may restrict a person's free exercise of religion only if government can show that such a restriction "(1) is essential to further a compelling governmental interest; and (2) is the least restrictive means of furthering that compelling governmental interest" standard. A constitutional challenge to this law reached the Supreme Court in June 1997 in the case of *City of Boerne v. Flores*,[55] and the

Court majority struck down the RFRA as reaching beyond the powers of Congress. The majority ruled that, whereas the Fourteenth Amendment grants Congress the power to enforce a constitutional right, the new law goes beyond enforcement and, in fact, alters the meaning of the right, thus infringing on the power of the judiciary and into the traditional prerogatives of states.

A reader more quantitative than I might count the number of governmental bodies making, remaking, and revising decisions on the compelling state interest standard initiated by the *Smith* case. The result is a patchwork of policy involving legislative bodies, administrative officials, and courts at both state and national levels.

Still the story did not end there. Several states adopted their own version of the RFRA, mandating the compelling state interest standard, and other state judges simply held it to be required under the language of existing state constitutions, which have force separately from the U.S. Constitution. Meanwhile, in 2000 Congress adopted the much more limited Religious Land Use and Institutionalized Persons Act of 2000 (RLUIPA),[56] which forbids the federal government from implementing land uses regulations that impose a substantial burden on the religious exercise of a person, or impose a substantial burden on the religious exercise of a person confined to an institution, "unless that action is in furtherance of a compelling governmental interest and is the least restrictive means of furthering that compelling governmental interest." Rather than resting on Fourteenth Amendment grounds as the RFRA had, this law was based on the commerce and spending clauses, and it therefore extends to all programs that receive federal money. In *Cutter v. Wilkinson*[57] (2005) this law was upheld against an Establishment Clause challenge as a permissible Free Exercise accommodation.

As a result of post-*Smith* developments, religious rights advocates and scholars have turned increasing attention to state courts for the vindication of religious freedom rights during the past decade.[58] This development somewhat mirrors similar shifts in civil rights advocacy, which experienced a similar move from federal to state venues after the federal courts began seriously retrenching civil rights protections in the 1980s. Whatever one may think about the substantive issues of religious and civil rights, the shifting points of access to government are exactly what Madison anticipated.

Comparisons, Concluding Reflections, and Normative Implications

These cases illustrate the extent to which constitutional conflicts over the accommodation of religion are tied up in institutional competition.

Both *Smith* and *Kiryas Joel* centered on religious accommodation. The *Smith* case debated when *courts may order other institutions* to accommodate the religious needs of individuals in the interests of religious free exercise; the *Kiryas Joel* case asks when other public officials *may voluntarily* accommodate religious needs without violating the Establishment Clause. Recall that most typical religious accommodations are made on an *ad hoc* basis by administrative officials such as school principals, military commanders, and social service agencies; many are written into legislation without much notice or conflict. Court intervention always indicates a failure to resolve accommodation issues administratively or legislatively. People resort to courts either when religious advocates have failed to achieve the accommodation they believe is warranted or when nonadherents believe that a particular accommodation conveys an unwarranted advantage on one or more religions and thus violates state or federal laws against religious establishment. Because we so often describe religious accommodation conflict as judicial narratives, we often forget that courts are last resorts after negotiation, lobbying, and the rest of the normal political process have failed to satisfy all interested parties.

Courts in the United States occupy the intersection of two different sets of expectations. On one hand, they are a branch of government, part of the political process, characterized by their own sets of influences, constituencies, and resources. On the other hand, their decisions are authoritative in a special way, and although individual judges and decisions are often criticized, the authority of courts is mostly legitimate. My own emphasis on judicial resolution does not presume that courts are the best decision makers in religion cases, although there are some good reasons for a limited optimism in that direction. As a student of the courts and their jurisprudence, I am persuaded that judicial decisions have one clear advantage, and that is that judges, especially appellate judges, must justify their decisions with respect to principles that are consistent with precedent and the text of statutes and constitutions.

Courts certainly do not always "get it right," but the practice of justifying decisions is perhaps a magnetic force in the direction of principled decisions. But far more significantly, I trust the system of redundancy built into our system. The Supreme Court (in my view and that of many scholars) got it wrong in the *Smith* Case. But Congress, state legislators, and state judges got a second, third, and fourth shot at the issue and ultimately reached a complex of reasonable solutions. This analysis has some clear normative implications. Above all, it requires preserving the independence of courts—an independence that has been gravely undermined over the past several years. Not only the constitutional guarantees regarding religion but all constitutional guarantees depend on an independent judiciary with both the power and the will to hold other decision makers accountable to them. Independent courts are critical, not primarily because of the wisdom of judges but because of both the integrity of law itself and because of the role courts play in the redundancy of our political system.

Divided government for Madison was an expedient to prevent tyranny. It is more than a preventer of harm, but also a positive good, important not only for what it prevents but for what it enables. The multiple points of access for citizens making demands on the political system have proven to be at least as important as the electoral system in promoting democratic responsiveness and accountability.

In addition to the conclusions we may draw from them about institutional pluralism, these cases also provide opportunities to reflect on the competing images of homogeneity, segmentation, and pluralism for maintaining harmony. The Amish in *Yoder* and the Satmar Hasidim in *Kiryas Joel* are both insular in the sense of living in separate communities and maintaining cultures dramatically different from the mainstream. And yet, neither was totally separate from the norms of surrounding communities. Michael McConnell understands the *Yoder* decision as a commitment to protect genuinely insular communities:

> The Supreme Court held unanimously that the Amish have a constitutional right to protection from being "assimilated into society at large." The legal system can accept the proposition that a religious community is a self contained unit with the right to set its own norms, so long as—in the Court's words in *Yoder*—it "interferes with no rights or interests of others."[59]

Like the Amish, the Satmar Hasidim of Kiryas Joel are an insular community seeking a seamless way of life. The citizens of Kiryas Joel, of course, have an undeniable constitutional right to educate their children in either public schools or private religious schools. But to insist on receiving public education on their own terms in order to preserve their insularity seems to ask for fragmentation and exclusivity rather than citizenship within a pluralistic society. Justice Souter, writing for the majority, explicitly addressed what I have called "segmentation," and he called "gerrymandering." He concluded that the Establishment Clause prohibits the drawing of governmental boundaries along religious lines in order to accommodate the needs of a religious community. Lines that today may be drawn benevolently may later be drawn maliciously. From a pluralist perspective, reinforcing lines of separation by making congruent religious and governmental boundaries violates the pluralist commitment to overlapping patterns of community and cleavage.

Bob Jones University could also be described as insular, but not in the same way as the Amish community. It actively recruited only students and faculty who shared its sectarian vision, and it scrupulously refused government support in order to avoid the accompanying regulations. But as a university, it engaged the wider culture, teaching students the skills to become leaders in—and we might say missionaries to—the outside world. Bob Jones University's constitutional challenge forced a choice between two contending pluralist values—the value of equality and inclusion for a long-oppressed minority, and the value of autonomy for a dissenting religious group to reject racial inclusion. The Supreme Court decision upholding the IRS demonstrates the conditions under which government chooses to exercise to the fullest its role as a meaning source, even to the point of denying financial advantages to those who pursue a contrary vision. And yet, there is the troubling sacrifice of genuine diversity in this decision. Justice Powell's concurring opinion captured it well:

> [The majority] ignores the important role played by tax exemptions in encouraging diverse, indeed often sharply conflicting, activities and viewpoints. As Justice Brennan has observed, private, nonprofit groups receive tax exemptions because each group contributes to the diversity of association, viewpoint, and enterprise essential to a vigorous, pluralistic society. Far from representing an effort to reinforce any perceived "common community conscience," the provision of tax exemptions to nonprofit groups is one indispensable means of limiting the influence of governmental orthodoxy on important areas of community life.[60]

Hard cases like *Bob Jones* force the state to confront its own certainty and commitment to a common vision. In a pluralist society, such instances should be few and far between. The sacrifice of alternate meanings is a heavy price in a pluralist society; this decision is one of the rare occasions when the normative commitments to equality and inclusion override the autonomy of a group with a contrary vision, so long as purely private options remain available. In light of America's history of racial exclusion, the policy of promoting inclusive common citizenship appeared to be truly compelling.

The situations of Capt. Goldman and of Smith and Black may represent the most common kinds of problems; the plaintiffs sought to maintain a distinctive practice of their religion while being fully engaged in the surrounding cultures and roles. Laws that forced them to choose between religious distinctness and social integration undermined their opportunities for overlapping identities and commitments.

Some readers will surely object to the value I have placed on overlapping meanings in the social mosaic. Their vision of a unified life is surely an attractive one, with a longer history than the pluralism. However, such a vision is ultimately not consistent with the American cultural and political heritage. In fact, this brief survey suggests that pluralism is ultimately not consistent with demands either for total insularity or for perfectionists who want to use the mechanisms of the state to transform the public agenda.

The survey of these cases does not illustrate any comprehensive principle for resolving the kinds of conflicts that arise under the religious clauses. Indeed, constitutional scholar Winnifred Fallers Sullivan, among others, argues that the range of religious practices and the concomitant burdens to them are so diverse that there simply is no First Amendment principle for resolving them.[61] I tend to agree that it is futile to search for the defining elements of religion or for a religiously neutral constitutional principle. Neither courts nor legislatures nor bureaucracies always get "right answers" because often there simply are no right answers. And yet, this need not be a pessimistic conclusion. Because multiple institutions have a chance at managing the conflict, the odds are good that somewhere along the line compromises are worked out and tensions are defused. And the fluidity of multiple coalitions of minorities means that the losers in any one episode are likely to move on to other issues and to seek other coalition partners. Thus, the fluidity and general messiness of both political institutions and the religious landscape are (pardon the pun) our saving grace.[62]

In the Introduction, I referred to our society's good fortune, rather than its political brilliance. But this fortuitous situation demands something of individuals. Every kind of social institution both requires and creates a kind of cultural requisite, and pluralism is no exception. Social and political pluralism are maintained by individuals who are able to live in an environment of multiple and crosscutting identities, meanings, and values. Pluralism requires us to accept the fragmentation of social roles and institutions as well as the ability to hold various identities and loyalties simultaneously. It is a poor fit for perfectionism.[63] None of this is easy. Asking people to live with such deep inconsistencies goes against our desire for a coherent existence. The desire for seamlessness will impel some people to withdraw into insular communities and others to join redemptive movements. Yet, the awkward gaps, overlaps, and shifting identities may be precisely the "glue" that binds together a pluralist society.

Political philosophers argue how much and what kind of consensus is required to hold a society together. In the view I have described, coherence is maintained not so much by an essential core of common beliefs as by the crosscutting patterns of cleavage, identity, conflict, and commitment among citizens. Without crosscutting and overlapping bonds, conflicts become mutually reinforcing. The need for cohesion reminds us of the fundamental difference between a genuinely pluralist society and a segmented one. That is why it is so important that religious minorities enjoy full freedom to engage in divergent practices *while* participating in the system at large. This pattern is the underlying "constitution" of pluralism.

The pluralism of American religions could not persist without a pervasively pluralist institutional context. It depends, profoundly, on governmental institutions that prevent the accumulation of power and provide political access for shifting coalitions of participants. Thus, pluralism requires both a commitment to sustaining the multiple systems of power inherent in the Madisonian structure of government and an appreciation of fluidity. Two final examples illustrate this fluidity. Before the 1990 *Smith* decision, most observers would have put faith in the federal courts, especially the Supreme Court, over state governments for protecting religious liberty. Less than a decade later, under numerous state RFRA laws, state courts seemed to be in the forefront of new religious protections. Similarly, religious conservatives, after a disappointing decade attempting to influence national public policy, recognized opportunities in local arenas, including school boards and city councils. These strategic changes illustrate the inherent fluidity of the pluralist system. The constitution of pluralism reminds us that any concentration of power is potentially dangerous, including concentrations in institutions that may be temporarily asserting the agendas with which we agree.

To the extent that these conditions of pluralism continue to be part of a cohesive whole, they give us cause for confidence in the extraordinary ability of the American polity to manage—if not solve—religious conflicts with relative harmony and peace. We are the inheritors of considerable good fortune both in the patterns of American religiosity and governmental structure, and although these patterns are reasonably stable, they are not guaranteed. The continuation of both kinds of pluralism ultimately requires the commitment of religious leaders, government officials at all levels, and citizens of all faiths.

Notes

1. Mark Lilla, "The Politics of God," *New York Times,* August 19, 2007. See also Mark Lilla, *The Stillborn God* (New York: Alfred A. Knopf, 2007).

2. Thomas L. Friedman, "War of the Worlds," *New York Times,* February 24, 2006, A23.

3. In 1998 I examined several of the most well-considered principles for understanding the Free Exercise Clause and proposed that it could be best understood as a strategy for fostering alternate sources of meaning in a society. I still consider this the best understanding of Free Exercise but am now less sanguine that it offers definitive and concrete guidance in hard cases. Bette Novit Evans, *Interpreting the Free Exercise of Religion: The Constitution and American Pluralism* (Chapel Hill: University of North Carolina Press, 1997).

4. This point and many subsequent ones were originally articulated in Evans, *Interpreting the Free Exercise of Religion.*

5. Nancy Rosenblum develops this point in "Faith in America: Political Theory's Logic of Autonomy and Logic of Congruence," chapter 12 in this volume.

6. Many observers make this point. See, for example, Melissa Rogers, "Symposium: Beyond Separation: Church and State: Traditions of Church-State Separation: Some Ways They Have Protected Religion and Advanced Religious Freedom and How They Are Threatened Today," *Journal of Law & Politics* 277 (Winter 2002).

7. This argument builds up an earlier work, "The Constitutional Context of Religious Liberty," in Mary Segers, ed., *Piety, Politics, and Pluralism: Religion, the Courts, and the 2000 Election* (Lanham, MD: Rowman & Littlefield, 2002).

8. The literature of political science is replete with interpretations of American pluralism. My own view takes its inspiration from one of the "fathers" of pluralist theory, Robert Dahl. Among Dahl's works, see especially *A Preface to Democratic Theory* (Chicago: University of Chicago Press, 1956); *Who Governs* (New Haven: Yale University Press, 1961); *Polyarchy* (New Haven: Yale University Press, 1971); *Dilemmas of Pluralist Democracy* (New Haven: Yale University Press, 1982), *On Democracy* (New Haven: Yale University Press, 1998), *On Political Equality* (New Haven: Yale University Press, 2006).

9. Leonard Levy, *The Establishment Clause* (New York: Macmillan, 1986).

10. See, for example, Diana Eck, *A New Religious America* (New York: Harper, 2001), and Robert Wuthnow, *America and the Challenges of Religious Diversity* (Princeton, NJ: Princeton University Press, 2005).

11. Michael Foley and Dean Hoge, *Religion and the New Immigrants* (New York: Oxford University Press, 2007).

12. Catherine Albanese, *America Religion and Religions*. 4th ed. (Belmont, CA: Thomson Wadsworth, 2007).

13. Roger Finke and Rodney Stark, *The Churching of America* (Piscataway, NJ: Rutgers University Press, 1992).

14. Will Herberg, *Protestant/Catholic/Jew* (New York: Doubleday, 1958).

15. Robert Wuthnow, *The Restructuring of American Religion* (Princeton, NJ: Princeton University Press, 1988).

16. See Donald Miller, *Reinventing American Protestantism* (Berkeley: University of California Press, 1997), and Scott Thumma and Dave Travis, *Beyond the Megchurch Myth* (San Francisco: Josey Bass, 2007). See also David Rozen and James Nieman, eds. *Church, Identity, and Change* (Grand Rapids, MI: Eerdmans, 2005).

17. Mark Noll, *The Old Religion in a New World* (Grand Rapids, MI: Eerdmans, 2002), 162.

18. James Davison Hunter, *Culture Wars: The Struggle to Define America* (New York: Basic Books, 1991).

19. Several of the chapters in this volume address the culture war thesis. See particularly Kenneth Wald and David Leege, "Mobilizing Religious Differences in American Politics," chapter 11, on the role of elites in exacerbating polarization; Geoffrey Layman, "Religion and Party Activists," chapter 7, on the role of political parties; and John Green, "Religious Diversity and American Democracy," chapter 2, for implications of recent polling data.

20. Alan Wolfe, *One Nation After All* (New York: Viking Press, 1998). The most convincing empirical studies leading to the optimistic conclusion are found in Morris Fiorina, *Culture War? The Myth of a Polarized America* (White Plains, NY: Pearson Longman, 2005), and The Pew Forum on Religion and Public Life, *US Religious Landscape Survey,* available at http://religions.pewforum.org/?gclid =CI3cg9So25QCFQsiIgodb14alA.

21. Thomas Luckmann, *The Invisible Religion: The Problem of Religion in Modern Society* (New York: Macmillan, 1967).

22. Robert Bellah, *Habits of the Heart* (Berkeley: University of California Press, 1985).

23. Alan Wolfe, *The Transformation of American Religion* (New York: Free Press, 2003).

24. See, for example, Robert C. Fuller, *Spiritual, but Not Religious* (New York: Oxford University Press, 2001), 8; Peter L. Berger, "Reflections on the Sociology of Religion Today," *Sociology of Religion Today* 62 (2001): 443, 446–47; Martin Marty, "The Widening Gyres of Religion and Law," 45 *DePaul Law Review* 45 (1996): 651, 664; Rebecca French, "Shopping for Religion: The Change in Everyday Religious Practice and Its Importance to the Law," *Buffalo Law Review* 51 (2003): 127, 164–65; Charles Taylor, *Varieties of Religion Today* (Cambridge, MA: Harvard University Press, 2002), 102–3; and Frederick Mark Gedicks and Roger Hendrix, "Religious Experience in the Age of Digital Reproduction," *St. Johns Law Review* 79 (2005), 127, 157. See data in Barry A. Kosmin, Egon Mayer, and Ariela Keyser, *American Religious Identification Survey* (New York: City University Graduate Center, 2001).

25. See, for example, Kenneth Wald and Allison Calhoun-Brown, *Religion and Politics in the United States*, 5th ed. (Lanham, MD: Rowman & Littlefield, 2007).

26. M. M. Slaughter has raised a provocative critique of this vision, noting that "pluralism diminishes the power of differences by treating all differences as equal when in terms of positionality, they are not." The point is that some of these differences convey power or its absence, and that is a difference that makes a difference. See M. M. Slaughter, "The Multicultural Self: Questions of Subjectivity, Questions of Power," in Michael Rosenfeld, ed., *Constitutionalism, Identity, Difference, and Legitimacy* (Durham, NC: Duke University Press, 1994), 369–80, esp. 378.

27. Nancy Rosenblum's chapter, "Faith in America: Political Theory's Logic of Autonomy and Logic of Congruence," chapter 12 in this volume, argues that the internal ideologies and structures of organizations within a pluralist democracy need not be consistent with the democratic norms of the society itself.

28. In 1998 I used the term "fundamentalist" to describe this view, and I still believe that the desire for seamless integration characterizes fundamentalisms of all types. Nevertheless, because the word has numerous and contested meanings and contexts, I shall avoid it here.

29. Frank Lechner, "Fundamentalism Revisited," in Thomas Robbins and Dick Anthony, eds., *In Gods We Trust,* 2nd ed. (New Brunswick: NJ: Transaction, 1990), 77, 80.

30. He makes this argument in a lengthy book titled *The Institutes of Biblical Law* (Phillipsburg, NJ: Presbyterian and Reformed Publishing Co., 1973).

31. Mark Lilla, "The Politics of God," *New York Times Magazine,* August 19, 2007.

32. One example may suffice for many. After failing to achieve its major goals nationally during the 1980s, the Christian coalition shifted its strategy to achieving electoral and policy goals at the state and local levels.

33. The classic description of this process is still Robert Dahl's *Who Governs?* (New Haven: Yale University Press, 1961).

34. Nancy Rosenblum develops this point in chapter 12 in this volume.

35. The most articulate spokesman for the representation-enhancing view of judicial review is John Hart Ely, *Democracy and Distrust* (Cambridge, MA: Harvard University Press, 1980).

36. James Madison, Federalist #51, in Hamilton et al., *The Federalist Papers* (originally published 1787–88) (New York: Bantam Books, 1982), 264.

37. James Madison, Federalist #10, *The Federalist Papers*, 48.

38. Gary S. Gildin, "Symposium: God's Law in the People's Law: A Discussion of Contemporary Issues Arising from Religion and the Law: The Sanctity of Religious Liberty of Minority Faiths under State Constitutions: Three Hypotheses," *University of Maryland Law Journal of Race, Religion, Gender and Class* 6 (Spring 2006), 21. Footnotes omitted. Data are from Barry A. Kosmin, Egon Mayer, and Ariela Keyser, *American Religious Identification Survey* (2001), 23.

39. The most famous works by Robert Dahl are cited in note 8.

40. 406 US 205 (1972).

41. *Goldman v. Weinberger* 475 US 503 (1986). The most famous critique of this decision is Michael Sandel, "Religious Liberty—Freedom of Conscience or Freedom of Choice," *Utah Law Review* (1989), 597.

42. Similar cases have arisen when Muslim school teachers have been forbidden from wearing head coverings (hijab) in public schools. Such rules undermine pluralism by forcing a person to choose between her religiously mandated head covering and her position as public school teacher rather than being able to operate in the crosscutting contexts of both roles and identities. More recently, a Florida appeals court ruled against a Muslim woman's request for accommodation under Florida's Religious Freedom Restoration Act when her insistence on maintaining her religiously required face coverings (niqib) came into conflict with state law requiring a full-face photo on identification photographs. *Sultaana Freedman v. State of Florida,* 924 So.2d 48 (Fla. App 5 Dist.2006).

43. See Rosenblum's discussion of consistency in chapter 12 of this volume.

44. 461 US 564 (1983). Two preliminary questions preceded the constitutional one. The first was a matter of statutory construction and administrative law: Had Congress authorized the IRS to withhold the tax deduction? The second dealt with an interpretation of the Internal Revenue Code: whether the long-standing requirement that charities must serve a public purpose in order to receive tax-deductible status also applied to tax exemptions in 501(c)(3). The Court answered both questions in the affirmative.

45. The procedural and institutional complexities of this case are far more complex than this summary indicates, including a reversal of policy by the IRS in 1981, a presidential appeal for congressional legislation, and turmoil within the Reagan administration. For a splendid account of the political background of this

case, see Louis Fisher and Neal Devins, *Political Dynamics of Constitutional Law* (St. Paul, MN: West, 1992), 52–67. On the university itself, see Quentin Schultze, "The Two Faces of Fundamentalist Higher Education," in Martin Marty and Scott Appleby, eds., *Fundamentalisms and Society* (Chicago: University of Chicago Press, 1993), 490–535.

46. In *Runyon v. McCray* 427 US 160 (1976), the Court had held that the Reconstruction era Civil Rights Act 42 USC 1981 forbade racial discrimination in private schools, but the issue of private religious schools was not addressed. It is interesting to contrast this case with a much earlier one, *Berea College v. Kentucky* 211 US 45 (1911), in which a private religious college was punished for violating a State's law *requiring* racial segregation.

47. Perhaps the most profound commentary on the *Bob Jones* case was that offered by Robert Cover in his "*Nomos* and Narrative," *Harvard Law Review* 97 (1983), especially pp. 62–67. In spite of Cover's great sympathy for insular religious communities, he ultimately concluded that a truly compelling public commitment may sometimes override that of a religious association. Cover would have accepted the university's defeat more readily had the majority opinion been phrased in terms of the government's profound commitment to racial equality. But Chief Justice Burger's opinion spoke merely of deference to congressional public policy—a goal insufficient, in Cover's view, to justify the sacrifice of its autonomy. Cover argues that the normative autonomy of Bob Jones University deserved more protection unless the court was willing to assert a much stronger commitment to racial equality—not merely a "public policy." The Court's decision took away too much from Bob Jones while giving too little to racial equality:

> It is a case that gives too much to the statist determination of the normative world by contributing too little to the statist understanding of the Constitution. . . . In the impoverished commitment of Chief Justice Burger's opinion, the constitutional question was not necessary, but the Court avoided it by simply throwing the claim of protected insularity to the mercy of public policy. The insular communities deserved better—they deserved a constitutional hedge against mere administration. And the minority community deserved more—it deserved a constitutional commitment to avoiding public subsidization of racism.

48. *Board of Education of Kiryas Joel School District v. Grumet,* 512 US 687 (1994).

49. *Aguilar v. Felton,* 473 US 402 (1985) and *Grand Rapids v. Ball*, 473 US 373 (1985).

50. 1989 N. Y. Laws, ch. 748.

51. *Grumet v. Cuomo,* 900 N.Y. 2d 57 (1997); 681 N.E. 2d 340 (1997).

52. *Agostini v. Felton,* 521 US 203 (1997).

53. My interpretation is consistent with, and much influenced by, such works as Robert Cover, "The Uses of Jurisdictional Redundancy: Interests, Ideology, and Innovation," *William & Mary Law Review* 22 (1981), 639; and Martha Minow, "Pluralisms," *Connecticut Law Review* 21 (1989), 965.

54. 494 US 872 (1990).

55. 521 US 507 (1997).

56. 42 U.S.C. sect. 2000cc et seq.

57. 544 US 709 (2005).

58. See, for example, Marci A. Hamilton, "Federalism and the Public Good: The True Story Behind the Religious Land Use and Institutionalized Persons Act," *Indiana Law Journal* 78 (Winter/Spring 2003), 311.

59. Michael McConnell, "Christ, Culture, and Courts: A Niebuhrian Examination of First Amendment Jurisprudence," *DePaul Law Review* 42 (1992), 191, 196. The most profound theoretical discussion of normative autonomy is still the classic commentary on the *Yoder* and *Bob Jones* cases by the late Robert Cover, in "Foreword: Nomos and Narrative," The Supreme Court 1982 Term, 1983 *Harvard Law Review*, 1, 1983.

60. Cover (1983), 609.

61. Winnifred Fallers Sullivan, *The Impossibility of Religious Freedom* (Princeton, NJ: Princeton University Press, 2005). This book describes the Florida case of *Warner v. City of Boca Raton* 887 S.2d 1023 (Fla.2004), in which mourners erected memorials in a city cemetery that prohibited such memorials but claimed that the monuments were religious in nature and thus protected under Florida's Religious Rights Restoration Act.

62. Perhaps the best example of the "new coalition partners" point is the cases of Rev. Sun Myung Moon. When Moon, leader of the very unpopular Unification Church, was expelled from the United States allegedly because of immigration irregularities, a large coalition of religious leaders from across the religious spectrum joined together of to protest on his behalf.

63. On the role of perfectionist groups in pluralist societies, see John Rawls, *A Theory of Justice: Restatement,* ed. Erin Kelly (Cambridge, MA: Harvard University Press, 2001).

PART II

Religion and Democratic Values

Chapter 5

THE POLITICAL CONSEQUENCES OF RELIGIOSITY

Does Religion Always Cause Political Intolerance?

JAMES L. GIBSON

FOR QUITE SOME TIME, social scientists have recognized that religiosity and political intolerance are closely intertwined, with those who are more deeply committed to religion tending toward greater intolerance. However, scholars have not been entirely clear about whether religious beliefs cause intolerance, whether intolerance causes religious beliefs, or whether intolerance and religious beliefs share a common antecedent, such as dogmatism and authoritarianism. Moreover, debate exists as to what precisely it is about being religious that fuels intolerance. Possible candidates include the belief in dogma, with clear and rigid distinctions between ideas that are "right" and "wrong," the tendency of those who are religious to define themselves as a clearly defined "in-group" distinct from various "out-groups," and the propensity (concomitant or not) to perceive threats from their political and ideological foes. Without a clear understanding of the precise interconnections between religiosity and intolerance, it is difficult to imagine how the intolerance of believers can be understood and, ultimately, tamed.

The purpose of this chapter is to investigate the relationship between intolerance and religiosity, based on a survey of a representative sample of the American mass public conducted in 2007. The survey is notable for (1) extensive measures of perceived intergroup threat and political intolerance, (2) broad indicators of religiosity and involvement within religious institutions, and (3) the ability to control for a variety of antecedent variables.

The analysis begins with a discussion of political tolerance, grounding this chapter in democratic theory and an empirical literature that is now more than a half a century old. I then focus on multidimensional indicators of religiosity, ranging from measures of self-identification, participation in religious organizations, and collateral beliefs about religion and politics. After testing for the simple interrelationship between religiosity and intolerance, I turn to trying to unravel the causal structure knitting the variables together. The chapter concludes with a discussion of how the propensity for intolerance among those who are religious might be tamed and put to better service for democratic politics.

Theoretical Background: The Role of Tolerance in Democratic Theory

Democracy is, of course, a system of procedures by which majorities tend to have their way: the majority rules. Liberal democracies require mechanisms of aggregating citizen preferences within majoritarian institutions, and this is perhaps the essence of the concept of democracy (e.g., Dahl 1989). But democracy—especially liberal democracy—is also a system in which institutionalized respect for the rights of political minorities to try to become a majority must exist. In particular, political minorities in a liberal democracy must be given the means of contestation—the right to try to convince others of the rightness of their positions. Setting up institutions of majority rule turns out to be a comparatively simple task; ensuring the right of unpopular political minorities to compete for political power turns out to be far more difficult.

Without guarantees of the right of all to participate in politics, the "marketplace of ideas" cannot function effectively. The idea of a marketplace is that anyone can put forth a product—an idea—for political "consumers" to consider. The success of the idea is determined by the level of support freely given in the market. The market encourages deliberation, through which superior ideas are found to be superior, and through which the flaws of bad ideas are exposed for all to see (almost as if guided by an invisible hand).[1] Liberal political philosophers (such as J. S. Mill) have long been attracted to this marketplace notion, and many consider it an essential element of democratic governance.

Many instances exist in which lack of confidence in the effectiveness of the marketplace of ideas has stimulated governments to place restrictions on the potential entrants to the arena. Some political systems prohibit, for instance, political parties based on religion; others ban all political parties not based on a particular religion. "Extremist" ideas are banned in some systems (as in laws prohibiting Holocaust denials), just as "radical" political parties are prohibited from participating in other systems (e.g., fascist parties in Germany). American policy makers in 1954 (and policy makers throughout much of the world as well) apparently had so little confidence in the ability of ordinary people to consider and reject Communism that they banned Communists from putting their ideas forward for consideration.[2] Perhaps most common throughout the world today, governments that have become accustomed to political power often seek to prohibit opposition groups from participating in the marketplace of ideas.[3] Without a willingness to put up with all ideologies seeking to compete for the hearts and minds of the citizenry, the market is likely to fail. Thus, a fairly simple theory is that democracies require the free and open debate of political differences, and such debate can only take place where political tolerance prevails.

Political tolerance in a democracy requires that all political ideas (and the groups holding them) get the same access to the marketplace of ideas as the access legally extended to the ideas dominating the system. This definition obviously precludes any form of violence, and therefore, I make no claim that political tolerance extends to the right of terrorists to engage in terror. It may, however, protect the speech rights of terrorists or, more precisely, those who advocate terrorism (e.g., defenders or advocates of suicide bombing).[4] The liberal democratic theory of political tolerance does not protect many forms of nonpolitical expression, such as pornography (except as enlisted in the service of politics) and most types of commercial speech. It does, however, extend the right of contestation to deeply unpopular ideas, such as the need for a violent revolution or racism or Communism or radical Islam.

Whenever the definition of tolerance is considered, critics question whether certain types of "extreme" speech must be protected. These discussions may be useful in principle but not in practice. From the point of view of empirical research on tolerance, the controversies that emerge do not have to do with the most extreme and unusual forms of speech but rather with the contestation rights of relatively innocuous ideas. In the case of the United States, for instance, even in the twenty-first century, 48 percent of the American people prefer that atheists (someone who is against all religion and churches, the typical way atheists are depicted in survey research) be denied the right to hold a public demonstration (see Gibson 2008). Similar findings have been reported from a Polish survey in 1993 (Karpov 1999). Only after ordinary people come to tolerate a range of even slightly unorthodox ideas should research then focus on tolerance of the views of the most extreme members of society.

Liberal democratic theory also provides some guidance as to what sorts of activities must be guaranteed to political minorities. Actions and behaviors related to efforts to persuade people and to compete for political power must be put up with. This might include giving public speeches, running candidates for public office, or even publicizing a group by removing trash from the freeways (and claiming credit for doing with so with a publicly erected sign). Obviously, illegal activity need not be countenanced, even if we acknowledge that the line between legal and illegal is often thin, given the power and propensity of majorities to criminalize political activities by the minority.[5]

This theory of the marketplace of ideas anticipates two important (and interconnected) restraints on freedom. First, as I have already mentioned, many fear that the government, typically under the guise of regulation, will usurp power and deny the expression of ideas threatening to the status quo (i.e., the power of the government of the day). Examples of such abuses of minority rights to participation are too widespread to even begin to catalog in this chapter.

A second constraint on freedom is more subtle: it originates in the political culture of a polity—the beliefs, values, attitudes, and behaviors of ordinary citizens. Restraints on freedom can certainly emanate from public policy, but they can also be found in subtle (and, on occasion, not so subtle) demands for conformity within a society's culture. To the extent that ordinary citizens are intolerant of views challenging mainstream thought, the expression of such viewpoints is likely to generate sanctions and costs. This can in turn create what Noelle-Neumann (1984) has referred to as a "spiral of silence": a dynamic process in which those holding minority viewpoints increasingly learn about how rare their views are, thereby leading to silence, which in turn makes the ideas seem to be even less widely held and therefore more dangerous or costly to express. Perhaps the most significant legacy of McCarthyism in the United States was not the limitations imposed on Communists and their fellow travelers—legal limitations that were often severe and included imprisonment—but instead was the creation of a "silent generation," a cohort unwilling to express views that might be considered controversial or unpopular. And, to complete the circle, mass political intolerance can be a useful form of political capital for those who would in turn enact repressive legislation. To the extent that a political culture emphasizes conformity and penalizes those with contrarian ideas, little tolerance exists, and the likelihood of political repression is high.

Conceptualizing and Measuring Political Intolerance

Tolerance thus requires that citizens and governments put up with ideas that are thought to be objectionable. Two components of this definition require further consideration: Which ideas must be put up with, and which activities must be allowed? The answers to both of these questions are intimately related not just to the conceptualization of tolerance but to its operationalization as well. From the viewpoint of empirical studies of political tolerance, measurement issues of whom and what have become concerns of great importance.[6]

In Stouffer's era,[7] the nature of the perceived threat to the dominant ideology of the time was clear[8]: it came from Communists and their "fellow travelers." Consequently, tolerance questions were framed around the right of Communists to compete for political power. To the extent that it is obvious which groups are potential objects of intolerance in a society, then at least part of the job of measuring mass political intolerance is easy.

For instance, the largest amount of data on political tolerance has been collected by the General Social Survey in the United States. This survey, begun in the early 1970s and continuing through today, routinely asks about people in five groups: someone who is against all churches and religion (atheists), a man who admits he is a Communist, a man who admits he is a homosexual, a person who advocates doing away with elections and letting the military run the country (militarists), and a person who believes that blacks are genetically inferior (racists). These particular groups are derived from Stouffer's research and are assumed to be representative today of the fringes of the American ideological continua.

The obvious limitation of these questions is that the replies of those who are themselves atheists, homosexuals, Communists, militarists, and racists cannot be treated as valid indicators of political tolerance.[9] The flaw with the Stouffer approach to measuring political intolerance was discovered by John Sullivan and his colleagues. *Tolerance is putting up with that with which one disagrees.* Consequently, it makes no sense to ask one who is a Communist whether Communists should be allowed to make speeches, and so forth.[10] Sullivan et al. (1982) argued that a valid measure of intolerance requires an "objection precondition," by which they meant that the stimulus presented to every respondent (the ideology or group representing the ideology) must be objectionable. To achieve this, the respondents must be allowed to identify the highly disliked group; the researcher does not specify which groups are asked about; rather the respondents must designate the group. So as to introduce some degree of comparability across respondents, each is asked to identify the group he or she *dislikes the most*; tolerance questions are then asked about this group. The technique has been named the "least-liked" measurement approach, even though this is a slight misnomer in that the group asked about is actually the most disliked, not, strictly speaking, the least liked.[11]

Levels of Intolerance in the Contemporary United States

How politically tolerant are the American people, and how have levels of tolerance changed? Unfortunately, answering these questions is confounded to some degree by differences in how political intolerance is measured.

It is certainly true the American people have become more tolerant of Communists since the McCarthy era (Gibson 2008). At the same time, however, intolerance of political activity by Communists is commonplace. More generally, in an analysis of intolerance from 1976 to 1998, Mondak and Sanders (2003, 501) draw the following conclusions:

"There is evidence that tolerance has increased marginally in that 82 to 85% of respondents were coded as intolerant for the years 1976–1989 versus 79 to 82% for the years 1990–1998." Thus, political intolerance within the political culture of the United States is relatively high and persistent.

At the same time, the empirical evidence suggests that what has changed over time in the United States is not levels of intolerance—which have remained approximately constant—but rather which groups are deemed the objects of intolerance. Gibson (2008) refers to this as "pluralistic intolerance," by which he means that intolerance is not focused on any particular group, but only in the sense that many groups, representing varying ideologies, are the objects of contemporary intolerance. The picture painted by most studies of contemporary public opinion in the United States is one shaded darkly toward political intolerance.

What Causes Some Citizens to Be Tolerant but Others Not?

Perhaps one of the most widely investigated questions in the tolerance literature has to do with the etiology of intolerance at the individual level. Many have contributed to identifying predictors of intolerance, ranging from Sniderman's work (1975) on self-esteem and social learning to Sullivan et al. (1982) on threat perceptions, democratic values, and psychological insecurity to Stenner's book (2005) on the personality trait authoritarianism. Nearly all agree that some sort of closed-mindedness or psychological rigidity contributes to intolerance, even if the precise label attached to the concept varies across researchers.

In virtually all studies, threat perceptions are one of the strongest predictors of intolerance. Not surprisingly, those who are more threatened by their political enemies are less likely to tolerate them. However, a number of surprises are associated with the threat-tolerance relationship. The strongest predictor of intolerance is the feeling that a group is threatening, but, ironically perhaps, it is not the direct threat to one's own personal well-being (egocentric threat perception) that is crucial, but it is instead perceived threat to the group and/or society (sociotropic threat perception) that is more likely to generate intolerance (e.g., Gibson and Gouws 2003; Davis and Silver 2004). Moreover, several studies have now reported that the perceived efficacy of a group (its power or potential for power) has few implications for the other aspects of threat perceptions or for political intolerance (e.g., Marcus et al. 1995; Gibson and Gouws 2003). It seems natural to suggest that intolerance flourishes where the threats of groups and ideas are highest, yet the various processes involved have been found to be fairly complex, and the simple relationship does not typically exist.[12]

It is also paradoxical that, even though one might expect perceptions of threat to be shaped by personality characteristics, in fact, little convincing evidence has been adduced on this point. The most concentrated effort to identify the personality precursors to threat is the research of Marcus et al. (1995), although many scholars have worked on this problem. If in fact threat perceptions are based on realistic factors (e.g., realistic group conflict), then there is no necessary requirement for psychological variables to be implicated. On the other hand, to the extent that groups represent sociotropic threats, one might well hypothesize that individual personality characteristics (e.g., authoritarianism and chauvinistic nationalism) are activated. Unraveling these relationships—or lack of relationships—is a research problem of considerable importance for the field.

In the original model of the origins of intolerance, Sullivan et al. (1982) demonstrated that tolerance is connected to a more general set of beliefs about democracy (even though the slippage between general commitments to democracy and specific applications to the rights of disliked groups is considerable). Gibson et al. (1992; see also Gibson 1995) have expanded this research to consider more specifically the connection between tolerance and support for democratic institutions and processes (see also Finkel and Ernst 2005). At least in Russia, such interrelationships are not strong, largely because of the difficulty of embracing tolerance of hated groups and ideas. In formerly dictatorial systems, people were denied majority rule; consequently, the majoritarian aspects of democracy are readily embraced because they lead to the empowerment of the people. Extending these rights to unpopular minorities requires more intellectual effort and political security than many can muster. Tolerance may be the most difficult democratic value of all; only among those with a fully articulated democratic belief system—which is especially uncommon among people not repeatedly exposed to democratic institutions and processes—do we see close connections between tolerance and the other democratic values.

Figure 5.1 depicts the simple model that has emerged from a few decades of research on the origins of mass political intolerance. This model is the starting point for my analysis of the influence of religiosity on intolerance.

The Role of Religiosity in Creating Political Intolerance

Empirically focused social scientists have also long been concerned about the connection between religiosity and political intolerance, beginning with Stouffer's efforts to understand intolerance during the McCarthy era. Generally, research has found a connection between religiosity and intolerance (e.g., Nunn et al. 1978; Beatty and Walter 1984; Wilcox and

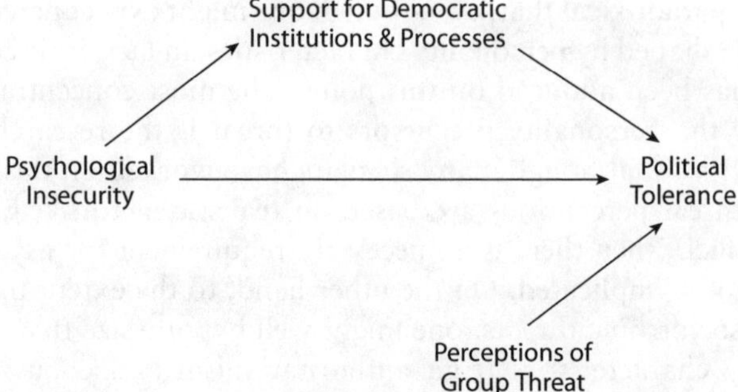

Figure 5.1. The conventional, cross-sectional model of the origins of political tolerance.

Jelen 1990; Green et al. 1994; but see Eisenstein 2006). However, several infirmities characterize extant research, including (1) the use of different measures of political tolerance (fixed group versus least-liked groups); (2) the use of varying measures of religion and religiosity (e.g., beliefs versus identities); (3) different understandings of exactly what it is about religion that contributes to intolerance (e.g., whether doctrinal beliefs of some sorts are the culprits); and (4) generally, uncertainty about the causal structure connecting religion to intolerance. As a result, clear conclusions about how and why religion and intolerance are connected are difficult to draw from existing research.

Summary

Thus, the specific purposes of this chapter are (1) to assess levels of political intolerance in the contemporary United States; (2) to determine which political groups and ideas are the most common targets of intolerance; (3) to measure the degree of threat posed by these groups and ideas; (4) to test the conventional hypotheses about the origins of intolerance; and, most important, (5) to investigate the degree to which religiosity contributes to intolerance, with particular attention to the causal processes involved in the connections between religion and intolerance. The analysis reported here is based on a nationally representative survey conducted in 2007.[13]

Contemporary Political Intolerance in the United States

To recap, political tolerance is, simply stated, putting up with that with which one disagrees. In the context of democratic systems, this means allowing one's opponents rights of political competition. A tolerant person, like a tolerant political system, will allow all ideas, even repugnant ones, to enter into the marketplace of ideas and compete for the hearts and minds of the citizenry.

Because politics is more complicated today than it was while under the influence of the Republican senator from Wisconsin in the late 1940s and early 1950s, it is prudent to allow the respondents to tell us which groups and ideas, if any, they find objectionable. As I have noted, the standard technology for accomplishing this is the "least-liked" measurement strategy. Developed by Sullivan, Piereson, and Marcus (1982), this approach allows all respondents to identify groups/ideas they dislike. Tolerance and threat questions are then asked about these groups. Thus, although the nominal group about which the questions are framed varies for each respondent, the questions are "content controlled" in the sense that all individuals are queried about groups they find highly objectionable. The least-liked approach to measuring intolerance has been used widely in tolerance research throughout the world (e.g., Gibson and Gouws 2003; Peffley and Rohrschneider 2003).

This approach to measuring intolerance in 2007 therefore began by asking the respondents to rate a variety of preselected groups in terms of how much they like or dislike the group. These affect questions were used in part as a means of getting the respondents to think broadly about groups, including those that might be considered by some to be on the fringes of American politics. The respondents were then told they could supplement this list with any other group they dislike a great deal. Next, they were asked to indicate which three groups from the list (as supplemented) they disliked the most.[14] The targets selected in 2007 are shown in table 5.1, as are the affect ratings (based on a 1 through 11 scale) for each of the groups.

The most commonly disliked group in America today is the Ku Klux Klan, with approximately one-third of the respondents naming the Klan as most disliked, and almost three-fourths putting the KKK on the list of the three most disliked groups. Apart from the KKK, no other group is targeted by a majority of Americans. Perhaps the single greatest surprise is that atheists (those who are against all religion and churches) would attract the ire of two in five Americans, a figure about equivalent to that for those who would do away with elections and let the military run the country and for radical Muslims.

This table also demonstrates that the disliked groups are indeed viewed quite negatively. The portion of the table labeled "Affect Thermometer" refers to the degree of warmth or coldness felt toward the group, on the conventional 100-degree thermometer. Among those naming the KKK as among their three most disliked groups, the average temperature

TABLE 5.1
Most Disliked Groups, United States, 2007

Group[b]	Nominated as				Affect thermometer[a]		
	Most disliked	2nd most disliked	3rd most disliked	Among 3 most disliked[c]	Mean	Std. dev.	N
Ku Klux Klan	35.5	25.4	12.3	71.7	4.2	10.6	647
Radical Muslims	15.0	13.2	10.0	37.2	8.4	14.5	335
Militarists	13.8	14.0	15.3	41.9	5.3	11.5	378
Atheists	12.2	11.8	17.0	39.8	9.6	19.5	359
Favor abortion	5.6	7.7	7.9	20.7	8.8	16.1	186
U.S. Communists	4.4	10.3	13.6	27.3	10.0	18.7	246
Other[d]	3.0	2.7	2.0	7.5	4.9	10.0	67
Gay rights activists	2.5	5.0	4.6	11.7	16.7	27.0	106
Don't know	1.8	0.8	0.7	3.2	—	—	—
Christian fundamentalists	1.5	2.0	3.9	7.2	11.7	17.2	65
Liberals	1.4	1.5	2.5	5.2	22.3	24.4	47
Against abortion	1.3	4.3	6.5	11.6	16.0	24.6	104
None	1.2	0.2	1.6	3.0	—	—	—
Conservatives	0.6	0.6	1.0	2.1	26.7	21.8	19
Society for a New America	0.3	0.5	1.1	1.7	19.3	24.2	16

[a] These are affect scores on a 0 to 100 degrees feeling thermometer only among those who named the group as among their three most disliked groups.

[b] The groups are ordered by the percentage of respondents naming the group as most disliked. The actual names used for the groups are these: Ku Klux Klan, members of the Ku Klux Klan; Radical Muslims, radical Muslims; Militarists, those who advocate doing away with elections and letting the military run the country; Atheists, people who are against all churches and religion; Favor abortion, those who would allow all abortions; U.S. Communists, members of the U.S. Communist Party; Gay rights activists, gay rights activists; Christian fundamentalists, Christian fundamentalists; Liberals, liberals; Against abortion, people who would prohibit all abortions; Conservatives, conservatives; Society for a New America, members of the Society for a New America (a fictitious group).

[c] This percentage does not necessarily total to the sum of the first, second, and third most disliked groups because of missing data on those variables. Instead, this is the percentage of all respondents in the survey who named the group as among her or his three most disliked groups.

[d] These are groups nominated by the respondents as supplements to the list presented to them.

TABLE 5.2
Political Intolerance, 2007

Group/activity	Percentages[a] Tolerant	Uncertain	Intolerant	Mean[b]	Std. dev.	*N*
Most disliked group						
Speak	49.1	7.6	43.3	3.01	1.38	459
Run for office	43.3	8.0	48.8	3.20	1.42	459
Demonstrate	42.0	9.9	48.2	3.22	1.29	459
Intolerance index[c]	—	—	—	3.16	1.13	459
Another highly disliked group						
Speak	54.9	9.8	35.3	2.80	1.32	481
Run for office	51.4	8.8	39.8	2.93	1.37	481
Demonstrate	53.0	10.3	36.7	2.86	1.23	481
Intolerance index[c]	—	—	—	2.86	1.12	481

[a] Note: Item percentages total to 100% (except for rounding error) across the three columns.
[b] The responses to these questions were collected on a five-point response set. The means reported here are based on the uncollapsed distributions.
[c] This index is the mean of the responses to the three tolerance items for each of the two groups.

assigned the group is 4.2 degrees, which is of course very close to the lowest point on the scale. The Klan is not distinctive, however. When these respondents identify groups as among their most disliked, they are indeed focusing on extremely disliked groups.

The respondents were asked three tolerance questions about the most disliked group and what I will refer to as another highly disliked group.[15] Following theories of liberal democracy (e.g., Dahl 1971), and extant research on political intolerance (e.g., Gibson and Gouws 2003), the queries concerned whether these groups should be allowed to speak, demonstrate, and run candidates for office. The results are reported in table 5.2.[16]

The data in this table document fairly widespread political intolerance in the United States today. Slightly less than one-half of the respondents would not tolerate political activity by their most disliked group; the figure for the other highly disliked group is somewhat more than one-third. Not a great deal of variation exists across the various activities, and surprisingly small differences can be found between the judgments of the most disliked group and another highly disliked group. Indeed, two-thirds (66.2 percent) of the respondents would not tolerate their most disliked group on at least one of the three activities, and a majority (55.2 percent) are similarly intolerant of the other highly disliked group (data not shown). By any accounting, intolerance appears to be fairly common in the United States today.

TABLE 5.3
Perceived Threat from Highly Disliked Groups, 2007

Group	Percentage at most threatening score	Mean	Std. dev.	*N*
Most disliked group				
Dangerous to society	49.2	8.0	2.7	459
Unwilling to follow democratic rules	36.6	6.4	3.5	457
Un-American	33.1	6.2	3.6	457
If got power, affect my freedom	50.3	7.8	3.0	459
If got power, affect my security	42.6	7.4	3.2	459
Dangerous to people	45.6	7.7	2.9	459
Angry	37.8	7.2	3.0	459
Hatred	17.0	5.6	3.1	459
Powerful	14.5	4.7	3.3	459
Affect how I live	21.3	4.6	3.9	459
Likely to gain power	13.7	3.9	3.4	458
Afraid	21.1	5.2	3.7	458
Another highly disliked group				
Dangerous to society	30.5	6.6	3.1	480
Unwilling to follow democratic rules	24.8	5.7	3.4	480
Un-American	22.9	5.5	3.3	477
If got power, affect my freedom	34.7	6.8	3.4	480
If got power, affect my security	33.5	6.4	3.6	480
Dangerous to people	26.1	6.4	3.1	480
Angry	27.9	6.1	3.5	480
Hatred	13.4	4.8	3.3	480
Powerful	10.0	4.3	3.1	480
Affect how I live	21.5	4.6	3.8	480
Likely to gain power	9.6	3.7	3.3	480
Afraid	15.8	4.4	3.7	480

Note: Higher mean scores indicate more of the attribute (e.g., more hatred, more afraid).

Threat Perceptions

Even though the groups/ideas about which we asked the tolerance questions are all highly disliked, they are not all equally threatening to the respondents. We therefore asked a fairly standard battery of questions assessing perceived threats from these groups. Table 5.3 reports the results.

The data in this table reveal that the disliked groups are not only disliked, but they are also seen as highly threatening to the American people. For instance, almost a majority place the most disliked group at the most extreme point on the scale measuring perceived danger to society. The other disliked group is generally not seen as being as threatening as the most disliked group, but it too scores high on most of these dimensions. Note should also be taken of a conventional finding in the tolerance literature: although these groups are threatening, they are perceived neither to be powerful nor to have much potential to become powerful in American politics. Perceptions of group efficacy are thus not a precursor to perceptions of group threat.

In order to create indices of perceived threat, these items were subjected to common factor analysis. Three significant factors were extracted,[17] and the factors generally conform to the three conventional subdimensions of threat: sociotropic threat, egocentric threat, and perceived group power and efficacy. Factor scores derived from this analysis will serve as the measures of perceived group threat.

Assessing the Religiosity Hypothesis

Measuring Religiosity in the Contemporary United States

We put to the respondents a number of questions about their religious attachments, attitudes, and beliefs. In addition to nominal religious traditions, we also asked about the importance to the respondent of membership in the religious group. Table 5.4 reports the traditions and strengths of attachments. Care must be taken with this table because some of the traditions have few adherents, and some are internally heterogeneous (i.e., the "other religion" category). Further, for ease of interpretation, I have collapsed the categories "not very important" and "not important at all" into a single group on the indicator of the importance of religious identities.

Responses to questions such as these will always be interpreted in light of expectations. From one perspective, these data seem to indicate *relatively weak attachments*. For roughly 20 percent of the respondents, the declared religious affiliation is only nominal; identification with the religion is minimal. At the other extreme, something less than one-third of the respondents claim their religious affiliation is extremely important to them. Even among those who call themselves "born again" (or evangelical Christians), that identity is extremely important to only 45.3 percent of the respondents (data not shown). For most Americans, their religious affiliations seem to be associated with fairly strong, but not overwhelming, identifications with the group.

We also asked the respondents three questions about their religious beliefs:

> Most of the problems of this world result from the fact that more and more people are moving away from God. (Agree strongly—Disagree strongly.)

TABLE 5.4
Religious Traditions and Strength of Religious Identities

	Importance of Religious Identity				
	Extremely important	Very important	Not important[a]	Total	*N*
Protestant	33.4	43.9	22.7	100.0%	476
Catholic	29.0	48.0	23.0	100.0%	200
Jewish	31.3	50.0	18.8	100.0%	16
Mormon	45.0	40.0	15.0	100.0%	20
Other	31.8	50.0	18.2	100.0%	66
None[b]	11.0	18.3	70.6	100.0%	109

Note: Rows total to 100 percent, except for rounding errors.

[a] This category includes those saying the identity is "not very important," "not important at all," and "don't know how important."

[b] This category includes atheists, nonbelievers, and agnostics.

We are also interested in what people like you think about some religious matters. Please tell me the statement that comes closest to your own personal opinion.

I know God really exists, and I have no doubts about it.
While I have doubts, I feel that I do believe in God.
I find myself believing in God some of the time, but not at all other times.
I don't believe in a personal god, but I do believe in a higher power of some kind.
I don't know whether there is a god, and I don't believe there is any way to find out.
I don't believe in God.

Next, tell me which statement comes closest to what you believe about the Devil.

I think it is completely true that the Devil exists.
I think it is probably true that the Devil exists.
I think it is probably not true that the Devil exists.
I think it is definitely not true that the Devil exists.

In earlier research, Nunn et al. (1978) found that although belief in God is not a particularly strong predictor of intolerance, belief in the Devil is. According to their argument, belief in the Devil is associated with the view that evil exists, that it represents an omnipresent threat, and that one must be ever-vigilant against it. Under such conditions, intolerance is perhaps a natural response.

Among these respondents, belief in God is quite widespread: 69.5 percent assert that "God really exists and I have no doubts about it." Belief in the Devil is less widespread, with only 51.5 percent expressing certainty that the Devil exists. Finally, a substantial majority of Americans (60.8 percent) agree that many of the problems of the world today result from people "moving away from God." By the criterion of the attitudes held, most Americans seem to be at least moderately strongly religious.

Finally, attending religious services is perhaps less common than one might predict. Only 40.9 percent attend religious services weekly, with another 19.9 percent (for a total of 60.9 percent) attending at least once a month. Conversely, about 40 percent of the American people attend religious services less than once a month (e.g., only on special holy days or never). Americans are less strongly committed to their religious institutions than to their religious beliefs themselves (a finding perhaps not surprising in light of the widespread scandals and criminal actions involving the Catholic Church).

The religious questions we asked represent something of a potpourri, ranging from the frequency of attending services to beliefs about the Devil. However, when these various indicators are factor analyzed (common factor analysis), a strongly unidimensional structure is revealed.[18] Overall, this pool of indicators exhibits extremely strong psychometric properties.[19] Factor scores from this analysis will therefore be used as an overall indicator of the degree of religiosity of the respondent. I will refer to this construct as "religious traditionalism."

For some analytical purposes, it is also useful to have a categorical indicator of religious traditionalism. I therefore created one by counting the number of highly religious responses to the six questions about religion and religious beliefs. The correlation of this index and the factor score is 0.89. Only a fairly small minority of the respondents (13.5 percent) registered a perfect score on the index; only 6.9 percent received a score of zero. I have further trichotomized this measure to yield a simple indicator of low, medium, and high levels of religious traditionalism. According to this indicator, 31.0 percent of the American people score high on traditionalism, whereas 34.7 percent score low.

Religious Traditionalism and Intolerance of Nonbelievers

Before turning to the analysis of the least-liked groups, it is useful to consider the simple relationship between religious traditionalism and intolerance of atheists, particularly because the questions about atheists were put to all respondents in the survey. We asked the respondents two questions about "those who are against all religion and churches" (hereinafter, by conventional usage, "atheists"). One question was a simple

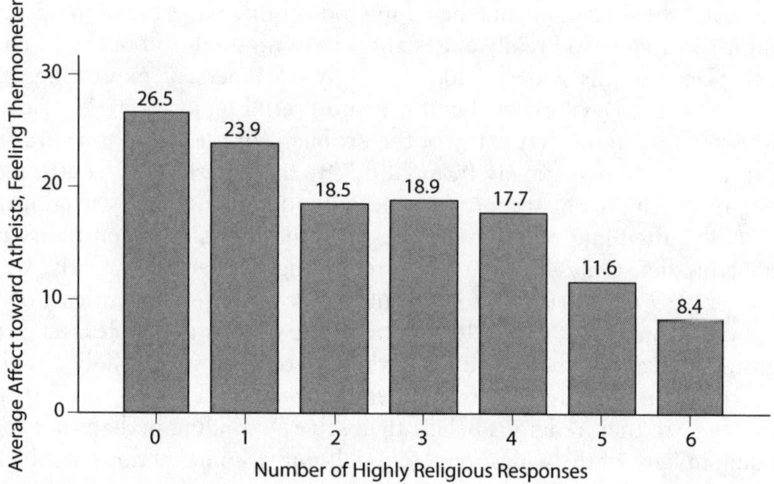

Figure 5.2. Affect toward atheists and respondent religious traditionalism. Entries are average scores on a 0 to 100 degrees feeling thermometer. $r = -0.21$, $p < 0.001$.

feeling thermometer measuring degree of affect toward the group and the other question asked: If a "group of people who are against all churches and religion were planning to hold public rallies and demonstrations in your community to advance their cause, how would you react to a ban by the authorities of a public demonstration by those against all churches and religion?" Overall, atheists are quite disliked by the American people (mean affect = 17.1 degrees, standard deviation = 24.8, median = 1 degree), with fully 45.4 percent of Americans rating atheists at the coldest point on the thermometer (zero degrees). Indeed, only 6.2 percent of the respondents assigned atheists a score above 50 degrees.[20] On the other hand, intolerance of an atheist demonstration is not nearly so widespread, with only one-third of the respondents supporting such a ban. Thus, despite considerable antipathy among most Americans toward atheists, at least some portion of the population is able to exercise forbearance and not support policies restricting the free speech and assembly rights of those against all religion and churches.

But are religious Americans more likely than the irreligious to express antipathy and intolerance toward atheists? Figure 5.2 reports the mean level of antipathy toward atheists according to levels of religious traditionalism; figure 5.3 reports the percentage of respondents willing to ban a demonstration by atheists, also according to levels of religious traditionalism.

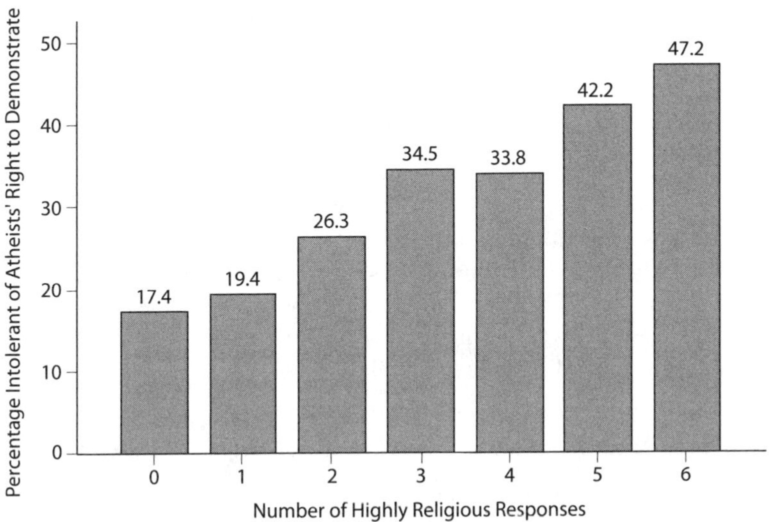

Figure 5.3. Intolerance toward atheists and respondent religious traditionalism. Entries are the percentages expressing intolerance of the rights of atheists. $r = 0.19$, $p < 0.001$.

Two aspects of figure 5.2 are noteworthy. First, as I have already observed, positive feelings toward atheists are quite rare among the American people. Second, the degree of negativity varies substantially according to the degree of religious traditionalism of the respondent.[21] The greater the degree of religious traditionalism, the less the degree of positive feeling toward atheists. This relationship would likely be stronger were there not a "floor effect" (i.e., the lowest affect score offered the respondents was zero degrees, and a significant proportion selected this score).

A relationship of equivalent strength exists between religious traditionalism and intolerance, as depicted in figure 5.3. Those who are more religious are considerably more likely to support a ban on demonstrations by those against all religion and churches.[22] However, it is worth noting that even at the highest level of religious traditionalism, no more than half of the respondents support a ban on the demonstration by atheists.

When the intolerance indicator is regressed on both religious traditionalism and group affect, both exert a statistically and substantively significant influence on intolerance: both coefficients (standardized regression coefficients) are 0.16. This indicates that those who dislike atheists are less likely to tolerate them ($\beta = -0.16$), but that even when affect is held constant, those more religious are more likely to be intolerant ($\beta = 0.16$).

So simple dislike of atheists seems to be an insufficient explanation of why religious Americans are unwilling to allow rights of speech and assembly to atheists.

The analysis to this point has been useful because all respondents were asked the two questions about atheists. However, a well-known and quite legitimate critique of this approach to intolerance is that intolerance can only be recognized when all respondents are presented with a group that is objectionable. In this analysis, those who are religious do indeed mostly (but not completely) satisfy this requirement. But the irreligious may not. Therefore, it is necessary to reconsider the question of intolerance from the point of view of the "least-liked" measurement approach, developed by Sullivan et al. (1982).

Religious Traditionalism and Intolerance of Highly Disliked Groups

Those who are religious are distinctive in respect to the groups they do or do not include among their three most disliked groups. They tend to include atheists ($r = 0.28$) and proabortionists ($r = 0.28$) and to exclude Christian fundamentalists ($r = -0.26$), militarists ($r = -0.21$), and antiabortionists ($r = -0.18$) (with a positive coefficient indicating that believers are more likely to select the group and negative coefficient indicating that they are less likely to name the group). On all other groups, the religious and the irreligious are indistinguishable.

But are those who are religious more intolerant than nonbelievers when it comes to tolerance as measured through the least-liked technology? Figure 5.4 reports the basic relationship.

The relationships depicted in this graph are moderate and negative: as religious traditionalism increases, tolerance decreases. For the most disliked group, the correlation with the religious traditionalism factor score is –0.19; for the other highly disliked group, the coefficient is –0.22. Thus, even when tolerance is corrected for the "objection precondition"—meaning that all respondents are reacting to a group they highly dislike—the religious are more intolerant than the irreligious.

This finding is not surprising in light of extant literature. But at this point, little confidence can be had in the finding because no controls for the other known causes of intolerance have been implemented. In particular, before any conclusion can be drawn about the causal relationship between religion and intolerance, controls for the factors indicated in figure 5.1 must be implemented. Multivariate analysis is essential.

For the multivariate equation, measures of support for democratic institutions and processes and dogmatism are necessary. Scales measuring these concepts have been created (see Appendix A for the measurement details). Dogmatism is measured via three items from Rokeach's scale of

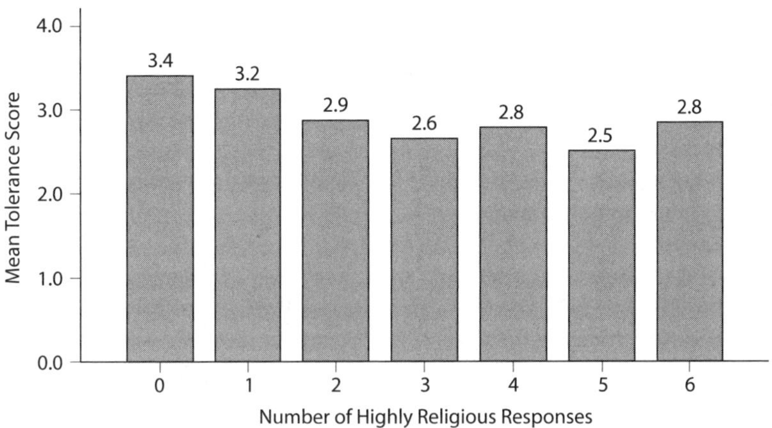

Another Highly Disliked Group

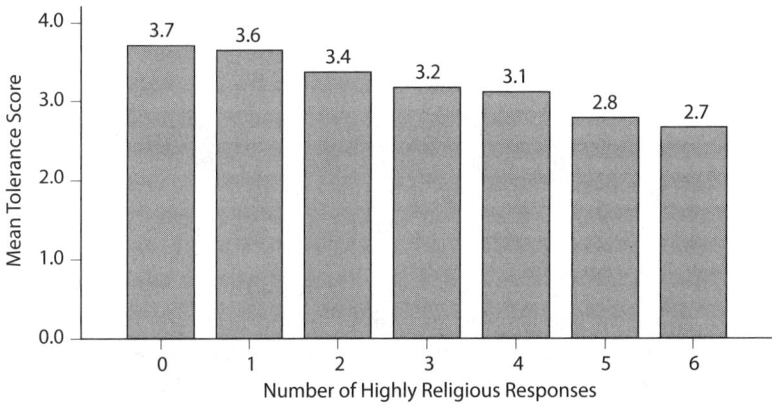

Figure 5.4. Tolerance of highly disliked groups by levels of religious traditionalism.

closed-mindedness. Support for democratic institutions and processes is indicated by multi-item measures of (1) support for the rule of law, (2) the relative valuation of order versus liberty, and (3) support for a multiparty system. Such indicators have been widely used in earlier research (e.g., Gibson 2007). Religious traditionalism is moderately related to dogmatism ($r = 0.27$) and to a preference for order over liberty ($r = 0.20$), is weakly related to support for a multiparty system ($r = 0.13$), and is completely unrelated to attitudes toward the rule of law ($r = -0.01$).

TABLE 5.5
Multivariate Analysis of Political Tolerance

Predictor	r	b	s.e.	β
Dogmatism	−0.36	−0.32	0.05	−0.23***
Value of order over liberty	−0.40	−0.24	0.06	−0.17***
Support for a multiparty system	−0.39	−0.18	0.06	−0.13**
Support for the rule of law	0.29	0.08	0.05	0.06
Threat: Sociotropic, system danger	−0.26	−0.23	0.05	−0.19***
Threat: Power	0.13	−0.04	0.04	−0.03
Threat: Egocentric	−0.16	−0.04	0.05	−0.03
Religious traditionalism	0.21	0.45	0.15	0.09**
Whether most disliked or other disliked group	0.15	0.15	0.03	0.13***
Intercept		2.56	0.09	
Standard deviation—dependent variable		1.14		
Standard error of estimate		0.95		
R^2				0.31***
N		881		

Significance of standardized regression coefficients (β): $***p < .001$; $**p < .01$; $*p < .05$.

Table 5.5 reports the multivariate results. In the equation are the traditional predictors of tolerance as well as the overall indicator of religious traditionalism. Several conclusions can be drawn from these data.

First, this analysis confirms virtually all of the conventional wisdom about the etiology of intolerance. Intolerance is grounded in dogmatism, lack of support for democratic institutions and processes, and perceptions of group threat. In this analysis, attitudes toward the rule of law have few consequences for intolerance, just as do perceptions of the power and power potential of the group. In terms of threat perceptions, the sociotropic indicator is dominant, as it virtually always is in models predicting intolerance.

The most important finding of this table is that, despite quite stringent controls, religious traditionalism nonetheless still has a significant effect on intolerance. As religious traditionalism increases, tolerance decreases. This indicates that the religious are more intolerant, but not because they are more threatened by their political enemies, nor because they are more dogmatic than other citizens, nor because their support for democratic institutions and processes is weaker. *Ceteris paribus*, greater involvement in religion is associated with more political intolerance. To reiterate, the effect is not great, but nor should it be expected to be in an equation as comprehensive as this.

The coefficients in table 5.5 represent the direct effects of the variables on tolerance. Indirect effects can also be important in assessing the impact of a variable such as religious traditionalism. I have already noted, for instance, that those who are more religious are likely to be more dogmatic. Thus, in addition to its direct effect, religious traditionalism influences intolerance via dogmatism.

I note, however, that little of the influence of religious traditionalism flows through perceptions of group threat. The correlations between religious traditionalism and sociotropic and egocentric threat are trivial, even though the correlation with perceived group power is 0.10. However, perceived group power has little influence on intolerance, so this pathway is insignificant as a cause of political intolerance. Indeed, on the individual threat items (i.e., the individual components of the threat factor scores), the maximum correlation between religious traditionalism and threat is a mere 0.10 (with perceived power). Religious traditionalism does not influence intolerance via some sort of connection to heightened or distinctive threat perceptions.

Finally, I have reestimated the equation in table 5.5 using the individual components of religious traditionalism rather than the factor score. This analysis allows me to zero in on the specific aspects of religious traditionalism that contribute to intolerance.[23]

In this expanded equation (data not shown), only a single indicator achieves statistical significance: Those who believe most of the problems of this world are the result of people moving away from God are, *ceteris paribus*, more intolerant. Of course, each of the individual components of religious traditionalism exhibits a substantial bivariate relationship with intolerance. But this belief seems to be the "active ingredient" by which religious traditionalism contributes to intolerance.[24]

This survey includes insufficient measures of the various attitudinal components of religious traditionalism to pursue this analysis any further. However, it may be telling that the single best predictor of intolerance is this statement about the relevance of religion for secular affairs. Those subscribing to "pie-in-the-sky" religious ideologies may not be more intolerant because of their acceptance of the world as it is and their belief in rewards in the hereafter, especially for those who have suffered. Perhaps the greatest danger of religiously based intolerance materializes when those who are religious feel obligated to try to conform the world to their ideologies. Exploring various aspects of religious ideologies should be a prime concern of future research on the connection between intolerance and religious traditionalism.

Discussion and Concluding Comments

Perhaps one might reasonably expect those who are religious to be intolerant of their principal foes, those who are against all religion and churches. But the evidence of this chapter is that the intolerance of believers is not confined to intolerance of atheists. Those who are religious are more intolerant than those who are not even when we confine the analysis to highly disliked groups of any sort and even when we impose strong statistical controls. The effect is not strong, but it is statistically significant and is manifest in both a direct effect on intolerance and indirect influences.

Still, these findings are particularly ominous for atheists in America. Atheists are widely disliked, and that antipathy readily translates into political intolerance. Other highly disliked groups might be characterized as "extremists" (e.g., the Ku Klux Klan), but it is difficult to imagine how those who are against all religions and churches could be viewed as outside the boundaries of legitimate debate in the United States. Those who casually admit their atheism in discussions over public policy (e.g., scientists who deny the existence of a god) ought to heed these findings and be cautious in revealing their beliefs (or lack thereof).

Of course, with any cross-sectional analysis, questions of causal flow arise, and that is certainly a legitimate complaint against the analysis reported in this chapter. I have shown that religious traditionalism and intolerance covary, but I cannot rule out entirely the possibility that both religious beliefs and intolerance stem from a common source. At the same time, however, that alternative source must be something other than dogmatism, support for democratic institutions and processes, or threat perceptions (the control variables included in table 5.5). For instance, even among the closed-minded, religious traditionalism is associated with enhanced intolerance. With these statistical controls and the use of the least-liked measurement technology, at least some confidence can be had in the conclusion that religious traditionalism contributes to intolerance.

Political scientists rely on a handful of stock solutions to the problem of citizens subscribing to antidemocratic views such as political intolerance. Typical palliatives include institutional design, citizen reeducation, efforts to mitigate threat perceptions, and enhancing pluralism and cross-cutting cleavages. Within this context, the intolerance of those who are religious might be neutralized by building institutional barriers to their participation in politics, by attempting to persuade believers of the importance of democratic values (even by appealing to traditions of liberalism and tolerance within some religious ideologies), by trying to enhance feelings of political security (particularly so that the down-and-out do not turn to the opiate of religious xenophobia out of their despair), and by highlighting multiple group memberships, especially in groups that are heterogeneous in their ideologies and values. Each of these possible solutions has been tried at various points within American politics, and each has most likely contributed to the diminution of intolerance among those who are religious. Whether there is any traction left in these various schemes is at present unclear.

It seems at least possible that the consequences of this connection between religious traditionalism and political intolerance will become more serious for American politics in the future. There are several elements to this argument.

Harkening back to the so-called Elitist Theory of Democracy (e.g., Gibson 1988), scholars have long argued that barriers to political participation tend to screen out of the political process those holding less democratic predispositions. Because level of education, political interest and knowledge, and other political resources are typically concomitants of political tolerance, the tolerant tend to be more engaged in the political process, the intolerant less so (e.g., Sullivan et al. 1993). Anything that widens participation therefore poses at least some threat to the democratic process.

Historically, religious traditionalists have tended to be disengaged from the political process. But this is likely changing and changing substantially (e.g., Green 2009) as the religious are increasingly seen as an untapped resource capable of having a substantial influence on American politics (e.g., the strong efforts made to mobilize the "religious right," which is most likely dominated by what I have referred to as religious traditionalists). To the extent that those with weaker commitments to democratic institutions and processes acquire influence in the political process, values such as political tolerance may be threatened.

A counter to this line of argument is that political participation tends to contribute to the development of democratic values. However, voting is not a very participatory type of political action when it comes to producing change in basic political attitudes and beliefs, and even deliberation in the United States tends to involve discussions of only like-minded people (e.g., Mutz 2006). It is not clear, therefore, that enhanced political participation will inculcate tolerant values among believers, especially those subscribing to the view that secular affairs should be guided by religious tenets and ideologies. These various processes are certainly complicated and consequently introduce some amount of uncertainty into whether the marketplace of ideas in American politics is secure.

What is clear, however, is that democratic politics requires that the marketplace of ideas in the United States must be vigilantly protected against those who would define some viewpoints as unacceptable. Pernicious proposals for speech restriction periodically percolate throughout American politics—from proposals to ban Holocaust deniers, to criminalize hate speech, to penalize incitement and disloyalty, and to constrain academic freedom to only acceptable viewpoints. A citizenry strongly committed to political tolerance may not be a sufficient condition for the protection of individual liberty, but it is most likely necessary, and it certainly contributes to strengthening democracy in the United States. Future research should therefore focus on methods by which citizens, those who are religious included, can be persuaded to value tolerance more highly.

Appendix: Measurement

Dogmatism

This concept was measured via three items drawn from Rokeach's research (1960) on closed-mindedness.

There are two kinds of people in this world: those who are for the truth and those who are against it.
To compromise with our political opponents is dangerous because it usually leads to the betrayal of our own side.
A group that tolerates too many differences of opinion among its own members cannot exist for long.

An index was created via common factor analysis, which revealed a strongly unidimensional structure to the items.

Support for Democratic Institutions and Processes

This concept is conceptualized as a multidimensional attitudinal syndrome involving the following subdimensions and indicators.

SUPPORT FOR THE RULE OF LAW

It is not necessary to obey a law you consider unjust.
Sometimes it might be better to ignore the law and solve problems immediately rather than wait for a legal solution.
The government should have some ability to bend the law in order to solve pressing social and political problems.
It is not necessary to obey the laws of a government that I did not vote for.
When it comes right down to it, law is not all that important; what's important is that our government solves society's problems and make us all better off.

SUPPORT FOR A MULTIPARTY SYSTEM

What our country needs is one political party, which will rule the country.
The party that gets the support of the majority ought not to have to share political power with the political minority.
Our country would be better off if we just outlaw all political parties.

RELATIVE VALUATION OF ORDER AND LIBERTY

Society shouldn't have to put up with those who have political ideas that are extremely different from the majority.

It is better to live in an orderly society than to allow people so much freedom that they can become disruptive.

Free speech is just not worth it if it means that we have to put up with the danger to society of extremist political views.

Common factor analysis almost perfectly supported the hypothesized three-dimensional structure. Indices of each of the attitudes are represented by the factor scores from this analysis.

Notes

Funding for this research was provided by the Weidenbaum Center on the Economy, Government, and Public Policy at Washington University in St. Louis. I especially appreciate the support for this research provided by Steven S. Smith. I am particularly indebted to John Green, who has enlightened me in numerous ways regarding religion and politics in general and this chapter in particular, and to Chris Claassen and Jesse Atencio, both of whom offered valuable comments on an earlier version of this chapter.

1. I do not discount the value of simply allowing all ideas—right and wrong—to have their say, to have what procedural justice scholars refer to as "voice" (e.g., Tyler and Mitchell 1994; Tyler et al. 1997). Procedural justice theories posit that allowing groups voice enhances the legitimacy of the democratic process, especially among those unable to win within majoritarian arenas.

2. See Gibson (1988) for examples of the types of restrictions put on Communists in the United States during the 1940s and 1950s. See also Goldstein (1978).

3. In the early part of the twenty-first century, examples of this phenomenon are too numerous to catalog. The efforts of Robert Mugabe to maintain his power in Zimbabwe provide an excellent exemplar.

4. As I write this, the British are considering new proposals to ban pure speech in support of such activities as suicide bombing. It remains to be seen whether such legislation will be acceptable to British judges and the British people.

5. This issue is actually a bit more complicated given that political minorities typically need access to specific tactics (e.g., public demonstrations) that the majority does not require or find useful. Thus, regimes sometimes invoke political equality when they ban all demonstrations, even if the effect of such bans falls quite disproportionately on different segments of the political community.

6. On the measurement of tolerance and other democratic values see Finkel, Sigelman, and Humphries (1999).

7. The modern era of empirical research on political intolerance began with Stouffer's classic study (1955) conducted in the heyday of McCarthyism in the United States.

8. Sullivan et al. (1985) make the same argument about Israel.

9. Note that Kuklinski, Cobb, and Gilens (1997) argue on the basis of a "list experiment" that roughly one-half of white males in the American South are racist.

10. Scholars have tried innovative methods for correcting for such bias (e.g., Wilson 1994; Mondak and Sanders 2003), but it seems likely that the utility of asking questions about these standard groups will continue to diminish over time.

11. One important drawback of the least-liked technology is that it is quite costly in terms of questions and interview time and is difficult to administer via telephone interviews.

12. That sociotropic threat perceptions are the most influential type of threat implies that social identity concerns may play an important role in this process. That hypothesis has been investigated, but the findings are too complicated to consider in this chapter. For research on the role of group attachments in shaping identities, see Gibson and Gouws (2000) and Gibson (2006).

13. This survey is based on a nationally representative sample. The survey, conducted by Schulman, Ronca, and Bucuvalas Inc. (SRBI), was fielded during the summer of 2007. Computer-assisted telephone interviewing was used. Within households, the respondents were selected randomly. The interviews averaged around twenty-five minutes in length. The AAPOR Cooperation Rate #3 was 43.8 percent, and the AAPOR Response Rate #3 was 29.5 percent (see AAPOR 2004), which is about the average of telephone surveys these days (Holbrook et al. 2007). The final data set was subjected to some relatively minor poststratification and was also weighted to accommodate variability in the sizes of the respondents' households. The initial questionnaire was subjected to a formal test and, on the basis of the results of the pretest, was significantly revised.

14. Only 7.2 percent of the respondents added a group to the list, and these groups were extremely varied. Only a tiny fraction of those nominating an extra group selected one of these supplemental groups as among their three most disliked groups. A split ballot with random assignment of respondents to either the most disliked group or another highly disliked group was employed.

15. The other highly disliked group is the third-most-disliked group if the respondent identified one; if not, the second-most disliked group was used.

16. The respondents were asked tolerance and threat questions about their most disliked group or another disliked group, with random assignment to type of group.

17. The eigenvalue of the fourth factor is a trivial 0.87.

18. The initial factor extracted explains 49.8 percent of the variance, and the eigenvalue of the second factor is a trivial 0.81. The strongest item loading is associated with belief in God (0.71), and the weakest is a dichotomy indicating whether the respondent is a nonbeliever. The reliability of the item set is also strong (Cronbach's alpha = 0.77).

19. In this analysis, I excluded the question about being "born again" because it was not asked of particular religious groups (e.g., Jews). However, the correlation between the factor scores produced by including and excluding this item is 0.99, indicating that no measurement traction whatsoever is lost by discarding this variable from the analysis.

20. Obviously, for most Americans, atheists satisfy the "objection precondition" for valid measures of intolerance.

21. The correlation between affect and the religious traditionalism factor score is –0.21, which is both statistically and substantively significant.

22. The bivariate correlation between the factor score and the categorical measure of intolerance is 0.19, which is statistically and substantively significant.

23. Care must be taken with this analysis because indices are typically more strongly correlated with other variables than are the individual components of the indices. This is because of the enhanced reliability of indices in comparison to single-item indicators.

24. When I create separate indices of the three religious attitudes and the indicators of religious behavior, I discover that only the attitudes influence political tolerance ($\beta = 0.13$, $p < 0.000$). This finding reinforces the view that it is not religious attachment per se that leads to political intolerance, but instead it is the collateral beliefs associated with some attachments and identifications that create intolerance. This conclusion is identical to our findings on group attachments in South Africa (e.g., Gibson and Gouws 2003; Gibson 2006).

References

American Association for Public Opinion Research. 2004. *Standard Definitions: Final Dispositions of Case Codes and Outcome Rates for Surveys*. Available at http://www.aapor.org/pdfs/standarddefs_3.1.pdf (accessed 9/22/2005).

Beatty, Kathleen Murphy, and B. Oliver Walter. 1984. "Religious Preference and Practice: Reevaluating Their Impact on Political Tolerance." *Public Opinion Quarterly* 48 (1, Spring):318–29.

Dahl, Robert A. 1971. *Polyarchy*. New Haven: Yale University Press.

———. 1989. *Democracy and Its Critics*. New Haven: Yale University Press.

Davis, Darren W., and Brian D. Silver. 2004. "Civil Liberties vs. Security: Public Opinion in the Context of the Terrorist Attacks on America." *American Journal of Political Science* 48 (1, January):28–46.

Eisenstein, Marie A. 2006. "Rethinking the Relationship between Religion and Political Tolerance in the US." *Political Behavior* 28 (4):327–48.

Finkel, Steven F., and Howard R. Ernst. 2005. "Civic Education in Post-Apartheid South Africa: Alternative Paths to the Development of Knowledge and Democratic Values." *Political Psychology* 26 (3):333–64.

Finkel, Steve, Lee Sigelman, and Stan Humphries. 1999. "Democratic Values and Political Tolerance," in John Robinson, Phillip Shaver, and Lawrence Wrightsman, eds., *Measures of Political Attitudes*, 203–96. San Diego: Academic Press.

Gibson, James L. 1988. "Political Intolerance and Political Repression during the McCarthy Red Scare." *American Political Science Review* 82 (2, June): 511–29.

———. 1995. "The Resilience of Mass Support for Democratic Institutions and Processes in the Nascent Russian and Ukrainian Democracies." In *Political Culture and Civil Society in Russia and the New States of Eurasia,* ed. Vladimir Tismaneanu, 53–111. Armonk, NY: M. E. Sharp.

———. 2006. "Do Strong Group Identities Fuel Intolerance? Evidence from the South African Case." *Political Psychology* 27 (5):665–705.

———. 2007. "The Legitimacy of the U.S. Supreme Court in a Polarized Polity." *Journal of Empirical Legal Studies* 4 (3, November):507–38.

Gibson, James L. 2008. "Intolerance and Political Repression in the United States: A Half-Century after McCarthyism." *American Journal of Political Science* 52 (1, January):96–108.

Gibson, James L., Raymond M. Duch, and Kent L. Tedin. 1992. "Democratic Values and the Transformation of the Soviet Union." *Journal of Politics* 54:329–71.

Gibson, James L., and Amanda Gouws. 2000. "Social Identities and Political Intolerance: Linkages within the South African Mass Public." *American Journal of Political Science* 44 (2, April):278–92.

———. 2003. *Overcoming Intolerance in South Africa: Experiments in Democratic Persuasion*. New York: Cambridge University Press.

Goldstein, Robert Justin. 1978. *Political Repression in Modern America*. Cambridge, MA: Schenkman.

Green, John C. 2009. "The Faith-Based Politics in American Presidential Elections: Trends and Possibilities." In *The Future of Religion in American Politics*, ed. Charles W. Dunn. Lexington, KY: University of Kentucky Press.

Green, John C., James L. Guth, Lyman A. Kellstedt, and Corwin E. Smidt. 1994. "Uncivil Challenges? Support for Civil Liberties among Religious Activists." *The Journal of Political Science* 22:25–49.

Holbrook, Allyson L., Jon A. Krosnick, and Alison M. Pfent. 2007. "The Causes and Consequences of Response Rates in Surveys by the News Media and Government Contractor Survey Research Firms." In *Advances in Telephone Survey Methodology*, eds. James Lepkowski, N. Clyde Tucker, J. Michael Brick, Edith D. de Leeuw, Lilli Japec, Paul J. Lavrakas, Michael W. Link, and Roberta L. Sangster, 499–527. New York: Wiley.

Karpov, Vyacheslav. 1999. "Religiosity and Political Tolerance in Poland." *Sociology of Religion* 60 (4):387–402.

Kuklinski, James H., Michael D. Cobb, and Martin Gilens. 1997. "Racial Attitudes and the 'New South'." *The Journal of Politics* 59 (2, May):323–49.

Marcus, Georges E., John L. Sullivan, Elizabeth Theiss-Morse, and Sandra L. Wood. 1995. *With Malice toward Some: How People Make Civil Liberties Judgments*. New York: Cambridge University Press.

Mondak, Jeffrey J., and Mitchell S. Sanders. 2003. "Tolerance and Intolerance, 1976–1998." *American Journal of Political Science* 47 (3, July):492–502.

Mutz, Diana. 2006. *Hearing the Other Side: Deliberative versus Participatory Democracy*. Cambridge: Cambridge University Press.

Noelle-Neumann, Elisabeth. 1984. *The Spiral of Silence: Public Opinion, Our Social Skin*. Chicago: University of Chicago Press.

Nunn, Clyde Z., Harry J. Crockett Jr., and J. Allen Williams Jr. 1978. *Tolerance for Nonconformity*. San Francisco: Jossey-Bass.

Peffley, Mark, and Robert Rohrschneider. 2003. "Democratization and Political Tolerance in Seventeen Countries: A Multi-level Model of Democratic Learning." *Political Research Quarterly* 56 (3, September):243–57.

Sniderman, Paul M. 1975. *Personality and Democratic Politics*. Berkeley: University of California Press.

Stenner, Karen. 2005. *The Authoritarian Dynamic*. New York: Cambridge University Press.

Stouffer, Samuel C. 1955. *Communism, Conformity and Civil Liberties*. New York: Doubleday.

Sullivan, John L., James E. Piereson, and George E. Marcus. 1982. *Political Tolerance and American Democracy*. Chicago: The University of Chicago Press.

Sullivan, John L., Michal Shamir, Patrick Walsh, and Nigel S. Roberts. 1985. *Political Tolerance in Context: Support for Unpopular Minorities in Israel, New Zealand, and the United States*. Boulder, CO: Westview Press.

Sullivan, John L., Patrick Walsh, Michal Shamir, David G. Barnum, and James L. Gibson. 1993. "Why Are Politicians More Tolerant? Selective Recruitment and Socialization among Political Elites in New Zealand, Israel, Britain, and the United States." *British Journal of Political Science* 23 (January):51–76.

Tyler, Tom R., Robert J. Boeckmann, Heather J. Smith, and Yuen J. Huo. 1997. *Social Justice in a Diverse Society*. Boulder, CO: Westview Press.

Tyler, Tom R., and Gregory Mitchell. 1994. "Legitimacy and the Empowerment of Discretionary Legal Authority: The United States Supreme Court and Abortion Rights." *Duke Law Journal* 43:703–815.

Wilcox, Clyde, and Ted Jelen. 1990. "Evangelicals and Political Intolerance." *American Politics Research* 18 (1):25–46.

Wilson, Thomas C. 1994. "Trends in Tolerance toward Rightist and Leftist Groups, 1976–1988: Effects of Attitude Change and Cohort Succession." *Public Opinion Quarterly* 58 (4, Winter):539–56.

Chapter 6

THE CHRISTIAN RIGHT AND CIVIC VIRTUE

CLYDE WILCOX

THE ISLAMIC REVOLUTION in Iran in 1979 and the rise of the Christian Right in the United States sparked an interest among political scientists in the power of religion to influence politics (Wald and Wilcox 2006). The Iranian revolution came as a surprise to a discipline that accepted the inevitability of secularization (Wolfe, chapter 1, this volume); Iran had been perceived as an exemplar of secular modernization. The establishment of a new regime where religious authorities had veto power and the use of apostasy trials to squelch dissent made clear the potential for illiberal religious movements to undermine and destroy democratic institutions (Wald et al. 2005).

As the Iranian revolution was gathering momentum, Christian conservatives in the United States were preparing for their own incursion into politics by building social movement organizations (Martin 1996). After Ronald Reagan's surprisingly easy victory in 1980, Rev. Jerry Falwell claimed credit on behalf of a network of Christian Right groups that had worked to mobilize fundamentalist and evangelical voters. The emergence of the Christian Right surprised journalists and scholars alike and set off an avalanche of research and writing.

Many academics saw similarities between this new Christian Right movement and the Islamist movement that had come to power in Iran and was active in other countries (Almond et al. 2003; Marty 2003). The media portrayed the members of the Christian Right as "largely poor, uneducated and easy to command" (Weisskopf 1993) and described in some detail the intolerance of movement activists. The successive waves of Christian Right mobilization that followed led many academics and political activists to fear that a horde of uncivil, uncompromising citizens were invading the body politic, winning control of the Republican Party, and pushing the nation toward intolerant policies.

Christian Right leaders fueled these fears with bold promises. In 1991 the Christian Coalition Board of Directors ratified a Ten Year Plan that proclaimed the goal of having "effective control of at least one political party" by the year 2000. The Coalition's founder Pat Robertson announced that year at the group's Road to Victory convention that he sought to win control of legislatures in 35 states and to eventually expand that to all 50 states. He promised to win control of Congress by 1996 and to "see the White House in profamily, Christian hands by 2000, if the Lord permits." To do this Robertson planned to identify ten precinct workers in each of the 175,000 precincts in the United States and to build a voter list of 50,000,000 conservative Christians.

Coupled with bold promises of political power were intolerant comments by movement leaders. Moral Majority leader Jerry Falwell proclaimed in 1980 that God did not hear prayer of Jews.[1] Christian Right leaders denounced gays and lesbians, feminists, civil liberties groups, and political liberals in religious language and frequently linked opposing views to the work of Satan. Direct mail solicitations by Christian Right leaders sought to build fear and hostility toward liberal groups.

Movement activists often failed to embrace democratic norms. Some local activists demanded that public libraries fire employees who displayed gay pride buttons and charged that teachers who claimed that a woman might win the presidency were teaching witchcraft (Rozell and Wilcox 1996a). Others demanded that books sympathetic to gays and lesbians be removed from public libraries and that school curricula teach that homosexuality was "abnormal, wrong, unnatural and perverse." In one school district, Christian Right activists objected to stories about women's equality, gun control, environmentalism, and even lightning as being anti-Christian (Bates 1993).

Liberal activists who wrote about the Christian Right during this period used their own uncivil and intolerant language and sought to instill fear of the Christian Right (Boston 2000; Hedges 2006). Direct mail fundraising letters by civil liberties groups charged that conservative Christians sought to establish an Iranian-style theocracy. But the comparison to the Iranian revolution fails on one central point—the Christian Right sought to gain power through elections and to influence policy through the normal political process. Indeed, most Christian Right activists see the hand of providence in the writing of the U.S. Constitution (Lienesch 1993).

There are, however, similarities between the U.S. Christian Right and moderate Islamist political parties that participate in electoral politics. Both seek to make law consistent with religious teachings and texts and to increase public acknowledgment of religion. Both seek to privilege traditional families by reducing opportunities for women and by allowing discrimination or even prosecution of sexual minorities. Christian Right groups and Islamist groups have worked together in international organizations on a variety of gender-related issues (Buss and Herman 2003).

The questions of whether to and how to involve illiberal religious movements and activists in democratic politics have sparked heated debate in political science. Political theorists disagree whether religious certainty is compatible with democratic deliberation and whether religious reasons are appropriate in the public square (see Rosenblum, chapter 12, this volume). Scholars debate whether involving religious parties and groups in electoral democracy is dangerous because it might allow illiberal religious groups to win power, or whether involvement in electoral politics might lead to greater commitment to democratic norms (Kalyvas 2000; Rosenblum 2003; Clark 2006; Schwedler 2006; Wittes 2008).

Some question the sincerity of commitment by various Islamic parties to democracy, pondering whether if they ever won an election they might abolish democratic institutions (Haqqani and Fradkin 2008). There is little doubt that the mainstream of the Christian Right is committed to democratic processes, although at the fringe some Christian reconstructionist thinkers advocate theocratic regimes. Moreover, the stability of U.S. political institutions and the diversity of religious sentiments in the United States guarantee that the movement could never come to dominate politics (see Evans, chapter 4, this volume). There is therefore little danger that the Christian Right would come to power and abolish electoral democracy.

A greater fear is that illiberal religious groups might limit the civil liberties of secular citizens, religious minorities, and other groups. Christian Right leaders have made many illiberal statements and have endorsed a limited view of pluralism. Pat Robertson promised to appoint only Christians and Jews if he won the presidency, and other leaders endorsed policies that would limit civil liberties for feminists, gays and lesbians, atheists, and other groups.

Yet it might also be that engagement in electoral politics might lead to greater support for democratic norms and values among religious activists. Democratic politics requires compromise and negotiation with other parties and groups, and winning elections in many political systems requires religious parties to appeal to a wider range of voters, frequently by using secular language. And the process of this engagement presumably leads to at least deliberation within the movement or party about priorities and about what types of compromise are acceptable.

Political engagement is also likely to lead at least some religious activists to deliberate with those outside the movement or party. By deliberating with others who do not share their religious certainty and who share only some of their policy preferences, activists may come to understand the rationale for opposing policies, to respect and even form personal connections with those with whom they disagree. In the process they may increase their levels of civic virtues such as mutual respect and trust, support for deliberation and compromise, and tolerance (Mutz 2002).[2]

Past studies have shown that Christian Right activists show high levels of dogmatism, authoritarianism or authority-mindedness, and intolerance (Johnson and Tamney 1984; Wald et al. 1989; Owen et al. 1991; Jelen 1991; Wilcox et al. 1995). But it is possible that these civic deficits come not from membership in the Christian Right but rather in the religious culture from which the Christian Right recruits its members. White fundamentalist and Pentecostal churches preach doctrine that may increase fear and hostility of political opponents, decrease trust and support for deliberation and compromise, and lower levels of tolerance.

Fundamentalist churches preach that humans are inherently sinful and that members should remain separate from sinners, a belief that lowers social trust of those outside the congregations (Ammerman 1987). They teach that there is one truth, which is revealed in the literal words of the Bible, which Christians must consistently espouse. The belief in a single truth makes deliberation and compromise morally suspect and makes it less important to maintain the marketplace of ideas that underpins notions of tolerance.

In addition, many of these churches preach an eschatology that depicts the world in an apocalyptic battle between the forces of Christ and those of Satan, who is a real sentient being who walks the earth and tempts Christians. They describe a coming final battle between the forces of good and evil, foretold in Scripture and fictionalized in the series of bestselling novels in the *Left Behind* series. Belief in the existence of Satan has been shown to be a powerful predictor of intolerance (Nunn et al. 1978). Thus, many of the fundamentalists, evangelicals, and Pentecostals believe that their opponents "threaten the well-being of humanity on a cosmic scale" (Green et al. 1994).

Religious ideas matter, and the theology of churches from which the Christian Right draws is a source of civic deficits.[3] Studies have repeatedly shown that those who believe in the literal truth of scripture are less tolerant than other Americans and more fearful of their political opponents (Beatty and Walter 1984; Wilcox and Jelen 1990; Guth and Green 1991; Reimer and Park 2001).

If Christian Right activists enter politics with a large deficit in civic virtues stemming in part from their religious attributes, then they may enhance those virtues through political engagement and still lag behind other political elites. And if Christian Right members do gain civic virtues through political participation, this has implications for broader discussions of the role of religious parties and religious debate in democracy.

In this chapter, I consider the impact of the Christian Right on the democratic values of its members, drawing on my own qualitative and quantitative research over nearly thirty years and performing new empirical tests using data from a survey of Republican presidential donors. First, however, it is important to consider theoretical reasons why membership in the Christian Right might not, or might, increase civic virtues.

The Passion of the Christian Right: Why the Movement Might Not Increase Civic Virtue

Membership in social movement organizations and other voluntary groups can have many types of positive effects on their members. It can increase the information of members and lead to higher levels of efficacy. Members of some types of groups may develop better political skills as they work within the organization, and perhaps deliberative skills as well as they discuss issues within the group. This might lead to greater civic virtues as well, including civility, the norms of compromise, and tolerance. All types of groups have the potential to have positive effects, but groups may differ in the types and magnitude of their impact.

Mark Warren (2001) has argued that organizations centered on exclusive social identity generally have limited capacity to build civic virtues such as civility, tolerance, and the norms of compromise. Deliberation is most enhanced by discussions with those with a different point of view (Mutz 2006), but exclusive identity groups focus primarily on shared identities and minimize potential disagreement. This is because such groups have relatively easy exit—members can vote with their feet and leave organizations where they feel uncomfortable.

Easy exit means that if members encounter significant disagreement, and if they find this unpleasant, they will simply shop around for another organization where there is greater consensus. There will be little reason to engage in deliberation that invoves real disagreement and therefore less opportunity to develop perspective-taking ability or political skills. Any deliberation is likely to be within an enclave and thus less likely to lead to greater moderation or tolerance (Sunstein 2000).

Warren singles out the Christian Right as a movement that is especially unlikely to have positive effects on the tolerance and deliberative skills of its members (p. 35) because its mobilization language demonizes outgroups. Although these kinds of groups can create strong bonding capital, they do so by making it more difficult to build bridges across differences (Putnam 2000; Warren 2001). As members come to fear liberals, feminists, and gay rights activists, they may even lower their levels of civic virtues such as social trust, deliberative skills, and tolerance.

There is little doubt that Christian Right groups have frequently demonized outgroups and sought to portray themselves as engaged in a culture war. Scholarly accounts of the movement frequently use and even recycle war imagery (Buell and Sigelman 1985; Wilcox et al 1991; Wilcox 1992a; Guth et al. 1995; Green 1996; Jelen and Wilcox 1997; Wilcox and Larson 2006; Campbell and Robinson 2007; Layman, chapter 7, this volume).[4] Activists have used this language as well; even the normally soothing Ralph Reed once called himself a guerilla fighter who traveled by night and left his opponents in body bags.[5]

It is common for all groups to caricature their political opponents in communications aimed at mobilizing members, and civil liberties groups have similarly sought to increase fear and distrust of Christian conservatives in their direct mail solicitations. But there are two things that are especially troubling about Christian Right materials. First, they are aimed at a population whose theology inclines them toward lower levels of tolerance and higher levels of fear of their opponents (Green et al. 1994). Second, these materials frequently portray the culture war as an apocalyptic rather than political struggle, one between good and evil, a frame that is particularly troubling for democratic deliberation (Smith 2008). Surveys of Christian Right activists have shown that many believe that their political work is part of a battle for the soul of America against Satanic forces (Wilcox et al. 1991).

Such beliefs make the potential constituency of the movement unusually responsive to messages that build fear and distrust against liberal and secular groups. And Christian Right organizations have been very willing to dispense such messages in fundraising and mobilization. The magnitude of the incivility in these messages is worth noting.

- One direct mail fundraising letter by the Moral Majority warned that schools that receive federal funds would "be forced to hire known, practicing and *soliciting* homosexual teachers." It also warned that the courts and Congress would protect smut peddlers, "so that they can openly sell pornographic materials *to your children*" (emphasis added).
- A fundraising letter from Focus on the Family warned that Christians would soon be barred from wearing religious pins on their coats or dresses or from carrying religious materials to read at lunch at work. Readers were warned that if they violated these provisions, they would lose their jobs.
- Pat Robertson warned in a fundraising letter that feminism was a "socialist, anti-family political movement that encourages women to leave their husbands, kill their children, practice witchcraft, destroy capitalism and become lesbians."
- A fundraising appeal by Concerned Women for America began by warning that "Your right to think and live as a Christian is in

deadly danger because of Tom Daschle, Ted Kennedy's new 'hate crimes' bill. You and I must do everything we can to stop this evil bill TODAY."
    - The letter goes on to warn that "your pastor could be jailed," "Christian schools could be shut down," "the whole pro-life movement could be outlawed."
    - "Like a scene from Nazi Germany, bonfires would fill the streets as liberal activists destroy Bibles and other sources of 'intolerance' and 'hate speech.'"
    - The mailing was enclosed in an envelope with a picture of the Bible, covered with the word CENSORED in bold red letters, and "CONTAINS HATE SPEECH" below (Berry and Wilcox 2007).
- An article on the Focus on the Family web page argued that the true agenda of the gay-rights movement was to "promote pedophiles as prophets of the New World Order."

The thought that your political opponents want to send soliciting homosexuals to your schools, have you fired for a religious pin, encourage your daughter to practice witchcraft, or have a marshmallow roast on a bonfire of Bibles does not increase appreciation for the values of deliberation and compromise. Moreover, the use of religious and biblical language in these communications adds additional salience to the message and in many cases casts them as part of a larger battle between good and evil.

Thus, it may be that membership in the Christian Right lowers levels of civic virtues by increasing fear and hostility toward political opponents. Those exposed to a steady stream of such communications may become less trusting, less willing to compromise or deliberate about political ideas, and less willing to allow their opponents to fully participate in democratic discourse.

Deliberation in the Christian Right: Why the Movement Might Increase Civic Virtues

It is also possible that the Christian Right has increased the democratic values of their members. I have interviewed Christian Right activists in Ohio in the 1980s and in Virginia and in Washington, DC, since the early 1990s. I have sat in on national and local meetings and listened in on strategy sessions. This qualitative work leads me to conclude that real deliberation occurs within the Christian Right.

Although in theory Christian Right groups should allow easy exit, in practice activists appear reluctant to leave local organizations because they are bound together by ties of friendship, neighborhood, and congregation. Like the prisoners in hell in Sartre's play, many feel obliged to discuss and debate even when free to leave (Sartre 1955). Moreover, many activists genuinely enjoy discussing, debating, and even arguing about politics—at least within the enclave.[6]

Often these discussions rely on religious reasons, but frequently this occurs on both sides of an internal debate. And although it is fair to say that many Christian Right activists do not enter these debates willing to consider any possible position, I have seen participants apparently convinced on arguments over when abortion might be permitted, what policies are appropriate with regard to sexual minorities, and especially in recent years, what policies are appropriate on immigration and even the death penalty.

Although these deliberations occur within social identity organizations as Warren notes, over time the Christian Right has gradually incorporated more religious diversity, forcing activists to discuss policies outside of their religious traditions.

Early Christian Right groups appealed to narrow religious constituencies: the Moral Majority was primarily comprised of independent Baptists, for example (Guth 1983). As the Christian Right has sought to build more inclusive social identities, it has sought to bridge previously deep theological chasms. The "bonding" capital of the Christian Right, especially in the 1990s, entailed building theological bridges to create the shared identity of "Christian conservatives." Divisions between fundamentalists and Pentecostals were once intense: early in the twentieth century one prominent fundamentalist pastor called Pentecostals the "last vomit of Satan."[7] In the 1980s the movement foundered on religious divisions, but by the 1990s pentecostals and fundamentalists worked together in the same organizations (Green and Guth 1988; Wilcox 1992b; Wilcox et al. 1996).

Similarly, the cooperation between conservative Catholics and evangelicals in the Christian Right of the early twenty-first century would have seemed impossible even in the early 1980s. Early studies showed that hostility toward Catholics was a powerful predictor of support for the Moral Majority (Kellstedt 1988; Wilcox 1989). At one Ohio Moral Majority meeting I attended in 1981, a sermon preceded the organizational session titled "Roman Catholic Church, Harlot of Rome."

By the early 1990s, fundamentalist activists told Mark Rozell and me that they had met Catholics who might actually be good Christians; by the late 1990s similar activists were telling us of having Catholic Christians in their homes for dinner (Bendyna et al. 2000). By the mid-2000s, Catholics and evangelicals were engaged in a serious dialogue in the Christian Right and other conservative networks over issues such as the death penalty, the environment, and natural family planning (Robinson

2008). Evangelicals spoke of "being in the listening boat" on various issues where Catholic doctrine differed from evangelical positions.

There were also somewhat less successful efforts to include African-Americans and Latinos in the Christian Right, and Ralph Reed wrote a serious critique of racism (Reed 1994). More recently the Christian Right has had more success in multiracial cooperation in political coalitions (Campbell and Robinson 2007), creating in the process at least some occasions to deliberate across racial lines. Christian Right groups have sought to build organizations that span class barriers as well. In terms of social capital, this may not constitute a full bridge to diversity, but for many activists who had not spoken seriously with Catholics or African-Americans before, it is at least a footbridge.[8]

It is not merely the expanded internal deliberation that might lead to greater civic virtues. Although the first wave of Christian Right organizations such as the Moral Majority did little to train their activists in democratic politics, in the 1990s new organizations spent considerable effort in teaching political skills, including compromise and negotiation. The Christian Coalition initially mounted an ambitious program to train state and local activists in how to reach out to those who might support at least some policies that the movement espoused. They focused on rhetorical self-restraint and on how to use language appropriate to the audience. Many Christian Right leaders seek to create bilingual activists, who can speak the language of accommodation and secular reasons when in the broader public sphere and a narrower and more extreme rhetoric in private (Moen 1994; Rozell and Wilcox 1996b).

In the few sessions that I attended, the focus was usually on utilitarian goals—how to reach different audiences and build winning coalitions. These sessions did not advocate true deliberation but rather trained activists in defending their policy preferences using a variety of arguments. Yet even these practical sessions may have had positive effects, for to win an audience you must understand its perspective. Research has shown that evangelical activists frequently lack perspective-taking ability (Robinson 2008) and that this ability is essential in order for deliberation to increase tolerance (Mutz 2002).

Finally, Christian Right organizations of the 1990s and 2000s have encouraged their members to be very active in Republican Party politics, which has exposed them to arguments of moderates and even libertarians. In many cases these initial interactions were remarkably hostile and uncivil—on both sides (Rozell and Wilcox 1995). But over time, many Christian conservatives have had to bargain with others in the party with different views, and in many states they have been more willing to support moderate candidates than moderates have been to support

Christian conservative candidates. Some activists in Virginia have told me of meeting gun enthusiasts at meetings of a local Christian Right group, then attending NRA meetings where they meet environmentalists. These crosscutting memberships have been posited to contain conflict and increase civility and tolerance (Truman 1951; Mutz 2006).

Thus, the Christian Right may have taken some citizens with little prior exposure to difference and encouraged them to interact with individuals who partially share their political preferences. At the minimum, we should expect this to lead to increased trust and tolerance toward those with whom they have forged a new bond, as past research has confirmed (Wilcox et al. 1996; Rozell et al. 1998). But some have argued that increased exposure to difference can generalize beyond the narrow bonds of a social group (Pettigrew 1997). Robinson has argued that Catholics might be the "gateway drug" that leads to greater evangelical tolerance of even out-groups (Robinson 2008).

Thus, my past qualitative research leads me to suspect that at least some Christian Right activists benefited from a broadening of the range of groups within their social bond and from the benefits of compromise and deliberation within the enclave. Recently Jon Shields has made a much stronger claim—that "civility is easily the most universally taught deliberative norm in the Christian Right." Drawing on his own interviews with activists in certain pro-life organizations, Shields claims these groups "labor diligently to moderate and inform the passions they have provoked by encouraging activists to embrace deliberative norms, especially the practice of civility, the rejection of theological appeals, and moral reasoning. . . . To violate these deliberative norms, then, is not just impolitic; it is also unfaithful" (Shields 2007). If the Christian Right has sincerely sought to inculcate love and civility in the "hearts and minds" of citizens, then it might well increase tolerance of its members (Gibson 1989).

It is likely, of course, that a full theory of the impact of the movement on its members would require many qualifiers. Activists enter politics with varying levels of perspective-taking ability and in their fear or openness to difference. Different Christian Right organizations reach different audiences and have crafted their messages to fit these niches. It may also be that the movement has a different effect on passive and active members. Passive members—especially those who primarily receive mail and magazines from the movement and who contribute money—may become more fearful and intolerant because of these communications. The most active members, however, may be exposed to training and discussions outside of the enclave and may therefore increase their civic virtues.

The Data

To partially test these possibilities I use data from a mail survey of a stratified random sample of donors to the primary campaigns of the Republican presidential candidates in 2000. The survey was mailed to both significant donors of more than $200 drawn from the Federal Election Commission (FEC) disclosure records and also smaller donors drawn from FEC matching fund requests and George W. Bush's campaign website.[9] The first wave of surveys was mailed in summer of 2001, with two to four follow-up mailings. The overall response rate was 50 percent, excluding undeliverable questionnaires, including 1008 donors of less than $200 and 918 contributors of more than that amount.

Because the survey was stratified by receiving candidate, there are significant oversamples of donors to Christian Right favorites Gary Bauer, Patrick Buchanan, Alan Keyes, and George W. Bush. Some 414 small donors were members of Christian Right groups, constituting 41 percent of all GOP primary donors. Fully 335 large donors were members of Christian Right organizations, comprising 37 percent of all donors of this size. To take full advantage of this large number of respondents, the data have not been weighted to reflect the population of all donors. The data constitute an elite sample that includes large numbers of Christian Right members but are not representative of political donors.[10]

Christian Right members are identified as those who said that they were either a member of a generic Christian conservative or pro-family group or who indicated that they were a member of any one or more of four specific groups: the Christian Coalition, Focus on the Family, Concerned Women for America, and the Campaign for Working Families (a PAC sponsored by Gary Bauer). In addition, for some analyses I divide Christian Right group members into active and passive members, distinguishing those who attend meetings or are otherwise active from those who merely receive materials and give money. I also divide members into those who entered politics before the Christian Right became active, those who were mobilized during the first wave of the movement (1978–1988), and those who were mobilized later.

The survey also includes a variety of questions that tap religious affiliation, identity, behavior, and belief. Evangelical denomination is coded 1 for all who attend denominations with evangelical, Pentecostal, or fundamentalist roots, 0 for all others. Catholics are similarly identified with a dummy variable. Evangelical identity is coded 1 if a respondent checked any of the following religious identities: Evangelical Christian, fundamentalist Christian, born-again Christian, Pentecostal Christian, or Charismatic Christian; otherwise it is coded as 0. Religiosity is a scale combining frequency of church attendance and personal religious salience. Finally, Bible views is a four-point question that measures belief in the authority of Scripture. Respondents could indicate that the Bible was literally true, that it had no errors but was not literally true, or that it was inspired but contained human error.

As dependent variables I include a range of questions designed to measure hostility toward and fear of social groups, an apocalyptic approach to politics, social trust, the norms of compromise, openness to deliberation, and tolerance.[11] In the analysis below, I first show the actual responses of Christian Right activists and other GOP donors, because the actual levels of hostility, trust, support for deliberation, and tolerance matter in how we estimate the Christian Right.

Next, I estimate multivariate models to see if Christian Right members are different from others who share their theology, religious affiliations and identities, and demographic characteristics. In these tables I will show coefficients only for Christian Right membership and for other religious attributes, holding constant other factors that are not shown to simplify the presentation. It will be possible to see the direct effect of religious affiliations, identities, behaviors, and beliefs on all Republican donors and then to compare Christian Right members with other Republicans who share these same religious attributes, along with other social characteristics.

Although the data were gathered in part to test the questions asked in this chapter, there are important limitations. First, all respondents are donors and therefore political activists. Second, most members of the Christian Right in this sample are also members of other organizations—including business groups, civic associations, or pro-gun groups—and thus receive political communications from many other sources. Indeed, Christian Right group members were slightly more likely to be members of other types of groups than other donors. Finally, in a single cross-sectional survey it is difficult to prove causation, a point that I explore more fully in the conclusion.

Group Affect and Apocalyptic Politics

If Christian Right direct mail solicitations encourage fear and hostility toward liberal groups, we would expect to find that group members are more hostile toward liberal groups than other Republicans and more likely to believe that liberal groups are powerful and active in their states. Table 6.1 compares the evaluations of social groups by Christian Right and non–Christian Right donors.

The top of the table shows the percentage of Christian Right members and other Republican donors who rate various social groups at 0 degrees—the coldest possible rating on a one-hundred-point "feeling

TABLE 6.1
Christian Right Membership, Group Affect, and Apocalyptic Politics

	Christian Right	Other donors
Affect toward groups: % who rate at 0		
Feminists	53%	32%**
Homosexuals	56%	27%**
ACLU	60%	32%**
Environmentalists	22%	13%**
Labor unions	23%	19%@
Muslims	31%	22%**
Jews	4%	4%
Catholics	4%	6%
Christian fundamentalists	4%	16%**
Percentage who see each group as very active in state		
Feminists	24%	17%**
Gay rights groups	37%	27%**
Christian conservatives	35%	25%**
Apocalyptic Politics		
U.S. Christian nation/Christian laws	94%	66%**
Attack on Christian schools is by Satan	65%	22%**
God works through elections and political parties	69%	22%**
N	749	1177

@$p \leq .10$; *$p \leq .05$; **$p \leq .01$.

thermometer." Majorities of Christian Right group members rated feminists, homosexuals, and the ACLU at 0 degrees—twice the figure for other Republican donors. Nearly a quarter rated environmentalists and labor unions at 0 degrees as well, in each case significantly greater than for other Republican donors. Clearly Christian Right members are more hostile toward their political opponents than are other Republicans. The degree of hostility is not consistent with admonitions to "hate the sin, love the sinner."

Christian Right activists are also more likely to rate Muslims at 0 degrees than were other Republican presidential donors, whereas nonmembers are more likely to give Christian fundamentalists a similarly low rating. This reminds us that it is not only the Christian Right that strongly dislikes its opponents.[12] There are no significant differences in ratings of

Catholics and Jews, with only a few donors in each camp clearly hostile to these religious groups.

The fact that Christian Right members are not significantly more likely to show hostility toward Jews is a notable and consistent finding in the literature, but the lack of hostility to Catholics represents a major change from studies in the 1980s. Early studies showed that anti-Catholicism was one of the strongest predictors of support for the Moral Majority, and that state chapters of the Moral Majority had virtually no Catholic members (Kellstedt 1988; Wilcox 1989).

Members of the Christian Right are also more likely than other GOP donors to perceive that feminist and gay rights groups are very active in their state, and also to believe that Christian conservative groups are active in their state. Thus, Christian Right members are more likely to perceive their state's politics to be characterized by a culture war.[13] The combined hostility toward liberal groups and the increased belief that they are active in the state suggests that Christian Right members would feel threatened by liberal groups, and the perception that Christian conservatives are also more active suggests a struggle between dangerous groups and the movement.

The data at the bottom of table 6.1 confirm that Christian Right members are more likely than other Republicans to see political struggles in apocalyptic terms. Nearly all Christian Right members believe that the United States is a Christian nation whose laws should conform to Christian teachings. More than two-thirds of all Christian Right members agree that the attack on Christian schools is led by Satan, and also that God works through elections and political parties. These attitudes suggest an orientation toward political debates that is antithetical to deliberation and tolerance.

Taken together, the data in table 6.1 suggest that we have reason to be worried about the democratic values of Christian Right members. More than half of all members are extremely hostile toward liberal groups, and more than two-thirds see politics as involving in part a contest between good and evil. And many believe that in their states there is an active political struggle between social liberals and Christian conservatives. But these descriptive data do not tell us whether Christian Right group members are distinctive when compared to others who share their religious and demographic characteristics, nor do they tell us how religion shapes these attitudes more broadly.

Table 6.2 shows the impact of religious variables and Christian Right membership on hostility to liberal groups and apocalyptic political views. The dependent variables are scales that combine questions from table 6.1.[14] Essentially these models compare Christian Right activists to other Republican donors who share their religious affiliation, identity,

TABLE 6.2
Multivariate Models of Group Affect and Apocalyptic Political Views

		b	β	*t*
Evaluation of liberal groups				
Bible		−1.91	−0.10**	−2.77**
Religiosity		0.10	0.01	0.18
Orthodox identity		0.75	0.04	0.20
Evangelical denomination		−4.09	−0.09	−3.01**
Catholic		−1.76	0.04	0.15
CR membership		−4.30	−0.10	−3.78**
N	1619			
R^2	0.36			
Apocalpytic political views				
Bible		0.32	0.33	13.30**
Religiosity		0.17	0.20	8.69**
Orthodox identity		0.11	0.11	4.98**
Evangelical denomination		0.17	0.08	3.49**
Catholic		0.04	0.02	0.80
CR membership		0.33	0.16	8.04**
N	1556			
R^2	0.59			

Notes: Affect toward liberal groups is an average of feeling thermometer ratings of homosexuals, the ACLU, and feminists. Apocalyptic political views is a factor score from common factor analysis of the questions shown in table 6.1.

Full model includes controls for big/small donors, education, income, age, gender, and south. @$p \leq .10$; *$p \leq .05$; **$p \leq .01$.

observance, and doctrine, and who also share their other characteristics. As a stronger test, I also hold constant political ideology in the model of evaluations of liberal groups because the most conservative Republicans are likely to feel the least warmth toward these organizations.

The data show that various religious factors influence evaluations of liberal groups and apocalyptic political views. The patterns are subtly different for the two sets of attitudes, revealing the complexity of religious influences. Hostility toward liberal groups is highest among those who attend evangelical denominations and those who believe that the Bible is literally true. But levels of religiosity per se do not predict hostility toward liberal groups, perhaps because some respondents frequently attend churches that preach tolerance.

An apocalyptic approach to politics is most strongly predicted by the belief in the literal truth of Scripture. Religiosity also strongly predicts apocalyptic political views, even controlling for theology, religious identity, and denomination. Additional analysis (not shown) shows that this effect is confined to a single group—those donors who believe in the literal truth of the Bible. Among that group, those who attend church more than weekly are quite different from those who attend less frequently. Among other Republican donors, religiosity does not influence apocalyptic political views. Evangelical denomination and orthodox religious identity also matter, although less than theology. Catholics are again not different from other donors.

Most importantly, Christian Right group members are distinctively more hostile toward liberal groups and more likely to see politics in apocalyptic terms than others who share the same theology, religious identity, religious affiliation, and religiosity. Christian Right membership is a stronger predictor of hostility toward liberal groups than any religious variable. Christian Right membership therefore appears to increase hostility toward liberal groups and to increase the tendency to view political battles in apocalyptic terms. Such a worldview—hostility toward enemies who are associated with Satan and who are opposed by the forces of God—is not one that is likely to increase civic virtues.

Civic Virtues and the Christian Right: Social Trust, Deliberative Norms, Compromise

Theorists differ in their ambitions for the kinds of civic virtues that might result from associational involvement. Nancy Rosenblum suggests the importance of modest accomplishments—such as the ability of militia groups to channel social pathologies that otherwise might undermine democracy (Rosenblum 2000, 57). Although some of the constituency of the Christian Right may lack various democratic norms, they do not share the social ills of militia members.

More ambitious democratic theorists hope that membership in associations might increase social trust, which plays an important role in democratic processes (Warren 1999). Membership might also provide opportunities for deliberation, which can help members understand their own and others' arguments, and to possibly understand those of their opponents (Price et al. 2002; Barabas 2004; Mutz 2006). Associations might also help their members develop norms of compromise and accommodation that are essential for pluralist democracies.

Table 6.3 shows the responses of Christian Right members and other Republican donors to questions designed to measure these orientations. Christian Right members are significantly less trusting than other Republicans, with only one in four agreeing that "most people can be trusted to do right," and a clear majority believing that "you can't be

TABLE 6.3
Civic Norms: Christian Right Contributors and Others

	Percentage who agree or strongly agree with each statement	
	Christian Right	Other donors
Trust		
Most people can be trusted to do right	24%	36%**
You can't be too careful with people	53%	42%**
Deliberation		
On most issues, one correct point of view	52%	22%**
Talking with others can change my mind	57%	68%**
I understand why others disagree on abortion	58%	79%**
I find it hard to respect those who disagree with me	24%	14%**
My political involvement helps me understand others' point of view	56%	60%*
My involvement helps me understand that some views are dangerous	86%	75%**
Compromise—General		
Better to hold out than compromise	39%	67%**
Compromise essential part of politics	65%	84%**
Sometimes work with those you disagree with	90%	91%
Compromise within party		
If party changed position on issues I would leave	73%	52%**
It is important to support nominee if disagree	17%	20%*
N	749	1177

[@] $p \leq .10$; * $p \leq .05$; ** $p \leq .01$.

too careful with some people." Both sets of Republicans seem relatively low in trust compared with the results of national surveys with similar questions, especially compared to other whites with high levels of education.[15]

Political theorists have traditionally set high standards for the types of deliberations that are most productive for democracy. Some have argued that deliberative citizens must be open to new arguments and evidence, uncertain of the truth (Gutmann and Thompson 1996). The data here show that a majority of Christian Right group members enter into any negotiations and deliberations convinced that there is a single correct point of view on most policy matters. This is hardly encouraging for open deliberation and debate.

But a majority also report that talking with others has at times changed their opinion. This is true even for a narrow majority of those who also said that there is one correct view in politics. This suggests that many Christian Right activists believe there is one truth but are sometimes swayed by others about what that truth might be.

A majority of Christian Right members also say that they understand why others disagree with them on abortion, and only a small minority find it hard to respect those with whom they disagree. Christian Right members and other Republicans are equally likely to say that their involvement in politics helps them understand others' points of view. But Christian Right members are significantly more likely to also agree that their involvement in politics has shown them the danger of some political views.

This suggests that many Christian Right group members are open to deliberation, argument, and evidence, at least within the enclave. Talking with other social conservatives (e.g., evangelicals talking with Catholics) may help to shift opinions on issues such as immigration. And Christian Right activists claim to understand why people disagree even on emotional issues such as abortion and to be able to respect those who disagree with them.

But they are also more likely to have become aware of the magnitude of danger in certain ideas, presumably especially those of liberal groups. As evangelical Christian Right members build bonds with conservative Catholics and other Republicans, they do so in part by sharing their fears of secular liberal Democrats. One Christian Right activist in Virginia told me that she came to trust Catholic conservatives when she realized that they shared common enemies—feminists, gay rights activists, and other liberal groups.

On more general norms of compromise, Christian Right members are far more likely than other Republican donors to value holding out for their values rather than compromising, and they are far less likely to agree that compromise is an essential part of politics. They are no different from other Republicans in being willing to work with those with whom they disagree, however. This presumably means that most Christian Right members are willing to work with those with whom they disagree so long as it does not involve compromise on principles.

Christian Right group members are also less likely to voice support for norms of compromise within the GOP. The difference is particularly large in the willingness to leave the party if it changed its positions on key issues.[16] But a majority of both sets of donors are willing to leave the party over principle and to withhold their support from nominees with whom they disagree.

Taken together, these data show that Christian Right activists do have lower levels of social trust and support for deliberation and compromise than other Republican donors. But the absolute levels of these civic virtues are higher than most critics of the movement would expect. The image of an unyielding cadre of religious zealots who brook no compromise is clearly overstated—Christian Right activists are willing to be persuaded in at least some political conversations and to engage in compromise that does not involve core principles. Once again, however, it is important to parcel out the effects of religious and social characteristics to see if Christian Right members are truly distinctive.

Table 6.4 shows the results of multivariate models of scales measuring the civic virtues shown as separate questions in table 6.3. As in table 6.4, the results hold constant demographic variables and whether the donor gave a large or small contribution. The questions in table 6.3 have been combined into five scales, measuring social trust, certitude in deliberation, the belief that deliberation reveals dangerous ideas, general norms of compromise, and compromise within the Republican Party.[17]

Once again different religious characteristics matter for each civic virtue. Evangelical denominations and identities both predict lower levels of trust, as does the belief that the Bible is literally true. Evangelical churches frequently stress the inherent sinfulness of humanity and focus on personal, individual salvation. But religiosity per se does not lead to decreased trust. Catholics are not distinctive in their levels of social trust.

Members of evangelical or Catholic churches, those with orthodox religious identities, and those who believe that the Bible is literally the word of God are all more likely to enter political conversations with great certainty of their positions. Once again, however, religiosity is not a predictor, for some churches emphasize moral certitude, whereas others emphasize the spiritual quest for truth. No religious attribute predicts the view that deliberation reveals dangerous ideas.

For both scales measuring support for compromise, Bible views, religious identity, and being Catholic are all associated with lowered levels of support. The impact of Catholicism is greatest in attitudes toward compromise within the Republican Party. Recall from table 6.3 that these items focus on the willingness to leave the party or not support candidates who do not support key issues. It may well be that conservative Catholics, as relatively late entrants to the GOP attracted primarily by social issues, are therefore more likely to indicate a willingness to leave the party if it changes its position on key issues. Their partisanship is more instrumental to begin with, based on certain key issues. Once again, religiosity does not predict willingness to compromise when denomination, identity, and doctrine are controlled.

Compared to others with the same religious beliefs, affiliations, and behaviors, Christian Right members have significantly lower levels of all five measures of civic virtues. They are significantly less trusting, less

TABLE 6.4
Multivariate Models of Civic Norms

	b	β	*T*
Social trust			
Bible	–0.07	–0.07	–1.71@
Religiosity	0.05	0.06	0.09
Orthodox identity	–0.07	–0.08	–2.21*
Evangelical denomination	–0.19	–0.09	–2.50*
Catholic	0.09	0.04	1.27
CR membership	–0.17	–0.08	–2.80**
Moral certitude and deliberation			
Bible	0.13	0.13	3.80**
Religiosity	–0.00	–0.01	–0.08
Orthodox identity	0.08	0.09	2.72**
Evangelical denomination	0.15	0.07	2.18*
Catholic	0.27	0.11	4.28**
CR membership	0.40	0.20	7.00**
Deliberation reveals dangerous ideas			
Bible	0.03	0.03	0.79
Religiosity	0.02	0.03	0.89
Orthodox identity	0.02	0.03	0.74
Evangelical denomination	0.08	0.04	1.22
Catholic	0.04	0.02	0.79
CR membership	0.17	0.09	3.02**
Norms of Compromise			
Bible	–0.10	–0.10	–2.83**
Religiosity	0.02	0.03	0.80
Orthodox identity	–0.08	–0.09	–2.62**
Evangelical denomination	0.02	0.01	0.76
Catholic	–0.12	–0.05	–1.78@
CR membership	–0.19	–0.09	–3.02**
Compromise in GOP			
Bible	–0.10	–0.10	–2.83**
Religiosity	0.02	0.02	–0.71
Orthodox identity	–0.10	–0.10	–3.13**
Evangelical denomination	–0.10	–0.04	–1.35
Catholic	–0.23	–0.10	–3.60**
CR membership	–0.20	–0.10	–3.39**

Full model includes controls for big/small donors, education, income, age, gender, and south. @$p < .10$; *$p < .05$; **$p < .01$.

deliberative, and less supportive of compromise in general and within the GOP than other Republican activists. Again there is little evidence here that the Christian Right increases civic virtues.

The Christian Right and Political Tolerance

Political tolerance is one of the most central of all civic virtues. To be tolerant, citizens need not meet in open-minded deliberation, trust their opponents, or compromise—they merely must allow them access to the public sphere. But as James Gibson notes in this volume (chapter 5), liberal democratic government requires that all groups be allowed to enter the marketplace of ideas and to have access to the public forums where they can attempt to sway opinion.

Respondents were asked whether members of various groups should be allowed to demonstrate "assuming that there is no threat of violence," and whether they would allow members of these groups to teach in the local public schools "assuming professional conduct." These questions therefore remove one of the most common objections to tolerance of public demonstrations and hiring teachers with diverse views.

The survey included a range of social and political groups, including feminists, homosexuals, atheists, and environmentalists—all disliked by Christian Right leaders, along with white power advocates, black nationalists, militia members, and Christian fundamentalists. Although the survey did not provide the content-controlled measures that are widely used in studies of tolerance (Sullivan, Piereson, and Marcus 1982), there is evidence that content-specified measures can provide useful estimates of tolerance (Gibson 1992). In particular, these items allow us to examine tolerance toward two sets of activities (Gibson and Bingham 1982) and toward most of those social groups especially disliked by the Christian Right.

Table 6.5 shows the responses to some of these items by Christian Right members and other GOP presidential donors. For all Republican donors, support for allowing groups to demonstrate is much higher than allowing their members to teach in public schools. All Republican donors were less supportive of the right to demonstrate for groups associated with violence, including militia members, white power advocates, and black nationalists, and other groups that they might dislike such as feminists and Christian fundamentalists. The exception to this rule is Christian Right member support for demonstrations by homosexuals, where support falls below 60% and is therefore lower than that extended to milita members and Black Nationalists. A majority of both sets of Republicans would allow demonstrations by members of each group, although these numbers are lower than those found in other surveys of educated elites.

TABLE 6.5
Christian Right Support and Membership and Tolerance

	Christian Right	Other donors
Would allow to demonstrate		
Atheists	72%	78%**
Homosexuals	59%	75%**
Environmentalists	86%	87%
Feminists	80%	85%*
Christian fundamentalists	90%	87%@
Militia members	66%	66%
White power advocates	58%	62%@
Black nationalists	65%	67%
Would allow to teach		
Atheists	42%	58%**
Homosexuals	24%	50%**
Environmentalists	64%	72%**
Feminists	44%	66%**
Christian fundamentalists	81%	67%**
Militia members	33%	33%
White power advocates	18%	23%*
Black nationalists	25%	28%@
N	749	1177

@$p < .10$; *$p < .05$; **$p < .01$.

Support for allowing members of these groups to teach in public schools was substantially lower. The data are not directly comparable to the General Social Survey, which asks about teaching in public universities. Even the most tolerant citizens might hesitate at the image of a white power advocate teaching seventh-grade U.S. history of the civil rights movement. Among donors who are not members of Christian Right groups, there is majority support for allowing all four liberal groups to teach, and for Christian fundamentalists as well, although fully one-third of other Republican donors would not allow them to teach.

Among Christian Right group members, support for allowing members of these liberal groups to teach is remarkably low. Majorities would deny the right of atheists, homosexuals, and feminists to teach in public schools, and a third would even deny this right to environmentalists. Nearly one in five would not allow Christian fundamentalists to teach—a figure concentrated primarily among Catholic and mainline Protestant members of the movement, but also to some extent among nonfundamentalist evangelicals. The intolerance of Christian Right activists extends to a certain degree to those who are within nearby enclaves.

It should not be surprising that Christian Right group members are especially intolerant of school teachers who are members of liberal groups. Christian conservatives have long been worried about schools that might inculcate their children with "wrong" values and beliefs. They believe that children are tempted by wrong ideas and must be sheltered. The Bible promises that conservative Christians can "train up your child in the way he should go, and when he is old he will not depart of it" (Proverbs 22:6). Christian Right groups have battled over public school curricula throughout the century, focusing on a variety of issues such as the teaching of evolution, sex education, values clarification, and "secular humanism." Many group members send their children to private religious schools to protect them against exposure to ideas that might lead them astray. These attitudes are deeply held within the religious communities that are mobilized by the Christian Right, and frequently local disputes begin without any organized support by movement organizations (Bates 1993). But the absolute level of support for allowing liberals to teach is disturbingly low.

Table 6.6 begins with the same basic models as in tables 6.2 and 6.4, with demographic variables and size of contribution again held constant. Because Christian Right groups are especially intolerant of liberal groups, the table explores only tolerance toward atheists, homosexuals, environmentalists, and feminists. Factor analysis confirmed an important distinction between allowing members of these groups to demonstrate and to teach, so separate equations are estimated for both types of behaviors.

In these tables, the strongest predictor of both measures of intolerance is belief in the literal truth of the Bible, a result consistent with those of previous studies. Catholics are somewhat less likely to support the right of minorities to demonstrate and significantly less likely to support their right to teach in public schools.[18] Members of evangelical denominations were somewhat less supportive of the right of liberal groups to teach in public schools. Both Catholic and evangelical congregations have been especially active in creating their own private schools.

Christian Right group members are not significantly less likely than other donors who share their theology and social backgrounds to allow groups to demonstrate, but they are significantly less willing to allow them to teach in public schools.[19] Separate models (not shown) show that Christian Right group members are especially intolerant of the rights of gays and lesbians, and of feminists, to teach in public schools.

The data in the top of table 6.6 show that Christian Right members are less tolerant of liberal groups teaching in public schools, but it does not show us why they are less tolerant. The data in tables 6.2 and 6.4

TABLE 6.6
Multivariate Models of Tolerance

	b	β	*T*
Liberal groups demonstrate			
Bible	−0.17	−0.17	−4.67**
Religiosity	0.03	0.04	1.10
Orthodox identity	0.03	0.03	0.91
Evangelical denomination	−0.00	−0.00	−0.06
Catholic	−0.12	−0.05	1.91@
CR membership	0.04	0.02	0.67
Liberal groups teach			
Bible	−0.23	−0.24	−6.52**
Religiosity	0.00	0.00	0.12
Orthodox identity	0.04	0.04	1.16
Evangelical denomination	−0.13	−0.06	−1.77@
Catholic	−0.15	−0.06	−2.33*
CR membership	−0.13	−0.07	−2.26*
Expanded model			
Liberal groups teach			
Bible	−0.12	−0.12	−3.06**
Religiosity	0.03	0.03	0.88
Orthodox identity	0.05	0.06	1.64
Evangelical denomination	−0.05	−0.02	−0.63
Catholic	−0.10	−0.04	−1.54
CR membership	0.00	0.00	0.05
Hostility to liberal groups	−0.65	−0.24	−7.96**
Liberal group threat	−0.08	−0.06	−2.42*
Apocalpytic political views	−0.11	−0.11	−2.69**
Certitude in deliberation	−0.14	−0.15	−4.97**
Social trust	−0.06	−0.06	−2.33*

Full model includes controls for big/small donors, education, income, age, gender, and south. @$p < .10$; *$p < .05$; **$p < .01$.

have established that Christian Right members are more hostile toward liberal groups, believe they are more active in their states, are more likely to perceive political conflict in apocalyptic terms, and are less trusting, less deliberative, and less willing to compromise than other Republican donors.

At the bottom of table 6.6, I include controls for attitudes and orientations that were shown in tables 6.2 and 6.4 to be distinctive among

Christian Right members. I control for affect toward liberal groups and perceived threat of liberal groups to see if the Christian Right is less tolerant primarily because they dislike and fear liberal groups more. I also control for apocalyptic political views, social trust, deliberative values, and support for compromise.[20]

The results show that the strongest predictor of intolerance toward liberal groups is hostility toward them and that perceived threat from these groups is also a significant predictor. Certitude in deliberation, an apocalyptic approach to politics, and social trust are also significant predictors. With these attitudes controlled, only one religious attribute remains a significant predictor of intolerance—the belief in a literal Bible.

After controls for these attitudes, Christian Right group members are no longer less tolerant than other Republican donors. But neither are they more tolerant. This model controls for nearly every attitude that could lead to intolerance—religious doctrine, hostility and fear of liberal groups, the tendency to see politics in apocalyptic terms, certitude in deliberation, and social trust. Even compared with donors with similar attitudes, Christian Right donors are no more tolerant. There is little support here for the idea that the Christian Right has increased the tolerance of their members.

Most importantly, the final equation tells us *why* Christian Right members are more intolerant of liberal groups. Christian Right group members are less tolerant because they are more hostile and threatened by liberal groups than are other Republican donors who attend the same churches and share the same doctrine. Christian Right group members are less tolerant in part because they are more likely to see politics in apocalyptic terms. They are less tolerant because they enter politics with greater certitude than others who share their theology. And they are less trusting than even others from the same churches. All of these beliefs are reinforced by Christian Right direct mail communications and by their publications.

Distinguishing among Christian Right Members

One way to make inferences about the impact of the Christian Right on its members is to compare those who have been active for the longest time with more recent recruits. If membership increases civic virtues, then those who have been active the longest time may be more trusting, deliberative, and tolerant. Some research has reported that Christian conservative activists who have been in politics the longest have higher levels of democratic values (Rozell and Wilcox, 1996a; Layman, chapter 7, this volume).

Yet these results do not themselves show that membership led to increased civic virtues because some members of the Christian Right withdraw from political engagement over time. It may be that the longest-active members are more deliberative and tolerant because they have acquired these attitudes through the political process, but it also may be because among those who joined 20 years ago, the least tolerant and deliberative have already dropped out of politics.

In these data, I identified those who first entered politics before the formation of the Moral Majority in 1978, during the first wave of mobilization between 1978 and 1989, and after the creation of the more ecumenical movements that sought to provide more training from 1990 on. I estimated a series of multivariate models similar to those in tables 6.2, 6.4, and 6.6 (not shown), including only members of Christian Right groups, and including dummy variables to identify when the activists first entered politics.

The results show that democratic values are lowest among those who were mobilized during the 1980s and higher among both those who entered politics before the formation of the Moral Majority and those who came of age after the more ecumenical groups had formed. Christian Right members who were mobilized before 1978 or after 1989 were significantly less likely to be extremely hostile to liberal groups, to have apocalyptic views of political debates, to be certain in their deliberations, to reject the norms of compromise, and to be highly intolerant of liberal groups.

The differences are statistically significant but substantively small. But the results are consistent with two different interpretations. First, it may be that the Christian Right of the 1980s mobilized the least-trusting and least-tolerant citizens and that the Christian Coalition and other later groups were able to reach a somewhat different set of Christians. Alternatively, it may be that the data show that the training of the Christian Coalition and other organizations paid off and that these organizations instilled greater civic virtues.

It is also possible that what matters for civic virtues is not *whether* someone is a member of the Christian Right but rather *how* he or she is involved in the organization. Those whose only contact with the movement is to read its direct mail and publications and to contribute money are exposed to a steady diet of passionate communications that demonize opponents and that claim that only a contribution can save the country from the terrible dreams of liberal groups. Perhaps those who attend local meetings, or who are active in organizations in other ways that maximize face-to-face contact, have increased their levels of trust, their support for the norms of trust and deliberation, and their tolerance.

The survey asked donors whether they were members of specific groups, including Christian Coalition, Concerned Women for America, Focus on the Family, and Campaign for Working Families, and several other groups outside of the Christian Right. Donors were then asked to name the group in which they were most active and to check any activities that they regularly engage in with that organization. More than 40 percent of those who indicated that they were members of abstract or concrete Christian Right groups selected one of these organizations as their most important membership; this resulted in 306 respondents.

From these questions, it is possible to compare those who are passive members—whose only activities are reading a newsletter and/or contributing money—with those who engage more actively in the organization—who attend meetings, participate in group activities or projects, or work with allied organizations. Nearly three in four donors who listed Christian Right groups as their most important membership reported that their only participation was reading materials or giving money.

There were no significant differences in tolerance or other civic virtues between passive and active members of the Christian Right. There were notable differences, however, between Christian Right members who worked through the movement with allied groups and all other members. Those who worked in allied groups were significantly less hostile toward liberal groups. They were also more trusting and more supportive of deliberation and compromise. This might suggest that those most open to compromise and deliberation choose to work with other organizations, or that taking part in deliberations with members of other organizations increases civic virtues.

Conclusion

These results first tell us something about the role of religion in shaping civic virtues among all Republican donors. How religious a citizen is appears to have no impact on his or her civic virtues, a finding reinforced by James Gibson's chapter in this volume (chapter 5). Deeply religious citizens attend churches with varying messages and find different inspirations in prayer and Bible reading. It is not how religious a citizen is that influences democratic values, but rather how he or she is religious.

The one consistent predictor of low levels of civic virtue is belief in a literal interpretation of the Bible. It is worth noting that it is only literalists who are distinctive—those who believe the Bible has no errors but is not literally true have the same levels of trust and tolerance as those who believe that it is a book that contains human errors. In many ways this may represent the power of an idea, for it is difficult to see the virtue of deliberation and compromise if the truth is contained in a single text.

But this is not to say that a belief in literal scripture is incompatible with democracy. As Glenn Tinder has noted, it is possible to believe that the Bible is literally true but that human interpretation of the text is so obviously fallible as to instill humility in those who seek to understand its message (Tinder 1989). Moreover, the political meaning of large religious texts such as the Christian Bible is socially constructed in communities that emphasize different interpretations.

The descriptive data on Christian Right members in tables 6.1, 6.3, and 6.5 reveal a somewhat mixed picture of the democratic values of the movement—one that is less worrisome than the movement's severest critics suggest but less benign than that painted by movement supporters. Christian Right members are very hostile toward groups that their movement most directly opposes—feminists, gays and lesbians, and the ACLU—with a majority giving them the lowest possible rating. They are less hostile toward environmentalists, union members, and even Muslims, and they are quite warm toward Catholics and Jews.

They are less trusting than other Republican donors, and they enter deliberations with more certainty and greater fear of dangerous ideas. And they are less supportive of compromise than other Republican activists. But majorities say that they have changed their minds after talking to others, that they understand why some people take pro-choice positions, and respect those who disagree with them. Majorities also say that compromise is essential to politics, and that it is essential to work with those with whom they disagree. In each case they have lower levels of openness and compromise than other Republicans, but they do not fit the profile of rigid and uncompromising citizens. On these questions certainly, the Christian Right members pass the bar for democratic inclusion easily.

They are less willing to allow members of liberal groups to teach in public schools than other Republicans, who are themselves rather intolerant compared to other studies of educated elites. There is widespread support for allowing liberal groups to demonstrate, but far less support for allowing them to teach in the public schools. The magnitude of the intolerance is striking. In response to a question with a preface "assuming professional conduct," only 24 percent would allow gays and lesbians to teach in public schools, only 44 percent would allow feminists, and fully a third would not allow environmentalists to teach.

The data in tables 6.2, 6.4, and 6.6 show that even when compared with others who believe that the Bible is literally true, who attend Catholic or evangelical churches, and who hold evangelical religious identities, Christian Right members consistently have lower levels of democratic values. Christian Right members are significantly more hostile toward liberal groups than others in their faith, and they are more certain that politics has apocalyptic consequences. They are less trusting, less deliberative, less willing to compromise, and less willing to allow liberals to teach than are others with religion and demographics held constant.

These data suggest that the Christian Right has done little to increase the civic virtues of its members, but they are not definitive proof. It is possible that the Christian Right was especially attractive to those evangelicals who most disliked and feared liberal groups, were the least trusting and deliberative, and were the most intolerant. That is, within a single congregation it may have been that those most lacking in civic virtues joined Christian Right groups, whereas those who were somewhat more trusting and tolerant chose not to join. To fully sort this out, we would need survey data from the same activists from before they joined Christian Right groups, but these survey data do not exist.

Based on my own interviews with activists over many years, I think that the Christian Right has had a mixed effect on the democratic values of its members. In the early days of the Ohio Moral Majority, movement activists frequently stood out in their congregations as the most hostile toward liberal groups, and the most likely to think that politics was a struggle between good and evil. Moral Majority county leaders were usually Baptist Bible Fellowship pastors, and they told me that they sought out the most receptive members of their congregations. Christian Right members probably had lower levels of civic virtues even when they entered politics than those in the same churches who did not join.

But I also saw ample evidence that exposure to Christian Right direct mail and other materials increased the fear and intolerance of many members. In interviews with Christian Right women in 1982, several women told me that before they had joined the Moral Majority, they had been unaware of the many dangers surrounding them. One woman said, "I lay awake at night now and fear for my son." One older man had become fearful about secular humanists in the schools. As we talked, he admitted that he had visited the local school recently and seen no evidence of secular humanism, and in telling this he showed some relief. But by the end of the interview his fear had returned.

The Christian Right of the 1990s sought to train their activist base in the rules of democratic debate and in bridging differences in ethnicity, race, religion, and class. My qualitative work and other quantitative work suggest that fundamentalists in the Christian Right have bridged barriers of theology, working now with Pentecostals and Catholics. The amount of anti-Catholic bias in early Moral Majority organizations is difficult to overestimate and also difficult to imagine today. A tiny step perhaps from one perspective, but it represents a giant leap from the early 1980s.

Moreover, the Christian Coalition in particular trained its members to enter into deliberations with African-Americans, Latinos, Catholics, Jews, and libertarian Republicans. They sought out activists who could be "bilingual"—talking the language of conservative faith in local meetings but a more secular language in public. And many who went through this training appeared to me to gain in their ability to understand diverse perspectives. In the survey data, the subset with the highest levels of civic virtures is that which entered politics in the 1990s and that also worked with allied groups.

This may well explain the distinctive findings of Jon Shields (2007). Shields calls Jerry Falwell and Randal Terry marginal fundamentalists and devotes considerable attention to the efforts of groups like "Stand to Reason" and pro-life organizations as the "true" Christian Right. These latter organizations train their members to persuade others and thus try to instill democratic norms and perspective-taking ability. I have no doubt that these groups do instill democratic norms, but I see these groups as peripheral to the movement. Shields's more optimistic conclusions depend on his selection of organizations, but they do remind us that Christian conservative activism is not incompatible with civility and mutual respect.

Thus, I conclude that Christian Right membership probably had diverse effects on its members, depending on which group they joined and how they were active. For that smaller subset of members who joined groups that provided training in the art of politics, and who entered into political deliberations with members of other groups, Christian Right membership led to an increase in civic virtues. In a few cases among those whom I have personally interviewed, the change was substantial. But for those who were merely exposed to direct mail solicitations and publications, membership increased hostility and fear and led to greater intolerance. These results have implications for the study of other illiberal religious movements as well. Islamist parties generally have dense networks of social organizations that involve face-to-face contact, which should maximize the benefits of democratic participation. But comparative politics scholars who debate criteria for deciding which parties will have democratic consequences appear to be justified, for some groups in the Christian Right had a different impact than others.

Meanwhile, there is evidence that a new generation of evangelical activists has higher levels of civic virtues and a broader policy agenda. Many Christian Right groups were formed by Republican activists, whose motive was to affect elections rather than to instill democratic values. Republican financial resources poured into evangelical groups that were the most willing to increase evangelical turnout through fear. Other, more moderate evangelical voices had difficulty being heard over the volume of Christian Right mobilization (for a discussion of the political mobilization of religion, see Wald and Leege, chapter 11, this volume).

Today's younger evangelicals remain committed in opposition to abortion and same-sex marriage but are far less hostile toward gays and lesbians, feminists, and other liberal groups. Perhaps most importantly, they are less fearful that a tide of liberalism is sweeping across America. They attend churches that are growing and perceive that evangelicals can affect policy. They enter into dialogue with a range of political actors. It seems likely that membership in these new evangelical organizations has a more profound positive effect on democratic values and civic virtues.

Notes

1. Falwell was endorsing a statement by Southern Baptist Convention president Rev. Bailey Smith. Falwell later reversed this statement after meeting with the leaders of Jewish groups in Washington. See Marjorie Hyer, "Evangelicalist Reverses Position on God's Hearing the Prayer of Jews." *The Washington Post* October 11, 1980, p. A02.

2. Political theorists refer to civil virtues, civic virtues, and even pre-civic virtues. Here I use the term to refer to those attributes that enable citizens to engage in democratic politics, including social trust and reciprocity, deliberative skills, and tolerance.

3. For other work showing that religious ideas matter, see Harris, chapter 8, this volume.

4. It is important to note that many of these authors, including me, do not argue that all Christian Right activists are intolerant or uncivil.

5. Norfolk *Virginian-Pilot*, November 9, 1991.

6. Recent studies show that real deliberations occur in many churches, which might be expected to be places of easy exit (Neilheisel et al. 2006).

7. More recently, Jerry Falwell proclaimed that those who spoke in tongues (a sacred experience for Pentecostals) had eaten too much pizza the night before.

8. Putnam notes that the bridging-bonding distinction is sometimes a matter of degree, although this has been largely ignored by scholars writing in the field. (Putnam 2000, 22–23.)

9. Steve Forbes did not disclose the identity of his modest set of small donors, so we were unable to sample from them. Large and small contributions are raised differently—large contributions are usually raised through personal networks, whereas smaller contributions are solicited through direct mail, telemarketing, and e-mail appeals that use more extreme language. Although every set of results presented below was run separately for large and small donors, the relationships were nearly identical. Therefore, I will combine the two groups to simplify the presentation.

10. Analysis that weighted the data to reflect the portion of donors to each candidate yielded substantively identical results.

11. Thanks to Mark E. Warren for extensive consultation in developing these items.

12. The surprising 4 percent of Christian Right members who rated Christian fundamentalists at 0 occurs among Catholics and nonfundamentalist Evangelicals.

13. This result holds true even when controlled for state of residence—that is, it is not merely that Christian Right members live in states where liberal groups and the Christian Right are objectively more active.

14. For details of scale construction, contact the author.

15. http://www.gallup.com/poll/18802/Gallup-Panel-People-Cant-Trusted.aspx, accessed October 6, 2008.

16. Interestingly, party moderates have a greater history of defecting from Christian Right nominees than vice versa.

17. The dependent variables are factor scores from common factor analysis, rotated to allow correlation among factors. For details of the items in each scale contact the author.

18. Catholics are distinctive toward only one group for demonstrations—gays and lesbians. Gay rights groups have sought permission to march in various parades of special interest to Catholics, so this issue may have a distinctive frame.

19. A separate model exploring only the right to demonstrate for gays and lesbians showed that Christian Right members are distinctively intolerant on this single measure.

20. Models were estimated with measures of support for compromise and the belief that deliberation exposes dangerous ideas, but these attitudes were not significant and created instabilities in the estimation.

References

Almond, Gabriel A., R. Scott Appleby, and Emmanuel Sivan. 2003. *Strong Religion: The Rise of Fundamentalisms around the World*. Chicago: University of Chicago Press.

Ammerman, Nancy Tatom. 1987. *Bible Believers: Fundamentalists in the Modern World*. New Brunswick, NJ: Rutgers University Press.

Barabas, Jason. 2004. "How Deliberation Affects Policy Opinion." *American Political Science Review* 98:687–701.

Bates, Stephen. 1993. *Battleground: One Mother's Crusade, the Religious Right, and the Struggle for Control of Our Classrooms*. New York: Poseidon Press.

Beatty, Kathleen Murphy, and Oliver Walter. 1984. "Religious Preference and Practice: Reevaluating Their Impact on Political Tolerance." *The Public Opinion Quarterly* 48:318–29.

Bendyna, Mary, John C. Green, Mark J. Rozell, and Clyde Wilcox. 2000. "Catholics and the Christian Right: A View from Four States." *Journal for the Scientific Study of Religion* 39:321–32.

Berry, Jeffrey M., and Clyde Wilcox. 2007. *The Interest Group Society*. New York: Pearson Longman.

Boston, Robert. 2000. *Close Encounters with the Religious Right: Journeys into the Twilight Zone of Religion and Politics*. Amherst, NY: Prometheus.

Buell, Emmett, and Lee Sigelman. 1985. "An Army That Meets Every Sunday? Popular Support for the Moral Majority in 1980." *Social Science Quarterly* 66:426–34.

Buss, Doris, and Didi Herman. 2003. *Globalizing Family Values: The Christian Right in International Politics*. Minneapolis: University of Minnesota Press.

Campbell, David C., and Carin Robinson. 2007. "Religious Coalitions for and against Gay Marriage: The Culture War Rages On." In *The Politics of Same-Sex Marriage*. Chicago: University of Chicago Press.

Clark, Janine A. 2006. "The Conditions of Islamist Moderation." *International Journal of Middle East Studies* 38:539–60.

Gibson, James L. 1989. "The Structure of Attitudinal Tolerance in the United States." *British Journal of Political Science* 19:562–70.

———. 1992. "Alternative Measures of Political Tolerance: Must Tolerance be 'Least-Liked'?" *American Journal of Political Science* 36:560–77.

Gibson, James L., and Richard D. Bingham. 1982. "On the Conceptualization and Measurement of Political Tolerance." *The American Political Science Review* 76:603–620.

Green, John C. 1996. "A Look at the 'Invisible Army': Pat Robertson's 1988 Activist Corps." In *Religion and the Culture Wars: Dispatches from the Front*, 44–61, ed. J. C. Green, J. L. Guth, C. E. Smidt, and L. A. Kellstedt. Lanham, MD: Rowman & Littlefield.

Green, John C., and James L. Guth. 1988. "The Christian Right in the Republican Party: The Case of Pat Robertson's Supporters." *The Journal of Politics* 50:150–65.

Green, John C., James L. Guth, Lyman A. Kellstedt, and Corwin E. Smidt. 1994. "Uncivil Challenges? Support for Civil Liberties Among Religious Activists." *The Journal of Political Science* 22:25–49.

Guth, James L. 1983. "The New Christian Right." In *The New Christian Right: Mobilization and Legitimation*, 31–49, ed. R. C. Liebman and R. Wuthnow. New York: Aldine Publishing Company.

Guth, James L., and John C. Green. 1991. "An Ideology of Rights: Support for Civil Liberties among Political Activists." *Political Behavior* 13:321–44.

Guth, James L., John C. Green, Lyman A. Kellstedt, and Corwin E. Smidt. 1995. "Onward Christian Soldiers: Religious Activist Groups in American Politics." In *Interest Group Politics,* 4th ed., 55–76, ed. B. A. Loomis and A. J. Cigler. Washington, DC: CQ Press.

Gutmann, Amy, and Dennis F. Thompson. 1996. *Democracy and Disagreement.* Cambridge, MA: Belknap Press.

Haqqani, Husain, and Hillel Fradkin. 2008. "Islamist Parties: Going Back to Origins." *Journal of Democracy* 19:13–18.

Hedges, Chris. 2006. *American Facists: The Christian Right and the War on America.* New York: Free Press.

Jelen, Ted G. 1991. "Politicized Group Identification: The Case of Fundamentalism." *The Western Political Quarterly* 44:209–19.

Jelen, Ted G., and Clyde Wilcox. 1997. "Conscientious Objectors in the Culture War? A Typology of Attitudes toward Church-State Relations." *Sociology of Religion* 58:277–87.

Johnson, Stephen D., and Joseph B. Tamney. 1984. "Support for the Moral Majority: A Test of a Model." *Journal for the Scientific Study of Religion* 23:183–96.

Kalyvas, Stathis N. 2000. "Commitment Problems in Emerging Democracies: The Case of Religious Parties." *Comparative Politics* 32:379–98.

Kellstedt, Lyman. 1988. "The Falwell Issue Agenda: Sources of Support among White Protestant Evangelicals." In *An Annual in the Sociology of Religion*, ed. M. Lynn and D. Moberg. New York: JAI Press.

Lienesch, Michael. 1993. *Redeeming America: Piety and Politics in the New Christian Right.* Chapel Hill, NC: University of North Carolina Press.

Martin, William. 1996. *With God on Our Side: The Rise of the Religious Right in America.* New York: Broadway Books.

Marty, Martin E. 2003. "Our Religio-Secular World." *Daedalus* 132:42–48.

Moen, Matthew C. 1994. "From Revolution to Evolution: The Changing Nature of the Christian Right." *Sociology of Religion* 55:345–57.

Mutz, Diana C. 2002. "The Consequences of Cross-Cutting Networks for Political Participation." *American Journal of Political Science* 46:838–55.

———. 2006. *Hearing the Other Side: Deliberative versus Participatory Democracy.* Cambridge and New York: Cambridge University Press.

Neilheisel, Jacob R., Paul A. Djupe, and Anand E. Sokhey. 2006. "Veni, Vidi, Desseri: Churches and the Problem of Democratic Deliberation." *American Politics Research* 20:1–30.

Nunn, Clyde Z., Harry J. Crockett Jr., and J. Allen Williams. 1978. *Tolerance for Nonconformity.* San Francisco: Jossey-Bass.

Owen, Dennis E., Kenneth D. Wald, and Samuel S. Hill. 1991. "Authoritarian or Authority-Minded? The Cognitive Commitments of Fundamentalists and the Christian Right." *Religion and American Culture* 1:73–100.

Pettigrew, Thomas F. 1997. "Generalized Intergroup Contact Effects on Prejudice." *Personality and Social Psychology Bulletin* 23:173–85.

Price, Vincent, Josepth N. Cappella, and Lilach Nir. 2002. "Does Disagreement Contribute to More Deliberative Opinion?" *Political Communication* 19:19–112.

Putnam, Robert D. 2000. *Bowling Alone : The Collapse and Revival of American Community.* New York: Simon & Schuster.

Reed, Ralph. 1994. *After the Revolution.* Dallas: Word Publishers.

Reimer, Sam, and Jerry Z. Park. 2001. "Tolerant (In)civility? A Longitudinal Analysis of White Conservative Protestants' Willingness to Grant Civil Liberties." *Journal for the Scientific Study of Religion* 40:735–45.

Robinson, Carin. 2008. "Doctrine, Discussion and Disagreement: Evangelical and Catholics Together in American Politics." PhD diss., Georgetown University, Washington, DC.

Rosenblum, Nancy L. 2000. *Membership and Morals.* Princeton, NJ: Princeton University Press.

———. 2003. "Religious Parties, Religious Political Identity, and the Cold Shoulder of Liberal Democratic Thought." *Ethical Theory and Moral Practice* 6:25–53.

Rozell, Mark J., and Clyde Wilcox. 1995. *God at the Grass Roots: The Christian Right in the 1994 Elections.* Lanham, MD: Rowman & Littlefield.

———. 1996a. *Second Coming: The New Christian Right in Virginia Politics.* Baltimore: Johns Hopkins University Press.

———. 1996b. "Second Coming: The Strategies of the New Christian Right." *Political Science Quarterly* 111:271–94.

Rozell, Mark J., Clyde Wilcox, and John C. Green. 1998. "Religious Constituencies and Support for the Christian Right in the 1990s." *Social Science Quarterly* 79:815–27.

Sartre, Jean-Paul. 1955. *No Exit, and Three Other Plays*. New York: Vintage Books.

Schwedler, Jillian. 2006. *Faith in Moderation: Islamist Parties in Jordan and Yemen*. Cambridge and New York: Cambridge University Press.

Shields, Jon A. 2007. "Between Passion and Deliberation: The Christian Right and Democratic Ideals." *Political Science Quarterly* 12:89–113.

Smith, Rogers M. 2008. "Religious Rhetoric and the Ethnics of Public Discourse." *Political Theory* 36:272–300.

Sullivan, John Lawrence, James Piereson, and George E. Marcus. 1982. *Political Tolerance and American Democracy*. Chicago: University of Chicago Press.

Sunstein, Cass R. 2000. "Deliberative Trouble? Why Groups Go to Extremes." *Yale Law Journal* 110:71–119.

Tinder, Glenn E. 1989. *The Political Meaning of Christianity: An Interpretation*. Baton Rouge: Louisiana State University Press.

Truman, David Bicknell. 1951. *The Governmental Process: Political Interests and Public Opinion*. New York: Knopf.

Wald, Kenneth D., Dennis E. Owen, and Samuel S. Hill Jr. 1989. "Habits of the Mind? The Problem of Authority in the New Christian Right." In *Religion and Political Behavior in the United States*, 93–108, ed. T. G. Jelen. New York: Praeger.

Wald, Kenneth D., Adam L. Silverman, and Kevin Fridy. 2005. "Making Sense of Religion in Political Life." *Annual Review of Political Science* 8:121–43.

Wald, Kenneth D., and Clyde Wilcox. 2006. "Getting Religion: Has Political Science Rediscovered the Faith Factor." *American Political Science Review* 100:523–29.

Warren, Mark E. 1999. *Democracy and Trust*. Cambridge and New York: Cambridge University Press.

Warren, Mark R. 2001. *Dry Bones Rattling: Community Building to Revitalize American Democracy*. Princeton, NJ: Princeton University Press.

Weisskopf, Michael. 1993. "Energized by Pulpit or Passion, the Public is Calling." *The Washington Post*, February 1, A1.

Wilcox, Clyde. 1989. "Evangelicals and the Moral Majority." *Journal for the Scientific Study of Religion* 28:400–14.

———. 1992a. *God's Warriors: The Christian Right in Twentieth-Century America*. Baltimore: Johns Hopkins University Press.

———. 1992b. "Religion and the Preacher Vote in the South: Sources of Support for Jackson and Robertson in Southern Primaries." *Sociological Analysis* 53:323–32.

Wilcox, Clyde, and Ted G. Jelen. 1990. "Evangelicals and Political Tolerance." *American Politics Quarterly* 18:25–46.

Wilcox, Clyde, Ted G. Jelen, and Sharon Linzey. 1995. "Rethinking the Reasonableness of the Religious Right." *Review of Religious Research* 36:263–76.

Wilcox, Clyde, and Carin Larson. 2006. *Onward Christian Soldiers: The Christian Right in American Politics*, 3rd ed. Boulder, CO: Westview.

Wilcox, Clyde, Sharon Linzey, and Ted G. Jelen. 1991. "Reluctant Warriors: Premillennialism and Politics in the Moral Majority." *Journal for the Scientific Study of Religion* 30:245–58.

Wilcox, Clyde, Mark J. Rozell, and Roland Gunn. 1996. “Religious Coalitions in the New Christian Right.” *Social Science Quarterly* 77:543–59.

Wittes, Tamara Cofman. 2008. “Islamist Parties: Three Kinds of Movements.” *Journal of Democracy* 19:7–12.

Chapter 7

RELIGION AND PARTY ACTIVISTS

A "Perfect Storm" of Polarization or a Recipe for Pragmatism?

GEOFFREY C. LAYMAN

FAR AND AWAY the dominant theme in recent observations about American party politics is that the two major parties are growing increasingly polarized, with the Republican Party moving in a conservative direction on nearly all major issues of public policy while the Democratic Party stakes out consistently liberal ground. Party polarization has been an exceedingly popular topic for journalists such as *New York Times* columnist Paul Krugman (2002), who contends that "Fundamental issues are at stake, and the parties are as far apart on those issues as they ever have been"; *Washington Post* commentator George F. Will (2004), who notes that "Never [has American] politics been more European, meaning organized around ideologically homogeneous parties"; and Ronald Brownstein (2007), who, in his book *The Second Civil War*, contends that "From Congress and the White House through the grassroots, the parties today are becoming less diverse, more ideologically homogeneous, and less inclined to pursue reasonable agreements" (2007, 11). Focusing on polarization has been no less fashionable among political scientists, who have produced a plethora of research showing a substantial and widening policy gap between the parties' leaders, elected officials, and mass coalitions (Rohde 1991; Abramowitz and Saunders 1998, 2005; Hetherington 2001; Stonecash et al. 2003; Jacobson 2005; McCarty et al. 2006; Sinclair 2006; Black and Black 2007). Moreover, scholars have shown that this fissure is expanding not just on newer issues or a particular issue agenda but in a host of policy domains—from cultural and lifestyle issues to race and to economic and social welfare issues (Poole and Rosenthal 1997; Layman and Carsey 2002; Layman et al. 2006; Brewer and Stonecash 2007).

Accompanying, and perhaps flowing from, the growing ideological divergence of the two major parties have been important and potentially negative changes in the style of American politics. Political rhetoric has become increasingly strident and personal not only in discussions on radio, television, and the Internet but also in debates on the House and Senate floors (Uslaner 1993; Jamieson and Falk 2000; Sinclair 2006). Political advertising is more and more negative, focusing on the personal and policy weaknesses of candidates' opponents rather than on their own strengths or ideas (Geer 2006; Sinclair 2006). Political campaigns seem to be placing greater emphasis on mobilizing their ideological and partisan bases and less weight on garnering the support of centrist swing voters (Sinclair 2006).

This combination of increased substantive differences between the parties and an increasingly strident, attacking, and base-focused political style clearly has important consequences for American democracy. Most observers, not surprisingly, see these consequences as negative, arguing that such a combination produces inflexible parties and elected officials who are unable or unwilling to compromise with each other to achieve policy goals (Brock 2004; Brownstein 2007). The resulting stalemate in policy making (Jones 2001; Binder 2003) leaves important societal needs unmet and thus diminishes levels of political engagement, trust, and participation among ordinary citizens—particularly those who occupy the political center (Dionne 1991; Shea 2003; Fiorina et al. 2005; Brownstein 2007). As a *Washington Post* (2004) editorial noted in the aftermath of the 2004 election, "Polarization is worrisome. . . . It can condemn Congress to gridlock . . . [and] it can alienate citizens from their government."

Not all political onlookers, however, take such a dim view of policy divergence between the parties. In fact, almost from their founding, the major criticism of the American parties has been not that they are too polarized but that they are too similar. Such complaints were heard in the 1830s, when the famous French political observer Alexis de Tocqueville wrote that "great political parties . . . more attached to ideas rather than to personalities . . . no longer exist[ed]" in the United States (Tocqueville 1966 [1835], 61), were reasserted in 1888 when British politician and intellectual James Bryce suggested that "neither party has any clean-cut principles, any distinctive tenets" (Bryce 1995 [1888], 699), and were offered most famously in 1968, when independent presidential candidate George Wallace allowed that "there's not a dime's worth of difference" between the two major parties. In political science, the most well-known of these laments was provided in 1950 by the Committee on Political Parties of the American Political Science Association. It argued that "alternatives between the parties are defined so badly that it is often difficult to determine what the election has decided even in broadest terms," and called for more programmatic and cohesive parties (American Political Science Association 1950, 3–4).

In keeping with such sentiments, recent research suggests that increases in party polarization may strengthen the parties in the electorate (Bartels

2000; Hetherington 2001), increase the ideological sophistication of citizens (Pomper and Weiner 2002; Layman and Carsey 2002), and perhaps even spur increases in voter turnout (Abramowitz and Saunders 2005). Moreover, ideologically distinct and internally cohesive parties may be more likely to keep their campaign promises and to act on policy issues in a coherent way after elections, thus making it easier for voters to hold the winning party accountable for its policy actions (Crotty 2001; Pomper 2003) and possibly enhancing policy representation in the American political process.

Whether positive or negative, it is clear that the growth of party polarization and the accompanying increase in stridency and dogmatism have fundamental consequences for the health of American democracy. The question for this chapter is the degree to which changes in the religious characteristics of party activists—political actors who play vitally important roles in choosing the parties' nominees, shaping their policy agendas, and providing funds and manpower for their general election campaigns—have contributed to these developments.

In particular, I address two possibilities. The first is that changes in the religious composition of the parties' activist bases—especially the growing presence of devout evangelical Protestants and other religious "traditionalists" among GOP activists and of secular (nonreligious) individuals and religious "modernists" in the Democratic activist corps—have contributed to party polarization and to political inflexibility and stridency. They may have increased polarization because the ascendant religious groups in each party may have more extreme issue positions than their fellow partisans—most notably on cultural and moral issues, but on a host of other policy agendas as well. They may have encouraged greater dogmatism in political discourse because these religious groups are more likely than other party activists to be political "purists," passionately committed to their policy positions and unwilling to compromise on those positions. Put differently, it may be that the manifestation of a religious cleavage known for its polarizing and impassioning tendencies among a set of political actors—party activists—notorious for their ideological extremity, unyielding policy commitments, and outsized influence on the parties has produced a "perfect storm" of polarization and dogmatism in American politics.

The second possibility is more encouraging from a normative standpoint. It is that although party involvement by groups at the extremes of the American religious spectrum may have pushed the parties to more polarized and unyielding policy positions, this very involvement also may encourage the members of those groups to adopt more pragmatic and flexible approaches to politics over time. In other words, the very nature of party politics, with its emphasis on electoral victory and coalition building, may provide something of a cure for its own disease.

To assess these possibilities, I turn to surveys of Democratic and Republican national convention delegates from 1972 through 2004. I use those data to examine change over time in the religious orientations of party activists and the consequences of that change for the policy positions and political norms of the parties' activist bases. I find support for both ideas. The growth of committed evangelicalism among Republican activists and of secularism among active Democrats has pushed the parties' policy positions toward the ideological extremes and increased support within the parties for a purist approach to politics. At the same time, long-term participation in party politics makes some groups of activists—committed evangelical Republicans, in particular—more pragmatic in their political styles.

Religion, Policy Polarization, and Political Norms among Party Activists

There are a number of culprits for the growth of party polarization and political stridency in American politics. However, outside of the political realignment of the South, the two that seem to be identified most often by scholars are the important and growing role of activists in party politics and the emergence of a new religious divide between the two major parties.

Activists as a Mainspring of Polarization

A number of scholars have identified party activists as the principal catalysts for the recent growth in ideological polarization between the Democratic and Republican Parties in government and in the electorate (Aldrich and Rohde 2001; Shafer 2003; Saunders and Abramowitz 2004; Fiorina et al. 2005; Layman et al. 2006). This is hardly surprising because theoretical work long has argued that party activists help to pull parties and candidates away from the political center and to create partisan differences on policy issues (Aranson and Ordeshook 1972; Aldrich 1983, 1995; Chappell and Keech 1986; Shafer and Claggett 1995; Miller and Schofield 2003).

Activists play such a role because they are disproportionately represented in the primaries and caucuses that determine party nominees in the United States (Ranney 1972; Aldrich 1995; Fiorina et al. 2005), because party nominees also need activists' financial support and manpower in order to win general elections (e.g., Miller and Schofield 2003), and because activists simply hold more ideologically extreme views than do ordinary voters or the rank-and-file members of their parties (Ranney 1972; Miller and Jennings 1986). The polarizing impulse that activists exert on the parties may have grown even further in recent decades as the presidential nominating process has grown more open, increasing the influence of activists relative to that of party leaders (Aldrich 1995); as substantial declines in congressional primary turnout have made party activists a more disproportionate share of those electorates (King 2003); and as activists themselves have grown more polarized on a range of policy dimensions (Saunders and Abramowitz 2004; Layman, Carsey, Green, Herrera, and Cooperman 2010).

Another characteristic of party activists that may promote party polarization also may encourage inflexibility—and perhaps incivility—in political deliberation. Activists tend to be motivated strongly by their policy preferences and thus to eschew compromise on those preferences. This has become more true over the last half-century as party "professionals" or "pragmatists" motivated by partisan victory and material gain increasingly have been replaced by "amateurs" or "purists" motivated primarily by ideology and unwilling to sacrifice their policy goals to the goal of party victory (Wilson 1962; Wildavsky 1965; Soule and Clarke 1970; Aldrich 1995; Fiorina et al. 2005).

The "Culture Wars" Divide and Party Polarization

The division of the Democratic and Republican Parties along the lines of a new cleavage in American religion has the potential to exacerbate these tendencies of party activists. Religious differences between the parties and their coalitions are, of course, not new. However, in recent decades, the traditional fault lines between the great faith traditions, with Catholics and Jews (along with black and southern Protestants) comprising the spiritual backbone of the Democratic coalition and Protestants (outside of the South) playing that role within the GOP (Berelson et al. 1954; Green 2007), may have given way to a new political divide both within and between these traditions.

This new fissure—referred to as a theological or religious "restructuring" in some works (Wuthnow 1988; Smidt et al. 2009) but most commonly known by the "culture wars" label given to it by James Davison Hunter (1991)—is based primarily on religious beliefs and behaviors and pits individuals who subscribe to traditionalist religious beliefs and engage in traditional religious practices against those who hold modernist beliefs and disavow traditional forms of worship. Several scholars document a growing division of the parties along traditionalist-modernist religious lines, with religious traditionalists—especially the most devout members of the theologically conservative evangelical Protestant denominations—gravitating toward the Republican Party, while the Democratic camp increasingly is comprised of religious modernists and seculars—those individuals with no religious affiliation at all (Kohut et al. 2000; Layman 2001; Green 2007; McTague and Layman 2009).[1]

Particularly relevant here is the fact that this new divide has emerged most clearly among the parties' activists, with committed evangelicals and other religious traditionalists becoming an increasingly large and influential force among GOP activists while seculars and religious modernists grow in numbers and importance among active Democrats (Layman 1999, 2001; Green and Jackson 2007; McTague and Layman 2009). In fact, although there is considerable debate about the degree to which the traditionalist-modernist divide has emerged within mass public opinion and partisanship, even the critics of the culture wars perspective acknowledge its clear significance for activist-level politics (e.g., Williams 1997; Fiorina et al. 2005).

The new religious divide between Republican and Democratic activists clearly may have contributed to levels of policy polarization between the parties, and it may have done so in both direct and indirect ways. The direct contribution lies in the simple fact that the policy perspectives of religious traditionalists on the one hand and religious modernists and seculars on the other hand tend to be quite divergent. The gap is widest on cultural issues such as abortion, gay rights, and prayer in the public schools (Kohut et al. 2000; Layman and Green 2006).

However, Hunter argues that the "rhetorical leadership" (1991, 281) of religious and political elites may extend the influence of the traditionalist-modernist cleavage beyond the moral and cultural issue agenda, thereby creating an "isomorphism between religious conservatism and political preservationism . . . and between religious liberalism . . . and political reformism" (1991, 128). Empirical work suggests that Hunter overstated the case but does find some connection between religious traditionalism and conservatism not just on cultural issues but also in social welfare attitudes, views on defense and foreign policy issues, and in general ideological identifications (Layman and Green 2006). Thus, as committed evangelicals and other religious traditionalists become a larger component of the Republican activist base and seculars and religious modernists become better represented among active Democrats, the policy differences between the two parties' activists should grow, and that rift should push the issue positions of the parties' candidates and platforms farther apart.

The growing representation of these religious groups among party activists may make a more-indirect contribution to policy polarization by influencing the participation decisions and policy attitudes of activists in other religious groups. One of the leading accounts of party activist change contends that individuals thinking about involvement in a political party—whether they are potential activists deciding whether or not to become involved or current activists deciding whether or not to remain involved—base their decisions on the overall policy views of the party's current activist corps (Aldrich 1983, 1995). Other work suggests that the policy attitudes of current party activists also are shaped by the views of other activists—individual activists may bring their policy outlooks into line with the predominant views of their fellow activists (Miller and Jennings 1986; Layman and Carsey 1998; Layman, Carsey, Green, Herrera, and Cooperman 2010). Increases in the representation of devout evangelicals within the GOP activist corps and of seculars among active Democrats should affect the participation decisions and policy attitudes of other activists in a way that should result in greater conservatism, in the aggregate, among the Republican activists from all religious groups and greater liberalism among Democratic activists from across the religious spectrum. In other words, the policy differences between the same religious groups in different parties should grow larger over time.[2]

The Religious Divide and Purist-Pragmatist Political Norms

The growing religious chasm between active Republicans and Democrats also may help to account for the increasingly strident and inflexible style of American politics. Because of the essential incongruity between the traditionalist and modernist moral visions, there is a tendency for those on each side to view the positions of the other camp as illegitimate and thus to see compromise with political opponents as morally bankrupt (Hunter 1991, 1994; Himmelfarb 1999; White 2003). Moreover, the ascendant religious cadres in the parties may bear the usual hallmark of new activist groups pursuing relatively new policy agendas—they may be "more concerned with victory for their position on the new issue than with their party's electoral success" (Sundquist 1983, 308). In fact, other research finds that secular Democratic activists and committed evangelical activists in the GOP tend to be political "amateurs" or "purists," displaying stronger commitments to their policy agendas than to the party and eschewing compromise on policy issues to improve the prospects of electoral victory (Kirkpatrick 1976; Freeman 1986; Layman 2001).

On the other hand, party activity itself may provide a remedy for the "ailment" of purist sensibilities and ideological dogmatism that traditionalist Republican activists and secular Democratic activists may have helped to infect in it. Because political parties exist primarily to win elections and shape public policy, involvement in them may, over the long run, instill in activists the pragmatism and willingness to compromise that are often necessary to achieve electoral victory or to fashion policy coalitions. In fact, past research has demonstrated a connection between length of involvement in party politics on one hand and commitment to party victory and political pragmatism on the other hand (Conway and Feigert 1968; Roback 1975; Abramowitz et al. 1983; Stone and Abramowitz 1983), and such a connection actually may grow stronger as the parties grow more ideologically polarized. As partisan policy differences increase, the idea of the other party gaining power may grow more repugnant to issue-motivated activists, thus making them more receptive to compromise on their party's nominees and platforms in order to keep that from happening. In short, the longer that religious traditionalists are involved in the GOP and religious modernists and seculars are active Democrats, the more likely they may be to adopt a "professional" and pragmatic approach to politics.

Such a pattern may be especially evident among committed evangelical Republicans because the Christian Right organizations that have worked to mobilize evangelicals into the GOP seem to have become more pragmatic as they have matured and their relationship with the party has strengthened (e.g., Oldfield 1996). Many of these organizations have started downplaying theological language and rationales for policy positions, building a more broadly ecumenical base of support, and broadening their issue agendas beyond the core moral issues. They have even been willing to accept compromise and incremental, rather than radical, change on some cultural issues (Oldfield 1996; Rozell 1997; Green et al. 2006; Rozell and Gupta 2006).[3] Situated not only in a political party but also in a maturing Christian Right movement, evangelical Republican activists may be especially likely to become more politically "professional" the longer they are active in the GOP.

Data

To examine changes over time in the religious orientations of party activists and their relevance for partisan policy polarization and activists' political norms, I turn to the Convention Delegate Studies (CDS), a series of surveys of Democratic and Republican national convention delegates and presidential campaign activists from 1972 to 2004. The CDS surveys from 1972 to 1992 were conducted by Warren E. Miller and other scholars.[4] The 2000 CDS was modeled after the earlier CDS surveys and included both a cross-sectional survey of year 2000 convention delegates and a panel survey of respondents to the 1992 CDS.[5] The 2004 CDS combined an online survey and a mail survey of delegates to the 2004 party conventions and included questions that were identical or similar to those in prior CDS surveys.[6]

The CDS provide the most appropriate data source for this inquiry for several reasons. First, the CDS is the only longitudinal study of national convention delegates to consistently contain indicators of religious orientations. Each of the CDS surveys includes questions about denominational affiliation and frequency of church or synagogue attendance, and the 2000 and 2004 surveys also asked respondents about their view of the

Bible and their religious identifications. Second, as the longest-running set of surveys of American party activists, the surveys allow me to document changes in religious and policy polarization between Democratic and Republican activists over the longest time span possible. Finally, national convention delegates are among the most visible and important groups of party activists. They help draft party platforms, often occupy party leadership roles, and, during the national conventions, receive more media coverage than other groups of party activists. Thus, they may have considerable influence on the parties' policy positions and may send a particularly strong signal about those positions to both potential party activists and ordinary voters. At the same time, the composition of the parties' convention delegations reflects the outcomes of a presidential nomination process in which activists at a more grassroots level participate and wield influence. Thus, although delegates may represent a relatively "elite" level of party activism, they may provide a useful indicator of the religious orientations, policy positions, and political norms of the grassroots-level activists who participate in presidential primaries and caucuses.[7]

Religious Change among Party Activists

To take a first look at the degree to which the traditionalist-modernist religious divide between party activists has grown over time, I use the 2000 and 2004 CDS surveys to examine the religious orientations of various delegate cohorts, defined by the year in which respondents were first national convention delegates. Following Green's representation of the American religious landscape in chapter 2, table 7.1 describes these cohorts in terms of both religious "tradition" and level of religious traditionalism.[8] In addition to the five major traditions in the United States—evangelical Protestants, mainline Protestants, black Protestants, Catholics, and Jews—and seculars, the table includes smaller traditions such as the Eastern Orthodox faiths, conservative nontraditional faiths such as Mormons, liberal nontraditional religions such as Unitarians, and other (non-Judeo-Christian) religions.[9] I divide the members of the three largest religious traditions (Catholics and evangelical and mainline Protestants) into three levels of religious traditionalism (traditionalist, centrist, and modernist) based on their view of the Bible, religious identifications, and frequency of worship attendance.[10]

The table reveals both important changes over time in the religious characteristics of Republican and Democratic delegates and sharp religious differences between the two parties' activist bases. The key development is the marked increase over time in the representation of traditionalist evangelicals among Republican activists and of seculars among active Democrats. Among individuals who first attended national

TABLE 7.1
Religious Orientations of Republican and Democratic National Convention Delegates by Delegate Cohort (in Percentages)

	First year as delegate				
	Pre-1992	1992	1996	2000	2004
Republicans					
Evangelical Protestants					
Traditionalist	12.3	22.0	28.8	24.5	25.8
Centrist	4.7	3.0	4.2	2.8	2.3
Modernist	0.4	—[a]	—	—	—
Mainline Protestants					
Traditionalist	23.3	16.1	22.9	17.5	8.6
Centrist	23.0	20.3	12.7	16.7	21.6
Modernist	0.7	2.1	—	1.4	1.6
Catholics					
Traditionalist	18.3	14.4	11.9	13.9	12.2
Centrist	5.7	7.2	5.9	8.0	11.7
Modernist	0.7	—	0.9	0.7	1.4
Black Protestants	0.3	0.9	2.5	1.7	5.3
Eastern Orthodox	1.0	0.9	0.9	0.2	0.5
Conservative nontraditional	1.0	4.2	3.4	2.8	3.6
Liberal nontraditional	0.3	0.9	—	0.7	0.9
Jewish	2.9	1.7	2.5	1.4	1.8
Other faiths	—	—	—	.5	.9
Secular	3.6	6.4	3.4	7.2	2.7
Democrats					
Evangelical Protestants					
Traditionalist	4.0	4.7	4.2	4.5	1.0
Centrist	4.6	4.1	2.8	4.1	1.8
Modernist	0.4	0.4	0.5	0.2	1.0
Mainline Protestants					
Traditionalist	3.7	2.8	5.1	4.3	2.3
Centrist	16.2	16.8	18.6	15.0	20.2
Modernist	3.3	3.9	2.8	2.5	3.0
Catholics					
Traditionalist	6.5	5.5	4.2	4.7	5.1
Centrist	17.9	18.0	17.7	18.4	13.6
Modernist	4.6	4.9	6.5	2.7	2.5
Black Protestants	11.0	5.3	7.4	8.5	6.3
Eastern Orthodox	0.4	1.6	1.4	0.5	0.5
Conservative nontraditional	0.6	0.6	0.5	1.0	1.0
Liberal nontraditional	6.0	7.3	3.7	9.3	4.0
Jewish	9.2	7.7	7.4	8.0	9.6
Other faiths	0.6	0.8	1.9	1.8	3.3
Secular	11.2	15.6	15.4	14.4	24.9

Source: 2000 and 2004 Convention Delegate Studies.

[a] Indicates that no delegates fell into this category in a particular year.

conventions before 1992, traditionalist evangelicals made up a noticeable, but relatively modest segment of the GOP activist base, and clear pluralities of delegates came from the ranks of traditionalist and centrist mainline Protestants. However, evangelical traditionalists markedly increased their presence in the GOP in the 1990s and 2000s and were the numerically dominant religious group among Republican activists in every year from 1992 to 2004. In the Democratic activist base, seculars were a noticeable presence among first-time delegates in the years prior to 1992.[11] Secular representation was somewhat greater in the 1992 cohort and remained at a similar level among first-time delegates in 1996 and 2000. In 2004, however, the presence of seculars among first-time Democratic delegates grew substantially, making secular delegates a plurality of the party's activist base.[12]

Three aspects of table 7.1 merit further attention. First, there has been some asymmetry in the growth of traditionalist evangelicalism in the GOP and in Democratic secularism. Evangelical traditionalists have constituted nearly a quarter of—and a plurality of—the Republican delegate cohorts in every convention year since 1992, whereas the representation of seculars within Democratic delegate cohorts only rose to that level in 2004. This may suggest that the rise of Democratic secularism occurred in response to circumstances particular to 2004—perhaps a reaction to President Bush's overt religiosity, his close ties to evangelicals and cultural conservatives, or his prosecution of the war in Iraq—and may not be sustained at the same levels as Republican evangelicalism. On the other hand, seculars have been a much stronger presence in Democratic cohorts than in Republican cohorts throughout this period, and the bottom line is that these religiously polarized activist groups—secular Democrats and traditionalist evangelical Republicans—were the plurality groups in their respective parties in 2004.

Second, the representation of traditionalist evangelicals among Republican activists and of seculars among active Democrats in 2004 was quite comparable to the contribution of these groups to the parties' electoral coalitions in 2000 and 2004 (see Green's table 2.7 in chapter 2). However, where there is evidence of greater religious polarization among activists than in the parties in the electorate is in the presence of each party's ascendant group in the other party. Among activists, there were virtually no secular Republicans (2.7 percent) or evangelical Democrats (3.8 percent) in 2004, whereas secular Republicans (9 percent) and evangelical Democrats (12.6 percent) are much better represented in the parties' mass coalitions.

Third, the ascendance of traditionalist evangelical Republicans and of secular Democrats has accentuated a broader and apparently longstanding traditionalist-modernist cleavage between the parties' activist

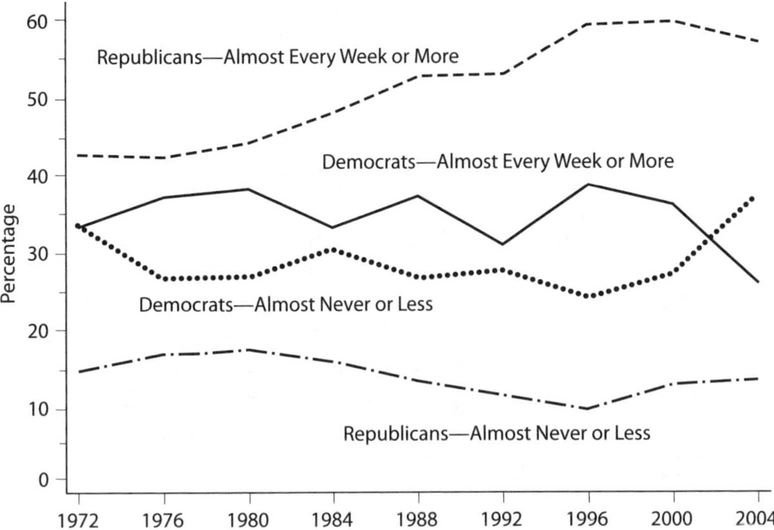

Figure 7.1. Worship attendance of presidential campaign activists, 1972–2004. Source: 1972–2004 Convention Delegate Studies.

bases. The percentage of all evangelicals among Republicans nearly doubles or more than doubles the same percentage among Democrats in all cohorts, and, as noted above, the percentage of seculars among Democrats is at least twice that among Republicans in all of the cohorts. There are much higher percentages of Jews and members of liberal nontraditional faiths—two groups with generally modernist religious and cultural tendencies—among Democrats than among Republicans in all cohorts. Finally, there are substantial percentages of mainline Protestants and Catholics in all of the cohorts for both parties. However, in most cohorts, a plurality or near plurality of Republican mainliners and Catholics hold traditionalist religious beliefs, practices, and identifications, whereas the Democrats in those traditions are more likely to have centrist or modernist orientations.

This pattern of clear and growing religious polarization between the parties' activists is also evident in levels of worship attendance among Republican and Democratic activists from 1972 through 2004.[13] Figure 7.1 shows that the difference in frequent attendance between Republican and Democratic delegates was relatively small in 1972 (9 percentage points) but had grown markedly (to over 28 percentage points) by 2004. The low-attendance part of the figure confirms the picture painted by other research of staunch secularism at the 1972 Democratic convention (Kirkpatrick 1976; Layman 2001). Over 30 percent of delegates to that convention almost never or never attended worship services, whereas fewer than 15 percent of 1972 Republican delegates fell into that category. That partisan gap grew smaller in 1976 with a sizable decline in low or nonattendance among Democrats. In 2004, however, it became even larger than it was in 1972, as over 37 percent of Democratic delegates (as compared to 13 percent of Republican delegates) claimed to never or almost never attend worship services.

As in table 7.1, figure 7.1 shows that the increase in religious traditionalism among active Republicans has been quite steady, whereas the growth of nonreligion among Democratic activists took shape rapidly between 2000 and 2004. However, the upshot again is a substantial and growing religious divide between the parties' activists. Religious traditionalists are becoming a larger presence among Republican activists, while seculars and other less-traditionally religious groups are increasing their ranks among active Democrats.

Religion and Policy Polarization

Has the mounting religious divide between Republican and Democratic activists contributed to the growth of ideological and policy polarization between the two parties? The evidence in table 7.2 suggests that it has, and not just on the moral and cultural issues most closely related to the traditionalist-modernist cleavage. In that table, I show the mean attitudes of 2000 presidential campaign activists in various religious groups on cultural issues, social welfare issues, racial issues, and federal defense spending as well as on liberal-conservative ideological identification.[14] Not surprisingly, Republican activists are much more conservative than Democrats in every issue domain and in ideology, and the divisions between Republicans and Democrats in the same religious category also are considerable. Less substantial, but still important, are the intraparty differences between religious groups. On virtually every measure, the traditionalist members of the largest faith traditions are at least slightly more conservative than their centrist and modernist counterparts within both parties. These gaps are largest on cultural issues but are present in each policy domain and in overall ideology.

Moreover, the ascendant religious groups among Republicans and Democrats are clearly positioned at the ideological extremes of their parties. Traditionalist evangelical Protestants in the GOP are the most conservative Republican group on every measure, whereas seculars are one of the most liberal Democratic groups in every category. Figure 7.2 highlights the fact that traditionalist evangelical Republicans are noticeably more conservative than all other Republican activists on every dimension, whereas seculars are more liberal than nonsecular Democrats on each

TABLE 7.2
Policy Attitudes and Ideology of 2000 Presidential Campaign Activists by Religious Tradition and Religious Traditionalism

	Cultural issues	Social welfare issues	Racial issues	Defense spending	Ideological identification
Republicans					
Evangelical Protestants					
Traditionalist	0.76	0.60	0.62	0.72	0.70
Centrist	0.34	0.46	0.54	0.66	0.40
Mainline Protestants					
Traditionalist	0.46	0.46	0.52	0.66	0.46
Centrist	0.20	0.40	0.44	0.58	0.28
Catholics					
Traditionalist	0.54	0.44	0.44	0.64	0.50
Centrist	0.22	0.42	0.42	0.58	0.28
Conservative nontraditional	0.44	0.46	0.46	0.52	0.52
Jewish	0.20	0.38	0.52	0.44	0.44
Secular	0.18	0.42	0.58	0.60	0.32
Democrats					
Evangelical Protestants					
Traditionalist	–0.16	–0.38	–0.06	0.12	–0.10
Centrist	–0.40	–0.50	–0.48	0.01	–0.34
Mainline Protestants					
Traditionalist	–0.30	–0.36	–0.12	0.20	–0.18
Centrist	–0.56	–0.48	–0.22	–0.06	–0.36
Modernist	–0.70	–0.62	–0.28	–0.16	–0.52
Catholics					
Traditionalist	–0.04	–0.34	–0.10	0.18	–0.14
Centrist	–0.44	–0.46	–0.22	–0.04	–0.32
Modernist	–0.66	–0.56	–0.26	–0.14	–0.50
Black Protestants	–0.36	–0.42	–0.60	–0.10	–0.34
Liberal nontraditional	–0.74	–0.60	–0.38	–0.24	–0.60
Jewish	–0.82	–0.54	–0.34	–0.10	–0.48
Secular	–0.72	–0.60	–0.40	–0.32	–0.60

Source: 2000 Convention Delegate Study.
Note: Entries are mean values on scales ranging from –1 for most liberal to 1 for most conservative.

dimension. These differences are statistically significant on every variable in both parties. In fact, although there may have been some asymmetry in the patterns of growth among traditionalist evangelical Republicans and secular Democrats, there is no irregularity in the policy extremity of the two groups. Democratic seculars are more liberal than their fellow partisans to about the same degree as traditionalist evangelicals in the GOP are more conservative than theirs. It clearly appears that the religious

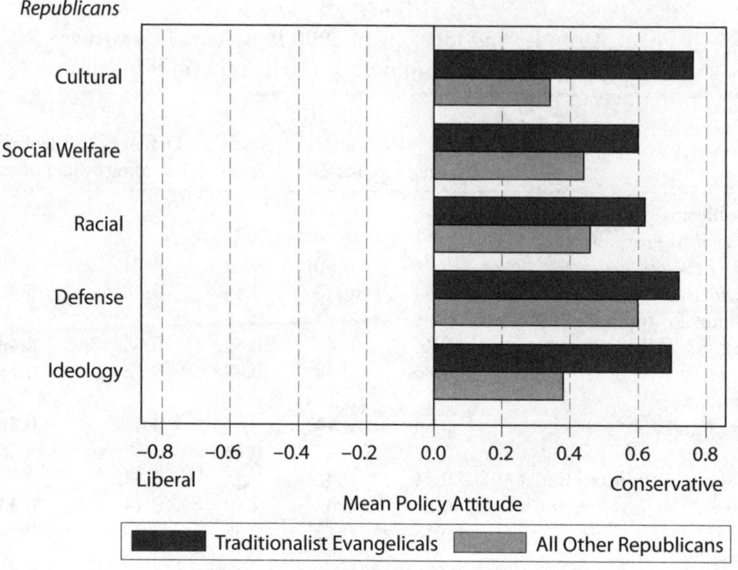

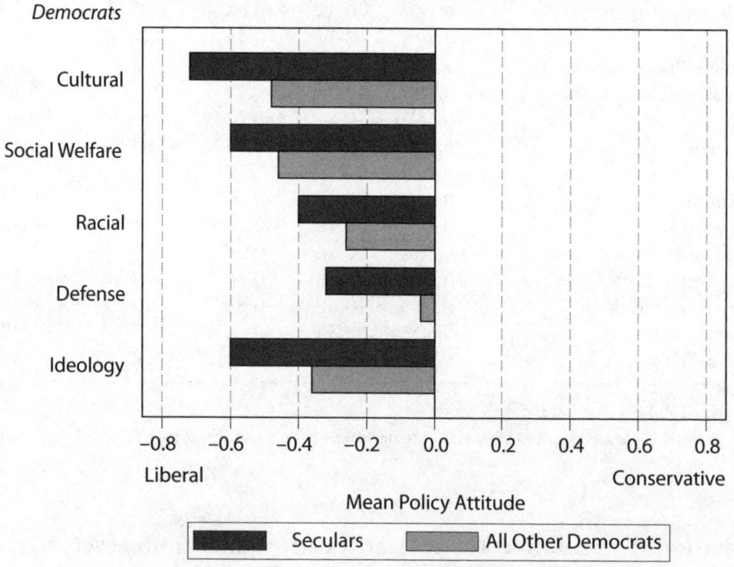

Figure 7.2. Policy attitudes and ideology: traditionalist evangelicals versus other Republicans and seculars versus other Democrats. Source: 2000 Convention Delegate Study. Note: Policy attitudes and ideology range from –1 (most liberal) to 1 (most conservative).

polarization and the ideological polarization of party activists have gone hand in hand.[15]

In fact, the degree to which the religious cleavage between party activists has helped to heighten ideological polarization between the parties may be both larger and more subtle than the relatively straightforward evidence of traditionalist evangelical conservatism in the GOP and Democratic secular liberalism suggest. As I noted above, the growing representation of committed evangelicals among Republican activists and of seculars among active Democrats may have helped to increase party polarization in the whole range of religious groups by affecting patterns of activist turnover and attitudinal conversion. These patterns of partisan religious change may make Republican activity more attractive to the more conservative members of various religious groups and less so for the more moderate members, whereas involvement in Democratic politics may become more appealing to the more liberal members of various faiths and less so to their more moderate members. They also may encourage continuing Republican activists to move their own policy attitudes and ideological orientations in a conservative direction and persuade continuing Democratic activists to convert toward more liberal positions.

These possibilities are examined in figures 7.3 and 7.4. Figure 7.3 shows the mean positions on abortion and the ideological identification scale of Democratic and Republican activists in six religious groups—frequent and infrequent church attenders within the evangelical Protestant, mainline Protestant, and Catholic traditions from 1972 through 2004—and demonstrates that partisan ideological polarization has increased within the whole range of religious groups.[16] The patterns on the abortion issue are especially striking. In 1972, the divisions on abortion were religious and not partisan. In all three traditions, frequently attending Republicans and frequently attending Democrats held more pro-life attitudes than did infrequent attenders in both parties, and there was virtually no difference between Republicans and Democrats in the same attendance group. The substantial attendance gap and the lack of a partisan gap were especially evident among Catholics, where Democrats who attended mass regularly were much more antiabortion than Republicans who attended infrequently. Moreover, comparison across the graphs for each tradition also revealed a gap based on religious affiliation in 1972. Frequently attending Catholics and evangelicals in both parties were more opposed to abortion than were the frequently attending mainline Protestants in both parties.

Over time, however, Republican activists in all of the religious groups tended, in the aggregate, to grow more pro-life while Democrats in the same categories became more pro-choice. Thus, by 2004, the cleavage on abortion was defined much more by party than by religion. Infrequently

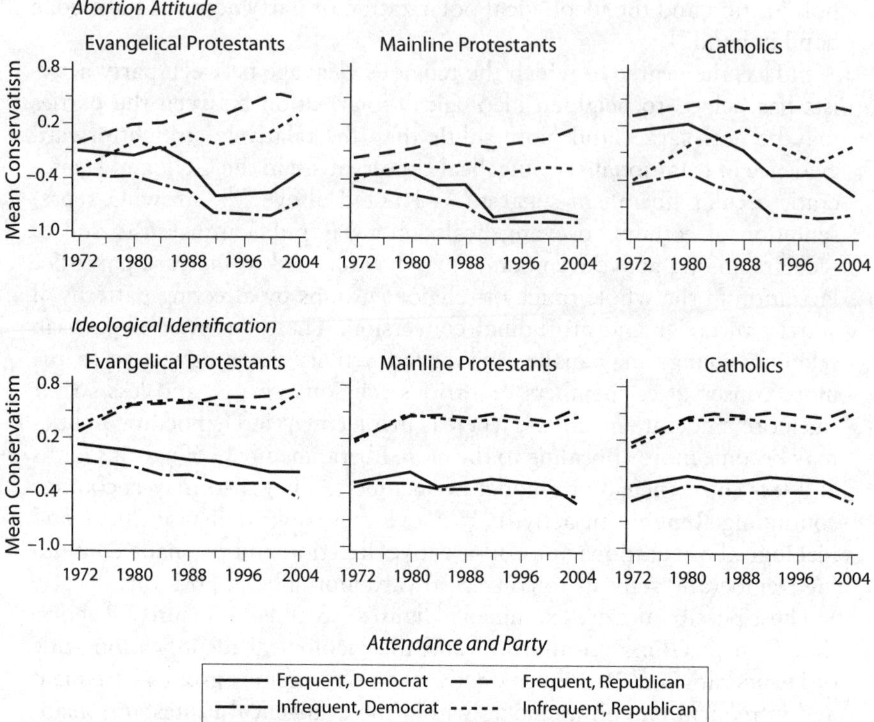

Figure 7.3. Mean abortion attitudes and ideological identifications of activists by religious tradition, worship attendance, and party, 1972–2004.

attending Republicans had become clearly more antiabortion than frequently attending Democrats, and that was true even among Catholics, where the attendance gap had been particularly wide in 1972. In fact, the influence of party on abortion views in 2004 was more important than not only that of church attendance within faith traditions but also the combined impact of religious tradition and church attendance. Infrequently attending Republicans affiliated with mainline Protestantism—the Christian tradition within which pro-life sentiments are least common—were noticeably more opposed to abortion (–0.30 versus –0.58 on the abortion scale, ranging from –1 to +1) than were frequently attending Democrats affiliated with Catholicism—the most pro-life faith tradition in 1972. Less devout mainline Republicans also were slightly more antiabortion than were frequently attending evangelical Democrats.

The trends for ideological identification are not as remarkable as those in abortion attitudes. However, Republican activists in all three faith traditions and in both attendance groups did increase their aggregate levels of conservatism, while Democratic activists in the same religious groups tended to grow at least slightly more liberal. Thus, the differences in the ideological proclivities of active Republicans and Democrats in the same religious groups were significantly larger in 2004 than they had been in 1972. In fact, in all of the groups except infrequently attending Catholics and mainliners (where the partisan difference increased from 0.60 in 1972 to 0.92 in 2004 and from 0.50 in 1972 to 0.88 in 2004, respectively), the partisan ideological difference was at least twice as large in 2004 as it had been in 1972.

The next step is to assess the argument that the growing presence of traditionalist evangelical activists within the Republican Party and of secular activists within the Democratic Party has encouraged this growing interparty ideological divide within religious groups. To do so, I take advantage of variation across states in the religious context of party activism. In the GOP, for example, there is, of course, a larger presence of committed evangelical activists in some state Republican Parties than in others. If the growing presence of committed evangelicals in the ranks of active Republicans has helped to make Republican activists from other religious groups more conservative in the aggregate (either by attracting a more conservative set of activists within those groups into the GOP or by encouraging continuing Republican activists from those groups to convert to more conservative policy positions), then we should see higher levels of conservatism among those Republicans who are most likely, by virtue of their state-level political context, to come into contact with committed evangelical activists. In other words, the larger the committed evangelical proportion of a state's Republican activists is, the more conservative the policy attitudes and ideological proclivities of the state's GOP activists from other religious groups should be. Following the same logic, the larger the secular proportion of a state's Democratic activists is, the more liberal the ideological orientations of the state's nonsecular Democratic activists should be.

In figure 7.4, I show the impact of the state-level religious context in which activists operate on their policy and ideological orientations in 2000 and on change in those orientations between 1992 and 2000. The effects on 2000 orientations represent the overall impact of state religious context on activists' ideologies and policy positions: its impact on activist recruitment and retention (i.e., the decisions of some nonactivists to become activists and the decisions of current activists about whether or not to remain active) and on ideological and policy conversion by individual party activists. The effects on change between 1992 and 2000 reflect the impact of state religious context just on ideological and policy conversion among those individuals who remained active in party politics over that eight-year period.

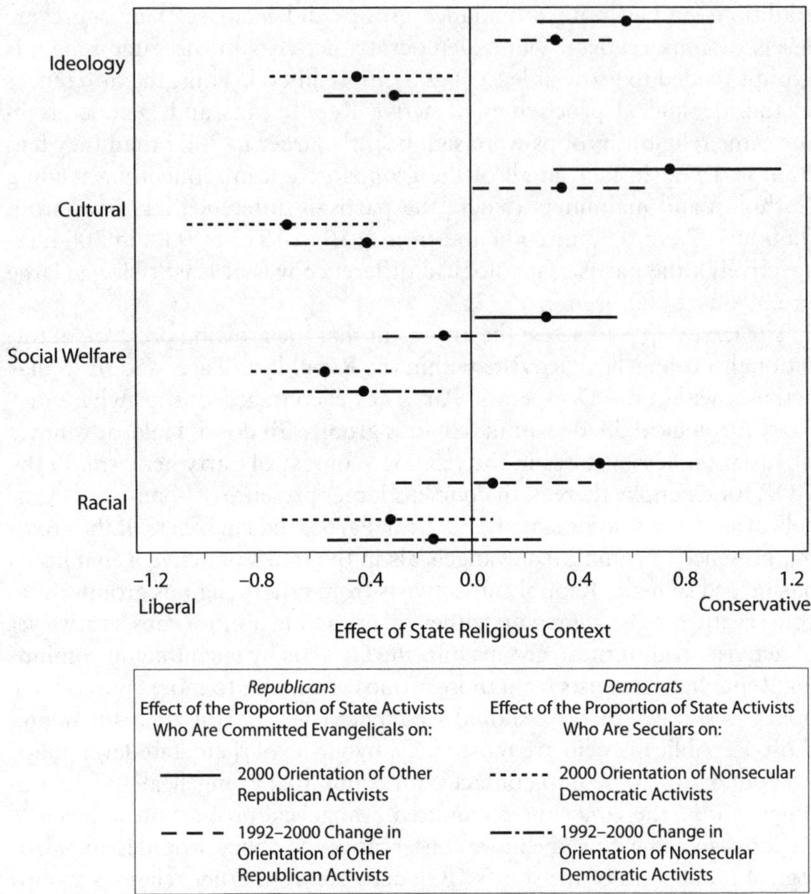

Figure 7.4. The impact of the religious context of state party activism on individual activists' policy and ideological orientations in 2000 and on change in policy and ideological orientations between 1992 and 2000. Source: 2000 Convention Delegate Study and 1992–2000 Convention Delegate Study Panel. Note: The circles on each line are the effect (unstandardized regression coefficient) of the religious context of state activists on the orientations of current activists or change in their orientations between 1992 and 2000. The lines represent the 90 percent confidence interval around the effect. When the lines do not intersect the zero value, the effect is statistically significant ($p < 0.10$).

For ideology, cultural attitudes, social welfare attitudes, and racial attitudes, the figure includes four different lines. The circle on each line represents the effect (estimated from a statistical model) of state religious context on activists' orientations or on the 1992–2000 changes. The line represents the confidence interval, or margin of error, around the estimated effect. The first line (solid) for each orientation is the effect of the proportion of Republican activists in a state who are religiously committed evangelical Protestants on the 2000 orientation of all Republican activists who are not in the committed evangelical camp. The second line (dashed and dotted) is the effect of the proportion of religiously committed evangelicals among state Republican activists on change between 1992 and 2000 in the orientations of all other Republican activists. The third line (dotted) represents the effect of the proportion of Democratic activists in a state who are secular on the 2000 orientations of nonsecular Democratic activists. The fourth line (dashed) represents the effect of this secular proportion on change between 1992 and 2000 in the orientations of nonsecular Democrats.[17]

The figure makes it clear that the religious context of state party activism does shape the policy and ideological orientations of Democratic and Republican activists. Beginning with the GOP, increases in the presence of committed evangelicals among a state's Republican activists are associated with greater conservatism in the ideological identifications and the cultural, social welfare, and racial policy attitudes of the Republican activists in other religious groups from that state.

These effects are associated not only with the aggregate orientations of a state's Republican activists but also with individual-level ideological change. The dotted and dashed lines indicate that residing in a state where there is a greater likelihood of interaction with committed evangelical activists leads individual Republican activists from other religious groups to move their own ideological orientations, cultural issue attitudes, and racial attitudes in a more conservative direction. The effect is not statistically significant for racial attitudes, but it is for ideology and cultural attitudes, and even for these variables, the effect is far from enormous. Moving from Connecticut, where none of the Republican activists were committed evangelicals, to South Carolina, with the highest proportion (0.57) of devout evangelicals among active Republicans, the difference in the average increase in cultural conservatism between 1992 and 2000 is only 0.12 (on the scale ranging from −1 to +1). However, it does appear that more interaction with committed evangelical activists may spur other Republicans to convert to more conservative positions themselves.

Among Democrats, greater contact with secular activists has just the opposite impact on the ideological orientations and policy views of nonsecular activists. The secular proportion of Democratic activists in a state is significantly and substantially related to greater liberalism in the ideological identifications and cultural, social welfare, and racial issue attitudes of 2000 Democratic activists. It also is related to change in a liberal direction between 1992 and 2000 in the ideological and policy perspectives of individual Democratic activists from outside the secular camp.[18] These effects are similar in magnitude to those on the Republican side.

The predicted difference in the average 1992–2000 increase in social welfare liberalism among activists from the state with the largest proportion of secular Democrats (Oregon at 0.32) and the state with the smallest proportion (Mississippi at zero) is 0.12.

It is clear that the increases in committed evangelicalism among Republican activists and of secularism among Democratic activists have helped to increase the level of ideological and policy polarization between the two parties. They have done so in two ways. First, because committed evangelical Republicans are more conservative than any other religious group in the GOP activist base whereas secular Democrats are more liberal than nonsecular Democratic activists on most issues, the growing presence of these groups simply means that there are more highly conservative activists in the GOP and more highly liberal activists in the Democratic Party. Second, and more subtly, they have helped to increase levels of interparty ideological polarization within the whole range of religious groups. The increasing representation of committed evangelicals among active Republicans appears to have attracted more conservative activists from other religious groups into Republican activism and to have encouraged continuing Republican activists to adopt more conservative cultural and ideological perspectives. The growing secularism of Democratic activists seems to have made Democratic activism more appealing to the more liberal activists from outside the secular camp and to have spurred nonsecular Democratic activists to move their own positions in a liberal direction.

Religion and Political Norms

Has the traditionalist-modernist religious divide between Republican and Democratic activists helped to make party politics not only more polarized but also more inflexible and strident? Put differently, are the activist groups at the extremes of the religious spectrum—traditionalist evangelicals in the GOP and secular Democrats—more committed than their fellow partisans to "purist" political ideals such as emphasizing policy commitments over partisan and electoral goals and demanding that party candidates honor those commitments? Are they less likely to accept "pragmatic" political norms such as compromise for the sake of electoral success, maximizing intraparty harmony, and selecting party candidates who have broad electoral appeal regardless of ideology?

I address these questions in figure 7.5 by showing the percentages, from the 2000 CDS, of traditionalist evangelicals and all other Republican activists and of secular and nonsecular Democratic activists taking the pragmatic position with regard to six statements about political norms: whether or not minimizing intraparty disagreement is important,

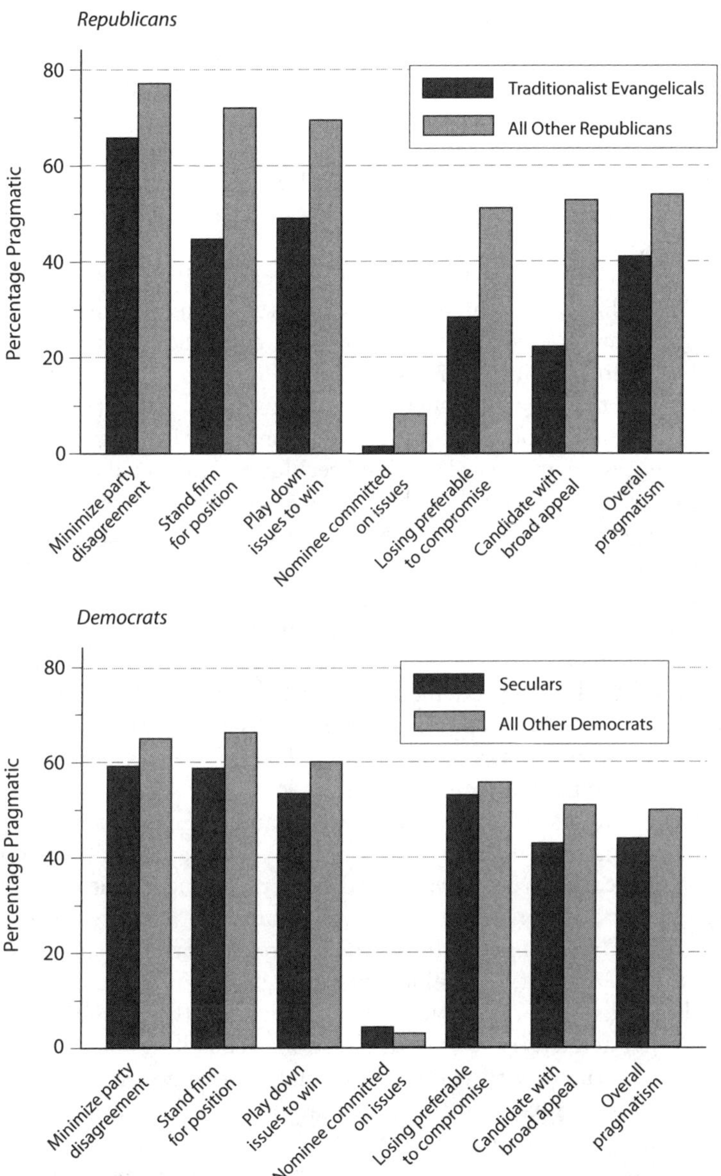

Figure 7.5. Activists' political norms: traditionalist evangelicals versus other Republicans and seculars versus other Democrats. Source: 2000 Convention Delegate Study. Note: The bars represent the percentage of each group providing the pragmatic response to each statement of political norms.

whether or not one should stand firm for a position even if it means resigning from the party, whether or not the party should play down policy issues in order to win elections, how important it is that the party's presidential nominee be committed on issues, whether or not losing elections is preferable to compromising on issues, and the importance of selecting candidates with broad electoral appeal. I also show the mean scores of the groups on an overall pragmatism score based on reactions to all six statements.[19]

The results are mixed for Democratic activists. Seculars are significantly more likely than nonsecular Democrats to agree with the purist statement that "one should stand firm for a position even if it means resigning from the party" and significantly less likely than nonseculars to agree with the pragmatic view that "choosing a candidate with broad electoral appeal is more important than a consistent ideology." However, the differences are not very large, and secular and nonsecular activists do not differ significantly on the other four statements. Seculars have significantly, but not substantially, lower scores on the pragmatism index than do nonsecular Democrats.[20] Seculars, in short, are more purist than other Democratic activists, but not by much.

The results are decidedly not mixed for Republican activists. Traditionalist evangelicals are more likely than every other Republican group to agree with all of the statements worded in a purist direction and less likely than every other Republican group to disagree with all of the statements worded in a pragmatic direction. The differences between traditionalist evangelicals and all other Republican activists are more than 20 percentage points on four of the six items and are highly significant on each statement and on the pragmatism index.[21] It appears that traditionalist evangelical activists have helped not only to make the Republican Party's policy positions more conservative but also to decrease the willingness of GOP elites and activists to compromise on those positions.[22]

At the same time, it is possible that the relationship between the norms of traditionalist evangelical activists and those of the Republican Party and its other activists runs in both directions. The GOP, like any political party, exists primarily to win elections and control government, and, in the American context, being successful at either of those things—at least over the long run—requires some willingness to compromise on policy issues and some attention to developing broad electoral and policy coalitions. Thus, the longer devout evangelicals are involved in the Republican Party, the more the pragmatic norms of party politics may rub off on them. The same logic, of course, may apply to secular Democrats and other groups of party activists. However, as mentioned above, it may be particularly true among traditionalist evangelical Republicans, not only because they start at such conspicuously low levels of pragmatism but

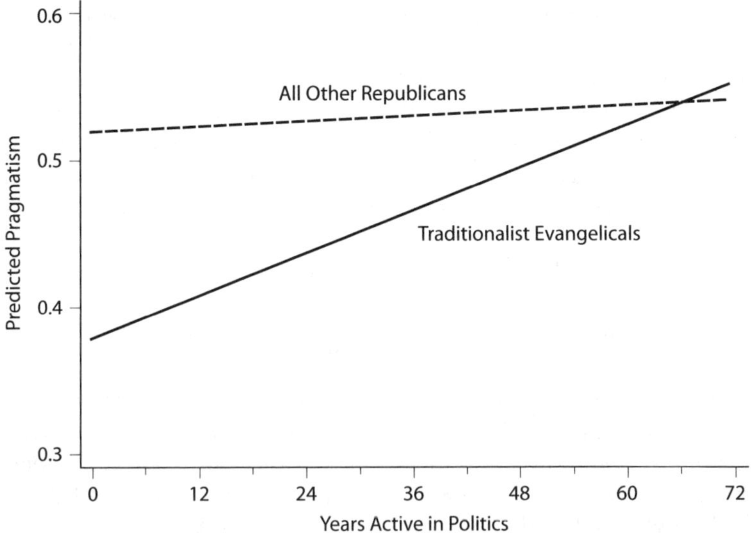

Figure 7.6. The impact of length of political activity on purist-pragmatist norms for traditionalist evangelical activists and other Republican activists. Source: Computed by the author from regression models using the 2000 Convention Delegate Study.

also because many of the Christian Right organizations that mobilize them into politics have grown more pragmatic over the last two decades.

To assess that possibility, I computed the correlation between the number of years that activists have been involved in party politics with the overall pragmatism score across the various partisan and religious groups. In keeping with existing evidence that activists grow more willing to sacrifice ideological orthodoxy for electoral victory the longer that they are involved in a party, the correlation was positive for nearly every group. However, it was generally quite small and statistically insignificant for most groups, including secular Democrats. The clearest exception to that pattern was traditionalist evangelical Republicans, where the correlation was modest (0.25) but larger than that for any other religious group within either party, and highly significant ($p < 0.01$). Traditionalist evangelical activists do bring policy commitments and purist political perspectives into their GOP involvement, but they are more likely than other Republican activists to become more pragmatic the longer they are involved in the party.

To better illustrate that, figure 7.6 shows the predicted levels of pragmatism for traditionalist evangelical Republicans and all other Republican activists by length of political activity.[23] The figure demonstrates that when they are relatively new to party politics, traditionalist evangelical activists have lower levels of political pragmatism than other Republican activists. However, as traditionalist evangelicals become more experienced in party politics, they become more accepting of pragmatic political norms at faster rates than do other Republican activists.[24] The figure suggests that it may be a rather long time before devout evangelicals are as pragmatic as other active Republicans. However, it is clear that GOP involvement does make these activists less averse to compromise and coalition building as they pursue their political and policy goals.[25]

Conclusion

Just as Green demonstrates a widening religion gap between the parties' electoral coalitions in chapter 2, this chapter has displayed a growing traditionalist-modernist religious divide between the parties' presidential campaign activists. If we assume that party polarization and growing inflexibility in political debate are detrimental to American democracy, then my analyses suggest that the growing religious divide has been normatively undesirable. The increasing representation of traditionalist evangelical Protestants among Republican activists and of seculars among Democratic activists has helped to create something of a "perfect storm" of party polarization and ideological dogmatism in American politics. These groups not only have brought very conservative and very liberal policy and ideological orientations into their respective parties but also have encouraged greater party polarization between Republican and Democratic activists from a host of other religious groups.

In addition to their ideologically extreme policy positions, traditionalist evangelical Republicans and secular Democrats tend to bring purist perspectives to their political activity. They are less willing than other activists to compromise on those positions to create intraparty harmony and to broaden their parties' electoral appeal. That is especially true of devout evangelical Republicans. Just as Gibson shows a connection between religiosity and political intolerance in chapter 5 and Wilcox finds a lack of tolerance and commitment to deliberative norms in chapter 6, I have shown that traditionalist evangelical activists in the GOP are less committed than their fellow partisans to the pragmatic norms that may be crucial not only for partisan success but also for democratic deliberation and policy making.

The blame for this religion-based party polarization and inflexibility, however, should not be placed entirely on religiously inspired activists and the groups that mobilize them into politics. At least some, maybe even most, of it should go to the parties themselves and their strategic politicians. As Wald and Leege convincingly argue in chapter 11 and in their earlier work (Leege et al. 2002), societal religious divisions do not translate naturally or automatically into religious and cultural cleavages between the political parties. They become manifest in party politics because some political entrepreneurs see in them potential political advantages for themselves and their parties and thus politicize religious fault lines by championing the issues and political symbols related to them. This politicization of the religious cleavage is what ultimately attracts activists on its opposite sides into party politics and thus spurs the growth of religious polarization between the two parties' activist bases.

In fact, I contend elsewhere (Layman 2001) that the principal catalysts for attracting secular activists into the Democratic Party and evangelical activists into the Republican Party were not religious leaders but strategic political leaders—namely George McGovern and his allies in the Democratic Party in the early 1970s and the leaders of the "New Right" wing of the GOP in the late 1970s—who were seeking to emerge from disadvantaged political positions. Moreover, once secular Democratic activists and traditionally religious Republican activists gained a foothold within their respective parties, other strategic politicians within the parties responded by moving their own positions on cultural and other issues to less centrist ground (see, for example, the movements in the 1980s of George H. W. Bush to a more pro-life position on abortion and of Jesse Jackson to a more pro-choice position as they developed campaigns for the Republican and Democratic presidential nominations, respectively, over the course of the 1980s), and this likely served to attract even more religiously polarized activists into party politics. Thus, the parties and their political leaders are certainly not passive responders to or pawns of growing religious polarization between the Democratic and Republican activist bases. In all likelihood, they actively shape and encourage it.

However, before casting aspersions on party politicians for this polarization, we should consider the possibility raised by Rosenblum in chapter 12, that religious involvement in politics actually may have some positive implications for the health of American democracy. Although the growing presence of committed evangelicals in the GOP may have hardened that party's issue positions and reduced its ability or willingness to negotiate or compromise on those positions, it also appears that participation in party politics may be acting to soften that very set of evangelical activists. There may be a general tendency for activists to grow more devoted to their parties and more pragmatic in their approaches to politics the longer that they are active (Roback 1975; Stone and Abramowitz 1983), but that tendency is particularly pronounced among traditionalist evangelical Republicans. As these activists grow more experienced in party politics, they become more supportive of pragmatic norms at a significantly faster rate than do other Republican activists. The reason simply may be that they have more ground to make up, given their initially very strong commitments to purist norms. However, it also may be that the Christian Right organizations that mobilize and, to some extent, train evangelical activists have grown more politically pragmatic since they first emerged (Rozell 1997; Green et al. 2006). The willingness of evangelical activists to compromise on policy issues and to build broad political coalitions may grow even more in the relatively near future. Younger evangelical leaders are displaying a more moderate and ecumenical approach to politics than the old guard of the Christian Right did, and younger evangelical congregants seem to have a broader and less consistently conservative set of political concerns than that of their older counterparts (Kirkpatrick 2007; Cox 2007; Gerson 2008).

Moreover, even the bad news of the religious divide between the parties' activists may not be entirely bad. As exemplified by *Toward a More Responsible Two-Party System* (American Political Science Association 1950), the 1950 report of the APSA "task force" that was far and away the most famous predecessor to this one, political scientists have long hoped for more programmatic and ideologically distinctive political parties. It appears that they now have them. The parties are, by many measures, more "responsible" now than they were in the 1950s (e.g., Green and Herrnson 2002). They offer clearer and more distinct policy programs to voters, and they seem to be more committed to the ideological principles contained in those programs. This increase in the philosophical distinctiveness and commitment of the parties has had some negative consequences, but some of its consequences may have been the positive ones envisioned in the 1950 report—stronger parties in the electorate, increased ideological sophistication in the mass public, and perhaps even greater electoral participation and policy representation.

The growing religious divide between Republican and Democratic Party activists has clearly helped to make the parties more "responsible," pushing them to more distinct ideological locations and placing more pressure on them to hold fast to their policy agendas. If there are some normatively positive aspects of responsible parties, then perhaps the growing connection between religion and party activism is, all in all, not so bad.

Notes

1. Political scientists studying religion and politics traditionally have defined "seculars" as all individuals without a religious affiliation and not just those who positively identify themselves as atheists, agnostics, or unbelievers (e.g., Green

2007; Kohut et al. 2000). However, recent research shows that the bulk of the contemporary growth in the proportion of Americans who are not affiliated with religion has been spurred by an increase in the number of people who believe in basic religious tenets but are religiously unaffiliated rather than an increase in the presence of true nonbelievers (Hout and Fischer 2002). This has prompted some scholars to distinguish between "unaffiliated believers" and the unaffiliated individuals who truly are secular, or unbelieving, much as Green does in chapter 2 of this volume.

This research, however, focuses on patterns in the mass public, whereas the religiously unaffiliated activists who have infiltrated the Democratic Party are much more likely than their mass-level counterparts to reject traditional religious labels and orientations (Kirkpatrick 1976; Layman 2001). This is seen in the responses to the religious questions that religiously unaffiliated Democratic respondents provided to the survey of 2004 national party convention delegates used in this chapter (see below for more details). When asked for their "religious preference," nearly 36 percent of the unaffiliated Democratic delegates in 2004 identified themselves as atheists, agnostics, secular humanists, or nonbelievers (as compared to only 1 percent of religiously unaffiliated respondents to the 2004 survey of the American National Election Studies (ANES), the leading academic survey of the American mass electorate (see http://www.electionstudies.org for details) who claimed agnostic or atheist as their religious affiliation). Nearly 76 percent of unaffiliated Democratic delegates said that the Bible is not the Word of God, and none of them said that the Bible is the "literal" Word of God (as compared to 13 percent of the unaffiliated respondents to the ANES agreeing that "the Bible is the actual Word of God and is to be taken literally, word for word," and 54 percent saying that the Bible is not the Word of God). Over 60 percent of unaffiliated Democratic delegates said that they never attend worship services, and none of them claimed to attend worship services more than a few times a year. Finally, when asked to choose terms describing their religious identities, 78 percent of the religiously unaffiliated Democratic delegates who claimed any religious identity at all described themselves as either "ethical humanists, "secular humanists," agnostics, or atheists (as opposed to choosing other response options such as "evangelical or fundamentalist Christian," "liberal/progressive Christian," or "born-again Christian"). In short, it appears that religiously unaffiliated Democratic activists are, by and large, quite secular. So, given that my discussion of seculars in the parties' activist bases focuses almost entirely on Democratic activists, I use the term "secular" to describe party activists with no religious affiliation throughout this chapter.

2. Consider, for example, the impact that a greater presence of devout evangelical Protestants among Republican activists might have on the participation decisions and policy attitudes of Republicans in a less devout and traditionalist religious category, say less devout mainline Protestants. As committed evangelicals become better represented among active Republicans and push the policy positions of both the typical Republican activist and of Republican candidates to the right, that will increase the attraction of Republican activity for the less devout mainliners who have highly conservative views on policy issues, making it more likely that the current activists in that group will stay involved in GOP

politics while those not yet active will become involved. However, it will decrease the appeal of GOP activism for the less committed mainliners who have more moderate policy views, making it more likely that they will either drop out of Republican activity or decide not to become involved. Moreover, the movement of Republican activists and candidates to the right may encourage or pressure less devout mainline Protestants who have remained active in the GOP to move their own policy positions in a conservative direction. A similar process should take shape among other Republican religious groups, and the growing secularism of Democratic activists should stimulate similar developments among nonsecular groups within the Democratic activist base.

3. It is less clear that the Christian Right has promoted deliberative democratic norms such as civility, tolerance, and respect for political opponents among its active members. Some scholarship (e.g., Shields 2007) contends that Christian Right organizations work to instill a commitment to democratic values in their members, but other work—such as that of Wilcox in chapter 6—shows that Christian Right membership often lessens such commitments.

4. See Miller and Jennings (1986), Herrera (1992), and Layman (2001) for more details about each of these surveys. There was no CDS survey conducted in 1976 or 1996.

5. Like all of the earlier CDS surveys, the 2000 CDS (conducted by Thomas Carsey, John Green, Richard Herrera, and Geoffrey Layman) was a mail survey. For the cross-sectional portion of the study, we mailed surveys to all of the delegates to the 2000 Democratic and Republican national conventions for whom we had correct address information (4284 Democrats and 2049 Republicans). The response rate was 39 percent, which is comparable to response rates for earlier CDS surveys. For the panel study, surveys were mailed to 1888 respondents to the 1992 CDS for whom there was correct address information, and the response rate was 48 percent, resulting in a panel of 911 respondents. Some of the respondents in the panel were also delegates to the 2000 conventions and are included in the 2000 delegate cross-section so that there are data on 1907 delegates to the 2000 Democratic convention and 985 delegates to the 2000 Republican convention. There are far more Democrats than Republicans in the sample because there were roughly twice as many delegates at the Democratic National Convention as there were at the Republican National Convention in 2000.

6. The 2004 CDS was conducted by Rosalyn Cooperman, John Green, Richard Herrera, and Geoffrey Layman. We sent e-mail messages to all of the 2004 national convention delegates for whom we had valid e-mail addresses (2730 Democrats and 605 Republicans), inviting them to participate in the online survey. The rather low response rates—21 percent among Democrats and 22 percent among Republicans—resulted in samples of 578 Democratic delegates and 134 Republican delegates. Because of the very small Republican sample, a follow-up mail survey of GOP delegates was conducted. Mail surveys were sent to all of the 510 Republican delegates for whom we had correct addresses and who had not responded to the online survey. Completed surveys were received from 260 of those Republicans, bringing the 2004 Republican sample to a total of 394 delegates. Despite the different (and mixed) format of this study and its rather low response rates, the distribution of basic demographic and political variables

in the 2004 CDS is, for both parties, quite similar to those in the 2000 CDS and in the surveys of 2004 national convention delegates conducted by CBS and the *New York Times*. Nevertheless, I make limited use of the 2004 data, using them only to provide a data point for the most recent presidential election year in assessments of longitudinal trends. I use the 2000 CDS for all of the cross-sectional analyses.

7. The CDS surveys allow me to examine a group of party activists that is a bit broader than just the delegates to a particular year's convention. Because the 1980, 1984, 1988, and 2000 CDS surveys all included panel components, they surveyed many individuals who, although delegates to earlier conventions were not delegates to that year's convention but were active in its presidential campaign. My analysis focuses on this larger set of presidential campaign activists.

8. The religious characteristics of all of the cohorts that first attended national conventions in 2000 or earlier are taken from the 2000 CDS. I examine differences across delegate cohorts with only the 2000 and 2004 CDS surveys rather than with the full series of CDS surveys because the 2000 and 2004 CDS included far more extensive batteries of religious questions and gauged religious affiliation very differently than did the earlier surveys (relying on an open-ended question about religious preference rather than the rather limited set of response options that appeared in earlier CDS surveys).

9. The evangelical Protestant tradition in table 7.1 includes nonblack members of denominations such as the Southern Baptist Convention, the Assemblies of God, Wisconsin and Missouri Synod Lutherans, Church of Christ, and the Presbyterian Church in America. The mainline Protestant group includes nonblack members of denominations such as the Episcopal Church, the United Methodist Church, the Evangelical Lutheran Church in America, and the Presbyterian Church in the U.S.A. The black Protestant tradition includes members of black Protestant denominations such as the African-Methodist Episcopal Church and the National Baptist Convention as well as all other African-Americans affiliating with Protestant churches (see Kellstedt and Green 1993; Steensland et al. 2000; and Layman and Green 2006 for more details on classifying Protestants into these three traditions). The secular category includes both respondents who claimed no religious affiliation and those claiming identifications such as agnostic, atheist, and secular humanist.

10. To do this, I first collapsed the indicators of view of the Bible, worship attendance, and religious identification into scales ranging from 1 to 3. The Bible question in the CDS surveys had four response options: (1) The actual Word of God, to be taken literally, word for word; (2) The inspired Word of God, with no errors but not to be taken literally; (3) The inspired Word of God, but it contains human errors; and (4) A good book but not the Word of God. I classified the fourth option as modernist, the third as centrist, and the first two as traditionalist. For worship attendance, I classified those respondents who "never" or "seldom" attend as modernist, those who attend "a few times a year" or "once or twice a month" as centrist, and those who attend "once a week" or "more than once a week" as traditionalist. For religious identification, I classified those respondents identifying themselves as "liberal/progressive Christian," "ethical humanist," or "liberal/progressive Catholic" as modernist; those identifying as

"mainline Christian" as centrist; and those identifying as "fundamentalist Christian," "evangelical Christian," "Charismatic/Pentecostal Christian," "born-again Christian," "conservative/traditional Christian," or "conservative/traditional Catholic" as traditionalist. I then took each respondent's mean value on each of the three scales on which he or she had nonmissing values. Finally, I classified all respondents with values at or rounding to one as "modernists," those with values at or rounding to two as "centrists," and those with values at or rounding to three as "traditionalists."

11. Using the CDS surveys from 1972 through 1992, Layman (2001) shows a high level of secularism among 1972 Democratic delegates but much smaller percentages of seculars at the 1976 and 1980 Democratic conventions.

12. Given the considerable importance of the South to recent changes in American party politics, it is interesting that the growth of traditionalist evangelicalism among Republican activists and of secularism among Democratic activists has been fairly symmetrical across the South and the non-South. Within the GOP, the percentage of traditionalist evangelicals grew from 7 percent in the pre-1992 cohort to 21 percent in the 2004 cohort among nonsouthern convention delegates and from 21 percent before 1992 to 41 percent in 2004 among southern delegates. Over the same period for Democrats, the percentage of seculars grew from 14 percent to 25 percent among nonsouthern delegates and from 4 percent to 11 percent among southern delegates.

13. This analysis employs all of the CDS surveys from 1972 through 2004 and includes all of the respondents to those surveys who said that they were involved in particular years' presidential campaigns. In the 1972–1992 CDS, the worship attendance variable had five categories: never, almost never, a few times a year, once or twice a month, and almost every week. In the 2000 and 2004 CDS, there were six categories: never, seldom, a few times a year, once or twice a month, once a week, and more than once a week. The category labeled "almost never or less" in figure 7.1 combines the bottom two levels of attendance in each year. The "almost every week or more" category is simply the top attendance level in the surveys from 1972 through 1992 and combines the top two levels in 2000 and 2004.

14. I only show the mean values of religious groups for which there are at least 15 observations on every variable. Attitudes toward cultural, social welfare, and racial issues are the scores from factor analyses of respondents' positions on multiple issues. These include cultural issues such as abortion, homosexual rights in jobs, school prayer, and parental consent for abortion; social welfare issues such as government services and spending, government providing health insurance, and federal spending on welfare and on programs to assist the unemployed; and racial issues such as government responsibility to help blacks and preferential hiring of racial minorities. All of the issue attitudes and ideological identifications range from –1 for most liberal to +1 for most conservative.

15. Of course, the cross-sectional evidence in table 7.2 is merely suggestive of a relationship between the trends over time in religious and ideological polarization between the parties' activists. To actually establish that such a relationship exists would require longitudinal analysis, something made very difficult by the fact that the CDS surveys prior to 2000 asked a small and inconsistent set of questions about both policy issues and religion. However, all of the CDS surveys

have included a question on abortion, and I measured the differences from one election year to the next in party polarization on abortion and the election-to-election changes in the percentage of seculars among Democratic activists plus the percentage of frequently attending evangelical Protestants among Republican activists. The correlation between these election-to-election changes is 0.51 and approaches statistical significance ($p = 0.10$). If the data begin with 1976 (excluding 1972, when the percentage of seculars among Democratic activists was quite high but with the *Roe v. Wade* decision yet to be issued and neither party platform making mention of abortion, abortion had not yet become a partisan issue), the correlation is a robust 0.73 and is statistically significant ($p = 0.03$) even in a sample of only eight time points. Changes in partisan religious polarization and party polarization on abortion clearly have been closely connected.

16. I focus here on abortion and ideological identification because they were the only policy or ideological questions asked in each of the CDS surveys from 1972 through 2004. Frequent church attendance is defined as attending "almost every week" in the 1972–1992 surveys and as attending "once a week" or "more often than once a week" in the 2000 and 2004 surveys. Infrequent attenders are all respondents not in the frequent attendance category.

17. To estimate these effects, I first pooled all of the CDS surveys from 1984 through 2000 and computed the proportion of each state's Republican activists made up by committed evangelicals (defined in each survey as evangelical Protestants who attend church almost every week or more frequently) and the proportion of each state's Democratic activists made up by seculars. I pooled the various surveys in order to have samples of both Republican and Democratic activists from each state that were of sufficient size for making inferences about the religious characteristics of all Republican and Democratic activists in that state. Pooling the 1984, 1988, 1992, and 2000 CDS produces samples of 30 or more Republican activists in all states except Delaware and West Virginia and samples of 30 or more Democratic activists in all states except Delaware and Vermont. Thus, Republican and Democratic respondents from Delaware, Republican respondents from West Virginia, and Democratic respondents from Vermont were dropped from the analyses. To gauge the effect of the state religious context on activists' orientations in 2000, I turned to the 2000 CDS and estimated a regression model of the state proportion of traditionalist evangelicals among Republican activists on the 2000 ideological identifications, cultural attitudes, social welfare attitudes, and racial attitudes of Republicans from outside of the committed evangelical camp, and a regression model of the impact of the state proportion of seculars among Democratic activists on the 2000 orientations of nonsecular Democrats. These models included controls for religious tradition and worship attendance (dummy variables for the various religious traditions and frequent and infrequent church attenders within the three largest traditions [evangelical Protestants, mainline Protestants, and Catholics]), income, education, age, union membership, gender, region (dummy variables for residents of the South, Midwest, and West), race, and state political ideology. I created the state ideology variable with data based on state-level election day exit polls, as discussed in Erikson et al. (1993) and provided in updated form by Gerald Wright on his Web site (http://mypage.iu.edu/~wright1/). To form my measure, I

subtracted the proportion liberal from the proportion conservative in each state and took the mean of that difference from 1984 to 2000 for each state.

In order to estimate the impact of state religious context on change in the attitudes and orientations of individual activists, I turned to the 1992–2000 CDS panel study and examined the impact of state-level activist religion on change between 1992 and 2000 in the ideological orientations and issue attitudes of individuals who were active in Republican or Democratic presidential campaign politics throughout that period. The dependent variables in these models are particular policy or ideological orientations of continuing party activists in 2000. The independent variables are those same orientations in 1992, the state-level religious context, and the control variables.

All of the policy attitudes and ideological orientations in both 1992 and 2000 are treated as latent variables with multiple observed indicators. The indicators of social welfare attitudes are responses to questions about government services and spending, government providing health insurance, and government spending on welfare programs, programs to help the unemployed, child care, and public schools. For racial attitudes, they are responses to questions about government help for blacks and government spending on programs for blacks. For cultural attitudes, they are position on abortion and feeling thermometer ratings of pro-life groups and pro-choice groups. For ideology, they are the ideological identification scale and thermometer ratings of liberals and conservatives. The models take into account measurement error in all of the observed indicators of the latent variables. To provide a scale for the latent variables, I constrain the factor loading for one observed indicator to be equal to 1.

I estimated the models using Amos 5.0, which computes full information maximum likelihood (FIML) estimates even in the presence of missing data (Andersen 1957). Wothke and Arbuckle (1996) describe the FIML procedure used by Amos and show that the estimates produced by it are more consistent and efficient than those produced by methods using pairwise or listwise deletion of missing observations.

18. The effects on both 2000 orientations and 1992–2000 change are statistically significant at $p < 0.10$ or lower for ideology, cultural attitudes, and social welfare attitudes. The effects for racial attitudes are not statistically significant.

19. I conducted a principal-components factor analysis of the six items for all 2000 activists. The analysis produced one factor with an eigenvalue greater than 1. It had an eigenvalue of 2.09 and explained 34.8 percent of the total variance in the six items. Five of the six items had factor loadings of 0.5 or greater. The sixth—"it is best to minimize disagreement within the party"—had a loading of 0.38.

20. I conducted tests of statistical significance on the individual norms items and on the overall pragmatism score. The tests were tests of difference in means between committed evangelicals and all other activists in the Republican Party and between seculars and all other Democratic activists on variables coded 0 for "disagree" and 1 for "agree." The difference between secular Democrats and all other Democrats is statistically significant at $p < 0.05$ on standing firm for a position, choosing a candidate with broad appeal, and on overall pragmatism.

21. The difference between traditionalist evangelical Republicans and all other Republicans is statistically significant at $p < 0.001$ on each norm and on overall pragmatism.

22. Of course, it is possible that the less pragmatic political approach of traditionalist evangelical activists does not flow directly from their religious orientations but results simply from their staunch ideological and policy conservatism. There is a strong relationship between ideological extremity and purist political norms (Wildavsky 1965), and traditionalist evangelicals are clearly more conservative than other active Republicans. To assess this possibility, I regressed the scores of 2000 GOP activists on the pragmatism index on a dummy variable for traditionalist evangelicals, ideological identification, attitudes on social welfare, cultural issues, racial issues, and defense spending in addition to several other factors that should be related to political pragmatism (the number of years in which individuals had been active in politics, age, dummy variables for activists who held party office at the time of the survey and for those who held public office at that time, the amount of contact that respondents said they had with people active in national, state, or local party affairs, the respondent's assessment of the strength of the party organizations in his or her state and local area, and a dummy variable for supporters of George W. Bush as the Republican presidential nominee in 2000). The strongest effects on pragmatism were those of ideological identification and cultural issue attitudes [statistically significant ($p < 0.001$) coefficients of –0.22 and –0.16, respectively]. However, even after these and other orientations had been controlled for, traditionalist evangelicals were noticeably less pragmatic than other Republican activists (0.07 less on a pragmatism index ranging from zero to 1), and the difference was highly statistically significant ($p < 0.001$). Thus, the steadfastly purist norms of evangelical traditionalists in the GOP do come from their cultural and ideological conservatism to some degree, but they also seem to emerge directly from their staunchly orthodox religious orientations.

23. The predicted values in figure 7.6 are from a model in which the overall pragmatism score was the dependent variable and number of years active in politics, a dummy variable for traditionalist evangelicals, an interaction term that is the product of that dummy and length of activity, and a variety of controls were the independent variables. The control variables were other factors that should be related to both pragmatism and political longevity, including age, dummy variables for activists who held party office and public office at the time of the survey, ideological identification, the amount of contact that respondents said they had with people active in national, state, or local party affairs, the respondent's assessment of the strength of the party organizations in his or her state and local area, and a dummy variable for supporters of George W. Bush as the Republican presidential nominee in 2000. The predicted values in the figure were computed by holding all of the control variables constant at their mean values.

24. All three components of the interaction between the variable for traditionalist evangelicals and length of activity had statistically significant ($p < 0.05$) regression coefficients. The significant coefficient on the traditionalist evangelical variable was negative, indicating that traditionalist evangelicals are less pragmatic than other Republicans when they first become active in party politics. The significant coefficient for length of activity was positive, indicating that other Republican activists become more pragmatic the longer they are involved in party politics. Finally, the significant coefficient on the interaction term was positive,

indicating that traditionalist evangelical activists grow more pragmatic at a significantly faster rate than do other Republican activists.

25. Another possibility is that rather than long-term party activity causing traditionalist evangelicals to become more politically pragmatic, it is activists' initial levels of pragmatism that cause some traditionalist evangelicals to stay active in the GOP for longer periods and others to drop out of party activity more quickly. In other words, perhaps the less pragmatic activists among traditionalist evangelicals are more likely than their more pragmatic counterparts to drop out of GOP activity—either because they dislike the compromise and pragmatism inherent in party politics or because they want to pursue other, more issue-focused, types of political involvement—meaning that the traditionalist evangelicals most likely to be left among long-term Republican activists are those who were more pragmatic in the first place. To assess that possibility, I turned to the 1992–2000 CDS panel study and compared the mean values on the pragmatism index of the traditionalist evangelical Republicans who were active in both the 1992 and 2000 presidential campaigns and the traditionalist evangelical Republicans who were active in the 1992 campaign but who had dropped out of party activity by 2000. The group that was active in both campaigns did have a slightly higher level of pragmatism than the dropouts (0.41 versus 0.37 on the zero-to-1 scale), but the difference between the two means did not approach statistical significance ($p = 0.56$). So, rather than traditionalist evangelicals self-selecting into and out of long-term party activity based on their initial levels of pragmatism, it appears that there is a causal impact of long-term party activity on the political norms of traditionalist evangelical Republicans.

References

Abramowitz, Alan I., John J. McGlennon, and Ronald B. Rapoport. 1983. "The Party Isn't Over: Incentives for Activism in the 1980 Presidential Nominating Campaign." *Journal of Politics* 45:1006–15.

Abramowitz, Alan I., and Kyle L. Saunders. 1998. "Ideological Realignment in the U.S. Electorate." *Journal of Politics* 60:634–52.

———. 2005. "Why Can't We All Just Get Along? The Reality of a Polarized America." *The Forum* 3 (issue 2): article 1, available at http://www.bepress.com/forum.

Aldrich, John H. 1983. "A Downsian Spatial Model with Party Activism." *American Political Science Review* 77:974–90.

———. 1995. *Why Parties? The Origin and Transformation of Political Parties in America.* Chicago: University of Chicago Press.

Aldrich, John H., and David W. Rohde. 2001. "The Logic of Conditional Party Government: Revisiting the Electoral Connection." In *Congress Reconsidered*, 7th ed., eds. Lawrence C. Dodd and Bruce I. Oppenheimer. Washington, DC: CQ Press.

American Political Science Association. 1950. *Toward a More Responsible Two-Party System: A Report of the Committee on Political Parties of the American Political Science Association.* New York: Rinehart.

Andersen, T. W. 1957. "Maximum Likelihood Estimates for a Multivariate Normal Distribution When Some Observations Are Missing." *Journal of the American Statistical Association* 52 (278):200–203.

Aranson, Peter H., and Peter C. Ordeshook. 1972. "Spatial Strategies for Sequential Elections." In *Probability Models of Collective Decision Making*, eds. Richard Niemi and Herbert Weisberg. Columbus, OH: Merrill.

Bartels, Larry M. 2000. "Partisanship and Voting Behavior, 1952–1996." *American Journal of Political Science* 44:35–50.

Berelson, Bernard R., Paul R. Lazarsfeld, and William N. McPhee. 1954. *Voting: A Study of Opinion Formation in a Presidential Campaign*. Chicago: University of Chicago Press.

Binder, Sarah A. 2003. *Stalemate: Causes and Consequences of Legislative Gridlock*. Washington, DC: Brookings Institution.

Black, Earl, and Merle Black. 2007. *Divided America*. New York: Simon & Schuster.

Brewer, Mark D., and Jeffrey M. Stonecash. 2007. *Split: Class and Cultural Divides in American Politics*. Washington, DC: CQ Press.

Brock, William E. 2004. "A Recipe for Incivility." *Washington Post* June 27:B7.

Brownstein, Ronald. 2007. *The Second Civil War*. New York: Penguin Press.

Bryce, James. 1995 (1888). *The American Commonwealth*. Indianapolis: Liberty Fund.

Chappell, Henry W. Jr., and William R. Keech. 1986. "Policy Motivation and Party Differences in a Dynamic Spatial Model of Party Competition." *American Political Science Review* 80:881–900.

Conway, M. Margaret, and Frank B. Feigert.1968. "Motivations, Incentive Systems, and the Political Party Organization." *American Political Science Review* 62:1159–73.

Cox, Dan. 2007. "Young White Evangelicals: Less Republican, Still Conservative." *Pew Forum* September 28, available at http://pewforum.org/docs/?DocID=250.

Crotty, William. 2001. "Policy Coherence in Political Parties: The Elections of 1984, 1988, and 1992." In *American Political Parties: Decline or Resurgence?* eds. Jeffrey E. Cohen, Richard Fleisher, and Paul Kantor, 122–37. Washington, DC: CQ Press.

Dionne, E. J. Jr. 1991. *Why Americans Hate Politics*. New York: Touchstone.

Erikson, Robert S., Gerald C. Wright, and John P. McIver. 1993. *Statehouse Democracy: Public Opinion and Policy in the American States*. New York: Cambridge University Press.

Fiorina, Morris P., with Samuel J. Abrams and Jeremy C. Pope. 2005. *Culture War? The Myth of a Polarized America*. New York: Pearson Longman.

Freeman, Jo. 1986. "The Political Culture of Democrats and Republicans." *Political Science Quarterly* 101:327–44.

Geer, John G. 2006. *In Defense of Negativity: Attack Ads and Presidential Campaigns*. Chicago: University of Chicago Press.

Gerson, Michael. 2008. "Faith without a Home." *Washington Post* February 27:A17.

Green, John C. 2007. *The Faith Factor: How Religion Influences American Elections*. Westport, CT: Praeger.

Green, John C., and Paul S. Herrnson, eds. 2002. *Responsible Partisanship?* Lawrence, KS: University Press of Kansas.

Green, John C., and John S. Jackson. 2007. "Faithful Divides: Party Elites and Religion." In *A Matter of Faith: Religion in the 2004 Presidential Election*, ed. David E. Campbell. Washington, DC: Brookings Institution.

Green, John C., Mark J. Rozell, and Clyde Wilcox, eds. 2006. *The Values Vote? The Christian Right and the 2004 Elections*. Washington, DC: Georgetown University Press.

Herrera, Richard. 1992. "The Understanding of Ideological Labels by Political Elites: A Research Note." *Western Political Quarterly* 45:1021–35.

Hetherington, Marc J. 2001. "Resurgent Mass Partisanship: The Role of Elite Polarization." *American Political Science Review* 95:619–31.

Himmelfarb, Gertrude. 1999. *One Nation, Two Cultures*. New York: Knopf.

Hout, Michael, and Claude S. Fischer. 2002. "Why More Americans Have No Religious Preference: Politics and Generations." *American Sociological Review* 67:165–90.

Hunter, James Davison. 1991. *Culture Wars: The Struggle to Define America*. New York: Basic Books.

———. 1994. *Before the Shooting Begins: Searching for Democracy in America's Culture War*. New York: Macmillan.

Jacobson, Gary C. 2005. "Polarized Politics and the 2004 Congressional and Presidential Elections." *Political Science Quarterly* 120:199–218.

Jamieson, Kathleen Hall, and Erika Falk. 2000. "Continuity and Change in Civility in the House." In *Polarized Politics*, eds. Jon R. Bond and Richard Fleisher, 96–108. Washington, DC: CQ Press.

Jones, David R. 2001. "Party Polarization and Legislative Gridlock." *Political Research Quarterly* 54:125–41.

Kellstedt, Lyman A., and John C. Green. 1993. "Knowing God's Many People: Denominational Preference and Political Behavior," In *Rediscovering the Religious Factor in American Politics*, eds. David C. Leege and Lyman A. Kellstedt. Armonk, NY: M. E. Sharpe.

King, David C. 2003. "Congress, Polarization, and Fidelity to the Median Voter." Working Paper, John F. Kennedy School of Government, Harvard University.

Kirkpatrick, David D. 2007. "The Evangelical Crackup." *New York Times* October 28:38

Kirkpatrick, Jeane J. 1976. *The New Presidential Elite*. New York: Sage.

Kohut, Andrew, John C. Green, Scott Keeter, and Robert C. Toth. 2000. *The Diminishing Divide: Religion's Changing Role in American Politics*. Washington, DC: Brookings Institution.

Krugman, Paul. 2002. "America the Polarized." *New York Times* January 4:A21.

Layman, Geoffrey C. 1999. "Culture Wars in the American Party System: Religious and Cultural Change among Partisan Activists Since 1972." *American Politics Quarterly* 27:89–121.

———. 2001. *The Great Divide: Religious and Cultural Conflict in American Party Politics*. New York: Columbia University Press.

Layman, Geoffrey C., and Thomas M. Carsey. 1998. "Why Do Party Activists Convert? An Analysis of Individual-Level Change on the Abortion Issue." *Political Research Quarterly* 51:723–50.

———. 2002. "Party Polarization and 'Conflict Extension' in the American Electorate." *American Journal of Political Science* 46:786–802.

Layman, Geoffrey C., Thomas M. Carsey, and Juliana Menasce Horowitz. 2006. "Party Polarization in American Politics: Characteristics, Causes, and Consequences." *Annual Review of Political Science* 9:83–110.

Layman, Geoffrey C., Thomas M. Carsey, John C. Green, Richard Herrera, and Rosalyn Cooperman. 2010. "Activists and Conflict Extension in American Party Politics." *American Political Science Review*. Forthcoming.

Layman, Geoffrey C., and John C. Green. 2006. "Wars and Rumours of War: The Contexts of Cultural Conflict in American Political Behaviour." *British Journal of Political Science* 36 (January):61–89.

Leege, David C., Kenneth D. Wald, Brian S. Krueger, and Paul D. Mueller. 2002. *The Politics of Cultural Differences: Social Change and Voter Mobilization Strategies in the Post–New Deal Period*. Princeton, NJ: Princeton University Press.

McCarty, Nolan, Keith T. Poole, and Howard Rosenthal. 2006. *Polarized America: The Dance of Ideology and Unequal Riches*. Cambridge, MA: The MIT Press.

McTague, John Michael, and Geoffrey C. Layman. 2009. "Religion, Parties, and Voting Behavior: A Political Explanation of Religious Influence." In *The Oxford Handbook on Religion and American Politics*, eds. Corwin E. Smidt, Lyman A. Kellstedt, and James L. Guth. Oxford: Oxford University Press.

Miller, Gary, and Norman Schofield. 2003. "Activists and Partisan Realignment in the United States." *American Political Science Review* 97:245–60.

Miller, Warren E., and M. Kent Jennings. 1986. *Parties in Transition: A Longitudinal Study of Party Elites and Party Supporters*. New York: Sage.

Oldfield, Duane M. 1996. *The Right and the Righteous: The Christian Right Confronts the Republican Party*. Lanham, MD: Rowman & Littlefield.

Pomper, Gerald M. 2003. "Parliamentary Government in the United States: A New Regime for a New Century?" In *The State of the Parties*, 4th ed., eds. John C. Green and Rick Farmer, 267–86. Lanham, MD: Rowman & Littlefield.

Pomper, Gerald M., and Marc D. Weiner. 2002. "Toward a More Responsible Two-Party Voter: The Evolving Bases of Partisanship." In *Responsible Partisanship?* eds. John C. Green and Paul S. Herrnson, 181–200. Lawrence, KS: University Press of Kansas.

Poole, Keith T., and Howard Rosenthal. 1997. *Congress: A Political-Economic History of Roll Call Voting*. New York: Oxford University Press.

Ranney, Austin. 1972. "Turnout and Representation in Presidential Primary Elections." *American Political Science Review* 66:21–37.

Roback, Thomas H. 1975. "Amateurs and Professionals: Delegates to the 1972 Republican National Convention." *Journal of Politics* 37:436–68.

Rohde, David W. 1991. *Parties and Leaders in the Postreform House*. Chicago: University of Chicago Press.

Rozell, Mark J. 1997. "Growing Up Politically: The New Politics of the New Christian Right." In *Sojourners in the Wilderness: The Christian Right in Comparative Perspective*, eds. Corwin E. Smidt and James M. Penning. Lanham, MD: Rowman & Littlefield.

Rozell, Mark J., and Debasree Das Gupta. 2006. "The Christian Right and the Politics of Abortion: The Triumph of Pragmatism?" Presented at the conference "Fundamentalism and the Rule of Law" at Cardozo School of Law, March 14–15, 2006, New York, NY.

Saunders, Kyle L., and Alan I. Abramowitz. 2004. "Ideological Realignment and Active Partisans in the American Electorate." *American Politics Research* 32:285–309.

Shafer, Byron E. 2003. *The Two Majorities and the Puzzle of Modern American Politics*. Lawrence, KS: University Press of Kansas.

Shafer, Byron E., and William J. M. Claggett. 1995. *The Two Majorities: The Issue Context of Modern American Politics*. Baltimore: Johns Hopkins University Press.

Shea, Daniel M. 2003. "Schattschneider's Dismay: Strong Parties and Alienated Voters." In *The State of the Parties*, 4th ed., eds. John C. Green and Rick Farmer, 287–99. Lanham, MD: Rowman & Littlefield.

Shields, Jon A. 2007. "Between Passion and Deliberation: The Christian Right and Democratic Ideals." *Political Science Quarterly* 122 (1):89–113.

Sinclair, Barbara. 2006. *Party Wars: Polarization and the Politics of National Policy Making*. Norman, OK: University of Oklahoma Press.

Smidt, Corwin E., Lyman A. Kellstedt, and James L. Guth. 2009. "The Role of Religion in American Politics: Explanatory Theories and Associated Analytical and Measurement Issues." In *The Oxford Handbook on Religion and American Politics*, eds. Corwin E. Smidt, Lyman A. Kellstedt, and James L. Guth. Oxford: Oxford University Press.

Soule, John W., and James W. Clarke. 1970. "Amateurs and Professionals: A Study of Delegates to the 1968 Democratic National Convention." *American Political Science Review* 64:888–98.

Steensland, Brian, Jerry Z. Park, Mark D. Regnerus, Lynn D. Robinson, W. Bradford Wilcox, and Robert D. Woodberry. 2000. "The Measure of American Religion: Toward Improving the State of the Art." *Social Forces* 79 (1):291–318.

Stone, Walter J., and Alan I. Abramowitz. 1983. "Winning May Not Be Everything, but It's More Than We Thought." *American Political Science Review* 77:945–56.

Stonecash, Jeffrey M., Mark D. Brewer, and Mack D. Mariani. 2003. *Diverging Parties: Social Change, Realignment, and Party Polarization*. Boulder, CO: Westview.

Sundquist, James L. 1983. *Dynamics of the Party System: Alignment and Realignment of Political Parties in the United States*. Washington, DC: Brookings Institution.

Tocqueville, Alexis de. 1966 (1835). *Democracy in America*. New York: Harper & Row.

Uslaner, Eric M. 1993. *The Decline of Comity in Congress*. Ann Arbor: University of Michigan Press.

Washington Post. 2004. A Polarized Nation? November 14:B6.
White, John Kenneth. 2003. *The Values Divide.* New York: Chatham House.
Wildavsky, Aaron. 1965. "The Goldwater Phenomenon: Purists, Politicians, and the Two-Party System." *Review of Politics* 27:393–99.
Will, George F. 2004. "America's Shifting Reality." *Washington Post* November 4:A25.
Williams, Rhys H., ed. 1997. *Cultural Wars in American Politics: Critical Reviews of a Popular Myth.* New York: De Gruyter.
Wilson, James Q. 1962. *The Amateur Democrat.* Chicago: University of Chicago Press.
Wothke, Werner, and James L. Arbuckle. 1996. "Full-Information Missing Data Analysis with Amos." SPSS White Paper, Chicago: SPSS.
Wuthnow, Robert. 1988. *The Restructuring of American Religion.* Princeton, NJ: Princeton University Press.

PART III

Political Diversity and American Religion

Chapter 8

ENTERING THE PROMISED LAND?

The Rise of Prosperity Gospel and Post–Civil Rights Black Politics

FREDRICK C. HARRIS

THE FUNERAL of Martin Luther King Jr.'s widow, Coretta Scott King, in February 2006 symbolically revealed the diminishing influence of the prophetic tradition in African-American politics and civic life. What surfaced in this ritual of remembrance and homage to Mrs. King, who for over thirty years kept the memory and the values of her husband's message of peace and social change in the nation's consciousness, was a nod to a theological worldview whose beliefs are antithetical to the prophetic tradition Dr. King embraced. Dr. King's funeral in 1968 had been held at the Ebenezer Baptist Church, which is surrounded by a poor neighborhood east of downtown Atlanta, but the final service for Mrs. King was held at New Birth Missionary Baptist Church—a suburban megachurch 15 miles outside of the city—whose minister, Bishop Eddie Long, is an ardent supporter of a theology that teaches the virtues of material prosperity.

Long had been criticized months before when a newspaper investigation revealed that he received compensation from the church's charity organization that included a million dollar plus salary, a $1.4 million mansion, and a Bentley automobile. When asked by a reporter about the compensation, Bishop Long responded: "We're not just a church, we're an international corporation." Informing the reporter that "Jesus wasn't poor," Bishop Long justified his compensation from the charity, pointing out that "we're not just a bumbling bunch of preachers who can't talk and all we're doing is baptizing babies. . . . You've got to put me on a different scale than the little black preacher sitting over there that's supposed to be just getting by because the people are suffering."[1]

The controversy did not end there. When the Interdenominational Theological Center (ITC), a predominately black Christian seminary in Atlanta, invited Bishop Long to speak at its commencement, students protested, an honorary degree recipient boycotted the ceremony, and a long-time trustee of the seminary expressed outrage. The honorary degree recipient was James Cone, a distinguished professor of theology at Union Theological Seminary, who is considered the "father" of black liberation theology. Cone objected to Long denigrating the prophetic tradition of the black church and distorting the legacy of Dr. King. "King devoted his life to the least of these," Cone remarked. "He could have been just like Bishop Long with all the millions he has, but he chose to die poor. . . . He would not use his own message or his own movement to promote himself."[2] ITC trustee Bishop John Hurst Adams of the African Methodist Episcopal Church was more direct in his criticism. Long, Adams argued, "substituted the pursuit of justice for the pursuit of prosperity."[3]

The tensions surrounding the prophetic legacy of the activist wing of the black church tradition and the emerging influence of the prosperity gospel in Afro-Christianity goes beyond the choice of a church for a funeral, a graduation speaker, or the misuse of a church charity. It points to fundamental differences in how black churches should go about eradicating racial inequality in American society. Although historically activist black churches developed both social and political strategies to combat poverty and discrimination, either by developing their own social programs, community economic development initiatives, or by pressuring government to help the poor and elect public officials supportive of social justice (Owens 2007), the growing influence of the prosperity gospel presents a challenge to what has been described as the "civic traditions of black churches" (Harris 2001). This tradition is steeped in black churches engaging in electoral politics and economic development efforts in their communities; ministers provide spiritual and political guidance to their congregants, and congregants are encouraged to use their talents and skills to foster social change in their communities.

This activist tradition may have met its strongest ideological challenge since the civil rights movement. Indeed, theologian Robert M. Franklin describes the prosperity gospel as the "the single greatest threat to the historical legacy and core values of the contemporary black church tradition" (Franklin 2007, 112). As a religious doctrine that supports a worldview that, according to Franklin, "permits and rewards extraordinary inequalities of wealth and power," critics claim that the theology neglects the concerns of the poor and the pursuit of social justice (Frankin 2007, 113). Although elements of the prosperity gospel in Afro-Christianity are not new, evidence suggests that its contemporary incarnation is more mainstream than marginal, attracting predominantly middle-class and working-class blacks to arena-sized churches where the virtues of living an "abundant life" of wealth, good health, and positive relationships are preached.

Prosperity gospel is not popular only among African-Americans but has strong appeal among white evangelicals and "unchurched" Christians in general who have recommitted themselves to their faith, which they now see as having more relevance and practicality to their lives than the churches they grew up in. With popular preachers such as the best-selling author Joel Osteen, who has one of the largest congregations in the country and attracts millions of people to his ministry through his special appearances around the country and weekly television program, the theology of prosperity has moved from the margins of Protestant Christianity toward the center. As one of the fastest growing faiths globally, second perhaps to Islamic fundamentalism, prosperity theology—or what has also been described as the Word of Faith Movement—has implications not only for the politics of black communities in the United States but throughout the world. Its global reach extends to Nigeria, Sweden, South Korea, Guatemala, and Brazil, and among other countries where followers see their faith as a means to enhance their opportunities for material success and healthy living (Coleman 2000, 27–28).

Although some might think that prosperity gospel is on the fringe of American religious life or that the social gospel holds little sway today, an opinion poll points to the theological tensions that exist among believers. In a 2006 Time/CNN Poll respondents expressed positions that reflect the social gospel tradition and the prosperity gospel. About 60 percent of Christians in the survey believe that "God wants people to be financially prosperous," slightly over 20 percent agreed that material wealth is a sign of "God's blessings," while a third reported that "if you give away your money to God, God will bless you with more money." Nearly half of the respondents agreed that "Jesus was rich and we should follow his example."

On the other hand, responses to some questions indicate support for values associated with the social gospel. Forty-four percent of the respondents rejected the idea of a rich Jesus, and 43 percent believed that churches were not doing enough to assist the poor, a response that would indicate support for the values of the social gospel tradition. Only half of the respondents were familiar with the prosperity movement, and a mere 17 percent reported that they were followers. However, the responses do indicate that a significant number of American Christians see their faith linked with material success even though fewer than 20 percent claim to be part of the prosperity gospel movement. Unfortunately, there are too few black respondents in the survey to provide reliable estimates of the differences in the responses to questions between blacks and whites on these questions. Nonetheless, anecdotal evidence suggests that blacks are among the strongest followers of the Word of Faith Movement in the United States and that black ministers such as Frederick K. C. Price and Creflo Dollar are among the leading proselytizers (Harrison 2005). As a result, the idea that prosperity gospel has a greater influence on Afro-Christians has far more political consequences for them than for white evangelicals, whose religious worldviews reinforce the core American value of individualism. For African-Americans, at least historically, the idea of the collective has been more central to their political values than the importance of individualism (Dawson 1994). Therefore, prosperity gospel represents a clash with core political values in the black church tradition.

This chapter explores the tensions between the two theological perspectives and considers the impact prosperity gospel may have on present and future directions in the politics of black communities. The prosperity gospel, with its emphasis on transforming individuals into prosperous and healthy Christians, and the prophetic tradition, with its commitment toward transforming poor and marginal communities, provide a context to explore the potential impact of the prosperity gospel on long-held religious values that have emphasized the importance of community above individualism in black political life.

As Michael Dawson explains in his theory of linked fate, blacks—rich and poor and of all religious persuasions—evaluate political preferences and policy initiatives based on their perception of how preferences and policies affect blacks as a group. Black churches have been central to nurturing those communalist values that contribute to a sense of linked fate, as well as fostering the political discussions and skills that connect congregants to electoral and community politics (Harris 1999; Harris-Lacewell 2004). The rich networks and institutions that are embedded in black churches are, alongside the black family, community organizations, and black media, responsible for reinforcing and enhancing a sense of solidarity among blacks by "crystallizing the shared historical experience of African-Americans into a sense of collective identity" (Dawson 2001, 11).

As the most extensive institution among African-Americans, black churches have the capability to reinforce the political saliency of racial interests and to provide information about the status of the race (Dawson 1995, 11). Thus, the influence of prosperity gospel, either through the proliferation of Word of Faith churches that draw black adherents or through the adoption of prosperity preaching in more traditional black churches, may have the effect of eroding or perhaps softening a sense of linked fate among blacks by adopting religious values that emphasize individualism and depoliticize church-based efforts that address racial inequality. On the other hand, prosperity gospel's emphasis on personal transformation as a strategy for economic mobility may foster the beginnings of an alternative style of politics in black communities, one that emphasizes the virtues of individualism, personal responsibility, entrepreneurship, and personal morality. An emphasis on those values is more closely aligned with mainstream American political values than the predominant focus on social justice that has been the hallmark of activist black churches for generations.

Afro-Christianity and the Struggle for Racial Equality

The evolution of black churches in American life has its roots in social and political protest. As a people who were enslaved and uprooted from their land and indigenous religious practices, blacks were Christianized in the New World, developing a religious worldview that both challenged and provided explanations for their enslavement. These worldviews opposed the ideology and the practices of white supremacist–infused Christianity that offered biblical justifications for the capture and enslavement of Africans and their descendents. Although black Christians shared the same fundamental views as white Christians about the birth, life, and resurrection of Christ, at the beginning, black Christians constructed alternative meanings of the life of Christ and biblical lessons that opposed society's interpretations of their oppressed conditions (Genovese 1974; Raboteau 1978).

African-American Christians, for instance, have historically placed greater emphasis on the lessons of the Hebrew Bible, the belief of the personal intervention of God in history, biblical perspectives on the suffering and the ultimate triumph of Christ, and the belief in equality and treatment for all Christians, no matter their race or economic circumstances (Lincoln and Mamiya 1990, 2–5).

The importance given to freedom in black religious traditions has also made black Christians distinct from the traditions of white Christians. Involving more than freedom from religious persecution, the themes of freedom that evolved in the black religious experience reflect the social and political struggles that African-Americans experienced during slavery, Reconstruction, and the struggle for full citizenship that took place for more than half of the twentieth century. Freedom has meant different things over time, but it meant collectively improving the lot of blacks in the United States. As C. Eric Lincoln and Lawrence H. Mamiya explain in *The Black Church and the African-American Experience*, "During slavery [freedom] meant release from bondage; after emancipation it meant the right to be educated, to be employed, and to move about freely from place to place. In the twentieth century, freedom means social, political, and economic justice" (1990, 4). As mentioned, the meaning of freedom in Afro-Christianity has placed less emphasis on individual freedom and greater emphasis on a collective-oriented sense of freedom that not only liberates African-Americans from political, economic, and social persecution in a white-dominated society but also liberates the nation from its failings as a truly democratic society.

This sense of freedom that developed in both secular and religious institutions, both at the center and the margins of black society, provided the leadership, networks, and language that guided African-Americans in their quest for equality. The institutional resources and symbolic power of Afro-Christianity's sense of freedom provided individual blacks with a means to understand their oppression and struggle, no matter the ideological tendency in a given historical moment. With the exception of black Marxism, which only during rare moments in history adopted Christian perspectives in efforts to appeal to African-Americans (Kelley 1990), ideological tendencies among African-Americans such as black versions of liberalism, nationalism, and conservatism were, and still are, influenced by Afro-Christianity.

The conflict between the prosperity gospel and social gospel/liberation theology is, from an ideological perspective, a debate on how best to advance the black community in the twenty-first century. This conversation is as old as Booker T. Washington's and W.E.B. Dubois's conflict over social and economic uplift versus civil rights at the turn of the twentieth century and Martin Luther King and Malcolm X's perspectives on integration versus separatism during the 1960s. Today the debate has turned to whether the lack of individual responsibility is the reason for the condition of the black poor or does racism continue to play a significant role in black American life.

Thus, the conflict between the social gospel/liberation theology wing of Afro-Christianity and its emerging prosperity gospel wing is at its core a theological *and* ideological debate about the best strategy for African-Americans to advance in American society. As Michael Dawson reminds us in his discussion about the historical tendencies in African-American political thought, "[t]he fact that two African Americans can believe their fate is linked to that of the race does not mean that they agree on how best to advance their own racial interests" (2001, 11).

In similar terms, the disagreements between the two theologies are partly over what God truly wants for the "destiny of the race" rather than doctrinal debates about which theology represents the best path to salvation. As prosperity gospel gains greater currency in Afro-Christianity, through both its Pentecostal roots as well as through its adoption in more traditional black churches, prosperity gospel may challenge the prophetic tradition in the black church movement, a tradition that coincides with both liberal and black nationalist political ideologies that have dominated the black political thought and practice. In a so-called postracial America, where race matters less than other identities and political commitments, adherents of the prosperity gospel may reflect more conservative political attitudes. These conservative tendencies might discourage black nationalist sentiments, promote political conservatism, engender apolitical views on activism, and, by default, soften support in black communities for liberal social policies targeted toward minorities and the poor.

The Prophetic Tradition and Prosperity Gospel: A Theological Civil War?

In the past few years there has been a theological "civil war" brewing among the ministers and theologians of the prophetic tradition and the gospel of prosperity. During the 2008 Democratic Party primaries, the sermons of Senator Barack Obama's former pastor, the Reverend Jeremiah Wright of the Trinity United Church of Christ in Chicago, highlight this tension. Reverend Wright came under scrutiny for his perceived anti-white views and unpatriotic critiques of American society. In a sermon that was delivered after the 9-11 terrorist attacks on the United States, Reverend Wright, in words of condemnation that reflect the style and the substance of prophetic preaching, criticized the United States for its militarism and foreign policy. His message declared that the United States was being "damned" by God for its military pursuits throughout the world and for its treatment of powerless people at home and abroad. As a minister who adheres to the teachings of black liberation theology and as a church that practices the social gospel tradition of assisting the poor through a variety of church-sponsored services, Reverend Wright and Trinity United Church of Christ provide but one of many examples of today's activist-oriented black churches.

However, not only did Reverend Wright come under attack by Senator Hillary Clinton's campaign, the media, and political conservatives, he also was criticized by some black ministers for having an outdated and impractical theological worldview, one that no longer, some thought, addressed the immediate needs of black communities. Other black ministers and liberal white ministers took offense at the idea that a minister would be criticized for speaking out against injustice. The undercurrent to the debate about Reverend Wright and his theological commitment to black liberation theology once again opened up a debate about what the priorities of black churches should be in the twenty-first century. For proponents of the social gospel/liberation theology traditions, this debate is intertwined with questions about the theological legitimacy of the prosperity gospel.

Reverend Frederick Haynes III of Dallas's Friendship-West Baptist Church accuses prosperity ministers of being "co-opted by American capitalism" and for "blaming the poor for their circumstances and praising the pursuit of earthy riches."[4] At the 2006 annual meeting of the National Baptist Convention, the largest black denominational body in the United States, Reverend Haynes accused prosperity ministers of abandoning the poor and deceiving followers for financial gain. "Black communities are suffering," Reverend Haynes proclaimed, "while the prosperity-pimping gospel is emotionally charging people who are watching their communities just literally dissolve."[5]

Prosperity gospel preachers, on the other hand, think that to not teach about the biblical virtues of prosperity is heresy and a barrier to bringing sinners to Christ. Their appeals are based more on biblical reinterpretations than on the more explicit ideological and political commitments that are more apparent in black liberation theology and the social gospel tradition. Frederick K. C. Price, a black pastor of a megachurch and one of the leading proponents of the prosperity gospel, argues in his book, *Prosperity on God's Terms*:

> It has to be a satanic deception for the Christian to speak against prosperity. Satan very well knows that if we become financially independent of our circumstances, he will no longer control our progress. "Poor-mouthing" Christians are not going to be credible witnesses of the goodness of God, nor will they influence very many people. But more importantly, they are not going to get the Gospel out. They are aiding the enemy—while rejecting the command of God Who told us to promote the gospel—and they don't even know it. (1990, 8–9)

As mentioned, this theological worldview, which emphasizes the virtues of good health and material gain to its adherents, is at odds with the prophetic tradition in Afro-Christianity. Whereas proponents of the social gospel and liberation theology recognize how structural inequalities in American society place barriers before minorities and the poor, proponents of the prosperity gospel see negative spiritual forces preventing the faithful from receiving financial blessings from God. The social gospel commands that Christians transform the communities of the poor and acknowledge the existence of racial inequality. The theology of liberation emphasizes that God sides with the oppressed and that the suffering of black people in particular indicated that God, Himself, is black. A look back at the development of the prophetic tradition in Afro-Christianity and the evolution of the prosperity gospel provides context to show these two theological perspectives support values that may have opposite effects on the future of church-based civic activism in black communities.

Social Gospel and Black Liberation Theology

The social gospel, a religious movement that evolved in the late nineteenth and early twentieth centuries, commands that the faithful uplift the poor and transform poor and disenfranchised communities through community uplift and political activism. As the religious arm of the Progressive movement, the social gospel tradition developed a theological worldview that the righteous should not only be concerned about the salvation of sinners—whose sins reflected the social environment in which they lived—but should also be concerned about the plight of the dispossessed here on earth. So to save sinners from damnation, the social gospel advocated improving their environment and saving the souls of sinners.

The founders of the movement reflected the sentiments of mainline white, middle-class Protestants and supported the settlement house movement, labor rights, civil rights, and later the peace movement. The tradition has not only included mainline Protestants but also, at least historically, Catholics and Jews. Led by urban black clergy, the social gospel tradition among blacks provided a morally sanctioned framework that justified and legitimized the church's involvement in the civil rights movement (McAdam 1982; Morris 1984). The social gospel tradition within black communities combined the perspectives of the social gospel, whose early supporters often overlooked the prevailing racism in American society, and the ideology of racial uplift, which promoted the idea that black elites and institutions were obligated to uplift the poor (Luker 1991).

Although uplift ideology and the biblical justification that supported it existed among black elites before the Civil War, its influence became hegemonic in black communities at the turn of the twentieth century, when black communities became economically and politically marginalized in the wake of Reconstruction's collapse (Gaines 1996). Using the biblical story of the Exodus, Afro-Christians saw themselves as an oppressed people, enslaved, liberated, and wandering in the wilderness of America's racist society. This view of Afro-Christians has its origins in slave religion, in which slaves who became Christians adopted the biblical story of the Exodus as a way to understand their bondage and their struggle for freedom. Where white Christians saw their conquest of the New World as manifest destiny and America as the land of "milk and honey," converted slaves saw America as Egypt, land of bondage (Raboteau 1994, 9; Glaude 2000).

Some traditions within Afro-Christianity, particularly Holiness and Pentecostal churches, primarily hoped for a better situation in the afterlife, but urban churches affiliated with the black "mainline" focused their energies on saving souls and improving the social environment of their congregants by building schools, orphanages, hospitals, and mutual-aide and burial societies. Thus, the work of redeeming the souls of the poor linked both sinners and the righteous in racially segregated communities. During the "great migration" North between the two World Wars, the social gospel of racial uplift was instrumental in supporting civil rights through support of the National Association for the Advancement of

Colored People and secularly based social uplift organizations such as the Urban League (Harris 2001).

One of the first texts, from a theological perspective, to interpret biblical scriptures and symbols in support of the idea that Jesus sided with the oppressed—and by extension African-Americans—is Howard Thurman's *Jesus and the Disinherited*, originally published in 1949. In Thurman's interpretation, the life of Jesus represented all disinherited people, and as such, the Gospel of Christ and the actions of Christians should reflect that viewpoint. Anticipating Martin Luther King's public theology of social justice, Thurman argued that

> the economic predicament with which [Jesus] was identified in birth placed him initially with the great mass of men on earth. The masses of people are poor. If we dare take the position that in Jesus there was at work some radical destiny, it would be safe to say that in his poverty he was more truly Son of man than he would have been if the incident of family or birth had made him a rich son of Israel. (Thurman 1996, 17–18)

Indeed, the theological perspective that God sided with the oppressed was appropriated by King and used as a biblical justification for blacks to actively resist segregation. In his first movement speech, delivered in December 1955 at the Holt Street Baptist Church in Montgomery, King preached, "we are determined here in Montgomery to work and fight until justice runs down like water and righteousness like a mighty stream," a command that was inspired by the Hebrew Bible prophet Amos. Referencing both Thurman's biblical interpretation of the oppressed and the story of the Exodus, King tells the audience "we, the disinherited of this land, we who have been oppressed so long, are tired of going through the long night of captivity." King would use the story of the Exodus and the idea that Christ sides with the oppressed throughout his many speeches. In his very last, delivered in Memphis at a mass meeting for striking garbage workers in 1968, the symbol of the Promised Land in the Exodus story was used to convey to African-Americans that their freedom was inevitable, whether he reached the Promised Land with them or not. Like the biblical Moses, who led the Israelites out of Egyptian slavery and received God's commandment on Mt. Sinai, King told this mostly black audience:

> But it doesn't matter with me now, because I've been to the mountaintop. And I don't mind. Like anybody, I would like to live a long life. Longevity has its place. But I'm not concerned about that now. I just want to do God's will. And He's allowed me to go up to the mountain. And I've looked over. And I've seen the Promised Land.

> I may not get there with you. But I want you to know tonight, that we, as a people will get to the Promised Land.

As a revolt against the interracial and nonviolent, turn-the-other-cheek philosophy of King's social gospel, black liberation theology saw the suffering of Christ as a context for the persecution of black people in the United States and argued for a more radical interpretation of the Bible and the life and death of Jesus. In his influential book *Black Messiah*, Detroit minister Albert Cleage (1993) argues that not only did God side with the oppressed but that Christ, because of the suffering he endured, was black. As an ideological challenge to the Nation of Islam's criticism of Christianity as the "white man's religion," Cleage justified support for building a separate black nation on the foundations of Christianity, a stance ideologically compatible with black nationalism. Reverend Cleage wrote that Christianity promoted communalist values and opposition against the status quo, virtues that he argued have historical links to Afro-Christianity. "Black Americans need to know," Cleage argued, "that the historic Jesus was a leader who went about among the people of Israel, seeking to root out the individualism and the identification with the oppressor which had corrupted them . . ." (Cleage 1993, 101).

The leading theologian of black liberation theology then and today is James Cone, a professor at Union Theological Seminary in New York. His works have influenced a generation of black seminarians throughout the country who have become ministers at traditional black churches and racially diverse mainline Protestant churches. Adopting the viewpoints of black nationalism, Cone in his work has contested the very meaning of Christianity in the United States. Because mainstream white churches were complicit in supporting slavery and racial segregation, Cone argues that a Christian worldview that does not consider the plight of the oppressed is a useless theology. "There can be no Christian theology which is not identified unreservedly with those who are humiliated and abused," Cone argued in the 1970s.

Furthermore,

> theology ceases to be a theology of the gospel when it fails to arise out of the community of the oppressed. For it is impossible to speak of God of Israelite history, who is the God who revealed himself in Jesus Christ, without recognizing that he is the God for those who labor and are heavy laden. (Cone 1970, 18)

Some empirical evidence suggests that the political significance of black liberation theology may have softened since the activist 1960s and 1970s. Calhoun-Brown (1999) reports that nearly a third of African-Americans believe in the image of a black Christ, a measure that would indicate support for black liberation theology. She finds that holding an image of a black Christ increases support for a form of black nationalism that advocates separation from American society—a finding that would support Cleage's theology of Christian black nationalism. The belief in a black Christ, however, did not enhance feelings of group solidarity or predict voting behavior or the belief that churches should be involved in politics, behaviors that would be more in line with the prophetic tradition that calls for social change. These findings suggest that the social mission of the black church may be more important for activist black churches than the theological viewpoints of black liberation theology.

The growing popularity of prosperity gospel among African-Americans may be partly attributed to the perceived failures of the prophetic tradition in dealing with the persistence of racial inequality in the post–civil rights era. Perhaps a theological worldview that centers on transforming the lives of blacks as individuals is more appealing to a generation of African-Americans who are less familiar with historic struggles against legalized segregation than a theology that focuses too much on the past. Thus, as the memory of the civil rights and black power movements fades, the story of the Exodus may have less appeal among a new generation of black Christians.

Prosperity Gospel

With its roots in Pentecostalism the prosperity gospel encourages believers to address personal problems—and by extension societal problems—by using faith and positive thinking to improve their health and material prosperity. Although most of the black Protestant churches evolved out of protest from the exclusion and discrimination of white Protestants, Pentecostalism evolved as a multiracial religious movement and is heavily influenced by religious practices indigenous to the black American experience. As a religious movement that developed around the same time as the social gospel movement, known colloquially in black communities at that time as "sanctified churches," mainstream black churches considered Pentecostal churches as part of a fringe movement, if not a cult. If there ever was a religious tradition that was associated with an otherworldly, pie-in-the-sky orientation, it is the Pentecostal movement, a movement that prepared its adherents for the biblical prophecy of the rapture, an event where the faithful will disappear from earth and ascend into heaven (Blumhofer 1993, 16).

Pentecostalism was inspired by the biblical account of the day of Pentecost, where the followers of Christ spoke in unknown tongues, which followers considered, along with the practices of faith healing and the ability to give and interpret prophesies, "gifts of the spirit." In the United

States the spread of Pentecostalism occurred through the Azusa Street Revival, an event where whites, blacks, Asians, and Mexicans, as well as people across social classes, gathered in revival services between 1906 and 1915 in Los Angeles to experience the "gifts of the spirit." Led by William Seymour, a black minister from Texas, whose biblical perspectives on Pentecostalism were taught to him by the white minister Charles Parham of Topeka, Kansas, the Azusa Street Revival was influenced by the charismatic black religious practices that remain a part of the movement today.

Adopting Negro spirituals and the preaching styles of black ministers of the day, the Azusa Street Revival was the first truly racially integrated and cross-class religious movement to develop in the United States. As one historian of the movement explains, the beginnings of Pentecostalism "meant loving in the face of hate—overcoming the hatred of a whole nation by demonstrating that Pentecost is something very different from the success-oriented way of life" (Hollenweger 1997, 20). Yet the dominant views of racism in society at the turn of the twentieth century disrupted the initial multiracial characteristics of the movement. Its theological founder, Charles Parham, sympathized with the Ku Klux Klan, racially segregated students at his Bible school in Topeka, preached against the intermingling of races, and believed that Anglo-Saxons were the master race, practices that ran counter to the Azusa Street experience (Hollenweger 1997).

Despite racism dividing the Pentecostal movement, the Assemblies of God, the predominately white and leading denomination of Pentecostals, acknowledges today the racially diverse origins of the movement. Writing nearly a hundred years after the birth of Pentecostalism in the United States, the Assemblies of God recognizes that:

> The Azusa Street revival witnessed the breakdown of barriers which normally divide people from one another: race, class, and gender, wealth, language, education, church affiliation and culture. . . . The mission had an integrated leadership and congregation—and although it was decades before the civil rights movement, had an amazing lack of discrimination. (quoted in Hollenweger 1997, 23)

Indeed, the interracial origins of the Pentecostal movement positioned Pentecostalism to become the most diverse religious movement in the United States today, a fact that came about because of the success of the civil rights movement, with which ironically Pentecostals, black or white, had little if any involvement.

Because of the lifting of racial barriers that separated racial and ethnic groups in the post–civil rights era, Pentecostalism has been able to spread its message to a diverse group of Christians without being hindered by the divisions that hindered its beginnings. But a more racially tolerant society is only part of the story of its success as a national and global religious phenomenon. The growth of neo-Pentecostalism in the 1960s and 1970s was also the result of a more this-worldly Pentecostalism where less emphasis has been placed on behavioral restrictions (avoiding provocative dress, social dancing, makeup, etc.), the virtuousness of forsaking material processions, and separation from the secular world and its culture.

No longer stigmatized as the religion of the oppressed, neo-Pentecostalism is popular among the working and middle classes in the United States (but less so in developing countries, where it is popular among the poor). These Pentecostalists see the embracement of popular culture as complementing their lifestyles and the teachings of the movement as practical guidance to matters of family and work. Consequently, less emphasis was placed on the "by-and-by" and more on receiving blessings and guidance in the "here and now." The theology of prosperity emphasizes self-actualization, in which individuals can alter the course of their lives by "naming and claiming" health and prosperity for themselves. This worldview operates on a principle of reciprocity between believers and God—the more they give to the ministry and positively confess their desires to God, the more they will be materially and spiritually rewarded with God's blessings. A person's lack of material success is attributed not to societal forces but to his or her lack of spiritual commitment.

Whereas the prophetic tradition is indigenous to the development of Afro-Christianity, the prosperity gospel has its modern origins in white, mid-twentieth-century Pentecostalism. Kenneth Hagin Sr., who is considered the "spiritual father" of prosperity gospel, has been distributing religious books and audiotapes on prosperity gospel since the mid-1960s (Harrison 2005). However, several scholars have noted that Hagin actually appropriated and plagiarized the writings of a little-known early twentieth century evangelist, E. W. Kenyon, whose perspective on prosperity blended Pentecostalism and New Thought metaphysics (Hollenweger 1997). Although on the fringes of Pentecostalism in the 1960s, Hagin popularized prosperity gospel through his radio broadcast, a magazine (*The Word of Faith)*, and through his Bible training schools.

The perspectives on the social gospel and liberation theology have been nurtured mostly in the corridors of seminaries. To the contrary, the Word of Faith Movement has disseminated its message broadly through a loosely formed network of nondenominational churches, Bible training schools and seminars, revivals, festivals, books, video and audio tapes, and especially through television cable networks such as the Trinity Broadcasting Network and the Word Network. Hagin's writings and sermons have influenced many of the contemporary prosperity gospel ministers, both black and white. Kenneth Copeland, a white minister from Forth Worth, Texas, and Frederick K. C. Price, a black minister from Los Angeles, have taken up Hagin's mantle as leading proselytizers of the doctrine, writing self-help-style books on prosperity that have mass appeal (Harrison 2005). With titles such as *The Laws of Prosperity* (first published by Copeland in 1974) and *Name It and Claim It! The Power of Positive Confession* (published by Price in 1992), the Word of Faith Movement has developed a cottage industry of Bible-based self-improvement books that provide guiding principles for the "abundant life."

Taking a page from the best selling book *Rich Dad, Poor Dad,* which provides readers instructions on how to become wealthy, John Avanzini's *Rich God, Poor God* offers a biblical parallel to enhance the riches of the righteous:

> As children of God, we have a heavenly father who "owns the cattle on a thousand hills" (Psalm 50:10). The rich God of the Scripture openly declares, "The silver is mine, and the gold is mine, saith the LORD of hosts" (Haggai 2:8). Everyone knows the real God has limitless assets. However, much too often His Children declare to the world by their diminished lifestyles that He should be classified as a poor God! They are constantly using every possible means to raise funds for their various programs, while they go without the things they need in their personal lives. The thinking folks of this world ask, and rightly so, "How is it possible that a truly rich Father would have so many poor children?" (2001, viii)

Just as the social gospel and liberation theology preachers interpret biblical icons and scriptures to argue that Jesus and God side with the oppressed, prosperity gospel preachers also use biblical stories and scriptures to convey to believers that Christians should pursue wealth. Another popular minister of the prosperity gospel, Creflo Dollar, argues that Jesus was born into wealth because "Kings brought Him gold" after his birth and that Jesus had a "treasurer who [kept] up (with his money)," which suggests that the image of Jesus as a liberator by the prophetic tradition is, for proponents of the prosperity gospel, a mischaracterization.[6] In a scripture that has been the cornerstone of prophetic teaching, Luke (4:18–19) proclaims:

> The Spirit of the Lord is upon me, because he hath anointed me to preach the gospel to the poor; he hath sent me to heal the broken hearted, to teach deliverance to the captives, and the recovering of the blind, to set at liberty them that are bruised, to preach the acceptable day of the Lord.

Dollar interprets this passage as a command to teach the poor to change their situation. Stating that "Jesus said that the poor will be with us always," Dollar proclaims that "Jesus takes the poor man who has no control over his life and puts him back in control of his circumstances when he receives this message (of prosperity)" (Dollar 1999, 4).

Kirbyjon H. Caldwell, who preaches the prosperity gospel at the majority black Windsor Village United Methodist Church in Houston, argues that Christians have misinterpreted the well-known biblical scripture that commands that it is more difficult for a rich man to ascend to the kingdom of heaven than for a camel to pass through the eye of a needle. While reading Joshua 1:8, which refers to prosperity for those who keep God's law, Caldwell got an epiphany about the meaning of prosperity for Christians:

> "Whoa!" I thought. "God wants me to be prosperous and have good success! God did not make provisions—whether it's stocks and bonds, nice cars and nice homes, or peace of mind, joy, and healthy self-esteem—for Satan's kids. God's provisions are for His children, if they're for anybody" (Caldwell 1999, 17).

T. D. Jakes, who has been dubbed the next Billy Graham and one of the most popular preachers in the United States, argues that the tactics of the activist black church of the 1960s hold less importance today. Rather than an emphasis on social justice, Jakes argues, there needs to be a greater focus on helping people obtain the good life:

> Jesus said, "I come that you might have life and have it more abundantly. . . ." I'm not against marching, but in the '60s the challenge of the black church was to march. And there are times now perhaps that we may need to march. But there's more facing us than social justice. There's personal responsibility, motivating and equipping people to live the best lives that they can really does help them live the scriptures and to bring them to life.[7]

Although the prosperity gospel is growing in popularity among black adherents, aspects of the doctrine are not new in Afro-Christianity. The first half of the twentieth century saw the emergence of "Negro cults" such as Charles Manuel "Sweet Daddy" Grace's United House of Prayer and Father Divine's Peace Mission (Weisbrot 1983; Dallam 2007). Although these religious leaders were known for their flamboyant lifestyles and were accused of taking advantage of their largely poor followers, both Grace and Divine provided social services for their members that included affordable housing, food pantries, and daycare centers for working parents. Indeed, they were directly involved in politics, which included supporting civil rights causes such as antilynching legislation and participating in electoral politics. However, unlike the prosperity ministers and their followers today, Grace and Divine's ministries were composed of people primarily on the margins (Weisbrot 1984; Dallam 2007).

A more direct line to the prosperity gospel in Afro-Christianity is found in the ministries of Reverend Frederick Eikerenkoetter (better known as Reverend Ike) of United Church and Science Institute in New York and Boston and the Reverend Johnnie Colemon of the Christ Universal Temple in Chicago. Both these ministers were known to teach the importance of prosperity and adopted New Thought metaphysics as part of their religious message, starting back in the 1970s and 1980s. Reverend Ike, who flaunted materialism, preached to his followers during his popular radio broadcast that the "lack of money is the root of all evil."

Hans A. Baer and Merrill Singer (1992) describe this religious perspective in Afro-Christianity as "thaumaturgical sects." These sects "maintain that the most direct way to achieve socially desired ends—such as financial prosperity, prestige, love and health—is by engaging in various magico-religious rituals or the acquiring of esoteric knowledge that provides individuals with spiritual power over themselves and others" (62).

Thaumaturgical sects undermine followers' participation in social reform and civic activism because they

> tend to hold the individual responsible for his or her present condition and stress the need to develop a positive frame of mind while at the same time overcoming negative attitudes. . . . Because of their individualistic orientation, such groups are largely apolitical and express little interest in social reform." (63)

Although followers of prosperity gospel do not practice magico-religious rituals or require their adherents to acquire esoteric knowledge, the prosperity gospel does practice positive confession as a way to acquire material prosperity, health, and positive family relationships. What is new about the emergence of prosperity gospel in the post–civil rights era is that its adherents are not on the margins of society, nor is the prosperity gospel viewed as a cult-like religion. Many of the followers are thought to be from the striving black working class and middle class rather than from poor, inner-city communities.

As a religious worldview that is anchored in individualism, prosperity gospel has the potential to undermine the civic traditions of black churches. One important study on the influence of the prosperity gospel in black churches notes that "instead of advocating protest marches, voting drives, and other forms of activism familiar to black church movements," the prosperity gospel "teach[es] members that poverty is the curse of the devil and the power to transform their oppression resides within the ability to appropriate their faith and take their rightful place in the Kingdom of God." This worldview not only appeals to the growing black middle-class, whose class status would have predicted that they would become less religious or join middle-class mainline denominations, it also appeals to "all poverty-stricken minorities stretching for a glimmer of hope" (Lee 2005, 103).

On the other hand, the prosperity gospel may be forming other new social bonds that can have long-term consequences for the politics of black communities. One of the most interesting developments in American Protestantism is the racial and ethnic diversity of the Pentecostal movement. Where Martin Luther King lamented in the 1960s that Sunday church services were the most segregated hour in America, the diversity found in Pentecostalism today outpaces the largely homogeneous liberal mainline Protestant and traditional black churches. These connections have the potential to create multiracial religious movements on the right, as we have seen around opposition to gay marriage and homosexual rights by coalitions of white and black evangelicals (Harris 1999).

Religious and Political Explanations of the Emergence of Prosperity Gospel

Although the prosperity gospel is not explicitly political in its orientation, as are the liberal theologies of social gospel and black liberation theology, its popularity emerged simultaneously with the rise of political conservatism in the 1980s. Since then the civil rights community has been under attack for its lack of new ideas for solving the problems of the poor and for continuing to believe that racial discrimination is the primary explanation for why many in the black community have not progressed. Social welfare programs were gradually dismantled. Civil rights initiatives, most notably affirmative action, and the social programs of the New Deal and Great Society have been challenged not only by conservatives but also by liberals. Part of the appeal of the prosperity gospel is that even if government cannot solve the problems of the poor, followers believe that God can bring about prosperity and good health despite the secular world's systems of poverty and racism.

To adherents of the prosperity gospel, positive thoughts and the practice of planting financial "seeds" through monetary contributions to ministries may have greater possibility for social mobility than the government policies for the poor or laws forbidding racial discrimination. No analysis of racism or "suffering" are part of prosperity's gospel, for

> racism is not important because the individual and the desire for money is all that is important. The poor are blamed for their poverty, the poverty itself seen as evidence that they do not fully believe in

Christ. With money, all seeming injustices can be corrected. Justice is just another commodity in their theologies. (Mitchem 2007, 82)

Indeed, the black community is divided on whether the lack of progress in black communities is mostly caused by racism or by the individual fault of blacks themselves, a perspective that would complement the individualist thrust of the prosperity gospel movement among Afro-Christians. In a survey commissioned by Columbia University's Center on African-American Politics and Society (CAAPS) and the ABC News Polling Unit, a plurality of blacks—44 percent—think that the lack of black progress is attributed to insufficient initiative among blacks themselves, whereas 37 percent believe that the reason that blacks have not moved forward is racism. This response is interesting in light of the fact that over three-quarters of blacks (76 percent) reported that they had personally experienced racial discrimination. Clearly for a large segment of blacks structural forces in American society have less impact on black progress than what can be gained by the virtues of individual responsibility.[8] Indeed, during the 2008 presidential election, Barack Obama often lectured majority black audiences about the need for blacks to take greater personal responsibility in their lives. In one speech, given at a Pentecostal church in Chicago on Father's Day, Obama urged black men to take greater responsibility for being fathers, a message that was positively received in black communities.

Another explanation of the rise in the popularity of prosperity gospel is one of the very successes of the civil rights movement—the rise of a visible black middle class, the largest in the nation's history. Like their white counterparts, the "mainline" black Protestant congregations are losing members to fundamentalist and charismatic churches, many of which are nondenominational and promote the gospel of prosperity. Whereas middle-class congregations of the past were rooted in the social gospel tradition, the poor and working-class Pentecostal congregations were more likely to be apolitical and "otherworldly." No longer considered cults or marginal to the African-American religious experience, neo-Pentecostalism has evolved in the post–civil rights era as a religion of respectability that appeals to the black middle class and to "strivers" who link their upward mobility to a spiritual worldview that rewards believers with wealth and good health.

Another possible explanation might be the realization that black political empowerment has not been accompanied by black economic success. Although the prophetic tradition served as a religious justification for the black power movement and helped to facilitate that movement's incorporation into electoral politics by promoting the belief that activist churches have an obligation to support candidacies that represent the interest of oppressed communities, blacks remain, as a group, on the economic margins of American life. Indeed, while the number of black elected officials has climbed in the past forty years, including unprecedented numbers of blacks elected to Congress and to city halls, local, state, and national governments, services to the poor have been severely cut back. Thus, perhaps for many followers of the prosperity gospel, the ideas and strategies of the social gospel tradition are perceived to be no longer legitimate (at least not solely) for "uplifting" black communities from poverty. Again, recent trends in black public opinion are instructive. When asked whether blacks should gain economic power or build political power, a clear majority of blacks—62 percent—believe that building economic power is more important than gaining political power (24 percent). Only 14 percent thought both were equally important.[9]

What's even more revealing is that most African-Americans believe that individual strategies are better for the material improvement of blacks as a group than collective group strategies. Although a majority of African-Americans—64 percent—feel that their fate is linked with other blacks, blacks are clearly divided over what is the best strategy for group progress. A majority of blacks believe it is better for blacks to improve their situation by working within the system (51 percent) than by engaging in protest (43 percent). And a slight plurality—49 percent—believe that blacks have to play down their racial identity rather than freely express their racial identity (46 percent) in order to get ahead in society. What is more, blacks are also divided over what is the best way for blacks to perceive themselves in society. A near majority (49 percent) agree that "blacks should stop thinking of themselves as a group and think more of themselves as individuals." Forty-eight percent of blacks disagreed.[10] Clearly, beliefs emphasizing economic strategies over political strategies, conventional politics over the politics of protest, and individualism over group solidarity would be receptive to the theological claims of the prosperity gospel. Future research in religion and African-American politics will have to systematically tease out the relationships between theological beliefs and social and political views on what are the best strategies for black progress.

Conclusion

The debate between the social gospel/black liberation theology and the prosperity gospel raises general questions about role of theology in a democracy. Although we see the two theological traditions dividing black religion, there are larger issues at play about how best to integrate religious citizens into a democracy. Should the faithful organize among themselves to have their preferences attended to in the polity, or should religion provide individuals with habits and beliefs that support democratic values? For African-Americans, a group whose political and religious values are rooted in a commitment to solidarity, this question is becoming ever more meaningful. The rise of the prosperity gospel in Afro-Christianity offers a departure from the group-oriented strategy. One could argue that, like the integrating forces of the Protestant ethic in nineteenth century Britain and the United States, the prosperity gospel equips its adherents to thrive in a market-driven economy and in a political system that privileges individuals over groups.

Indeed, the popularity of the theology itself might be a reflection of the larger changes that are occurring in the politics of black communities. In a period in which racial identities are competing with other social identities—class, gender, sexuality, and religion—the social gospel tradition and black liberation theology in particular may be running its course in a so-called postracial society.

The battle between the gospel of prosperity and the social gospel/liberation theology tradition presents several possibilities for the future of religion and African-American political activism. As Alan Wolfe explains in this volume's introduction, not only is there religious diversity, a fact that is the foundation of our understanding of the role of religion in American public life, but there is also political diversity in American religion. What this analysis of religion and politics in black communities points to is the increasing diversity—or greater divergence—of theological perspectives in Afro-Christianity. Although black Americans, particularly in wake of Barack Obama's ascendancy to the White House, are solidly attached to the Democratic Party, there are differences among blacks about how blacks should go about socially, economically, politically, and, yes, religiously improving themselves and black communities.

Here are some possibilities of the political impact that prosperity gospel might have on the future of black politics. Strong adherence to the gospel of prosperity could lead to a return to political quiescence among a large segment of the black religious community, or at least a decline in church-based activism. Believers might be less inclined to participate in civic and political life oriented toward community action because of their focus on individual concerns and material desires. On the other hand, because of the Pentecostal origins of the prosperity gospel, the nature of church-based activism among some blacks may shift from a social justice focus to activism centered on moral issues such as abortion and gay marriage. The seeds for that type of activism are present. Although over 90 percent of African-Americans in California voted for Barack Obama in the 2008 general election, 70 percent of blacks also voted in favor of Proposition 8, a ballot measure that overturned the California Supreme Court's legalization of same-sex marriage.

But it is also possible that believers may develop a mixed theological worldview that incorporates elements of both the social gospel tradition and the gospel of prosperity. Afro-Christians may simultaneously be committed to individual transformation as well as the need for community transformation through social and political action. However, mixed theological perspectives might still produce less civic engagement than there would be for a theological perspective that solely embraced the social gospel tradition or liberation theology, two religious worldviews that are by their definition committed to social and political change. It is unclear whether prosperity gospel will win out or fade or whether the social gospel tradition will remain as an important theological justification for the need for social change in black communities. But what is clear is that the social and political changes in contemporary black life, especially the widening social class gap among blacks, present a new challenge for Afro-Christianity in the twenty-first century.

Notes

1. John Blake, "Bishop's Charity Generous to Bishop," *Atlanta-Journal Constitution* August 28, 2005.

2. In 2007 the Senate Finance Committee launched an investigation of Bishop Long and other prosperity gospel ministers. The committee is looking into whether particular ministries are operating more like for-profit institutions than nonprofit institutions that are tax exempt. Senator Chuck Grassley (R-IA), the ranking minority leader of the Senate Finance Committee, has requested financial documents from various ministers and churches. Other ministers under investigation include Kenneth and Gloria Copeland, Creflo Dollar, Benny Hinn, Joyce Meyer, and Paula White.

3. John Blake, "Long Not Welcomed by All at Seminary, Graduation Provokes Protest," *Atlanta-Journal Constitution* May 11, 2006.

4. "Black Leaders Blast Mega Churches, Say They Ignore Social Justice," Associated Press, June 29, 2006.

5. "Black Baptist eschew 'prosperity preaching,'" Transcript, WFAA TV, Dallas, September 7, 2006.

6. John Blake, "Was Jesus Rich? Swanky Messiah Not Far-fetched in Prosperity Gospel," *Atlanta-Journal Constitution*, October 22, 2006.

7. Quoted from transcript, "Prosperity Gospel," *Religion and Ethics*, August 17, 2007.

8. See Fredrick C. Harris, "Survey on Race, Politics, and Society," Center on African-American Politics and Society, Columbia University, September 2008.

9. See Harris, "Survey on Race, Politics, and Society" (2008).

10. "Blacks' Political Engagement Spikes, Though Racial Divisions Remain Deep," ABC News/USA Today/Columbia University Poll: Blacks, Politics, and Society," September 23, 2008, http://abcnews.go.com/PollingUnit/Politics/story?id=5831483&page=1.

References

Avanzini, John. 2001. *Rich God, Poor God: Your Perception Changes Everything*. Tulsa, OK: Abel Press.

Baer, Hans A. and Merrill Singer. 1992. *African-American Religion in the Twentieth Century*. Knoxville, TN: University of Tennessee Press.

Blumhofer, Edith L. 1993. *Restoring the Faith: The Assemblies of God, Pentecostalism, and American Culture*. Urbana, IL: University of Illinois Press.

Caldwell, Kirbyjon, with Mark Seal. 1999. *The Gospel of Good Success*. New York: Simon & Schuster.

Calhoun-Brown, Allison. 1999. "The Image of God: Black Theology and Racial Empowerment in the African-American Community." *Review of Religious Research* 40:197–212.

Cleage, Albert B. Jr. 1993. "The Black Messiah." In *Black Theology: A Documentary History,* Vol. 1: *1966–1979,* eds. James H. Cone and Gayraud S. Wilmore. Maryknoll, NY: Orbis Press.

Coleman, Simon. 2000. *The Globalisation of Charismatic Christianity*. Cambridge: Cambridge University Press.

Cone, James H. 1970. *A Black Theology of Liberation*. Philadelphia and New York: J. B. Lippincott.

Copeland, Kenneth. 1999 [1974]. *The Laws of Prosperity*. Tulsa, OK: Harrison House.

Dallam, Marie. 2007. *Daddy Grace: A Celebrity Preacher and His House of Prayer*. New York: New York University Press.

Dawson, Michael. 1994. *Behind the Mule: Race and Class in African-American Politics*. Princeton, NJ: Princeton University Press.

———. 2001. *Black Visions: The Roots of Contemporary African-American Political Ideologies*. Chicago: University of Chicago Press.

Dollar, Creflo A. 1999. *Total Life Prosperity: 14 Practical Steps to Receiving God's Full Blessing*. Nashville, TN: Thomas Nelson Publishers.

Franklin, Robert M. 2007. *Crisis in the Village: Restoring Hope in African-American Communities*. Minneapolis, MN: Fortress Press.

Gaines, Kevin. 1996. *Uplifting the Race: Black Leadership, Politics, and Culture in the Twentieth Century*. Chapel Hill, NC: University of North Carolina Press.

Genovese, Eugene. 1974. *Roll, Jordan, Roll: The World the Slaveholders Made*. New York: Vintage Books.

Glaude, Eddie S. 2000. *Exodus! Religion, Race, and Nation in Early Nineteenth-century America*. Chicago: University of Chicago Press.

Harris, Fredrick C. 1999. *Something Within: Religion in African-American Political Activism*. New York: Oxford University Press.

———. 2001. "Black Churches and Civic Traditions: Outreach, Activism, and the Politics of Public Funding of Faith-Based Ministries." In *Can Charitable Choice Work? Covering Religion's Impact on Urban Affairs and Social Services*, ed. Andrew Walsh. Hartford, CT: Pew Program on Religion and the News Media and Greenberg Center for the Study of Religion in Public Life, Trinity College.

Harris-Lacewell, Melissa. 2004. *Barbershops, Bibles, and B.E.T.: Everyday Talk and Black Political Thought*. Princeton, NJ.: Princeton University Press.

Harrison, F. Milmon. 2005. *Righteous Riches: The Word of Faith Movement in Contemporary African-American Religion*. New York: Oxford University Press.

Hollenweger, W. J. 1972. *The Pentecostals: The Charismatic Movement in the Churches*. Minneapolis, MN: Augsburg Publishing House.

Kelley, Robin D. G. 1990. *Hammer and Hoe: Alabama Communists during the Great Depression*. Chapel Hill, NC: University of North Carolina Press.

Lee, Shayne. 2005. *America's New Preacher: T. D. Jakes*. New York: New York University Press.

Lincoln, C. Eric, and Lawrence H. Mamiya. 1990. *The Black Church in the African-American Experience*. Durham, NC: Duke University Press.

Luker, Ralph E. 1991. *The Social Gospel in Black and White*. Chapel Hill, NC: University of North Carolina Press.

McAdam, Doug. 1982. *Political Process and the Development of Black Insurgency*. Chicago: University of Chicago Press.

Mitchem, Stepanie. 2007. *Name It and Claim It? Prosperity Preaching in the Black Church*. Cleveland, OH: The Pilgrim Press.

Morris, Aldon. 1984. *The Origins of the Civil Rights Movement*. New York: Free Press.

Owens, Michael Leo. 2007. *God and Government in the Ghetto: The Politics of Church-State Collaboration*. Chicago: University of Chicago Press.

Price, Frederick K. C. 1990. *Prosperity on God's Terms*. Tulsa, OK: Harrison Press.

———. 1992. *Name It and Claim It! The Power of Positive Confession*. Los Angeles: Faith One Publishing.

Raboteau, Albert J. 1978. *Slave Religion: The "Invisible Institution" in the Antebellum South*. New York: Oxford University Press.

———. 1994. "African-Americans, Exodus, and the American Israel." In *African-American Christianity: Essays in History*, ed. Paul E. Johnson. Berkeley: University of California Press.

Thurman, Howard. 1996 [1949]. *Jesus and the Disinherited*. Boston: Beacon Press.

Weisbrot, Robert. 1984. *Father Divine and the Struggle for Racial Equality*. Urbana, IL: University of Illinois Press.

Chapter 9

THIS FAR BY FAITH?

Religion, Gender, and Efficacy

ALLISON CALHOUN-BROWN

Faith is the substance of things hoped for, the evidence of things not seen.
—Hebrews 11:1 NKJV

EARLY IN 2008, I went to a women's meeting with a friend at a local church not too far from where I live. Those in attendance at the meeting fully reflected the rich mosaic of African-American religious life. In the same room there were medical doctors, attorneys, engineers, psychologists, and college professors fellowshipping somewhat seamlessly with others who in social scientific language would be classified as "the underclass"—women with no or low-paying jobs, some from housing projects, others with miraculous testimonies of survival—all sharing the word of faith. There were young women and old, married women and single, some with children and some without, all assembled to learn how to be more effective—as women—in their lives.

Before the service, in the informal network that was my pew, I heard (and participated in) a rich debate about whether it was more logical and advantageous to support Hillary Clinton to be the first female president or Barack Obama to be the first African-American president. There was even one woman in the row who suggested the Republican agenda of John McCain might be more consistent with the principles of our faith. The only clear consensus that emerged from that conversation was that these were exciting times and that everyone should get involved and participate politically.

The service began. A female minister (women can be ordained at this church) spoke for about an hour on the power women can possess if they understand the role of authority in their lives. Indeed, the minister explained that if women remain submitted to God as our Father, submitted to our husbands, and submitted to ministerial leadership, then we will remain in a position to be blessed. In the next segment we learned some fashion tips. Right before the service was dismissed, we were reminded to get out and vote in the political primary that was coming up soon.

By the end of the meeting, as a political scientist, I felt once again as if I had been hit in the middle of the intersection of religion, gender, politics, and race, all paths that structure my life. I came home and returned to this chapter while asking myself the questions: Is religion empowering for women? Is it empowering for me? When democratic impulses are communicated in a patriarchal environment, what is the net effect?

Of course I am not the first to reflect on issues related to the equality of men and women in religious environments. This is not unique to the African-American experience. For religious women, the very faith that is the source of strength and comfort for them, foundational to the choices they make, and essential to eternal life, too often in a fundamental way devalues or at least discriminates against them because of who they are as women. This is true in nearly all faith traditions, among all races and ethnicities. Although race and ethnicity certainly influence the dynamic, the broader issues of religion and empowerment are ones most religious women face sooner or later. My experience at an African-American church that evening was the impetus to evaluate in this chapter the more general question of how religion, gender, and efficacy are related in the lives of American women. The message of authority and submission that was communicated that night is communicated in various ways in churches, synagogues, mosques, and temples all over the country. The hymns that are sung in the service may take on a traditional, gospel, country, or contemporary flair, but the context with regard to gender issues and inequality is strikingly familiar.

There is no doubt that religion is a highly gendered sphere. Nearly every faith tradition is patriarchal—often citing and celebrating sacred texts as holy justification for subordination. Even today in most congregations the clergy are male, God is Father, and "His" way is the norm for church, family, and life. In a recent book another professor tells of standing happily with her mother and daughters in an Orthodox synagogue in Jerusalem for prayer when she was interrupted by her eldest daughter and asked: "Mommy how can you stand behind this *mechitza* and teach feminism?"[1] She approached the rabbi about reconfiguring the seating so that the women's section would be next to the men's rather than behind it. The rabbi refused her request and asked "aren't women treated with respect in other aspects of synagogue life?" (Hartman-Halbertal 2002).

This experience presents more than just a personal dilemma but has consequences for democratic politics and the role that religion and religious institutions play in facilitating it. What does it mean to have opportunities to learn civic skills, to be encouraged to vote, to develop social capital, to be politically informed and mobilized in a context that condones, supports, and in many cases promulgates inequality? Today, politicized religious movements like that of the religious right are often represented as a backlash against the successes of feminism in the late 1960s and 1970s. Marshalling the forces of the traditionalist faithful, these movements are portrayed as being dominated by men with the interest of women falling victim to male subjugation. The problem with this portrayal is that the congregations of the religious right are filled with women. Women are more religious than men on every indicator of religiosity and devotion. For generations women have been more likely than men to belong to religious organizations, to attend them regularly, to donate money to churches, to engage in volunteer activities through them, and to provide religious reasons for doing the work. It is ironic that these facts persist despite the fact that men are more likely to be in positions of authority (Burns et al. 2001, 89) and that the doctrine and practice of many of these religious organizations relegate women to supportive if not subordinate roles. Rather than victims of fundamentalist beliefs, many women have been active agents of these ideas. Several studies find that well-educated women are as likely to join patriarchal religious groups as those who do not have access to economic and educational resources (Davidman 1991; Kaufman 1991; Dufour 2000).

Although we may applaud the myriad ways religious institutions support democratic values and processes, it is insufficient if we do not also examine how participation and attendance in these institutions affect women. Not only political empowerment but personal empowerment is fundamental to female agency. As Jane Junn notes in a recent article, "political action is a double edged sword; it has potential for liberation and transformation, but it is also a uniquely powerful tool for the development of false consciousness" (2007, 131). Just as more women in government does not always mean better government, women participating in churches—developing social capital and civic skills and being politically mobilized through religious networks—does not necessarily produce better citizens, alter the nature of political or religious power, or change the effects that this power has on individual agency. From Islam to Judaism, Christianity to Hinduism, the greater part of religious experience is associated with the subservience of women, even while scholars highlight the value of religion to female political empowerment and women within these traditions claim to be liberated by their faith. Such disparate characterizations of the relationships among religion, political empowerment, and gender suggest that there is still much to learn about the nature of their intersection.

The main purpose of this chapter is to examine the ways religiosity affects feelings of personal and political empowerment in women. This sense of empowerment or efficacy is a self-appraisal of capabilities. It is an important gauge of the well-being of a democracy. Research consistently indicates the link between efficacy and participation (Campbell et al. 1960; Rosenstone and Hansen 1993). The more effective people feel, the more likely they are to engage the political process. There are many studies that examine the impact of religion on political participation[2]; far fewer examine religion's effect on antecedent political motivations such as efficacy. The basic findings of this study support the need to examine religious effects separately for men and women and to appreciate the multidimensionality of religious experience.

For women, frequent church attendance was a positive predictor of political efficacy, but it was negatively associated with feelings of personal empowerment. Diminishing personal efficacy—the personal agency of women—undermines their psychological resources in ways that men do not experience. Internalized and personal expressions of religion such as religious salience in this study had no impact on women but increased feelings of political efficacy in men. Just as people's religious experiences are often gender specific, the effects of religiosity on efficacy are also gender specific. As one observer remarked, religion offers a "mixed blessing" for the empowerment of women, simultaneously enhancing their competence and esteem but doing so within the constraints of a highly gendered religious domain (Hegland 1997).

Religious Institutions and Political Engagement

Contemporary political science research has recognized the significant place that churches occupy in supporting America's democratic capacity (Bellah et al. 1985; Verba et al. 1995; Putnam 2000). "Faith communities in which people worship together are arguably the single most important repository of social capital in America" (Putnam 2000, 66). Participation in these religious institutions produces the friendship networks, norms, and social trust that are beneficial to democratic governance. This works because the nonpolitical orientation of much religious activity can "spill over" to political activity because of the similarities and applicability of tasks (Peterson 1992). In addition to developing social capital, churches are excellent environments in which to learn civic skills. Religious institutions offer people opportunities to learn leadership, communication, and organization in ways that are not as easily available in other places. The man who drives the sanitation truck can be a deacon in the church; the woman who works in food service at the local diner can be the chair of the pastor's anniversary committee.

The relatively equal opportunity that churches provide to learn civic skills is reason to applaud their democratic vigor. Specifically, churches offer a way for women and minorities to compensate for deficits they may have in other socioeconomic resources. Moreover, churches can impact the politics of parishioners more directly through exposure to political stimuli, informal discussions, and leadership cues. As I experienced at the women's meeting, churches are places where friends talk politics and hear political messages, and people are socialized based on a particular perspective. All this is done in an environment infused with the transcendence that defines religious life. It can be a powerful combination.

Most studies that examine the relationship between religion and political engagement focus on how religious practices contribute to civic skills and social capital without more fully considering how such practices can directly affect the strength and confidence of those active in religious life. Believing that God is with you can be its own source of motivation and encouragement. "Blessed assurance" can provide strong incentives for participation (Harris 1999, chapter 5). There is a good deal of research focusing on African-American politics that demonstrates that this is the case. Not only do narratives of activists during the civil rights movement emphasize the importance of religiously induced efficacy to political action (Garrow 1986; MacLeod 1991; Williams 2002), empirical studies have also documented the relationship. Research shows that belief systems and religiosity serve to promote the psychological resources that are associated with political participation and collective action among African-Americans. Harris (1994, 1999) finds that religiously inspired political efficacy is not an opiate but a catalyst for greater political engagement. Calhoun-Brown (1996) elaborates on how attending political churches positively affects political motivation among blacks by increasing efficacy, interest, and consciousness. Indeed, there are many studies confirming the relationship among belief systems, religiosity, and psychological resources in the African-American community (Shingles 1981; Allen et al. 1989; Wilcox and Gomez 1990; Ellison 1991; Brown and Wolford 1993; Reese and Brown 1995; Harris-Lacewell 2004). However, less research has been devoted to this dynamic beyond minority communities.[3]

Gender, Religion, and Political Engagement

This oversight is particularly telling in the case of women. Contextualizing the religious domain is important (Djupe and Gilbert 2006). Research demonstrates that there are differences in how civic skills are developed between religious traditions (Brady et al. 1995; Djupe and Grant 2001; Cavendish 2000), between blacks and whites (Verba et al. 1993; Cavendish 2000; Musick et al. 2000), between women and men (Schlozman et al. 1994), and between church environments that are politically oriented and those that are not (Verba et al. 1995). If the nature of the religious context matters for the development of civic skills, it likely also matters for how resources such as efficacy are developed there. As Smidt observes, models that accentuate the link between associational life and civic engagement may underemphasize the role that social and structural antecedents play in the process (2003, ch 1).

For religious women one of the most important structural antecedents is the gendered nature of the religious domain. Institutionally, organized religion is complicit in the perpetuation of traditional gender roles. Reflecting on this fact more than a hundred years ago, Elizabeth Cady Stanton observed, "All the religions of the earth degrade her, and so long as women accept the position they assign her, emancipation is impossible."[4] Feminist scholars have long coupled their critique of a male-dominated society with a critique of religion.[5] Feminist calls for equality between the sexes have clashed sharply with traditional religion's ideas about a "God-ordained" hierarchy in family life. The God-ordained family structure is constituted by a husband, who is the primary breadwinner, decision maker, and authority; his wife, who is the primary homemaker; and their children, who are in humble subjection to the parents. The God-ordained unit mirrors the "ideal Beaver Cleaver type family" of the American cultural schema. As was observed in a recent article, "In the United States religion and family have been intertwined and interdependent institutions and the construction of familism, or morally sanctioned ideals of family, has been central to religious life and to official religious discourse" (Edgell and Docka, 2007). Traditional religion contributes to the social construction of gender. In the traditional conception only men have a public role, while women in their private role are keepers of hearth and home. Politics and other external conditions are outside the scope of a woman's responsibilities.

Today of course, what is considered an "appropriate" gender role is contested territory. Even in the most conservative communions there are "feminist sensibilities." Although conservative religious discourse still reflects very traditional gender roles, domestic practice is far more equivocal (Hunter 1987; Bartkowski 2001; W. Wilcox 2002). The continuing challenge and problem is that although traditional religions make both practical concessions and adaptations to the modern social trends that affect them just as do the rest of society, their notion of ideal family structure—what really "should" be—remains unchanged. For instance, it is a very different thing for evangelical Christians to disavow patriarchy altogether than to justify its continuance by calling on husbands to be nurturing, sensitive "servant leaders" (Gallagher 2003).

Distinctive gender roles also continue to be reflected in religious institutions. In churches men and women often operate and excel in separate spheres on the basis of conservative religious interpretation. Although some suggest that the autonomy of these separate spheres can be empowering (Kaufman 1991; Gilkes 1997; Brasher 1998), religious feminists criticize the damage done to women's identity by a masculine image of God and a paternal image of leadership (Daly 1973; Schussler-Fiorenza 1984; Ruether 1985; Plaskow 1990). In religious organizations the one great opportunity space for women is "churchwork." In many ways because "churchwork" is often largely a female sphere, it is not surprising that women are able to succeed and develop civic and organizational skills there. Still, many other aspects of religiosity are not as equitable. These nonequitable areas may be particularly relevant when it comes to psychological involvement in politics, where the gap between men and women persists. In their comprehensive study of the origins of participatory differences between the sexes, Burns et al. (2001) demonstrate that a weaker psychological orientation toward politics is one of the major reasons why men participate more than women.[6] They suggest that men and women have different "tastes for politics" largely because politics is perceived to be a man's game and that the gross disparities in the representation of men and women among visible political elites have implications for political participation. The psychological engagement of women with politics is therefore influenced by the gender composition of the political environment.

If this is true at the national level, the socialization that takes place in religious environments where there is often an even more complete absence of women in positions of authority might also be expected to have deleterious effects on perceptions of a woman's role, a woman's place, and a woman's capacity to engage in public life. If this absence is based on a justifying theology and set of beliefs about proper activities and roles for women, not only political engagement but personal engagement might also be undermined. In other words, for women, religiosity might be a negative indicator of personal and political efficacy even without consideration of the otherworldly orientations stereotypically associated with religious beliefs (Marx 1967). Still, these effects must be evaluated because there is a good deal of qualitative research that indicates religiosity increases efficacy in women (Kaufman 1991; Brasher 1998; Faver 2000; Griffith 2002). Some explain that even though patriarchal religious environments can be uncomfortable for them, women are willing to cope with the inequality in part because inequality is only peripheral to their faith experience (Ozorak 1996). Women have shown a tremendous capacity to "sift out" what is offensive from their religious traditions (Dufour 2000). It is important to remember that the "faith experience" is broad and multidimensional. It may not always produce consistent effects.

It is entirely possible that some aspects of religiosity lower feelings of efficacy and others increase it. Because religious institutions are disproportionately patriarchal, organizational aspects of religiosity such as church attendance may depress efficacy even while more personal aspects of religion such as religious salience or prayer and Bible reading might be expected to enhance it. It is also important to estimate effects of religion on both personal and political efficacy and not to assume somehow that increases in political efficacy reflect or are consistent with increases in personal efficacy. When democratic impulses are communicated in environments of gender inequality, does it make sense to expect that both the political and personal efficacy of women will still increase? As women of the religious right are mobilized politically, is their power really increased? Agency operates in the context of power relations. Recent research has applauded the opportunities that religious institutions provide to enhance the social capital and civic skills of women in particular. Although this may be a good thing, what are the normative consequences for women in American public life of gaining greater resources on these terms? Because of the gendered nature of most religious contexts and the traditional gender roles associated with them, my expectation is that, for women, church attendance increases political efficacy but decreases personal efficacy. Conservative religious beliefs decrease both personal and political efficacy; however, internal measures of religiosity such as religious salience are expected to increase them because believing one is working with a divine force is powerful motivation regardless of what those beliefs are.

Data and Measures

The data used to evaluate the relationships between religion and efficacy examined in this chapter come from Verba, Schlozman, Brady and Nie's 1990 American Citizen Participation Study (CPS). The study was designed to examine political and nonpolitical civic participation in the United States. It asks a considerable number of questions related to the religious orientations of respondents. It also has detailed measures of both personal and political efficacy.

Personal and Political Efficacy

Efficacy has two related components. The first component focuses on perceptions of personal ability; the second focuses on the government's responsiveness. As Lane explained in his classic study (1959), political efficacy "contains the tacit implication that an image of the self as effective is intimately related to the image of democratic government as responsive to the people." He continues, people "who have feelings of mastery and are endowed with ego strength tend to generalize these sentiments and to feel that their votes are important, politicians respect them, and elections are, therefore, a meaningful process" (149). Contemporary measures of political efficacy that distinguish between feelings of personal political effectiveness (internal efficacy) and government responsiveness (external efficacy) reflect this logic.[7] Personal efficacy is a particularly important concept to evaluate when looking at the impact of religion on the political engagement of women. Personal efficacy is a fundamental to female agency. As indicators of personal efficacy, individuals were asked to agree or disagree with the following statements: I usually count on being successful at everything I do; I like to assume responsibility; I like to take the lead when a group does things together; I enjoy convincing others of my opinions; I often notice I serve as a model for others; I am good at getting what I want; I am often a step ahead of others; I often give others advice and suggestions. Responses to these statements were combined into an additive index.[8]

The measures of political efficacy in the CPS largely tap its external dimension. Respondents were asked if they felt the national and local governments would pay attention to their complaints as well as whether they believed they had influence over government decisions in national and local matters. These four questions were combined to form a single indicator.[9]

The CPS data confirm the well-known fact that there are significant differences between men and women in terms of efficacy. Women had lower self-appraisals of their capabilities both personally and politically than men. Both the personal and political efficacies of men were higher than those of women. Men had a higher sense of personal agency as well as more confidence about their ability to impact politics when compared to women in the study.[10]

Religion in the CPS

Because religion is a multidimensional concept encompassing individual beliefs and behaviors as well as institutional orientations and activities, multiple measures must be employed to assess its impact. The first indicator of institutional religiosity used in this study is frequent church attendance. Women who attend places of worship regularly have more opportunities for exposure to the effects of religious institutions as gendered domains. This study compared individuals with very regular patterns of attendance, those who report that they go to church nearly every week or more, to those who do not go as often. Church attendance as an organizational or institutional expression of religiosity is likely to depress personal efficacy because in these contexts women are more likely to experience inequality than through more personalized religious expressions.

Unfortunately, no direct measure of the level of gender inequality someone faced in church was available in the CPS. Inclusion of such a measure would have been preferred.

Still, religious traditions vary in the number of women in positions of authority as well as how integral patriarchy is to church organization and teachings about family and social life. In an effort to capture this dynamic and as an additional measure of institutional religiosity, major American religious traditions are examined individually.[11] Denominational affiliation is but a blunt indicator of the gendered nature of the religious domain. It may not incorporate the high level of diversity that can exist in belief and between faith and practice in individual churches even within the same denominational family. Although certainly some religious traditions are more equitable than others, organized religion is not associated with female equality. The expectation is that the messages conveyed through institutionalized religion differ significantly from the messages one gets through personal prayer or meditation. In the organizational church environment, a minister interprets what is sacred; in personal contexts, an individual does the interpretation and decides what aspects of religion are relevant to his or her life. Similarly, because political socialization likely takes place at an organizational rather than the individual level, church attendance for women is expected to increase political efficacy because it is in church that respondents are exposed to political cues and democratic norms.

The second overall measure of religiosity included in this study is religious salience. Respondents were asked how important religion was to their lives. This study compares those who reported religion was very important to those who indicated it was less than very important in their lives. Religious importance is an individual expression of religious devotion. It is an indicator of the "blessed assurance" that religion may provide. Because such assurance can be a powerful source of motivation, it may increase both personal and political efficacy.

The third measure of religiosity in this study is an indicator of fundamentalist beliefs. This study compares those who believed the Bible was God's Word to those who did not express this conviction.[12] Fundamentalist beliefs may reflect the kind of conservative gender ideas that are expected to depress both personal and political efficacy. Fundamentalist beliefs, of course, are not associated with the empowerment of women because they reflect traditional gender roles. They may also influence levels of religious involvement (Peterson 1992; McKenzie 2001).[13]

The CPS data confirm a gender gap in the faith practices of men and women. On each of the measures of religiosity women were more devout than men. Almost 50 percent of women said that they went to church nearly every week or more. Only a third of men had this level of attendance. Nearly two-thirds of women reported religion was very important in their lives. Only about 40 percent of men expressed this sentiment. A majority of women believed that the Bible was God's Word; only 37 percent of men shared this opinion. There are obviously significant differences in the behavior and attitudes of men and women toward religion.[14]

In order to develop a clear picture of religions' influence on personal and political efficacy, additional factors must be examined to evaluate their part in this dynamic. For instance, it is well established that the development of civic skills and norms facilitates political engagement. In evaluating the impact of religiosity on efficacy, this study takes into account the level of civic skills that a person has. Civic skills can be developed at church, at work, or as a result of belonging to an organization. Each of these is a place where an individual might have written a letter, planned a meeting, exercised decision-making skills, or given a speech. Such activities increase competence and are easily transferrable to the political realm. An additive index of skills exercised in any of these contexts is included in the model. Earlier research suggests that differences in efficacy may in large part be rooted in life circumstances (Verba et al. 1997). Thus, this study controls for education, family income, marital status, organizational membership, preschool children, amount of job training, race, and the amount of free time an individual said he or she had. Finally, because knowledge is also supposed to breed confidence, the study includes an indicator of a person's general level of knowledge measured by the number of vocabulary words that he or she answered correctly.[15]

Results

Table 9.1 details the bivariate relationship between religious attendance and the components of personal and political efficacy for men and women. The bivariate relationship describes how differences in religious behavior or practice are reflected in personal and political efficacy. Men who attended church nearly once a week or more were distinguishable from those who went less frequently on two indicators. Specifically, men who went to church regularly were more likely to report that they liked to take the lead in a group and that they often serve as a role model than those who attended less frequently. In both of these instances church attendance was associated with a gain in personal efficacy. This was not the case for women. Like men, women who went to church very frequently were more likely to report that they served as a role model. However, unlike men, frequently attending women had lower levels of personal efficacy on several indicators. Significantly lower numbers of these women indicated that they liked to assume responsibility, that they liked convincing others, that they believed they were often a step ahead of others, or that they often gave advice. The negative relationship between frequent church attendance and these aspects of personal efficacy for women is particularly interesting in light of the clearly positive relationship that church attendance has on the political efficacy of this group. Table 9.1 records that on every aspect of political efficacy frequently attending women had higher mean responses than those with more sporadic attendance patterns. This relationship did not exist for men. No statistically significant differences in political efficacy were seen between men who went to church very often and those who did not attend as much.

Table 9.1 also displays the bivariate relationship between view of the Bible and the components of personal and political efficacy. As expected, on several indicators women who held the most fundamentalist position on biblical interpretation had lower levels of personal and political efficacy. Those who said that the Bible was God's Word scored lower on half of the variables that comprised the personal efficacy scale. Fundamentalist men scored lower on two of the indicators: being good at getting what is wanted and often being a step ahead of others. However, unlike the positive association between church attendance and political efficacy, view of the Bible was a negative predictor of political efficacy for women. Women who held the fundamentalist perspective had statistically lower means on their perceived influence on the local and national government and the amount of attention they believed their complaint would receive at the local level. Although fundamentalist women were distinctive, the political efficacy of men who had this view of the Bible was indistinguishable from that of other men in the CPS. Salience, the third indicator of religiosity, was not strongly associated with personal efficacy for women in this data set (not shown). Two relationships were statistically significant. Those who thought religion was very important were more likely to view themselves as role models, but they were less likely to think that they were a step ahead of others. Salience was also not a strong bivariate indicator of political efficacy in women, although in men it was associated with stronger feelings of efficacy toward national affairs.

Do the bivariate relationships suggested by these data persist when additional factors are taken into account? Does frequent church attendance hurt the personal efficacy of women even though it helps their political efficacy? Is it really a fundamentalist view of the Bible or other socioeconomic factors that predict feelings of personal and political empowerment, particularly in women? Table 9.2 displays the multivariate determinants of political efficacy for men and women. The multivariate analysis displays the impact of all the factors simultaneously. Two

TABLE 9.1
Religiosity and Components of Efficacy

	Church attendance			
	Men		Women	
	<Weekly	Weekly	< Weekly	Weekly
Personal efficacy (percentages)				
Counts on being successful	86	87	82	81
Likes to assume responsibility	90	90	89*	85
Takes lead in a group	51	56*	39	38
Likes convincing others	63	63	57**	50
Often serves as role model	45	56***	46	54***
Good as getting what is wanted	66	63	60	62
Often step ahead of others	58	56	53***	46
Often gives advice	78	82	78*	74
Political efficacy (means)				
Influence on local govt.	2.5	2.6	2.3	2.4*
Influence on national govt.	1.9	2.0	1.8	1.9*
Attention to local complaint	2.7	2.7	2.5	2.7***
Attention to national complaint	2.3	2.4	2.1	2.4***

	View of Bible			
	Men		Women	
	Not Word	God's Word	Not Word	God's Word
Personal efficacy (percentages)				
Counts on being successful	86	87	84	80
Likes to assume responsibility	88	92	89	86
Takes lead in a group	54	51	43***	34
Likes convincing others	62	64	53	55
Often serves as role model	47	52*	53*	46
Good as getting what is wanted	68***	58	67***	56
Often step ahead of others	59*	53	56***	44
Often gives advice	79	80	77	76
Political efficacy (means)				
Influence on local govt.	2.5*	2.4	2.5***	2.2
Influence on national govt.	1.9	1.9	1.9**	1.8
Attention to local complaint	2.7	2.6	2.7**	2.5
Attention to national complaint	2.4	2.3	2.3	2.3

Data: 1990 Citizens Participation Study. All tests of significance $^{*}p < .05$, $^{**}p < .005$, $^{***}p < .0005$.

TABLE 9.2
Determinants of Political Efficacy Regression Coefficients

Variable	Model 1 Men	Model 1 Women	Model 2 Men	Model 2 Women
Education	0.09***	0.16***	0.09*	0.16****
Free time	–0.01	0.04	0.01	0.00
Organizational membership	0.16***	0.18***	0.18***	0.15***
Vocabulary	0.11***	0.14***	0.12***	0.14***
Family income	0.08	–0.06	0.13*	–0.09
Civic skills	0.06*	0.10*	0.04*	0.12*
Married	0.24	0.34*	0.22	0.33*
Preschool children	–0.20	0.14	–0.28	0.23
Job training level	–0.02	–0.05	–0.04	–0.05
Race (white)	0.42	0.03		
Bible God's Word	**0.11**	**–0.08**		
Religion very important	**0.35***	**–0.11**	**0.38***	**–0.05**
Very regular church attend.	**–0.29**	**0.55*****	**–0.26**	**0.52*****
Latino Christians	**0.31**	**–0.24**		
Mainline Protestants	**0.17**	**–0.11**		
Black Protestants	**–0.08**	**0.02**		
Evangelical Protestants	**0.02**	**–0.20**		
Catholics	**–0.49***	**0.25**		
(Constant)	6.21***	5.43***	6.50***	5.5***
R^2	0.14	0.16	0.15	0.16
N	991	1086	916	1017

Data: 1990 Citizens Participation Study. In all tests of significance $*p < .05$, $**p < .005$, $***p < .0005$.

Note: Diagnostics indicate that multicollinearity is not a big issue in these models. In these models no tolerance was lower than 0.53, and no variance inflation factor was greater than 1.9. In Model 2 race is omitted from the analysis because much of the racial dynamic is expressed in denominational affiliation. Because view of the Bible is also associated with religious tradition, this variable is not included in Model 2.

models are reported on the table. The first model includes all the sociodemographic factors with the three indicators of religiosity: frequent attendance, religious salience, and view of the Bible. The second model displays the same information but substitutes specific religious traditions for the view of the Bible.

Overall, the results reported conform to expectations. The variables that have been previously associated with political efficacy predicted feelings of empowerment. For both men and women higher levels of education, a more comprehensive vocabulary, being a member of a civic organization, and exercising civic skills each augmented a sense of political efficacy. Not surprisingly, race was associated with higher levels of political efficacy for white men, although this same racial dynamic was not predicted in women. Differences in marital status affected the political efficacy of women but not men.

Particularly significant for this study were the different ways that the religious variables impacted a sense of political efficacy for men and women. Church attendance, measured as going to church nearly every week or more, was a strong positive predictor of political efficacy in women. It was about as robust an indicator as belonging to a civic association or acquiring civic skills. This was expected. What was not expected was that very frequent church attendance did not have a similar effect in men. The religious factor that did increase political efficacy in men was religious salience. Men who reported that religion was very important in their lives felt more politically empowered than those who did not. Although internal religiosity can be a source of strength and motivation, these data suggest that it is men who get a political boost from private religious commitment.

Bivariate analysis suggested that view of the Bible might be a significant indicator of political efficacy for women. However, the multivariate models indicate that this relationship is driven by other socioeconomic factors. Once variables such as education, organizational membership, civic skills, and marital status were introduced, view of the Bible had no effect.

Table 9.2 Model 2 examines whether the positive impact that very regular church attendance had on the political efficacy of women is attributable to variation among faith traditions. The data indicate that, after taking into account other factors, there were no significant differences between unaffiliated women and those who were part of a denominational family. Denominational variation did not explain or moderate the positive relationship between regular church attendance and the political efficacy of women. Regardless of faith tradition, going to church a lot helped the political efficacy of women. When other factors were controlled for, there was no relationship between going to church frequently and the political efficacy of men. Moreover, for both men and women no significant interaction effects were found between religious tradition and frequent attendance.

Is personal efficacy predicated by the same factors as political efficacy? Table 9.3 displays these results. For the most part, similar things increase the personal efficacy of both men and women. Education, civic skills, and higher levels of job training all increased a sense of individual agency. Having less free time also predicted higher levels of personal efficacy, as busy people who are engaged in many tasks probably engage in the

TABLE 9.3
Determinants of Personal Efficacy Regression Coefficients

	Model 1		Model 2	
Variable	Men	Women	Men	Women
Education	0.09***	0.10***	0.10***	0.11***
Free time	−0.08***	−0.05***	−0.08***	−0.05***
Organizational membership	0.02	−0.04	0.03	−0.02
Vocabulary	−0.03	−0.07	−0.05	−0.08*
Family income	0.18***	0.13*	0.14*	0.09*
Civic skills	0.14***	0.22***	0.14***	0.22**
Married	−0.02	−0.24	−0.07	−0.24
Preschool children	−0.33	0.03	−0.40*	−0.02
Job training level	0.09*	0.12***	0.10*	0.10*
Race (white)	−0.74***	−0.48		
Bible God's Word	0.08	−0.11		
Religion very important	0.07	0.17	0.01	0.17
Very regular church attend.	−0.17	−0.32*	−0.17	−0.40***
Latino Christians			0.82*	0.48
Mainline Protestants			−0.40	0.31
Black Protestants			0.52	0.94**
Evangelical Protestants			−0.45*	0.08
Catholics			0.02	0.62*
(Constant)	4.00	3.74	3.71	3.10
R^2	0.19	0.16	0.20	0.16
N	987	1097	913	1027

Data: 1990 Citizens Participation Study. In all tests of significance $^{*}p < .05$, $^{**}p < .005$, $^{***}p < .0005$.

Note: Diagnostics indicate that multicollinearity is not a big issue in these models. In these models no tolerance was lower than 0.53, and no variance inflation factor was greater than 1.9. In Model 2 race is omitted from the analysis because much of the racial dynamic is expressed in denominational affiliation. Because view of the Bible is also associated with religious tradition, this variable is not included in Model 2.

tasks because they feel competent to do so. It is interesting that race was a negative indicator of personal efficacy for white men and women compared to the minority groups. Although perhaps unanticipated, this finding is consistent with many empirical studies that show blacks and other minorities have self-esteem equal to or greater than that of whites (Hughes and Demo 1989). Whites score higher than minority groups only when indicators of personal efficacy tap the level of control they feel they can exert over their lives. Thus, race increased the political efficacy of white men in the earlier political efficacy model. Because the measure of personal efficacy utilized in this study is a more basic assessment of personal worth and value, it is not unusual that race would be associated with lower levels of efficacy for whites on this measure.

Still, what is surprising is that frequent church attendance is associated with a decrease in feelings of empowerment for women. Women who went to church very frequently had lower levels of personal efficacy. The relationship for men was not statistically significant. It is striking that church attendance and not fundamentalist doctrine was associated with lower feelings of personal empowerment. Believing the Bible was God's Word was not a significant predictor of political or personal efficacy.[16] For women, however, frequent church attendance had an opposite effect on personal efficacy than it had on political efficacy.

The second model on table 9.3 indicates that religious traditions are of some consequence in developing feelings of personal efficacy. Compared to the unaffiliated, both Catholic and black Protestant women reported higher levels of personal empowerment. Black women scored almost a full point higher, and Catholic women nearly two-thirds of a point higher, than women who did not belong to a faith tradition. What is particularly interesting though is that, even taking into account denominational variation and the positive effect that religious traditions had on this indicator, frequent church attendance remained a strong negative determinant of personal efficacy for women. Those with very regular attendance patterns scored almost a half point lower on the personal efficacy scale than women who did not go to church as often.

A different pattern emerged for men. Church attendance was not a statistically significant indicator of personal efficacy for them. Of the religious variables, only evangelical tradition and Latino Christian had a notable effect on personal efficacy. Evangelical men were nearly a half point less efficacious, while Latinos scored almost a point higher than men with no stated religious affiliation.

Understanding that frequent church attendance is negatively associated with the personal efficacy of women gives us an opportunity to develop a more comprehensive picture of the gendered effect religion has on politics. Both personal and political efficacy increase political participation. If church attendance helps with one but hurts the other, what is the net effect? Figure 9.1 presents a path model that describes the positive and negative ways frequent church attendance influenced the nonelectoral political participation of women.[17] This kind of analysis evaluates indirect effects. How did church attendance, operating through personal and political efficacy as well as civic skills, ultimately impact participation? When basic sociodemographic factors were taken into account, frequent church attendance did not have a direct influence on participation. It did, however, have indirect influence through civic skills and personal and

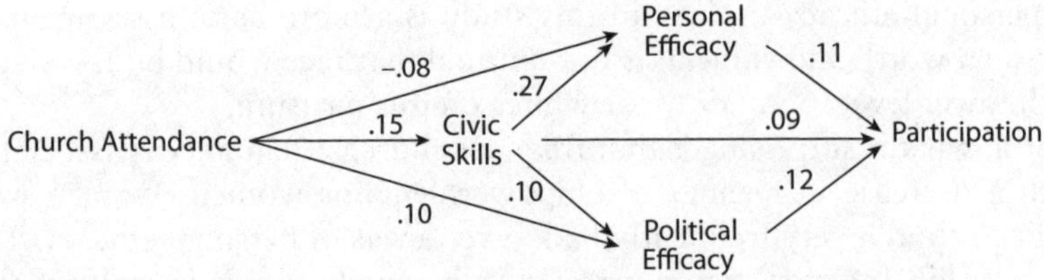

Figure 9.1. Path model of the effects of church attendance on political participation for women. Paths from exogeneous variables are controlled for education, income, race, organizational membership, and job training. All path coefficients significant at the $p < 0.05$ level or greater.

political efficacy.[18] Although the total indirect effect of church attendance on participation was modest, it is important to note that the total positive indirect effect was diminished by a fourth when the negative impact of church attendance on political efficacy was taken into account.[19] Although the effect is small, it nonetheless demonstrates the complicated and not always positive ways that church attendance effects the participation of women. It is also worth noting that for women frequent church attendance hurt personal efficacy nearly as much as church attendance helped their political efficacy. Not even the generation of civic skills fully compensated for this negative effect. The indirect positive effect church attendance had on personal efficacy through civic skills (0.04) only cut in half the overall negative direct effect that frequent church attendance had on personal efficacy (–0.08).

Religion, Gender, and Efficacy

There are several conclusions that can be drawn from this analysis. First, the importance of separately estimating models for men and women is abundantly clear. There are important differences in the way religion affects the two groups. Because the religious experiences of men and women are distinct, any expectation that the socialization they receive in religious contexts would be the same is problematic. Religion is a gendered sphere and produces gendered effects. Considering the importance of religion to women and the significance of religion to politics, in many ways the nature of the relationship among women, religion, and politics is both undertheorized and underinvestigated. Few studies examine the intersection of religion, politics, and gender, although at that intersection much can be learned about the complex nature of inequality and how beliefs, behaviors, institutions, and communities interact both to sustain and challenge the systems of stratification in which we all live.

Second, it is important to remember the multidimensional nature of religiosity and begin to appreciate its complex and sometimes inconsistent effects. There is a rich literature that documents how people gain civic skills through church. This is clearly important and beneficial to both efficacy and participation. However, everyone at church will not gain civic skills; everyone in the church will not engage to that degree. As anyone who has ever been a part of an organization knows, only a minority of people really do any work. But all women experience the gendered nature of the religious domain. Taking into account the effect of civic skills—does religiosity help or hurt the empowerment of women? This study reveals that it does both. Going to church frequently increased a woman's sense of political efficacy, but overall it decreased her sense of individual agency even after taking into account the effect of civic skills. It is entirely possible to feel more effective politically without feeling more effective personally. Religious institutions can energize women politically, then, without necessarily empowering them individually. This effect may be particularly salient when women are engaged politically in religious contexts that do not embrace the full equality of men and women. Scholars are examining these issues in democratizing nations and in Muslim countries; they are no less relevant here in the United States.

These issues were on dramatic display when John McCain chose Sarah Palin as his Republican running mate in the presidential campaign of 2008. In a political change up, traditionalist "family values" Republicans made feminist-oriented arguments about Palin's abilities to manage governing with family responsibilities, while gender-sensitive Democrats flirted with sexism and questioned the Alaskan Governor's judgment, experience, and values. Palin's selection illustrated the complexity of the relationship between religiosity and female empowerment. As a governor she was a modern religious woman who advocated traditional and conservative moral cultural ideas. She mobilized the Republican religious base, engaging the churches and political networks of Christian and social conservatives. For these cultural warriors her nomination was politically mobilizing in large part because she articulated social conservative values. Religious conservatives were mobilized by Palin's nomination because she was a champion of their ideas. However, they were mobilized politically without significant departure from the way these religious ideas have historically privileged gender inequality and diminished personal efficacy. For these religious conservatives, political mobilization was an entirely separate issue from whether women were personally empowered by the orientation of the faith. This distinction is especially salient because women often receive conflicting messages in religious environments about what are appropriate roles for them.

The third significant finding from this study is that it was frequency of church attendance, not a fundamentalist view of the Bible, that was negatively associated with personal efficacy. Some caution must be exercised in interpreting this effect and in concluding that fundamentalist ideas have no effect on the personal agency or efficacy of women. In the CPS, people were asked whether they believed the Bible was God's Word, inspired by God, written by men, or just a book written long ago. Other data sets allow for a clearer differentiation between those who take the Bible literally and those who do not. Still, the fact that church attendance was a negative predictor for women even after doctrine had been taken into account suggests that there is something in the institutional religious experience that produces its own negative effects on feelings of personal empowerment in women.

At first it appears curious that religious tradition does not better explain variation in the personal efficacy of women. If religious traditions differ in the nature of their patriarchal orientation, it is logical to expect that traditions that have restrictive practices such as forbidding the ordination of women might be more likely to diminish personal efficacy than religious traditions that are not as exclusionary. Still, it is important to remember that religious traditions are only a very rough indicator of the teaching and experience of women in individual churches. For example, although many Pentecostal denominations would be classified as evangelical, in some of these faith traditions women can be ordained and preach. Although Catholics do not allow female ordination, many Catholic congregations are effectively "pastored" by women (Wallace 1992). Moreover, having women in leadership positions is not necessarily an indicator of gender equality. Chaves (1997) found that formal denominational rules about ordination were only "loosely coupled" with the real-life experience and influence of women in the pews and pulpit. Thus, although both black Protestant and Catholic churches are formally very hierarchical and often gender exclusionary, both faith traditions facilitated not frustrated increases in the personal efficacy of women.

The data suggest that the act of going to church very frequently was a significant negative predictor of female empowerment. Women who went to church a lot were more similar in terms of efficacy than other women, regardless of denominational background. What is it about frequent church attendance that would present such a drag on personal efficacy? The answer may lie in the fact that religion as an institution is gendered. Although the level of inequality may vary across traditions, gender inequality is incorporated in the religious establishment of the Judeo-Christian tradition. A number of studies have found that religiousness hurt initiative in women. For example, devoutness has been associated with gender role stereotyping (Morgan and Scanzoni 1987), lower levels of motivation (Chusmir and Koberg 1988), diminished interest in career as opposed to family (Jones and McNamara 1991), and social inequality (Dhruvarajan 1990)—for women but not for men. The belief systems of American traditions are oriented toward male leadership with male prophets, male disciples, and a masculine image of God. Debates about gender-inclusive language notwithstanding, for most of the Western world religion remains structured and shaped by gender inequality.

Much of the scholarship on religion and politics for the past few decades has recognized how being religious shapes cultural and political cleavages in American politics independent of the faith tradition toward which the religiousness is directed (Hunter 1991; Kohut et al. 2000; Fiorina et al. 2005). According to this line of analysis, the religiously observant have tended to be more traditional in their worldview and consciously reject many "modern" ideas. Although these kinds of culture war classifications are an oversimplification, the negative relationship between frequent church attendance and political efficacy in women may reflect the ambivalence that the very religious—regardless of tradition—have toward the empowerment of women. It may reflect the distance that we have to go toward more egalitarian gender interpretations in the religious domain.

Still, this does not explain why female political efficacy was positively associated with church attendance. Why did going to church predict political empowerment when it did not predict personal empowerment? In many ways female political participation represents a more thoroughly modern and nontraditional role for women than the indicators of personal empowerment. The positive relationship between religion and political empowerment is a function of the cues and messages that people receive through their churches. Women who attend very often have more opportunities to receive these cues and interpret their political relevance. For women the communal nature of the religious experience is particularly important. Although religious men are likely to focus on their own spiritual discipline, women are likely to emphasize relationships with others in the religious community. Explaining why well-educated women participate in religious systems that are patriarchal in both faith and practice, many scholars highlight the sense of connectedness and support that being part of a religious community can provide (Davidman 1991; Ozorak 1996). Women benefit from these relationships and are willing to deal with the cognitive dissonance of the mixed messages they receive. Many women choose to "defect in place," remaining in their congregations even while they reject the aspects of faith that are objectionable (Winter et al. 1994).

Politically, this has consequences. Norms of participation and political engagement permeate today's religious communities. Religious messages communicate these norms, and they are reinforced through the religious, social, and participatory networks of frequently attending women. Women are confident of their ability to affect the political system. However, the norms related to appropriate roles for women and how individuals are to negotiate the contemporary conflicting challenges of family, work, and faith are much less clear. Even women in liberal faith traditions struggle with what personal empowerment means and how it is to be obtained. The gendered history of religion complicates and structures this dynamic. Traditionally religion has denied the full equality of women, and today it at best does not provide clear direction. Therefore, it is not altogether surprising that frequent church attendance was a positive predictor of political efficacy but a negative indicator of personal efficacy for women.

Democratic Implications

The paradox of being politicized through undemocratic institutions is particularly pertinent under the terms of cultural political conflict that Wald and Leege explain in chapter 11. As political elites attempt to exploit religious fault lines, female religious traditionalists enter the public square to defend the kind of conservative values that some think are at odds with their true interests. They become powerful politically to publically ensure the traditional gender roles that have historically defined inequality between the sexes. Is this a false consciousness? Is the mobilization of religious women in this circumstance somehow less politically authentic? On normative terms I am concerned about the idea of false consciousness. It is problematic to conclude that conservative religious women cannot define what is in their own interest and that religion somehow fundamentally compromises their judgment. Discussing false consciousness in chapter 11, Wald and Leege suggest that such allegations presuppose inferiority because inherent in the assertion is that one person can speak with authority about what is best for another. Still, to the extent that both religion and politics promulgate systems of stratification and inequality, it is disturbing that church attendance could compromise personal agency for women even while it appears to empower the confidence they have politically to engage the political arena on these unequal terms.

The main conclusion here is not that religion cannot increase personal efficacy in women. That idea is probably not right. Many qualitative studies suggest that it can. There are other aspects of religiosity and of spirituality that may result in the kind of personal motivation that "blessed assurance" likely produces. This study could not evaluate what activities like prayer and Bible reading might do. However, what is clear is that church attendance alone does not help; indeed it appears to hinder women's beliefs about their own capacity among those who attend most regularly. Even given this result relative to personal efficacy, it is significant that for women religion did not directly depress political engagement in any way. To the contrary, church attendance increased feelings of political empowerment for them. This confirms again that religion is indeed a political resource for women even beyond the generation of civic skills. However, as this study indicates, the influence of this resource is not entirely positive.

Overall, the finding that frequent church attendance hurts female personal efficacy seems to confirm, at least in part, the feminist critique of the relationship between religion and politics for women. The fact that church attendance undermines the personal efficacy of women is of consequence. Personal efficacy is fundamental to individual empowerment. It is important to remember that whatever political benefits accrue to women on the basis of religion are themselves tempered by the costs of receiving these benefits in a gendered and often discriminatory context.

Is this a problem for democracy? In chapter 12 Nancy Rosenblum asserts that it is not necessary to have principles of equality operating in every area of life—including in religious organizations—to produce the kinds of democratic dispositions that support political life. Indeed, as research by Wilcox in chapter 6 and Layman in chapter 7 confirm, nondemocratically oriented groups can still cultivate democratic values, although these values are often a byproduct of their political engagement and not the primary result. Politics is a prime venue for the law of unintended consequences. Historically, religiously infused movements such as abolition, temperance, and progressive era reforms empowered women in a time when neither the political nor religious arenas recognized their full participatory rights.[20] However, just because there are helpful unintended consequences does not mean we can overlook the way power and hierarchy structure inequality in both religion and politics. In treating religious institutions as though they are gender neutral, we miss the influence of the context and reduce politics to an individual phenomenon in a way that denies the structured reality in which individuals exist.

Notes

1. The *mechitza* is partition erected in the seating section of an Orthodox synagogue to prevent the mixing of men and women.

2. This literature is vast. For an example please see Wald et al. (1993), Verba et al. (1995), McVeigh and Smith (1999), Cassel (1999), Harris (1999), Ayala (2000), Jones-Correa and Leal (2001).

3. Few studies outside of African-American politics have looked explicitly at the relationship between religion and efficacy, interest, or knowledge. For a

notable exception see Hougland and Christenson (1983). They find church attendance to be positively related to political efficacy.

4. Quoted in the Elizabeth Cady Stanton, 1985. *Women's Bible*, abridged edition, 12. Glasgow and Bell.

5. For a good summary of this literature please see Linda Woodhead's chapter on "Feminism and the Sociology of Religion," in Richard K. Fenn's *The Blackwell Companion to the Sociology of Religion* (2001).

6. Other factors that they identify that help to explain why men participate more than women include resources (time, money, and civic skill), and recruitment (involvement in a social network that provides opportunities for recruitment to political activity).

7. For an excellent review of the literature on efficacy and how its measurement has developed please see Abramson (1983).

8. The alpha coefficient for the personal efficacy index was 0.72. The index ranged from 0 to 8. The indicators of personal efficacy included "I usually count on being successful at everything I do," "I like to assume responsibility," "I like to take the lead when a group does things together," "I enjoy convincing others of my opinions," "I often notice that I serve as a model for others," "I am good at getting what I want," "I am often a step ahead of others," and "I often give others advice and suggestions."

9. The alpha coefficient for the political efficacy index was 0.78. The indicators of political efficacy included four questions: how much influence the respondent thought he or she had over national and local government decisions, and whether the respondent believed a complaint about the national or state government that he or she took to a representative would be addressed. The scale ranged from 4 to 16.

10. On the personal efficacy index men scored 5.3 compared to the women's score of 4.9. On the political efficacy index men scored 9.5 compared to the women's score of 9.1. All differences were significant at the 0.0005 level.

11. The religious traditions examined here included mainline Protestants, evangelical Protestants, Catholics, Latino Christians, and black Protestants. Dummy variables were created for each of the traditions. The group of religiously unaffiliated individuals served as the comparison category. There were too few Jews in the CPS to conduct a meaningful analysis. Latino Protestants and Catholics were combined because of the small numbers in each of these categories. Other faith traditions and other Christians were not included in the models because they are composite categories and thus do not represent a unique theological or organizational perspective.

12. The other response categories for these questions included the Bible is inspired by God, the Bible is written by men, and the Bible was written long ago. The vast majority of respondents (83 percent) indicated the Bible was either God's Word or inspired by God. The more fundamentalist position is that the Bible is God's Word, and thus, that is the measure included in the analysis. Still, it is unclear that conceptually respondents drew bright distinctions between the Bible as God's Word and the Bible inspired by God. For this reason caution must be exercised in the interpretation of these results relative to fundamentalist beliefs.

13. Some readers may be concerned that these variables do not express a unique dimension of religiosity. Although there is some overlap between them, the variables are conceptually and empirically distinct. The correlation between

true Bible and frequent church attendance was 0.28. The correlation between true Bible and very important religious salience was 0.39, and the correlation between religious salience and church attendance was 0.55. Thus, although the variables are related, the correlations demonstrate that none of these variables is just a surrogate for another, and each may have its own distinctive effects.

14. In the CPS 41 percent of men and 60 percent of women said that religion is very important, 33 percent of men and 46 percent of women frequently attended church, and 37 percent of men and 52 percent of women said that the Bible is God's Word.

15. For a complete description of variables please see Verba, Schlozman, and Brady's 1995 book, *Voice and Equality*. In this analysis mean substitution is used for the family income and civic skills variables to account for missing responses. Although this substitution increased the number of cases evaluated in the model, the analysis was also conducted without mean substitution for these factors. No significant differences resulted.

16. Some caution must be exercised in concluding that fundamentalist ideas have no effect. Respondents were asked whether they believed the Bible was God's Word, inspired by God, written by men, or written long ago. More than 83 percent of respondents indicated that they believed the Bible was either God's Word or inspired by God. Believing the Bible is God's Word is the more fundamentalist position. However, it is unclear that reporting the Bible is inspired by God is that different from the Bible being God's Word. Other data sets such as the American National Election allow a clearer differentiation between those who take the Bible literally and those who do not.

17. The measure of political participation utilized here includes six acts: working in a campaign, contributing to a campaign, protesting, contacting a public official, participating in informal community activity, and attending community council or board meetings.

18. Analysis was performed to assess whether or not church attendance indirectly influenced participation through organizational membership. This relationship was indicated for women. Organizational membership was included as a control in the path model.

19. The total indirect effect of church attendance on political participation was 0.03. The total positive indirect effect was 0.04. The negative impact of church attendance on political efficacy was 0.01. These results are for women only.

20. For a good discussion of the role of religion and politics for women, see Wald and Calhoun-Brown (2007), chapter 11.

References

Abramson, Paul. 1983. *Political Attitudes in America*. San Francisco: W. H. Freeman and Company.

Allen, Richard, Michael Dawson, and Ronald Brown. 1989. "A Schema Based Approach to Modeling and African American Racial Belief System." *American Political Science Review* 83:421–22.

Ayala, L. 2000. "Trained for Democracy: The Differing Effects of Voluntary and Involuntary Organizations on Political Participation." *Political Research Quarterly* 53:99–115.

Bartkowski, John. 2001. *Remaking the Godly Marriage: Gender Negotiation in Evangelical Families*. New Brunswick, NJ: Rutgers University Press.

Bellah, Robert, Steven Tipton, William Sullivan, Richard Madsen, and Ann Swidler. 1985. *Habits of the Heart: Individualism and Commitment in American Life*. Berkeley: University of California Press.

Brady, Henry, Sidney Verba, and Kay Schlozman. 1995. "Beyond SES: A Resource Model of Political Participation." *American Political Science Review* 89:271–294.

Brasher, Brenda. 1998. *Godly Women: Fundamentalism and Female Power*. New Brunswick, NJ: Rutgers University Press.

Brown, Ronald, and Monica Wolford.1993. "Religious Resources and African American Political Action." *National Political Science Review* 4:30–48.

Burns, Nancy, Kay Schlozman, and Sidney Verba. 2001. *The Private Roots of Public Action*. Cambridge, MA: Harvard University Press.

Calhoun-Brown, Allison. 1996. "African American Churches and Political Mobilization: The Psychological Impact of Organization Resources." *Journal of Politics* 58: 935–53.

Campbell, Angus, Philip Converse, Warren Miller, and Donald Stokes. 1960. *The American Voter*. New York: John Wiley.

Cassel, C. 1999. "Voluntary Associations, Churches, and Social Participation Theories of Turnout." *Social Science Quarterly* 80:504–17.

Cavendish, James. 2000. "Church Based Community Activism: A Comparison of Black and White Congregations." *Journal for the Scientific Study of Religion* 39:371–84.

Chaves, Mark. 1997. *Ordaining Women: Culture and Conflict in Religious Organizations*. Cambridge, MA: Harvard University Press.

Chusmir, L., and C. Koberg. 1988. "A Look at Sex Differences in the Relationship between Religious Beliefs and Work Related Attitudes." *Journal of Social Behavior and Personality* 3: 37–48.

Daly, Mary. 1973. *Beyond God the Father: Toward a Philosophy of Women's Liberation*. Boston: Beacon.

Davidman, L. 1991. *Tradition in a Rootless World: Women Turn to Orthodox Judaism*. Berkeley: University of California Press.

Dhruvarajan, V. 1990. "Religious Ideology, Hindu Women and Development in India." *Journal of Social Issues* 46:57–69.

Djupe, Paul, and Christopher Gilbert. 2006. "The Resourceful Believer: Generating Civic Skills in Church." *Journal of Politics* 68:116–27.

Djupe, Paul, and Tobin Grant. 2001. "Religious Institutions and Political Participation in America." *Journal for the Scientific Study of Religion* 40:303–14.

Dufour, Lyn Resnick. 2000. "Sifting Through Tradition: The Creation of Jewish Feminist Identities." *Journal for the Scientific Study of Religion* 39:90–107.

Edgell, Penny, and Danielle Docka. 2007. "Beyond the Nuclear Family: Familism and Gender Identity in Diverse Religious Communities." *Sociological Forum* 22:26–51.

Ellison, Christopher. 1991. "Identification and Separatism: Religious Involvement and Racial Orientations among Black Americans." *Sociological Quarterly* 32:477–94.

Faver, Catherine. 2000. "To Run and Not Be Weary: Spirituality and Women's Activism." *Review of Religious Research* 42:61–78.

Fiorina, Morris, Samuel Adams, and Jeremy Pope. 2005. *Culture War? The Myth of a Polarized America*. New York: Pearson Longman.

Gallagher, Sally. 2003. *Evangelical Identity and Gendered Family Life*. New Brunswick, NJ: Rutgers University Press.

———. 2004. "The Marginalization of Evangelical Feminism." *Sociology of Religion* 65:215–37.

Garrow, David. 1986. *Bearing the Cross: Martin Luther King Jr. and the Southern Christian Leadership Conference*. New York: Morrow.

Gilkes, Cheryl Townsend. 1997. "The Roles of Church and Community Mothers: Ambivalent American Sexism or Fragmented African Familyhood?" In *African American Religion: Interpretive Essays in History and Culture*, eds. Timothy Fulop and Albert Raoteau. New York: Routledge.

Griffith, R. Marie. 2002. "The Generous Side of the Christian Faith: The Successes and Challenges of Mainline Women's Groups." In *The Quiet Hand of God: Faith-Based Activism and the Public Role of Mainline Protestants*, eds. Robert Wuthnow and John Evans. Berkeley: University of California Press.

Harris, Fredrick. 1994. "Something Within: Religion as a Mobilizer of African American Political Activism." *Journal of Politics* 56:42–68.

———. 1999. *Something Within: Religion in African American Activism*. New York: Oxford University Press.

Harris-Lacewell, Melissa. 2004. *Barbershops, Bibles and BET: Everyday Talk and Black Political Thought*. Princeton, NJ: Princeton University Press.

Hartman-Halbertal, Hova. 2002. *Appropriately Subversive: Modern Mothers in Traditional Religions*. Cambridge, MA: Harvard University Press.

Hegland, Mary Elaine. 1997. "A Mixed Blessing: The Majales-Shi'a Women's Rituals of Mourning in Northwest Pakistan." In *Mixed Blessings: Gender and Religious Fundamentalism Cross Culturally*, eds. Judy Brink and Joan Mencher. New York: Routledge Press.

Hougland, James, and James Christenson. 1983. "Religion and Politics: The Relationship of Religious Participation to Political Efficacy and Involvement." *Sociology and Social Research* 67:405–20.

Hughes, Michael, and David Demo. 1989. "Self Perceptions of Black Americans: Self Esteem and Personal Efficacy." *American Journal of Sociology* 95:132–59.

Hunter, James. 1987. *Evangelicalism: The Coming Generation*. Chicago: University of Chicago Press.

———. 1991. *Culture Wars: The Struggle to Define America*. New York: Basic Books.

Jones, B., and K. McNamara. 1991. "Attitudes toward Women and Their Work Roles: Effects of Intrinsic and Extrinsic Religious Orientation." *Sex Roles* 24:21–29.

Jones-Correa, Michael, and David Leal. 2001. "Political Participation: Does Religion Matter?" *Political Research Quarterly* 54:751–71.

Junn, Jane. 2007. "Square Pegs and Round Holes: Challenges of Fitting Individual Level Analysis to a Theory of Politicized Context of Gender." *Politics and Gender* 3:124–34.

Kaufman, Debra. 1991. *Rachel's Daughter: Newly Orthodox Jewish Women*. New Brunswick, NJ: Rutgers University Press.

Kohut, Andrew, John Green, Scott Teeter, and Roberth Toth. 2000. *The Diminishing Divide: Religion's Changing Role in American Politics*. Washington DC: Brookings Institution.

Lane, Robert. 1959. *Political Life: Why and How People Get Involved in Politics*. Glencoe, IL: Free Press.

MacLeod, Jay, ed. 1991. *Minds Stayed on Freedom: The Civil Rights Struggle in the Rural South, an Oral History and Cultural Center*. Boulder: Westview Press.

Marx, Gary. 1967. "Religion: Opiate or Inspiration of Civil Rights Militancy among Negroes." *American Journal of Sociology* 81:139–46.

McKenzie, Brian. 2001. "Self Selection, Church Attendance and Local Civic Participation." *Journal for the Scientific Study of Religion* 40:479–88.

McVeigh, R., and C. Smith. 1999. "Who Protests in America: An Analysis of Three Political Alternatives—Inaction, Institutionalized Politics, or Protest." *Sociological Forum* 14:685–703.

Morgan, M., and J. Scanzoni. 1987. "Religious Orientations and Women's Expected Continuity in the Labor Force." *Journal of Marriage and Family* 49:367–79.

Musick, Marc, John Wilson, and William Bynum Jr. 2000. "Race and Formal Volunteering: The Differential Effects of Class and Religion." *Social Forces* 87: 1539–70.

Ozorak, Elizabeth. 1996. "The Power, but Not the Glory: How Women Empower Themselves through Religion." *Journal for the Scientific Study of Religion* 25:17–29.

Peterson, Steven A. 1992. "Church Participation and Political Participation: The Spillover Effect." *American Politics Quarterly* 20:123–39.

Plaskow, Judith. 1990. *Standing again at Sinai: Judaism from a Feminist Perspective*. San Francisco: Harper & Row.

Putnam, Robert. 2000. *Bowling Alone: The Collapse and Revival of American Community*. New York: Simon & Schuster.

Reese, Laura, and Ronald Brown. 1995. "The Effects of Racial Messages on Racial Identity and System Blame among African Americans." *Journal of Politics* 57:23–43.

Rosenstone, Steven, and John Mark Hansen. 1993. *Mobilization, Participation and Democracy in America*. New York: Macmillan.

Ruether, Rosemary Radford. 1985. *Women and Church: Theology and Practice of Feminist Liturgical Communities*. San Francisco: Harper & Row.

Schussler-Fiorenza, Elisabeth. 1984. *In Memory of Her: A Feminist Theological Reconstruction of Christian Origins*. New York: Crossroads.

Schlozman, Kay, Nancy Burns, and Sidney Verba. 1994. "Gender and the Pathways to Participation: The Role of Resources." *Journal of Politics* 56:963–90.

Shingles, Richard. 1981. "Black Consciousness and Political Participation: The Missing Link." *American Political Science Review* 75:76–91.

Smidt, Corwin, ed. 2003. *Religion as Social Capital: Producing the Common Good*. Waco, TX: Baylor University Press.

Verba, Sidney, Nancy Burns, and Kay Schlozman. 1997. "Knowing and Caring about Politics: Gender and Political Engagement." *Journal of Politics* 59:1051–72.

Verba, Sidney, Kay Schlozman, and Henry Brady. 1995. *Voice and Equality*. Cambridge, MA: Harvard University Press.

Verba, Sidney, Kay Schlozman, Henry Brady, and Norman Nie. 1990. American Citizens Participation Study. [computer file] ICPSR 06635-v1. Ann Arbor, MI: Interuniversity Consortium for Political and Social Research [distributor], 1995.

———. 1993. "Race, Ethnicity and Political Resources: Participation in the United States." *British Journal of Political Science* 23:453–97.

Wald, Kenneth, and Allison Calhoun-Brown. 2007. *Religion and Politics in the United States*, 5th ed. Lanham, MD: Rowman & Littlefield.

Wald, K. D., L. A. Kellstedt, and D. C. Leege. 1993. "Church Involvement and Political Behavior." In *Rediscovering the Religious Factor in American Politics*, eds. D. C. Leege and L. A. Kellstedt, 121–38. Armonk, NY: M. E. Sharpe.

Wallace, Ruth. 1992. *They Call Her Pastor: A New Role for Catholic Women*. Albany: SUNY Press.

Wilcox, Clyde, and Leopoldo Gomez. 1990. "Religion, Group Identification and Politics among Blacks." *Sociological Analysis* 51:271–85.

Wilcox, W. Bradford. 2002. "Religion, Convention and Parental Involvement." *Journal of Marriage and Family* 64:780–92.

Williams, Johnny. 2002. "Linking Beliefs to Collective Action: Politicized Religious Beliefs and the Civil Rights Movement." *Sociological Forum* 27:203–22.

Winter, Miriam, Adair Lummis, and Allison Stokes. 1994. *Defecting in Place: Women Claiming Responsibility for Their Own Spiritual Lives*. New York: Crossroad.

Woodhead, Linda. 2001. "Feminism and the Sociology of Religion." In *The Blackwell Companion to the Sociology of Religion,* ed. Richard K. Fenn, 67–84. Oxford: Blackwell.

Chapter 10

RELIGION AND THE POLITICAL AND CIVIC LIVES OF LATINOS

David L. Leal

Introduction

This chapter explores the role of religion in Latino[1] political and civic lives. It addresses not only how religion affects traditional measures of political participation but, more importantly, how the support of religious institutions and the inspiration of faith have contributed to the preservation and empowerment of Latino communities in the past and the present.

The role of religion in Latino communities is not well known. Although most political scientists have a vague sense of Latinos as a Catholic population with some Protestant adherents, there is little understanding of how religious organizations and belief have shaped Latino political life. In fact, the more common view is that religion is an impediment to Latino participation rather than an important lens for understanding the past and present. For others, religion is simply irrelevant. As Stevens Arroyo (1998, 163) noted, "The study of religion among Latinos and Latinas has often suffered from unstated sociological premises. Sometimes it was approached as an anachronistic religious expression doomed to assimilation; at other times, it was viewed in a romantic light as folk customs without importance to religion in the United States."

For political scientists, one of the challenges is that much of the writing on Latinos, religion, and politics is outside of the discipline. The extant literature is largely the product of sociology, religious studies, history, and theology. The primary goal of this chapter is therefore to introduce political scientists to this broader literature. Although a single chapter cannot include all relevant topics and references, it can provide an overview of the subject as well as serve as the starting point for an exploration of this growing literature.

Espinosa et al. (2005) discuss the almost complete absence of religion in accounts of Latino history and politics. They note that "people are often surprised to see how crucial religious faith was to [César] Chávez's struggle for social justice" (4). They contrast this to the scholarship on the African-American political experience, where religion is a central focus.[2] Espinosa et al. also suggest that activists and academics are more comfortable with a secular perspective on Latino activism, which is reflected in the omission of religion from most of the scholarly literature on Latinos. They conclude that

> Latino religious ideology, institutions, leaders, and symbols have played a crucial role in Latino political, civic, and social action in the United States. In fact, the evidence in this volume suggests that they have served as the ideological glue for some of the most important struggles in the Latino community over the past 150 years. (5)

What explains this lack of research on Latinos, politics, and religion? One reason is that religion has played a complex role for Latinos that is often difficult to detect. Religion, and the Roman Catholic Church in particular, has played multiple—and often uncoordinated—roles in Latino political life. For instance, the leadership of the Chicano Movement did not derive from the pulpit, and in some places the Church[3] was opposed to social change. This stands in marked contrast to the black church, which produced individual leaders and crucial organizational support for the civil rights movement. Religion has also played a variety of other roles for individual Latino activists and specific movements and organizations. Leaders and organizations received practical assistance from parishes and religious officials; priests, nuns, and bishops played direct roles as organizers and indirect roles as thinkers; religious faith and symbols, such as *La Virgen de Guadalupe*, played an inspirational role; and despite the common image of Catholic and Protestant churches competing for Latino congregants, they sometimes cooperated in defense of Latinos or pursued similar goals.

Historically, the Catholic Church was not an indigenous institution for Latinos. During the Spanish colonial empire, the Church was reluctant to ordain native priests and nuns. Throughout the nineteenth and even twentieth centuries, clerics from Ireland and France were often sent to Hispanic parishes in the American Southwest. This does not mean that the church was unimportant to Latinos. Religious identity and community were key resources for Mexican-American communities attempting to survive in the decades after the Mexican-American War. Catholic and Protestant churches in the Southwest would also come to provide important educational opportunities for many individual Latinos.

As a result, there is no such thing as a "Hispanic church" that parallels the black church. Latinos have never controlled church institutions, Catholic or Protestant. Although many Catholics are Latino, and most Latinos are Catholic, this does not necessarily imply that Latinos have had or presently have prominent or influential roles in the institutional

Church. On the contrary, Sandoval (2006, xv) observed a "social distance between them and mainstream Catholics. They still lack a voice in the decision-making of the church, still lack a proportionate presence in all categories of institutional church leadership, and still have the sense they are seen as interlopers." Even in places that have largely been Hispanic in population and culture, the Church was historically wary of Latinos, suspicious of their beliefs, focused on serving the white and influential, and recruited foreign priests to serve as bishops. Today, Latinos still have little institutional power within the Catholic Church, either as clergy or in parish governing structures. Even within the same parish, Latinos often worship at different times and even in different locations than do Anglos (non-Hispanic whites) (Levitt 2002; NCCB/USCC 2000).

Recent years have seen a growing understanding of the role of religion in Hispanic communities across the nineteenth and twentieth centuries (see Stevens Arroyo 1980; Steele et al. 1998). For instance, Díaz Stevens and Stevens Arroyo (1998) propose the Emmaus paradigm:

> Taking as analogy the scriptural episode of Emmaus in which Jesus walked unrecognized alongside his disciples . . . after nearly a century of unrecognized presence, the nation's more than 25 million Latinos and Latinas began, in 1967, to use religion as a major source of the social and symbolic capital to fortify their identity in American society.

More generally, Sandoval (2006, xi) found that "The struggle of Hispanic Americans to maintain their cultural-religious character has gone hand in hand with the socio-economic political struggle."

The organizational efforts by and on behalf of Latinos in the Church are also receiving more attention. For instance, Hispanic priests organized in 1969 for social justice and to create change within the Church through the creation of PADRES (Martinez 2005). The political movement organized by Saul Alinsky, which is not explicitly ethnic but has proved useful for many Latino communities, was founded and sustained over the decades with important assistance from Church officials and parishes. The sanctuary movement for unauthorized immigrants in the 1980s involved both Catholic and Protestant churches, and the Catholic Church is a rare advocate on behalf of contemporary immigrants. The ministries of the Church along the border also provide practical assistance to immigrants, and the Church's general interest in social justice is important to low–socioeconomic status (SES) Latino communities. Religion also provides both inspiration and comfort to people at the margins of American society. Elizondo (2000) discusses Hispanic theology and proposes the "Galilee principle" based on Mark 12:10, "The stone which the builders rejected has become the Cornerstone." Latinos in the United States, not always appreciated and sometimes rejected (through segregation, discrimination, and deportation), can draw inspiration from the parallel.

Stevens Arroyo (1998) saw such trends as part of a new Latino religious resurgence. This signals not only a statistical transformation but also a qualitative change in American religious life. He reports that Latinos are developing a distinct religious life. No longer considered inferior, their unique linguistic and cultural features are finding permanent spaces across the religious landscape, and Latinos are more confident about their religious identities. For instance, it is increasingly common for Spanish liturgical texts to not simply translate English texts but to speak directly to the Latino experience.

Joining this sociological, historical, and theological work is a small body of recent political science research that investigates how religion affects political participation and vote choice. This chapter will bring together this quantitative research with the historical, sociological, and theological literatures to show how religion provides—both in the past and the present—material and spiritual resources for Latino political and civic engagement.

Background: Latinos and Religion in the United States

After decades of neglect, the study of Latinos is increasingly found in political science and other disciplines (see de la Garza and Leal forthcoming). This largely reflects the stunning growth in the presence of Latino/Hispanic peoples in the United States over the last few decades. Although people we would now call Hispanics have long been present in what is now the United States—with Spanish settlements in New Mexico founded nine years before the English landing at Jamestown, and St. Augustine settled forty-two years before Jamestown (not to mention the longstanding presence of native populations)—only recently have the Hispanic "forgotten people" (Sanchez 1940) gained national attention.

In terms of population share, Latinos are now the nation's largest minority group. The 2000 U.S. Census showed Latinos were 12.5 percent of the population, which increased to 14.8 percent by 2006. This reflects a population that grew from 35.3 million to 44.3 million in just over half a decade. From 2000 to 2006, Hispanics accounted for half of all U.S. population growth and had a growth rate three times higher than that of non-Hispanics. The Census estimates that the Latino share of the United States population will grow to 24 percent in 2050 and to 33 percent by 2100 (see table 10.1).

More generally, minorities constitute about one-third of the U.S. population, and in four states Anglos (non-Hispanic whites) are now the plurality instead of the majority (California, Hawaii, New Mexico,

TABLE 10.1
Hispanic Population Growth and Projections, 1970 to 2050

Year	Hispanic population (millions)	Hispanic population (percentage)
1970	9.6	4.7
1980	14.6	6.4
1990	22.4	9
2000	35.3	12.5
2010	47.8	15.5
2020	59.7	17.8
2030	73	20.1
2040	87.6	22.3
2050	102.6	24.4

Source: U.S. Census Bureau. http://www.census.gov/population/www/socdemo/hispanic/files/Internet_Hispanic_in_US_2006.pdf.

and Texas). Not only will this demographic shift require more scholarly attention to Latinos, but it will necessitate a change in the traditional black-white paradigm of understanding racial and ethnic politics.

In terms of religious affiliation, DeSipio (2007, 163) noted that the Catholic share of the Latino population may have declined slightly over the last two decades—from about 77 percent in 1989 to 70 percent today (see also Perl et al. 2006). About four in ten Catholics are Hispanic,[4] and although the number of Latinos reporting themselves as simply "Christian" or other religious tradition grew in the 1990s, Latinos will be increasingly central to the Catholic Church in the years to come. For instance, the 2002 *Catholic Almanac* stated that Latinos will constitute 86 percent of all U.S. Roman Catholics by the mid-century. Although such projections are difficult and contingent, it should not be controversial to state that American Catholicism will become increasingly Hispanicized throughout the twenty-first century. In addition to a relatively high degree of Catholic affiliation, Latinos are also highly religious in general, with over 90 percent identifying with a specific religion (Suro and Lugo 2007).

Although various Protestant denominations have made inroads among Latinos in recent years—primarily evangelical and Pentecostal churches—the overall percentage of Catholic Latinos has remained in the 70 percent range. This is because Latin American immigrants are largely Catholic, despite Protestant conversions throughout the Americas in the twentieth century. Much of the Latino Protestant affiliation is the result of conversions, which become more likely with time spent in the United States. For instance, the Protestant or other Christian share for Latinos is 15 percent for the first generation, 20 percent for the second, and 29 percent for the third (Espinosa et al. 2003).

The Hispanic Churches in American Public Life (HCAPL) National Survey in 2000 found that 39 percent of Latino evangelicals are former Catholics, 26 percent of mainline Protestant Latinos are former Catholics, but fewer than 10 percent of Catholics are converts from other traditions. However, about a quarter of Latino Catholics report a born-again experience, which is usually associated with evangelicals or Pentecostals (Espinosa et al. 2003). More generally, the 2006 Pew Hispanic Religion survey found that about 20 percent of Latinos report a conversion experience that led them to change religion or to drop religious identification.

Although some of these evangelical or Protestant gains reflect deeply felt spiritual changes, sometimes other factors are involved. For instance, some individuals may prefer the smaller and more intimate atmosphere of many storefront evangelical and Pentecostal churches. In addition, such churches are often led by Latino ministers, in comparison to the mostly Anglo Catholic priesthood. This is because the barriers to entry for such ministers are low—years of theological training are not necessary, nor are vows of poverty, chastity, or obedience. In addition, some immigrants see Protestant conversion as part of the Americanization process and a way to further the personal transformation that began with migration.

Table 10.2 includes some important facts about Latinos and the Roman Catholic Church. Not only are many Latinos Catholic, but many Catholics are Latinos. The number of parishes with Hispanic ministry or a majority Hispanic presence are large, but the number of Latino priests and the share of Latino seminarians are fairly small. Furthermore, the number of native-born Hispanic priests is limited (about 500 individuals), and the ratio of Hispanic Catholics to Hispanic priests is over eight times larger than the overall ratio of Catholics to priests. Although the figures for Hispanic seminarians and ordinations are approximately parallel to those of the overall Hispanic population in the United States, they are far below that of the Hispanic Catholic population.

The percentage of Hispanic bishops is similarly small, although this may prove less difficult for the Vatican to change in the future than the lack of vocations more generally. However, a shortage of Hispanic priests will limit the pool of potential Hispanic appointees to bishoprics.

History: Latinos and Religion in the United States

The footprints of Christianity are found all across Spanish North America. From San Francisco (St. Francis) to Los Angeles (the angels) to Santa

TABLE 10.2
Hispanic Ministry at a Glance

Percentage of U.S. Catholic population growth who are Hispanic since 1960	71%
Percentage of U.S. Catholics who are Hispanic	39%
Percentage of Hispanics who are Catholic	72.6%
Approximate number of U.S. parishes with Hispanic ministry	4000
Percentage of U.S. parishes with majority Hispanic presence	20.6%
Number of Hispanic priests in the United States	2900
Number of U.S.-born Hispanic priests (approximate)	500
Percentage of Hispanic priests in the United States	6.3%
Catholics per U.S. priest	1230
Hispanic Catholics per Hispanic priest	9925
Hispanic percentage of seminarians	13%
Percentage of Hispanic priests ordained in 2002	15%
Number of active U.S. bishops	281
Number of active Hispanic bishops	25
Ratio of U.S. bishops to general Catholic population	1:231,000
Ratio of U.S. Hispanic bishops to U.S. Hispanic Catholic population	1:1 million

Source: United States Conference of Catholic Bishops. http://www.usccb.org/hispanic affairs/demo.shtml#3.

Fe (holy faith) to San Antonio (St. Anthony) to Florida,[5] there is no avoiding the conclusion that the various adventurers, soldiers, priests, administrators, and settlers brought with them a collective evangelical fervor that went hand in hand with military conquest.

Modern skeptics will question how two such apparently opposite views coincided. The English "black legend" emphasizes Spanish cruelty while turning a curiously blind eye to similar—and perhaps more destructive—English imperial practices (Restall 2003). In this view, faith is only a veneer over conquest. However, we need to understand the spiritual and temporal worlds as the Spanish saw them in 1492. Fresh from a multicentury *reconquista* of the Iberian peninsula from Islam, the Spanish tended to view the world in religious terms. Contrary to our own contemporary divisions, Hanke (1975, ix) noted that "Generally speaking, there was no true racial prejudice before the fifteenth century, for mankind was divided not so much into antagonistic races as into 'Christians' and 'infidels.'" In the "New World," Spain saw not only a source of wealth but a people in need of the gospel.

The Spanish did not simply desire a conquest, however. According to Hanke (1975, 107), "no other nation made so continuous or so passionate an attempt to discover what was the just treatment for the native peoples under its jurisdiction than the Spaniards." An instructive example is the famous debate in Valladolid in 1550 between Bartolomé de las Casas and Juan Ginés de Sepúlveda about the nature of the natives of the New World. The Spanish Crown and the Council of the Indies ultimately decided to view them as fully human, the position argued by las Casas, and not as Aristotle's "natural slaves," as argued by Sepúlveda. Hanke sees this as a milestone event in the creation of the contemporary notion of human rights—certainly not the popular view of the fruits of the Spanish Empire. All this indicates that we must take seriously the religious underpinnings of the Spanish Colonial Empire, which would set in motion the creation of the Hispanic peoples of the United States.

Abalos (2007, 138) found that the Church served as an "institutional buffer" for the native and mestizo peoples of New Spain against the colonial administration. The Church saw its role as protecting indigenous people from the worst excesses of empire, but they did so "without questioning the hierarchical system that oppressed them" (138). He finds that the Church therefore became part of the problem, laying the groundwork for future anticlerical efforts by more liberal revolutionaries after the end of empire. He finds a parallel with contemporary Latinos, who "are not antireligious or antichurch, but there is a growing resistance to the efforts of the hierarchy to consider themselves the final arbiters of the sacred" (138).

The specific form of Catholicism carried over to the Americas was "filled with popular rituals such as saint devotions, pilgrimages, and special devotion to Mary" (Walsh 2004, 12–13). This individual and community focus, as opposed to an institutional church focus, was accentuated when the latter became associated with Spanish rule during the revolutionary period in Latin America. The prevalence of "popular religiosity," especially in the more thinly populated northern region of Mexico, would have implications for the postwar (1848–present) relationship between the Church and a Hispanic population "whose marginalization constituted its primary sociohistorical experience" (Walsh 2004, 13).

In the land that is now the American Southwest, the population was small, and religious oversight was fairly minimal in terms of personnel and jurisdictional organization. Before the American conquest, several events lowered the institutional presence of the church in the Southwest. These included the expulsion of the Jesuits in 1767, the expulsion of the Franciscans from Arizona and New Mexico in 1821, the "secularization"[6] of the missions in the 1830s, and the independence of Mexico from Spain in 1821.[7] The territory now known as the U.S. Southwest was under the jurisdiction of Mexican dioceses, and only rarely did bishops visit. Before the Mexican-American War, only one diocese and one vicariate existed within this territory.

With the Church rather thin on the ground, forms of popular religiosity developed. The best known are the *Penitentes*, officially the *Fraternidad Piadosa de Nuestro Padre Jesús*. They practiced religious ceremonies and rituals in the absence of priests, taught the young, reenacted the crucifixion, practiced penances such as scourging, and engaged in some charitable and community activities. They may have kept the faith alive during times of official neglect, in this sense operating as a "parallel church." Bishop Jean Lamy (discussed below) and others opposed and sanctioned the *Penitentes*, who were not fully reconciled with the Church until 1974. With roots in the community, however, the *Penitentes* could not be suppressed by the bishop and exist to this day. For instance, when Bishop Lamy denied communion to *Penitentes* and denied religious status to the organization, it was made a benevolent society by the New Mexico legislature.

When the Church created dioceses in the Southwest, the new bishops were not necessarily sympathetic toward the Hispanic populations. The most famous individual is Jean Lamy, the first bishop, later archbishop of the Diocese of New Mexico. A Frenchman, he preferred to recruit priests and nuns from other parts of the United States and Europe. He also suspended or excommunicated several popular Hispanic priests, denied the sacraments to those who would not tithe, admitted to ruling through fear, squashed an incipient tradition of Hispanic vocations, and imported French architectural styles. Today his statue stands outside his French Romanesque creation, St. Francis Cathedral, incongruously located in Santa Fe.[8] Perhaps he simply reflected Church opinion; he was officially sent to a *partibus infidelium*, but such a designation "was clearly an affront to the Catholicism that had existed in New Mexico for 250 years" (Sandoval 2006, 44). According to Sandoval (2006, 47), "But for heirs of an austere Iberian spirituality who had experienced neither the Protestant Reformation nor the Catholic Counter-Reformation, it was not what one knew but how one lived that made all the difference."

Other religious complained about Hispanic ignorance of the faith and saw superstition in their beliefs. Church leaders often saw popular religiosity as "misguided at best and 'pagan' at worst," which led to attempts at correction "with more than an air of superiority and paternalism" (Walsh 2004, 14). Some clergy in the nineteenth century were reluctant to serve in the Southwest—one referred to a position in Brownsville as "the worst sentence that could have been given me for any crime" (Sandoval 2006, 45). This same individual, Bishop Dominic Manucy of Brownsville, once refused to accept twenty-two Mexican nuns who were fleeing Mexico despite the almost complete lack of Church personnel in

Texas—and the promise of local residents to pay their living costs. Such attitudes were particularly problematic because all the senior Church officials in the Southwest were European or of European descent. In California in 1900, for instance, all the bishops were Irish.

Not all Mexican-American efforts to resist unfriendly clergy failed, however. In 1904, residents of Taos petitioned the Archbishop of Santa Fe to remove a local priest because of his disrespectful behavior; the man was ultimately transferred to Milwaukee (Matovina 2005, 25). Matovina (2005) also described several instances where Mexican Americans used their long-standing Catholic heritage to combat Anglo claims that they were foreign and depraved—"they expressed an identity as Catholics whose preconquest heritage merited their ethnic, religious, and political legitimation" (27).

Part of this Church antagonism was concern about what Anglos would think of Catholicism. In the 1890s, a bishop in Arizona criticized Mexican-American religious processions because he thought they stirred anti-Catholic sentiment among Anglo Protestants. The same dynamic helps to explain Church opposition to the *Penitentes* in New Mexico. The Church was also under pressure to "Americanize" immigrants in the nineteenth and early twentieth centuries, and popular religious practices among Hispanics were therefore seen as problematic (Walsh 2004, 14).

This was also part of a larger dynamic whereby the Church was often silent in the face of the discrimination and subjugation that Hispanics sometimes faced in the decades after American rule came to the Southwest. This included violence, even lynching, but "if bishops and clergy spoke out in defense of the victims, no record was kept. More likely, they stayed silent out of desire to be accepted by secular society. This was not an era when the church distinguished itself in its defense of the oppressed" (Sandoval 2006, 51). As Walsh (2004, 16–17) similarly observed, the Catholic "clergy seemed to be more preoccupied with having the church become part of the establishment than with serving the community . . . and failed to look at the systemic social ills that contributed to the marginal status of many Mexicans and Mexican Americans"

Hispanics would take action to defend themselves in New Mexico, even if the Church would not. The *Penitentes* exercised political power in heavily Hispanic northern New Mexico and southern Colorado despite Church opposition. A different approach was adopted in the late nineteenth century by *Las Gorras Blancas*, riders wearing white hoods, who emerged to fight land grabbing and fencing practices in New Mexico. They cut fences and destroyed property, seeking to intimidate Anglos and Hispanics alike whom they saw as enemies (Arellano 2000). As Sandoval (2006, 53) noted, "The church that Lamy created had no contact with, control over, or sympathy for these fighters for justice." Matovina (2005,

22–23) pointed out that some foreign clergy were sympathetic to Hispanics, or at least did not actively seek to suppress their religions practices, but "criticism and conflict frequently marked the relations between established Hispanic Catholic communities and the Catholic religious leaders who arrived in the wake of U.S. conquest."

More generally, Sandoval (2006, 53–54) noted that Hispanics at the beginning of the twentieth century had no influence in the institutional Church, had few advocates within the Church, and the few remaining Hispanic priests had been intimidated into submission. In the face of ignorance and condescension, the Hispanic laity turned within, to their own religious traditions and practices. This parallels the status of Hispanics more generally in the Southwest in the decades after the Mexican-American War. They had become "the forgotten people" (Sanchez 1940), and some politicians did not believe that Hispanics existed in settled communities in the United States. Others believed that Hispanics would eventually disappear. Sandoval (2006, 55) notes that the church seemed to view Hispanic ministry as temporary; it prioritized ministry to Anglos and European immigrants, and some French clergy were happy to see Hispanic emigration from Texas to Mexico.

One consequence of this Church neglect was the declining importance of the parish in Mexican-American political and communal life. In the years between the world wars, Latinos would build a new array of civic organizations, many of which would merge into the League of United Latin American Citizens (LULAC).

However, this does not mean that religion provided no resources for the Mexican-American people in the last half of the nineteenth century. Matovina (2005, 19) noted that the historical conventional wisdom regards religion as providing few defensive resources for this community; sees religion as either ignoring Hispanics or acting as a means of social control; and confines religion to a private, domestic sphere. However, he finds that "Catholicism buttressed the conquered Mexicans' spirited defense of their dignity and rights" (20). Communities also "asserted their Mexican Catholic heritage in the public spaces of civic life through their long-standing rituals and devotions" (27). Anglos often sought to ban such activities, but in light of the many political and economic reverses of the Mexican-American people in the late nineteenth century, such public rituals became increasingly important (Matovina 2005, 27–28).

A sudden surge of migration from Mexico would change this situation dramatically in terms of both politics and religion. First, the land policies and politics of Mexican dictator Porfirio Diaz, the resulting Mexican Revolution, and the subsequent Cristero War drove hundreds of thousands of Mexicans to the United States. Slowly, haltingly, and inconsistently, the Church began to turn some attention to this population, which was visibly gaining in numbers rather than disappearing. For instance, when nuns and priests fled Mexico because of anticlerical violence, they now appear to have been accepted in Texas and allowed to engage in ministry. Sandoval notes some efforts to find Spanish-speaking priests, as well as incipient efforts at social justice ministry (one such effort took place in Crystal City in 1930, which would be a key setting for the Chicano Movement in the 1960s). Hispanics also benefited from the various hospitals, schools, and orphanages the Church was constructing, although these institutions were not necessarily created with Hispanics in mind.

This did not mean that Hispanics were welcome in parishes that served Anglo Catholics. New churches were built for Mexican immigrants, and the Church encouraged Hispanics to create their own religious organizations (such as the Association of Our Lady of Guadalupe, the *Guadalupanas*). Sandoval (2006, 57) called the result a "separate church."

The Church also began in the early twentieth century to create offices that specifically addressed Hispanic spiritual and temporal needs. In earlier decades, despite violence against Hispanics across the Southwest, the Church did not protest (Sandoval 2006, 65). During the mass deportations during the Depression, which included some American citizen children, there is no record of Church protest. During a pecan-shellers strike in San Antonio in 1938, the Archbishop of San Antonio denounced the strikers as communists. At best, this time was a precursor to the changes that would take place after World War II.

An early effort was the establishment by the Catholic bishops of an immigration office in El Paso in 1921. More important, the Church would formally and institutionally incorporate Hispanic issues and concerns through an office that rose in stature over the course of the twentieth century. In 1945, the Bishops' Committee for the Spanish Speaking (BCSS) was opened in San Antonio and led by Archbishop Robert E. Lucey. It was meant to address the social and spiritual needs of Mexican Americans in Texas. Despite an initial plan to rotate among regional offices in the Southwest, the BCSS never left Texas.[9] Despite criticism from more conservative elements, the BCSS engaged in activities ranging from the unionization of bus drivers to involvement with migrant farm workers to child-care programs. It denounced the *Bracero* program, which brought temporary laborers from Mexico to the United States, as a form of slavery. With the assistance of the BCSS, local priests were able to conduct naturalization classes, create employment agencies, lobby on behalf of migrant workers and antipoverty programs, and organize lay groups such as the Catholic War Veterans.

In 1969, this committee was transformed into the Division for the Spanish Speaking and moved to Washington, DC, as part of the National

Conference of Catholic Bishops. The name was changed to the Bishops' Committee for Hispanic Affairs. In 1974, the division was elevated to a Secretariat of Hispanic Affairs under the auspices of the NCCB, which is now the United States Conference of Catholic Bishops.

Sandoval (2006, 62–63) suggests this more activist and positive approach reflected a change of heart by the bishops, who felt they should not focus only on the spiritual realm, and who may have also seen the inconsistency of organizing Irish Catholics in the East to fight injustice while ignoring Hispanic parishioners.

There were some limits to this renewed World War II–era interest in Hispanics, however. Many Hispanics were second-class citizens in the Church, relegated to church basements and organized into separate religious and social organizations. Although the BCSS developed a pastoral plan that advocated a combination of religious instruction, sacramental activities, and social services, implementation was inconsistent and could founder on lack of funds and clergy disinterest (Levitt 2002, 152). On the other hand, this arms-length treatment reinforced a Latino tradition of separate formal and informal religious practices; allowed lay leaders (including women) to gain a more prominent religious role; and allowed Latino communities to include more elements of popular religiosity than might have been the case if the congregation had been under greater scrutiny (Levitt 2002; Díaz Stevens 1998).

After World War II, there were few Hispanic priests, and Hispanic lay persons were not present in leadership positions across the range of Church institutions (including colleges and universities). By contrast, the African-American community could point to many religious as well as civic and business leaders—important precursors to the civil rights movement (McAdam 1982). Why were so few Hispanic Church leaders developed? Part of the explanation is the low levels of educational achievement by Hispanics, which meant they did not qualify to attend seminaries. But there was also hostility to Hispanic seminarians and a sense that "Hispanics were of such weak faith that they could not be priests. . . . The priesthood, like the officer class in the Armed Forces, was for whites only" (Sandoval 2006, 78). In addition, the few Hispanic religious were often prevented from working in their own communities or refused permission to offer masses or confession in Spanish. Regardless of the reason, most priests were non-Latinos and "were unable to serve as ethnic leaders in times of political need, and the Catholic Church did not provide a resource for leadership development and upward mobility among Mexican-American youth (DeSipio 2007, 166).

The result was that some left the Church, but others would confront the Church from within. In 1969 a new group was formed by fifteen Mexican-American priests essentially to lobby the Catholic hierarchy.

Named PADRES, or Priests Associated for Religious, Educational, and Social Rights,[10] it initially presented twenty-seven resolutions to the National Council of Catholic Bishops. According to Sandoval (2006, 83), "PADRES made clear that it would be the voice of the voiceless Hispanics." Among other issues, PADRES asked for the appointment of Hispanic priests and bishops in Hispanic areas, financial support for poor parishes, Church support for striking agricultural workers, and the recruitment of Hispanic religious. More generally, as noted by Mario García (2004, 77), "one of the key issues overlooked in Chicano history, as well in contemporary Chicano studies, is the major part that many Chicano priests have played and continue to play in their communities."[11] Understanding the story of PADRES helps to better understand this long-standing dynamic (see Martinez 2005 for a comprehensive account).

In 1971, a group of fifty nuns met to form a parallel group, *Las Hermanas*. With "faith in a God that seeks political, social, and ecclesiastical justice" (Medina 2004, 98), this group defied stereotypes and was active on behalf of many political and social causes. Another consequence of clergy activism was the Mexican American Cultural Center (MACC) in San Antonio, which would train thousands of Hispanic and Anglo individuals for pastoral work with Hispanics as well as for work in Latin America (see Castañeda-Liles 2004). Ríos (2004) similarly studied the social justice activism of Puerto Rican Pentecostal women in New York City, activities that run counter to religious, gender, and ethnic stereotypes.

The Church began to change institutionally through Vatican II. This multifaceted and much-debated event saw, inter alia, a re-emphasis of the role of the laity in the Church.[12] Individuals began to reconceptualize their relationship with a Church that many had seen as bureaucratic and ritualistic. For instance, Abalos (2007, 138–39) found "a growing consciousness in the community following the spirit of Vatican II that the Church is not constituted by the official hierarchy or only the clergy, but that the Church is the people of God, laity and clergy together." For Latinos, Vatican II meant reforms such as the virtual disappearance of the Latin mass and the widescale adoption of vernacular masses (including Spanish); a deemphasis of Americanization as part of Hispanic ministry; and a new role for the Church in the world, as exemplified by the policy of a "preferential option for the poor." Latino identity and culture was no longer a problem for the post–Vatican II Church.

The Chicano Movement is usually described in very secular terms, a Hispanic counterpoint to the civil rights movement but without an equivalent to the black church. This ignores the religious issues at stake and the religious motivations of some of the key participants. For instance, in 1974, members of the Brown Berets took over a church in Brighton, Colorado, refusing to leave until the priest agreed to offer mass in Spanish.

One illustration of the changing Church views of Latinos is the 1970 ordination of the first Hispanic bishop in the United States. Patricio Flores was appointed an auxiliary bishop in the Archdiocese of San Antonio and later became Bishop of El Paso and Archbishop of San Antonio. César Chávez, the leader of the United Farm Workers of America, read a Bible passage at the ceremony. By contrast, the first African-American bishop in the Roman Catholic Church, James Augustine Healy, was ordained in 1875. The appointment of Flores was not only symbolic. He used his position to support the creation of the Alinsky group COPS (Communities Organized for Public Service) and the National Hispanic Scholarship Fund.

By 2006, twenty-three Hispanic or Latin American/Spanish bishops were in office. As with elected officials, the fact of common ancestry does not necessarily lead to agreement. The bishops were sometimes divided by ideology, class, national origin group, and ecclesiology. In a similar dynamic, the members of the Congressional Hispanic Caucus do not always agree, and descriptive representation does not necessarily imply substantive representation. In addition, just as Latino legislators are underrepresented in terms of their population share, so are Latino bishops in the Catholic Church. The bishops also changed over time. A newer generation was less radical, less influenced by the passions of the Chicano Movement and the early struggles for acceptance and voice in the Church. Again, this reflects larger dynamics in the Latino community, as the Chicano Movement peaked and a newer generation of Latinos adopted less confrontational ideas and tactics.

Perhaps the most important event during this time period was the *Encuentro* movement. *Encuentros* were convened by the Catholic bishops and designed to be broadly inclusive discussions of the needs of Catholic Hispanics in the United States. The First National Hispanic *Encuentro* was held in 1972 in Washington, DC, a meeting of male and female lay and religious leaders that many saw as a chance to air grievances against the Church. True to 1960s form, the *Encuentro* ended with seventy-eight demands and conclusions. Some would be adopted, such as Spanish sections in diocesan newspapers and a greater institutional presence in the Church, such as a new Hispanic committee of the National Conference of Bishops. Others were not, such as training all novitiates in Spanish and ordaining women as deacons.

This was followed by an additional national *Encuentro* in 1977. It was also held in Washington and was preceded by a survey of over 100,000 Latino Catholics about the Church. The result was a 1983 pastoral letter—*The Hispanic Presence: Challenge and Commitment*. The letter saw the NCCB clearly stating that "At this moment of grace we recognize the Hispanic community among us as a blessing from God." It "noted that Mexican Americans and other Hispanics exemplify values that uplift church and society, such as respect for the dignity of each person, profound love of family life, a deep sense of community, an appreciation of life as a precious gift from God, and pervasive and authentic devotion to Mary, the mother of God" (Matovina and Riebe-Estrella 2002, 12). It also signaled a movement away from "the Americanization trends of the past and finally affirmed the differences that Latinos brought to the church as positive developments rather than customs to be changed" (Walsh 2004, 23).

However, it was also a disappointment in some circles. According to Pulido and Vega (2004, 243), the adopted pastoral plan for Hispanic ministry was approved but without funding, so "some Hispanic leaders compared it to a beautiful new car without wheels." In the view of Abalos (2007, 139), it was "a very cautious, almost apologetic, statement that can at best be charitably described as a beginning." He reports that the Latino bishops worried that a more forceful statement would lead to its rejection by the other bishops.

This document did lead to a third *Encuentro* in 1985, where "the Latino community found its voice" (140). It called for the greater involvement of Hispanics at all levels of the Church as well as for structures that would promote ministries to Hispanics. The participants endorsed preferential options for the poor, the importance of education for transforming society, and the role of women. It also sought to replace the Church policy of assimilation with that of pluralism, a view that has taken root today. The resulting document, the *National Pastoral Plan for Hispanic Ministry*, concluded that:

> Integration is not to be confused with assimilation. Through the policy of assimilation, new immigrants are forced to give up their language, culture, values, and traditions. . . . By integration we mean that our Hispanic people are to be welcomed to our church institutions at all levels. They are to be served in their language when possible, and their cultural values and religious traditions are to be respected. Beyond that, we must work toward mutual enrichment through interaction among all our cultures. *(NPPHM #4)*[13]

In addition, the *Encuentros* had political implications for individual participants. During the third *Encuentro*, according to Sandoval (2006, 104), "many local leaders received invaluable training." We therefore see how church participation can increase the civic skills noted by Verba et al. (1995) as crucial to political participation, especially for those without education or occupational advantages.

Another Hispanic program with civic implications was the *Cursillos de Cristiandad*. This was a weekend spiritual experience that was imported from Spain to Waco, Texas in 1957. It was designed to counteract the perceived indifference of many men to the Church. According to Sandoval (2006, 105), "Many of the Hispanic leaders of the 1970s owed their social conscience to the *Cursillo*, including César Chávez and many of the farm workers in his union." With roots in a Spanish version of Catholicism, it emphasized the transformation of cultural Catholicism into everyday faith practices (Levitt 2002, 152). Walsh (2004, 20) noted that it promoted "a personalized Catholicism that reaffirmed the need for a conversion-like experience." Put differently, "it presented a vision of Christianity as a life of 'conscious and increasing grace' rather than the *beatería* (pious old-ladyism) which many men associated with devotion" (Vidal 2004, 58). Pulido and Vega (2004, 242) saw it as "the first movement within the church to stress the leadership potential of the Mexican American community." Influential community leaders such as César Chávez, Willie Velasquez, and Ernie Cortés were active participants in the program. In addition, the restoration by Vatican II of the permanent diaconate allowed many men who had experienced the *Cursillo* movement to play a more formal role in the Church.

A wide variety of other Church groups have arisen in recent decades, some new and some Spanish-language versions of existing organizations. All undoubtedly provide opportunities for the development of religious devotions as well as the organizational and leadership skills that are so well developed in small group settings.

Latinos, Religion, and Political Activism

Latino Farm Workers and the Chicano Movement

The church in the 1950s was slow to fully embrace the cause of migrant farm workers. Part of the difficulty was that many growers were themselves Catholic; a Church long focused on increasing its social standing and ministering to the advantaged was wary of angering these more established parishioners. As noted by Barvosa-Carter (2004, 274), "both sides wished to have their cause endorsed by the church." According to the priest who headed the Catholic Rural Life Conference, "Church authorities are frozen with fear that if they take a stand with the workers the growers will punish them in the pocketbook."[14]

Individual religious would sometimes take action, but the position of the institutional Church was ambivalent at best. In 1949, four priests received permission from the Archbishop of San Francisco to work with farm workers, which included the discussion of labor rights. The growers counterattacked by suggesting that the Church should lose its tax-exempt status, and they convinced other California bishops to criticize this effort. For instance, the Archbishop of Fresno (the site of many farms) denounced the priests as leftists with communist ideas, and the Bishop of San Diego said that this kind of social justice work was an improper church activity (Sandoval 2006, 121). This specific ministry ended in 1962, but it helped to set the stage for later efforts. Among the people who were included in the outreach effort was the future farm labor leader César Chávez.

Despite some early Church assistance, César Chávez noted that many of the religious who initially came out to support him were Protestant. He said "Why do the Protestants come out here and help the people, demanding nothing and give all their time to serving the farm workers, while our own parish priests stay in their churches where few people come and feel uncomfortable?" (Sandoval 2006, 122).[15] Walsh (2004, 19) noted that in California, "Priests were warned about becoming politically involved in the burgeoning migrant farm worker cause" and that growers threatened to withhold money from the Church. Although the Church would not initially endorse the grape boycott, it did mediate some union jurisdictional disputes, created a Bishop's Committee on Farm Labor, and the bishops would later endorse a grape and lettuce boycott.

The increase in Church involvement was caused in part by Chávez's example. Chávez was "a man of deep Catholic faith. For him the connection between his political and labor organizing and his faith was a close one" (Barvosa-Carter 2004, 273). He emphasized nonviolence, attended mass daily, made all his important decisions while fasting, and exemplified the spirit of St. Francis. His introduction to organizing began when he met Father Donald McDonnell while working in a lumber mill in San Jose, California. Fr. McConnell urged him to read the papal encyclicals on labor and books about St. Francis of Assisi and Gandhi. Chávez also worked with the Industrial Areas Foundation, which is discussed later in this chapter and itself had some Catholic antecedents.

Chávez also used religious symbols adroitly. During the celebrated March from Delano to Sacramento in 1966, the banner of *La Virgen de Guadalupe* led the marchers, followed by the American and Mexican flags. Chávez envisioned the march as a type of religious pilgrimage, and it ended on Easter Sunday. In the spring of 1968, he embarked on a twenty-five-day fast. The fast was broken during a mass attended by Robert Kennedy. As the two men sat together in a field while mass was said from the back of a truck, "few images could more vividly illustrate how effective the intermingling of politics and Latino/a religious expression could become" (Barvosa-Carter 2004, 275). This event, as well as the sight of thousands of supporters praying and singing during a court appearance in Bakersfield during his fast, was televised nationally. The Plan de Delano, which was written by Luis Valdez, was filled with religious content: it quoted Pope Leo XIII, who criticized "the greed of speculators" who exploit workers for their own enrichment. According to León (2004, 61), "Political action was not only inspired or informed by mystical or religious faith: for the UFW, political revolt was a sacred action itself."

This religious aspect to the life and work of Chávez is not well known, however. According to Lloyd-Moffett (2004, 35), the struggle to define the legacy of Chávez was initially won by those who sought to define him as a secular activist:

> Seeking to co-opt Chávez and his cause, those who defined his early legacy—the liberal intelligentsia and Chicano activists—embarked on a conscious, consistent, and comprehensive agenda to secularize Chávez and substitute their own values for his stated motivations. In the process, they erased the spiritual basis of his public record, thereby creating the "Christ-less" Chávez of popular perception.

However, this secular view of Chávez is not accepted by many Latinos, for whom "he is venerated not as a social activist but as a socially minded Messiah who operated under God" (46). Lloyd-Moffett (2004) believes that more recent efforts by academics and Latino Catholics are leading to a more comprehensive understanding of the man who once said he was motivated by "faith in God and our choice to follow His son." In doing so, "the unspoken myth that Latino religion has had little influence on civic engagement will inevitably be challenged" (47).

In addition to Chávez, many of the leaders of the Chicano Movement were lay Catholics or otherwise religiously motivated. If Chávez is the popular icon of the movement, then Reies López Tijerina stands as a counterexample who illustrates important features of religion and politics in America. Tijerina was the leader of the Aliania Federal de Mercedes Reales, a confrontational activist group that operated largely in New Mexico in the 1960s. It sought to return land to Mexican Americans that the group thought was promised by old Spanish land grants but stolen by Anglos and the U.S. government.

Tijerina was a Pentecostal minister who later returned to the Catholic Church. Busto (2004) notes not only how his unique "magical-literalist" style was deeply intertwined with his political activism but also that his style put him outside the boundaries of Robert Bellah's "American Civic Religion." He is contrasted with leaders like Chávez, "whose careful orchestration of vernacular Mexican Catholic symbols and ritual action overlapped with the larger American meaning of religious sacrifice and sainthood . . . whose otherwise 'radical' messages were delivered in ways digestible for political liberals" (72). Busto finds that Bellah and others "prefer minority leaders who do not threaten or disrupt the hegemony of a 'common' (read: assimilationist) set of public values" (73). Although undoubtedly motivated by Christianity, Tijerina's individualistic and confrontational movement was ultimately ineffective, although it did prove inspirational to some in the Chicano Movement.

Immigration and Immigrants

Churches, especially the Roman Catholic Church, are often associated with support for immigrants, but this is a relatively recent development. During the Great Depression, when hundreds of thousands of Mexicans were strongly "encouraged" to leave the United States, the Church did little.

The position of the Church on migration issues can be contradictory. It would come to oppose the *Bracero* program as well as unauthorized immigration, in part because both impeded union organizing. On the other hand, the Church supports the right of individuals to migrate when necessary.

During the 1980s, hundreds of thousands of Central Americans fled civil wars and moved to the United States. Many entered clandestinely and were faced with arrest and deportation. The Reagan administration saw them as economic and not political migrants; to claim otherwise might be interpreted as blaming our Cold War allies in Central America. In response, the sanctuary movement emerged to provide shelter and protection to these migrants. Hundreds of religious congregations would participate, its members risking arrest for harboring immigrants without legal status.

The Church would not officially endorse these actions, undertaken both by individual priests and nuns as well some parishes and religious congregations, as this was against the law. Hispanic bishops were largely silent on the matter, although some provided aid to individual groups. When Pope John Paul II visited the United States in 1987, he praised the "great courage and generosity" of those who sheltered Central American refugees. When this was subsequently interpreted as an endorsement of the sanctuary movement, he clarified his statement to add that he did not condone law breaking (María García 2004, 166). Although only a relatively small number of refugees were housed by the movement, "the public debates that resulted from sanctuary ultimately facilitated the legal changes that gave Central Americans certain protections" (María García 2004, 168) as well as brought to public attention issues such as church and state relations and civil disobedience.

In 1986, Ronald Reagan signed the Immigration Reform and Control Act (IRCA). A compromise measure, the bill enhanced sanctions against employers who hired the undocumented, but it also created a legalization program for longer-standing unauthorized residents. The United States Catholic Conference (now named the United States Conference of Catholic Bishops) opposed the former but supported the latter and therefore did not oppose the bill. The USCC, through its Migration and Refugee Services Department, subsequently provided assistance to the undocumented who wished to apply for legal status.

One growing area of study in the immigration field is transnationalism, and the Catholic Church is playing a key role in promoting such ties. As Levitt (2002) noted, this has been in process since the 1800s through missionary campaigns, educational institutions, pilgrimage shrines, the sending of church personnel across the globe, and otherwise global initiatives—"a vast, interconnected network of activities throughout the world" (157). In addition, while Vatican II led to a greater recognition and valuing of the diverse elements in the Church body, it also "rehomogenized" certain religious thoughts and practices across the globe and within a framework that continued to be centered in Rome (Hervieu-Léger 1997). Although migrants have long been able to find branches of home-nation religious institutions in the United States, Levitt (2002, 158) suggested that Pope John Paul II and the Church were deemphasizing political borders by emphasizing a "religious transnational civil society" whereby members can feel at home in multiple locales.

Levitt discusses the religious experience of Dominicans in the United States, which had multiple cross-border dynamics. Many Dominican migrants in Massachusetts became increasingly involved in the formal Church, for reasons that ranged from social comfort to social mobility. The Dominican religious experience previously emphasized popular religiosity, but the migrants became more attuned to formal experiences, which in turn influenced Dominicans back home. Ideas and money flowed from Massachusetts to the island, and subsequent arrivals to the United States were better able to adapt because they had already been exposed to U.S. Church practices.

In general, membership in transnational church institutions can take the form of an organization with branches in multiple nations, such as the Roman Catholic Church, or national churches in alignment, as between Protestants groups with the same faith heritage (for example, Baptist) in Latin America and the United States. In either case, these immigrants are not truly strangers in a strange land because they are connected to institutions with some power that advocate for the rights and dignity of migrants. Levitt (2002) noted that through such group memberships the migrant can solve problems and voice concerns.

Community Organizing

In 1940, Saul Alinsky founded an organization in Chicago named the Industrial Areas Foundation (IAF). With the financial assistance of department store heir Marshall Field III, the group sought not to impose an ideology or outside leadership on community actions. Instead, its goals included identifying and training potential community leaders and launching a local organization that would decide its own priorities. The IAF sends trained organizers to a locale and cooperatively develops issue priorities and strategies for confronting power. The hallmarks of the IAF are a focus on practical issues, not theories, and a persistent determination to publicly confront elected officials and bureaucrats and hold them accountable for results. IAF groups have achieved notable local successes in many places.

Although not officially a Hispanic organization concerned with Hispanic issues, the IAF has provided a vehicle for community improvement that many Hispanics have found useful.[16] This is in marked contrast to many nonprofits and nongovernmental organizations, which sometimes impose individuals, priorities, and goals on a community regardless of local desires and needs.

Unlike many organizers, Alinsky actively sought the assistance of religious groups. In Chicago, it was a Catholic priest who introduced him to Marshall Field. In the late 1970s, when grassroots organizations seemed to be sputtering, IAF efforts were reinvigorated by religious organizers, who "transformed Alinsky's model by linking it much more intimately with the religious congregations and faith commitments of participants" (Wood 2004, 146).

Nowhere was this more successful than in San Antonio, Texas. In 1973, Ernie Cortés experienced IAF training in Chicago and returned to San Antonio to organize a group. He looked for members and leaders among parishes and Church-related organizations, such as the Holy Name Society, and he also attracted the support of local religious figures. He eventually created COPS, a network of dozens of Catholic and some Protestant groups. The spokesman was Al Benavides, a young priest. The group would go on to win significant political victories, ranging from changing the electoral system (from at-large to ward) to $100 million in civic improvements in the *barrios*. Cortés drew many religious figures to his work and used scripture to help inspire activism. He said, for instance, that Moses and Paul were among the great organizers in history (Barvosa-Carter 2004, 272–73). The result "deeply transformed formerly Anglo-controlled politics in San Antonio (Wood 2005, 146). Similar groups were organized in Los Angeles (UNO), the Texas Rio Grande Valley (Valley Interfaith), and elsewhere, although success in Hispanic communities could vary accord to local context (Skerry 1993).

In addition to the Church helping to secure political victories, IAF organizations also helped to reinvigorate parish life. According to Sandoval (2006, 129), "Social involvement, rather than conflicting with spiritual concerns, enhanced all aspects of the parish's programs."

One of the better-known organizing efforts in the post–Chicano Movement era is the Mothers of East Los Angeles (MELA) protest against the placing of a state jail and toxic waste incinerator in a residential Hispanic neighborhood. The story begins when state authorities, having consulted the political science literature, decided to locate waste incinerators in low-SES communities because the residents would be less likely to protest. In the case of the prison, the state selected a location near Boyle Heights in East Los Angeles, a lower-middle-class Mexican-American neighborhood. Thirty-four schools were located within 2 miles of the proposed project, but the state sought to avoid an environment impact statement or a community hearing.

MELA was one of the groups that emerged to protest the decision, and it included about four hundred Mexican-American women, largely committed Catholics who were previously active in parish-based organizations. The network also worked with Catholic priests and Mexican-American elected officials. For instance, critical to spreading the word about the proposal were not only Assemblywoman Gloria Molina but also Father John Moretta of Resurrection Catholic Parish. They tapped into existing networks to build an opposition movement, and they wanted to involve women's voices in what had been a lobbying effort by a relatively small and elite group of businessmen. Father John, for example, asked the women in the parish to meet after mass to discuss the jail, and he named the group after the women in Argentina who publicly protested the disappearance of their children during the military regime. Father John also encouraged leaders to emerge, and many participants expressed a religious dimension to their efforts. Pardo (1997, 151–52) noted that this effort "illustrates how these Mexican-American women transform 'traditional' networks and resources based on family and culture into political assets to defend the quality of urban life. . . . Religion, commonly viewed as a conservative force, is intertwined with politics." She also noted that such efforts were not unique to Los Angeles "but are repeated in Latin America and elsewhere" (151).

Religious festivals and rituals can also play a role in establishing a visible Latino presence in urban areas. As Goizueta (2002, 127) observed, "Mexican American popular traditions bring religion into the public square, thereby breaching the boundary between private life and public life and challenging another epistemological dichotomy." For a people who have long occupied a liminal civic space, religion provides an opportunity to symbolically reclaim public spaces, proclaim a community presence, and reinforce a spiritual identity.

In their account of *Día de los Muertos* celebrations in Los Angeles, Medina and Cadena (2002) find political as well as spiritual significance in the popular revival of a ritual that until the 1970s was largely a private practice. Spiritually, this tradition represents a Mesoamerican worldview that defies "mainstream attempts to silence a culture and a spirituality" (72–73). Attended by both Catholics and non-Catholics, it reflects indigenous thought by emphasizing the honoring of the dead, which is contrary to contemporary Western religious views that largely divorce the dead from the living. However, it does reflect some traditional Spanish conquest–era practices involving All Saints Day (*Todos los Santos*) and in this way reflects the Catholic-Mesoamerican religious syncretism discussed below.

The popularization of this day began in the early 1970s, in part as a result of the efforts of a Roman Catholic nun, Franciscan Sister Karen Bolallero. She helped start a Latino art center called Self Help Graphics, and at the suggestion of two Latino artists, the center began to celebrate *Día de los Muertos* in 1972. Four years later, thousands of people were in attendance. Today, such celebrations have spread throughout the United States and take on political significance. According to Medina and Cadena (2002, 86), "For a historically subordinated population, publicly honoring their ancestors takes on political meaning. . . . Claiming public space to honor these 'others' is 'an ultimate act of resistance against cultural domination.'"[17]

Matovina (2002) explored the role of religion for Mexican Americans in San Antonio, Texas. San Fernando Cathedral became the "Mexican church" because of the refusal of Anglo parishes to accept Hispanic parishioners. Aside from its religious life, the cathedral was important to the community because the pious societies that developed also promoted leadership development, social networking, and community support. For instance, both immigrant and native-born women were allowed to play roles in pious societies, a rare opportunity for personal development outside the home.

Perhaps most importantly, the parishioners began to assert a symbolic presence in the city through the revival of public processions in honor of the Virgin of Guadalupe. Beginning in the early twentieth century, and supported not only by the bishop but also by Mexican and Spanish priests in residence, the events became more elaborate and public over the decades. Much of the impetus was the presence of Mexican nationals in exile because of the Mexican Revolution, and the events served a Mexican nationalist purpose. However, these events also served the purpose of "symbolically reversing the racism they encountered in the world around them" (37) by Mexican Americans publicly parading the brown-complexioned Virgin. The presence of clergy—ranging from archbishops to parish priests—"confirmed the value of their language, cultural heritage, and religious traditions" (37). As interpreted by Matovina (2002, 40), "Guadalupan devotion at San Fernando was far more than an expression of Marian devotion. It encompassed patriotism and political protest, divine retribution and covenant renewal, ethnic solidarity and the resistance of a victimized people. . . ."

Davalos (2002, 42) describes how Latinos in the Pilsen neighborhood of Chicago use the *Via Crucis* to combat "the architecture of domination." Started in 1977 by Father James Colleran and St. Vitus parish, the *Via Crucis* is a reenactment of the crucifixion experience of Jesus—including the Stations of the Cross—in which community members play roles such as Mary, Jesus, the two thieves crucified with Jesus, and Roman soldiers. Fr. Colleran was an activist who organized a number of protest activities on behalf of Latinos and immigrants, but *Via Crucis* was a uniquely spiritual attempt to achieve parallel goals. For the participants, the suffering of Jesus is seen as a metaphor for the suffering of the neighborhood and its residents. The marches are considered a collective protest against political, social, and economic injustices—which are sometimes specifically named during the event. For instance, in 1994 the march stopped at a tortilla factory to pray for its employees, an act that resulted in a change in working conditions. In the midst of everyday poverty, discrimination, and exclusion, the experience therefore provides "a claim to space. It is a public event in which Mexicanos momentarily position themselves at the center—displacing a 'minority' or 'alien' status and the sanctioned racialized landscape of Chicago" (42).[18]

Beyond Mexican Americans and Catholicism

Puerto Ricans

Puerto Ricans in the United States have characteristics of both migrants and natives. Although the Jones Act of 1917 bestowed citizenship on all Puerto Ricans, just in time for World War I, the experience of moving from Puerto Rico to the mainland United States would not be completely unfamiliar to someone migrating from Latin America. Puerto Rican migration was particularly strong after World War II, when about a half-million people moved from the island to the mainland.

Despite the fact that "push" was more responsible than "pull" for many of these migrants, the Church "chose not to acknowledge Puerto Rican migrants as a colonized people displaced by an imposed economic restructuring" (Barvosa-Carter 2004, 263). Instead, it saw them as voluntary migrants who would acculturate in the European pattern by eventually giving up Puerto Rican linguistic and cultural features.

At this time, the Church also decided to integrate migrants into existing parishes. The previous policy was that of "national parishes," whereby a particular parish would cater to one specific ethnic group. Created around the turn of the twentieth century in response to large-scale immigration from Europe, this was largely intended as a stop-gap measure. Although these parishes would feature non-English services and incorporate foreign cultural traditions, the ultimate goal was for the immigrants to "pray like Americans" (Levitt 2002, 151). Archbishop Spellman of New York City was particularly enthusiastic about the new "Americanization" plan, and New York was the primary destination of Puerto Rican migrants.[19] Although canon law prevented Spellman from closing existing national parishes without Vatican permission, he decided in 1939 that no further Spanish-language parishes would be established. Thus, "the Puerto Ricans, and later the other Latino groups, were the first Catholic immigrant groups in the United States to be denied churches of their own" (Vidal 2004, 53).

When the Church directed Puerto Ricans to Anglo parishes, the existing parishioners were not necessarily very enthusiastic. In fact, many Puerto Ricans received the clear message to stay away. Priests were also unfamiliar with Spanish and Puerto Rican culture. When the Great Migration began, there were very few Puerto Rican priests in New York City. Even in the 1970s, only three native-born Puerto Ricans were priests. However, Archbishop Spellman did create an Office of Hispanic Apostolate and require many priests to study Spanish, eventually in Puerto Rico itself. Nevertheless, Barvosa-Carter (2004) noted that the motivation was as much political as spiritual, as Spellman thought that drawing Puerto Ricans into the U.S. Church would combat potential communist influence in the community. In addition, many migrants were more interested in retaining their cultural identity and ultimately returning to the island—and not in following the pattern of turn-of-the-century Europeans. This created conflicts between the Church and Puerto Rican parishioners. Despite the "integrated parish" model, Puerto Ricans would create distinct communities within parishes, which created opportunities for the development of lay leadership. Conflict would ultimately abate, however, as the Church began to revise its approach to Hispanic parishioners in the 1960s, as discussed previously.

More recently, Vidal (2004, 58) noted that the *Cursillo* movement was critical to keeping alive Catholicism among Puerto Ricans who were a minority of the U.S. population and denied national churches. Many who experienced *Cursillo* training would later become deacons in the Church after Vatican II, when the permanent diaconate was created. Their presence proved so important to the community that Vidal (2004, 63) called Puerto Rican deacons the "native clergy" of the community.

Religion also plays a political role on the island of Puerto Rico itself. Since 1999, religious personnel and institutions were key participants in the campaign to stop U.S. Navy bombing practice on the island of Vieques. The Ecumenical Coalition of Churches for Vieques included eight Christian denominations, and its efforts helped to defeat the pro-statehood government in the 2000 local elections, which had opposed church activism in this area. In addition, many Catholic and Protestant activists and clergy worked together to protest, set up camps, and disrupt Navy activities on Vieques. Hundreds of protesters were arrested, but in 2003 the Bush administration agreed to cease Navy operations (McGrath-Andino 2004).

Cuban Americans

After Castro's revolution ended in success in 1959, several waves of Cubans migrated to the United States. The first few years brought over 200,000 refugees, and a second wave brought nearly half a million. A third wave, the Mariel boatlift, brought an additional 125,000 individuals.

Contrary to the lack of effort made on behalf of Puerto Ricans, the Church engaged in a sustained and costly operation to accommodate the Cuban refugees fleeing the Castro revolution. Most of these early arrivals were practicing Catholics (up to 80 percent, according to one estimate), and the Church organized the initial foster care for the children sent to the United States by their parents through *Operación Pedro Pan* (Operation Peter Pan; see Torres 2003).

To create a religious life in the United States for Cuban refugees, the Church promoted Spanish language acquisition among Anglo priests. Parishes began to offer Spanish-language masses, new parishes were created for the refugees, and Cuban priests and nuns opened three high schools in 1961. By the end of the 1980s, Cubans comprised almost two-thirds of Catholics in Miami, and two auxiliary bishops were born in Cuba.

Cuban migrants in the United States also use the church to proclaim connections to the island of Cuba. Levitt (2002, 158) notes how Miami Cuban-Americans created a shrine to the patron saint of Cuba. The exiles would bring their newborns to the shrine as a way to symbolically assert a form of transnational citizenship in the island. This may relieve some of the pain of exile and also indicate political claims on the future of the island.

More generally, De La Torre (2004a, 75) wrote about how each of the various Cuban exile communities over the centuries in the United States (1850, 1890s, 1930, and 1960s) "equates religious morality with nationality." Today, he finds that many in the Cuban community interpret their exile in religious terms, as a people chosen by God who are struggling against diabolical forces. Their success in the United States confirms their God-given role to "bear witness against the evils of communism in general and Castro in particular" (78). This lens of "*la lucha*" or "*la causa sagrada*" turns a political movement into a crusade, "complete with a

Christ (Martí), an antichrist (Castro), a priesthood (Cuban American National Foundation), a promised land (Cuba), and martyrs (those who gloriously suffer in the holy war against the evil of Castro)" (80).

Barvosa-Carter (2004, 270) noted that the Elian Gonzales crisis included "political discourse heavy with religiously charged rhetoric." De La Torre (2004a, 81) similarly observed that "the merging of ultra-rightwing political views with Christianity can be seen" in this incident. Some from the exile community surrounded the house where Elian was harbored, frequently prayed, and said the Rosary, and some claimed to have seen the Virgin Mary hovering over the house. As these events began weeks before Christmas, it is not surprising that some Cuban Americans saw Elian as the Christ child and his mother as Mary. Some Cuban-American followers of Santería believed that the sea god had originally spared Elian's life and that returning him to Cuba would be tantamount to giving him to Satan (De La Torre 2004a, 81–82).

Although the Church in Miami took no official position, local priests were actively involved. Elian was staying in the house of his great-uncle, and one priest said mass in the house six days a week for the family. Another organized the prayer vigils outside, and an auxiliary bishop compared Castro to King Herod.

From the non-Cuban perspective, this episode could be confusing. However, the "metamorphosis of Elián into a sacred symbol was not the Machiavellian formulation of a few with political power; rather, it was a joint effort of the Exilic Cuban community, who attempted to comprehend the will of a Deity who had seemed silent during the past forty years of their Babylonian captivity in Miami" (De La Torre 2004b, 251).

What are the political implications of this episode? When federal agents raided the house in April, several months before the 2000 presidential election, it might have cost Vice President Al Gore the election. Without the raid, which was widely condemned by the Cuban-American community, the Democrat might have retained enough votes to make the Palm Beach County butterfly ballot controversy irrelevant. Because the Cuban-American community has long been a key political constituency in Miami-Dade and Florida, its religious interpretation of political events cannot be ignored or dismissed.

Protestants

Anglo migration brought Protestantism to what is now the southwestern United States. Although Mexican law required conversion to the Church, this was in practice ignored. After the Mexican-American War, some Hispanics converted as part of a desire to assimilate, but for many years Hispanics would not be included in leadership positions. Protestant churches emphasized social services, opening schools and community centers, although some did this from religious fervor, and others saw "Americanization" as a duty and part of a larger battle against communism and anarchy (Sandoval 2006, 153). Parallel to the Catholic Church, however, Protestant denominations did not protest the forced repatriations of the Great Depression or address the structural factors that marginalized Latinos economically, socially, or politically.

Abalos (2007, 139) noted several reasons for the success of contemporary Protestant evangelizing efforts: that many ministers are themselves Latino and "share the daily hardships of the community," speak Spanish, and employ a more egalitarian church service that emphasizes scripture instead of ritual. Barvosa-Carter (2004) suggests that Protestant gains may not ultimately have significant political implications. For instance, some research suggests that only limited parallels can be drawn between the voting patterns of Latino and Anglo evangelicals and Pentecostals. In addition, Latinos are already balancing some conservative social beliefs with relatively liberal views toward government activism. Furthermore, many Latinos may become Protestants because of the opportunity to exercise greater religious leadership and to participate in smaller-scale religious settings. If so, this would not necessarily have political consequences. In addition, it is possible that a growing Latino presence in Protestant churches could affect how non-Latinos view Latinos and policy issues relevant to many Latinos, such as immigration reform.

Several important figures of the Chicano Movement were Protestants: Reies Lopez Tijerina was at one point a Pentecostal minister, and Corky Gonzalez was a Presbyterian. However, the most important Hispanic dynamic within Protestantism is the growth of Pentecostalism, which is traditionally viewed as apolitical and more interested in personal than in political transformations. Sandoval (2006, 161) notes that this can be interpreted as either fulfilling the Marxian "opiate" claims of religion or a "powerful mode of protest to systemic oppression."

However, Ramírez (2004, 178) has noted "the dismissal of Pentecostal and Evangelical congregations as sites of political empowerment." If public life is defined broadly, and by looking beyond traditional political activities such as voting and campaigns, we can find a variety of ways in which such communities are playing micro- and macro-level civic roles. He notes that "For a marginal proletariat on the move, U.S. Latino congregations serve not only as anterooms to the public square but also as critical sanctuaries where transnational identities are forged and where intergenerational and intraethnic ties are strengthened" (178). For instance, Ramírez relates the story of how an evangelical church arranged for the unauthorized return of a member who was unexpectedly deported from the United States. He asks, "Given the far-off possibilities of formal political enfranchisement for many like Efren, our inquiry into Latino religious and civic life should press the point: Was the rescue, embrace, and empowerment of a marginal laborer by a marginal faith community any less relevant than the community's formal engagement at the various levels of civic life?" (188). In another example, a character reference from a Latin American congregation to an American congregation may be a key document (for the otherwise "undocumented") on arrival in the United States. Ramírez concludes that while political scientists are busy studying more elite political actors, surely there is room for the study of how religion plays a role in the interior life of subaltern communities.

Scholarly Approaches

Theology and Community

According to Ford (1999, 3), "Theology at its broadest is thinking about questions raised by and about the religions." Far from debating how many angels can dance on the head of a pin, theology addresses issues centrally important to the human experience. For communities on the margins of society, theology can be especially important. As noted by De La Torre and Aponte (2001, 3), "In a very real sense theology, and especially Hispanic theology, is the province or property, not solely of the theological specialist, but of the whole community." They further observed that "The study of Hispanic theology is simultaneously personal, communal, historical, contextual, creative, and essential for the common good of society. Hispanic theologies nurture people spiritually and culturally, both as individuals and a community. Not simply an academic articulation, Hispanic theology is a means and expression of survival and meaning at the grassroots level" (5). According to Abalos (2007, 155), "Theology at its best is a reflection of the lived faith experiences of a people as they confront the political and historical situation."

One might reasonably ask how theology can vary by racial, ethnic, and cultural groups. Do Latinos and Anglos think about the same Christian God in different ways? De La Torre and Aponte (2001, 6) provide an example of how sin is recognized and defined in ways that privilege one cultural understanding over another. In seminary, De La Torre notes that "sloth" was taught as one of the four foundations of sin. To a young Hispanic seminarian, this seemed to reflect a North American and European celebration of the "Protestant work ethic." He reflected that "Would not a culture whose salient characteristic is hyperindividuality produce a list of sins void of any communitarian dimension? . . . While the Eurocentric theologies I was studying in seminary taught me to categorize sin as an essentially private affair, Latin American theologians such as Gustavo Gutiérrez and Jon Sobrino showed how sin always negatively affects the whole community" (6). He argues that all study of God and the Bible occurs within a specific context and that "complete 'objectivity' is a myth" (7).

Hispanic theology, or thinking about God from the Hispanic perspective, is necessarily derived "from the underside of U.S. economic structures. From the bottom, their voices provide a needed critique of the status quo" (De La Torre and Aponte 2001, 27). For most scholars, this thinking will call to mind "liberation theology," a Roman Catholic concept that originated in Latin America.

Ford (1999, 19) points out that the most common theological labels "are borrowed from politics: conservative theology, liberal theology, and radical theology." Although Latin American liberation theology is a well-known but not necessarily well-understood concept in the United States, it is far from the only thinking about God that has emerged in the Americas. In fact, liberation theologians encouraged American Hispanic theologians to develop their own ideas and not simply apply Latin American formulations. Sandoval (2006, 130) observed that Hispanic theologians see themselves as occupying a space between the first and third worlds, between the United States and Latin America. Although liberation theology has significantly influenced contemporary U.S. Hispanic religious thought, "one must not confuse U.S. Hispanic theologies with Latin American liberation theologies, or vice versa" (De La Torre and Aponte 2001, 35).

Hispanic theology as a distinct approach began with Father Félix Varela. He was writing about faith and political freedom in Cuba, which was part of the Spanish Empire during his lifetime (1788–1853). His thinking nevertheless parallels the roots of contemporary Hispanic theology, specifically its foundation in social, cultural, political, and economic realities. In the twentieth century, Father Virgil Elizondo developed the idea of *mestizaje* as the way to understand the contemporary Hispanic experience. As *Time* magazine noted, Elizondo "has taken the stigma of Hispanic otherness and transformed it into a triumphant Catholic theology."[20] *Mestizaje* reflects the complexity of Hispanic cultures—not simply Spanish or Mesoamerican but a combination with additional elements that forms a new reality.[21]

Elizondo wrote that "the borderlands between the U.S. and Mexico form the cradle of a new humanity."[22] Key to understanding this dynamic are the two conquests—first by the Spanish, then by the United States. The first gave rise to "a centuries-long historical process of *mestizaje*" (Matinova and Riebe-Estrella 2002, 8), whereas the second produced pressures to assimilate. Although most scholars discuss the continuity of religious traditions as a means of protest against the dominant culture,

Elizondo also discussed a second *mestizaje* that results from influences in the United States. Given that the political and cultural contexts of the United States and Mexico differ, it seems logical that Hispanic religious traditions and thoughts will change in the United States as they respond to or adapt to unique contexts.

To what degree is a Hispanic theology relevant to diverse Hispanic communities that have a number of denominational and national-origin group differences? Abalos (2007, 155) wrote that "A Latina/Latino theological reality is emerging within the community and is one that transcends religious denominations identified as a mestizo consciousness." Despite the diversity within and across Hispanic communities, De La Torre and Aponte (2001, 43) note that "some common themes do recur in the shared attempt to understand God."

Theological views have had important political and cultural consequences from the beginning of the Spanish conquest. Sandoval noted that the Church originally feared or disdained native beliefs, even seeing them as satanic. Sacred texts were burned, thereby destroying a large portion of the written records of the preconquest Americas. Only a small number of codices survived this process of cultural destruction.[23] With the reconquest of Iberia in the minds of the conquistadors, the Spanish were eager to fight perceived evils and spread Christianity. However, the Spanish might have done better to study these records and understand native theology. Evangelization efforts might have been more effective, for instance, if Spanish priests had found "redemptive parallels" in indigenous religions. Instead, because the Spanish simply destroyed the visible aspects of religion in the Americas (codices, priests, and temples) and imposed Christianity, many natives retained preconquest religious beliefs while participating in the formal, ritualistic aspects of Christianity. In some cases, the result was syncretism, whereby Christian thoughts and symbols were used to represent native beliefs. For instance, Abalos (2007, 145) notes that "Mary and the saints were often revered as gods and goddesses who substituted for the regional deities, that is, local deities were baptized by being given a Christian name."

Today, theologians are more likely to see parallels between the "cosmovision" (Carrasco 1990) of Mesoamerica and traditional Christian beliefs. In 2002, Pope John Paul II canonized Juan Diego, the Náhuatl Indian who reported seeing the Virgin Mary in 1531. This appearance took place on a site revered as religious by the native population well before the arrival of Christianity. This Virgin, the Mexican equivalent of many such national Virgins, is portrayed with dark skin and represents a deeply held and widespread form of religious syncretism. To Catholic theologians, this could be seen as either harmlessly symbolic or the smuggling of theological impurities into the true faith. Canonization therefore served as recognition that the indigenous contribution to Christianity was positive and enriching.

For instance, Carlos Fuentes (1992) observed that Amerindian faith sees the world as holy, which corresponds to a contemporary Church theology that is beginning to see environmental destruction as a sin (Thavis 2008). As Sandoval (2006, 9) noted, this may be "the foundation for a new theology of the environment." Laura Pérez (1998, 43) argued that native thoughts that deemphasize the boundaries between this life and the afterlife are "ultimately at odds with the reigning capitalist culture of extreme exploitation of the planet and human beings, hierarchically ordered according to degrees of difference with respect to the dominant."[24] Even today, Mesoamerican ideas are still found in Hispanic religious thought. For instance, Daniel Groody, CSC, observed pre-Columbian religious elements in the contemporary religious thoughts of migrant farm workers.[25]

David Abalos (2007, 137) noted that "The Spanish did not introduce the sacred. They contributed a particular, historical, although very important, manifestation of the sacred as found in the Catholic religion." Sandoval (2006, 32) noted that Catholicism and Mesoamerican thought "created not only a new people but also a new religion, one with the essentials of Catholicism but also with the spirit and some of the religious traditions of the indigenous peoples." This Catholicism is therefore a different blend than that found in other parts of the United States, or indeed the world.

Theological ideas continue to play a role in politics, although they do not necessarily reflect the simplistic "red state versus blue state" divisions emphasized by the media. In "Theology Finds Its Way into a Debate over Unions," the *New York Times* discussed the role of religious thinking in a California labor debate (Freedman 2008). The Sisters of St. Joseph of Orange are the sponsors of a health care system with fourteen hospitals that employ 20,000 workers. The Service Employees International Union sought to organize about 9000 of the (mostly Hispanic) nonprofessional staff, but disputes emerged about the recognition of the election. With the support of many priests, the union held protest rallies and worship services and appealed to Catholic bishops. The nuns were unhappy that their commitment to social justice was in question. Nuns from this order had been arrested in 1973 in support of the organizing efforts of César Chávez, and the order currently sponsors a range of social service activities. Although the papal encyclical *Rerum Novarum* gave Church support to labor-organizing efforts, the hospital system argues that the Catholic concept of the dignity of the individual gives workers the right to refuse to join the union. The nuns believe that no union is necessary and will not agree to election rules proposed by the union. With God on both sides, the nuns feel betrayed and the activists see hypocrisy.

Social Science Research

A small but growing literature is now examining the political implications of religion for Latino political engagement. In terms of partisanship, Latinos are more likely to vote for Democrats than Republicans in national elections by a two-to-one ratio. Recent research suggests that a key determinant of Latino partisanship is religious denomination. Catholics are much more likely to vote for Democrats than are non-Catholics (Espinosa et al. 2003; Lee and Pachon 2007; Leal 2007), and such differences are greater than any other demographic or socioeconomic status differences. The one exception is national-origin group, where Cuban-Americans are the GOP outlier (see Leal et al. 2005, 2008). Underlying this denominational dynamic are policy and ideology; Latino Protestants are more likely to identify as conservatives than are Latino Catholics, and the former hold more conservative views of abortion, school prayer, and same-sex marriage (Espinosa et al. 2003). Using the HCAPL 2000 survey, DeSipio (2007) found that Latino non-Catholics are about 40 percent more likely to be Republicans than are Latino Catholics.

Although Republicans have hoped to capitalize on such relatively conservative Latino opinions on social issues, this does not appear to be a workable strategy. This is a population with high levels of unmet socioeconomic needs, and the Democratic policy agenda is more in line with community priorities. A parallel dynamic exists for African-Americans, who also hold some socially conservative religious views but are even stronger Democrats. In addition, although Latino evangelicals are twice as likely to be Republican as Latino Catholics, their GOP identification is less than that of Anglo evangelicals. Suro and Lugo (2007) found that for registered voters, about a third of Latino evangelicals are Republicans, whereas the corresponding figure for Anglos is 50 percent. For Latino Catholics, only 18 percent identify with the GOP. More generally, Lee and Pachon (2007, 268) observed that "Latino evangelicals have not yet been closely connected to the politics of their Anglo evangelical brothers and sisters."

Another way that religion may affect Latino political engagement is through encouraging or discouraging participation. Political science research shows that levels of participation are highly correlated with socioeconomic status; the higher the status, the greater the odds of participation. For Latinos, this is a key explanation—in addition to citizenship status and a relatively youthful population—for the disparities between Latino and Anglo voting. More recently, Verba et al. (1995) argued that another dimension to turnout is the civic skills of individuals. For many, such skills are developed in the workplace, in schools, and at home. They are also developed in voluntary organizations, and for many lower-SES individuals, the Church can serve as a venue—and perhaps the only such venue—for learning such skills. Although the Church is not formally a political body, the skills developed during nonpolitical religious volunteerism are relevant and applicable to political participation.

Verba et al. (1995) further argued that one reason for relatively low Latino participation rates is their Catholic affiliation. They argued that the Roman Catholic Church was less likely to develop civic skills than were Protestant churches. This proposition was tested by Jones-Correa and Leal (2000), who examined the Latino National Political Survey and American National Election Study data. They hypothesized that if denomination affected participation across race and ethnicity, it should also be associated with variation in participation within racial and ethnic groups. However, they found no evidence that Anglo or Latino Catholics were less likely to participate than Anglo or Latino Protestants. In fact, according to some measures of participation, Latino Catholics were more likely to participate than were Latino Protestants. One variable that was more consistently significant was church attendance, which therefore suggests that the key explanatory factor was the associational role of churches, which can serve as sources of information, scenes of recruitment, and therefore spurs to participation.

A somewhat contrary finding is by Lee and Pachon (2007), who examined these questions using a 2000 Tomás Rivera Policy Institute Survey. They found no evidence that church attendance was associated with participation, although born-again status was statistically significant. In addition, they did not discover any denominational effects. Lee et al. (2002) also found that political mobilization and the development of civic skills are no more likely to be found in Protestant than Catholic churches. They generally found few denominational differences in various types of political activities, but they did note that Catholics were more likely to vote than evangelicals.

Using the HCAPL 2000 survey, DeSipio (2007) found that Catholics are almost a third more likely to vote than non-Catholics, which is additional evidence against the Verba et al. (1995) thesis. He also found that Latino Catholics were more likely than Protestants to report that their churches have become more involved in social and political issues.

Conclusions

Over several centuries, the relationship of the Church to the Latino-Hispanic-Hispano residents of what is now the United States has changed significantly. Until the mid-1920s, despite a few individual efforts, the institutional Church was not interested in ministering to Hispanics, let alone advancing social justice causes. Bishop Ricardo Ramirez (Sandoval 2006, xii) observed that it was only by the 1940s that the Church "began to recognize its role and participate in the struggle." Sandoval (2006, 119) pointed out that a priest in Albuquerque in the 1970s refused to allow a Spanish-language mass in a parish that was 98 percent Hispanic, but he did offer a Polish mass.

However, the demographics of the United States are changing, and this has significant religious implications. By midcentury, Hispanics will constitute approximately a quarter of all residents of the United States and a much larger share of Roman Catholics. One estimate suggested that Latinos would constitute up to 86 percent of all Catholics by 2050, but regardless of the exact level of growth, we can confidently state that American Catholicism will become increasingly Hispanicized throughout the twenty-first century.

In response to such transformations, the Church in 1992 began requiring all seminarians in the United States to have some Spanish language training and undergo training in sensitivity to Latino cultures. In addition, from 1990 to 1998, Church expenditures on Hispanic ministry rose by 80 percent, and the presence of such ministries in parishes grew by almost 50 percent (Levitt 2002, 155).

This change in perspective is striking. According to Bishop Arthur N. Tafoya, Chairman of the Bishops' Committee on Hispanic Affairs, "Hispanic Catholics in the United States have gone from virtual anonymity to the very center of Church life."[26] More generally, Matovina and Riebe-Estrella (2002, 5) pointed out that the Church is no longer an immigrant church or an Americanized church—it is an increasingly Mexican, other Latino, Asian, and African church—although it is administered by a largely middle-class, European-American priesthood.

One reason for this change in approach is competition. As noted by Levitt (2002, 150), the Catholic Church is working hard to attract Latinos. This reflects not only the declining membership of white ethnics but also the increased competition for Latino allegiance by Protestant churches. It will be increasingly difficult to understand Catholic, evangelical, or Pentecostal religious faith and communities without reference to Latinos. Choice and competition, central to so many aspects of American economic and cultural life, are unavoidable in the study of American religion.

Although some may be alarmed at such statistics, Maryknoll Father Donald Hessler predicts that Latinos will in fact renew the U.S. Catholic Church. Sandoval (2006, 168) also sees Hispanics as modeling positive behaviors and orientations: living simply, less materialistic, more focused on family and community than the individual, attuned to diversity, and with a faith less mediated by materialistic and secular American culture.

Following these numbers are scholars who seek to better understand the Latino religious experience. Largely pioneered by researchers outside of political science, and often outside of the social sciences, this new work is rediscovering the importance of religious faith and institutions to Latino communities. However, there is still a "secular narrative" that ignores religion or emphasizes the negative. For example, Lloyd-Moffett (2004, 42) worried that "the electronic and textual mediums that will transmit Chávez's legacy erase his spiritual basis from the historical record and perpetuate a stereotype of a split between faith and action for Latino civic leaders." Such a perspective is increasingly difficult to maintain. According to Barvosa-Carter (2004, 275), "In the political work of César Chávez, Ernesto Cortés, and others, grassroots politics and religion are so intertwined that politics not only plays a formative role in Latino/a religious experience, but conversely, religious experience can help to shape the course of Latino/a politics." Furthermore, as observed by Mario García (2004, 77), "one of the key issues overlooked in Chicano history, as well in contemporary Chicano studies, is the major part that many Chicano priests have played and continue to play in their communities. This gap also reflects the lack of emphasis by scholars on the contributions of Catholic parishes in providing both organization and a sense of community among Chicano Catholics."

Matovina and Riebe-Estrella (2002, 3) find that "historical treatments often subsume Hispanics into an Americanization paradigm presumed to hold true for all Catholics in the United States." This history of "national" and then "interethnic" parishes tells a story of European immigrants becoming American with the help of a Church that initially emphasized separation. However, this story may not apply to a Latino population that began not as "immigrants but enduring communities of faith that survived the U.S. takeover" following the Mexican-American War. After this political incorporation, both laity and clergy used religious rituals and customs to "maintain the unity of the Mexican population and permit them to resist, to a certain extent, the invasions of the Anglo-Saxon race."[27] As Mexican migration increased during the Mexican Revolution, World War I, and the Cristero Revolt, the effects were to repopulate and reinvigorate existing Mexican-American communities as well as establish new communities. Whereas European migration was largely curtailed by World War I, the Great Depression, and World War II, Mexican migration continued and, in fact, became more important to the U.S. economy. While European traditional ritualistic and devotional practices gradually changed in the United States, Latino traditions remained alive and the subject of some revival.

There is also evidence that the Church is shifting its ministry and political involvements in reaction to the growing Latino presence. Abalos saw the pastoral letters of the 2000s—the *Encuentro and Mission* (an addendum to the National Pastoral Plan) and *Strangers No Longer* (the joint letter by Mexican and U.S. bishops)—as more explicitly political in their discussion of the relationship of the Catholic Church to Latinos. The former statement, for instance, states that "Issues of immigration, education, human rights, border concerns, voter registration, and dialogue with labor union leaders are all issues relevant to the Hispanic community."[28]

Nevertheless, there still remains the potential for disagreements between the Church and Latinos. As noted earlier, Abalos (2007, 138) found that Latinos "are not antireligious or antichurch, but there is a growing resistance to the efforts of the hierarchy to consider themselves the final arbiters of the sacred." For instance, Matovina and Riebe-Estrella (2002, 1) describe a conflict between the priests and parishioners at St. Leander Church in California—the very church where this chapter author was baptized. Because of a liturgical scheduling conflict, the church wanted to cancel the annual Guadalupe celebration. When Hispanic parishioners complained, the priests agreed to hold the Guadalupe mass at 5 a.m. Despite expectations of few parishioners, the mass was standing room only. The lesson is that "Such instances of misunderstanding, disagreement, and at times even open conflict are not uncommon as the Hispanic presence in U.S. Catholicism continues to expand rapidly" (1).

Another change is that lay leaders are becoming increasingly prominent, including women. As noted by Levitt (2002, 154), women "continue to be the unofficial ministers of the family-centered traditions that are at the core of Latino religious dynamics." Matovina and Riebe-Estrella (2002, 14) wrote that women can play empowered roles in Mexican-American religious traditions, but such traditions can also promote patriarchy within the larger community. How such roles will be viewed by the entirely male Catholic, and largely male Protestant, religious leadership is unclear.

In addition, as the Pew Forum noted, "Latino Catholics are helping to reshape the Catholic Church in the U.S. not only through their sheer numbers but also through their distinctive forms of worship."[29] The report noted that Latino Catholics are four times more likely to identify as charismatics than are Anglo Catholics; twice as likely to have seen or experienced a divine healing; twice as likely to have seen or experienced an exorcism; and 19 percentage points more likely (31 percent vs. 12 percent) to have directly experienced a revelation from God. In addition, over 60 percent attend masses that sometimes feature "the kind of exuberant atmosphere that is more characteristic of Pentecostalism or other forms of charismatic or renewalist Christianity."[30]

Research on Latinos and religion will also enrich related fields of study. More generally, Levitt (2002, 150) noted that "Religious institutions have always helped immigrants integrate into the countries that receive them and enabled them to stay connected to the countries they came from." The Latino experience provides another example of this dynamic. Religious studies research will also benefit from a closer examination of Latinos. According to DeSipio (2007, 161), "traditional analysis of American Catholicism neglects the important role that Latinos are playing in revitalizing the faith and building its numbers."

Last, is the "civil religion" discussed by Bellah (1967) being challenged by the new Latino migrants? Although mostly Catholic and Christian, Latin American immigrants arrive with new spiritual ideas and practices. Will they assimilate, as previous Europeans groups have done, or will they instead transform Christianity in their image? Although new groups have long arrived in the United States, our fourth great wave of migration is adding significant diversity to our understanding of Christianity, but we cannot predict the political and societal changes this will bring.

Notes

1. This chapter is largely based on the growing literature on Latinos and religion. I am particularly indebted to Moises Sandoval, who wrote the groundbreaking book that serves as the foundation for much of my historical discussion.

This chapter uses the words Hispanic and Latino interchangeably. Although some scholars and activists prefer one word or the other, the average person sees little difference. In some regions, Hispanic is more commonly used (for example, Texas), whereas in other places, Latino is more often heard (as in California). New Mexicans sometimes uniquely use the words "Hispano" or "Spanish" to describe themselves, which reflects the unique historical experience of New Mexico. However, there is little evidence that such nomenclature has deep political implications. Latino institutions use both Hispanic and Latino—i.e., the Congressional Hispanic Caucus, National Association of Latino Elected and Appointed Officials, United States Hispanic Chamber of Commerce, and the National Institute for Latino Policy.

2. For a comparative discussion of African-American and Latino religious leadership, see Pulido and Vega (2004).

3. In this chapter, I refer to the Roman Catholic Church as the "Church." This apparent privileging reflects realities on the ground; over two-thirds of Latinos are currently Catholics; the Latino share of Catholics may reach 50 percent by the year 2020 (Abalos 2007, 138); and the future of the American Catholic Church is by all accounts a Hispanic future. The Catholic Church is therefore intertwined with Latinos in a way paralleled by no other religious institution in the United States.

4. Rieff (2006). The Pew report "Changing Faiths: Latinos and the Transformation of American Religion" estimated the 2006 figure at 33 percent. See http://pewforum.org/newassets/surveys/hispanic/hispanics-religion-07-final-mar08.pdf.

5. Ponce de Leon named it for the Spanish Easter feast, "La Gran Pascua Florida."

6. Meaning the administration of the missions not by the Franciscan order but by the regular diocesan, or "secular," clergy.

7. Which event led many religious to return to Spain (in this context, the word "religious" refers to men and women in holy orders).

8. Although perhaps less incongruously before the "Spanish Colonial" design aesthetic began to take root in the early twentieth century (see Wilson 1997).

9. "Bishops' Committee for Hispanic Affairs." *The Handbook of Texas Online*, Texas State Historical Association, available at http://www.tshaonline.org/handbook/online/articles/BB/icb5.html.

10. In Spanish, PADRES stood for Padres Asociados para Derechos Religiosos, Educativos y Sociales.

11. He notes three types: community activists, community organizers, and cultural workers.

12. "For many centuries, a sharp distinction prevailed between clergy and laity, as if there were two classes of Christians. Even today, many people ignore the fact that all the baptized make up the Church, and speak of 'the Church' when they mean only the bishops and priests. Vatican II insisted that *all* the baptized constitute the People of God and are equally called to holiness and to participate in the mission of the Church" (O'Collins 2008, 91; emphasis in original).

13. http://www.usccb.org/hispanicaffairs/rememberingpast.shtml.

14. Quoted in Sandoval (2006, 115).

15. Barton (2004) notes that some mainline Protestant Hispanics who played a role in the Chicano Movement would later serve as bridges connecting these institutions with activist elements in Mexican-American communities. Some individuals would ultimately take leadership roles in their denominations.

16. Wood (2004, 149) reported a survey that suggests about one-fifth of churches that participated in faith-based community organizing are a majority Hispanic.

17. The quotations are from Mesa-Baines (1993).

18. Page and Thomas (1994, 111) refer to "white public space" that is not a specific location but a collection of institutions, experiences, practices, and performances that "routinely, discursively and sometimes coercively privilege European Americans over nonwhites." Quoted in Davalos (2002, 65).

19. Americanization was also applied to the Church in Puerto Rico itself (Vidal 2004) and was carried out by the American bishops who were appointed to the island until the 1960s (although in ecclesiastical terms, the island was, and still is, officially part of Latin America).

20. Cited in De La Torre and Aponte (2001, 1).

21. See also Gracia (2000) and Anzaldua (1999) for more on the theology of *mestizaje* and the borderland.

22. Elizondo (1988, x). Cited in De La Torre and Aponte (2001, 37).

23. Although as Carrasco (1990, xv) notes, "In spite of the human devastation and cultural transformation brought on by the conquest and European colonialism, significant versions of the native images of space, time, the cosmos, social and economic relations, and the underworld are available to us."

24. Quoted in Matovina and Riebe-Estrella (2002, 87).

25. Sandoval (2006, 4–9).

26. http://www.nccbuscc.org/comm/archives/2000/00-044.shtml.

27. Bishop Henry Granjon, 1902, quoted in Matovina and Riebe-Estrella (2002, 4).

28. http://www.usccb.org/hispanicaffairs/encuentromission.shtml.

29. The Pew Forum on Religion and Public Life, "A Portrait of American Catholics on the Eve of Pope Benedict's Visit to the U.S." http://pewforum.org/docs/?DocID=294.

30. Although the report noted that "It is important to point out that the adoption of some key features of Pentecostal or charismatic Christianity by Hispanic Catholics does not appear to be undermining their commitment to Catholicism."

References

Abalos, David T. 2007. *Latinos in the United States: The Sacred and the Political.* South Bend: University of Notre Dame Press.

Anzaldúa, Gloria. 1999. *Borderlands/la frontera: The New Mestiza.* San Francisco: Aunt Lute Books.

Arellano, Anselmo. 2000. "The People's Movement: Las Gorras Blancas." In *The Contested Homeland: A Chicano History of New Mexico,* eds. Erlinda Gonzalez-Berry and David R. Maciel. Albuquerque: University of New Mexico Press.

Barton, Paul. 2004. "*¡Ya Basta!* Latino/a Protestant Activism in the Chicano/a and Farm Workers Movements." In *Latino Religions and Civic Activism in the United States,* eds. Gastón Espinosa, Virgilio Elizondo, and Jesse Miranda. New York: Oxford University Press.

Barvosa-Carter, Edwina. 2004. "Politics and the U.S. Latina and Latino Religious Experience." In *Introduction to the U.S. Latina and Latino Religious Experience*, ed. Hector Avalos. Boston and Leiden: Brill Academic Publishers.

Bellah, Robert. 1967. "Civil Religion in America." *Daedalus* 96:1–21.

Busto, Rudiger V. 2004. "'In the Outer Boundaries': Pentecostalism, Politics, and Reies López Tijerina's Civic Activism." In *Latino Religions and Civic Activism in the United States,* eds. Gastón Espinosa, Virgilio Elizondo, and Jesse Miranda. New York: Oxford University Press.

Carrasco, Davíd. 1990. *Religions of Mesoamerica: Cosmovision and Ceremonial Centers.* Long Grove, IL: Waveland Press.

Castañeda-Liles, Socorro. 2004. "Spiritual Affirmation and Empowerment: The Mexican American Cultural Center." In *Latino Religions and Civic Activism in the United States,* eds. Gastón Espinosa, Virgilio Elizondo, and Jesse Miranda. New York: Oxford University Press.

Davalos, Karen Mary. 2002. "'The Real Way of Praying': The Via Crucis, Mexicano Sacred Space, and the Architecture of Domination." In *Horizons of the Sacred: Mexican Traditions in U.S. Catholicism*, eds. Timothy Matovina and Gary Riebe-Estrella. Ithaca, NY: Cornell University Press.

De la Garza, Rodolfo O., and David L. Leal. Forthcoming. "Latino Politics." In *The Encyclopedia of Political Science*, ed. George T. Kurian. Washington, DC: Congressional Quarterly Press.

De La Torre, Miguel A. 2004a. "The Cuban American Religious Experience." In Hector Avalos (ed.), *Introduction to the U.S. Latina and Latino Religious Experience*. Boston and Leiden: Brill Academic Publishers.

———. 2004b. "Pray for Elián: Religion and Politics in Miami." In *Latino Religions and Civic Activism in the United States,* eds. Gastón Espinosa, Virgilio Elizondo, and Jesse Miranda. New York: Oxford University Press.

De La Torre, Miguel A., and Edwin David Aponte. 2001. *Introducing Latino/a Theologies*. Maryknoll, NY: Orbis Books.

DeSipio, Louis. 2007. "Power in the Pews? Religious Diversity and Latino Political Attitudes and Behaviors." In *From Pews to Polling Places: Faith and Politics in the American Religious Mosaic*, ed. J. Matthew Wilson. Washington, DC: Georgetown University Press.

Díaz Stevens, Ana-María, and Anthony Stevens Arroyo. 1998. *Recognizing the Latino Resurgence in U.S. Religion*. Boulder, CO: Westview Press.

Elizondo, Virgilio P. 1988. *The Future Is Mestizo: Life Where Cultures Meet.* Oak Park, IL: Meyer-Stone Books.

———. 2000. *Galilean Journey: The Mexican-American Promise*. New York: Orbis Books.

Espinosa, Gastón, Virgilio Elizondo, and Jesse Miranda. 2003. *Hispanic Churches in American Public Life: Summary of Findings*. Notre Dame, IN: Institute for Latino Studies.

———. 2005. "Introduction: U.S. Latino Religions and Faith-Based Political, Civic, and Social Action." In *Latino Religions and Civic Activism in the United States,* eds. Gastón Espinosa, Virgilio Elizondo, and Jesse Miranda. New York: Oxford University Press.

Ford, David F. 1999. *Theology: A Very Short Introduction*. Oxford: Oxford University Press.

Freedman, Samuel G. 2008. "Theology Finds Its Way into a Debate over Unions." *New York Times* August 9, B10.

Fuentes, Carlos. 1992. *The Buried Mirror: Reflections on Spain and the New World*. New York: Houghton Mifflin.

García, María Christina. 2004. "'Dangerous Times Call for Risky Responses': Latino Immigration and Sanctuary, 1981–2001." In *Latino Religions and Civic Activism in the United States,* eds. Gastón Espinosa, Virgilio Elizondo, and Jesse Miranda. New York: Oxford University Press.

García, Mario T. 2004. "PADRES: Latino Community Priests and Social Action." In *Latino Religions and Civic Activism in the United States,* eds. Gastón Espinosa, Virgilio Elizondo, and Jesse Miranda. New York: Oxford University Press.

Goizueta, Roberto S. 2002. "The Symbolic World of Mexican American Religions." In *Horizons of the Sacred: Mexican Traditions in U.S. Catholicism,* eds. Timothy Matovina and Gary Riebe-Estrella. Ithaca, NY: Cornell University Press.

Gracia, Jorge J. E. 2000. *Hispanic/Latino Identity: A Philosophical Perspective.* Malden, MA: Blackwell.

Hanke, Lewis. 1975. *Aristotle and the American Indians: A Study of Race Prejudice in the Modern World*. Bloomington: Indiana University Press.

Hervieu-Léger, Danièle. 1997. "Faces of Catholic Transnationalism: In and Beyond France." In *Transnational Religion and Fading States*, eds. Susanne Hoeber Rudolph and James Piscatori. Boulder, CO: Westview Press.

Jones-Correa, Michael A., and David L. Leal. 2000. "Political Participation: Does Religion Matter?" *Political Research Quarterly* 54:91–123.

Leal, David L. 2007. "Latinos and Religion." In *A Matter of Faith: Religion in the 2004 Presidential Election*, ed. David E. Campbell. Washington, DC: Brookings Institution Press.

Leal, David L., Matt Barreto, Jongho Lee, and Rodolfo O de Garza. 2005. "The Latino Vote in the 2004 Election." *PS: Political Science and Politics* 38:41–49.

Leal, David L., Stephen A. Nuno, Matt Barreto, Jongho Lee, and Rodolfo O de Garza. 2008. "Latinos, Immigration, and the 2006 Midterm Elections." *PS: Political Science and Politics* 41:309–17.

Lee, Jongho, and Harry Pachon. 2007. "Leading the Way: An Analysis of the Effect of Religion on the Latino Vote." *American Politics Research* 35:252–68.

Lee, Jongho, Harry P. Pachon, and Matt Barreto. 2002. "Guiding the flock: Church as vehicle of Latino political participation." Paper presented at the annual meeting of the American Political Science Association. Boston, MA, August 29–September 1, 2002.

León, Luís. 2004. "César Chávez and Mexican American Civil Religion." In *Latino Religions and Civic Activism in the United States*, eds. Gastón Espinosa, Virgilio Elizondo, and Jesse Miranda. New York: Oxford University Press.

Levitt, Peggy. 2002. "Two Nations under God? Latino Religious Life in the United States." In *Latinos: Remaking America*, eds. Marcelo M. Suárez-Orozco and Mariela M. Páez. Berkeley: University of California Press; Cambridge: David Rockefeller Center for Latin American Studies.

Lloyd-Moffett, Stephen R. 2004. "The Mysticism and Social Action of César Chávez." In *Latino Religions and Civic Activism in the United States*, eds. Gastón Espinosa, Virgilio Elizondo, and Jesse Miranda. New York: Oxford University Press.

Martinez, Richard Edward. 2005. *PADRES: The National Chicano Priest Movement*. Austin: University of Texas Press.

Matovina, Timothy. 2002. "Companion in Exile: Guadalupan Devotion at San Fernando Cathedral, San Antonio, Texas, 1900–1940." In *Horizons of the Sacred: Mexican Traditions in U.S. Catholicism*, eds. Timothy Matovina and Gary Riebe-Estrella. Ithaca, NY: Cornell University Press.

———. 2005. "Conquest, Faith, and Resistance in the Southwest." In *Latino Religions and Civic Activism in the United States*, eds. Gastón Espinosa, Virgilio Elizondo, and Jesse Miranda. New York: Oxford University Press.

Matovina, Timothy, and Gary Riebe-Estrella. 2002. "Introduction." In *Horizons of the Sacred: Mexican Traditions in U.S. Catholicism*, eds. Timothy Matovina and Gary Riebe-Estrella. Ithaca, NY: Cornell University Press.

McAdam, Doug. 1982. *Political Process and the Development of Black Insurgency, 1930–1970*. Chicago: University of Chicago Press.

McGrath-Andino, Lester. 2004. "Intifada: Church-State Conflict in Vieques, Puerto Rico." In *Latino Religions and Civic Activism in the United States*, eds.

Gastón Espinosa, Virgilio Elizondo, and Jesse Miranda. New York: Oxford University Press.

Medina, Lara. 2004. "The Challenges and Consequences of Being Latina, Catholic, and Political." In *Latino Religions and Civic Activism in the United States*, eds. Gastón Espinosa, Virgilio Elizondo, and Jesse Miranda. New York: Oxford University Press.

Medina, Lara, and Gilbert R. Cadena. 2002. "Días de los Muertos: Public Ritual, Community Renewal, and Popular Religion in Los Angeles." In *Horizons of the Sacred: Mexican Traditions in U.S. Catholicism*, eds. Timothy Matovina and Gary Riebe-Estrella. Ithaca, NY: Cornell University Press.

Mesa-Baines, Amalia. 1993. "Curatorial Statement." In *Ceremony of Spirit: Nature and Memory in Contemporary Latino Art*. San Francisco: The Mexican Museum.

National Council of Catholic Bishops/United States Catholic Conference (NCCB/USCC). 2000. "Hispanic Ministry at the Turn of the New Millennium: A Report of the Bishop's Committee on Hispanic Affairs." Washington, DC: Author.

O'Collins, Gerald. 2008. *Catholicism: A Very Short Introduction*. Oxford: Oxford University Press.

Page, Helán, and R. Brooke Thomas. 1994. "White Public Space and the Construction of White Privilege in U.S. Health Care; Fresh Concepts and a New Model of Analysis." *Medical Anthropology Quarterly* 8:109–16.

Pardo, Mary. 1997. "Mexican American Women Grassroots Community Activists: 'Mothers of East Los Angeles.'" In *Pursuing Power: Latinos and the Political System*, ed. F. Chris Garcia. South Bend: University of Notre Dame Press.

Pérez, Laura. 1998. "Spirit Glyphs: Reimagining Art and Artist in the Work of Chicana Tlamatinime." *Modern Fiction Studies* 44:36–76.

Perl, Paul, Jennifer Z. Greely, and Mark M. Gray. 2006. "What Proportion of Adult Hispanics are Catholic? A Review of Survey Data and Methodology." *Journal for the Scientific Study of Religion* 45: 419–36

Pulido, Alberto López, and Santos C. Vega. 2004. "'The Lord Requires Justice': Lessons on Leadership from the African American Church for Mexican American Catholics." In *Latino Religions and Civic Activism in the United States*, eds. Gastón Espinosa, Virgilio Elizondo, and Jesse Miranda. New York: Oxford University Press.

Ramírez, Daniel. 2004. "Public Lives in American Hispanic Churches: Expanding the Paradigm." In *Latino Religions and Civic Activism in the United States*, eds. Gastón Espinosa, Virgilio Elizondo, and Jesse Miranda. New York: Oxford University Press.

Restall, Matthew. 2003. *Seven Myths of the Spanish Conquest*. New York: Oxford University Press.

Rieff, David. 2006. "The Hispanicization of American Catholicism." *New York Times Magazine*, December 24.

Ríos, Elizabeth D. 2004. "'The Ladies Are Warriors': Latina Pentecostalism and Faith-Based Activism in New York City." In *Latino Religions and Civic Activism in the United States*, eds. Gastón Espinosa, Virgilio Elizondo, and Jesse Miranda. New York: Oxford University Press.

Sanchez, George I. 1940. *Forgotten People*. Albuquerque, NM: University of New Mexico Press.

Sandoval, Moises. 2006. *On the Move: A History of the Hispanic Church in the United States*. New York: Orbis Books.

Skerry, Peter. 1993. *Mexican Americans: The Ambivalent Minority*. Cambridge: Harvard University Press.

Steele, Thomas J., SJ, Paul Rhetts, and Barbe Awalt (Editors). 1998. *Seeds of Struggle/Harvest of Faith*. Albuquerque, NM: LPD Press.

Stevens Arroyo, Anthony. 1980. *Prophets Denied Honor: An Anthology on the Hispano Church of the United States*. New York: Orbis Books.

———. 1998. "The Latino Religious Resurgence." *The Annals of the American Academy of Political and Social Science* 558:163–76.

Suro, Roberto, and Luis Lugo. 2007. *Changing Faiths: Latinos and Transformation of American Religion*. Washington, DC: Pew Hispanic Center.

Thavis, John. 2008. "Social effects of sin greater than ever, says Vatican official." *Catholic News Service* March 10. http://www.catholicnews.com/data/stories/cns/0801336.htm. Accessed August 2, 2008.

Torres, Maria de los Angeles. 2003. *The Lost Apple: Operation Pedro Pan, Cuban Children in the U.S., and the Promise of a Better Future*. Boston: Beacon.

Verba, Sidney, Kay Lehman Schlozman, and Henry E. Brady. 1995. *Voice and Equality: Civil Voluntarism in American Politics*. Cambridge, MA: Harvard University Press.

Vidal, Jaime R. 2004. "The Puerto Rican Religious Experience." In *Introduction to the U.S. Latina and Latino Religious Experience*, ed. Hector Avalos. Boston and Leiden: Brill Academic Publishers.

Walsh, Arlene Sánchez. 2004. "The Mexican American Religious Experience." In *Introduction to the U.S. Latina and Latino Religious Experience*, ed. Hector Avalos. Boston and Leiden: Brill Academic Publishers.

Wilson, Chris. 1997. *The Myth of Santa Fe: Creating a Modern Regional Tradition*. Albuquerque: University of New Mexico Press.

Wood, Richard L. 2005. "*Fe y Acción Social*: Hispanic Churches in Faith-Based Community Organizing." In *Latino Religions and Civic Activism in the United States*, eds. Gastón Espinosa, Virgilio Elizondo, and Jesse Miranda. New York: Oxford University Press.

PART IV

Religion and Cultural Conflict

Chapter 11

MOBILIZING RELIGIOUS DIFFERENCES IN AMERICAN POLITICS

Kenneth D. Wald

David C. Leege

When the principal association of political scientists in the United States convenes a Task Force on Religion and American Democracy, the action suggests that religion matters in American public life. This assumption, reinforced by an outpouring of published research over the last thirty years, has not always been widely accepted by political scientists. Indeed, the prevailing attitude toward religion in the discipline has traditionally been characterized by indifference, a tendency to regard religion as a minor political force that arises occasionally and often with baleful consequences for the political system (Wald and Wilcox 2006). In terms of scholarly attentiveness to religious issues in American politics, this volume and others of its kind attest that we are living in something of a golden age (see, e.g., Layman 2001; Wald and Calhoun-Brown 2006; Campbell 2007; Wilson 2007).

The waxing and waning salience of religious influence in American political life naturally raises questions about the conditions and circumstances that encourage the political mobilization of religious forces. How are religious values, organizations, and communities mobilized in American politics? How do religious issues reach the political agenda in the United States? These questions assume that religious engagement in politics is problematic, that religious controversies or religious communities are not inevitably part of the political agenda. Part of our task in this chapter is thus to examine the processes by which the religious factor has gained political relevance in the contemporary United States. In addition to that goal, we also want to confront the widespread fear that religion is a particularly dangerous and divisive political force, a toxic element with the capacity to undermine stable polities and democratic governance. Therefore, apart from attempting to explain how religious issues are politicized, we further assess how such an upsurge in religiously based politics has affected the tenor of political life in the United States. What are the normative consequences for American public life of the engagement of religious forces in conventional politics? Do these forces threaten to unleash dangerous passions that may undermine the political system?

In the first section of the chapter, we address the questions of *how* and *why*. This section draws on the theory of cultural political conflict we developed in Leege et al. (2002), discussing the distinctive nature of religiously based political cleavages and their translation into partisan political forces. In answering the *to what effect* questions about the impact of this political style on American public life, we consider the danger signs about culturally based political conflict and the factors that may tend to regulate them in the American context. Given the fragility of the social and political order, only a fool would offer confident predictions about whether the American political system can cope well with the kind of cultural tensions that have undermined other apparently stable polities. After all, Americans fought a civil war over slavery that was fueled in part by conflicting religious values (Miller et al. 1998). Despite the hazards of prediction, we think the signs are currently propitious that the United States can accommodate such political conflicts without succumbing to widespread political violence and disorder or to its correlate, sustained political repression by the state.

Religious Conflict as Cultural Politics

When it is converted from a noun to a verb, "othering" refers to the process by which members of a group define their own identity by emphasizing what distinguishes them from another group. Othering is typically utilized to make a group feel pure by painting its opponents as impure—a quality that can range from merely dirty and unattractive to dangerous and demonic. Capturing the reflexive nature of the process, Littlewood and Lipsedge (1997, 27) wrote "To confirm our own identity we push the outsiders even further away. By reducing their humanity we emphasize our own." According to James Morone (2003), the distinction between a virtuous *Us* and a vice-ridden *Them* who need to be reformed runs through American political history.

This process is seldom benign. Rather, by making such rigid distinctions between itself and another community, a group may justify excluding the Other from full participation in social, economic, and political life. Because religion is so often a central marker of group identity, we frequently see othering employed during political competition. That is, candidates and campaign organizations try to paint their opponents as religiously and morally threatening by emphasizing their outsider status (see Wilcox, chapter 6 in this volume, on how this is accomplished by direct mail appeals from Christian conservative organizations). For much of American political history and ending in 1960, Catholics were the

Other excluded from the White House. But in the nomination campaigns for the 2008 American presidential election, the dynamic of the Other was also on display.

During the presidential campaign of 2008, some opponents of Senator Barack Obama utilized religion to delegitimate him, insisting that Obama, a professed Christian, was, variously, a Muslim, a hidden Muslim, a graduate of an Indonesian *madrassa* (religious academy) that taught extremist Islam, a sworn enemy of Judaism and Israel, and, most incredibly, a devotee of al-Qaeda (Mosk 2008). As Jamal's contribution to this volume (chapter 3) illustrates, the othering of Muslims in post–9-11 America provided fertile ground for these beliefs, prompting many Americans to associate the moderate Islam practiced in the United States with the more radical varieties that exist elsewhere. Other critics argued that the Christianity Obama learned at his South Side Chicago congregation was a racist, Afrocentric, anti-American faith.

Mitt Romney, a Mormon, faced a similar kind of attack during the GOP primaries. When Senator John McCain expressed a voter's preference for the presidency to be held by a Christian, he gave impetus to those evangelical Protestant clergy who consider Mormonism a dangerous, anti-Christian cult and who therefore counseled their flocks not to vote for Romney on religious grounds. This enabled McCain, who had neither the lifestyle nor the political priorities of conservative Christians, to outpoll the socially conservative Romney among white evangelicals in many GOP primaries. Both Obama and Romney were thus portrayed as religious outsiders and therefore unworthy of a presidential nomination.

How does a candidate's religious affiliation—real or imagined—become grist for the political mill? The next section attempts to unpack the politics that encourages activists to utilize religion as a political weapon.

Mobilizing Cultural Tensions in American Political Life

In *The Politics of Cultural Differences* (Leege et al. 2002), we argued that religious questions should be subsumed under a general theory of cultural political conflict. Like other domains of culture (Wildavsky 1987), religion addresses the central existential concerns of human action—Who am I (identity)? What should I do (action)? How should I react to the Other (boundaries)? Americans embrace religious institutions precisely because these traditions provide resources that help people work out responses to such fundamental puzzles about the human order (Fowler 1989). The answers that people develop to questions about identity, action, and boundaries—their sense of the "moral order" (Wuthnow 1987)—are likely to structure their political attitudes and behavior in critical ways.

This approach differs in two important respects from the most widely cited theory of culture in American politics, James Davison Hunter's (1991) "culture war" model. First, Hunter is essentially silent on the question about how cultural concerns are politicized, largely embracing an undertheorized teleological linkage, namely, behind policy is politics, behind politics is culture, and behind culture is religion. To the extent that it appears in the work of Hunter and other culture war theorists, politics is essentially an environment that passively receives inputs from the social order without making any significant contribution to the development of cultural conflict. To the contrary, we contend that politics is in fact critical to the mobilization of cultural tensions.

Apart from divergent approaches to the political process, the two accounts of cultural politics also differ in how they define cultural conflict. To Hunter, cultural politics simply denotes a specific set of issues that engage religious passion. By contrast, Leege et al. emphasize that culture is manifested in several domains, implicating the moral orders defined by race, gender, and nationalism as well as by religion. These moral orders provide fertile territory for political mobilization because they involve deeply felt social values that undergird personal identity and imbue individuals with a powerful sense about which groups are worthy and unworthy, what policies are right and wrong. Hence, in this formulation, cultural conflict is less a particular set of issues and more a style of campaigning that draws on subcommunal tensions by means of elite efforts to politicize such cleavages. It differs in tenor from campaigns where candidates attempt to portray themselves as more competent than their opponents at achieving consensual goals ("valence" issues in the language of Campbell et al. 1960) or campaigns built on "character" traits such as experience or consistency of belief.

Drawing heavily on the observation of political consultants and perceptive journalists (Barone 1990; Edsall and Edsall 1992; Freedman 1996; Schnur 2007), the theory of cultural politics we advanced contends that the translation of religious ideas/grievances/concerns into politics relies on four key steps:

1. Ambitious political elites constantly scan the horizon in search of cultural tensions and fault lines. They identify developments or events that appear to disturb the moral orders of various cultural communities.

Public controversies are usually stimulated by issue entrepreneurs, activists who find "hot button" issues with the capacity to alter the political universe in their favor. In many cases, such entrepreneurs locate a potential issue and then work with elected public officials or candidates to raise an outcry about the matter. As with most human action, the motives for such efforts encompass normative commitment to a philosophy, organizational self-interest, and political ambition. For the elected official, embracing the issue may offer an opportunity to achieve national prominence by becoming the champion of a popular cause and to be elected to higher office.

An issue is considered suitable for mobilization if it has the potential to upset what members of a target audience consider the rightful order of society. Consider the case of "partial birth abortion," an issue that has been on the public agenda since the 1990s. On the surface, this subject concerns a rarely used medical procedure typically employed in the second trimester to terminate a pregnancy. How did such a matter become ripe for political mobilization?

The medical procedure known by various names came to the attention of the National Right to Life Committee in 1995 (Rovner 2006). The leaders of this antiabortion organization christened it "partial birth abortion," a term that was soon incorporated in a bill sponsored by U.S. Representative Charles Canady (R-FL) to prohibit the procedure. The idea behind the label was to further politicize the debate over abortion and move the American public firmly into the pro-life camp. The procedure, especially when performed late in the second trimester, involved a potentially viable child and raised the specter of infanticide. As such it was offensive to public sensibilities, and it was seen as a tool likely to foster opposition to abortion on humanitarian grounds. Twelve years of acrimonious debate later, the United States Supreme Court finally upheld bans on the procedure, signaling an important victory for the opponents of abortion. For the first time since *Roe v. Wade*, the Court moved symbolic attention away from privacy rights—"a women's right to choose"—to "the right of a child to live."

2. Elites politicize these issues by framing them as threats, using "efficient symbols" that pack powerful meaning in tangible, compact form. Symbols are instruments intended to engage the emotions of voters. Accordingly, this style of politics invokes powerful emotions—often fear and anger, sometimes hope and optimism—as explicit tools of political campaigning.

In the 1988 presidential campaign, Republicans faced a challenging candidate in the person of Massachusetts governor Michael Dukakis. As Dukakis was little known nationally, the Republican campaign set out to find a way to link him to unpopular Democratic policies. They found the perfect tool in the person of a Massachusetts convict, Willie Horton, who had committed a rape while on work-release from a Massachusetts prison during Dukakis' tenure as governor. It did not matter that the work-release program was the brainchild of Dukakis' predecessor as governor, a Republican, or that it had been deployed in federal corrections under the Reagan watch. Willie Horton was a symbol that successfully fused concerns about black crime, dangerous black males, and

Democratic timidity (Mendelberg 1997). Republican campaign organizations accordingly created television advertisements that stoked voter anger by suggesting that Dukakis was responsible for the breakdown of law and order by pursuing liberal policies. Although formally disavowed by the Bush campaign, the television ads, featuring "a big black rapist" (in the words of Bush campaign manager, Lee Atwater), were a key element in the ultimately successful effort to drive up Dukakis' negatives and cut into the Democratic base.

"Tax and spend" and "welfare queen," phrases often wielded by Republican candidates in the 1980s, combined notions of an unjust, distant (federal) redistributive state under the control of unelected elites ("pointy-headed intellectuals," "effete snobs"), relative deprivation, unworthy blacks, and immoral lifestyles (Sears and Citrin 1982; Edsall and Edsall 1992). Still another negative slogan, "theocracy on both ends of Pennsylvania Avenue," was developed by Democrats to raise fear among moderate Republicans about the capture of their party by conservative Christian evangelicals. These symbols become staples of negative political advertising and are understood in the political science lexicon as "easy issues" (Carmines and Stimson 1989) or "morality politics" questions (Meier 1994). Whereas other types of issues prompt candidates to assert that they could do a better job than the opposition in achieving a consensual goal—reducing crime, raising employment, cutting taxes—cultural issues enable the candidates to claim the moral high ground and associate the opposition candidate with policies that are repugnant.

3. These symbols become tools wielded by partisan elites in their attempts to control the size and composition of winning electoral coalitions. Depending on the party's status, it may use these symbols to encourage turnout by its normal supporters ("mobilize the base") and/or to promote either defection or nonparticipation by elements of the opposing party's core vote. Thus, to understand the effects of religion on American democracy, we must devote considerable attention to issue framing by politicians.

In the calculus of electoral politics, the goal of the party is to create an electoral majority sufficient to win the contest. For the majority party, the challenge is to hold together its various factions as a cohesive force. The minority party, on the other hand, has to (a) stimulate its partisans to vote and (b) somehow chip away at the majority coalition. This means either converting partisans on the other side to their position, which is difficult, or simply talking the other side's partisans into staying home. Abstention, the behavior that underlies demobilization, is often easier to achieve than conversion.

Hence, the minority party will often strive to raise doubts in the mind of the other candidate's partisans about whether their party's nominee truly reflects their own values, sowing uncertainty, anxiety, and anger among the opposition's supporters (Leege and Wald 2007). In the post–New Deal electoral system, a period that began in the 1960s, the GOP has to great effect deployed cultural issues to demoralize particular groups within the Democratic majority coalition. Racial resentment became a powerful theme aimed alike at white southern segregationists, many of whom were devout evangelicals and considered racial separation divinely inspired, and urban dwellers in the North, many of whom were working-class ethnic whites who regarded blacks as competitors for jobs and neighborhoods and as threats to the social order (Rieder 1985; Valentino and Sears 2003). In the 1970s and 1980s, fears about threats to the moral order from feminists, gays, antiwar activists, recreational drug users, and proponents of abortion inspired the use of new symbols to detach traditionalist Democrats from their partisan moorings. In each case, the message was that Democratic candidates no longer upheld the values of the party, and disaffected Democrats were better represented by the GOP.

4. With advances in campaign technology and changes in communication channels, it has become easier and more common for parties to wield cultural tools and thus to undertake culturally based political campaigns. The practice known as microtargeting has allowed the customizing and delivery of scientifically targeted campaign appeals. However, like all electoral strategies, these tools are available to both parties and may not work or work as intended.

In the era of partisan newspapers and sharply limited broadcast outlets, parties and candidates tended to reach out to voters with fairly broad and generic political advertisements. Narrower targeting was possible but extremely expensive and quite inefficient. Over the past twenty years, however, the channels of access to voters have exploded (Hillygus and Shields 2008). Based on lists purchased from magazines, interest groups, clubs, and other organizations with particular partisan leanings, and consumer firms that monitor and classify Internet hits, target voters may be reached by fax, e-mail, text messages, highly targeted mailings, closed-circuit broadcasts, and advertisements customized for particular narrowcast outlets (e.g., Fox News channel, MTV). Parties may and do station outreach representatives in religious congregations, service clubs, other voluntary associations, and youth entertainment venues. Voters thus find themselves inundated with messages that are much harder, more specific, and more emotive than the campaign appeals of yesteryear, yet narrowly enough targeted to avoid raising a public clamor.

In 2004, for example, the Republican National Committee (RNC) mailed out carefully crafted pamphlets to voters in conservative Christian churches in a few states, including mailings that insisted that Democrats wanted to ban the Bible (Kirkpatrick 2004). Although this mailing drew a bit of press scrutiny, most such efforts fly beneath the radar of campaign observers. Careful empirical studies of the 2004 election by Monson and Oliphant (2007) document the appeals that the RNC made to twenty-four microtargeted categories, both among vulnerable Democrats and in the Republican base. Many of these appeals "treated outsiders . . . as morally wrong, un-American, or godless" (Leege 2007, 263). Campbell and Monson (2007) illustrate the strength that microtargeted antigay material had in battleground Electoral College states in 2004. They argue, simply, it worked. Cultural appeals are thus easier to utilize in the current information climate.

The primary campaign attacks on Obama and Romney in 2008 (see discussion above) illustrate how religion can be incorporated into the four-step cultural politics scenario. As part of opposition research on Obama and Romney, supporters of opposing candidates identified potential vulnerabilities that could be exploited. By using powerful symbols as codewords—*madrassa* (which conjures up images of suicide bombers) or cult (which associates the respectable Church of Jesus Christ of Latter-Day Saints with groups like the Branch Davidians or Moonies)—they politicized the latent differences. The attacks on both candidates were aimed at undermining the partisan loyalties of various core constituencies in both the primaries and general election. Most of these charges were circulated by such classic microtargeting tools as e-mail campaigns, targeted mailings, blogs, and commentary by campaign surrogates.

We have painted this process in broad strokes because of space limitations and need to add some nuance to the general portrait. As President Obama's victory would seem to demonstrate, there is no guarantee that cultural appeals work simply because there are multiple issue frames available to the electorate. Parties may offer dueling cultural images that offset each other or compete for influence in defining the national agenda.

When a party misreads the cultural climate, its attempt to imbue a political issue with a particular meaning may backfire spectacularly. We may consider as a case in point the tale of Terri Schiavo, the young Florida woman in a persistent vegetative state whose husband decided to permit her to die by withholding sustenance under Florida's "death with dignity" act. Schiavo became a cultural symbol that could support alternate templates in the 2002 political campaign (Wald et al. 2006). To Republicans, she was meant to symbolize the plight of the helpless human in the face of soulless medicine and a patent disregard for human life by arrogant, unelected judges. Many Democrats (and not a few Republicans) understood Schiavo instead as a poster child for the unwanted and unwarranted intrusion of government into the most intimate realm of family affairs. As images do, the meaning of Terri Schiavo extended beyond the case itself to ongoing disputes about human reproduction (abortion), medicine (stem-cell research), and the ethics of an elite profession. Although the Republican Party leadership in Washington embraced efforts by the biological family to force continued feeding, the net effect probably hurt the GOP by contributing to its image as a party too eager to use the state to advance its own conception of morality.

Is Cultural Politics Dangerous?

Religiously based political mobilization in the United States may be disquieting because it raises concern about whether American politics may come in time to resemble those of Lebanon, Iraq, India, or Bosnia. The emergence of violent sectarian conflicts around the globe has sometimes been understood as the outcropping of deep, primordial cleavages that lurk just beneath the surface of perpetually divided societies (Isaacs 1975). Yet an alternative perspective suggests that societies politically riven by communal conflict are not all that different from apparently stable polities such as the United States. This "constructivist" approach insists that cultural differences are always "available" for mobilization, even in seemingly integrated states, and can be mobilized as a basis for political action by the explicit efforts of elites. As one important component of the cultural domain, religion is a resource that can be deployed by determined politicians as a means to fashion social and political identity. The bloody conflict in the Balkans during the 1990s exemplifies the process.

Long before communism emerged as the dominant political movement in the aftermath of World War II, the population of the Yugoslavian state was divided among Catholicism, Orthodox Christianity, and Islam. Despite the absence of overt confessional cleavage from the public square during the Tito years, however, religion remained an important component of cultural identity that linked individuals to ethnic groups. Such identity typically includes a symbol system that comprises, among other elements, "collective myths of origin, the assertion of ties of kinship or blood . . . , a mythology expressive of the cultural uniqueness or superiority of the group; and a conscious elaboration of language and heritage" (Bates 1974, 458). When the Yugoslavian state collapsed amid a legitimacy crisis in 1989, it provided ripe conditions for the emergence of religion as a basis of national and territorial identity (Iveković 2002, 534). This potential was realized by virtue of the efforts of political and religious leaders who both spearheaded this very public recovery of ethnoreligious awareness and took advantage of the heightened group consciousness as a means of achieving and maintaining power (Gagnon 1994; Vrcan 1994; Cohen 1997). The bloody civil conflicts that subsequently broke out in Bosnia-Hercegovina in 1991 were not religious wars in the sense of competition over faith claims but rather conflicts over land, power, and ideology that were often legitimated in the name of religion and fought between combatants defined by religious affiliation.[1]

Politicized religious symbols were critical in the effort to mobilize populations on the basis of ethnoreligious identity. Michael Sells (2003, 312) recounts how Serbian nationalists drew on a pivotal nineteenth-century battle with the Ottoman Empire to amplify a sense of ethnonationalism defined by opposition to Islam. The "Serbian Golgotha," an emotive term transfiguring the fate of Serbian Orthodox martyrs against Islam into the narrative of the passion of Christ, became a dominant theme in the discourse among the community and was represented concretely by staged reenactments throughout the province. Serbians reinforced their own identity by portraying Bosnian Croats (Roman Catholics) and Muslims as irreducibly genocidal populations who posed an ongoing existential threat to Christian Orthodoxy. Some Orthodox priests toured the provinces, publicly blessing war criminals and justifying the destruction of Catholic and Muslim holy sites (Iveković 2002, 525).

Not to be outdone, Croat Catholics and their militias prominently featured a famous international pilgrimage site where visions of the Virgin Mary, staples of Catholic folk religiosity, were tied to Croat nationalism (Cohen 1997, 489). Observing public rituals, a journalist noted an even more expressive example of the linkage between religious identity and nationalism:

> The cross of Christ stands next to the Croatian flag, the Croatian bishop next to the Croatian minister of state. . . . This was truly again a real war for the "honoured cross and golden liberty," for the return of Christ and liberty to Croatia. The church is glad for the return of its people from the twofold slavery—Serbian and communist. (Quoted in Powers 1996, 221)

Bosnian Muslims do not seem to have mounted similar displays, perhaps because that identity was always understood as principally cultural and national rather than religious (Iveković 2002, 530; Sells 2003, 310). Nonetheless, there was evidence of increased public displays of Muslim religiosity during the war and some efforts to extend identification with Muslim resistance movements around the globe (Iveković 2002, 531; Cohen 1997, 493–95).

Despite differences in the nature of mobilization across the three traditions, all such efforts shared a disposition to partition the universe between Us and Them, the hallmark of othering. Vrcan (1994, 418) noted

> a pervading and systematic Manicheism . . . portraying the opposed parties on one side as the angelic or quasi-angelic personification of

> the Good and, on the other side, stigmatizing the other as the diabolic or quasi-diabolic incarnation of Evil as such, or depicting one side as God's and stigmatizing the other as Satan's. . . .

This Manicheism lent a particular savagery to the Bosnian conflict (Vrcan 1994, 420).

Could it happen here? Although the Bosnian experience seems light years away from the American political situation, there are striking parallels. In both places, religious affiliation has become for many people a highly politicized form of social identity that entails the adoption of symbol systems that motivate public behavior. As in the Balkans, this development in the United States has been midwifed by political elites who sponsor social movements that serve their ambitions for power and higher office. In such mobilization campaigns, the goal is to create psychological distance between Us and Them and paint "Them" as a feared and despised Other. Although this strategy is pursued in the United States principally through election campaigns rather than paramilitary actions, some observers of the American scene regard culture wars as the potential precursor to shooting wars. At the very least, as Gibson demonstrates in chapter 5 of this volume, Americans who regard members of a particular group as threatening to their own social group or to the broader social order are appreciably more willing to deny that group fundamental political rights. The next section will thus examine three normative issues raised by a political style where elites consciously heighten cultural tensions by deploying powerful symbols as staples in campaigns and elections.

Threat to Political Stability

Our theory of cultural political conflict assumes a political life where elites engage rationally and effectively in identifying and intensifying cultural differences, fashion and wield symbols that invoke strong emotions, demonize political opponents as enemies, and consciously attempt to divide the electorate into blocs united by anger and resentment against the Other. It is a style built on Richard Nixon's underutilized aphorism that the secret of politics is knowing who hates whom. Clausewitz famously defined war as the continuation of politics by other means. Cultural political conflict seemingly inverts the definition, making politics a continuation of war by other means. Although we think culture war theory is conceptually deficient, likening politics to war certainly identifies a danger that this cultural political style will unleash dark and irrational forces, polarize people, and inject unhealthy levels of fanaticism and extremism into the body politic.

Such fears about incendiary "single issue politics" undergird the common assertion that polities with predominantly religious/ethnic cleavages are much less stable than nations with other kinds of political divisions (Rose and Urwin 1969). The problem according to some scholars is that conflicts rooted in basic matters of identity—religion, language, ethnicity—may not admit compromise solutions that are necessary to maintain stable societies. No doubt persuaded by the Balkans war discussed above, some scholars believe that religion is inherently prone to encourage intergroup hostility and violence because it divides the world into good and evil, sanctioning any means necessary to subdue those against God's side.[2] Certainly, the murderous rages fueled by a sense of divine entitlement—on display in the American Civil War, for example (Woodworth 2001)—make this threat appear tangible. Anecdotally, even in the contemporary American context, it is not hard to find instances where culture warriors have used language that denies the humanity of their opponents (see Wald et al. 1989) or to identify murderous violence traced directly to cultural groups with polarized world views (Aho 1991). The appearance of groups attempting to negotiate such divides, organizations named "Common Ground" or "JustLife," also suggest that some activists have recognized the danger of such polarization and tried to transcend it. Wilcox (chapter 6, this volume) notes that leaders of Christian conservatism have attempted to moderate the sometimes Manichean views of organizational activists by teaching the values of compromise, empathy, and civility.

One way to understand such culturally based conflict is through Max Weber's discussion of value rationality. This phrase seems jarring because it juxtaposes concepts commonly posed as opposites: politics based on values or convictions, on the one hand, is distinguished from politics rooted in interests, derived not from passion but from cool, cerebral calculation of costs and benefits. Indeed, in *Economy and Society*, Weber distinguished between instrumental rationality, defined as action that adjusts objectives in response to costs, and rationality based on values held so strongly that they do not change regardless of the costs of obtaining them. Although these are perceived as opposing ideal types, qualitatively different types of behavior, they may in fact coexist in a social movement. Studying movements for nationalist mobilization by ethnic groups, Varshney (2003, 94) made an important distinction between ends and means. Whereas somebody motivated by value rationality would not compromise on ultimate ends, he or she is quite likely to consider multiple means to a deeply held end:

> The fact that my identity gets tied up with my group does not mean that I accept as right everything that the group (i.e., its leadership on

> behalf of the group) does. I may have a different version of group objectives and may even try to convince my group that my version is right. My *identity* may be tied up with my group, but my *views* may not be. Such intra-ethnic clashes on what is valuable and what means are appropriate to achieve those goals allow for a great deal of volition, intragroup strategizing, and struggle. Indeed, if I have leadership ambition, I may even try to retrieve my group's history purposively to show that I am historically more authentic than are my adversaries in the group, while both my adversaries and I seek group betterment.

It is important not to read more into this statement than Varshney intended. He is careful to note that the strong passions that underlie culturally based group identity may indeed promote a willingness to engage in violent behavior against seemingly innocent civilians. Yet this outcome is not inevitable but contingent. It depends on the arguments, perspectives, and persuasiveness of those engaged in internal debates on the ends of the movement. This admits the possibility that people can wield cultural values rationally without necessarily resorting to socially destructive political tactics.

There is evidence that the American political system can indeed manage and contain such tensions (Tesh 1984). Perhaps the acid test is the abortion controversy in which one side portrays abortion as nothing less than murder and the other sees it as the inalienable choice of the pregnant woman. Early research summarized by Steiner (1983) found that stark differences between the two sides were effectively moderated by the American political system. The norms of the legislative process tended to isolate those with extreme positions and leave the matter to be resolved by negotiation, compromise, and the judicial process. Although this may well have frustrated the extremists, encouraging the isolated cases of violence against abortion providers, these acts only underscored their impotence by branding such vigilante behavior as criminal conduct.[3] Elizabeth Oldmixon's research on Congressional decision making (2005) suggests that the patterns detected by Steiner continue to operate. In the House of Representatives, profound differences over abortion have been accommodated to the routines of the budgetary process. Much the same has happened in the ongoing battle over stem-cell research. Congressional debate during the Bush era centered on President Bush's decision to freeze federal funding for research using stem cells harvested from embryos destined to be discarded as they lose viability. This transforms the question from life and death to a debate over spending and federalism, the constitutional provision that reserves authority to the states in areas not under federal jurisdiction. Although often cast as a partisan debate at the national level—Democrats pro, Republicans con—California, Massachusetts, Missouri, and other states with Republican governors invested heavily in this area of medical research. Many morality issues may be transformed into thoroughly conventional distributive issues (Wald et al. 2001).

As elites play the key role in identifying and politicizing cultural conflicts, they may be equally important in managing them within the rules of the political game. The literature of plural societies emphasizes the role of interelite bargaining to obtain concessions that prevent deep cleavages from destroying the political system (Lijphart 1977). By virtue of participation in policy making, elites may develop strong respect for the system that permits them to achieve progress. Several studies of newly mobilized religious political activists in the United States have suggested precisely such a scenario, noting that most "true believers" who are unable to compromise gradually drop out in frustration at their inability to effect change (Rozell and Wilcox 1996; Conger and McGraw 2008; Layman, chapter 7, this volume), ceding leadership to pragmatists who accept the rules of the game and simply attempt to turn them to their own use. There are enough counterexamples (e.g., Wald and Corey 2002) to suggest that this outcome, too, is a contingency rather than a certainty. The political system is crucial both in generating cultural conflict and in producing conditions that manage it.

One of the most important structural characteristics of the American political system that encourages "secular reformist gradualism" (Lipset 1959, 61) is multiple points of access. If movement elites cannot gain the whole loaf in one branch of government or one level of government, they can get slices of it by changing the venue to a different branch or level. On the abortion debate, many evangelicals and Catholics embraced the 1980 campaign rhetoric of Governor Ronald Reagan (ignoring his strongly pro-choice behavior as California governor) and came to expect that he would successfully lead the effort to pass a constitutional amendment banning abortion. Saddled with a Democratic majority in the House of Representatives, Reagan lacked both votes and gumption. But he did embark on a program of appointing federal judges who would restrict the circumstances where abortion was permissible. Control of courts became more important than majorities on Capitol Hill. Eventually the *Webster* decision (1989) and the *Casey* decision (1992) shifted the abortion venue to the states. Regulation of health and well-being was often a focal point. Conflict now surrounded state legislative elections where statutes and constitutional amendments would limit or outlaw abortion. Generally in a democracy a venue close to people of similar demography is easier to control than a national venue that begs compromise among disparate sectors of the population. With abortion, in particular, far more states would potentially limit or ban it than states would permit it. Thus, multiple points of access provided a safety valve to moral partisans who might be tempted, like John Brown with slavery, to take the law into their own hands.

False Consciousness

Harkening back to the Marxist conception of false consciousness, some writers condemn culturally based political conflict as inauthentic, a tool by which individuals are encouraged to ignore their *real* interests by pursuing "artificial" questions. This approach contends that cultural political conflicts promote concern about secondary matters, displacing more important issues on the political agenda. As expressed in Thomas Frank's *What's the Matter with Kansas?* (2004), cultural issues are stirred up with the connivance of economic elites as a means of distracting workers from the way their economic interests are being savaged by conservative policies. In effect, Frank argues, workers are collaborating in their own political repression. (In much the same way, Calhoun-Brown notes in chapter 9 in this volume that the participation of women in patriarchal churches appears to undermine the sense of personal efficacy that might otherwise enable them to seek political solutions for their subordination in society and the polity.)

Frank is correct to note that cultural defense issues may be potent determinants of political action to workers with low levels of education and income security, people who would seem to have an objective interest in better pay and generous public welfare benefits. Indeed, in talking about the social changes that had occasioned political conflict since the watershed 1960s, Everett Carll Ladd (1976) identified an "inversion" of the typical cleavage pattern in American politics. On cultural issues involving sexuality, gender roles, drug use, and the like, the traditional supporters of the Democratic Party, members of the working class, had actually been drawn to the defense of moral traditionalism that was championed by the Republicans, whereas social and economic elites, the traditional mainstay of the GOP, were closer to the Democratic position.

We are not persuaded that this constitutes a legitimate criticism of cultural political conflict. On normative terms, we reject the claim that culturally based political conflict is somehow inauthentic. Such a claim rests at base on the idea that one group of observers can somehow speak with authority about what issues should matter to another group. Individuals in any group have the autonomy to decide for themselves what political issues are salient without having such a preference ordering imposed on them by fiat. More broadly, we reject the idea that cultural conflict is limited to overt religious issues. Consider the debate over welfare reform, a policy area that was contested in terms of conflicting moral values—a belief that individuals are ultimately responsible for their own economic status by virtue of the choices they make versus the equally compelling argument that the state has a moral obligation to insure that all citizens enjoy at least a minimal standard of living (Kennedy and Bielefeld 2006, ch 1). As the example illustrates, economic issues may implicate the moral order no less than questions about sexuality, gender roles, or other issues with overt religious dimensions.

Historically, scholars have recognized that opposition to slavery by northern workers (or its defense by their southern counterparts) was not simply a matter of economic advantage. Rather, antislavery politics pursued by many urban workers reflected views about the morality of the southern way of life. To northerners, slavery permitted moral degradation of human beings and was an offense against God and nature (Oestreicher 1988). Southerners saw the "peculiar institution" instead as a beneficent arrangement ordained by God that supported a righteous society. As Abraham Lincoln acidly noted in his famous Second Inaugural, both sides were confident in their moral supremacy. Rather than consider such positions as illustrative of "false" consciousness, we consider them political opinions with no more or less integrity than popular views on any other policy area.

The claim of false consciousness itself points to the challenge of the American left in facing up to strong normative claims based on religion. In recent presidential elections, Democratic nominees Walter Mondale, Michael Dukakis, and John Kerry (as well as Republicans Bob Dole and George H. W. Bush) were notably discomfited by the demands for "God talk" on the campaign circuit. When they spoke of how their faith informed their political positions, these candidates seemed inauthentic, as if they were pandering to a special interest group rather than speaking from the heart.[4] The same reluctance to speak about ultimate values seems to handicap progressive organizations generally. Stephen Hart's (2001) detailed study of two organizations, Amnesty International and Milwaukee Innercity [*sic*] Congregations Allied for Hope (MICAH), a faith-based community-organizing coalition, noted a huge difference in styles of engagement and public discourse between the two movements. The former drew almost entirely on classic liberalism and rights talk, while the latter was deeply anchored in an ecumenical language of hope and redemption. The MICAH example indicates to Hart how a more expansive style of discourse, rooted in American's cultural heritage, enables activists to reach out and encompass a more diverse constituency than does classic liberalist individualism. We heard echoes of that communal style in the 2008 campaign rhetoric of Barack Obama, a candidate whose political education was profoundly shaped by community organizing among churches in Chicago's South Side.

The thorny and complex relationship between liberalism and religion makes simple conclusions inappropriate. Scholars have struggled to find ways to reconcile the tenets of liberalism and illiberal cultural values (Swaine 2001), and some have begun to suggest ways to synthesize the two styles in the context of American political life (McGraw and Formicola 2005). Cultural political conflict is not going to go away, making such efforts more urgent.

Group Privilege

The larger implications of this campaign style intersect recent debate about multiculturalism and identity politics (cf. Pickett 2006). Religious identities run deep and may reinforce caste-like cultural divisions. For example, to be an evangelical white southerner was, for the most part, to be a prejudicial and segregationist Democrat through the first half of the twentieth century and, more recently, to be an anti–federal government Republican. To be an African-American evangelical or a Jew, both of whom incorporate group liberation themes in their theology, was to be perforce a civil rights Democrat. Does this simply reduce politics to a matter of identity politics? When political issues revolve around identity, there are dangers that groups will insist that their values alone be privileged by the state or, alternatively, that they maintain the right to exit from obligations that are otherwise binding on the rest of society. In the context of religion, these alternatives are manifest today in movements to "Christianize" American society or alternatively to hold certain sectarians exempt from rules governing public education, employment law, and the like. Earlier in American history, such efforts were acute when Protestants tried to enforce their hegemony over Roman Catholics by demanding that Catholic children be educated in public schools that reflected a Protestant ethos rather than parish schools intended to socialize young Catholics in the faith.

If there is one normative assumption that knits together practitioners of what Bernard Crick once called the American science of politics, it is precisely this commitment to the norms of liberal democracy. Although there are varying traditions of citizenship within liberalism, it has usually been understood to include "nonrevocable rights to free speech, association, assembly and property *for individual citizens who are the irreducible unit of the polity*" (Katznelson and Milner 2002, 6, emphasis ours). This concept is so deeply woven into the fabric of contemporary liberalism that even efforts to justify the use of religious language in public debate on Lockean grounds note that such rights inhere exclusively in religious individuals and not in religious collectivities (McGraw 2003). From this perspective, efforts to enshrine a particular conception of human personhood in the law can be contested as a form of religious establishment that violates the free exercise rights of individuals seeking abortion (Wenz 1992). This renders problematic political conflict conducted through the lens of religious doctrine.

Although identity-based political conflict presents challenges to liberal norms of governance, we do not see culturally based political conflict as necessarily fitting the charge. First, even though religious identities are salient to individuals, they are not the only basis of social identification. Rather, such identities are but one of many conflicting holds on the life of believers and may not be consummatory. Individuals typically belong to multiple groups, and these multiple allegiances may induce cross-cutting cleavages that mitigate the excesses of identity politics. Even in 1960, when Catholics in large numbers rallied around their co-religionist who was the Democratic presidential nominee, some Catholics voted for Richard Nixon because they valued being a Republican or an anticommunist more than supporting a fellow Catholic.

Second, many religious values are *prescriptive*, that is, models of the good life to be emulated, rather than *proscriptive*, that is, values to be violated only at threat of eternal perdition. Proscriptive moral teaching finds it hard to tolerate a society perceived to violate God's will with abandon and anticipates apocalyptic punishment from God unless the state can transform the society. By contrast, prescriptive values allow for vigorous debate over how various policies meet the moral imperative without declaring one position alone as just and all others illegitimate. For example, members of Conservative Jewish congregations recite a weekly prayer for the United States, beseeching God to teach the "insights of Your Torah" to the nation's leaders so that "they may administer all affairs of state fairly, that peace and security, happiness and prosperity, justice and freedom may forever abide in our midst" (*Siddur Sim Shalom* 1985, 415). In the Jewish tradition, there is ample room for debate on how to understand the Torah's commandments. In like manner, the comprehensive pastoral letter about nuclear war prepared by the Catholic Bishops of the United States (National Conference of Catholic Bishops 1983) did not assert that there was only one legitimate option but recognized that the inherent complexity of nuclear weaponry required paying attention to various streams of Catholic social thought. Even at that, the pastoral letter did not command assent to specific recommendations but invited Catholics to ponder Church teachings as they considered questions of war and peace.

Third, to restate a claim made earlier, many policy options are treated as alternate means toward a just end; the religious believer may approach these through a complex moral calculus rather than as a zero-sum game. For example, the "seamless garment of human life" teaching developed by the late Cardinal Joseph Bernardin presented a complex calculus to devout Catholics across a wide range of issues where human life, life chances, dignity, and development were at stake, rather than the single issue of abortion. In a subsequent pastoral letter on economic matters, *And Justice for All*, the bishops acknowledged that reliance on vigorous markets may be a more effective strategy than redistributive taxation for alleviating human need.

Fourth, Americans have grown accustomed to "a wall of separation between church and state" that may be breached if common sense suggests that religious values are consensual and appropriate for the solution of a social problem. For years, ready-made religious organizations have used public funds in nonproselytizing ways to address human need. Long before the development of Charitable Choice and the White House Office of Faith-Based Initiatives, organizations such as Catholic Relief Services, Catholic Charities, Lutheran World Relief, and other denominationally based organizations were major players in providing both domestic and international social services, funded partially by tax dollars, and these did not seem to undermine the neutrality of the state (Wineburg 2000).

Finally, Martin Marty (1976) has characterized Americans as more a nation of *behavers* than *believers*. By this he means that faith commitments are firm but less important than affiliation and practice. We wear our religion on our sleeves, but as Tocqueville argued, its primary purpose is to show that we are moral and trustworthy people. Dwight Eisenhower embodied that spirit when he observed in 1954 that American democracy required "a deeply felt religious faith—and I don't care what it is" (Henry 1981). This is hardly the stuff of sectarianism. Crusades quickly spend themselves of zeal and are followed by normality and pragmatic ways to order our community life.

These observations about social mechanisms help to explain why religion, an incredibly powerful force in American life, has nonetheless seldom provoked fundamental challenges to the democratic order. Mark Lilla (2007) reminds us that the coincidence of strong religious values with a stable polity is possible in the United States only because of the "great separation" that confines religiously inspired political debate to specific matters of policy rather than to the legitimacy of a political system based on human reason rather than biblically revealed truths. This reinforces what Nancy Rosenblum (chapter 12, this volume) describes as the tendency of religious politics in the United States to remain well within the parameters of constitutional democracy, eschewing demands "for guaranteed political representation and quotas . . . or for differential private laws of marriage and divorce based on sacred law interpreted and enforced by religious authorities."

Although it has the potential to undermine democratic values and demean the tenor of public life, we do not think that religion invariably has such consequences. Indeed, religion can perform as a helpful component of policy deliberations that injects higher goals and transcendent values into what might otherwise be a strictly utilitarian process. That was the common ground we find in the correspondence between strict Puritan John Adams and rational deist Thomas Jefferson (Cousins 1958). That is also the reason social historian Alexis de Tocqueville felt the American form of democracy had a greater future than the French form.

Conclusion

Every contributor to this volume acknowledges that religious issues have joined the contemporary American political agenda. In this chapter, we have argued that such issues can most profitably be approached through a cultural theory of politics that puts political processes at the center of attention. The prominence of religious factors is in no small measure created by ambitious elites who perceive political gain from highlighting and mobilizing cultural tensions that include (but are not limited to) a religious dimension. They do so by politicizing cultural tensions through the manipulation of powerful symbols that accentuate the emotions and stimulate an Us-versus-Them perspective.

Although the roots of debilitating religious cleavages may be present in the populace, they may not surface unless cultivated by ambitious politicians with the help of the press who frames the story. When the scurrilous literature that claimed Senator Barack Obama was really a Muslim circulated during the Democratic primaries, Senator Hillary Clinton repudiated it. When Senator John McCain was introduced by a Southern Ohio talk-show host who again and again made reference to Barack *Hussein* Obama, McCain angrily denounced him. But when selected clips of sermons by Obama's United Church of Christ pastor, Jeremiah Wright, appeared continuously on the Internet, Senator Obama felt compelled to deliver a major address on race, religion, and politics. Obama discussed deep constitutional values, the American credo, the history of race relations in the United States, and the prophetic role of African-American churches. He repudiated the offensive anti-American comments of his pastor, but he would not totally disown a man of God who had brought him deeper into the Christian faith, performed his marriage, and baptized his daughters. The chattering class immediately pronounced that the denunciation had not gone far enough, keeping the story alive for weeks. Senator Clinton allowed that she would have withdrawn from the church. Senator McCain renewed his faith in America, overlooking the fact that a televangelist whose support he had solicited (Jerry Falwell) had also cursed the United States following 9-11. Clearly the fear of the presumed religious Other resonates with a sector of the voting public sufficiently to be nudged along by political opponents. And an interesting footnote is found in Obama's eventual disowning of Wright when it was clear that his former pastor kept the controversy blazing so that he could sell his forthcoming book.

As we noted at the outset, the same processes characterized the period leading to the civil war that wracked Bosnia from 1992 to 1995. By contrast with the real war in the Balkans, talk of "culture war" in the American context may seem ridiculously overblown. Nonetheless, the mechanism that stirred conflict in Bosnia bears a close resemblance to the dynamic of cultural conflict that we have observed in the United States. Unlike the "primordialist" school that regards the Bosnian civil war as the inevitable consequence of deeply felt group animosities that have festered for centuries, social constructionists emphasize instead the key role played by entrepreneurs who perceived ethnoreligious tension as a path to power in a democratizing society. In fanning the flames, they made deadly use of various symbols deeply tied to religious history and group identity.

The case of Bosnia is a sobering reminder that religious enthusiasm in politics may all too easily spill over into real war if a society lacks the mechanisms to constrain and contain such tensions. As we argue, there are encouraging signs that the United States possesses a variety of qualities that will prevent religiously inspired cultural differences from destroying the political system. As in other divided societies, the attitudes that characterize political elites and the incentives and structure of political opportunity may work to soften the level of political polarization. Religion can supply both the seeds of violent political conflict and the resources for reconciliation (Little 2007).

What is the future of cultural politics in the United States? Although it is hazardous to forecast the political future, we think it likely that this style of campaigning will persist as long as it is judged likely to pay dividends to ambitious political elites. That is, we anticipate no diminution in the *frequency* of culturally based campaign appeals but do expect them to vary in *effectiveness* from one campaign to the next.

The 2008 presidential election reminds us once again that cultural appeals do not invariably trump a campaign strategy based on valence issues. In 1992, the principal aim of Democratic campaign managers was to avoid fighting the election on cultural grounds by positioning candidate Bill Clinton squarely in the mainstream and thus shifting the debate to Republican responsibility for the slumping economy. Senator Obama's general election campaign in 2008 seems to have been cut from the same cloth. In a televised ad run extensively in both key battleground states and some targeted Republican-leaning states shortly after he clinched the nomination, Obama evoked his "heartland" heritage, love of country, deep religious faith, respect for family, and other core values of the

American creed (Finnegan 2008). Although the ad no doubt had multiple goals, one aspect was certainly an attempt to "immunize" him from Republican attacks on those grounds so he could instead render the election a referendum on Republican management of the economy and foreign policy, issues likely to cut in his favor in November. Similarly, to blunt or forestall arguments that he was hostile to gun rights, a factor that had seriously damaged the last two Democratic presidential nominees in key states, Senator Obama applauded the Supreme Court's discovery of an individual's right to gun ownership while he emphasized the need for communities to protect their children against gun violence.

With its "Summer of Love" commercial released in July shortly after the Obama ads began running, the GOP deployed campaign appeals that recycled prominent cultural themes from past elections. This ad drew a striking contrast between displays of hedonism, self-indulgence, and drug use among disaffected youth in the summer of 1967 and, half a world away, Senator McCain's demonstrated love of country and loyalty to comrades in the face of torture and barbarity during his captivity in North Vietnam. Although Senator Obama was a small child at the time, political operatives dug through his biography, preparing to highlight his admissions of youthful drug use, lax school attendance, and other flaws to associate the Democratic nominee with the counterculture and unfavorable images of African-Americans from the 1960s (Edsall 2008). The goal of these efforts was to reinforce doubts about Senator Obama's fitness for the presidency among white working-class Democrats, the same constituency that has frequently deserted Democratic presidential candidates over their departure from valued cultural norms. Although these kinds of appeals are not overtly religious, they draw on a traditionalist moral order with special resonance to many Protestants and Catholics. The outcome of the 2008 election told us that the cultural politics strategy did not succeed in its short-term objective. Nonetheless, we have not seen the last attempt to politicize cultural values in American public life.

Notes

1. As Sells (2003) notes, religion did determine the identity of the victims of ethnic cleansing.

2. This was captured nicely by Garrison Keillor's observation that members of the fictional Sanctified Brethren of Lake Woebegone entered each theological conflict certain that "God was standing right behind them, smiling and holding their coats."

3. To our knowledge, there was no organized effort to save Paul Hill, the defrocked minister convicted of murdering an abortion provider and his escort in Florida. Hill's death warrant was signed by an avowed pro-life Republican,

Governor Jeb Bush. Under a variety of presidents with differing views on cultural issues, the resources of the U.S. government have been deployed against the "Patriot" movement, which merged Christian fundamentalism with extreme antistate rhetoric and action.

4. If this problem is not unique to Democrats, neither do all Democrats have the problem of speaking authentically about the role of faith in their political lives. In 2005, Tim Kaine withstood virulent charges that he opposed the death penalty by explaining to voters that his opposition was formed by his religious experience:

> I wanted to explain to people how my faith and my heart for public service, formed while serving as a missionary in Central America, inspire me to seek public office. As a law student at Harvard 25 years ago, I found myself with a lot of options but little direction. I decided to take off a year and work with Catholic missionaries in Honduras. I was the principal of a small vocational school, teaching carpentry, religion, and academics to children who had no other educational options. Second only to becoming a father, that experience was the most formative of my life. It has influenced everything I have done since—from my career as a civil rights attorney to my service in local and state offices. (Kaine 2006)

This strategy succeeded, and Kaine won the Virginia governorship because, as campaign consultants put it, Kaine had the biography to back it up. That is, having referred often to these experiences over the course of his career in politics, Kaine had built up credibility that prompted voters to accept his explanation and thus neutralize the charges. For evidence of similar efforts by Democrats to deal with religious values, see Kirkpatrick (2006).

References

Aho, James A. 1991. *The Politics of Righteousness: Idaho Christian Patriotism.* Seattle: University of Washington Press.

Barone, Michael. 1990. *Our Country: The Shaping of America from Roosevelt to Reagan.* New York: Free Press.

Bates, Robert H. 1974. "Ethnic Competition and Modernization in Contemporary Africa." *Comparative Political Studies* 6:457–84.

Campbell, Angus, Phillip E. Converse, Warren E. Miller, and Donald Stokes. 1960. *The American Voter.* New York: John Wiley.

Campbell, David E., ed. 2007. *A Matter of Faith: Religion in the 2004 Presidential Election.* Washington, DC: Brookings Institution Press.

Campbell, David E., and J. Quin Monson. 2007. "The Case of Bush's Reelection: Did Gay Marriage Do It?" In *A Matter of Faith: Religion in the 2004 Presidential Election,* ed. David E. Campbell. Washington, DC: Brookings Institution Press.

Carmines, Edward G., and James A. Stimson. 1989. *Issue Evolution: Race and the Transformation of American Politics.* Princeton, NJ: Princeton University Press.

Cohen, Lenard J. 1997. "Prelates and Politicians in Bosnia: The Role of Religion in Nationalist Mobilisation." *Nationalities Papers* 25:481–99.

Conger, Kimberly H., and Bryan T. McGraw. 2008. "Religious Conservatives and the Requirements of Citizenship: Political Autonomy." *Perspectives on Politics* 6:253–66.

Cousins, Norman, comp. 1958. *In God We Trust: The Religious Beliefs and Ideas of the American Founders.* New York: Harper & Brothers.

Edsall, Thomas B. 2008 (July 8). "The Struggle to Define Barack Obama." *Huffington Post*, http://www.huffingtonpost.com/2008/07/08/the-struggle-to-define-ba_n_111334.html.

Edsall, Thomas Byrne, and Mary D. Edsall. 1992. *Chain Reaction: The Impact of Race, Rights, and Taxes on American Politics.* New York: W. W. Norton.

Finnegan, Michael. 2008. "Obama ad stresses values and patriotism." *Los Angeles Times*, June 20, available at http://www.latimes.com/news/politics/la-na-obama20-2008jun20,0,3715994.story.

Fowler, Robert Booth. 1989. *Unconventional Partners: Religion and Liberal Culture in the United States.* Grand Rapids, MI: William B. Eerdmans.

Frank, Thomas. 2004. *What's the Matter with Kansas? How Conservatives Won the Heart of America.* New York: Metropolitan Books.

Freedman, Samuel G. 1996. *The Inheritance: How Three Families and America Moved from Roosevelt to Reagan.* New York: Simon & Schuster.

Gagnon, Vernon P. Jr. 1994. "Ethnic Nationalism and International Conflict: The Case of Serbia." *International Security* 19:130–66.

Hart, Stephen. 2001. *Cultural Dilemmas of Progressive Politics.* Chicago: University of Chicago Press.

Hillygus, D. Sunshine, and Todd G. Shields. 2008. *The Persuadable Voter: Wedge Issues in Presidential Campaigns.* Princeton, NJ: Princeton University Press.

Hunter, James Davison. 1991. *Culture Wars: The Struggle to Define America.* New York: Basic Books.

Isaacs, Harold. 1989. *Idols of the Tribe.* Cambridge, MA: Harvard University Press.

Iveković, I. 2002. "Nationalism and the Political Use and Abuse of Religion: The Politicization of Orthodoxy, Catholicism and Islam in Yugoslav Successor States." *Social Compass* 49:523–36.

Kaine, Tim. 2006 (February 9). "How I Won," *Blueprint*, available at: http://www.dlc.org/ndol_ci.cfm?kaid=132&subid=193&contentid=253714.

Katznelson, Ira, and Helen Milner. 2002. "American Political Science: The Discipline's State and the State of the Discipline." In *Political Science: The State of the Discipline,* eds. Ira Katznelson and Helen Milner, 1–32. New York: W. W. Norton.

Kennedy, Sheila Suess, and Wolfgang Bielefeld. 2006. *Charitable Choice at Work: Evaluating Faith-Based Job Programs in the States.* Washington, DC: Georgetown University Press.

Kirkpatrick, David D. 2004. "Republicans Admit Mailing Campaign Literature Saying Liberals Will Ban the Bible." *New York Times,* September 24, 22A.

———. 2006. "Consultants Help Democrats Embrace Faith, and Some in Party Are Not Pleased." *New York Times,* December 26.

Ladd, Everett Carll Jr. 1976. "Liberalism Upside Down: The Inversion of the New Deal Order." *Political Science Quarterly* 91:577–600.

Layman, Geoffrey. 2001. *The Great Divide: Religious and Cultural Conflict in American Party Politics.* New York: Columbia University Press.

Leege, David C. 2007. "From Event to Theory: A Summary Analysis." In *A Matter of Faith: Religion in the 2004 Presidential Election,* ed. David E. Campbell. Washington, DC: Brookings Institution Press.

Leege, David C., and Kenneth D. Wald. 2007. "Meaning, Cultural Symbols, and Campaign Strategies." In *The Affect Effect: Dynamics of Emotion in Political Thinking and Behavior,* eds. George E. Marcus, W. Russell Neuman, Michael MacKuen, and Ann M. Crigler. Chicago: University of Chicago Press.

Leege, David C., Kenneth D. Wald, Brian S. Krueger, and Paul D. Mueller. 2002. *Politics of Cultural Differences: Social Change and Voter Mobilization Strategies in the Post–New Deal Period.* Princeton, NJ: Princeton University Press.

Lijphart, Arend. 1977. *Democracy in Plural Societies: A Comparative Exploration.* New Haven, CT: Yale University Press.

Lilla, Mark. 2007. *The Stillborn God: Religion, Politics and the Modern West.* New York: Knopf.

Littlewood, Roland and Maurice Lipsedge. 1997. *Aliens and Alienists: Ethnic Minorities and Psychiatry.* Third edition. London: Routledge.

Lipset, Seymour Martin. 1959. *Political Man.* Garden City, NY: Doubleday-Anchor.

Little, David, ed. 2007. *Peacemakers in Action: Profiles of Religion in Conflict Resolution.* New York: Cambridge University Press.

Marty, Martin. 1976. *A Nation of Behavers.* Chicago: University of Chicago Press.

McGraw, Barbara A. 2003. *Rediscovering America's Sacred Ground: Public Religion and Pursuit of the Good in a Pluralistic America.* Albany, NY: SUNY Press.

McGraw, Barbara, and Jo Renee Formicola, eds. 2005. *Taking Religious Pluralism Seriously: Spiritual Politics on America's Sacred Ground.* Waco, TX: Baylor University Press.

Meier, Kenneth J. 1994. *The Politics of Sin: Drugs, Alcohol, and Public Policy.* Armonk, NY: M. E. Sharpe.

Mendelberg, Tali. 1997. "Executing Hortons: Racial Crime in the 1988 Presidential Campaign." *Public Opinion Quarterly* 61:134–57.

Miller, Randall M., Harry S. Stout, and Charles Reagan Wilson, eds. 1998. *Religion and the American Civil War.* New York: Oxford University Press.

Monson, J. Quin, and J. Baxter Oliphant. 2007. "Microtargeting and the Instrumental Mobilization of Religious Conservatives." In *A Matter of Faith: Religion in the 2004 Presidential Election,* ed. David E. Campbell. Washington, DC: Brookings Institution Press.

Morone, James A. 2003. *Hellfire Nation: The Politics of Sin in American History.* New Haven, CT: Yale University Press.

Mosk, Matthew. 2008. "An Attack That Came out of the Ether." *Washington Post,* June 8, available at http://www.washingtonpost.com/wp-dyn/content/article/2008/06/27/AR2008062703781_pf.html.

National Conference of Catholic Bishops. 1983. *The Challenge of Peace: God's Promise and Our Response.* Washington, DC: United States Catholic Conference.

Oestreicher, Richard. 1988. "Urban Working-Class Political Behavior and Theories of American Electoral Politics, 1870–1940." *Journal of American History* 74:1257–86.

Oldmixon, Elizabeth. 2005. *Uncompromising Positions: God, Sex and the U.S. House of Representatives.* Washington, DC: Georgetown University Press.

Pickett, Brent L. 2006. "Multiculturalism, Liberalism, and Philosophy." *Polity* 38:134–50.

Powers, Gerald F. 1996. "Religion, Conflict and Prospects for Reconciliation in Bosnia, Croatia and Yugoslavia." *Journal of International Affairs* 50:221–52.

Rieder, Jonathan. 1985. *Canarsie: The Jews and Italians of Brooklyn against Liberalism.* Cambridge, MA: Harvard University Press.

Rose, Richard, and Derek Urwin. 1969. "Social Cohesion, Political Parties, and Strains in Regimes." *Comparative Political Studies* 2:7–67.

Rovner, Julie. 2006. "'Partial-Birth Abortion:' Separating Fact from Spin." Available at http://www.npr.org/templates/story/story.php?storyId=5168163.

Rozell, Mark J., and Clyde Wilcox. 1996. "Second Coming: The Strategies of the New Christian Right." *Political Science Quarterly* 111:271–94.

Schnur, Dan. 2007. "The Affect Effect in the Very Real World of Political Campaigns." In *The Affect Effect: Dynamics of Emotion in Political Thinking and Behavior,* eds. George E. Marcus, W. Russell Neuman, Michael B. MacKuen, and Ann Crigler. Chicago: University of Chicago Press.

Sears, David O., and Jack Citrin. 1982. *Something for Nothing: Tax Revolt in California.* Berkeley: University of California Press.

Sells, Michael A. 2003. "Crosses of Blood: Sacred Space, Religion, and Violence in Bosnia-Hercegovina." *Sociology of Religion* 64:309–31.

Siddur Sim Shalom. 1985. New York: Rabbinical Assembly, United Synagogue of America.

Steiner, Gilbert Y., ed. 1983. *The Abortion Dispute and the American System.* Washington, DC: Brookings Institution Press.

Swaine, Lucas A. 2001. "How Ought Liberal Democracies to Treat Theocratic Communities?" *Ethics* 111:302–43.

Tesh, Sylvia. 1984. "In Support of 'Single-Issue' Politics." *Political Science Quarterly* 99:27–44.

Valentino, Nicholas, and David Sears. 2003. "Cracking the White 'Solid South' with the Nexus of Race and Religion: The 1960s as Transition?" Paper presented to the annual meeting of the American Political Science Association, Philadelphia, PA.

Varshney, Ashutosh. 2003. "Nationalism, Ethnic Conflict, and Rationality." *Perspectives on Politics* 1:85–99.

Vrcan, Srdjan. 1994. "The War in Ex-Yugoslavia and Religion." *Social Compass* 41:413–22.

Wald, Kenneth D., James W. Button, and Barbara A. Rienzo. 2001. "Morality Politics vs. Political Economy: The Case of School-Based Health Centers." *Social Science Quarterly* 82:221–34.

Wald, Kenneth D., and Allison Calhoun-Brown. 2006. *Religion and Politics in the United States,* 5th ed. Lanham, MD: Rowman & Littlefield.

Wald, Kenneth D., and Jeffrey C. Corey. 2002. "The Christian Right and Public Policy: Social Movement Elites as Institutional Activists." *State Politics and Policy Quarterly* 2:99–125.

Wald, Kenneth D., Dennis E. Owen, and Samuel S. Hill Jr. 1989. "Habits of the Mind? The Problem of Authority in the New Christian Right." In *Religion and Political Behavior in the United States,* ed. Ted G. Jelen, 93–108. New York: Greenwood Press.

Wald, Kenneth D., Richard K. Scher, Matthew DeSantis, and Susan Orr. 2006. "So Close and Yet So Far: The Christian Right in Florida Politics." In *The Values Campaign: The Christian Right in the 2004 Elections,* eds. John C. Green, Mark J. Rozell, and Clyde Wilcox, 158–78. Washington, DC: Georgetown University Press.

Wald, Kenneth D., and Clyde Wilcox. 2006. "Getting Religion: Has Political Science Rediscovered the Faith Factor?" *American Political Science Review* 100:523–29.

Wenz, Peter. 1992. *Abortion Rights as Religious Freedom.* Philadelphia: Temple University Press.

Wildavsky, Aaron. 1987. "Choosing Preferences by Constructing Institutions: A Cultural Theory of Preference Formation." *American Political Science Review* 81:3–21.

Wilson, J. Matthew, ed. 2007. *From Pews to Polling Places: Faith and Politics in the American Religious Mosaic.* Washington, DC: Georgetown University Press.

Wineburg, Bob. 2000. *A Limited Partnership: The Politics of Religion, Welfare, and Social Service.* New York: Columbia University Press.

Woodworth, Steven E. 2001. *While God Is Marching On: The Religious World of Civil War Soldiers.* Lawrence, KS: University Press of Kansas.

Wuthnow, Robert. 1987. *Meaning and Moral Order: Explorations in Cultural Analysis.* Berkeley: University of California Press.

Chapter 12

FAITH IN AMERICA

Political Theory's Logic of Autonomy and Logic of Congruence

NANCY L. ROSENBLUM

POLITICAL THEORY STARTLED INTO THOUGHT

American institutions and political thought reflect the historically momentous separation of government from theology and divine revelation. We have imperfect separation of church and state. But we do not have anything like separation of religion and politics. Americans' religiosity is measurable and intense,[1] and so are the political participation of citizens qua believers, advocacy by religious groups, and constitutional litigation on behalf of religious claims. The past several decades of religious politics in the United States and abroad have startled political theorists into thought,[2] jogging us to contemplate the significance of politically active religion for democracy. In this chapter, I take a step back from the immediate questions asked by political scientists: whether and how religion fuels the current partisan divide, for example. Instead, I focus on the foundational questions political theorists pose. I speak of "questions" in the plural because political theorists have arrived at divergent judgments of the urgent question before us. Is it whether democracy in America is hospitable to flourishing religious pluralism? Or is it whether religion is compatible with robust democracy here? Political theorists are divided about what should be our orientation and guiding concern—making democracy safe for religion or making religion safe for democracy?

Those who think that the challenge is American democracy's will to ensure a generous, supportive environment for religion begin with the idea of autonomous religious communities and assign religious membership equal standing if not priority over citizenship. This parity is captured in the thought that Americans are "dual citizens." On these grounds, theorists justify religious exemptions from general laws and accommodation of religious activities, public funding of religious schools and programs, and full-voiced political engagement by religious activists on behalf of their causes. I call this position "the logic of autonomy." In contrast, self-described "muscular" democratic theorists rank the obligations of citizenship over the demands of faith. They resist compromising democratic norms of fairness and equality, and they would enforce these principles and practices in every sphere and "all the way down," regulating the internal lives of religious associations, prohibiting religious exemption from general laws, restricting government funding and support, and constraining the manner in which religious activists participate in politics. I call this the "logic of congruence." The logic of autonomy and the comprehensive logic of congruence mark the poles of contemporary American thought on the subject. Readers will recognize the outlines of these two orientations in everyday political debates about the style, scope, and political influence of religious activists advancing their claims.

In the first half of this chapter I set out the background conditions that give rise to contemporary political theorists' interest in religion and democracy and to their divergent judgments about whether the priority concern is insuring flourishing religious pluralism or robust democracy.[3] I go on in broad brush strokes to set out the logic of autonomy and the logic of congruence, their assumptions and prescriptions. I argue that both "logics" suffer from stringency and excess. Solicitude for the ambiguity of citizenship experienced by believers as "dual citizens" concedes too much to religion, and solicitude for citizenship as an undiluted political identity concedes too little.

This chapter's second half proposes a more modest *political congruence* as an addition to political theory's repertoire.[4] Political congruence means following the institutional "rules of the game," of course. But as important as political behavior is, political congruence is a moral register. I identify two core elements of political congruence: a tempered version of the philosophic notion of "public reason" and democratic identity as a political majority or minority. When it comes to religion and democracy in America, I argue, political congruence suffices. It provides a justifiable regulative ideal, and empirical political science (including task force essays in this volume) shows that it is adhered to by religious actors in practice.

Where We Are Today: Comparative Political Moderation

It is important to observe at the outset that in comparative terms religious politics in the United States today is moderate[5] and that political theorists startled into thought are not compelled to focus anxiously on securing political peace and stability. Against the background of comparative moderation, we see that both the logic of autonomy and the logic of congruence are extravagant responses to religious politics in America; they conjure threats and magnify what is necessary to defend against them. At the same time, moderation is almost certainly a condition for the political congruence I recommend. For my purposes, then, a brief overview of comparative moderation is helpful.

When Maurice Duverger warned that political partisanship can take on a "truly religious form" and that "the term party includes veritable churches with their clergy, their faithful, their belief, their orthodoxy, their intolerance," he was referring to "political religions"—to Jacobinism and Bolshevism.[6] In parts of the world, the force of the analogy has been reversed, and Islam is called "the new Marxism."[7] Today, "political religion" refers not to secular ideology infused with religious fervor but to the force of religious belief and authority in politics. It is marked by extremism, religious mobilization, and sometimes by violent conflict. America has been spared both full-blown Marxism and fundamentalist Islam. More generally, neither comprehensive political ideologies nor affirmations of religious integralism—the conviction that divine revelation and religious authority should guide every aspect of social and political life for the nation as a whole—define the political landscape here. In the United States, agitation by religious groups for autonomy does not amount to wholesale challenges to the obligations imposed by democracy, and it is not a prelude to claims that a particular doctrine or clerical authority should rule. Religious groups in the United States are nonviolent and unarmed. Public policy is not driven by the need to negotiate a working relationship between government and religions hostile to the basic arrangements of church and state. Indeed, no politically active religious group rejects constitutional democracy.[8]

Within the parameters of constitutional democracy, too, religious politics is comparatively moderate. The United States does not suffer the strains experienced by other democracies, in large part because religious pluralism here is not state sponsored. European mergers of church and welfare state provoke religious groups (notably Muslims and other non-Christian immigrant groups) to struggle to be included on the list of officially recognized national religions, which affords an array of state-sponsored benefits often including direct public funding of religious schools and salaries for clergy. We are spared having to confront the contentious question of whether to extend legal parity and state support to every faith. Religious groups in the United States do not agitate for guaranteed political representation and quotas either, or for differential private laws of marriage and divorce based on sacred law interpreted and enforced by religious authorities.

Last, religious politics today is moderate in comparison to other moments in American history. Religious hatred has sometimes been a driving force in U.S. political life, but at present we are spared the challenge of maintaining workable relations among groups.[9] Religious pluralism is viewed in approving terms overwhelmingly in surveys, and Americans' religiously diverse social networks reflect that.[10] Some Americans may rue that fellow citizens of other faiths or nonbelievers are not saved, but they typically allow that they are moral, and good citizens. The crusade against a woman's right to abortion is intense and divisive, but less so than past mobilization over slavery, war, drinking, prostitution, and education.[11] Religion has been at the heart of political crises and movements for radical change in the United States, pressing for civil rights on one hand and resisting civil and social equality on the other,[12] a reminder that religious political goals today may be contested but that with few exceptions they are comparatively conventional and benign.

If we take our cues from contemporary theology rather than from actual politics, religion does appear in a guise that is more challenging to democracy, sometimes verging on hostile alienation. Some American theologians aggressively assert the absolute priority of faith and insist that religious citizens must be able to answer Jeffrey Stout's question in the affirmative: "is it not possible to see . . . some reflection of God's redemptive activity in modern democratic aspirations?"[13] For theologians like Stanley Hauerwas the concern is precisely that too often the facile answer is "yes." He opposes the thought that there is a comfortable fit between religion and democracy in America. His charge to Christians is to refuse to "domesticate the Gospel" in order to make it credible to its cultural detractors; to stop trying to "fit American values into a loosely Christian frame"; to cease policing their convictions for their compatibility with social order; to reject the common view that the church's task is "running errands" for democracy and offering up faith as a "helpful if complaining prop for the state."[14] For Hauerwas, the [Christian] church is "an alternative polis," and believers should accept that they live in the world as "resident aliens." That said, American theologians who question the compatibility between religion and democracy are themselves comparatively moderate. They are not radical rejectionists or quietists; the church is unalterably of and in the world, a participant in public life. And nothing in "resident alien" mandates political extremism.

I hold by moderate as a fair description of religious politics here. I mean that the basic framework of constitutional democracy is accepted as a stable commitment not just a modus vivendi. I mean religions' self-description, certainly the political face of religious organizations, is typically populist rather than sternly authoritarian or hierarchical. I mean that religious groups claim that their politics redounds to the benefit of nonbelievers as well as believers and cast their values and programs as the property of the nation rather than of a particular church.

In comparative historical terms, the response of contemporary democratic theorists to these moderate expressions of religion in politics is tempered too. This deserves mention because historically political theory has often been virulent on the subject. Enlightenment thinkers promoted religious toleration, but at the same time many cast faith as inimical to reason and progressive thought and represented religious institutions and authorities as enemies of liberalism and later of democracy. Today, we rarely hear religion characterized as the opiate of the people, a product of fear or ignorance, or a device for appeasing common pain and misery. Political theorists do not represent religion as a futile, infantile, or unphilosophical quest for meaning by those who cannot endure uncertainty or the truth of meaninglessness.[15] Atheism is no more avowed or applauded in democratic theory than in electoral politics.[16] Noticeably absent, too, are hostile anticlericalism and the charge that a church's ability to control voters ("to arrange their obedience") is based on punitive authority.[17]

If religious politics is comparatively moderate and political theorists are not strident antagonists of religion as the enemy of enlightened citizens and governments, what fuels the contesting views that American democracy is insufficiently hospitable to religion and that religion is a serious challenge to democracy? What drives defenders of democracy to advocate a severe, comprehensive logic of congruence and defenders of religion to propose a logic of autonomy?

Over the course of the last several decades, demands by religious activists for greater political sustenance, both symbolic and substantive, are the background for the emergence of theorists' divergent responses. These changes in religious politics, quite apart from specific controversial crusades such as opposition to women's right to obtain an abortion or teaching creationism in public schools, are the context for the wave of political theory on the subject.

First, classic appeals by marginal groups for protection for their religious liberty and relief from the "strain of commitment" democracy imposes on believers (the Jehovah's Witnesses on symbolic issues such as the flag salute or Quaker conscientious objection) have been eclipsed by demands from powerful, mainstream religious groups for exemption from a virtually unlimited array of laws and regulations. These include, for example, civil rights laws in the area of employment, as when a religious school maintains its right to fire a pregnant teacher because she violates their belief that mothers of young children should not work outside the home, or a church asserts its right to fire a janitor working in a gym open to the public because he has lapsed from certain articles of faith. The Religious Freedom Restoration Act was Congress's attempt to address these widespread and wide-ranging demands for accommodation wholesale.

Escalation of claims for accommodation and exemption from state interference is compounded by a second change, as religious groups activate to win positive government recognition and material support. They want to be full beneficiaries of the ever-increasing scale and scope of assistance doled out at the discretion of local, state, and national governments acting not just as sovereign but as patron. Activists on behalf of religion agitate for funding for schools and programs, for grants and loans, and for beneficial tax status. They advocate for church-state partnerships, what John DiIulio calls "government-by-proxy,"[18] which requires both a tax structure designed to encourage private donations to religious associations and direct public funding. Religious groups reinforce their claims by arguing that their programs are uniquely successful because of their virtuous grounding in faith.

In all this, religious activists' overarching aim goes beyond securing a particular item of funding or latitude for religious expression. The goal is to retrieve for religion what has been lost when prayer was eliminated from public schools and challenges to the public display of religious symbols were successful. Restoration of crèches or crosses or prayer may be impossible, but religious groups still agitate to recover the status that comes with official recognition for the unique value of religion. Their goal is to secure the generous, hospitable environment religion *is owed* in appreciation not for its "truth" (pluralism does not permit that claim) but for its contributions to the virtue and public life of the nation.

Religious activists resisting settled expectations of privatization, organizing to set political agendas, agitating for influence, and pressing new symbolic and substantive demands startled political theorists into thought. These political developments, as much as partisan politics or particular divisive issues such as abortion, provoked theorists to identify and justify what they take to be the right relation between religion and democracy in America. They have marked out divergent paths—the logic of autonomy and the logic of congruence.

The Logic of Autonomy: Believers as Dual Citizens

Strong defenders of religious autonomy justify "liberty-enhancing governmental accommodation," a "unified, across-the-board deferential approach in church-state matters," and a rejection of key elements of separation.[19] They urge expanded religious accommodation for mainstream as well as minority faiths and argue for an end to Establishment Clause inhibitions on public aid. These arguments are made on behalf of religions generally, with assurance that exemption and funding should be nonsectarian, should not amount to a de facto national establishment, and should not lead to religious uniformity. The aim is government support for flourishing religious pluralism.

Defenders of religious autonomy are pluralists, then, but this position should not be confused with political science's interest group pluralism.

In interest group theory, religious associations are one advocacy group among others. Religious groups *do* operate as ordinary interest groups in practice, of course. They organize and advocate, acquire "access" to legislators, write bills, and obtain favorable treatment. Interest group politics is not the correct framework, however, when the goal is winning public recognition and support for religion as a unique and incommensurable "interest" with special status, as the logic of religious autonomy assumes.

Often enough the case for exemption, accommodation, and funding is made in the conservative terms I described: restoring religious liberty from what is seen as unjustifiable infringements and correcting religion's diminished public standing. But the theoretical justification is positive and assertive not defensive, and it amounts to an innovation in American political thought. I call it the logic of autonomy because it claims for religion a sort of semisovereignty. Defenders of religion's special status characterize the United States as a community of communities, a nation comprising autonomous communities of faith. Religious communities are *constitutive* of political order in this view, and citizens are properly seen as "dual citizens" with obligations imposed by both spheres. Without accommodation and support "dual citizens" burdened by both the obligations of citizenship and demands of faith are unequal citizens. (Note that "dual citizenship" challenges both the idea of a unitary citizen identity and a more variegated notion of individuals' identities and obligations.) From this standpoint it is wrong to see religion as just one beneficiary of discretionary government support; public recognition and accommodation of religion are not just permissible but required.

It is not hard to see what is radical in the logic of autonomy. The intrinsic importance of religious community represents a challenge to the supremacy of the state. The position is reminiscent of another tradition of pluralism, the British idealist tradition of Maitland, Figgis, and Laski, who opposed Leviathan and defined sovereignty as shared among the self-governing sources of law. This theoretical affinity is important because it shows that the logic of autonomy does not rest on a particular theology of Catholic subsidiarity or Calvinist supremacy of church over state. Instead, it is grounded in a political account of the status of religion and on a particular interpretation of American constitutionalism. From this standpoint: "The concern of the Religion clauses is with the preservation of the autonomy of religious life," and "The First Amendment . . . undermines any claim by the state to ultimate normative authority."[20]

The provocation of the logic of autonomy becomes clear if we take a concrete case—government funding of religious education—and contrast the justification offered by theorists of autonomy with other reasons for urging public support for sectarian schools. Liberal egalitarians sometimes justify state aid to religious schools in order to equalize educational opportunities for students condemned to failing public schools. In contrast, advocates of support for religious pluralism do not argue for funding for parochial schooling in terms of fair choice or as compensation for background inequalities; their standpoint is the public obligation to maintain flourishing religious communities for "dual citizens." For their part, multiculturalists concerned to empower minority cultural groups relegated to the margins sometimes advocate public funding, arguing that groups suffering exclusion and discrimination cannot sustain themselves unless they are able to provide their members with the full range of "extensive life-cycle services." In this view, public support for the "meat and potatoes" of welfare, security, and education is warranted.[21] Again in contrast, advocates of the logic of autonomy are not particularly concerned with the viability of fragile groups suffering prejudice and poverty; they urge public aid to powerful religious communities as well as weak ones. The point is not survival but, to repeat, a public commitment to religious flourishing.

Theorists of religious autonomy inch in the direction of European models of state-sponsored religious corporatism, with its public agreements that government will support officially recognized churches. The difference is that American advocates of religious autonomy do not have history on their side. In Europe, government support for religion preserves a historic formula that brought public order. In addition, the European welfare state is built on mergers between church and state, and public funding is a foundation for the provision of social services. Neither condition holds for the United States, and the argument for support for religious groups is based not on institutional reasons to award material benefits but on the desire for official public acknowledgment of religion's unique status and contributions to public life.[22]

Theorists of religious autonomy are single-mindedly preoccupied with one-way protection for faith and not with the reciprocal concern whether religion is safe for democracy. Indeed, the formulation "making democracy safe for religion" is too weak to capture this position, for once again the problem is establishing what theorists see as the public obligation to secure religious autonomy and flourishing. Theorists of religious autonomy are impatient with political wariness about exemption and funding; they vigorously deny that accommodation will produce political competition among faiths for government support or conflict with opponents (including some religious opponents) of official public solicitude for religion. They do not allow that enhancing public recognition and support for faith is likely to excite hostility or unravel the "community of communities." But if necessary, theorists of religious autonomy are willing to recommend structural changes to American democracy: alterations in the terms of federalism or devolution of programs to semiautonomous communities. To illustrate: although the U.S. Supreme Court has opened the way for school voucher programs, many state constitutions explicitly prohibit government funding for religious schools, and in cases like these, theorists would mandate federal supremacy.

Above all, the logic of autonomy is radical in its insistence on the parity between obligations of citizenship and demands of faith and on the essential ambiguity of citizenship. "Dual citizens" are not like hyphenated Americans, with ethnicity to the left of the hyphen and civic identity to the right.[23] Rather, both religious identity and citizenship dictate political rights and obligations. That explains why theorists are at home with the thought that "dual citizenship" "dilutes the concept of citizen."[24] And dilution is precisely what the logic of congruence guards against.

The Logic of Congruence: Fairness and Democratic Reproduction

With its prescriptions for exemption, accommodation, and public support for religious pluralism, the logic of autonomy stands in opposition to the dominant orientation in democratic theory today: the logic of congruence, with its single-minded concern to ensure that religion is safe for democracy. Congruence theorists do not espouse the more aggressive view that American democracy must be made safe *from* religion, but they do see demands by religious activists as potentially subversive of democratic principles and robust citizenship. The bedrock of this standpoint is captured in the assertion that religious groups must "endorse a constitutional regime even when their comprehensive doctrines may not prosper under it, and indeed may decline," even if laws undermine the group's "fundamental interest in maintaining a certain degree of success and of influence for its own view."[25]

Solicitous of strong democracy, the logic of congruence calls for the enforcement of democratic principles of fairness, due process, nondiscrimination, and democratic organization "all the way down" and in every area of the life of religious associations. Case by case, the logic of congruence rebuts arguments for religious exemption and accommodation. Religious groups should not be exempted from educational requirements, and theorists disapprove of the Supreme Court's ruling in favor of the Amish in *Yoder*. They disapprove of exemption from everything from antidiscrimination law to municipal zoning rules. Justice Scalia ruled in the 1990 Supreme Court case *Employment Division v. Smith* that accommodation of religion is not constitutionally required, and advocates of comprehensive congruence agree. But they dissent from the Court's further ruling that discretionary accommodation by federal and state legislatures is constitutionally permissible, which invites religious groups to organize political alliances to press for concessions. The logic of congruence opposes religious exceptions to laws and regulations whether the decision is made by courts or democratic majorities.

The logic of congruence also opposes most public support for religion. For example, theorists of religious autonomy see tax exemption for religion as acknowledgment of the intrinsic value of communities of conscience. From the standpoint of theorists of congruence, in contrast, the category "nonprofit" reflects a conditional public judgment of the worthiness of the group as measured by its conformity to democratic values and its provision of public goods to the public generally. Theorists of congruence agreed with the IRS when it withheld tax exempt status for Bob Jones University because of the school's religiously based policy against interracial dating. In the same spirit, congruence dictates prohibiting or withholding public support (licenses, tax status, grants) from the activities of religious groups if they engage in religious, much less racial or gender, selectiveness in hiring; it forbids "publicly funded discrimination."[26] Rigorous advocates of comprehensive congruence challenge even the ministerial exception and would withhold tax exempt status from churches that do not admit women or gays into the ministry.[27]

The principle of fairness is one foundation for the stern, comprehensive logic of congruence, and we can appreciate the force of this reasoning. Uniform application of general laws is a bulwark against invidious partiality and discrimination, and historical experience warns that religion has been an agent of entrenched privileges and prejudicial burdens on particular faiths. The logic of congruence also rests its case on fairness when it says that religious belief, practices, and authority should not be treated with more deference than nonreligious beliefs, practices, and authority. Where advocates of religious autonomy insist that religion is special, advocates of congruence deny that there are principled grounds to distinguish religious claims from the intense preference-based desires of nonreligious groups or the demands of faith from the obligations assumed by committed members of nonreligious associations.

Why shouldn't fairness in the distribution of rights, obligations, and benefits be satisfied by accommodating both religious and nonreligious claims on the basis of "ultimate ethical commitments," say, as is the case for conscientious objection to military service?[28] Why does the logic of congruence oppose latitudinarian exemption and accommodation in acknowledgment of the strains of commitment that arise when obligations of many kinds of membership come into conflict with particular general laws? For one thing, theorists predict a slippery slope: abandoning uniformly enforced general laws would result in arbitrariness and arrant particularism. Another answer reveals more about theorists' assumptions about the significance of uniformity. Even if differential rights and responsibilities are benign rather than prejudicial, and even if they are arrived at for reasons that can be justified, uniformity has independent value. It is a tutelary force, a necessary tool of public education in fairness and equality. Congruence is imperative for cultivating democratic citizens.

Undergirding the proposition that democratic principles should apply everywhere and "all the way down," then, is the perennial concern to reproduce democratic citizens. Democracy depends on the presence of a distinct complement of dispositions and capacities, the argument goes; these are said to be cultivated in secondary associations as well as public institutions; and they must be reinforced and reiterated to have effect.[29] The logic of congruence sees every association as a potential boot camp of citizenship and every incongruent group as potentially corrosive. Put succinctly, "Modern liberal democracy needs the right sort of civic culture, and religious communities *of the right sort* are an important part of that culture." The logic of congruence affirms "the supreme political importance of constituting diversity for liberal ends."[30]

I part company with this anxious preoccupation with making religion safe for American democracy. A lot would be lost if demands for congruence were undiluted and democratic norms were strictly enforced against religious groups (and others) in every sphere. For one thing, there are fundamental liberty grounds for opposing comprehensive congruence and for leaving the internal lives of groups undisturbed: freedom of association above all. The logic of congruence is also vulnerable on its own terms because it rests on unwarranted assumptions about both the institutions required to reproduce democracy and the dynamics of character development. It relies on the proposition that religious associations whose internal lives and practices do not conform to democratic principles cultivate errant beliefs and practices that undermine democracy and, further, that individuals are of a piece—incapable of holding different values and exhibiting different conduct in different spheres. This unitary view of moral personality finds support neither in moral psychology nor in introspection and what we know about ourselves. Prized democratic dispositions do not have to be cultivated or exhibited everywhere to be practiced in political life.

Other complications undermine the comprehensive logic of congruence. Incongruent groups do often cultivate democratic dispositions indirectly and do shape members who are also good citizens. As Clyde Wilcox shows (chapter 6, this volume), presumptively incongruent groups such as those on the Christian Right affect members in unanticipated ways and may generate positive democratic traits. Geoffrey Layman (chapter 7, this volume) notes that over time participation in party politics inclines even strident, traditionalist evangelical activists to practice compromise and reciprocity—to engage in a sort of practical liberalism.

Moreover, if we think that specifically democratic virtues are not the only valuable ones, then we should recognize that incongruent religious groups often cultivate desirable noncivic norms and dispositions. They may also circumscribe vices, serving as a safety valve for irrepressible illiberal and undemocratic dispositions. In other work I have discussed the uses of pluralism and why consistency is inimical to the full range of dispositions and capacities any modern society values.[31]

The empirical and dynamic grounds for resisting the logic of congruence as moral psychology do not detract from political theorists' principled concern for fairness and nondiscrimination. But they do undercut the logic of congruence as a program of political reproduction. Again, the logic of congruence is comprehensive, and in their single-minded anxiety to make religion safe for democracy, theorists demand too much.

Political Congruence 1: Public Reason

A more modest political congruence suffices for democracy in America, I argue. I propose not only that political congruence is a sufficient regulative ideal for religion in politics but also that there is empirical evidence that these elements of political congruence are accepted practice. Political congruence entails the obvious—playing by the democratic "rules of the game"—and there are practical, institutional reasons why participation by religious activists in electoral politics, interest group politics, protest politics, and "popular constitutionalism" (organization for and against the Supreme Court's constitutional interpretation, as around *Roe*) conforms to familiar, accepted patterns, as other task force essays show. Beyond political behavior there is the deeper matter of commitment in political life to democratic ideals and taking on democratic political identity. Political congruence plays in a moral register. In this section and the next I discuss two core elements of the moral face of political congruence: "public reason" and democratic identity as a political majority or minority.

One element of political congruence concerns the language and reasons religious groups employ in their attempts to win exemption from laws and regulations, obtain public funding, or advance or oppose public policy. Political philosophers draw a bright line between politics based on appeals to particular canons of faith, clerical pronouncements, or revelation on one hand and politics based on reasons and experiences implicit in democratic political culture on the other. "Public reason" is the term they have coined to refer to the kind of argument that is legitimate in democratic deliberation. It is the name for reasons and justifications that can be understood by men and women regardless of their particular moral or religious doctrines, reasons that other citizens could reasonably accept.[32]

I place adherence to the constraints of public reason at the heart of political congruence for several reasons. For one thing, under conditions of religious pluralism, appeals to irreconcilable and mutually incomprehensible doctrines and authorities are likely to be divisive; hostilities "are bound in time to assert themselves."[33] Public reason does not eliminate intense political conflict, much less ordinary disagreement, of course, but it does increase the chances that citizens understand why they disagree. More fundamentally, public reason is "part of the idea of democracy itself."[34] When in the course of making claims, exercising influence, and coming to political decisions citizens appeal to common, mutually understandable political principles and experiences, they signal mutual respect.

Public reason is a regulative ideal, not a policy prescription, and political philosophers rarely propose gag rules or censorship. Even so, many versions of public reason are too restrictive to serve my account of political congruence. For some philosophical advocates, public reason entails stern "epistemic abstinence"; only certain kinds of reasons are legitimate, and lacking discursive and argumentative character, religious reasons in particular cannot count as rational.[35] As this suggests, public reason is vulnerable on its own moral terms. After all, reciprocity and respect for others are ordinarily demonstrated by respect "for another person in his or her particularity."[36] In the context of democracy, respect requires giving individuals and groups "effective means for bringing their views before the public," which may include communicating in religious terms and imagery rather than hewing to philosophers' bright line of separation.[37] Otherwise, public reason is like the mandatory flag salute and risks compelling professions of political faith. It fails to take the demands of multiple memberships and obligations seriously.

Stringent public reason can be loosened, as John Rawls did with his notion of "wide public reason," and this is the view of public reason I point to as an element of political congruence. Widened public reason allows that religious reasons and imagery are admissible in political forums provided religious activists at the same time or in "due course" (and in good faith) offer public reasons in support of their favored principles and policies. Indeed, the wide view acknowledges that appeal to what are seen as the sacred roots of public authority can motivate commitment to constitutional order and that public ideals may be defended more persuasively and obligations motivated more dependably on religious than civic grounds. To repeat the standard example, Martin Luther King's religious appeal on behalf of civil rights was a proxy for democratic justifications of civic equality and citizens' obligations to one another.

In making wide public reason an element of political congruence, I agree with the foundational argument that public reason exhibits respect and reciprocity. With less confidence I concede that the constraints of public reason may improve mutual understanding and perhaps political deliberation. But I do not agree that religious language and imagery, belief and authority, are justified in public arenas only "as long as such an appeal is necessary to strengthen the ideal of public reason itself."[38] I include wide public reason in my account of political congruence less out of concern to identify and police the bounds of legitimate reasons in democratic politics and still less to mandate a certain type of argument; rather, my concern is to accommodate citizens' multiple ties and obligations. My objective is to avoid where possible asking citizens to decide (and to publicly demonstrate) where their primary obligations lie. (Note that neither the logic of autonomy nor the comprehensive logic of congruence appreciates the significance for democracy of multiple memberships and obligations; the former makes allowance only for religious identity, the latter defends undiluted civic identity.) The wide public reason I commend is latitudinarian and invites styles of argument and persuasion including a strong dose of common democratic ideas and experience. This position concedes something to the demands of faith, acknowledging that the political claims advanced by religious groups may be first, best, and necessarily expressed in religious terms. It imposes a moderate democratic obligation on religious activists to self-consciously acknowledge and adhere to some constraints in advancing their claims and, when they do not, to appreciate the significance for themselves and for others of relying exclusively on their own particularist grounds.

All this is abstract, and my assertion that political congruence suffices requires more than justifying the work public reason does and defining its wide contours. The question for any regulative ideal is whether it is possible to abide by, to reasonably try to attain, even if imperfectly. Is public reason an artifact of political philosophy or a widely recognized element of political congruence in American politics? Is public reason the practice of religious activists here?

Survey research fails to yield an answer to the first question. Polls tell us that only the most unreligious tenth of the population objects to the influence of religion on American life, but that public opinion on the influence of religion in politics specifically is more wary.[39] Something like 50 percent of respondents agree that "religious people should stay out of politics," but for this response to be meaningful we need to know to whom the phrase "religious people" refers and why those polled believed they should stay away. Does the objection apply to political activity by religious authorities speaking as authorities or to religiously identified citizens broadly? Survey data do not tell us whether the imperative that "religious people should stay out of politics" amounts to a call to strip actors of their religious markers or whether avowed religious identity and invocation of faith are acceptable if accompanied "in due course" by reasons rooted in democratic principles and experience.

What we *can* say with confidence is that public reason is well understood. To take a recent example, as Democratic presidential candidate Barack Obama articulated plainly:

> Democracy demands that the religiously motivated translate their concerns into universal, rather than religion-specific values. It requires that their proposals be subject to argument, and amenable to reason. . . . In a pluralistic democracy, we have no choice. Politics depends on our ability to persuade each other of common aims based on a common reality.[40]

We can also say that public reason or its semblance is common practice on the part of religiously identified political actors. Early opposition to abortion by Catholics invoked creedal objections, but a more politically attuned opposition led by evangelical Protestants moved beyond scripture and the "sanctity of life" to the language of health and civil rights.[41] These activists put abortion on the political agenda by tying it to a general conservative program of family values and acceptable sexual roles. Similarly, Kenneth Wald (chapter 11, this volume) describes a shift on this issue and others from a style that evokes religious identity and values to a focus on the regulation of health and well-being.

What should we make of moves away from arguments from within a system of religious beliefs to arguments that are generally accessible? It seems inadequate to disparage the shift as self-serving hypocrisy or self-censorship ("a theocrat in a necktie")—as if authentic political religion must be creedal or pronouncements of clerical authority. To be sure, there are examples of the wolf in sheep's clothing, casting "intelligent design" as a nonreligious alternative to evolution, for one.[42] For the most part, however, it is rightly seen as a semblance of public reason rooted in understanding of the sorts of arguments that are politically effective under conditions of religious pluralism and secular institutions.

> Each denominational or faith tradition . . . has, *in the very process of accepting the invitation*, modified its own self-understandings and the way it presents its beliefs to its own members and to the larger community. . . . To insist that one's creedal or denominational theology . . . defines and occupies the entire content and space of the religious spirit is to pay high costs in a religiously pluralistic and democratic society.[43]

Thus, the imagery used in support of causes such as prohibition of abortion or end-of-life procedures are not the Cross or the Virgin Mary, which appeal to a particular religion's theology, but symbols that are generally morally accessible even to nonbelievers, as in the case of Terri Schiavo.[44] True, religious activists, like others, also engage in "narrow-casting"—crafting messages in creedal terms or invoking religious authorities and addressing these messages to followers and others judged responsive on a particular issue. But religious groups typically enter politics for influence, not just self-expression, a motivation that militates in favor of public reason. This applies to the selection of issues as well as to how they are framed; as Wilcox argues (chapter 6, this volume), "parties and social movement organizations choose issues based on political opportunity, not theology."

Almost certainly, the terms and arguments generally employed by religious groups are more than just a semblance of public reason. They reflect respect for other citizens and thus engage the moral basis of this element of political congruence. Where we disagree about religious tenets and interpretive authority, and about the political implications of belief, democratic participation obligates us to speak to others in terms that make disagreement comprehensible and agreement possible. Public reason is not just the way in which the claims of religious groups and invocations of religion are presented in political areas. It is also the way religious activists ordinarily present themselves.

We see this vividly in now familiar political references to "religion" in general. Nothing is more curious historically or more characteristic of religious politics in the United States today than references to "faith" rather than to one or another faith. Instead of religious pluralism producing appeals to creedal specificity, appeals are made by and on behalf of religion in general. We might criticize political theorists' diffuse references to "religion" as errant philosophical abstraction or blamable indifference toward the nature of religions and religious experiences. We might even see it as the equivalent of militant atheists' tendency to view religion as all one single thing and an apology for any of its forms as "helping to sustain the whole."[45] However, religious activists themselves commonly speak of "religion" abstracted from theology, authority, and practices. Appeals to "religion" are made by advocates of religion in politics today and are best understood as a fair reflection of the nonsectarian, nontheological self-presentation of religion in political contexts.[46] It is not the case, then, that "only social scientists believe in something called 'religion.'"[47] (In fact, as this volume shows, political scientists employ nuanced categories; see Green, chapter 2, this volume.) It may be that "no one can coherently claim that religion in general is true,"[48] but it *is* coherent to claim that religion in general can be a serviceable political category. One reason "faith" is serviceable, of course, is the fact that religious pluralism in the United States is marked by ceaseless denominational division, the astonishing proliferation of faiths, and the sheer voluntariness of individuals entering and exiting religions at will (one estimate is that 25 percent switch).[49]

My point is not that religions in the United States have become undifferentiated—that assessment is the business of theologians and sociologists. My point is that the abstract self-designation "religion" in political life exhibits political congruence. Most obviously, "religion" in general is generally understood; it is a category inclusive enough to be accessible to most citizens; it serves the purposes of public reason. (And "faith" points beyond institutional religion to individuals as believers; in this respect too, it appeals to common American experience and conforms to the demands of public reason.) Also, by invoking "religion" in political contexts, participants disclaim any suggestion that their politics is rooted exclusively in the particulars of their own theology or practice. They disavow the political significance of denominations or sects, of religious segmentation or pillars, and demonstrate their inclusive intent. For just this reason some religious leaders self-protectively avoid political arenas; they fear the presumptive godlessness of national politics less than its ecumenical spirit.[50]

Political Congruence 2: Majority and Minority Political Identity

Public reason is a standard concept in political theory, and adherence to a wide version is common practice. A second element of political congruence is less appreciated. Majority and minority are the basic units of political life in the United States, and they are basic terms in political science, but they rarely figure in contemporary democratic theory. I propose adding them to the repertoire. Their significance is not limited to the practical fact that many political institutions require numerical majorities to reach decisions. Majoritarianism, I argue, is more than a decision rule, and minority is more than a losing count. In American democracy at least, majority and minority are political identities that shape the ways in which political actors, religious actors included, see and present themselves. And they do so in a moral register. In short, when undifferentiated "religion" is broken down by religious activists for political purposes today, it is not into this or that particular religion but into the basic democratic categories majority and minority.

Before advancing my own understanding of the significance of majority/minority identity for religion in American politics, it is useful to recall its institutional side: the "rules of the game." Democratic institutions often require the construction of majorities in order to reach decisions. At certain moments "religion" is a resource for creating electoral majorities, and "issue entrepreneurs" build organizations and invent tactics for mobilizing religiously identified voters, as several task force essays discuss in detail. Of course, religious identity waxes and wanes as an important predictor of political strength; other social identities are actually more stable. Nevertheless, periodically, religious identity and the social networking of religious groups provide a resource for building political majorities. We know too that religiously identified participants in party politics are more likely than participants in single-issue groups to see themselves acting as citizens rather than as advocates for a special interest.[51] In any case, the practical requirements of majoritarianism explain at least in part why strategies of religious polarization and appeals to purists often give way over time to what is necessary to reach out for the 51 percent. As one interview reports:

> One of the things I've learned is that there's a difference in politics between temporary and permanent coalitions. And you're building majorities for specific issues at specific times. You can have temporary coalitions with people you would not be working with under any circumstances for any reason, except that, you know, like, the feminists can often be in the same venue against obscenity and pornography.[52]

Political scientists focus on the political behavior and attitudes that conform to democratic rules of the game in the course of influencing the political agenda, forming alliances, and constructing majorities. They are led to the sanguine conclusion that "the American political system can indeed manage and contain" the tensions that arise from religion.[53] I agree. But majoritarianism is more than a decision rule, and I want to draw attention to another dimension. In assuming the political identity of majority or minority, religious actors cast themselves in basic democratic terms and, as important, evoke certain widely shared moral echoes of these terms. I turn very briefly to several expressions of this deeper dimension of political congruence that comes into play when religious groups identify themselves, as they do, as a majority or minority.

The normative weight of majority stems from the fact that it resonates with "we the people." In Tocqueville's terms, the majority is "the great body of the people," whose values and projects are not those of the victors only but belong to the nation. Religious groups share this understanding and adopt this mantle. The Moral Majority, to take an obvious literal example, was "a moment of ecumenical fervor"[54] when religious activists asserted that qua believers, citizens comprise a previously silent majority of Americans. The designation brought the moral weight of majority to bear on their cause. The Religious Freedom Restoration Act, to take another example, invoked not the free exercise rights of a vulnerable religious minority but the rights of the vast majority of Americans who are believers. Adding to the significance of majority as a democratic identity is the fact that in the United States the absence of a categorical religious majority, the fact that every faith is a minority, means that like any political majority, any religious majority has to be created. It is a political identity, not a numerical count. It has to be politically constructed and acknowledged. As such, it is bolstered by the moral resonance of the claim to represent "the great body of the people."

Religious groups may also present themselves as a minority, and this political identity too has moral echoes. American political thought is ambivalent about majoritarianism and imposes limits on the prerogative of the greater number.[55] When religious groups charge that they are deprived of some right or benefit, they typically identify themselves as a politically powerless minority suffering unfairly at the hands of the majority. The status of political minority is more compelling than the status of a particular religious minority, and religious groups direct our attention to their diminished standing as "second-class citizens." This is, clearly, democratic self-representation as a political identity. It is no surprise that the group most in agreement with the view that "rights of the religious people need protection" is black Protestants (see Green, chapter 2, this volume).

The fate of the Jehovah's Witnesses' petition for exemption from saluting the American flag captures this translation of religious minority into the democratic status of political minority. The Witnesses brought their theological objection to pledging allegiance to an inanimate object to court but lost this free exercise claim in *Gobitis,* where Justice Frankfurter ruled that the need to enforce behavior "society thinks necessary for the promotion of some great common end" outweighed their particular claim to religious free exercise.[56] Three years later, however, Justice Jackson sided with the Witnesses in *Barnette*, writing, "to sustain the compulsory flag salute we are required to say that a Bill of Rights which guards the individual's right to speak his own mind, left it open to public authorities to compel him to utter what is not in his mind."[57] The case does more than remind us that litigation by religious groups exhibits (and generates) commitment to constitutionalism and that they are often at the center of constitutional politics.[58] Its deeper significance is the shift in reasoning that justified this extension of civil liberty: from free exercise protection for a specific religious minority to free speech for a political minority. The case directs attention to a quintessential *democratic* right of the politically powerless.[59]

"Minority" has more than one valence in the United States and plays in more than one moral register. The minority that seized the attention of the Founders was not the powerless few but the politically influential few, "aristocrats." The notion of minority as a sinister interest, an antipopular elite subversive of the people's own understanding of its interests, remains standard fare. Public opinion today is overwhelmingly opposed to the idea that it is "perfectly proper for religious leaders to try to persuade people how to vote,"[60] and religious activists' tendency to disclaim a political role for clerical hierarchy and to assert religious populism comes in part from a desire to avoid the negative historical resonance of minority. Similarly, when religious activists inveigh against "secular elites," the "elite" part of the phrase is as important politically as the accusatory "secular."[61] The majority has religiosity in common, and "elite" evokes a sinister minority exerting undue influence.

Neither a religious nor a political majority exists spontaneously in the United States, ready to be activated or contested for. Majorities are created in the course of drawing lines of political division. The minority is not a designated corporate group either (no "titles of nobility" here). Majority and minority are labile and stand in dynamic relation to one another. Without identifying a particular majority, it is impossible to assign genuine political meaning to an "elite." At the present moment religious majority versus "secular elite" is a common political divide. But there is little reason to think that this will be an enduring basis for claims to majority status; "secular elite" is already fading. What is certain is that, periodically, religious activists in conjunction with nonreligious ones will create not just a numerical voting majority on the side of a single issue but a majority political identity with the moral weight of "the great body of the people," and in the process accuse some minority of exercising "undue influence."

Consider the dynamic of majority/minority political identity in action. If every faith in the United States is a minority, and any religious majority is a pluralist amalgam of faiths, it should give us pause that so many Americans think that laws should reflect the religious views of the majority. We can understand why Jews, other non-Christians, and nonbelievers might be in the dissenting 50 percent. But who *is* agreeing with the proposition? And with what phantom religious majority are they identifying? One interpretation of the meaning of this response is consistent with minority as "sinister elite": individuals believe the laws should *not* reflect the religious views of a religious minority. Another explanation is that each respondent is identifying with the particular majority that has formed around a political principle or policy meaningful to her, or with the imagined majority that might form. This survey response reflects how labile religious identity, and even more religious *political* identity, is here. It underscores congruence with the basic terms of democratic politics and the fact that religious groups go about shaping a majority or minority political identity for themselves.

In sum, the majority/minority distinction is important for religion in politics not only as evidence of adaptation to democratic institutions but also because it provides the terms in which religious actors assume and act out basic democratic political identities. It confirms both the comparative moderation and the constitutional commitment of religious politics here. For in the end, majority/minority operates only if there is an implicit orientation to the cohesion of the whole and to its priority over *both* majority and minority factions.

> The majority principle is psychologically binding . . . because the dissenting minority considers itself as belonging to the same community as the majority. . . . Should such a bond of unity . . . not exist, . . . then the majority principle would no longer function as a method of unifying in cooperation the wills of the citizens, but would become a mere condition of the fact of rulership.[62]

These terms are accepted and played out over and over by religious groups in American political life.

Political Congruence: Two-Way Influence

As I have presented it, political congruence refers to conformity to democratic practices, adherence to regulative ideals such as wide public reason, and adoption of democratic political identities. Public reason seems to require one-way accommodation by religion to democracy; that is, "in the very process of accepting the invitation" to enter politics, religious groups must modify their arguments, self-presentation, and even self-understanding. The same holds for religious self-identification as a majority or minority. The conclusion that "democracy shapes Christianity [and other faiths] more than the other way around" seems to get the direction of influence right.[63] That said, the other way around operates too. In electoral politics, protest politics, and constitutional politics, religiously identified actors are not simply adaptive. They refresh democratic politics and sometimes innovate, leading the way to challenges and reforms (on behalf of civil rights, to name a beneficial example) and providing models of political organization. Precisely because religious pluralism and democratic institutions are reciprocally influential here, political congruence is particularly strong.

A simple illustration of the influence of religion on the shape of democratic politics is changing forms of political organization. As one historian observed, "what is cause and what is effect is never completely clear."[64] The parallel between early congregationalism and expectations that political groups should be similarly organized for nonhierarchical, nonoligarchic decision making is one example. The influence of religious populism and revivalism on Jacksonian democracy is standard political history; evangelical rallies were crucial for the rise of mass party mobilization. Religious associations are also the acknowledged origin and model of voluntary association generally, and in the Progressive Era they were templates for burgeoning civic associations and advocacy groups. Today, the organizational innovation of megachurches is seen as a touchstone for building grassroots support for political parties. Like membership in megachurches, the thought goes, party identity is initially "thin and weak," with a low threshold for entry, no emphasis on theology, small group meetings, and a volunteer structure—all allowing for a gradual ramp-up of commitment of time and money, and personal identification as a partisan.[65] Political congruence is importantly, if episodically, a two-way dynamic.

I have pointed to affinities between the self-presentation of religion in politics and the public norms of American democracy. I have also argued that political congruence is a sufficient answer to the questions political theory poses about whether democracy is safe for religion and religion safe for democracy. Political congruence is modest and tempered compared to both the logic of autonomy and the comprehensive logic of congruence. The logic of autonomy and the logic of congruence are platforms of principle from which to justify or oppose the outcomes of democratic politics, but each is alarmist, single-minded in its concerns, and too radical in its implications to serve as a regulatory ideal for democratic politics in practice. True, political congruence operates at a different level than the logics of autonomy and congruence. It does not provide principles for determining whether or when to grant or withhold religious exemption from general laws or to supply public funding. The principles at work are imported from a range of democratic theories and strengthened by democratic experience. But political congruence suffices if we think that the claims brought by religious groups and the brakes imposed by others will be worked out, as they have been, in ongoing democratic politics. Political congruence is assurance that we normally reach decisions in a way that demonstrates that here, at least, religion is safe for democracy, and democracy is safe for religious pluralism.

Is my account of political congruence Pollyanna-ish? No; there is empirical support for the fact that the regulative ideal of political congruence is ordinarily respected and that democratic political identity is authentic. Still, political congruence is bounded by certain conditions. The moderation of religious politics in the United States that I described earlier is almost certainly a condition, and we can imagine changes that would upset it. Advocates of religious autonomy might find "dual citizenship" intolerable and retreat to political quiescence, avowing their alien status; or they might escalate claims that depend for their force solely on theology or clerical authority and try to impose sectarianism on the nation as a whole. Advocates of comprehensive congruence might slip over into an even more defensive resistance against any compromise of strict norms of fairness and nondiscrimination, say, and insist on safety from religion, which they portray as incongruent per se. Mutual provocation is certainly conceivable. But I have suggested good reasons to think political congruence is strong and will be sustained, even if—as is always the case—political outcomes are not to the satisfaction of advocates of autonomy or comprehensive congruence, or even if outcomes that are satisfactory to defenders of autonomy or congruence are not produced or justified for reasons internal to their logic.

Political congruence is not cause for triumphalism, however, and I end by observing the dark underside of the mutual reinforcement of religion and democracy in America.

Faith in America

"Faith in America": the phrase is a useful double entendre and cautionary note. Moral self-confidence is characteristic of American political life. Periodically, American democracy suffers from egregious moral hubris, from complacency rooted in self-righteousness. Certainty of the moral goodness and sincerity, the innocence and virtue of Americans and their government has been called "spiritual pride."[66] Religion in politics reinforces moral hubris.[67] Narratives of American identity are so infused with religion[68] and with echoes of a chosen people that Connor Cruise O'Brien called this country "God Land." Moral hubris fueled by faith makes a particularly dangerous appearance when America is at war.

To be clear: not all religious politics suffers from an absence of moral doubt. Nor is self-certainty unique to religious advocacy; after all, political ideologues of all stripes are "true believers" who see political accommodation as perverse or futile, compromise as capitulation, and brand even fellow partisans as heretics and traitors if they are insufficiently enthusiastic in support of an item of political faith. Still, certainty of political rightness, which is the vice of ideologues and extremists, is not the same as confidence in goodness, which is the distinctive feature of persistently moralized American politics.[69]

We have seen some of the factors that lead religion to fuel Americans' moral hubris. Precisely because religious advocacy in the United States lauds "religion" in general and because people of faith comprise a vast majority, religion is liable to reinforce the assumption that Americans are good, their intent virtuous. It generates "true believers" in this nation of believers. Religion also reinforces moral hubris because of the democratic habit of saying that faith-based politics redounds to the benefit of the nation rather than to a particular church. More speculatively, the eclipse of theology, in particular grim doctrines of unredeemable sin, and the infusion of religion with democratic optimism may play a part in fanning moral self-certainty. True, religious Jeremiahs see America falling from grace and characterize national trials as punishment for sin, but even here America can return to goodness. The right policies, the just war, will be redemptive.

Democratic theorists propose ways of injecting skepticism into politics in order to puncture self-certainty about the rightness of a course of action. They advocate more and better democratic deliberation or Deweyan pragmatism. But if certainty about the rightness of national action is not a matter of the correctness of a political policy but rather of unshakeable confidence in Americans' goodness and virtuous intent, skepticism is not much help. Tempering moral hubris is a matter of questioning our own good faith. Personally and individually believers may know that faith does not mean an absence of doubt, but this does not seem to translate into doubt about ourselves collectively. The only antidote to moral hubris is a genuinely harsh self-discipline, which acknowledges that "while America is an unusually fortunate nation, it is not a distinctively virtuous nation."[70]

I have argued that political congruence is assurance that religious pluralism and democracy are safe for one another. In that respect, faith in American politics is warranted. Faith in our unerring goodness is not.

Notes

I want to thank members of the task force for providing such an engaged and informed working group and for their helpful comments on this essay. Special thanks to John Green, Ira Katznelson, and Alan Wolfe for their specific suggestions.

1. See Robert D. Putnam and David E. Campbell, *American Grace: The Changing Role of Religion in American Public Life* (New York: Simon & Schuster, forthcoming).

2. A benchmark of political theory "startled into thought" is the arc of John Rawls's work. *A Theory of Justice* (Cambridge, MA: Harvard Univeristy Press, 1971) was concerned with distributive justice in a well-ordered society; *Political Liberalism* (New York: Columbia University Press, 1993) was concerned with how to reason about democratic decisions under conditions of disagreement, in particular divergent moral and religious systems of belief.

3. This is not a literature review, and the two "logics" I discuss are not as sharp in the work of any single theorist as I present it here. Still, this is a fair summary of two main principled views on the subject and their implications for politics and policy. My concern is political theory; I do not discuss contemporary American theology. These authors too were "startled into thought" at the same time, for many of the same reasons. The idea of the "public church" provoked arguments over its meaning and value.

4. See Nancy L. Rosenblum, "Religious Parties, Religious Political Identity, and the Cold Shoulder of Liberal Democratic Thought." *Ethical Theory and Moral Practice: An International Forum* 6, no. 1 (March 2003): 23–53.

5. The character of religious doctrine and authority is outside my purview, which is political congruence. It seems clear enough that there is no automatic relation between theology and authority on the one hand and political conduct and identity on the other. Indeed, the "translation" of one into the other is said by critics to be a regrettable "accommodationist" stance by "apologists" for the "public church," giving in to the temptation to see religion as support for democracy. Documenting and countering this are the burdens of Stanley Hauerwas and William H. Willimon, *Resident Aliens* (Nashville, TN: Abingdon Press, 1989). The authors do not commend withdrawal from "the world"; instead, they urge Christians to "join a countercultural phenomenon, a new *polis* called church," and "The church is the only community formed around the truth, which is Jesus Christ," 30, 77. Hauerwas targets Neibuhr in particular, for "policing" Christianity to conform to the requirements of sustaining democracy, in *Dispatches from the Front* (Durham, NC: Duke University Press, 1994), 103. Hauerwas writes, "Does that mean I do not support 'democracy'? I have to confess I have not got the slightest idea, since I do not know what it means to call this society 'democratic,'" 105.

6. Maurice Duverger, *Political Parties: Their Organization and Activity in the Modern State* (New York: John Wiley & Sons, 1963), 61–62.

7. Islam in Europe has been taken up as "an ideology of the downtrodden," Craig S. Smith, "Europe's Muslims May be Headed Where the Marxists Went Before," the *New York Times*, December 26, 2004, WK 7.

8. That is the occasional position of religious enclaves in retreat from the world.

9. When a televangelist calls the Catholic Church "the Great Whore" and "a false cult system," it is newsworthy, and the pastor feels obliged to apologize and say his remarks are misconstrued; see the piece on Rev. John Hagee, "Sen. McCain's Agents of Intolerance," editorial, the *New York Times*: http://nytimes.com/2008/05/24/opinion/24sat2.

10. Putnam and Campbell, on file with the author.

11. *McDaniel v. Paty*, 435 U.S. 618 (1978) 43.

12. One exception is opposition to civil rights for gays, including but not limited to marriage. Occasionally democratic theorists react shrilly, too; liberal constitutional theorists demonstrate "Roe rage," holding the Supreme Court's decision responsible for what they see as "sweeping right wing backlash." Robert Post and Reva Siegel, "Roe Rage: Democratic Constitutionalism and Backlash," *Harvard Civil Rights–Civil Liberties Review*, 42, no. 2 (Summer 2007): 373–434.

13. Jeffrey Stout, *Democracy and Tradition* (Princeton, NJ: Princeton University Press, 2004), 104.

14. Hauerwas and Willimon, 17, 24, 32, 38, 46.

15. A contemporary exception among democratic theorists is George Kateb in *Patriotism and Other Mistakes* (New Haven, CT: Yale University Press, 2006), 359.

16. "Militant atheism" has recently reemerged, but with the exception cited above and a few others, not in democratic theory. For popular examples see Sam Harris, *Letter to a Christian Nation* (New York: Knopf, 2006); Richard Dawkins, *The God Delusion* (London: Bantam Press, 2006); and Christopher Hitchens, *God Is Not Great: How Religion Poisons Everything* (New York: Twelve Books, 2007).

17. The exception is sermons by fundamentalist rabbis and Islamic clerics interpreted as commands for political action. See Yael Tamir, "Remember Amalek: Religious Hate Speech," in Nancy L. Rosenblum, ed., *Obligations of Citizenship and Demands of Faith* (Princeton, NJ: Princeton University Press, 2000).

18. John J. DiIulio, *Godly Republic: A Centrist Civic Blueprint for America's Faith-Based Future* (Berkeley: University of California Press, 2007).

19. Mary Ann Glendon and Raul F. Yates, "Structural Free Exercise," *Michigan Law Review* 90 (1991): 477–550 at 523, 530, and note 259.

20. Michael McConnell, "Accommodation of Religion: An Update and Response to Critics," *George Washington Law Review* 60 (March 1992): 690, 739.

21. Michael Walzer, *Politics and Passion: Toward a More Egalitarian Liberalism* (New Haven, CT: Yale University Press, 2004), 82.

22. Of course, public funding in America is complicated by entanglement of religious groups and government at the local and state levels and by the variability of accommodation. Not surprisingly, advocates of religious autonomy want *national* policies of exemption, recognition, and support. This national focus on the part of theorists of religious autonomy is the counterpart of congruence theorists' insistence that national standards of equality and due process should be applied everywhere and all the way down.

23. Jytte Klausen has collected data on self-identification: "In the predominantly Christian [European] countries, only 14–16% in Russia, France, and Spain said they were Christians first. In Germany, 33% said 'Christians first.' The US was the exception, with 42% saying Christians first." "Europe's Uneasy Marriage of Secularism and Christianity since the 1960s and the Challenge of Religious Pluralism," 10. Unpublished paper prepared for the 2007 Annual Meeting of the APSA, on file with the author.

There is other evidence that close to half of religious believers in America choose religion as a primary marker of identity over "American first," although this survey response is simply reported and not linked to either policy or a political theory of dual citizenship. Amaney Jamal reports that a national survey of Muslim Americans finds them "well-integrated even while they remain devout and committed to their identities." Asked whether they consider themselves "Muslims first" or "American first," the proportion choosing religion as a primary identity marker is similar to that among Christians in the general population: 47 percent of Muslims compared to 42 percent of Christians in the general population, 8.

24. McConnell, "Believers as Equal Citizens" in Rosenblum, ed. *Obligations of Citizenship and Demands of Faith*. 105.

25. John Rawls, "The Idea of Public Reason Revisited," in *The Law of Peoples with "The Idea of Public Reason Revisited"* (Cambridge, MA: Harvard University Press, 1999), 132, 149–50, 151.

26. For a recent overview of the state of the law, see Martha Minow, "Should Religious Groups be Exempt from Civil Rights Laws?" unpublished paper on file with the author. For an extended discussion of the preoccupation with equality and fairness in religious law interpretation, and a canvass of the multiple values that should inform constitutional debate, see Steven Shiffrin, "The Pluralistic Foundations of the Religion Clauses," *Cornell Law Review* 90 (September

2004): 9–96. Principled opposition to aid to religious schools is reinforced by the history of flight to evangelical schools as end runs around public school desegregation. Wariness is reflected in practice, for example, in the political difficulty of enacting school voucher plans even after constitutional objections have been dismissed. And voucher plans are at least potentially universal and neutral; most public funding is discretionary.

27. Of course, the scope and stringency of proposals for legislating and enforcing democratic principles and practices are variable. For example, "the logic of congruence" sees public schools as essential for democratic socialization and as symbols if not guarantors of equal opportunity, but few proponents of congruence would mandate exclusively public schooling, prohibiting sectarian private education.

28. The phrase is Amy Gutmann's in *Identity in Democracy* (Princeton, NJ: Princeton University Press, 2003), 153.

29. We recognize this as a version of the argument, not easily dismissed, that the enforcement of morals by censorship or regulation is necessary to prevent attitudes and behavior that corrode society, to ward off the informal ways in which political society may be undermined or radically redefined. T. M. Scanlon, "The Difficulty of Tolerance," in *The Difficulty of Tolerance* (Cambridge: Cambridge University Press, 2003).

30. Stephen Macedo, "Transformative Constitutionalism and the Case of Religion: Defending the Moderate Hegemony of Liberalism," *Political Theory* 26, no. 1 (February 1998): 56–80 at 73.

31. Nancy L. Rosenblum, *Membership and Morals: The Personal Uses of Pluralism in America* (Princeton, NJ: Princeton University Press, 1998).

32. For Rawls's tripartite division of the scope of public reason, see 133–34. Rawls takes pains to answer his religious critics by saying that secular comprehensive doctrines too are excluded. Arguments for congruence vary in stringency and scope. Some democratic theorists impose severe "epistemic abstinence" and admit only public reasons in public life. Some apply the constraints of public reason only to deliberation on constitutional essentials and matters of basic justice rather than all laws and policies. Some apply the constraints only to public officials and political candidates, others to citizens when they vote or engage in political advocacy in the public political forum.

33. "The Idea of Public Reason Revisited," *Law of Peoples* (1999): 150, 174ff. In many parts of Europe and other democracies there are statutory and constitutional bans on appeals to religion in public life. See Nancy L. Rosenblum, "Banning Parties: Religious and Ethnic Parties in Multicultural Democracies," *Journal of Law and Ethics of Human Rights,* 1 (2007): 17–75.

34. Rawls, 131.

35. In some accounts, public reason also marks philosophical and historical enlightenment: Habermas, for example, does not relent in the "quest to *aufheben* religion's moral teachings within the postconventional procedures of communicative action." Jurgen Habermas, "A Genealogical Analysis of the Cognitive Content of Morality," in *Inclusion of the Other* (Cambridge, MA: MIT Press, 1998), 44.

36. Stout, 72–73.

37. Scanlon, 189, 198.

38. Veit Bader, "Religious Pluralism: Secularism or Priority for Democracy?" *Political Theory* 27, no. 5 (October 1999), 598. "The priority for democracy . . . should explicitly allow for all religious or theological arguments compatible with liberal democracy," 617. Presumably philosophers are the judges of compatibility.

39. Putnam and Campbell document wariness toward "religion in politics" and religious leaders persuading people how to vote but positive attitudes when it comes to elected leaders being deeply religious, as evidence of good character.

40. Barack Obama, "Call to Renewal Keynote Address," June 28, 2006: http://www.barackobama.com/2006/06/28/call_to_renewal_keynote_address.php.

41. Reva Siegel, "The New Politics of Abortion: An Equality Analysis of Women-Protective Abortion Restrictions," *Illinois Law Review* (2007): 991. Post and Siegel, 48. Ronald Dworkin argues that "sanctity" of human life is an "essentially religious" value in *Life's Dominion* (Cambridge, MA: Harvard University Press, 1971), 155.

42. Alan Wolfe notes that the movement for intelligent design argues "for revelation in the guise of liberal ideas of fairness and pluralism of viewpoints," in this case, a subterfuge, but nonetheless an example of the tabling of revelation and recourse to the terms of public reason. Is it a wolf in sheep's clothing or transformative? "Whose Christianity? Whose Democracy?" Response to Hugh Heclo, *Christianity and American Democracy* (Cambridge, MA: Harvard University Press, 2007), 204–5.

43. Eldon J. Eisenach, *The Next Religious Establishment; National Identity and Political Theology in Post-Protestant America* (New York: Rowman & Littlefield, 2000), 40. In the same vein, Wolfe argues that the chief force for secularism is American culture, which "has so thoroughly shaped religion that, rather than constituting a danger to democracy, religion in order to survive has little choice but to adopt the trappings of modern democratic cultural life," 200.

44. Phillip Jones, Comment at the conference "Religion and Politics," sponsored by the Center for American Political Studies, Harvard University, May 2, 2008. Unpublished paper on file with the author.

45. Anthony Gottlieb, "Atheists with Attitude": http://www.newyorker.com/arts/critics/books/2007/05/21. This differs, of course, from theological pluralism, which is opposed by theologians like Hauerwas, who defends the label "sectarian" and a focus on the particulars of "what we believe," in Hauerwas and Willimon, 41.

46. We have passed beyond Protestant versus Protestant and Protestant versus Catholic, beyond generic Christianity and "Judeo-Christian," to generic faith. Eisenach marks the changes: Protestant (vs. Catholic) and its disestablishment, generic Christian-Judeo, and now secular or postreligious, 2–3.

47. Hugh Heclo, *Christianity and American Democracy* (Cambridge, MA: Harvard University Press, 2007), at 187.

48. Kent Greenawalt, "Five Questions about Religion Judges Are Afraid to Ask," in Nancy L. Rosenblum, ed., *Obligations of Citizenship* (Princeton, NJ: Princeton University Press, 2000), 198.

49. "Americans typically do not stay in one church long enough to learn that much about its theology and its history." Wolfe, 197.

50. Stout, 63, 72.

51. Kimberly Conger and Bryan McGraw, "Religious Conservatives and the Requirements of Citizenship," *Perspectives on Politics* 6 (2008), 261.

52. Cited in Conger and McGraw, 261.

53. Wald, 17.

54. Post and Siegel, 52.

55. Benjamin Constant, *Principles of Politics Applicable to All Government*, ed. Etienne Hofmann (Indianapolis: Liberty Fund, 2003), 32.

56. *Minersvile School District v. Gobitis*, 593, 594.

57. *West Virginia v. Barnette*, 632, 634.

58. "Citizen engagement in constitutional conflict may contribute to social cohesion in a normatively heterogeneous polity," Post and Siegel, 5.

59. Gordon Silverstein, "Precedent and Popular Constitutionalism: How the Supreme Court Shapes Political Discourse," APSA, August 2007, unpublished paper on file with the author. From Chapter 3 of Gordon Silverstein, *Law's Allure: How Law Shapes, Constrains, Saves and Kills Politics* (New York: Cambridge University Press, 2009). A host of religious claims have been reframed in terms of free speech. To take one example, religious groups used free speech claims to successfully mandate use of university facilities and financial support for religious publications.

60. Data in Putnam and Campbell, *American Grace*.

61. Jeffrey Stout shows the error of defining secular as a comprehensive worldview hostile to religion. The charge assumes secularism as an ideology of disbelief, identified with liberalism, and a theory of its spread. The discourse of modern democracies is secularized in the sense that "discourse is not framed by a theological perspective taken for granted by all those who participate in it," but secularization does not reflect commitment to secularism, meaning denial of religious beliefs or their expulsion from the public sphere, 93, 97.

62. Gerhard Leibholz, *Politics and Law* (Leiden: A. W. Sythoff, 1965), 27.

63. Wolfe, 193.

64. R. L. Moore, *Selling God: American Religion in the Marketplace of Culture* (New York: Oxford University Press, 1994).

65. Putnam and Campbell.

66. The phrase "spiritual pride" is Reinhold Niebuhr's, cited in William Galston, "When in Doubt," *Journal of Democracy* (Summer 2007): 31–37, at 35.

67. Nancy L. Rosenblum, "Centrism and Extremism and an Ethic of Partisanship" in *On the Side of the Angels: An Appreciation of Parties and Partisanship* (Princeton, NJ: Princeton University Press, 2008).

68. For example, Rogers Smith, *Stories of Peoplehood: The Politics and Morals of Political Membership* (Cambridge: Cambridge University Press, 2003). "There simply is no stronger basis for making a membership seem both unquestionably intrinsic and morally worthwhile than to have it assigned by God or the gods. No purely biological, ancestral, cultural, linguistic, or historical account can provide quite the same degree of sanctification that divine authorship bestows," 66.

69. I owe this conclusion to the brilliant short essay by William Galston, "When in Doubt," *Journal of Democracy* (Summer 2007): 31–37, at 36.

70. Galston, 36.

CONCLUSION

Reflections on Religion, Democracy, and the Politics of Good and Evil

IRA KATZNELSON

THE AMERICAN EXPERIENCE contradicts once-widespread expectations that religion would decline and become ever more contained in the private sphere of conscience and association under modern conditions, where religion is a choice rather than an imperative.[1] Over time, religious adherence has grown. Fewer than two in ten Americans formally belonged to a church in 1776, just over four in ten did by 1890, and nearly two in three do today.[2] In aggregate and on average, the American people testify to more belief (with well over 90 percent persistently affirming a belief in God[3]) and possess more widespread attachment to organized religion than any other classic candidate for theses about modernity and secularization. Individual religious experiences, church belonging and attendance, and the extent of belief exhibit great vitality.

Religious life in the United States seems more varied and more vital than at any time since World War II. American Protestantism, especially, has been marked by a host of revitalization movements, including Pentecostalism, charismatic movements, and megachurches, whose gains have surpassed losses by long-established Protestant denominations. Even in these mainline forms, as H. Richard Niebuhr put the point a half-century ago, Protestantism has been characterized by "re-evangelization, and by the evangelization of the Nation. The tendency to equate the gospel with the democratic social faith has been balanced by the effort to Christianize the democratic mind."[4] New post-1965 immigrant streams, moreover, have vastly extended the scope of religious belief and activity, well beyond the Protestant-Catholic-Jew triad identified in Will Herberg's 1983 "essay in American religious sociology." In Los Angeles, where Muslims outnumber Episcopalians, there are more than 600 identifiable faiths. There, and elsewhere, newcomers have refreshed and renewed long-established churches with declining attendance, notably in urban Catholic parishes.[5]

This vibrant plurality has not been restricted to civil society. Religious organizations and convictions of many types[6] have come to play an increasingly vigorous and visible role in political life in the past quarter-century.[7] American politics is charged with tight, if complex and contingent, links between personal faith and patterns of religious membership, on the one side, and political preferences and identities, on the other. Such identities often provide persons with political confidence to overcome barriers to political participation and collective action, but they also can become sources of anxiety that interject potentially potent forms of anger into public affairs when connected to feelings that particular commitments and ways of life are being either suppressed or threatened.[8]

Patterns of mobilization based on religious conviction are more than sources of intervention in public affairs. They reshape the words and practices of democratic politics. The country's political speech utilizes prayer, invokes God in its pledge of allegiance, routinely summons biblical references, and offers religious justifications a good deal more than is thought appropriate in most other liberal democracies.[9] Constituting some central features of American democracy, a political system premised on the existence of a modern state that is uncommonly permeable to the preferences of members of civil society, these fonts of political activity introduce elements of passion and widen the vector of policies debated in the media, in state and national legislatures and courts, and within many levels of public discourse.

A half-century ago, most political interventions by theologians, churches, and religiously motivated Americans were associated with liberal antiwar, social reform, and civil rights political positions. While often acting as critics of American culture, they rarely questioned the way the boundaries between church and state had developed, in practice or in jurisprudence.[10] Today, an even more prominent role for religious actors and views has become identified with conservative political argument, especially regarding deeply felt cultural questions associated with gender and sexuality, and with claims that too radical a separation of church and state constitutes an unacceptable measure of hostility to religion, arguing that it facilitates the policy triumph of anticlerical and secular viewpoints held by a modest minority of the population and provides insufficient scope for the public expression of religious convictions.[11] Altering the content of the Protestant center and periphery, this shift has produced what the sociologist of religion Robert Wuthnow has called "the great fracture in American religion" that divides fundamentalists, evangelicals, and self-described religious conservatives from religious liberals, humanists, and secularists. As mainline churches in the second camp have yielded their majority status within Protestantism to the first, the former, in turn, have crafted alliances on shared concerns with the Catholic Church in what only a short time ago was an unthinkable association.[12]

Both the vibrant place religion occupies in American life and the shift of the center of gravity toward religious assertiveness in the public sphere have provoked the contributors to this volume to chart, both empirically and normatively, the pitfalls and promise of religious faith and activism for democracy. They register a growing diversity and intensity, observe challenges to toleration, portray a sometimes uncomfortable collision of secular and religious perspectives, and identify the ways American politics and jurisprudence have coped with dilemmas inherent in the relationship of religion and democracy. Rejecting any automatic association of religion either with democratic foundations or antidemocratic instigations, they probe the borderlands of religion and democracy to discover the implications of their complex interactions—for political parties and voting, for degrees of broadmindedness, for the accommodation of multiple faiths, theologies, and denominations, for the meaning of politically relevant identities, for the character of law, and for deliberation and compromise. They wonder about the implications of religious, as distinct from secular, motivations for political activism; about the growing diversity of American religiosity and theology; about the interplay of religion and gender, ethnicity, class, and race; about the legal resolution of controversies about the imbrication of religion and public affairs; and, most broadly, about dangers and opportunities posed by the country's religious patterns for American democracy.

I

With these themes, this book's authors join a long lineage of discussion and dispute. The links they draw between the extraordinary pluralism of religion in America and questions that concern proper terms of engagement between religion and liberal democracy resonate with debates in colonial America and the early Republic. These concern the status of Christianity as a foundation for liberty, the role of established churches and the meaning of neutrality, rules of transaction governing relations of church and state, restrictions on blasphemy, and religious tests for office even before the Constitution's First Amendment specified how "Congress shall make no law respecting an establishment of religion, or prohibiting the free exercise thereof."[13] Whereas in revolutionary France, "the Enlightenment [was] configured as a *freedom from belief*," in the United States "the Enlightenment become something very different: not a freedom from belief, but a *freedom to believe*."[14] Whether, in addition, the First Amendment built what Thomas Jefferson famously denoted in a letter to the Danbury Baptist Association in 1802 as "a wall of separation between Church and State," and what the implications are for this partition have been subjects of great debate ever since the Founding, especially as the relationship between the Establishment and Free Exercise clauses is inherently charged with ambiguity. Nor were the terms of participation and membership in the polity by religious actors settled by George

Washington's earlier declaration to the Hebrew Congregation of Newport in August 1790 that "the citizens of the United States of America have a right to applaud themselves for having given to mankind examples of an enlarged and liberal polity," for

> it is now no more that toleration is spoken of as if it were the indulgence of one class of people that another enjoyed the exercise of their inherent natural rights, for happily, the Government of the United States, which gives bigotry no sanction, to persecution no assistance, requires only that they who live under its protection should demean themselves as good citizens in giving it on all occasions their effectual support.[15]

For well over two centuries, the tensions inherent in the Constitution's Establishment and Free Expression imperatives, and questions concerning the scope and character of religious toleration, have been constitutive features of American political development. As a democracy in a religious country, as a democracy that both curbs and induces forms of religious organization, speech, and action, and as a democracy that recurrently has had to discover standards of engagement to canalize its relations with religious organizations and passions, the United States has regularly debated the signals and conventions, the understandings and expectations, and the rules and standards of engagement the chapters in this volume address. When does religion strengthen civil society and buttress democratic institutions and behavior, and when, by contrast, does it fragment, polarize, and erode civility and thus make democracy more coarse and less secure? Tocqueville famously argued that widespread involvement in religious organizations and the mores advanced by Christianity (broadly and thinly understood) strengthened American democracy.[16] Recent empirical studies demonstrate that religious membership and activity provide the single greatest spur to political participation by individuals in what mostly is a relatively low-turnout, low-participation political system.[17]

At the core of this volume is a persistent probing of these questions: What are the implications of the range of diversity in American religion for the public sphere? How do the hard-wired and reinterpreted rules about establishments and expression shape how citizens think and act, organize and mobilize, politically? How do America's patterns of political participation, when motivated by religious conviction, affect the tone, content, and scope of the democratic process? Does the organized mobilization of religious principles and persuasions improve or detract from desirable qualities within American democracy and its politics of policymaking? With so much diversity of conscience and ways of life, and with so many contesting controversial ideas, how, further, can the polity discover toleration for views and behavior thought by others to be wrong, repugnant, or even sinful?[18]

These issues reverberate across the array of chapters, including the empirical designations of the remarkable heterogeneity of religious expression and organization in the United States. As John Green, Amaney Jamal, Frederick Harris, David Leal, and Allison Calhoun-Brown mark and measure this diversity, they do much more than chronicle its variety, for they highlight linkages to political attitudes and behavior, always bearing in mind the wider implications. In turn, as Bette Evans summarizes the charged history of jurisprudence, as James Gibson confronts the fragility of support for toleration, as Clyde Wilcox, Geoffrey Layman, and Kenneth Wald and David Leege examine the dimensions of religious mobilization at an elite and mass level, and as Rosa DeLauro offers an account by a leading political figure of the role played by religion in Congress, they seek to identify and understand how the political and politicized shapes and shadings of religion affect, and are affected by, American democracy.

Read together, they remind us that there has been a dominant solution in the United States to problems of religion and politics that, elsewhere, often has produced curbs on liberty and organized intolerance and even widespread violence. This orientation is the one Nancy Rosenblum's essay calls "political congruence"—the implicit requirement that religious groups respect democratic rules and practices, present themselves in public life not by appealing to religious meanings or revealed truths but to public reason, and strategically pursue the creation of political, not doctrinal, majorities, thus respecting the basic rule for social choice of finding 50 percent plus one in circumstances of religious pluralism where no single denomination can come close to possessing such a majority. Political congruence, she persuasively argues, is both the result and a producer of religious moderation. Americans tend not to assault or kill each other for their faith. In turn, political participation can moderate religiously motivated desires and demands, opening possibilities for compromise. Congregational experiences prod political participation and prepare citizens for a democratic give and take. Vibrant religious expression and a public sphere that is democratic can go hand in hand provided there is a recurring discovery of arrangements that refuse both the option that the state actively promote religion and the alternative of a stark separation of church and state that too effectively limits the presence of religious associations and claims in public life.

At the heart of this position are distinctions John Rawls underscored in *Political Liberalism*, his philosophical account of how democracy can be strengthened when its citizens are deeply divided along religious and ethical lines. The modern state, he argued, must not be conceptualized as an association or a community. Associations are partial and voluntary. Sovereign states are inclusive and compulsory. Associations have particular ends and aims. Democratic states only have ends that all free and equal citizens can share. Its particular aims are not fixed or settled but are negotiated and temporarily resolved. Communities are homogeneous. They are composed by people who share identities and comprehensive views. When membership is restricted only to persons who hold their particular understandings and commitments, basic democratic principles are violated by the imposition by one community of an inclusive set of values on all. Democratic states, he insisted, must incorporate and recognize pluralism, a "fact that is crucial for a well-ordered society's idea of public reason."[19]

Rawls also set apart political conceptions of justice like the U.S. Constitution from the often incommensurable ethical positions found in a society that is religiously heterogeneous. Rawls understood a political conception to be a guide for how public institutions "fit together into one unified system of social cooperation from one generation to the next." Such a conception for "the political culture of a democratic society" is free-standing; it cannot be reduced to any single comprehensive set of religious and cultural views that are held, often fiercely held, by different sets of citizens. "The problem," Rawls noted, "is how to frame a conception of justice for a constitutional regime such that those who support, or who might be brought to support, that kind of regime might also endorse the political conception provided it did not conflict too sharply with their comprehensive views."[20]

The formula for political congruence identified by Rosenblum—a willingness to play in the in-between, not settle things conclusively, and try to make the interaction of religion and democracy a positive-sum game—pursues just this goal and is based on just these differences. The alternative that seeks more robust public support for religious institutions, faiths, and practices risks mistaking a democratic state for an association or a community by politicizing religion in ways that threaten common citizenship despite great diversity. The option that wants the wall of separation to grow higher, more secure, and more difficult to breach, in turn, risks a lack of regard for persons of faith by imposing restrictions on their capacities, even rights, of free expression and thus offers a kind of ersatz universalism that also mistakes a democracy for an association or a community.

The "sweet spot" of political congruence thus beckons. These concluding remarks comment on this position, with which I am in agreement. I first retrace steps Rawls took to elaborate how democracy can be strengthened when its citizens are deeply divided along religious and ethical lines, especially his attempt to distinguish reasonable from unreasonable pluralism, and his identification of the "overlapping consensus" as the most desirable mechanism with which to account for how people with strong, different, and incompatible beliefs about truth and falsehood, good and evil, nonetheless can converge to back democratic institutions and support toleration. Bearing in mind this framework and analysis, I then highlight some features of the engagement of religion and democracy, bearing in mind H. Richard Niebuhr's observation that "in America the primary companion with which [religion] has had to deal as friend and rival and foe has been democracy."[21]

II

At stake is a two-sided challenge. What conditions best sustain a democracy in which, as President Washington put things, "every one shall dwell in safety under his own vine and fig tree and there shall be none to make him afraid"? What, in turn, is asked of the "not afraid" when they bring their beliefs, doctrines, and values into the public political arena?

Questions like these, which rest on the premise of a population composed of groups of persons with often deeply distinct and ethically competing worldviews that advance contending versions of truth, were missing in the most important work of twentieth-century liberal political thought, *A Theory of Justice* by Rawls.[22] There, he argued that a stable and decently organized democracy must be based on a shared single conception of justice, characterized by equal liberty and by limitations placed on social and economic inequalities, so that all have fair equality of opportunity, and inequality itself must benefit the least advantaged. These principles, he further contended, are those that would be chosen when negotiated by persons who are ignorant of their own particularity, including not just their economic position or native talents but their goals, identities, and views of the world. Behind this veil of ignorance, rational but unaware individuals would select the core principles for a just liberal democracy because they would be deciding on a design without knowing how these arrangements would affect them specifically. They would leap into the realm of the universal, bypassing their particular circumstances, practices, cultures, and beliefs. Legitimated by such an abstract and hypothetical bargaining situation, this single comprehensive doctrine would become the basis for a decent democratic polity. Each person "has a similar sense of justice and in this respect a well-ordered society is homogeneous. Political argument appeals to this moral consensus."[23]

Organized religion plays no role in this great book. It finds no mention, nor does personal faith or collective belief. Here, the polity is constituted as a single political community that consensually affirms a single and inclusive political doctrine. Some two decades later, Rawls recanted. In

Political Liberalism, he acknowledged that a "conception of social unity is excluded by the fact of reasonable pluralism; it is no longer a political possibility for those who accept the constraints of liberty and toleration of democratic institutions."[24] It is thus important to conceive of unity "in a different way," because, he now reflected, the idea "that all its citizens endorse this conception on the basis of what I now call a comprehensive philosophical doctrine" was an "unrealistic idea of a well-ordered society." It failed to appreciate how "a modern democratic society is characterized not simply by a pluralism of comprehensive religious, philosophical, and moral doctrines but by a pluralism of incompatible yet reasonable comprehensive doctrines. No one of these doctrines is affirmed by citizens generally."[25]

However desirable a comprehensive doctrine for democratic political life might be, it "can be maintained only by the oppressive use of state power"; that is, state power that one or another minority experiences as repression and subjugation.[26] In a key passage, Rawls observed how

> Religious and philosophical doctrines express views of the world and of our life with one another severally and collectively, as a whole. Our individual and associative points of view, intellectual affinities, and affective attachments, are too diverse, especially in a free society, to enable those doctrines to serve as the basis of lasting and reasoned political agreement. Different conceptions of the world can reasonably be elaborated from different standpoints, and diversity arises in part from our distinct perspectives. It is unrealistic—or worse, it arouses mutual suspicion and hostility—to suppose that all our differences are rooted solely in ignorance and perversity, or else in the rivalries of power, status, or economic gain.[27]

More positively, Rawls now stressed that there need not be a fatal contradiction between deep religious and ethical pluralism and political liberalism and free thought, for "a plurality of reasonable yet incompatible comprehensive doctrines is the normal result of the exercise of human reason within the framework of free institutions of a constitutional democratic regime."[28] This "diversity of reasonable comprehensive religious, philosophical, and moral doctrines found in modern democratic societies," he recognized, "is not a mere historical condition that may soon pass away; it is a permanent feature of the public culture of democracy."[29] If democracy is to thrive in the face of an irreducible and often religious pluralism, then it must find a foundation that citizens can share without recourse to a single and consensual comprehensive ethical basis for politics.

Yet once a particular and shared underpinning for democracy no longer is to be relied on because people hold very different versions of value and truth, matters of stability, finding a basis for a collective and mutual public life, deciding how to conduct public discourse, and identifying a distinction between reasonable and unreasonable doctrines arise as sharp and contested problems. How can people whose varying perspectives are rooted firmly in different and often competing structures of belief share a common democratic space? Is it possible to formulate and sustain political conceptions of justice like the Constitution of the United States that define how citizens should conduct political argument and reach collective decisions in circumstances marked by religious plurality, each with its own combination of practices, beliefs, and institutions that shape preferences and motivate actors who possess competing understandings of the good?

These questions demand the discovery of "fair terms of social cooperation between citizens characterized as free and equal yet divided by profound doctrinal conflict," that is, conditions that can secure liberty and democracy when diversity runs deep, and where different views and practices are thought not just to be better or worse but good or evil.[30] In such circumstances, the ways religious commitments, allegiances, and obligations enter public political life, he instructed, are crucial for the viability of a zone of democratic public reason and social choice.

This quest for mutual accommodation relies on the ability to draw a line between unreasonable and reasonable pluralism. Both types are deep; both transcend rationality. Persons who hold different positions will not yield their most cherished views as an outcome of rational argument. In the realm of such values and beliefs, "what is obvious to some persons and accepted as a basic idea is unintelligible to others." What makes pluralism reasonable is a willingness to discern and act on what Rawls identified as standards of fair cooperation despite such substantial differences. What defines the reasonable is a willingness, despite serious differences, to work within and advance a shared framework for political life. Reasonableness thus is marked by a capacity and will to enter the domain of public reason where reciprocity among equal citizens is a basic principle. "We enter as equals into the public world of others and stand ready to propose, or to accept, as the case may be, fair terms of cooperation with them."[31]

Reasonable pluralism, he insisted, does not require "a society of saints." Rather, it identifies a world in which associations and communities, including those with a religious basis, "have their own rational ends they wish to advance, and all stand ready to propose fair terms that others may reasonably be expected to accept."[32] Persons who hold quite different fundamental and comprehensive views "set out principles" in the public sphere that are drawn from these distinct bases, specifying and sharing their reasons in civic forums, and adjudicating their disagreements by practicing what Rawls called burdens of judgment. Sharing public space, reasonable pluralists are citizens who practice democracy notwithstanding their conflicting priors and despite the inability of reason to persuade people with such convictions to abandon them. Reasonable pluralists affirm different sets of stable and comprehensive religious beliefs, doctrines, and practices but do not expect to impose these on others, even when their commitments are passionate. Democracy thus rests on conceptions, institutions, and behaviors that all citizens, despite irreducible differences, might endorse in light of their own particular ideals. Reciprocally, if the common polity does not simultaneously draw on different doctrines and commitments, it cannot authentically qualify as a legitimate liberal democracy.[33]

What is critical, from this perspective, is the existence of mechanisms that can harness fervent religious belief and moral diversity on behalf of democracy in the absence of an overarching and singular moral consensus. "How then," the political theorist Joshua Cohen asked in an appreciative overview of *Political Liberalism*, "is it possible to achieve consensus on a conception of justice suited to a democratic society of equal citizens and to reap the benefits of that consensus, given the pluralism of comprehensive moralities that inevitably marks such a society?"[34] How can the requirements for democracy and toleration not only survive deep pluralism and the absence of a congruence of views but build agreement on these disparate foundations? To be robust, such a consensus must be more than a modus vivendi, more than a balance of forces between competing views, and should draw on resources from within distinct views of the good without imposing any one such comprehensive position on other members of society; and it must do so without eliminating the prospect that persons can pursue particular beliefs and ways of life they value highly.[35]

For this to happen, the conceptions and arrangements of liberal democracy have to be independent from, yet supported by, various religious and moral positions. The core idea is that there is no single pathway to liberal democracy and toleration. "Each citizen affirms both a comprehensive doctrine and the focal political conception, somehow related."[36] A wide array of people with highly disparate beliefs and practices, associations and communities, nonetheless can come to political agreement and share broad political commitments based on, not despite, their particularity. Different comprehensive religious and moral views can generate reasons—different reasons—that support the same ideas and arrangements about political rights, liberal institutions, and democratic procedures that moderate rivalries and determine matters of public policy. This "overlapping consensus" —"a consensus of reasonable (as opposed to unreasonable or irrational) comprehensive doctrines"—offers a means by which

> all those who affirm the political conception start from within their own comprehensive view and draw on the religious, philosophical, and moral grounding it provides. The fact that people affirm the same political conception on those grounds does not make their affirming it any less religious, philosophical, or moral, as the case may be, since the grounds sincerely held determine the nature of their affirmation.[37]

III

We should not underestimate what is at stake in securing reasonable pluralism and an overlapping consensus, especially because this combination is more challenging—ethically and practically—than simpler positions. This middle zone, marked by a political realm that is sustained by intersecting commitments, is inherently charged with tensions that are impossible to permanently resolve and thus must be managed and contained. In making demands for toleration for disliked positions, in finding room for forms of private and political expression that make others anxious, and in not crisply resolving whether, and when, the partition dividing the secular and religious realms is permeable or impermeable, the political congruence position is inherently unstable. All the more impressive, then, that the United States has achieved a combination of elements that have sheltered religious pluralism, found space for institutional and mostly congregational self-governance, and protected liberties of conscience, albeit often grudgingly and sometimes violated, while managing to keep American democracy as a site not dominated by any particular denomination, not based on rigid religious corporatism, and not inhospitable to persons with thin or nonexistent religious commitments.

But this has not been a placid or steady accomplishment. The junction of religion and democracy is inherently challenging. Democracy is a political system based on an oscillation of rulers and on the idea that policy outcomes are provisional rather than fixed once and for all. Religion, by contrast, concerned as it is with good and evil, commits to specific versions and corollaries of truth. Not all doctrines and normative commitments are equal. In labeling some as "reasonable," Rawls considered others to be "unreasonable and irrational, and even mad," so that "the problem is to contain them so that they do not undermine the unity and justice of society."[38] It is one thing to pronounce such a principled desire but quite another, however, to grapple with four particularly vexing issues, each difficult to resolve.

First is the question of pluralism itself. Viewed from within the perspective of the half of the country who today are Protestants in mainline, evangelical, African-American, or predominantly Latino churches, the

United States appears remarkably heterogeneous. The history of American Protestantism, under conditions of unprecedented freedom, has been a fractionalized history of many schisms and divisions, including regional and racial partitions, but also reunions of once-estranged churches. Protestant denominations in the United States include the churches of the Reformation, the churches of the Puritan Revolution, the churches of the eighteenth-century Awakening, the churches of the nineteenth-century Revivals, and the megachurches of twentieth- and twenty-first-century technology and suburbanization. Not only is this religious location exceptionally diverse across and within categories of belief and practices, but affiliated Protestants also are aware that nearly a quarter of the population is Roman Catholic, that nearly as many are unaffiliated or secular, and yet others belong to smaller minorities of Muslims and Jews. Most Protestants, even the more fervent, are attuned to this heterogeneity and are willing to moderate expectations for the affirmation of their preferences in public life. But not all, and not those who come to constitute clear majorities in particular locations, especially evangelical Protestants in some southern states, for whom pluralism is more akin to a millet system where one religion is hegemonic, though it tolerates the others. Further, from the perspective of minority religions in some historical circumstances—including both Catholics and Jews during the period of mass migration from 1880 to 1924—the internally diverse Protestant population appears as a dominating monolith. It defined public policy in areas that included Prohibition, religious curricula and prayers in the public schools, Sunday shop closings, and many other areas, some enforced by civil society coercion and violence with public authority looking the other way.[39] Further, when minority forms of worship have overlapped with racial categorization, as it has for Latino Catholics in predominantly Protestant locations, the character of pluralism has not resembled anything like a model of peaceful or equal coexistence. Pluralism is not just a fact of demography and attachments but of cultural, social, and symbolic power.

Second is the matter of reasonable pluralism, both its identification and taxonomy. The very concept implies participation in public reason and thus the shaping and securing of a common public realm. But in circumstances of unequal religious standing, some groups retreat, and others come forward. For much of the twentieth century, evangelical Protestants, especially after the Scopes Trial stigmatized their antievolution stance as primitive and ignorant, largely withdrew from the political realm. Conversely, the active presence of other groups in public democratic politics, especially mainline Protestants who dominated political speech, assumed this absence. When evangelicals returned to political activity, they were almost immediately tarred as unreasonable, especially for their staunch resistance to secular positions in culture wars, when in fact their patterns of participation and adjustment were not so simple to classify. When brought down from abstract definitions to specific historical circumstances, the distinction between reasonable and unreasonable pluralism seems too crisp and demanding, especially when facts on the ground area almost always are more uneven, complex, and often tied to the substantive preferences of those who do the judging. There is always the danger that deep and thick religious commitments will be adjudged as unreasonable a priori, rather than actually put to the test Rawls persuasively elaborates concerning requirements for public reason and deliberation in the give and take of democratic politics. There have been more than a few occasions in American history when the putatively reasonable have been willing to participate on these terms only when the putatively unreasonable have been left out. The gag rule that restricted debate in Congress so as to exclude abolitionist views that were largely promoted by strong believers is a clear case in point.

Third is the problem of making, discerning, and reproducing an overlapping consensus. There is a danger of circularity. If only the reasonable can legitimately help fashion such agreement, and if there is no fixed agreement about who is a reasonable player, the boundaries between those inside and outside can grow rather than diminish. There is a large literature on secular interest group politics, including classic work by David Truman, which insists that it is both unrealistic and unnecessary for groups to do more than pursue their own particular preferences, rather than bear in mind something that might be identified as a public interest.[40] By contrast, the Rawlsian position seems to judge "views unconcerned with common ground as unreasonable."[41] Otherwise, it is thought, religious and cultural issues will be adjudicated by power and majority rule alone. This is a plausible, perhaps even attractive, position, but it requires clarity about why certain matters of substance and allegiance require more willingness to compromise in advance than other kinds of questions and memberships. What, more exactly, is required from religious citizens and institutions when they engage with difficult public issues and seek to affect public policy about such charged matters as school prayer and abortion?[42] And who will judge whether they have appropriately adjusted to be candidates to contribute to an overlapping consensus?

Fourth is the closely related matter that not all issues are the same. They do not lie on the same dimension. Some are matters of more or less, but others generate passionate feelings about good and evil. Slavery and Jim Crow were arrayed on this kind of axis, dividing those who were certain they were just, even divinely ordained, from those who were sure they were wicked violations of God's will. For many Americans today, abortion plays this divisive role. For sure, there is something of a middle ground between *Roe v. Wade* and subsequent reductions and qualifications that most citizens support, but for large minorities the two positions are incommensurable and irreconcilable. We may ask, as Mark Graber does in a provocative book about the infamous 1857 Dred Scott decision that validated slavery in the territories and refused access to American citizenship to black residents, free as well as slave, how much accommodation to injustice is tolerable, and perhaps even required, within the framework of liberal democracy. Graber calls this the problem of constitutional evil, "the practice and theory of sharing civic space with people committed to evil practices or pledging allegiance to a constitutional text and tradition saturated with concessions to evil."[43] As the Civil War demonstrated, this dilemma defines and inhabits a zone of great moral uncertainty. How does one weigh up the choice between the eradication of slavery and the saturation of the country in the blood of some 600,000 dead by battle and disease, or, for that matter, the death of 36,000 (one in five) black Union troops? Is it not hopelessly credulous to think that any overlapping consensus—whether in ideas, norms, or institutions—can adjudicate such matters, let alone peacefully?

It is important not to make assumptions about political claims and arguments that are too fixed or unyielding. Over the course of American history, the content, character, and language of subjects that have generated religious involvement and stimulated religious passions has varied, reminding us that there have not been permanent religious positions on the range of questions that concern the relationship of religion and democracy. Over time, religious liberty arguably has increased as the meaning of disestablishment has clarified.[44] One result has been a shift in the content of disputes about the First Amendment itself. Another has been a series of changes to the location of conflict. Those matters that once primarily pitted some groups of Protestants against other Protestants shifted to disputes between Protestants and Catholics, then between Christians and members of minority religions. Today, such disagreements mainly take a secular versus religious form.

The combination of a ban on an established church and the encouragement of free expression likewise designates a charged zone. How the constitutional arc of the First Amendment should govern the character and boundaries of religious practices in public life has never become entirely settled. As a framework, the dual constitutional stipulation ruling out the existence of an official church while disallowing barriers to free religious expression is inherently marked by a challenging ambiguity. Issues concerning borderlands of church and state, how expressive faith and doctrinal ardor intersect instrumental calculations and strategic negotiations, and the ways religious commitments and organizations play a causal role in public affairs, arise with uncommon force precisely because the constellation of indispensable elements that compose an American formula for democratic religiosity offers no single or permanent solutions that resolve their inherent strains or satisfy all the society's varieties of comprehensive religious commitments.

Recurring contests about the meaning and implementation of the core rules established at the Founding have found expression within each branch of government, especially the federal courts. Almost as a matter of routine, American democracy has been marked by continual conflict about the level of distinction that is required between the government and religious institutions and activities to insure "the elimination of favoritism toward people or groups because of their religious identity," and to protect the public realm in a polity based on popular sovereignty from distortions imposed by the symbolic and institutional power of particular religious institutions, convictions, and ritual practices.[45]

On some matters there is widespread agreement, as, for example, regarding how there should be a clear distinction between the personnel and functions of the government and those of religious institutions, or that free religious expression is not limited to a Christian majority and, at least in that sense, that the United States is not a Christian nation. But there is robust disagreement about how public impartiality can best be reconciled with an appreciation of the significance of religion in the lives of most Americans. There are no fixed assessments of what constitutes acceptable and unacceptable degrees of entanglement between religion and the state, when governmental support for religious institutions and expression go too far, when laws can acknowledge the demands of religion, how devotion can be expressed in public settings, whether religious affiliations can be taken into account in implementing social policies such as adoption practices, whether religious associations that benefit from public funds can practice exclusionary hiring practices, or even what counts as a religious matter.[46]

Shaped over the course of more than two centuries by changes to demography, the composition of religious majorities and minorities, and the intensity and scope of doctrinal convictions and religious practices, these debates and transformations teach a dual, and not entirely consistent, lesson. They make an appreciation of democratic toleration and reasonable pluralism more pressing both for secularly oriented citizens, whose appreciation of religiosity tends to be wooden and dogmatic, and for religious activists, whose appreciation for the great span of religious belief and practice, and sometimes for the imperatives of democracy, likewise tends to be wooden and dogmatic. But they also remind us that religion and democracy do not neatly engage with each other, that distinctions between the reasonable and the unreasonable are not easy to establish, that the public arena is not just a zone of discussion but of power and imposition.

Given the beliefs and institutional behavior of its citizens, American democracy cannot thrive unless it persistently explores these concerns, and unless it discovers appropriate means in given historical circumstances that are consistent with the First Amendment's dual injunction. Solving the conundrum for liberal democratic politics posed by Rawls when he asked "how is it possible for there to exist over time a just and stable society of free and equal citizens, who remain profoundly divided by reasonable religious, philosophical, and moral doctrines"[47] requires persistent attention both to the character of religious pluralism and to the means through which an overlapping consensus can be sustained. Neither is easy. But both are necessary if democracy is to thrive without being grounded in a single, rather than many, patterns of belief and ways of life; and if, in turn, democracy does not ask so much of its participants that they have to sacrifice commitments that give their lives shape and meaning.[48]

Notes

1. With belief and religious practice having lost their compulsory status, Charles Taylor recently has written, we have been taken "from a society in which it was virtually impossible not to believe in God, to one in which faith, even for the staunchest believer, is one human possibility among others. . . . Belief in God is no longer axiomatic. There are alternatives." Charles Taylor, *A Secular Age* (Cambridge, MA: Harvard University Press, 2007), 3. For a consideration of the variety of religious forms of expression within this sense of secularization, see Ira Katznelson and Gareth Stedman Jones, eds., *Religion and the Political Imagination* (Cambridge: Cambridge University Press, 2010).

2. Roger Finke and Rodney Stark, *The Churching of America, 1776–2005. Winners and Losers in Our Religious Economy* (New Brunswick, NJ: Rutgers University Press, 2005), 23.

3. Gallup data since the 1930s to this effect are cited in Jeffrey K. Hadden, "Desacralizing Secularization Theory," in Jeffrey K. Hadden and Anson Shupe, eds., *Secularization and Fundamentalism Reconsidered: Religion and the Political Order* (New York: Paragon House, 1989), III: 16.

4. H. Richard Niebuhr, "The Protestant Movement and Democracy in the United States," in James Ward Smith and A. Leland Jamison, eds., *The Shaping of American Religion* (Princeton, NJ: Princeton University Press, 1961), 66. This edited collection, with such notable contributors as Oscar Handlin and Perry Miller, offers both a historical overview and a noteworthy portrait of the landscape of American religion a half-century ago.

5. Will Herberg, *Protestant-Catholic-Jew: An Essay in American Religious Sociology* (Chicago: University of Chicago Press, 1983). There are many discussions of religious vitality in the United States. Two of the best remain Kenneth Wald, *Religion and Politics in the United States* (New York: St. Martin's Press,

1987); and Robert Wuthnow, *The Restructuring of American Religion: Society and Faith since World War II* (Princeton, NJ: Princeton University Press, 2008). More recent overviews of the ways American religion has been changing include Alan Wolfe, *The Transformation of American Religion: How We Actually Live Our Faith* (Chicago: University of Chicago Press, 2005); Frank Lambert, *Religion in American Politics: A Short History* (Princeton, NJ: Princeton University Press, 2008); and Paul Harvey and Philip Goff, eds., *The Columbia Documentary History of Religion in America since 1945* (New York: Columbia University Press, 2005); on Los Angeles, see 427. American religious diversity remains primarily Christian, with about three in four Americans classifying themselves this way.

6. There also are a growing number of nonreligious persons who abjure any religious identification and some who, in small numbers, advance a sometimes militant atheism.

7. A particularly useful recent overview, with chapters on religion and voting behavior, past and present, public opinion, social movements, interest groups, the media, and legislative and judicial politics is Corwin E. Smidt, Lyman A. Kellstedt, and James L. Guth, eds., *The Oxford Handbook of Religion and American Politics* (New York: Oxford University Press, 2009).

8. I borrow this point from Charles Taylor, *Varieties of Religion Today* (Cambridge, MA: Harvard University Press, 2002), 114–15.

9. In a summary overview of long-term trends in American religion that salutes a recent historiographical turn away from a highly focused treatment of Puritanism, John F. Wilson concluded by observing how

> American society at the beginning of the twenty-first century embodies a cultural life that includes a spiritual or religious dimension. That is to say, America operates in terms of a set of assumptions through which the cosmos is regularized and explained and that offers an instrumental means of engaging with it. At the same time, as a society, America has permitted Old World religious traditions as well as new spiritual initiatives the space for a flourishing life. For this the most modern of nations to prove to be so hospitable to ancient preoccupations and traditions is remarkable, If nothing else, it has made those easy assumptions about the inevitability of secularization, taken for granted by several generations of intellectuals in the last century, seem disconnected from the gritty and grainy world we actually inhabit.

John F. Wilson, *Religion and the American Tradition.* Athens: University of Georgia Press, 2003, 73–74.

10. For a longer-term view, see John Herman Randall Jr., "The Churches and the Liberal Tradition," *Annals of the American Academy of Political and Social Science* 256 (March 1948): 148–64. This essay appeared in an issue devoted to "Organized Religion in the United States," thus providing a valuable snapshot at midcentury. Other notable contributions included essays on Judaism by Bernard Harrison and on the Catholic Church by John Courtney Murray. On the distinct role played by African-American churches in the struggle for equal rights, see Mark A. Noll, *God and Race in American Politics: A Short History* (Princeton, NJ: Princeton University Press, 2008).

11. For an elaboration of the view that an interpretation of the First Amendment as requiring separation goes too far in the direction of constraining religion, especially on the rights of clerics to exercise free speech in the political realm, see Philip Hamburger, *Separation of Church and State* (Cambridge, MA: Harvard University Press, 2002), 13, 93, 107, 120, 178, 280, 308, 490. Hamburger also underscores how the rhetoric of separation was invoked to justify a set of anti-Catholic practices (193–251). For an argument that liberalism permits too little scope for religious argumentation, see Jonathan Chaplin, "Beyond Liberal Restraint: Defending Religiously Based Arguments in Law and Public Policy," *University of British Columbia Law Review*, 33, no. 2 (2000): 617–46.

12. Robert Wuthnow, *The Struggle for America's Soul: Evangelicals, Liberals, and Secularism* (Grand Rapids, MI: William B. Eerdmans, 1989), 21–26. These liberal-conservative divisions also run through the denominations within Protestantism and among Jews, Catholics, and Muslims.

13. For a discussion of the diversity of colonial religion and its status on the eve of the making of the Constitution, see A. James Reichley, *Religion in American Public Life* (Washington, DC: Brookings Institution, 1985), 53–114; Sanford Cobb, *The Rise of Religious Liberty in America: A History* (New York: Cooper Square Publishers, 1968 [1902]); and Anson Phelps Stokes and Leo Pfeffer, *Church and State in the United States. Revised One-Volume Edition* (New York: Harper & Row, 1964), 3–103. An interpretation of early American religiosity as the completion of the Reformation under the impact of the Revolution as a popular movement is offered by Ernest Sutherland Bates, *American Faith: Its Religious, Political, and Economic Foundations* (New York: W. W. Norton, 1940). Also see Michael W. McConnell, "The Origins and Historical Understanding of Free Exercise of Religion," *Harvard Law Review*, 103 (May 1990): 1409–1517; and Sidney E. Mead, "From Coercion to Persuasion: Another Look at the Rise of Religious Liberty and the Emergence of Denominationalism," *Church History* 25 (December 1956): 317–37.

14. Grace Davie, "Religion in Europe in the 21st Century: The Factors to Take into Account," *Archives Euorpéennes de Sociologie* 47 no. 2 (2006): 289.

15. For an early twentieth-century retrospective on the controversial relationship between religion and democracy, see Carl Zollman, "Religious Liberty in American Law, I," *Michigan Law Review* 17 (March 1919): 355–77; and Carl Zollman, "Religious Liberty in American Law, II," *Michigan Law Review* 17 (April 1919): 456–78. Zollman stresses both the remarkable degree of religious liberty in America in tandem with an argument that the country has been from the start, and remains, a Christian country, governed under a penumbra of Christian hegemony. Also see Thomas J. Curry, *The First Freedoms: Church and State in America to the Passage of the First Amendment* (New York: Oxford University Press, 1986); and Frank Lambert, *The Founding Fathers and the Place of Religion in America* (Princeton, NJ: Princeton University Press, 2003).

16. For discussions of Tocqueville's views about religion in *Democracy in America*, see Sanford Kessler, "Tocqueville on Civil Religion and Liberal Democracy," *Journal of Politics* 39 (February 1977): 119–46; Cushing Strout, "Tocqueville and Republican Religion: Revisiting the Visitor," *Political Theory* 8 (February 1980): 9–26; Peter Dennis Bathory, "Tocqueville on Citizenship and Faith: A Response to

Cushing Strout," *Political Theory* 8 (February 1980): 27–38; Catherine Zuckert, "Not by Preaching: Tocqueville on the Role of Religion in American Society," *The Review of Politics* 43 (April 1981): 259–80; and Cynthia J. Hinckley, "Tocqueville on Religious Truth and Political Necessity," *Polity* 23 (Autumn 1990): 39–52.

17. Sidney Verba, Kay Lehman Schlozman, and Henry Brady, *Voice and Equality: Civic Voluntarism in American Politics* (Cambridge, MA: Harvard University Press, 1995).

18. These matters are not limited in significance to subjects that concern students of American politics. Students of international relations may wish to adjudge how the place of religion in American democracy has influenced the nation's global role and foreign policies. Students of comparative politics, in incorporating the American experience, might have to rethink their hypotheses about religion and modernity. Students of political theory will have to consider when, under what conditions, and how religious liberty and toleration become constitutive features of liberal and democratic polities and what frictions ensue, both inherently and contingently, when they do.

19. John Rawls, *Political Liberalism. Expanded Edition* (New York: Columbia University Press, 2005), 43. For a consideration, see Daniel A. Dombrowski, *Rawls and Religion: The Case for Political Liberalism* (Albany: State University of New York Press, 2001). It should be noted that the ways Rawls deals with religious divisions in American society is not to be above the fray but to take positions within contemporary arguments about religion. For examples of a critique of Rawls from the perspective of revelation rather than reason, see Robert P. George, "God's Reasons: The Role of Religious Authority in Debates about Public Policy," Remarks at the 1998 American Political Science Association Annual Meeting, http://www.orthodoxytoday.org/articles/GeorgeGodsReasons.php; and Alan Bloom, "Justice: John Rawls vs. the Tradition of Political Philosophy," in Chandran Kukathas, ed. *John Rawls: Critical Assessments of Leading Political Philosophers* (New York: Routledge, 2002), especially 226.

20. Rawls, *Political Liberalism*, 40.

21. He wrote of Protestantism, not religion generally. Niebuhr, "The Protestant Movement," 48.

22. John Rawls, *A Theory of Justice* (Cambridge, MA: Harvard University Press, 1971).

23. Ibid., 235.

24. Rawls, *Political Liberalism*, 201.

25. Ibid., xvi.

26. Ibid., 37.

27. Ibid., 58.

28. Ibid., xvi, 36, 37.

29. Ibid., 37.

30. Ibid., xxv.

31. Ibid., 53, 54.

32. Ibid., 57.

33. Ibid., 143.

34. Joshua Cohen, "A More Democratic Liberalism," *Michigan Law Review* 92 (May 1994): 1521.

35. Rawls, *Political Liberalism*, 39.

36. Ibid., 132–72, xix.

37. Ibid., 148.

38. Ibid., xvi–xvii.

39. A useful overview of the impact of Protestant confessionalism and the anti-Catholic tradition in public life can be found in E. R. Norman, *The Conscience of the State in North America* (Cambridge: Cambridge University Press, 1968), 75–102.

40. David B. Truman, *The Governmental Process* (New York: Alfred A. Knopf, 1951).

41. Cohen, "Democratic Pluralism," 1539.

42. Some issues that once had this status, notably divorce, have lost their charge. For a discussion, see Mark A. Smith, "Religion, Divorce, and the Missing Culture War in America," *Political Science Quarterly* 125 (Spring 2010).

43. Mark A. Graber, *Dred Scott and the Problem of Constitutional Evil* (Cambridge: Cambridge University Press, 2006), 1. Also see Mark A. Noll, *The Civil War as a Theological Crisis* (Chapel Hill: University of North Carolina Press, 2006).

44. This is a position argued by Mark DeWolfe Howe, *The Garden and the Wilderness: Religion and Government in American Constitutional History* (Chicago: University of Chicago Press, 1965).

45. Kent Greenawalt, "History as Ideology: Philip Hamburger's *Separation of Church and State*," *California Law Review* 93 (January 2005): 373. Also see Douglas Laycock, "The Many Meanings of Separation," *University of Chicago Law Review* 70 (Fall 2003): 1667–1701.

46. For sustained reasoning elucidating these issues, see the remarkable collection of essays by Kent Greenawalt on *Religion and the Constitution.* Volume 1 deals with *Free Exercise and Fairness*; Volume 2 with *Establishment and Fairness* (Princeton, NJ: Princeton University Press, 2006, 2008).

47. Rawls, *Political Liberalism*, 4.

48. The United States is sufficiently distinctive that it offers no catechism of questions and answers that simply can be transported to other places. But it has become ever more urgent to explore the conditions and standards that underpin America's combination of energetic religion, vibrant democracy, and religious toleration as other countries, including some long thought to be on the road to a secular future, face global and local revivals of religion, and as the movement of people has introduced religious diversity to sites that were more comfortably homogeneous just a short time ago.

INDEX